Psychological Theory

THE MACMILLAN COMPANY
NEW YORK · BOSTON · CHICAGO
DALLAS · ATLANTA · SAN FRANCISCO

MACMILLAN AND CO., LIMITED
LONDON · BOMBAY · CALCUTTA
MADRAS · MELBOURNE

THE MACMILLAN COMPANY
OF CANADA, LIMITED
TORONTO

Psychological Theory

CONTEMPORARY READINGS

Arranged and Edited by

Melvin H. Marx

ASSOCIATE PROFESSOR OF PSYCHOLOGY
UNIVERSITY OF MISSOURI

New York

THE MACMILLAN COMPANY

PREFACE

THIS BOOK OFFERS a collection of recent papers on problems of scientific theory construction in psychology (Part One), and an anthology of representative writings from the most prominent contemporary psychological theorists (Part Two). Coordinate with this division into sections on method and content, its major objectives are 1) to encourage a more critical understanding and a sounder utilization of the principles of theory construction, and 2) to give the advanced student a certain amount of first-hand experience with the work of the various men who have laid the theoretical foundations for contemporary psychology within the past two decades.

These objectives require little justification. Although many psychologists have become increasingly alert within recent years to the basic problems of theory construction, unfortunately there does not seem to have been a comparable general improvement in the actual construction of psychological theories. The need for the development of a deeper appreciation and a wider application of basic principles is being increasingly recognized, for graduate students in clinical and applied as well as theoretical-experimental areas.

It is hoped that the book will help to fill a gap in available textbooks. At the present time there is no source that offers a diversified approach to problems of theory construction. Nor is there available an anthology of contemporary theoretical positions over a wide range of subjects. Furthermore, books on systematic psychology typically approach contemporary problems from the point of view of the old schools, or systems, which are today important mainly in an historical sense. The stimulus to preparation of the present volume was the recognition of this textbook need during the development, over a period of years, of a course in contemporary psychological theory. The necessity of regular assignments of readings from diverse sources, mostly with library circulation restrictions, suggested the desirability of a single collection of the most useful and representative papers.

The book is intended for any advanced undergraduate or graduate course in psychological theory, systems, or history. In general, the somewhat more difficult material in Part One will be of more value in graduate courses in theory construction, or related topics; the material in Part Two will be more useful in advanced undergraduate or graduate courses in systematic and history. However, it should be noted that no hard and fast line can be drawn between the two parts of the book. A certain amount of theoretical content is unavoidably present in selections of the first part, and some of the selections of the second part contain methodological implications.

In addition to its use as a text, the book should be of some service as a general reference source for the present period, since it may be considered to document the development in psychology, within the past two decades, of a genuinely scientific type of theory construction.

A few words of explanation as to the criteria of selection are in order. The basic pattern of the book follows the general plan which I have developed in the teaching of the course in contemporary theory. This consists, briefly, of a series of seminar-type discussions on problems of scientific method and theory construction, followed by critical reports by students on major contemporary theorists. Most of the selections of Part One have therefore been used in class, and have been found to be effective aids to discussion as well as important sources of information. A reasonable degree of representativeness has been a definite objective, in the belief that presentation of a variety of points of view is not only intrinsically desirable but also might help to serve as an antidote to systematic inbreeding tendencies in graduate training programs.

In choosing material for Part Two an attempt was made to obtain selections that present basic systematic approaches, rather than detailed technical accounts, of the theoretical positions which have been most generally influential within the past two decades. For this reason some of the selections are among the earliest important papers published by the various theorists. They are meant to serve mainly as general background materials and as starting points for further, more intensive investigation. Also, selection of older and better established theorists should certainly not be interpreted as an indication of lack of appreciation for either younger theorists or well established experimentalists whose work has not been generally influential in a systematic sense. The former will have their representation in some future anthology; the latter belong more appropriately at the present time in volumes organized primarily around specific subject matters. For these reasons the selections for Part Two should not be considered to reflect the editor's judgment as to the quality or ultimate scientific significance of contemporary theoretical-experimental psychologists. Nor should they be taken to indicate his belief that those theorists chosen necessarily best exemplify the principles of theory construction presented in Part One. Selection has been purely on the basis of general systematic influence over a period of years.

Certain general matters of editorial method remain to be mentioned. A minimum of editorial comment has been included. It was thought desirable, however, to introduce each chapter with a brief orienting statement. The introductory paper, which was written for the book, contains material on the major general points on which I have found the typical beginning graduate student to be most deficient.

Space limitations have necessitated the cutting of some of the selections, especially in Part Two. This was done as simply as possible, with a minimum of disturbance of the original material.

References have been numbered in a separate sequence for each selection and placed immediately following the selection. It is expected that this method will facilitate their use. A brief set of suggested further readings is appended, by chapter titles, at the end of the book. For Part One these have been centered around the particular problems treated; for Part Two they refer mainly to the individual theorists.

I should like to acknowledge the kindness of the various authors, editors and publishers whose reproduction permissions made this volume possible. Specific permission citations will be found at the bottom of the first page of each selection. I should also like to acknowledge my general indebtedness to my students and colleagues at the University of Missouri for their critical evaluations during various phases of the preparation of the book. Special thanks are due to Fred McKinney for his encouragement during the early planning of the book, to Felix Goodson for his aid in the final preparation of the manuscript, and to my wife for her assistance throughout all phases of the planning and preparation of the book.

University of Missouri   *Melvin H. Marx*

CONTENTS

CONTENTS

PART ONE

Theory Construction

CHAPTER I

INTRODUCTION

IT IS THE PURPOSE of this introductory paper to present a general picture of scientific theory construction, with special reference to certain of the major methodological problems which apply particularly to psychology. In the interest of generality it is necessary to avoid extended consideration of many basically important but more specialized problems, a large number of which are covered in the selections that follow. The discussion has been influenced most directly by the arguments and conclusions of the operationists and the logical positivists, which are given a more detailed treatment in Chapters II and III.

1 THE GENERAL NATURE OF THEORY CONSTRUCTION

Melvin H. Marx

I Introduction

Direct empirical measurement is generally agreed to be the fundamental task of natural science. An impressive array of highly reliable and useful scientific knowledge has been accumulated in this way. However, it is not always possible to answer scientific questions *simply* by means of direct observation and measurement. Many phenomena appear to be too remotely and too tenuously related to the immediately observable variables to permit so direct an approach. Furthermore, there are problems of underlying general relationships between apparently unrelated phenomena that can not easily be attacked by strictly empirical methods. For these reasons all modern natural sciences have developed a large number of theories, or abstract explanatory principles, which are ultimately based upon but by no means entirely reducible to bare empirical measurements.

A number of problems involving the relationship between the empirical and the theoretical components of science have arisen in the rapid scientific emergence of psychology, with its long-time philosophical orientation and its intimate connection with matters of great practical significance. The actual use of theory in psychology does not appear to have kept pace with the formal recognition of the principles of theory construction. The following discussion aims at exposing the common ground that all theory construction shares, in the hope of stimulating more effective general consideration of the basic problems.

II Basic Assumptions

The arguments that follow depend upon the acceptance of certain assumptions, the implications of which are often overlooked in contemporary theory construction and theory criticism. They tend, unfortu-

Prepared for this volume.

nately, to be accepted in principle but ignored in practice. They may be briefly stated as follows:

1. The ultimate aim of all natural science is explanation and *understanding* and not simply prediction and control in a practical sense, as is often assumed. Brown (2) has pointed out that inability to predict or control earthquakes has not prevented the significant scientific development of seismology, and has argued that human behavior is probably in the same situation. In both cases "the causes are too obscure, intricate and inaccessible" for exact prediction. It is nevertheless true that we can investigate and understand these phenomena, and so modify our behavior accordingly. Theory, or general explanation, is the ultimate objective of science.

2. In the development of any scientific theory it is impossible to avoid direct dependence upon *empirical* operations. That is, any scientific theory, as distinguished from less rigorous "speculation," must refer back to previous empirical reports as well as point forward to new observations. It must be recognized, in addition, that some kind of bias, whether or not it is explicitly recognized, underlies all empirical measurements, regardless of how automatic and mechanical they may appear. It is thus not possible to separate completely the empirical from the theoretical components of scientific inquiry. For methodological purposes, however, it is desirable to delimit as clearly as possible the avowedly theoretical and the more strictly empirical, or observational, components.

3. All scientific investigation has one essential characteristic whose implications psychologists are particularly prone to overlook. It is *sociolinguistic behavior*. That is, it demands communication to others. "Observations" therefore always imply report, or *verbal statements,* and the same is of course even more obviously true of constructs and hypotheses (although other forms of symbolic expression than words may sometimes be used). The fact that psychology has developed, historically, as a science of "experience" *and* "behavior" should not be allowed to confuse the issue. The observer who wishes to make a scientific introspective analysis of his own experience, or "consciousness," must invariably produce a verbal protocol of some sort for communication to others. These protocols may then be treated, by the observer himself and by others, in essentially the same manner as any other reports of observations. If the introspective observer neglects to state clearly the details of his observation, and attempts to proceed directly to conclusions based

upon the observations, he thereby reduces the scientific value of his work in the same manner as the clinician who is unable or unwilling to produce protocols concerning his observations. From this point of view the special status of "private experience" or "consciousness" as a uniquely psychological subject matter—the problem of "existentialism" —is not regarded as a scientific question, since an answer one way or the other does not make any difference in the kind of scientific work that needs to be done.

III General Characteristics of Theories

Scientific theorizing is always an attempt to overcome the local limitations of direct observations, and to generalize beyond the immediate data. Several general characteristics of theories may now be described.

1. All theories aim at explanation, which means the establishment of *functional relationships between variables*. These must be stated in words or other symbols, and may thus be considered to be descriptive statements, or propositions, at varying levels of abstraction and comprehensiveness.

2. A theory is both a *tool* and an *objective*. Which of these functions is emphasized largely depends upon the degree of confidence—or social acceptability, and thus "factualness"—that it has achieved. It should be emphasized that no final or absolute theories (or laws) are to be expected in science. The best example of this is probably the sudden and revolutionary changes which occurred in physical theory towards the end of the last century. In this connection, however, it should also be recognized that classical Newtonian mechanics was not refuted, but was rather re-evaluated, as a result of the development of quantum and relativity theories.

When a theory is regarded only as an objective, the danger is that its provisional, tool-like character will be overlooked. This condition has been prominent in recent psychological history, as evidenced in the overly zealous polemic generated on the basis of very preliminary and provisional alternative theoretical positions.

3. Theories are always *relative* to the bias not only of the theorist, but also of the various observers upon whose empirical reports he has depended (cf. 3, 5). It may again be emphasized that some selectivity or bias in this general sense is inevitable in all observations. A common error is to talk and act as though theories somehow transcend the limitations of direct observation and logical inference, and so either are or

are not "true," or truly representative of "reality." This point of view seems to overlook the necessarily man-made nature of the more or less abstract propositions that we call theories and laws. All problems of ultimate "reality" are entirely extra-scientific questions, or "metaphysical" ones, as the logical positivists would say.

4. It follows that alternative theoretical approaches can be directly compared, scientifically, only if they make *different predictions* within the same observational framework. Scientifically, their value is a matter of empirical test, rather than philosophical or logical test, or even practical application. The various a priori biases which in actual practice account for much of the polemic and invective generated in psychological controversies ought to be recognized more clearly and explicitly as just such, and not disguised as the apparent functions of purely scientific analyses.

IV Major Elements of Theory Construction

Theory construction depends upon three major types of verbal statements, or propositions. Although their nature is often somewhat obscured by variations in usage, they may be most usefully differentiated as:

1. *Empirical* propositions. These are statements of "fact," of what has been observed.

2. *Hypothetical* propositions. These are statements of supposition, or conjecture, of what is predicted in observation.

3. *Theoretical* propositions. These are more or less general statements, of varying degreees of abstractness and comprehensiveness, concerning functional relations among variables.

There has been some apparent disagreement in psychology as to whether we have too few or too many of one or the other of these types of propositions. For example, Leeper (6) has commented that we have enough fact but insufficient theory, and Brown (2) that we have too much theory and too little fact. Analysis of many such opinions indicates, however, that what is really meant is that we have too little relationship between facts and theories. More adequate relating of the empirical and the theoretical components of psychology is a major contemporary problem.

It is the hypothetical type of verbal proposition that forms the link between the empirical propositions, or facts, and the theories. The implications of a theory can be tested only by means of specific predictions, or experimental hypotheses. These are questions which must be answered empirically. The hypothesis is thus the backbone of all scientific theory construction; without it confirmation or rejection of theories would be impossible. Establishment of empirical propositions is referred to as *inductive,* in contrast with the complementary development of the logical implications of theories, or the *deductive* phase of scientific investigation.

The closeness of relation between hypotheses and each of the two terminal types of propositions varies widely. This has resulted in a considerable amount of ambiguity in the meaning of the term "hypothesis." For example, certain types of hypotheses carry a minimum of relation to theories but are very closely related to empirical propositions. Such relatively restricted hypotheses may eventually lead to the establishment of so-called "empirical laws" (e. g., water expands in freezing) which have a certain amount of generality but contain little in the way of specific theoretical implications. On the other hand, the term hypothesis is often used as nearly synonymous with theory itself, to refer to any tentative and relatively untested type of theoretical proposition, especially if it involves a restricted range of phenomena. In this usage, hypotheses become theories after a reasonable amount of verification, modification, and amalgamation. Theories may then in turn become "laws," or explanatory principles of wide generality in which the highest degree of confidence is placed.

Theoretical and empirical propositions are characteristically tied together, in hypotheses of varying degrees of remoteness from direct observational test, by means of logical inferences called *symbolic constructs.* These are a special type of concept, or symbol, and serve the same general function as the theory itself; that is, they help to fill in the gaps which must always exist in the empirical data.

As Pratt (7) has clearly pointed out, all concepts contain both *more than* and *less than* the empirical data from which they are derived. The concept "dog"—"dog in general," that is—is at the same time more meaningful than the observation of any particular dog since it summarizes in a single word or other symbol the essence of an infinite number of observations, and less meaningful since it invariably loses in concreteness and individuality. Dangerous as concept-formation therefore is, it is nevertheless an absolutely essential step in the formation of scientific theory.

The example of "dog" represents a type of concept which can be *directly* reduced, by means of a relatively simple pointing operation, to particular observations (that is, experiencing a concrete dog). The dangers of concept-formation are even more pronounced, however, when a more complex type of concept is attempted. This is the type which is *constructed* on the basis of observations. Thus, the concepts—or, more specifically, the constructs—"motive," "habit," "gene," and "atom" cannot be built on observations in the same relatively simple and direct manner that the concepts "dog," "food pellet," and "chair" can be. Symbolic or logical constructs are *inferred* on the basis of observed relationships between objects and events. This characteristic results in an *construct* unfortunate tendency toward ambiguity which is especially marked in *validity* a complex field like psychology. It also suggests the importance of a careful analysis of such constructs, which are necessarily involved in theory construction, whether or not they are explicitly and formally recognized.

The three basic elements of theory construction are schematically shown in Figure 1. The characteristic of each element which is considered most essential, scientifically, is indicated along the continuum from practical affairs to science. The three continua may be considered in turn.

1. With regard to the empirical foundation of science, it may be freely granted that the everyday type of observation constitutes the groundwork for both the origin of scientific problems and the preliminary conceptual and theoretical formulations. However, notwithstanding the ability and ingenuity of some especially keen observers and reporters in literature, art, and related fields, some degree of *control* must be developed if science is to advance. This simply means a reduction in the ambiguity of the data, through naturalistic or experimental techniques, and their assignment as functions of definitely known variables. Further consideration of this important problem is beyond the scope of the present discussion.

2. *Operational validity,* or the open and clearly stated relationship of the construct to its empirical basis in operations producing the data, is the most essential characteristic of construct-formation. Animistic concepts and others with what Reichenbach (8) has called "surplus meaning" may be tolerated in the early, pre-scientific development of a field but their replacement by constructs more closely and necessarily tied to the data must occur for scientific advance.

The *intervening variable,* as first proposed by Tolman, offers an ideal

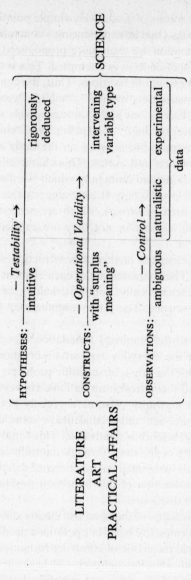

Figure 1 The three basic elements of scientific theory construction

opportunity for this kind of conceptual development. Most effectively used, it *means* nothing more than certain stated empirical operations. For example, Hull's construct of habit strength ($_sH_R$) quite literally *equals* (that is, is identical with) whatever empirical data result from variation in the four stated determinants: number of reinforcements, amount of reinforcing agent, time between stimulation and response, and time between response and reinforcement. Once the problem of some particular dependent variable has been settled, these four operations completely delimit what is meant by habit strength. Of course, there still remains the problem of relating *this* "habit strength" to other versions of the same general concept; but that is by no means a unique problem, and the important advantage in this case is that one can at least tell directly what the theorist or experimenter means by "habit strength." Furthermore, if the particular construct—that is, the particular operations which define it—proves to be experimentally ineffectual or otherwise inadequate, appropriate modifications can be readily made. Such operationally controlled flexibility is an enormous advantage in the clarification of the construct and its relation to empirical data.

It should be recognized that this extremely close coupling of constructs to empirically manipulable variables is not essential to operational validity. However, some degree of reduction of conceptual terms to equivalent empirical sentences is needed. This point will be elaborated in a later section.

3. *Testability* is the absolutely essential characteristic of any scientifically useful hypothesis. Obviously an explanation that cannot be tested in some way cannot be given an empirical evaluation. It is necessary to note that the scientific test cannot be intuitively made, and thus rest on unknown bases, as is common in everyday life. Intuition and insight are required throughout the course of any scientific development, but as science advances they should be progressively restricted to the preliminary formulations of constructs and hypotheses and not also be involved in the formal relations of these to the data. They are not to be considered as substitutes for the rigorous deduction of empirical implications from the scientifically fruitful hypothesis.

It follows from the foregoing considerations that scientific progress is marked by a progressive shift from left to right in the diagram in Figure 1 for all three phases of theory construction. In each case there is a reduction in ambiguity of relations between the various components, and an increasingly clear and often formal differentiation of their respective functions. The fact that scientific progress results in increasingly less natural and less lifelike concepts and theories obviously increases the difficulties of popularization and translation into practical action, but is hardly avoidable [cf. Pratt (7) for an especially good discussion of this point]. It is instructive to note, in this respect, how even Lewin, who may be considered to have been perhaps the most responsive of recent leading theorists to important human problems, was compelled to translate such problems into the highly "artificial" terms and concepts of topological and vector psychology. Even in the case of popular vs. technically coined terminology, there may be only an apparent advantage to using already familiar terms in new scientific, and unnatural, settings. As Thouless (10) has recently observed, the use of popular, familiar terms may actually be disadvantageous in spite of its superficial appeal because it is likely to result in a false and misleading sense of popular understanding, based upon the old but now inadequate meanings. This then simply increases the difficulties of popularization and re-translation.

v Objections to Operationism

There has been a great deal of misunderstanding and confusion with respect to the problem of operationism and its relation to intuitive functions. Some of this may be traced to certain kinds of pressures and motives which tend to restrict scientific work to the left side of the diagram in Figure 1. For example, there is the tendency to ask highly general, practically important but experimentally meaningless questions, and the attempt to translate these too directly into theory construction and research programs. These problems come, of course, out of everyday life situations but must be broken down into simpler and experimentally more meaningful questions before they can be effectively handled. It is the large, philosophically-oriented type of problem with which the older schools or systems were most directly concerned. Probably this helps to account for much of their failure to be scientifically more fruitful. The discouragement of such questions except in preliminary formulations and long-range goals, and their replacement or at least supplementation by more specific and productive questions, seem to be necessary prerequisites for scientific advance in psychology. The large generalizations will then follow as factual knowledge and empirically-related theory are built up on a more solid basis.

The pressure for quick, useful solutions to urgent practical problems and the alleged artistic and literary bias of some psychologists have also been regarded as detrimental influences so far as scientific progress in theory construction and research is concerned. It should be pointed out that, whatever merit these charges may have, they are not meant, or at any rate should not be meant, to be depreciatory of practical applications or literary and artistic pursuits per se. The latter interests in particular, however, are regarded as being at the opposite end of the scale from scientific methods (cf. Figure 1) and are considered to be no more appropriate in a strictly scientific endeavor than the purely objective and experimental point of view is appropriate or desirable in the realm of art and literature. In this connection William James' well-known distinction between the "tough-minded" and the "tender-minded" is often cited, and Boring (1) has presented an interesting elaboration of this notion emphasizing the basic temperamental differences that account for differences in approaches.

A more serious misunderstanding of the demands of operationism has apparently resulted from an overly literal interpretation, encouraged perhaps by the somewhat uncritical acceptance of the principle in the early days of its formalization. Thus Israel and Goldstein (4, p. 186) ask "How will the thoroughgoing operationist get started upon the investigation of a problem . . . ?" In the light of the preceding discussion it should be obvious that the answer to this type of objection is simply that problems and questions are originally formulated in relatively non-operational terms, but that if scientific progress is to occur they must ultimately be operationally refined. The difficulty seems to be that too many theorists fail to recognize the need for such refinement.

In answer to criticism of operationism on the ground that too much is demanded, it should be emphasized that operationism is primarily a more or less formal attempt to *stimulate critical evaluation* of the relationship between logical constructs and their supporting empirical data. All concepts do not need to be defined literally in terms of the precise physical operations involved. But it is fair to ask that the observational basis of any concept be made as explicit as possible—that, at least, this particular problem be recognized as a problem and not simply ignored, as is very often the case. If this is not adequately done the concept is certainly open to serious question, as are any conclusions based upon its use.

The need for careful operational analysis is greatest in just those areas of psychology where it is most difficult to apply. This situation has no doubt been responsible for a certain amount of the resistance to operationism that has appeared. Inner needs, phenomenological fields, personality structures, and the like become scientifically productive concepts only in so far as their observational bases can be directly evaluated in some way or the other. Throwing the spotlight of critical inquiry upon many such concepts would certainly reveal an embarrassing lack of clarity—and probably very often evoke a strong emotional reaction in the theorist—but there does not seem to be any other way of testing their validity if science is to be a public and communicable enterprise.

In summarizing this discussion, it may be well to stress the fact that all scientifically useful concepts in psychology are derived, ultimately, from observations. Failure to identify and localize the intuitive aspects of theory construction has been a major methodological defect in many of the higher-level types of theoretical work. Without some degree of willingness to subject all concepts to a critical, operational analysis the essential self-correcting processes in science can hardly function effectively. It is in just such a tight and exclusively speculative atmosphere that cultlike and antiempirical tendencies thrive.

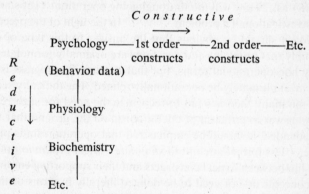

Figure 2 Two types of scientific explanation

VI Types of Explanation

All scientific theories, as attempted explanation, may be regarded as descriptions of functional relations between variables. Two major types of scientific explanation may be differentiated:

1. The *reductive*—by means of which particular phenomena are functionally related to other phenomena at a different level of description.

2. The *constructive*—by means of which the phenomena are described in terms of more abstract, or higher-order, constructs and hypotheses.

The two types of explanation are shown diagrammatically as they apply to psychology in Figure 2. Let us suppose that the behavior datum which we want to explain is a fairly simple one, say a description of an animal being presented with a certain type of food and eating. The chain of *reductive* explanation would then go approximately as follows: the eating behavior occurs because of certain stomach contractions and neurophysiological events, and these in turn occur because of certain biochemical conditions, etc. The *constructive* type of explanation would start with the same behavior, and might proceed along the following line: the eating behavior occurs because of food deprivation (construct of hunger drive) which under similar conditions previously has been paired with the giving of food (construct of reinforcement) to produce a certain behavior tendency (higher-order construct of habit), etc.

It may be noted that in each case explanation proceeds through an interlocking of the variables that are being described. When the variables which are used to explain are drawn from observations of a sort arbitrarily assigned to another level of description (for example, the physiological, if organ system functions are directly concerned), the explanation may be considered to be of the reductive type. When the variables are drawn from observations made on the same level of description (the psychological, if behavior is involved), the explanation may be considered to be of the constructive type. In either case the explanation proceeds to a more basic level of description—more basic in the sense that the original behavior data are found to vary systematically as functions of the changes in the other variables introduced.

A certain amount of controversial discussion has arisen over the relative merits, within psychology, of these two types of explanation. On the one hand it may be argued that the constructive type is *methodologically* more fundamental than the reductive, in the sense that it is only after a certain degree of successful constructive explanation has been achieved that the various descriptive levels may be readily related. On the other hand, it may be argued that the *ultimate* objective of science is explanation of the reductive type. Without attempting to evaluate these claims it may simply be stated that whatever type of explanation seems to be most useful should be adopted, and as a matter of fact it would often be very difficult to separate the two types in actual practice.

They are complementary, rather than mutually exclusive, and ought to be regarded as such.

vii Levels of Explanation

A somewhat related and equally sterile controversy has developed within recent years in regard to the relative merits of the *field-theoretical* and the *stimulus-response* types of theoretical and experimental approach. It seems necessary to emphasize that these types of theoretical approaches are also to be regarded as supplementary, if not actually complementary, rather than mutually exclusive. Whether one prefers to stress theory at the most molar levels of description, or to work upwards, so to speak, from the relatively molecular and simplified levels of description, appears to be a function of a number of factors. Among these may be mentioned personal, temperamental influences, types of problems being investigated, etc. It ought to be evident to any detached bystander that many kinds of scientific attacks are possible upon different levels of complexity, or molarity, which however measured must always be regarded as upon a continuum. It is therefore a most unfortunate fact that these two particular types of approaches, or any other two for that matter, should be so often and so emotionally opposed to each other. Claims of exclusive excellence from either side and premature extrapolation of conclusions based upon the present meager and tenuous store of scientific knowledge in psychology may be seen as having little basis in fact. The only scientific test of any type of theoretical approach is its ability to generate fruitful experiments or other observations and to lead to more satisfactory and more comprehensive theories. No scientific development in the field of psychology today justifies the enthusiastic acceptance of any single type of theoretical-experimental orientation.

A glance at the situation in physiology may be helpful in pointing up comparable problems in psychology. The physiologist may concentrate upon more and more detailed and refined analysis of highly technical problems within any one organ system, which has been the orthodox procedure as a matter of fact; or he may concern himself with more molar inter-relations of the various systems, as Cannon has done in his work on "homeostasis." There seems to have been no wholesale or concentrated effort within physiology to dispense with either approach, or even to treat them as in any way opposed to each other. They are recognized as complementary and necessary functions. There likewise seems to be no essential reason why the same calm acceptance of different purposes and approaches should not occur within psychology.

The problem of "reductionism" (e. g., 9), stimulated within recent years by the increasing popularity of the field-theoretical or holistic type of approach, has produced a great deal more heat and confusion than light and understanding. There is only one possible answer, scientifically, as to whether so-called emergent behavioral functions can be successfully "reduced" to more primary and less complex ones within the same field. The answer must be a pragmatic one, entirely dependent upon the extent to which such reduction eventually occurs. There is, again, at the present time no reliable scientific basis upon which to make any very definite statement on this problem. Physical and biological analogies or emotionally biased beliefs in either direction have little support in scientific evidence, and ought to be labelled more clearly for what they are—dubious analogies and emotionally grounded beliefs.

In this connection a certain amount of criticism has been directed within recent years against the various well-developed programs of theory construction based upon research with infrahuman animals. Again, a glance at a well-established and highly successful scientific field may be helpful in clarifying the situation. The research geneticist's primary, and many times practically exclusive, concern is with fundamental genetic functions, wherever they may occur. He has so intensively studied the fruitfly for the same reasons that the psychologist has so intensively studied the rat—convenience, ease of experimental control, large amount of previous work, etc. It would be difficult if not impossible to point to a single fundamental genetic discovery based upon human research, or for that matter upon many other animal forms than *Drosophila*. There seems to be no reason why the behavioral scientist should not be allowed an equally unimpeded opportunity to employ infrahuman animals in the same general way and for the same general purpose—the investigation of basic animal functions, regardless of the degree to which the results may ultimately be related to human problems.

In conclusion, it may again be emphasized that a diversity of interests and approaches is not only desirable but inevitable in as complex and heterogeneous a field as modern psychology. More rather than less experimental research and empirically-oriented theory is needed at all levels of explanation—the strictly molecular as well as the broadly molar. However, it must also be emphasized that regardless of the level of complexity, or molarity, worked at the psychologist is obliged to follow the general principles of scientific theory construction, as outlined in the preceding sections. One of the most immediate needs in contemporary psychology is for a more realistic attitude towards these general methodological requirements. A major obstacle to more effective scientific progress seems to be a general disinclination to submit constructs and theories to a critical and rigorous operational analysis (whether or not that particular term is used) and a corresponding failure explicitly to recognize the invidious infiltration of emotional beliefs and extra-scientific value throughout all phases of theory construction. A more careful distinction between scientific and extra-scientific elements is necessary to keep both kinds of values in their proper place. The essential neutrality of scientific methodology cannot be sacrificed, no matter how urgent the immediate needs for knowledge and action may be, without a corresponding loss of the effectiveness of science as a uniquely successful tool for the establishment of objective explanatory propositions of a high degree of empirically-tested probability.

VIII Summary

This paper has been concerned, in a more or less general way, with a variety of problems involving the relationship between the empirical and the theoretical components of scientific work. Special reference has been made to the particular problems which psychology, as a newly emerging science, has had to face. The general characteristics of theories were outlined, and an analysis of the basic elements of theory construction was presented. These were seen as 1) *control* of observations, 2) *operational validity* of constructs, and 3) *testability* of hypotheses. Particular attention was given to the problem of operational validity, especially with regard to certain of the major objections to operationism. Two types of scientific explanation were described: 1) the *reductive,* involving functional relationships between variables at different levels of description, and 2) the *constructive,* involving description of phenomena in terms of more abstract constructs. Finally, the problem of different levels of explanation was discussed. It was concluded that theoretical-experimental attacks upon the problems of behavior are needed at all levels of explanation, and that regardless of the level at which the theory is constructed the general principles of scientific theory construction must be followed.

References

1. Boring, E. G. Human nature vs. sensation: William James and the psychology of the present. *Amer. J. Psychol.*, 1942, *55*, 310-327.
2. Brown, W. Facing the facts. In *Proc. 25th Anniv. Celebr. Inaug. Grad. Stud.* Los Angeles: Univ. South. Calif. Press, 1936, 116-121.
3. Cohen, M. R. and Nagel, E. *An introduction to logic and scientific method.* New York: Harcourt, Brace, 1934.
4. Israel, H. E. and Goldstein, B. Operationism in psychology. *Psychol. Rev.*, 1944, *51*, 177-188.
5. Johnson, H. M. Pre-experimental assumptions as determiners of experimental results. *Psychol. Rev.*, 1940, *47*, 338-346.
6. Leeper, R. W. The experiments by Spence and Lippitt and by Kendler on the sign-gestalt theory of learning. *J. Exp. Psychol.*, 1948, *38*, 102-106.
7. Pratt, C. C. *The logic of modern psychology.* New York: Macmillan, 1939.
8. Reichenbach, H. *Experience and prediction.* Chicago: Univ. Chicago Press, 1938.
9. Sloane, E. H. Reductionism. *Psychol. Rev.*, 1945, *52*, 214-223.
10. Thouless, R. H. Some problems of terminology in psychological theory. *Brit. J. Psychol.*, 1949, *40*, Part I, 41-46.

CHAPTER II

OPERATIONISM AND LOGICAL POSITIVISM

AMONG THE MOST significant general scientific developments of this century has been the increasingly critical attention paid, by both scientists and philosophers, to the nature of science and scientific method. In this development the two most important formative influences have been the movement called operationism, *directly instigated by P. W. Bridgman's* The logic of modern physics, *and the broader philosophical position most commonly called* logical positivism, *primarily originating in the famed "Vienna Circle" of philosophers. Operationism represents an attempt by scientists to improve the rigor of scientific language by requiring that concepts be defined in terms of the operations that produce them. Logical positivism, or scientific empiricism as it is also often called, represents an attempt by philosophers to rid philosophy of its so-called "pseudo-problems"—those for which no empirical answers are available—and thus align it more closely with modern science. One of the first psychologists to recognize the psychological implications of these movements was S. S. Stevens. The first selection of this chapter presents his comprehensive treatment of the relationship of both these influences to psychology.*

Although operationism refers primarily to the problem of definition of scientific terms and concepts, as a general methodological movement it has very close connections with related problems of theory construction—that is, with the nature of the use to which terms and concepts are put by scientists. The selection by Gustav Bergmann and Kenneth W. Spence provides a useful general treatment of the relationship between operationism and theory construction.

20

2 PSYCHOLOGY AND THE SCIENCE OF SCIENCE

S. S. Stevens

The scientist has always been proud of his hard head and his tough mind. When William James (29) sat in judgment and divided the universe of temperaments into the tough- and tender-minded, the scientist knew where he belonged. He was happy to run with the goats, for he was an empiricist and he loved facts in all their crude variety. He was skeptical and cautious of word, and to "isms" of all kinds he was peculiarly unresponsive. The tender-minded were the rationalists. They had faith in intuition and were awed by the power of the mind. It was their opinion that by taking thought they could discover absolute principles of truth answering to the criteria of coherence and consistency and that, armed with these principles, they could legislate the bounds of science. They were the sheep whose wool shone white under the light of reason. They were most numerous in departments of philosophy.

Undoubtedly these two types are still with us, but it is the purpose of this review neither to shear the sheep nor tame the goats. Instead, its purpose is simply to invite attention to some recent developments in what we might call the Philosophy of Science.

The tough-minded scientist has always known that he could screen his integrity against the seductive pipings of the rationalist by ignoring philosophy. The tender-minded philosopher, gifted with his superior dialectic, has usually despaired at the stubborn naïveté of the scientist and has determined to leave the unrefined fellow to grovel alone, while he, the philosopher, calmly demonstrated the impossibility of proving anything by induction. Suddenly, however, we find, on the one hand, a coterie of philosophers plying us with what, if it is not science, is certainly not the brand of stuff we have ordinarily pigeonholed as philosophy; and, on the other hand, we are beset by a host of scientists of all disciplines campaigning for what, if it is not philosophy, is surely not the science we are used to.

From S. S. Stevens, Psychology and the science of science, *Psychol. Bull.*, 1939, *36*, 221-263. Reprinted by permission of the author, the *Psychological Bulletin*, and the American Psychological Association.

The philosopher, Benjamin (3), says of these scientists:

They begin with science, they talk about science, and they end with science, yet they do not conform at all to the tradition of scientific writing. . . . Their repeated reference to philosophical issues tempts one to classify them with this group, yet the writings approach these problems in a new spirit and with a new method, which seem quite foreign to traditional philosophy.

And concerning the widespread groups of philosophers participating in this movement, Reichenbach (52) observes:

Though there is no philosophic system which unites these groups, there is a common property of ideas, principles, criticisms, and working methods. . . . It is the intention of uniting both the empiricist conception of modern science and the formalistic conception of logic . . . which marks the working program of this philosophic movement.

So numerous and insistent are the words of those who have been seized by the spirit of this movement that they swell the pages of several new journals—journals whose subject matter defies simple classification.[1] There are articles by philosophers, mathematicians, and scientists. But it is more than a mere scrambling of the sheep and the goats. A common spirit animates most of these writings. The common theme, despite its fundamental simplicity, despite differences of interpretation by newborn enthusiasts, and despite the disparagement of misunderstanding, is probably to be esteemed as a truly great advance in the Philosophy of Science, or the Science of Philosophy.

Numerous phrasings of this central theme have been cast by authors interested in various aspects of it, but they all assert essentially that *science seeks to generate confirmable propositions by fitting a formal system of symbols (language, mathematics, logic) to empirical observations, and that the propositions of science have empirical significance only when their truth can be demonstrated by a set of concrete operations.* There are thus two separate realms of discourse: the *formal* (or rational) and the *empirical*. It is the business of the philosopher to labor with the formal and discover and perfect the rules of the scientific

---

[1] Some representative journals are: *Erkenntnis,* begun in 1930; *Philosophy of Science,* begun in 1934; and *International Encyclopedia of Unified Science,* begun in 1938. The advisory boards of these last two publications read like a who's who in science and philosophy. It would be a passionate optimist, however, who would expect such a band of hardy individualists to be entirely of one mind. Many of them have not yet spoken.

language, and it is the business of the scientist to apply the formal symbolic model to the observable world in such a way that the concepts he generates will satisfy the rules of operational criticism.

Elementary as these notions may appear, the development of their implications has commanded the interest of both tough- and tenderminded. The movement has proved disastrous for metaphysics, challenging for logic, and salutary for science. Philosophers and scientists in essential agreement are astonishing enough, but here we have them pleading for a common method. In this strange harmony we are witnessing the birth of a new discipline: the Science of Science. It is a triumph for self-consciousness. The science-makers are asking themselves how they make science and are turning on that problem the powerful empirical weapons of science itself; while at the same time a tough-minded outcropping among the philosophers is carefully combing the metaphysics out of logic in order to investigate more easily the common linguistic structure of science. In this quest the philosophers, like the scientists, resort to empirical methods. Witness the spirit of philosophy as exemplified by Nagel (44):

It is difficult for me to take seriously the various attempts made historically by philosophers to legislate to the sciences just what they can and cannot investigate . . . on the basis of a deductive theory of mind and nature. . . . Furthermore, it seems to me an integral character of skilled workmanship to insist upon the fact that no statement or proposal has any meaning apart from the methods which are or may be employed to establish or execute them.

In succeeding pages we shall see how operationism, beginning at one end in the laboratories of scientists, evolved an enterprise coördinate with that of Logical Positivism, Physicalism, and Scientific Empiricism which, beginning at the other end in the armchairs of philosophers, settled on the problem of the proper scientific use of logic. And we shall see how the natural issue of this mating came to make up the unifying principles of the Science of Science. We shall see how this movement concords with "behavioristics," which is a behavioristic psychology tuned up to keep pace with a fast-moving logical criticism. And finally, we shall see what the impact of this movement means for some specific problems in psychology, and what is indicated as the future rôle of psychology in this scheme.

Operationism

Ten years ago Professor Bridgman, the expert on high-pressure phenomena, wrote a book [2] called *The logic of modern physics* (11). It has been judged an excellent book, animated by the single idea that "in general, we mean by any concept nothing more than a set of operations; *the concept is synonymous with the corresponding set of operations.*" This dictum stands forth in what many have found to be objectionable nakedness, but, throughout more than 200 well-stocked pages, Bridgman demonstrates what he means by analyzing the operational meaning of the basic concepts of physics. There is nothing rationally a priori in his method (at least he honestly *tries* to exclude metaphysics). His introductory confession is: "The material of this essay is largely obtained by observation of the actual currents of opinion in physics." In this empirical spirit he observes the behavior of his colleagues and finds that what is considered an *explanation* "consists in reducing a situation to elements with which we are so familiar that we accept them as a matter of course, so that our curiosity rests." The reduction of the "situation" is made in terms of operations, but do we thereby arrive at exact and certain knowledge? No. "We never have perfectly clean-cut knowledge of anything, but all our experience is surrounded by a twilight zone, a penumbra of uncertainty, into which we have not yet penetrated," and consequently "no empirical science can ever make exact statements." The degree to which any of the laws of science wear the penumbrous halo can be told only by inspecting the operations which the laws are intended to generalize.

Bridgman's book is rich in example but poor in precept. That its author has occasionally been misunderstood has perhaps been due largely to this fact. The book gives numerous examples of operational method without prescribing explicitly what operational method is; it talks of "operations" without giving an explicit definition of the term; and it discourses on natural laws without pointing out how we get from particular operations to generalizations. In short, it is a thoroughly inductive enterprise, and the reader is often allowed to make the induction by himself. Nevertheless, the spirit of the book is unmistakable and its message is simple and powerful.

Philosophers rose to protest, or sometimes to defend, the notion of

[2] For additional comments on some of the books and papers cited in this review see the "Bibliography." [In the original publication.—Ed.]

"operational meaning" because it assures the automatic elimination of even the choicest propositions of metaphysics: "If a specific question has meaning," says Bridgman, "it must be possible to find operations by which an answer may be given to it." No operations, no meaning! And so, as we have said, philosophers, and others, rose to protest. Finally, the pressure pushed Bridgman temporarily from his Harvard laboratory and on to the lecture platform at Princeton where he spoke what became another book: *The nature of physical theory* (13).

To say that this second book pleased all who were disciples of the first book is perhaps not quite true. The author had been able to say in his first book that fortunately he would "be able to get along with a more or less naïve attitude toward" psychology and epistemology, but in his second work he boldly lays hold on thought, language, and experience. Bridgman's discussion of these concepts was what the world had been waiting for, but once out of the well-charted sea of physics and adrift in epistemology, the author's bark, if we are to believe the critics, appears to have lost its rudder. One cannot avoid the impression that criticism of this second book has been of unmerited severity, but perhaps severe criticism is what must be expected by a man who challenges us with issues as vital as those proposed by Professor Bridgman. Objection has been made to such statements as: "In the last analysis science is only my private science." "What," asks editor Malisoff (35), "can an operationist mean by a 'last analysis'?" Bridgman says his purpose in sailing the epistemological waters is "to map out the possibilities and limitations of the human mind in dealing with the problems presented to it." "Our complaint," criticizes A. F. Bentley (6), "is not that he makes this inquiry, but that in it he employs all the bad devices he had ejected from physics." Some of his devices are assertions crutched on such terms as "essentially," "absolutely," and "intuitively." Nevertheless, Bridgman's critics agree that his discernment in physics remains as fine as ever—he is still simple and hardheaded. In physics he is an operationist, and it is in physics that we should judge him, if we are to presume to do so.

Just as Bridgman had set out to apply and make explicit the principles by which Einstein shattered the physicist's notion of the absolute, so did others seize upon the opportunity to try out these principles in other fields. Psychologists, long self-conscious of their own self-consciousness, were particularly alert to this budding self-inspection on the part of the modern masters of physics. If the physicists could examine the methods of their science-making and evolve helpful principles, perhaps psychologists could do likewise. Such, at least, was the attitude of those who were happy to confess blindness to any fundamental dichotomy between the methods of psychology and physics.

Operationism in Psychology

But psychology is more difficult than physics—at least psychologists often find it easier to get themselves into a mess in their field than physicists do in theirs. Of course, when the physicist strays into psychology, the result is apt to restore the psychologist's ego-level, but if the physicist fumbles it only serves to show that when doing open-field running among psychological concepts the critic must hold the ball more tightly. In view of the difficulty of keeping a grip on the operational principle, it is not surprising to find evidence of dissension among the psychological apologists [Professor Bills (7) calls them "apostles"]. In spite of much scattered writing, the case for operationism in psychology has perhaps never been adequately briefed, but a few of its consequences have been made explicit, and some interesting applications have appeared.

We all remember Tolman's *Purposive behavior in animals and men* (61). Whatever dismay we may have felt at the superabundance of his glossary, the fact remains that in coining the words of his new language he appealed most directly and explicitly to experimental operations. The book is a monument in the methodology of definition. In much the same spirit, Professor Tolman has more recently prepared for us "an operational analysis of 'demands'" (62). In his own field of expertness we find McGeoch making a critical inquiry into the possibility of "learning as an operationally defined concept" (38). Boring treats of "temporal perception and operationism" (10) in a short, poignant demonstration of how a classical problem turns out to be specious when its defining operations are made explicit. Seashore and Katz propose to bring order to the chaotic discipline of abnormal psychology by "an operational definition and classification of mental mechanisms" (55). Lundberg, the sociologist, would do the same for the social sciences by replacing spineless intuitionism by "quantitative methods in social psychology" (34), the foundation for which would be concepts operationally defined. And finally, Kantor examines "the operational principle in the physical and psychological sciences" (30) and concludes that the principle, properly enlarged, can be employed to the psychologists' advantage. Now, these are not all of those who have taken notice of Bridgman's proposals. Nor do all these commentators see eye to eye with Bridgman or with each other regarding certain fundamentals. Furthermore, it is becoming alarmingly obvious that the phrases "operationally defined" and "operationally sound" are acquiring the sort of positive valence which leads to their being bandied about in indiscriminate fashion by writers who suppose that they can meet the operational test by announcing good intentions. Operationism is being threatened by its friends—largely, perhaps, because of the inherent difficulty of making a rigorous formulation of it.

What, then, are we to understand by operationism? All that any one man can do is to present his own version, and this I did in a series of articles in 1935 and 1936 (57, 58, 59). There are some points there which invite revision, but, in general, the sins appear to be those of omission. The statement there needs expansion, but obviously this review is not the place for it. A résumé is more in order.

First, however, it must be emphasized again that the development of operational principles is properly an empirical undertaking. What do the science-makers do? What methodology has the maximum survival value? When do propositions have empirical validity? In short, operational principles are induced generalizations rather than a priori fiats. They are therefore subject to the usual hazards and uncertainty of inductive propositions. This empirical aspect of operational criticism has never been sufficiently stressed, and it is not surprising that operationists have sometimes been regarded as self-appointed legislators who try to prescribe rather than discover.

These, then, are some of the generalizations which I propose as verifiable:

1. Science, as we find it, is a set of empirical propositions agreed upon by members of society. This agreement may be always in a state of flux, but persistent disagreement leads eventually to rejection. Bridgman does not agree to this social criterion of knowledge and it was against this notion that he aimed a part of his Princeton lectures (13). We must ask him, however, to produce the negative case. A physical law to which only Bridgman agreed would not be a part of physics— not, at least, until he won converts, and then there would be agreement.

2. Only those propositions based upon operations which are public and repeatable are admitted to the body of science. Not even psychology

knows anything about private experience, because an operation for penetrating privacy is self-contradictory.

3. What becomes acceptable psychology accrues only when all observations, including those which a psychologist makes upon himself, are treated as though made upon "the other one." Thus, we make explicit the distinction between the experimenter and the thing observed. This distinction is obvious in physics; in psychology it is equally valid.

4. Although a particular experimenter may himself become the object of study by another experimenter, and he in turn by still another, at some stage of such a regress an independent experimenter *must be* (i.e., is always) assumed. The recognition of this "experimenter-regress" unravels many knots in psychology.

5. A term denotes something only when there are concrete criteria for its applicability; and a proposition has empirical meaning only when the criteria of its truth or falsity consist of concrete operations which can be performed upon demand.

6. When we attempt to reduce complex operations to simpler and simpler ones, we find in the end that discrimination, or differential response, is the fundamental operation. Discrimination is prerequisite even to the operation of denoting or "pointing to," because whenever two people reduce their complex operations for the purpose of reaching agreement or understanding, they find that unless they can each discriminate the same simple objects or read the same scales they still will not agree. Agreement is usually reached in practice before these most elementary operations are appealed to.

7. There are two types of propositions: *formal* and *empirical*. The formal propositions are arrays of symbols without empirical reference. They are language, mathematics, and logic *as such*. Empirical propositions are those in which these arrays of symbols have been identified with observable events. Sometimes the two types of propositions intermingle and trouble results. For avoiding the obscurity of pseudo problems this distinction between the formal, syntactical model (symbols) and the operations for which it is made to stand is of prime importance. Hypotheses, for example, can be only formal statements—operationally empty—until they are demonstrated (see Appendix II).* Within the formal realm we speak sometimes of mathematical operations, but here we mean the manipulation of symbols carried out according to certain conventional rules. These are not the operations of operationism.

* In the original publication.—Ed.

Although we shall have more to say later about the contrast between the formal and the empirical, at this point we might do well to see how history occasionally sets them off from one another and thereby emphasizes their distinctive natures. Historically, the algebra of complex numbers (numbers of the form $x+iy$, where x and y are real numbers and i is the square root of -1) was developed from the purest of purely mathematical motives. The rules for the manipulation of these numbers (their addition, multiplication, division, etc.) were worked out in conformity with the conventional laws of ordinary algebra and interesting relations were discovered. Gauss, for example, set a landmark in algebra by proving that every algebraic equation in 1 unknown has a root and that all roots of such equations are complex numbers (see Bell, 2, p. 232). In Gauss's time these numbers were simply abstract symbols which could be combined according to the rules of the game we call algebra. They proved nothing about the empirical world or about science: they constituted, as they still do, a purely *formal* system. Then, with the advent of alternating electric currents, came also the need for a simple, effective "model" to represent electric circuits; and the electrical engineers discovered that if they let x stand for resistance, iy for inductive reactance, and $-iy$ for capacitative reactance, they could manipulate these symbols according to the rules of complex algebra and obtain new combinations of the symbols which they could then identify with some measurable aspect of an electric circuit. In other words, this formal system was found useful as a model, and out of its utility has grown the modern intricate theory of alternating currents. Therefore, when we can identify these complex numbers with various aspects of a circuit, we can say that the propositions containing these symbols are *empirical* propositions, testable by concrete operations.

These seven bald assertions about operationism are perhaps too brief to be convincing, but they may recommend the fuller development in the three papers already referred to. In the meantime we might profit by considering what operationism is not—still, of course, in only one man's opinion. Misunderstandings have been numerous and many of them could have been headed off had someone signaled what is nonoperational. Let us, then, look at a few of operationism's contrasts.

What Operationism Is Not

1. It is obviously not a new school of psychology. Rosenzweig (53) presented an admirable argument to show that the schools of psychology

are really more complementary than antagonistic, but he was worried about operationism. He should stop worrying.

2. It is not a set of rules telling how to be a bright and original scientist. It does not even tell how experiments should be carried out. It has no precepts. At the risk of breeding disappointment we must say of operationism, as James (29) said of pragmatism, that, "at the outset, at least, it stands for no particular results. It has no dogmas, and no doctrines save its method." Furthermore, its method is one which is applied *after* the scientific proposition has been made: it provides criteria for determining whether what *has been* said is empirically meaningful. In short, it tests inventions, but does not tell how to invent.

3. It is not opposed to hypotheses, theories, or speculation. It seeks merely to discover criteria by which these things may be detected and labeled. It is not opposed to poetry, art, or religion. It wants only to know the difference between these things and science. It wants to know under what conditions the consorting of science with metaphysics breeds pseudo problems. Scientists as people may be opposed to pseudo problems, but operationism's business, as a principle of criticism, is to discover them.

4. It is not a guarantee of agreement as to tastes or theories, but it points out how agreement as to facts is achieved by men capable of making the same fundamental discriminations. Operationism wants, most of all, to discover the bases of such agreement. What are the procedures which compel agreement among those engaged in open-minded pursuit of science? As to compelling agreement on tastes—that is probably a job in applied eugenics.

5. It is not positivism. The blemish on positivism was that in its reaction against rational metaphysics it pretended to base *everything* in science on experience. Operationism, however, acknowledges the rôle of the rational methods of mathematics and logic—formal disciplines which do not appeal to experience for verification, but only to conventions. Science uses these formal systems as models for representing its data. To deny them is to cure the disease by burying the patient.

When it is a matter of the significance of *empirical* rather than of *formal* propositions, needless to say, operationism adopts an uncompromising positivistic attitude.

6. It is not behaviorism. Like positivism, behaviorism erred in denying too much. Operationism does not deny images, for example, but asks: What is the operational definition of the term "image"? Of course

there are different behaviorisms, and some of the renovated brands are truly operational. Tolman (63) has a variety which he dubs explicitly "operational behaviorism"—and perhaps it is. It is certain that the behavioristic emphasis has served capably in blasting a path through subjectivity, and without this path an objective Science of Science could not march.

7. It is not monism. It asks only whether any operational meaning can be given the proposition that there is but one irreducible substance or attribute. Can the truth or falsity of this proposition be put to experimental test? If not, we face a pseudo problem.

8. It is not dualism. Here again the problems raised are pseudo problems, because the propositions are not testable. As Bills (7) so aptly says, "Parallelism would automatically reduce to a double-aspect formula, because where two sets of defining operations coincide perfectly they become identical operationally." Of course there can be no quarrel, except on the grounds of utility, with any arbitrary dividing or classifying of facts, but pseudo problems can be avoided only provided we remember that these classes are arbitrary.

The division of concepts into the categories of subjective and objective is justifiable—if at all—only on pragmatic grounds, and only *provided* both types of concept answer the operational test. Bills believes that "mentalistic" concepts like percept, image, and idea can be operationally defined. So do I. Kantor, however, is disturbed. He detects dualism. But Bills "cannot agree with Kantor that there is any necessary dualism implied in Stevens' position." Neither can Stevens. If we admit to our store of empirical science only those concepts which are operationally founded, can we not classify them according to our purposes?

Kantor (30) would appear to supplant dualism with a kind of realism. Now, realism is a metaphysical doctrine, and perhaps Kantor did not intend a realism. Nevertheless, he appears to defend the proposition: Nature is not the same as our knowledge of nature. Operationism must here again pose its perhaps tiresome, but necessary, question: Can any operations be formulated which will either prove or disprove this proposition? If not, it is operationally meaningless, however much "emotional meaning" it may pack.

9. Finally, operationism is not pluralism. It should be apparent by now that operationism is not consonant with any "ism" which asserts something about the ultimate nature of reality.

The Problem of Generality

There is one more criticism we must take seriously before we continue. It has been urged that operationism reduces to a vicious particularism; that there is no provision for generalization; that instead of unification in science a strict servility to the operational principle nourishes an ever-expanding multiplicity of concepts. Here is what the critics say:

Margenau, in "Causality in modern physics" (36), which he addressed to the philosophers, states that operationism "cannot be tolerated as a general directive. For, in the first place, it would, if carried to its consequences, dissolve the world into an unmanageable variety of discrete concepts without logical coherence."

Lindsay, in "A critique of operationalism in physics" (32), says: ". . . logically the operational method . . . implies that each concept is tied to a definite operation."

Lindsay and Margenau together, in their book, *Foundations of physics* (33)—a book which has brought them merited high praise—state: "On the basis of purely operational definitions, all concepts are strictly empirical and isolated" (p. 412).

Bills, in his excellent address on "Changing views of psychology as science" (7), says: "One of the ideals of scientific concept-makers is to reduce all concepts to a few fundamental ones. . . . Yet this is not, by any means, the likely outcome of operationally defined concepts. . . . For there is no universal set of operations."

Waters and Pennington, in their careful criticism of "Operationism in psychology" (64), assert: "The fact that the concept, for Bridgman, is *synonymous* with a corresponding set of operations cannot be overemphasized. The slightest change in any aspect of a set of operations would mean, therefore, a new concept and would demand, likewise, a new symbol for its designation. A multiplicity of concepts could scarcely be avoided."

Since Bentley (the critic, not the psychologist), in his flashy tirade on "Physicists and fairies" (6), has a point to make here, we will let him speak first. He refers to Lindsay and Margenau when he says: "By distorting Bridgman grossly enough, either man can, of course, readily destroy what he has distorted. Both men distort alike; first by insisting 'operations' must be all hands and no mind; second by alleging that no operation in this world can have anything to do with any other operation, not even with its own repetitions of itself."

Whether there is distortion or not, the fact that so many have pounced on this supposed snare in operationism means that the rules and procedure for generalizing from operations must sometime be made explicit. These rules obviously can be stated, because science does generalize, and operationism seeks only to discover how scientists do what they do.

The process of generalization proceeds on the basis of the notion of classes. All objects or events satisfying certain criteria we call members of a class and to that class we assign a name or symbol. Common nouns originate in precisely this fashion, and it is apparent at once that no empirical proposition is ever without some element of generality. Classification can proceed only when we have criteria defining the conditions for class-inclusion, and these criteria are essentially operational tests. Thus the statement, "Dobbin is a horse," asserts that Dobbin is a member of a class. This proposition is empirically meaningful only provided its truth or falsity can be demonstrated by concrete procedures. Does Dobbin satisfy the criteria of the class, *horse?* If he is a certain size and shape, is covered with hair, feeds on oats and hay, etc., we are happy to acknowledge him as a full-fledged horse. But how do we know he meets our tests? Here we resort to that fundamental operation we have already called discrimination. If we can discriminate crucial differences between Dobbin and other animals we have named horses, we reject Dobbin as something not horse. In other words, we "correlate" our discriminations—those made on Dobbin with those made on other objects—and the "goodness" of the correlation determines where we shall classify the beast.

It may be objected that we can always tell Dobbin from other horses, i.e., discriminate differences, but we still would resent the suggestion that he is not a horse. The answer is that a certain latitude is always allowed—we seldom resort to j.n.d.'s in a case like this—and the amount of the latitude determines the precision of the concept. As Bridgman has insisted, no concept is without its halo of uncertainty, its penumbra. No empirical class is ever watertight; we can always plague the taxonomist with the borderline case.

On the basis of elementary discriminations, then, we make our first rudimentary classes and in doing so we have made the first step toward generalization. From there we advance to form classes of classes [3] and to discover the relations between classes—always, at the empirical level, in keeping with operational criteria. Occasionally we find that from a certain point of view two classes satisfy the same criteria, or are related by a simple law, so that we are enabled to combine them into a more inclusive class under a more generic tag. Nevertheless, in all of these classifications and combinations the same simple rule is followed: We combine operations when they satisfy the criteria of a class; and the concept of that class is defined by the operations which determine inclusion within the class.

The matter can be illustrated by referring again to that example which appears to have been the jumping-off place for the critics: the concept of length. Bridgman's argument is that we measure the length of the table and the distance to a star by two different sets of operations and we have, therefore, two different concepts of length. True enough. And Bridgman proceeds thence to show that when dealing with very large distances or very minute ones, or with distances where velocities are involved, we do well to keep in mind the differences in our defining operations. However, in his concern for the perils of promiscuous class-matings he forgot to tell us when combining is legitimate. Length measured with a rod is different from length measured with a transit, but under certain statable conditions we can muster operations to determine the relation of these two sets of measurements, and, if they meet the proper criteria, we combine them to form a larger class defining length. Of course, if we had no operations for comparing the two lengths, we should have to veto their combination. In short, then, we can and do generalize the concept length, but we do it with operational sanction.

The Philosophical Movement

Just ten years ago, the year Bridgman published his *Logic of modern physics,* there appeared in Vienna a company of scholars bound together by mutual admiration and a common *Weltauffassung*—a scientific philosophy. Their discussions under the leadership of Professor Schlick accomplished a unitary enthusiasm which came to concrete

---

[3] This *empirical* process of forming classes of classes should not be confused with the *logic* of classes, in which the provision for an infinite hierarchy of classes led to the antinomies discovered by Russell. The empirical process has no *necessary* relation to a formal system of logic.

form in the organization of *Der Wiener Kreis*.[4] The avowed intention of this "Circle" was to replace philosophy by the systematic investigation of the logic of science which, for Carnap, is "nothing other than the logical syntax of the language of science." There are but two kinds of acceptable propositions: *formal* and *empirical*. Formal propositions concern syntax. They state the rules and procedure for combining words or symbols and have no empirical reference. Empirical propositions are assertions about the observable world and their truth or falsity can be tested by means of observational procedures. Since metaphysics consists of statements not susceptible to empirical test, it is either an array of syntactical (formal) sentences or else it is technical nonsense. Mostly it is nonsense. Philosophy must be purged of it; and, once purged, it becomes the business of philosophy, says the Circle, to investigate the rules of the language we use in formulating our scientific propositions. The goal of such philosophical research is to provide a secure foundation for the sciences.

This movement was not, of course, without its antecedents. Its most immediate point of departure was the famous *Tractatus logico-philo-*

[4] Some of the members of the Vienna Circle follow:

Moritz Schlick (1882–1936) fathered the group. Under his professorial paternalism the Circle met, discussed, and found its unity. (Schlick's unfortunate death, at the hand of a crazed student, occurred as he was climbing the steps of the lecture hall.)

Otto Neurath (b. 1882) contributed his own brand of enthusiastic originality. His spirited support of radical new theses provided important inspiration. Neurath coined the designations "Physicalism" and "Unity of Science."

Rudolph Carnap (b. 1891) labored with the problem of syntax—the logical rules of language. His energetic attack on the problem of the actual construction of a fundamental syntax for the "physical" language has created a whole new field of inquiry.

Philipp Frank (b. 1884), a theoretical physicist, applied the new theory of knowledge to the problems of physics.

Hans Hahn (1879–1934), a mathematician, investigated the foundations of mathematics and exact science in the light of the scientific *Weltauffassung* of the Circle.

Friedrich Waismann distinguished himself with an investigation of the logical foundations of mathematical thinking.

In addition to these members of the Vienna Circle there were other groups whose scientific philosophy was so similar as to be scarcely distinguishable. In fact, one of the impressive aspects of this recent philosophical movement is the manner in which a common *Weltauffassung* appeared almost simultaneously among widely scattered groups of scientists, mathematicians, and philosophers. There was the Warsaw Circle, which boasted such able logicians as Tarski (b. 1901) and Lukasiewicz (b. 1878). At Berlin, prior to the recent cultural eclipse, there was another Circle whose outstanding advocate was Reichenbach (b. 1891). Logicians Russell (b. 1872) and Frege (1848–1925) fall into the same tradition, and in America C. W. Morris (b. 1901) is perhaps the best known expositor of the common program. For a more complete listing of names, see Neurath's "Historische Anmerkungen" (45).

sophicus (66) by Russell's pupil, Ludwig Wittgenstein. The "Tractus" exhibited the close connection between philosophy and syntax; it made clear the *formal* nature of logic and showed that the rules and proofs of syntax should have no reference to the meaning (empirical designation) of symbols; and it showed that the sentences of metaphysics are pseudo propositions. But the roots of these notions can be traced even back beyond Wittgenstein. All who, like the positivists, struck out at metaphysics; all who, like Kant, sought to conciliate analytic (formal) methods with the synthetic (empirical); and all who, like the British empiricists, assaulted philosophy with logical weapons have something in common with the Vienna Circle. Hume, in particular, except when he was assuming the existence of a transempirical world, caught the spirit. He winds up his "Enquiries concerning human understanding" (28) with this counsel:

If we take in our hand any volume; of divinity or school metaphysics, for instance; let us ask, *Does it contain any abstract reasoning concerning quantity or number* [formal questions]? No. *Does it contain any experimental reasoning concerning matter of fact and existence* [empirical questions]? No. Commit it then to the flames: for it can contain nothing but sophistry and illusion.

A philosophy as distinctive as that of the Vienna Circle must inevitably become an "ism," and its disciples, Blumberg and Feigl (8), lost no time in introducing the Circle's program to American scholars under the title of "Logical Positivism." A. F. Bentley (5) promptly raised the question as to whether Logical Positivism is either logical or positive, but in spite of some obvious disadvantages, the name is not entirely unreasonable. Bentley, as his readers know, loves a *bon mot* and has a low threshold for alarm—he is aroused to criticism easily but not unpleasantly. The name Logical Positivism quite properly suggests the union of the formal and the empirical—a union which, in a well-ordered scientific household, is possible and legitimate.

Logical Positivism proposes to tell us how such a household should be run. A certain division of labor is required. The scientist, in his special field, continues to investigate the empirical relations among the variables he has at hand and these relations he represents by some form of symbolic language. The philosopher complements the scientist by probing the nature and the rules of this symbolic language. Statements about the empirical domain are called object-sentences; statements about language-forms are syntactical sentences. In any special science, such as psychology, both types of sentences frequently occur, because the psychologist must tell us not only about his facts, but also how he intends to use his words and symbols—he must provide his own definitions (see Appendix I).* The philosopher, on the other hand, can point out the logical implications of the psychologist's language and help him guard against the vicious combinations of the two types of sentences which lead to pseudo propositions.

Under this program it is not, however, the task of the philosopher to legislate for science. Science can use any logic it finds useful. Carnap (22), at this point, proposes a Principle of Tolerance to allay our fears: "It is not our business," he says, "to set up prohibitions, but to arrive at conventions." *"In logic,"* he continues, *"there are no morals.* Everyone is at liberty to build up his own logic, i.e., his own form of language, as he wishes. All that is required of him is that, if he wishes to discuss it, he must state his methods clearly, and give syntactical rules instead of philosophical arguments." Consequently, he who sets out to scrutinize the logic of science must renounce the proud claim that his philosophy sits enthroned above the special sciences. He works in the same field as the specialist, only with a different emphasis. He ponders the logical, formal, syntactical connections. He studies rules which are basically nothing other than conventions and matters of free choice. Hence the labors of the philosopher in that which is his only legitimate domain, the logic of science, are bound to be barren unless they are pursued in close coöperation with the special sciences.

Logical Positivism, then, seeks 1) to clarify the language of science, and 2) to investigate the conditions under which empirical propositions are meaningful. The language of science (including syntax, logic, and mathematics) consists of arrays of words or symbols which we assemble according to certain rules. The analytic propositions of syntax and mathematics are absolutely necessary and certain, once the rules of the game have been laid down. These propositions neither tell us anything about the empirical world, nor can they be confuted by experience. They can no more be proved "true" than can the conventional rules of the game of chess (see below). They simply record our determination to use words and symbols in a certain fashion.

Mathematics, under this view, is a completely rational and deductive system and nothing is contained in one formula which is not implicit in all formulas. This, to many, is a fearful thought. Poincaré (48) voiced

---

* In the original publication.—Ed.

his apprehension by asking: "If all the propositions it enunciates can be deduced one from the other by the rules of formal logic, why is not mathematics reduced to an immense tautology? . . . Shall we admit that the theorems which fill so many volumes are nothing but devious ways of saying that A is A?" The answer appears to be that regardless of how inventive mathematical discoveries may appear to be, they contain nothing not already implicit in the fundamental postulates of the system. The outcome of our symbol-juggling surprises and delights us and fills us with the illusion of discovery, simply because of the limitations of our minds. A man of sufficient intellect would disdain the use of logic and mathematics, for he would see at a glance all that his postulates and definitions implied. He would be aware of all possible discoveries under the rules. The rest of us, however, must continue to do our mathematics stepwise, proceeding from one tautological transformation to the next, and being surprised at the result.

The second aim of Logical Positivism—to discover the conditions of empirical meaning—leads to the notion that an object-sentence is one which is verifiable by means of some concrete procedure. At this point operationism and Logical Positivism are essentially indistinguishable and we shall say no more about them, except to note an error.

This is an error which the Logical Positivists themselves have acknowledged and corrected (cf. Carnap, 21, p. 11), but since the slip was made in what is commonly regarded as psychological territory, we had best have a look at it. The Vienna Circle committed the all too common fallacy: It claimed to find a difference between *knowledge* and *immediate experience* (see Blumberg and Feigl, 8). Knowledge is communicable, but the immediately given is private and noncommunicable. This from the mouth of a Logical Positivist! Indeed, by all the rules they have proposed, this sentence is not a testable proposition, for how shall we demonstrate the existence of the noncommunicable? But, as already indicated, the Logical Positivists have not been stubborn about insisting that it makes sense to talk of the private content of immediate experience as being different from the discriminable and reportable relations between experiences. Their past lapse in this regard is interesting only because it shows how easy it is for even the well-intentioned to talk nonsense when they invade this field of psychology. In "The operational definition of psychological concepts" (58) I have tried to demonstrate that an empirical (operational) definition of immediate experience is

possible provided we note precisely what its advocates do when we ask
them to indicate an example of it. Almost invariably they point to a
situation involving an elementary discrimination such as: "I see red."
Elementary discriminations, then, are what is meant by the immediately
given, and discriminatory reactions, of course, are public and communicable.

Physicalism

As thoroughgoing empiricists the Logical Positivists hold that all
meaningful scientific propositions are derived from experience. More
precisely, all such propositions are reducible to *protocol-sentences*—
sentences relating to the simplest elements of experience. This notion,
I take it, is equivalent to the operationist's view that complex propositions are shown to be meaningful when they can be reduced to simpler
propositions for which there are operational tests. The simplest propositions of all would be those relating to elementary discriminations.
Now, if all scientific propositions are reducible in this fashion, including propositions expressed in what is called *physical language,* it must
follow that *all* propositions are translatable into the physical language
—a language similar to that of contemporary physics. This is the thesis
of Physicalism.[5]

Physicalism was christened by Neurath (cf. 46). Contrary to what
the name suggests, it is not a metaphysical doctrine asserting that everything is physical, for such a proposition can have no testable meaning.
It is, on the other hand, a thesis relating to language: The physical
language is a universal language of science and the individual languages
used in any subdomain of science can be equipollently translated into
the physical language. Innocent as this assertion about language may
appear, it is charged with far-reaching implications for psychology. In
fact, the examples used to illustrate Physicalism make it appear that

[5] This is a somewhat oversimplified statement of Physicalism. Furthermore, Carnap
(21) has recently introduced extensive qualifications and changes into the original views
of the Vienna Circle regarding the relation of the various "languages" of science. His
reasons for preferring the physical to the psychological language (pp. 9 ff.) do not appear to me to be binding, especially if the psychological language is made operational.
If that is done, the choice becomes one based on convention or convenience. We could
express all physics in psychological language, but that would be more traumatic to tradition than if we were to express all psychology in the physical language. The name
Physicalism justifiably appeals to many as an unhappy designation, because it arouses
prejudices by suggesting the primacy of a materialistic physics.

the doctrine was aimed directly against psychology—at least against the kind peddled by philosophers.

Physicalism makes it clear that the traditional but somewhat antiquated problem of psychophysical dualism is exclusively a problem of syntax. Using the common "material mode" of speech we might say: To every psychical state there is a corresponding physical state of the body and the two are lawfully connected. Couched in this form, such a sentence is a veritable gold mine for pseudo problems. Physicalism would throttle these problems by saying: All sentences purporting to deal with psychical states are translatable into sentences in the physical language. Two distinctly separate languages to describe physics and psychology are therefore not necessary. And in this assertion we have Physicalism's denial of metaphysical dualism. It is the Logical Positivist's way of saying that psychology must be operational and behavioristic.

The philosopher, Hempel (27), calls this kind of psychology *logical behaviorism*. It differs from the primitive American stamp in that it does not prescribe that research shall be limited to stimulus-response connections. It is not, properly speaking, a theory *about psychology* at all, but only a logical theory about psychological sentences. The psychologist may study anything he pleases, but any verifiable psychological proposition he may utter is equivalent to some proposition in the physical language. An operationist would certainly agree to this notion. In fact, an operationist would point out that this view is correlative with his own dictum that any meaningful psychological proposition, even though it pertains to a toothache, is reducible to public, concrete operations.

The Unity of Science

How we get from Physicalism to the thesis of the *unity of science* is obvious indeed. If every sentence can be translated into the physical language, then this language is an all-inclusive language—a universal language of science. And if the esoteric jargons of all the separate sciences can, upon demand, be reduced to a single coherent language, then all science possesses a fundamental logical unity.

This idea of a unified basis for science, introduced into the Vienna Circle by the imaginative originality of Neurath, has launched a whole new movement in scientific philosophy. The newly-begun *International Encyclopedia of Unified Science* is tangible testimony to the vigor and

seriousness of the enterprise.[6] Annual congresses provide a forum where
the thesis is developed (Fifth Annual Congress to be held at Harvard
University, September 5-10, 1939); and out of this intellectual ferment
there is emerging a substantial basis for an empirical and universal
Science of Science. But before we inspect this newest of sciences—one
which is obviously still warm in the womb of its philosophy-mother—
let us look backward a few centuries.

How many men, since ancient Thales proposed that all is water,
have dreamed the dream of a universal science is beyond a guess. The
dream has taken many forms—mostly impracticable—for the history of
science is a story of diversification and specialization proceeding almost
geometrically with time. If there is unity in so much arborescence, where
are we to find it? Certainly not in subject matter where differentiation
is the rule. Perhaps, then, in method and logic.

In 1666 the twenty-year-old Leibnitz (2) dreamed his own dream
about the unity of science and recorded it in *De Arte Combinatoria.*
He himself called it a schoolboy's essay, but in it he proposed to create
*"a general method in which all truths of reason would be reduced to a
kind of calculation. At the same time this would be a sort of universal
language or script, but infinitely different from those projected hitherto;
for the symbols and even the words in it would direct the reason; and
errors, except those of fact, would be mere mistakes in calculation."*
How long would it take to create this logistic? Leibnitz thought a few
chosen men could turn the trick within five years. But chosen men were

---

[6] Neurath (47) describes *unified science* as *encyclopedic integration.* The new
"Encyclopedia" is to be constructed like an onion. The heart of the onion will be two
introductory volumes consisting of twenty pamphlets, and in these volumes will be
laid the foundations for a logical unity which will make possible future integration of
scientific disciplines. The first layer of the onion enclosing the heart will be a series of
volumes to deal with problems of systematization in special sciences, including logic,
mathematics, the theory of signs, history of science, classification of the sciences, and
the educational implications of the scientific attitude. Still outer layers will concern even
more specialized problems. The encyclopedia will not be an alphabetical dictionary and
its creators hope, quite piously, that it will not become a mausoleum but remain a
living intellectual force.

At the present writing only three numbers (1, 2, and 5) of the "Encyclopedia" have
appeared, but it is already clear that, although there is great community among the
contributors, detailed unanimity is absent. As to the problem of unity in science, for
example, Carnap finds as yet *no unity of laws* in science, but only *unity of language;*
Lenzen finds a basis for unity in the fact that all science starts from experience; Neurath
would get his unity by means of *encyclopedic integration;* Russell says the unity is
essentially one of method; and Dewey hopes for unity by promulgating what he calls
the scientific attitude.

not at hand and two centuries passed before the creation of a universal symbolic logic was even begun. Almost another century of labor has been needed to lay a foundation in logic and syntax so tangible that many men together could vision the unity of science.

Leibnitz, though, if any single man, was father to the idea. He hoped for a universal logicalization of human thinking by means of a general calculus and a general terminology. He conceived a formal discipline to include a theory and art of forming signs to represent ideas and a general calculus giving a universal formal method of drawing consequences from the signs. Then, if two men were to find themselves in disagreement as to anything except matters of observation, they would settle their argument by calculating the right answer. Leibnitz' inspiration is perhaps not without its utopian aspect, but it cannot be denied that the modern logic of science has made progress towards Leibnitz' goal.

Perhaps our progress has not always been of the sort that would have delighted the boy of twenty, for metaphysics was no triviality in 1666. Today, however, it is clear that the unhappy symphonies of pseudo propositions that are metaphysics have all too frequently thwarted our efforts at clarification. Logical analysis has unmasked metaphysics; at least that is one of the boasted achievements of the recent philosophical movement. Opinion will probably never be unanimous on this issue, but disclosure of the empirically meaningless aspects of metaphysics is intimately bound to the other advances claimed by the Logical Positivists. By way of review at this point, these are some of the achievements of the modern movement:

1. It has been demonstrated that a unified language of science is possible. The syntax of this language is to be discovered by careful analysis of linguistic usage in science. And what unity there is in science is to be found in the unity of its logic and syntax.

2. Linguistic analysis has revealed the all-important distinction between the *formal* and the *empirical* aspects of science. Formal science consists of the analytic statements established by logic and mathematics; empirical science consists of the synthetic statements established in the different fields of factual knowledge.

3. The statements of logic and mathematics derive their validity from conventions, and, from the point of view of empiricism, they are materially empty and constitute a closed system of tautologies. Logic deals with language only—not with the objects of language. Likewise,

mathematics deals with symbols—not with the objects which the symbols represent.

4. Empirical propositions have meaning when there exists a concrete procedure (a set of operations) for determining their truth or falsity. Empirical significance attaches only to testable or confirmable sentences.

5. What we have called the "truth" of an empirical proposition is something which can never be absolute. Repeated tests of an object-sentence can add to its probability but never clinch its certainty. Induction, as Hume pointed out, is not a watertight method of proving anything empirical.

6. The notion that all scientific sentences are translatable into a common form—the physical language—requires of psychology a behavioristic approach. Psychology so conceived is called *behavioristics*.

These alleged achievements of the philosophers have been attained in the same spirit professed by the operationists: an empirical study of the actual doings of science-makers. Little wonder, then, that the two groups, although differing in emphasis, have arrived at substantially the same generalizations. Furthermore, these studies investigating the science-makers are the beginnings of a Science of Science. Like all other sciences, this one began before it was founded. Its founding and christening are of very recent date. They coincide with the harvesting of its first fruits.

The Science of Science

These first fruits of the Science of Science, it would appear, are the positive advances of operationism, of Logical Positivism, and of all who have looked seriously into the rules under which science is created. Except for these fruits, of which many are still green and some may even turn out to be wormy, the Science of Science comprises little more than an optimistic program. The fullest account of this program is supplied by C. W. Morris in his excellent essay on the "Foundations of the theory of signs" (43).

Morris is a philosopher at Chicago, and many will want to ask: What good is a science in the hands of philosophers? The obvious retort is that all our major sciences passed their childhood in the mansion of philosophy and only after they had grown tough and empirical were they bold enough to desert the tender-minded parent. It may be that once again a band of curious men have turned up in some unsuspected corner a new science with which they will charm away a few hardy scholars and leave the parental mansion tenanted by the tender-minded.

Let us turn now to an outline of the scientific study of science. Morris calls it "Metascience" or "Scientific Empiricism." Morris is enthusiastically full of new terms; in fact, a difficulty with his account is that he is overly generous in his willingness to enrich our vocabulary. Much of his coinage, however, is choice and merits more extensive circulation. Morris defends the thesis that *it is possible to include without remainder the study of science under the study of the language of science, because the study of that language involves not merely the study of its formal structure but its relation to the objects it designates and to the persons who use it.* Language is a system of signs or symbols and the general science of signs is to be called *Semiotic.* Semiotic has a double relation to the other sciences: It is both a science among the sciences and an instrument of the sciences. It is not a "superscience" but rather a common science among the others. Every scientist at some stage of his work must embody his results in linguistic signs, and consequently he must be as careful with his linguistic tools as he is in designing his apparatus or in making his observations. In his enterprise, the scientist unites empiricism with methodological rationalism, and Semiotic studies how this marriage is consecrated.

The study divides itself into three dimensions or levels, which we shall discuss in turn:

1. Syntactics is the study of the relation of signs to signs.
2. Semantics is the study of the relation of signs to objects.
3. Pragmatics is the study of the relation of signs to scientists.

Syntactics refers to the formal disciplines commonly called logic, mathematics, and syntax, where the relation of signs to one another is *abstracted* from their relation to objects and to users or interpreters. At present this is the best developed branch of Semiotic, but in the field of the logical syntax of language there is still great labor to be done. The investigation of language from the syntactical point of view is at once both complex and fruitful. It has been possible accurately to characterize primitive, analytic, contradictory, and synthetic sentences, and to show that many sentences which are apparently object-sentences (and so concern things which are not signs) turn out under analysis to be pseudo object-sentences which must be interpreted as syntactical statements about language. An astonishing number of the scientist's sentences are syntactical in this sense (see Appendix I).* They are propositions without material content.

Ayer (1, p. 63) gives us a "striking instance" of the way in which propositions which are really linguistic are often expressed in such a way that they appear to be factual. At first glance, the proposition, "A material thing cannot be in two places at once," looks quite empirical, but critical inspection shows that "it simply records the fact that, as a result of certain verbal conventions, the proposition that two sense-contents occur in the same visual or tactual sense-field is incompatible with the proposition that they belong to the same material thing." The proposition, then, is a definition—it records our decision as to how we shall use the term "material thing." As this example suggests, the scientist frequently couches in the material idiom the propositions which he really intends as definitions, and thereby he tends unwittingly to generate pseudo problems out of his use—or misuse—of signs.

Of course, science is not the only activity in which we use signs. The artist, the musician, and the traffic cop are notable sign-users. What their various signs express or designate concerns semantics; what the effect of these signs is on society and the individual concerns pragmatics; but we can also inquire under what rules the signs are made, combined, and transformed, and that is syntactics.

Semantics refers to the rules determining under what condition a sign is applicable to an object or situation. Thus, the operational rule [7] laid down by Bridgman for determining the meaning of a term is, I take it, essentially a *semantical rule*. And the so-called "applicational definitions" used by the Logical Positivists to state when a term shall apply to an object come under this heading (cf. Blumberg and Feigl, 8). Within the study of these rules belong all the problems relating to the correlation between the signs which comprise a scientific treatise and the dis-

---

* In the original publication.—Ed.

[7] In discussing operationism I have used the words *term* and *proposition, applicability* and *truth* (Stevens, 58, 59). In keeping with the spirit of Semiotic I ought perhaps to say that *terms* have *applicability* under semantical rules when the criteria governing their use are operational criteria. Then, sentences formed by combining these *semantically* significant terms into propositions are *empirically* significant (have truth-value) when their assertions are confirmable by means of operations. In other words, there is a justifiable distinction between the operational meaning of words and symbols (semantical significance) and the operational meaning of empirical propositions. I am not certain, however, that Morris would distinguish between empirical and semantical propositions in the same way.

criminable aspects of the physical world to which the signs are meant to apply. The simplest semantical rule is that governing an *indexical* sign. Such a sign designates what is pointed at at any instant. The denotation of the sign is based upon the operation of pointing, which in turn, of course, involves an act of discrimination. We have already noted that discrimination is the simplest and most basic operation performable.

Many of the problems of semantics belong to psychology. Morris sees in the experimental approach made possible by behavioristics great promise for determining the actual conditions under which certain signs are employed. Unfortunately, rules for the use of sign-vehicles are not ordinarily formulated by the users of a language; they exist, rather, as habits of behavior, and semantics wants to know what these habits are and how they come to be established. Many pertinent experimental studies have already been made by psychologists seeking the conditions of concept formation and judgments of similarity, but more are in order. Tolman's discovery of sign-gestalts functioning in the life of the rat discloses semantics among the rodents, and Lashley's effort to discover what range of patterns are considered equivalent by the rat when he uses them as signs for food directs attention to the problem of functional substitutivity (to use Professor Boring's term) among symbolic forms.

The game of chess is frequently suggested (cf. Carnap, 18, and Reichenbach, 52) as an example of a system of conventional formal rules applicable to concrete objects and situations. Perhaps at this point we can better illuminate Semiotic by examining this ancient pastime. First let us consider a set of signs. We shall use 3 groups of symbols: 1) the letters *a, b, c, d, e, f, g,* and *h;* 2) the numbers 1, 2, 3, 4, 5, 6, 7, and 8; and 3) certain other signs such as Kt, B, Q, K, etc. Next we shall set up conventional rules for manipulating these symbols by allowing only combinations in which 1 sign from each of the 3 groups appears, such as, for example, Kt *c* 4. This combination shall be transformable into other combinations, depending upon the first symbol, Kt. Thus:

$$\text{Kt } c\ 4 \longrightarrow \text{Kt } e\ 5.$$

But we shall not be allowed to write:

$$\text{Kt } c\ 4 \longrightarrow \text{Kt } d\ 5.$$

Now, when we have stated all the rules governing these signs, what do we have? Quite plainly, what we have is a formal system—a set of signs governed by syntactical rules. We are engaged in the pursuit of syntactics.

Anyone who is a chess player will have guessed by now that these syntactical rules were *abstracted* from the game of chess. The point is that we can abstract them in this way and study them with no reference to anything beyond themselves. On the other hand, we can use them as a "model" to describe chess. In order to use them in this way we proceed to set up *semantical rules*. We say: Let the letters stand for the rows and the numbers for the columns of a chess board; let Kt stand for a particular small object (called a knight) which sits on a square of the board; then define Kt *c* 4 as equivalent to the statement that there is a knight on the square of coördinates *c* and 4; and define Kt *c* 4 ⟶ Kt *e* 5 as equivalent to the statement that the knight is moved from *c* 4 to *e* 5. These semantical rules are statements about the use of language—they merely record our decisions as to how we shall use certain signs—and as semantical rules they are not empirical propositions. (This distinction between semantical and empirical statements was not made sufficiently explicit in operationism, but it needs to be stressed.)

We create an empirical statement as soon as we say that Kt *c* 4 is true, i.e., that there is, in fact, a knight on *c* 4, because this statement can be operationally verified. We can look to see whether our knight is there on *c* 4, or elsewhere. If the knight is on *c* 4 the statement is confirmed as true and if the knight is not on *c* 4 the statement is unconfirmed and is false. On the other hand, the statement "Kt *c a*" can never be considered an empirical proposition, because this combination of signs violates the rules of syntax and is meaningless—it cannot be tested operationally.[8]

From our game of chess we can abstract still another dimension or aspect. We can ask: What is the relation of these rules to chess players? Is the game hard or easy? What is its place in society, etc.? Here we are broaching pragmatical questions.

Pragmatics, as a part of Semiotic, studies the relation of signs to scientists. Here belong the problems as to how the scientist, as a behaving organism, reacts to signs; how science, as a social institution, interacts with other social institutions; and how scientific activity relates to other activities. This, indeed, is the aspect of Semiotic most challenging to the psychologist. It is the problem of the interpretation of signs. What

---

[8] Note the similarity between the statement "Kt *c a*" and Ayer's example discussed above. To say that a knight cannot be on *c* and *a* at the same time is very like saying that an object cannot be in two places at once. Both statements follow directly from the rules of our syntax and are therefore nonempirical sentences.

is their effect on the man who sees or hears them? How do they determine behavior? How are they used and abused in shaping human destiny? A nebulous problem, one might complain, and overwhelmingly complex. "Yes, but none the less real and pressing," must be the answer.

The term "pragmatics" obviously suggests the philosophy known as pragmatism. The word was deliberately chosen to be thus suggestive. (In Semiotic we should say that the *pragmatical* aspect of the word is one of suggestiveness.) Pragmatism, more effectively than ever before, directed attention to the relation of signs to their users and assessed this relation as an aid in understanding intellectual activities. Pragmatics, as part of Semiotic, pays tribute to the achievements of Peirce, James, Dewey, and Mead, but it must not be thought identical with pragmatism as a philosophy.

Both pragmatism and pragmatics agree that the interpreter of a sign-vehicle is an organism whose "taking-account" of the sign consists in a *habit to respond* to the vehicle as it would to the thing designated by the sign. We thus find the problem of pragmatics cast in such a form that it can be handled by behavioristics—we deliberately avoid talking about the subjective effects of signs unless these effects are disclosed by public operations. Not only do we react to the signs appearing in sober scientific propositions, but our habits of response carry over to situations where signs obey neither semantical nor syntactical rules. We are often delighted by senseless jingles and moved to strong emotions by what analysis shows to be gibberish. In propaganda, where syntax is usually not violated, but where semantical relations are sometimes distorted, the pragmatical effects (the induction of some form of behavior) may be profoundly disturbing. Clearly, psychology has a stake in the solution of all these problems arising in pragmatics.

One more facet of this many-sided problem deserves our interest. What Morris calls *descriptive pragmatics* occurs when a sign used by a person is employed as a means of gaining information about the person. The psychoanalyst studies dreams for the light they throw upon the dreamer, not to discover whether there are actually any situations which the dreams denote. Likewise, we may study the statements of newspapers and politicians, not as empirical propositions, but for their ability to disclose the faction whose interest is being served by this form of propaganda. And in much the same spirit, the psychiatrist inspects the signs used by his patient in order to diagnose an abnormality. The pragmatical aberrations found among the psychoses are extremely illuminating, for occasionally a patient lets his system of signs displace completely the objects they once stood for; the troublesome world of reality is pushed aside and the frustrated fellow gets his satisfaction in the domain of signs, oblivious to the restrictions of syntactical and semantical rules. The field of psychopathology thus holds great promise as a place to apply Semiotic and discover some of its laws.[9]

There can be no doubt that in the realm of human behavior the concept of sign holds a key place. And if, as the pragmatists contend, mental phenomena are to be equated to sign-responses, psychology bears an intimate relation to the science of signs. The theory of signs—being the coördinated disciplines of syntactics, semantics, and pragmatics—is the core of a unified science. "Indeed," exclaims Morris (43), "it does not seem fantastic to believe that the concept of sign may prove as fundamental to the sciences of man as the concept of atom has been for the physical sciences or the concept of cell for the biological sciences."

Epilogue

That then, in all too brief review, is the manner in which the Science of Science has been staked out. Whoever would probe the making of science can learn all the answers by inspecting thoroughly the language of science. The investigator must remember, however, that *this language is an intersubjective (public) set of sign-vehicles whose usage is determined by syntactical, semantical, and pragmatical rules*. By making the Science of Science coextensive with the study of the language of science we have set spacious bounds to this field of inquiry—there is ample room for a variety of talents, and to bring all the diverse areas under cultivation will require coöperation among the specialties.

Three features of this lusty embryonic science stand out with particular prominence.

First, the rational and the empirical elements in science are disentan-

---

[9] Count Alfred Korzybski has written a bulky work called *Science and sanity* (Lancaster: Science Press, 1933), in which he contends that in the miseducation of our youth we teach them semantical rules based upon static Aristotelian classifications which they must then use in dealing with a fluid dynamic universe. Such semantical habits are enough out of tune with reality to drive many people crazy. Korzybski would cure the resulting insanity by renovating the patient's semantics. Whatever our opinion about this etiology and cure, it is plain that much of Korzybski's concern is with what Morris would call pragmatics—the effect of signs upon the users of signs.

gled and then reassembled according to a straightforward, workable plan. The formal, rational, analytic, a priori, deductive side of creative thinking, which has always been so dear in the hearts of James's "tender-minded," neither rules nor is ruled by the empirical, synthetic, a posteriori, inductive wing. Neither side can be called a usurper when both are understood, for they are not even in competition. Their union is achieved, not after the manner of Kant, who held out for a bastard hybrid which he called the "a priori synthetic judgment," but in conformity with the relation of sign to object.

Secondly, it is proposed that in our study of the science-maker we begin with the *products* of his activity—his finished propositions—rather than with his "experiences" or any other phase of his earlier behavior. This is a sensible place to begin. If we were to study the manufacture of any product, such as automobiles, we should probably find it useful first to ascertain what an automobile is and then to discover the conditions under which it comes into being. Science manufactures sentences, and we, as curious mortals, ask: What is a sentence and how is it made? The *complete* answer to this question is the Science of Science.

Thirdly, does it not appear that the Science of Science must go directly to psychology for an answer to many of its problems? Is it not also plain that a behavioristic psychology is the only one that can be of much help in this enterprise? A sign has semantical significance when an organism will react to it as it would to the object which the sign supplants. The psychologist works out the laws under which different stimuli evoke equivalent reactions. Signs, as stimuli, can be combined and utilized extensively in the control and direction of behavior, both individual and social. The entire activity of the scientist as a sign-using organism constitutes, therefore, a type of behavior for which behavioristics seeks the laws. If there is a sense in which psychology is the propaedeutic science (cf. Stevens, 59), it is undoubtedly in its ability to study the behavior, *qua* behavior, of the science-makers.

Perhaps we are too close to this young Science of Science either to judge its value or see clearly how it came to be. We shall forego the value-judgment, since it would merely disclose the author's particular prejudice (already clear, no doubt), but an observation about the movement's immediate ancestry is not entirely out of order. It now appears, in retrospect, that the Science of Science emerged as the reasonable outcome of revolutions in the three major fields: physics, psychology, and philosophy. These revolutions occurred almost independently, but a general community of spirit among them led directly to extensive cross-fertilization. Operationism as a revolution against absolute and undefinable concepts in physics, behaviorism as a revolution against dualistic mentalism in psychology, and Logical Positivism as a revolution against rational metaphysics in philosophy were the three forces whose convergence into a common effort is effected by the Science of Science.

Finally, the purpose of this review has been to call the attention of those of us who are psychologists to the critical principles involved in scientific method as evolved in recent scientific and philosophic movements. We have had little to say concretely about psychology or its facts, and undoubtedly many will be impatient with so much non-experimental discourse. "Who cares about philosophy?" they will say. "What matters is the product of the laboratory." While such robust empiricism is admirable, we must ask the indulgence of these tough minds. We must ask them to bear with us while we inspect our logical tools as carefully as we do our other apparatus. And we must ask them to weigh the implications for psychology of this statement by Quine, the logician (49):

The less a science has advanced the more its terminology tends to rest upon an uncritical assumption of mutual understanding. With increase of rigor this basis is replaced piecemeal by the introduction of definitions. The interrelationships recruited for these definitions gain the status of analytic principles; what was once regarded as a theory about the world becomes reconstrued as a convention of language. Thus it is that some flow from the theoretical to the conventional is an adjunct of progress in the logical foundations of any science.

References

1. Ayer, A. J. *Language, truth and logic.* London: Gollancz, 1936.
2. Bell, E. T. *Men of mathematics.* New York: Simon & Schuster, 1937.
3. Benjamin, A. C. *An introduction to the philosophy of science.* New York: Macmillan, 1937.
4. Benjamin, A. C. The operational theory of meaning. *Phil. Rev., N. Y.,* 1937, *46,* 644-649.
5. Bentley, A. F. The positive and the logical. *Phil. Sci.,* 1936, *3,* 472-485.
6. Bentley, A. F. Physicists and fairies. *Phil. Sci.,* 1938, *5,* 132-165.
7. Bills, A. G. Changing views of psychology as science. *Psychol. Rev.,* 1938, *45,* 377-394.

8. Blumberg, A. E. and Feigl, H. Logical positivism. *J. Phil.*, 1931, *28*, 281-296.
9. Boas, G. and Blumberg, A. E. Some remarks in defense of the operational theory of meaning. *J. Phil.*, 1931, *28*, 544-550.
10. Boring, E. G. Temporal perception and operationism. *Amer. J. Psychol.*, 1936, *48*, 519-522.
11. Bridgman, P. W. *The logic of modern physics*. New York: Macmillan, 1928.
12. Bridgman, P. W. A physicist's second reaction to Mengenlehre. *Scripta math.*, 1934, *2*, 3-29.
13. Bridgman, P. W. *The nature of physical theory*. Princeton: Princeton Univ. Press., 1936.
14. Bridgman, P. W. Operational analysis. *Phil. Sci.*, 1938, *5*, 114-131.
15. Brunswik, E. Psychology as a science of objective relations. *Phil. Sci.*, 1937, *4*, 227-260.
16. Bures, C. E. The concept of probability. *Phil. Sci.*, 1938, *5*, 1-20.
17. Campbell, N. R. *Physics: the elements*. Cambridge: Univ. Press, 1920.
18. Carnap, R. On the character of philosophic problems. *Phil. Sci.*, 1934, *1*, 5-19.
19. Carnap, R. *Philosophy and logical syntax*. London: Kegan Paul, 1935.
20. Carnap, R. Les concepts psychologiques et les concepts physiques sont-ils foncièrement différents? *Rev. Synthèse*, 1935, *10*, 43-53.
21. Carnap, R. Testability and meaning. *Phil. Sci.*, 1936, *3*, 419-471; 1937, *4*, 1-40.
22. Carnap, R. *Logical syntax of language*. London: Kegan Paul, 1937.
23. Dingle, H. *Through science to philosophy*. Oxford: Clarendon Press, 1937.
24. Einstein, A. On the method of theoretical physics. *Phil. Sci.*, 1934, *1*, 163-169.
25. Feigl, H. The logical character of the principle of induction. *Phil. Sci.*, 1934, *1*, 20-29.
26. Feigl, H. Logical analysis of the psycho-physical problem. *Phil. Sci.*, 1934, *1*, 420-445.
27. Hempel, C. G. Analyse logique de la psychologie. *Rev. Synthèse*, 1935, *10*, 27-42.
28. Hume, D. *Enquiries concerning the human understanding and concerning the principles of morals*. Oxford: Clarendon Press, 1902 (2nd ed.).
29. James, W. *Pragmatism*. New York: Longmans, Green, 1914.
30. Kantor, J. R. The operational principle in the physical and psychological sciences. *Psychol. Rec.*, 1938, *2*, 3-32.
31. Lewin, K. The conceptual representation and the measurement of psychological forces. *Contr. psychol. Theor.*, 1938, *1*, No. 4, 1-247.
32. Lindsay, R. B. A critique of operationalism in physics. *Phil. Sci.*, 1937, *4*, 456-470.

33. Lindsay, R. B. and Margenau, H. *Foundations of physics*. New York: Wiley, 1936.

34. Lundberg, G. A. Quantitative methods in social psychology. *Amer. sociol. Rev.*, 1936, *1*, 38-54.

35. Malisoff, W. M. The universe of operations (a review). *Phil. Sci.*, 1936, *3*, 360-364.

36. Margenau, H. Causality in modern physics. *Monist*, 1931, *41*, 1-36.

37. Margenau, H. Methodology of modern physics. *Phil. Sci.*, 1935, *2*, 48-72; 164-187.

38. McGeoch, J. A. Learning as an operationally defined concept. *Psychol. Bull.*, 1935, *32*, 688 (abstr.).

39. McGeoch, J. A. A critique of operational definition. *Psychol. Bull.*, 1937, *34*, 703-704 (abstr.).

40. McGregor, D. Scientific measurement and psychology. *Psychol. Rev.*, 1935, *42*, 246-266.

41. Menger, K. The new logic. *Phil. Sci.*, 1937, *4*, 299-336.

42. Morris, C. W. Scientific empiricism. *Int. Encycl. unif. Sci.*, 1938, No. 1, 63-75.

43. Morris, C. W. Foundations of the theory of signs. *Int. Encycl. unif. Sci.*, 1938, No. 2, 1-59.

44. Nagel, E. Some theses in the philosophy of logic. *Phil. Sci.*, 1938, *5*, 46-51.

45. Neurath, O. Historische Anmerkungen. *Erkenntnis*, 1930, *1*, 311-314.

46. Neurath, O. Physicalism: the philosophy of the Viennese Circle. *Monist*, 1931, *41*, 618-623.

47. Neurath, O. Unified science and its encyclopedia. *Phil. Sci.*, 1937, *4*, 265-277.

48. Poincaré, H. *The foundations of science*. New York: Science Press, 1913.

49. Quine, W. Truth by convention. In *Philosophical essays for Alfred North Whitehead*. New York: Longmans, Green, 1936. P. 90.

50. Rashevsky, N. Foundations of mathematical biophysics. *Phil. Sci.*, 1934, *1*, 176-196.

51. Rashevsky, N. Physico-mathematical methods in biological and social sciences. *Erkenntnis*, 1936, *6*, 357-365.

52. Reichenbach, H. *Experience and prediction*. Chicago: Univ. Chicago Press, 1938.

53. Rosenzweig, S. Schools of psychology: a complementary pattern. *Phil. Sci.*, 1937, *4*, 96-106.

54. Schlick, M. De la relation entre les notions psychologiques et les notions physiques. *Rev. Synthèse*, 1935, *10*, 5-26.

55. Seashore, R. H. and Katz, B. An operational definition and classification of mental mechanisms. *Psychol. Rec.*, 1937, *1*, 3-24.

56. Somerville, J. Logical empiricism and the problem of causality in social

sciences. *Erkenntnis,* 1936, *6,* 405-411.

57. Stevens, S. S. The operational basis of psychology. *Amer. J. Psychol.,* 1935, *47,* 323-330.

58. Stevens, S. S. The operational definition of psychological concepts. *Psychol. Rev.,* 1935, *42,* 517-527.

59. Stevens, S. S. Psychology: the propaedeutic science. *Phil. Sci.,* 1936, *3,* 90-103.

60. Struik, D. J. On the foundations of the theory of probabilities. *Phil. Sci.,* 1934, *1,* 50-70.

61. Tolman, E. C. *Purposive behavior in animals and men.* New York: Appleton-Century, 1932. [See Selection No. 29 in this volume.]

62. Tolman, E. C. An operational analysis of 'demands.' *Erkenntnis,* 1936, *6,* 383-390.

63. Tolman, E. C. Operational behaviorism and current trends in psychology. *Proc. 25th Anniv. Celebr. Inaug. Grad. Stud.* Los Angeles: Univ. S. Calif. Press, 1936, 89-103. [Selection No. 5 in this volume.]

64. Waters, R. H. and Pennington, L. A. Operationism in psychology. *Psychol. Rev.,* 1938, *45,* 414-423.

65. Weinberg, J. R. *An examination of logical positivism.* London: Kegan Paul, Trench, Trubner, 1936.

66. Wittgenstein, L. *Tractatus logico-philosophicus.* New York: Harcourt, Brace, 1922.

67. Woodger, J. H. *The axiomatic method in biology.* Cambridge: Cambridge Univ. Press, 1937.

3 OPERATIONISM AND THEORY CONSTRUCTION [1]

Gustav Bergmann and Kenneth W. Spence

I

During the last decade psychologists have become increasingly aware of the methodological problems of their science. This trend of thought has been but a part of the larger movement of Scientific Empiricism, which in turn gained momentum through the integration of the ideas

[1] This article is an elaboration of two papers read by the authors in a symposium on Current Aspects of Behavior Theory at the 1940 meeting of the Midwestern Branch of the American Psychological Association in Chicago.

From G. Bergmann and K. W. Spence, Operationism and theory in psychology, *Psychol. Rev.,* 1941, *48,* 1-14. Reprinted by permission of the authors, the *Psychological Review,* and the American Psychological Association.

developed in England (Russell) and on the continent (the Vienna Circle) with the pragmatist tradition in this country. In psychology, as in other sciences, these methodological analyses have stressed two different aspects of scientific enterprise. A number of psychologists, Tolman (17), Skinner (13), and Stevens (14), stimulated by the writings of Bridgman (3, 4), have centered their efforts largely on the *empirical component* of scientific method. Under the watchword of operationism, they have carefully considered and laid down the requirements that scientific concepts must fulfill in order to insure testability and thus empirical meaning. The second aspect, the *formal (theoretical) component* of scientific endeavor has been brought to the forefront in psychology principally through the writings of Hull (6, 7, 9) and Lewin (11, 12). By his persistent attempts to fit articulate theoretical structures to certain realms of behavioral data, the former has tried to show the essential rôle that formal systematization plays in scientific explanation. The latter has likewise emphasized the rôle of theory in his writings but has not as yet attempted rigorous theory construction.

In the broader framework of Scientific Empiricism the complementary nature of these two components of scientific method has been clearly recognized. It might even be said that one of the main achievements of this philosophic movement has been the methodologically correct evaluation and allocation of the respective rôles of these two modes of scientific thinking. Unfortunately in psychology there has not always been a proper appreciation of the incompleteness of an approach which neglects either one of these supplementary procedures in science. The present paper deals with some of the problems which have arisen in psychology with attempts to develop these two aspects of scientific method.

II

No body of empirical knowledge can be built up without operational definition of the terms in use. This basic methodological requirement is clearly recognized by the present writers. We should like, however, to call attention here to a certain tendency to use this "operational criterion" illegitimately as a means of criticizing theoretical attempts which are, at least, *methodologically* sound. Very often the real basis of such criticism has been nothing but a healthy skepticism as to the scientific value of the theories under examination. There should, of course, be no hesitation at voicing such doubts whenever the generalizations of a scientist seem overdrawn or if his theories do not look promising. But to express such doubts as a methodological argument only confuses the issue. Even sterile or rash theories should be eliminated by proper means, for otherwise there is the danger that promising theories will also be ruled out for no good reason at all. At the present state of the discussion, therefore, it might be useful to restate rather carefully the limits and the legitimate scope of operational analysis.[2]

Even before a scientist can set out to study some aspects of the phenomena he is interested in, e.g., animal maze learning or human rote learning, he must have at least some tentative ideas as to what the "relevant factors" might be, that is to say, as to what the determinants of the phenomena studied are. These ideas, of course, are drawn from his knowledge and his theoretical frame of reference. In a more advanced state, if such a relevant factor has become quantifiable, it is called a variable. Sometimes the term "condition" is also used in this context, and we speak of the conditions under which the phenomena occur. One important point that must be made here is that there is no methodological principle, no "operational recipe" which guarantees that no relevant factor has been overlooked. A statement such as this, then: Operationism requires that all the conditions be taken into account, can be quite misleading. For a construct which unwittingly leaves out a relevant factor (or determining condition) just leads to a different formulation of the empirical laws. For example, by telling us what manipulations he performs, what pointers he reads (weighing and measuring cubic content), and what computations he carries out with the numbers thus obtained (division, W/V), a primitive physicist would give us a methodologically correct definition of his *empirical construct* "density of a liquid." And this in spite of the fact that he might not have given any attention to the temperature in his laboratory, one of the conditions upon which, as we know, and as he might not know at that state of his investigation, the result of his manipulations and computations depends. The point is that we are able to trace back the terms of his language to the immediately observable. He has laid down all the conditions under which he is going to say: "This liquid has the density 1.3." Therefore, we know what he means, and that is

[2] Stevens' recent paper (15) on the subject is distinguished by a very cautious and circumspect attitude in this respect. The paper's main concern, however, is to integrate the methodological discussion within psychology with modern philosophy of science, a subject taken up by one of the present writers (1, 2).

all general methodology can insist upon at this level of the so-called *operational definition of empirical constructs.*

Historically and psychologically, then, the creation of helpful concepts is a very essential part of a scientific achievement. From the standpoint of methodological analysis, however, if the scientist has defined his concepts, he has only prepared his tools. Explanatory work proper starts, and can start, only after the empirical constructs have been laid down. And this work, of course, consists in nothing else but finding the *empirical laws,* i.e., the functional relationships between the variables. "Finding" in this context means inductive generalization from observation and experimentation. In this way, our hypothetical physicist, for instance, might become aware of the fact that the density of liquids, as defined by him, varies with temperature. He will then set out to establish the functional relationship between these two variables. But whether a more complete law would have to be established between his two variables and the further one of pressure, is again a pragmatic and no methodological question. We add two further remarks in elaboration of this cardinal point.

First, it must not be overlooked that many empirical laws consist just in the finding that different "classes of operations" lead, within certain ranges, to the *same* result. The operations are then said to define the *same* empirical construct. The classical example for such an empirical law is furnished by the alternative ways of measuring length either with a yardstick or by triangulation. Operational analysis has made us alert to the tentative and empirical character which such "identification," often uncritically and sometimes unjustifiably assumed, shares with any other empirical finding.[3]

Secondly, suppose that the scientist of our example, still ignorant of the relation between temperature and density, desired to ascertain whether his empirical construct "density" could be employed as an identifier of liquids. Upon discovery of the fact that the "same" liquid gives different "density-values" under different temperatures he would

---

[3] In order to comply with the more rigorous distinctions of Scientific Empiricism, one should speak here of "reduction chains" (Carnap) rather than of "classes of operations." A further prosecution of these points, however, leads directly into the investigation of the rules governing our use of "thing-names" and of the spatio-temporal frame of reference. Fascinating as this problem is, it does not seem that methodological clarification in psychology needs to go so far back into epistemology and logical analysis proper; the less so, as practically all psychologists agree that only physical phenomena are the material that psychology, like any other natural science, is concerned with.

realize that this cannot be done. But then he might try to identify liquids by recording their density at a given standard temperature. Strictly speaking, this "standard density" is a new construct.[4] The point is that, even if this new construct proves satisfactory for our physicist's present purposes, he has not yet stated all the conditions simply because there is always, at least theoretically, an infinite number of them. He might, however, have got hold of all the factors relevant for his purpose: i.e., within the range of specification and variation determined by his experiments and their intended generalization. The proof of the pudding is in the eating and not in any particular operational criterion. We see that even at the level of the empirical laws the scientist cannot derive any help from operationism. He will have to rely upon his own ingenuity and whatever help he might be able to get from an articulate theory.

Having formulated this limitation of operationism so strongly, it is only fair to state the real and sound scientific basis of the demand for careful consideration of "all the conditions." In the less complex and more mature fields of natural science (physics, chemistry) we are reasonably confident that we know and control *practically* all the variables necessary for the complete functional description attempted. In the biological and social sciences, on the other hand, this is not the case. Here, complexity of the situation and insufficiency of knowledge tend to preclude successful segregation of a set of variables which is reasonably complete. This is a shortcoming which limits the importance of most of the "empirical laws" and of theorizing in these fields at their present stage of development. The difficulty should be clearly recognized and it is to the credit of the operationists in psychology that they insist upon ultra-cautiousness and skepticism in these matters. But again it must be emphasized that the difficulty is not a methodological one. The question whether the individual variables are adequately and

---

[4] It is worth while mentioning, though, that these two constructs are in an hierarchical relation, i.e., that the class of operations (reduction chain) leading to one of them is a subclass of that leading to the other. The same holds true for concepts in psychology like learning criterion and retention criterion. There is, of course, a manifold factual interdependence between constructs and laws. Still we believe that the sharp analytical distinction between empirical constructs and empirical laws made in this paper is justifiable within scientific methodology, and might prove especially helpful for a clear appreciation of the operational viewpoint in present day psychology. At the level of logical analysis, however, the disentanglement of the thoroughgoing interdependence between the terms and the whole system of hypotheses constitutes one of the main tasks of scientific philosophy.

properly defined should be carefully distinguished from the question as to whether a set of variables sufficiently complete for a satisfactory functional description has been ascertained.

Before turning to the discussion of theory, there is still one further point to be made regarding the definition of "empirical constructs," the only aspect with which, as we have seen, operationism is properly concerned. The language of any science contains a whole hierarchy of interlocked empirical constructs—mass, acceleration, momentum, energy, or stimulus trace, excitatory potential, and so on. None of these particular constructs, of course, is "observable," in the sense in which a physical thing is observable. Nevertheless they are just as empirical as length, duration, weight, stimulus and all other such terms as are sometimes exclusively thought of as being operationally defined. All scientific terms are derived terms, derived from and retraceable to what one might call "the hard data," the "immediately observable," or what Stevens calls the "elementary operation of discrimination." [5] Any attempt then to divide this hierarchy of constructs into sheep and goats, i.e., operational constructs and theoretical constructs, is of necessity arbitrary. Actually much of what is usually called theorizing in empirical science consists, as will be discussed later, in the creation of these organizing empirical constructs during the search for the empirical laws. And for this reason some of them are sometimes referred to as theoretical constructs. This is all that can be meant by this distinction.

III

Turning now to the discussion of the theoretical aspects of scientific method in psychology, one of the most important tasks would seem to be the clarification of the terms "hypothetico-deductive method" and "postulational technique." A certain amount of confusion is apt to arise, and indeed has arisen, from an ambiguity in the meaning of these terms. In logic and mathematics they have reference to a formal language system developed as the consequence of a basic set of relations (called postulates or implicit definitions) between otherwise undefined terms. Hilbert's Axiomatics is an outstanding example of such a formal system. Interpretation by means of co-ordinating definitions relating

[5] Again, in the stricter language of Scientific Empiricism, all these expressions are rather objectionable and would have to be replaced by the syntactical term "primitive predicates." On this level of analysis the names of physical things themselves can be considered as "derived terms." For all these problems Carnap's *Testability and Meaning* should be given as a general reference (5).

the formal terms with empirical constructs makes this method a feasible one for scientists.

That is to say, the theoretical scientist can start from a set of undefined terms, *a, b, c,* state his postulates (implicit definitions) which relate them, and then show that by virtue of these few postulates, the terms *a, b, c* themselves or certain compound terms *x, y, z,* defined by means of them, fulfill exactly the formulæ which represent the empirical laws. This formal system may then be "interpreted" by co-ordinating a basic class of empirical constructs (experimental variables) either to the original terms *a, b, c* (phenomenological theory), or to the compound terms *x, y, z* (non-phenomenological theory). Actually there are few, if any, instances of such a method being exclusively relied upon in the development of the empirical sciences. As a matter of fact, even in geometry, the postulational method was a late achievement, born out of the need for systematic organization and epistemological clarification.

In actual scientific practice and particularly in recent psychological discussions (Hull) the term "mathematico-deductive" has been used in a meaning different from that of the formal logico-geometrical term just defined, although the distinction has not always been apparent. As the scientist usually understands the term, mathematico-deductive method consists in making guesses or hypotheses as to the choice of constructs (variables) and the mathematical relationships holding between them, and the further notion, not always followed in actual practice by psychologists, of strict and complete deductive elaboration of the consequences implied in these assumed relationships. Obviously, such a procedure is not necessarily hypothetico-deductive in the first sense.

This distinction is especially important for a proper understanding of the theoretical systems put forward by Hull, which we will therefore use as an exemplification of the general principles laid down in the preceding paragraphs. One can find the most divergent statements concerning various aspects of Hull's theories. Thus one writer (12) states that Hull's terms (concepts) are more or less well defined operationally, but that they are lacking in conceptual properties. At the other extreme one hears that his constructs are too highly theoretical and completely lacking in any empirical reference. These conflicting points of view appear to have arisen from Hull's terminology, particularly from his use of terms like "mathematico-deductive," "undefined concepts," and "postulates."

Misunderstanding might have been avoided if there had always been clear recognition of the fact that Hull's theorizing is hypothetico-deductive only in the second meaning outlined above. Hull does not begin with a set of purely formal terms, having no other meaning than that imparted to them by a set of implicit definitions, from which are then derived new terms and theorems made testable by means of co-ordinating definitions. Instead he actually begins with terms directly operationally defined. Unfortunately, he called them "undefined concepts," and thus created the erroneous impression that he started with purely formal terms which are never given the necessary co-ordinations to empirical constructs. A careful examination of these so-called "undefined concepts," however, will show that they are nothing but what one would call in a less sophisticated language the basic experimental variables, i.e., the variables manipulated and observed in the laboratory.[6]

The essential point to be noted, however, is that Hull's postulate systems do not contain implicit definitions relating these initial variables (concepts). Indeed, his postulates are nothing but definitions which define new constructs by stating them as mathematical functions of the initial variables (concepts). For example, in a recent modified formulation of his theory of simple adaptive behavior, Hull (8) gives as a postulate, what is really a definition of his term stimulus trace (s):

[1] $$s = a \log S(1 - e^{-hT}) \, e^{-kT'},$$

where S is the intensity of the physical stimulus; T the time of duration of S; T' the time since the termination of S; a, h, and k being empirical constants. Here the term stimulus trace has been newly created out of

[6] In the recent monograph on rote learning Hull (9) uses the terms "undefined concepts" and "definitions" (defined concepts). Both undefined and defined concepts consist largely in what might be described as directly operationally defined concepts and there is no essential methodological difference between them. Apparently the idea underlying Hull's distinction between these two categories is that the undefined concepts are those most directly point-at-able, i.e., involve the shortest defining sentences. Having selected these, he employs them in the definitions of the more complex defined notions. The whole system of definitions and postulates exhibits the mixture of explicit definitions and reduction chains characteristic of empirical science.

It should be mentioned that U6, U7 and U8 should not have been included among the undefined concepts of the rote learning monograph. They are elucidations regulating the use of derived terms defined later in the postulates. This has been recognized by Hull, himself, in a later section of the monograph (p. 306). By and large, however, operationists will correctly interpret Hull by substituting "operationally defined" for his expressions "undefined concepts" and "definitions."

the independent variables S, T, and T' by means of a mathematical technique.[7]

Several questions now arise concerning the scientific status of such "postulates," the answers to which will reveal a characteristic feature of psychological theory. Are these formulæ guesses as to the empirical laws of psychology? Obviously not in the same sense as the gas law or Newton's attraction formula, for there is no independent empirical referent, so far, for the newly defined variable. What then is the possible use of such a priori constructions?

For a satisfactory answer to this latter question we must examine the basic task of psychology. Like every other science, psychology conceives its problem as one of establishing the interrelations within a set of variables, most characteristically between response variables on the one hand and a manifold of environmental variables on the other. Or, in the usual mathematical denotation:

[2]
$$\frac{y_1 = f_1(x_1 x_2 \cdots x_n)}{y_m = f_m(x_1 x_2 \cdots x_n)}$$

The problem here is twofold: 1) the obtaining of the empirical curves and 2) the determination of their mathematical form, i.e., the specific nature of functions $f_1, f_2 \cdots f_m$. In solving this problem, physics is able to start out with assumptions as to the specific form of the f's describing elementary situations, i.e., situations of simple structure with a very limited number of variables, for it is possible to generalize or hypothesize these functions from experimental observation. More complex situations can then be adequately handled by deduction from and combination of these basic formulæ. In the course of this elaboration the physicist sometimes finds it convenient to employ new auxiliary terms (e.g., force in mechanics) defined out of the original variables.

In psychology, on the other hand, the number of variables entering into even the simplest behavior situation that can be experimentally produced is so great and the structure of their interrelationship is so complex that we are unable to make even a first guess as to the mathematical form of the equations directly from the empirical data without

[7] It should be clearly understood that, in spite of the use of such terms as stimulus trace, excitatory potential, etc., no physiological referents for these arbitrarily defined terms are implied. Attention should also be called to the point that by this very procedure these derived terms become themselves empirical constructs, or, if one prefers, they are indirectly operationally defined. They are methodologically comparable to the physicist's concepts of momentum, energy, etc.

some auxiliary theoretical device.[8] *The terms defined by Hull's postulates provide just such a device.* They attempt to bridge the gap between the two sets of variables, those manipulated by the experimenter and those measuring the observed responses. Technically, they aim at providing the means for ascertaining a rational fit to the empirical curve.

This aspect of our analysis can perhaps be best illustrated by a brief consideration of Hull's most recent formulation of simple behavior theory (8). The figure attempts to give a graphic representation of the hierarchic order of the terms involved. The basic (directly operationally defined) variables from which the construction starts, as shown at the left, are:

$T_1 =$ the time of duration of S_1,
$S_1 =$ the intensity of a physical stimulus, e.g., buzzer, lever,
$S_2 =$ reinforcing (goal) stimulus, e.g., food,
$T_2 =$ starvation time,
$T_3 =$ time between response to S_1 and occurrence of S_2,
$N\ \ =$ number of presentations of $S_1 - S_2$ sequence, i.e., trials.

Moreover there are the various measurable aspects of the response shown at the right:

$R_1 =$ amplitude of response,
$R_2 =$ latency of response, etc.

Hull now proceeds to the task of specifying the mathematical form of the empirical laws relating these two classes of variables. He attempts to do this by defining new terms out of the original variables so that in the final formulation of the empirical laws only the end members of this chain of intervening variables appear. This is accomplished in the manner schematically illustrated in the figure. The dotted lines indicate that these intervening variables, shown on the bridge, are derived in stepwise fashion from each other. To go into any detail would be beyond the scope of this paper. It is sufficient to indicate here that the final rational equations would express the response variables as a function of the just preceding intervening variable, excitatory potential ($\bar{E}$). It will also be noted that the response variables appear twice in the diagram; once on the bridge as derived, intervening constructs ($r_1\ r_2$) and once as independently operationally defined variables ($R_1\ R_2$).

---

[8] The securing of empirical data under concomitant variation of several variables is only beginning in psychology.

These two sets of formally different terms (r's and R's) are then identified and the success of the construction depends upon whether this identification is borne out by the experimental data. If so, the gap at the right end of the bridge is closed and the desired formulation of the empirical law has been attained. Finally, to complete the description of the diagram, the wavy lines leading down to the base symbolize the

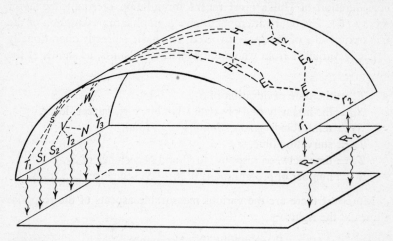

completion of the operational tie-up with the "immediately observable." [9]

For the sake of methodological completeness attention should be called here, perhaps, to a point of considerable importance (one somewhat obscured by the present emphasis) in regard to the determination of the final and complete rational form of the empirical law. By "final and complete" is meant the precise specification of each and every function connecting the two sets of variables. However, many deductions as to shapes and trends of behavior curves can be drawn if only some of the mediating functions (postulates) are specified, provided that the remaining non-specified functions hold to the general pattern assumed. As a matter of fact, many of the testable deductions made by Hull from this particular set are of this kind, for so far he has only roughly indicated the type of functions beyond the term H in the above scheme.

[9] This latter feature of the diagram follows the method of graphical representation suggested by Feigl and Koch in their clarification of the relation between empirical and formal language in psychology (10).

IV

In concluding this analysis it may be of some interest to indicate how this theoretical structure of Hull's relates to the conception of the nature of psychological theory outlined by Tolman in his presidential address (18) and earlier papers (16, 17). Tolman begins with equation system (2) and like Hull and any other methodological behaviorist conceives the task of psychology as one of determining the form of the functions (see page 63). In his scheme the independent variables $(x_1 \, x_2 \ldots x_n)$ are split into two classes, environmental and individual-difference variables, and the dependent variables are some aspects of behavior. As to the form of the functions, he states that "It is in fact so complicated that we at present seem unable to state it in any single simple statement. We find, rather, that we have to handle it by conceiving it as broken down into successive sets of component functions. These component functions connect the independent variables to logically constructed 'intervening variables,' and then connect these intervening variables in their turn to one another and to the final dependent behavior" (17, p. 91).

Clearly this description is fully in line, indeed identical, with the picture of Hull's actual procedure as outlined by our preceding analysis, and it is to Tolman's credit that he has been one of the first in psychology to outline this general methodological scheme. His actual theorizing, however, has always moved on a very general, programmatic level and has not gone beyond suggesting and cataloguing the various possible intervening variables and showing how they provide for the definition and use of mental terms (demands, hypotheses, etc.) in a behavioristic psychology. Such essential convergence between two theoretical viewpoints which are often regarded as being far apart strongly suggests that essential agreement on this level of general methodology is about to be reached in psychology. The most imperative task would now seem to be the persistent pursuit of attempts to formulate articulate theories in closest contact with the experimental data.

References

1. Bergmann, G. On some methodological problems of psychology. *Philos. Sci.*, 1940, 7, 205-219.
2. Bergmann, G. The subject matter of psychology. *Philos. Sci.*, 1940, 7, 415-433.

3. Bridgman, P. W. *The logic of modern physics.* New York: Macmillan, 1928.

4. Bridgman, P. W. *The nature of physical theory.* Princeton: Princeton Univ. Press, 1936.

5. Carnap, R. Testability and meaning. *Philos. Sci.,* 1936, *3,* 419-471; 1937, *4,* 1-40.

6. Hull, C. L. Mind, mechanism, and adaptive behavior. *Psychol. Rev.,* 1937, *44,* 1-32.

7. Hull, C. L. The problem of stimulus equivalence in behavior theory. *Psychol. Rev.,* 1939, *46,* 9-30.

8. Hull, C. L. Memoranda concerning behavior theory. (On file in Yale University Library.), 1940-41.

9. Hull, C. L.; Hovland, C. I.; Ross, R. T.; Hall, M.; Perkins, D. T.; and Fitch, F. B. *Mathematico-deductive theory of rote learning.* New Haven: Yale Univ. Press, 1940.

10. Koch, S. The logical character of the motivation concept. M. A. Thesis, State Univ. of Iowa, 1939.

11. Lewin, K. The conceptual representation and the measurement of psychological forces. *Contr. psychol. Theory.* 1938, *1,* No. 4.

12. Lewin, K. Formalization and progress in psychology. *Univ. Ia. Stud. Child Welf.,* 1940, *16,* No. 3.

13. Skinner, B. F. The concept of the reflex in the description of behavior. *J. gen. Psychol.,* 1931, *5,* 427-458. [See Selection No. 31 in this volume.]

14. Stevens, S. S. The operational definition of psychological concepts. *Psychol. Rev.,* 1935, *42,* 517-527.

15. Stevens, S. S. Psychology and the science of science. *Psychol. Bull.,* 1939, *36,* 221-263. [Selection No. 2 in this volume.]

16. Tolman, E. C. Psychology vs. immediate experience. *Philos. Sci.,* 1935, *2,* 356-380.

17. Tolman, E. C. Operational behaviorism and current trends in psychology. *Proc. 25th Anniv. Celebr. Inaug. Grad. Stud., Los Angeles:* Univ. of S. Calif. Press. 1936, 89-103. [Selection No. 5 in this volume.]

18. Tolman, E. C. The determiners of behavior at a choice point. *Psychol. Rev.,* 1938, *45,* 1-41.

CHAPTER III

THEORETICAL CONSTRUCTS

THE PROBLEM of the kind of theoretical constructs to use in the development of useful scientific theories is obviously of major importance and has attracted considerable attention within the past two decades. The increasingly explicit recognition of the need for exact, operationally adequate logical constructs to represent intra-organic functions has been one of the most promising developments in recent psychological history. In the first selection of this chapter the various types of theoretical constructs employed by psychologists are reviewed by Kenneth W. Spence, who as a leading proponent of Hullian behavior theory has been one of the most active and influential of the so-called "neo-behaviorists." The second selection is an important early paper of Edward C. Tolman, who provided the first systematic treatment of this problem and introduced the concept of the intervening variable. The third selection concerns the problem of the extent to which such intervening logical constructs are operationally valid—and are thus true "intervening variables" in Tolman's original sense; or are loaded with "surplus meaning"—and are thus "hypothetical constructs," in the terminology proposed by Kenneth MacCorquodale and Paul E. Meehl. In the last selection M. H. Marx reviews the relationship between hypothesis and construct and proposes more explicit formal use of the so-called "E/C" type of intervening variable, as a complement to the orthodox type and an alternative to the "hypothetical construct." For a further consideration of the problem of the orthodox type of intervening variable Selection No. 13 by Hull may be consulted.

4 TYPES OF CONSTRUCTS IN PSYCHOLOGY [1]

Kenneth W. Spence

1 Introduction

The task of the scientist has been described as that of attempting to discover ever more generalized laws by which the observable events within his field of study may be brought into interrelation with one another. To this end he develops and refines (mainly in the direction of quantitative representation) his concepts or variables, arranges highly controlled (experimental) conditions of observation and introduces theoretical constructions. While it is not the primary purpose of this paper to attempt a methodological analysis of these components of scientific method, it is necessary to begin our discussion by calling attention to two somewhat different roles or functions that one of them, construction of theory, plays in different fields of science or in the same field at different stages of development.

In some areas of knowledge, for example present day physics, theories serve primarily to bring into functional connection with one another empirical laws which prior to their formulation had been isolated realms of knowledge. The physicist is able to isolate, experimentally, elementary situations, i.e., situations in which there are a limited number of variables, and thus finds it possible to infer or discover descriptive, low-order laws. Theory comes into play for the physicist when he attempts to formulate more abstract principles which will bring these low-order laws into relationship with one another. Examples of such comprehensive theories are Newton's principle of gravitation and the kinetic theory of gases. The former provided a theoretical integration of such laws as Kepler's concerning planetary motions, Galileo's law of falling bodies, laws of the tides and so on. The kinetic theory has served

[1] The writer is greatly indebted to Dr. Gustav Bergmann for reading the manuscript and making valuable suggestions.

From K. W. Spence, The nature of theory construction in contemporary psychology, *Psychol. Rev.,* 1944, *51,* 47-68. Reprinted by permission of the author, the *Psychological Review,* and the American Psychological Association.

to integrate the various laws relating certain properties of gases to other experimental variables.

In the less highly developed areas of knowledge, such as the behavior and social sciences, theory plays a somewhat different role. In these more complex fields the simplest experimental situation that can be arranged usually involves such a large number of variables that it is extremely difficult, if not impossible, to discover directly the empirical laws relating them. Theories are brought into play in such circumstances as a device to aid in the formulation of the laws. They consist primarily in the introduction or postulation of hypothetical constructs which help to bridge gaps between the experimental variables. Examples of such theoretical constructs are legion in psychology, e.g., Tolman's "demand," Hull's "excitatory potential," Lewin's "tension system," and a host of other mentalistic and neurophysiologically-sounding concepts. It is the purpose of this paper to examine the attempts of psychologists to discover general laws of behavior, particularly the auxiliary theoretical devices they have employed in doing so.

II Theoretical Constructs in Psychology

Like every other scientist, the psychologist is interested in establishing the interrelations within a set of experimental variables, i. e., in discovering empirical laws. At the present stage of development the variables (measurements) studied by the psychologist and between which he is attempting to find functional relations appear to fall into two main groups:

1. R-variables: measurements of the behavior of organisms; attributes of simple response patterns (actones), complex achievements (actions) and generalized response characteristics (traits, abilities, etc.). These are sometimes referred to as the dependent variables.

2. S-variables: measurements of physical and social environmental factors and conditions (present and past) under which the responses of organisms occur. These are sometimes referred to as the independent, manipulable variables.

While not all laws are quantitative, science typically strives to quantify its constructs and to state their interrelations in terms of numerical laws. The numerical laws the psychologist seeks may be represented as follows:

$$R = f(S).$$

The problem here is twofold: 1) to discover what the relevant S variables are, and 2) to ascertain the nature of the functional relations holding between the two groups of variables.

In general, two radically opposed positions have been taken by scientists, including psychologists, as to the best procedure to follow in solving this problem. On the one hand are those who propose the introduction of theoretical constructs as described above. On the other there are the more empirically minded persons who attempt to refrain from the use of such inferred constructs and try to confine themselves entirely to observable data. An excellent defense of this latter viewpoint, along with a constructive proposal as to how such an approach can hope to discover general quantitative laws in psychology, is contained in the recent presidential address of Woodrow to the American Psychological Association (23). We shall leave consideration of the method proposed by Woodrow until later; certain criticisms he offers of the theoretical approach provide an excellent introduction to this method of discovering laws.

Beginning with the conception, more or less the same as that expressed at the start of this paper, that explanation in science consists in nothing more than a statement of established relationships of dependency (for psychology in terms of laws between measurements of environment and behavior), Woodrow goes on to protest that most psychologists seem to have been entirely too interested in postulating intermediate events occurring within the organism to explain the obtained measurements. The difficulty with such speculative constructs, he thinks, is that they cannot be measured because it is not possible to observe the interior of organisms. The result is that their specification must be left to the imagination. And as he says:

. . . our imaginations have not failed us. The things we have stuck within the organism in the hope thereby of explaining behavior are almost without limit in number and variety. They include mental sets and cortical sets, traces, residues, synaptic resistances, inhibitory and excitatory substances, inhibitory and excitatory tendencies, determining tendencies, mental attitudes, sentiments, wishes, tensions, field forces, valences, urges, abilities, instincts, and so on and on. Very popular indeed is the animistic type of explanation (23, p. 3).

While it must be admitted with Woodrow that many of the theoretical constructs employed by psychologists have never been too satisfactorily specified, one must protest the lumping together of all theoretical constructs in such a completely indiscriminate manner. As a matter of fact, Woodrow has included in his list certain conceptions which were never meant to be explanatory concepts. Thus such terms as set, attitude, sentiment, and in some instances drive, are what Carnap (3) has termed *dispositional predicates or concepts,* because they refer to the disposition of an object to a certain behavior under certain conditions. They usually serve as names for events which do not appear in observable experience but instead are introduced into the scientist's language in terms of conditions and results which can be described in terms that refer directly to observable experiences. Such concepts are prevalent in all fields of science and serve a useful purpose.

Then, again, Woodrow has failed to distinguish in his list between what turn out upon analysis to be very different kinds of theoretical constructs. While some of them are little better than the animistic notions of primitive man, others have qualified as quite satisfactory in the sense that they have led to the formulation of behavioral laws. We turn now to the consideration of the different kinds of theories (theoretical constructs) that have been proposed in psychology.

III Four Types of Theoretical Constructs

Theoretical constructs are introduced, as we have said, in the form of guesses as to what variables other than the ones under control of the experimenter are determining the response. The relation of such inferred constructs (I_a) to the experimental variables, measurements of S and R, is shown in the following figure. Here we have assumed an over-simplified situation for purposes of exposition.

S-variables	I-variables	R-variables
X_1	I_a	R_1

Figure 1 Intervening variables

If under environmental conditions X_1 the response measure R_1 is always the same (within the error of measurement) then we have no need of theory. Knowing that condition X_1 existed we could always predict the response. Likewise if, with systematic variation of the X variable, we find a simple functional relation holding between the X values and the corresponding R values we again would have no problem, for we could precisely state the law relating them. But unfortunately things are not usually so simple as this, particularly in psychology.

On a second occasion of the presentation of condition X_1, the subject is very likely to exhibit a different magnitude of response, or in the second example there may be no simple curve discernible between the two sets of experimental values. It is at this point that hypothetical constructs are introduced and the response variable is said to be determined, in part by X_1, and in part by some additional factor, or factors, $I_a, I_b \ldots$, i.e., $R = f(X_1, I_a, I_b \ldots)$. The manner in which these theoretical constructs have been defined by different psychologists permits a grouping of them into four categories: 1) animistic-like theories in which the relations of the construct to the empirical variables are left entirely unspecified, 2) neurophysiological theories, 3) theories involving constructs defined primarily in terms of the R variables and 4) theories involving constructs intervening between the S and R variables.

1. *Animistic conceptions.* Little need be said about such instances of psychological speculation. They are included here merely for the purpose of completing the record. The invoking of such general concepts as the "soul," "mind," "élan vital," "entelechy," "idea," "libido," not to mention many more specific instances (e.g., insight, instinct [2]) in order to account for the apparent capriciousness of the behavior of organisms has been all too prevalent in psychology. When not safe from disproof by reason of the fact that their locus is usually specified to be in some region within the organism unaccessible to observation, these concepts are rendered invulnerable by failure to specify what relations they might have either to the S or R variables. While such vagueness renders them unverifiable, it does insure them a vigorous and long career among certain types of thinkers. Needless to say, such vague conceptions receive little attention today among scientific-minded psychologists.

2. *Neurophysiological theories.* The extent to which neurophysiological concepts, defined in terms of the operations and instruments of the neurophysiologist, are employed in psychological theorizing is not nearly so great as is sometimes thought. As a matter of fact, if we employ such variables to help us out in our formulation of behavior laws we are not, strictly speaking, theorizing for such concepts are not hypothetical, but are empirically defined. In such instances we have stated a law interrelating environmental, organic and behavioral variables. As yet we do not have very many such laws, except in the case

[2] Such terms, of course, when used as dispositional predicates serve the useful function of providing a name for the phenomenon.

of the simplest kinds of behavior (sensory responses, reflexes, etc.).

There are, of course, many theoretical constructs in psychology which are supposed to represent hypothetical neurophysiological processes, but whose properties are defined either in terms of the response variables (type 3 theory), in terms of environmental factors and the response variables (type 4 theory), or just assumed to be operating without making any specification of their relations to either the environmental or response variables (type 1 theory). Examples of these are Köhler's construct of brain field (12) to explain perceptual and memory phenomena (type 3), Pavlov's constructs (16) of excitatory and inhibitory states (type 4), and certain neural trace theories of learning (type 1).

It will be seen that this category really cuts across the other three. Further consideration of some of these theories will be given in our discussion of the final two classes of theory.

3. *Response-inferred theoretical constructs.* The fact that the behavior of organisms varies even though the objective environmental condition remains unchanged has led some psychologists to assert that the laws of such behavior cannot be formulated in terms of objective environmental variables even though additional hypothetical constructs are employed to bolster the effort. These writers have insisted that behavior must be accounted for in terms of the psychological situation. Thus Lewin (13) in his book *Dynamic theory of personality* refers to what he describes as the complete failure of such German writers as Loeb, Bethe and other objectivists to develop an adequate theoretical interpretation of behavior in terms of the objective situation, i.e., the physical situation as described by the operations of measurement of the physicist and/or the objective social situation as described by the sociologist. It is always necessary, he insists, to describe the situation as the subject sees or perceives it, i.e., in terms of what it means to him. Typical quotations from Lewin's writings indicate the positive tone taken by such writers:

For the investigation of dynamic problems we are forced to start from the psychologically real environment of the child (13, p. 74). Of course, in the description of the child's psychological environment one may not take as a basis the immediately objective social forces and relations as the sociologist or jurist, for example, would list them. One must rather describe the social facts as they affect the particular individual concerned (13, p. 75).

One of the basic characteristics of field theory in psychology, as I see it, is the demand that the field which influences an individual should be described not in "objective physicalistic" terms, but in the way in which it exists for that person at that time (15, p. 217).

As Lewin implies in the last quoted excerpt it would seem that this type of "psychological" approach to the theoretical constructs of psychology is characteristic of the self-styled field theorists or Gestalt psychologists. Thus Koffka (10) makes use of the construct of "behavioral environment" and the more inclusive construct of "psychophysical field" which includes the former and the physiological field, while Köhler (11, 12) refers to "phenomenal field" and to "brain field." Koffka and Köhler differ slightly from Lewin in that they introduce a physiological terminology in the description of the properties of some of their behavior-determining fields whereas Lewin does not. The methods of determining the structure and properties of these fields whether "brain field," "behavioral environment" or "life space" are, however,

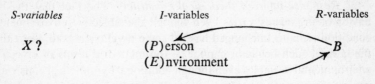

Figure 2 Lewin's theoretical constructs

essentially the same, and as we shall see later, involve extensive use of the phenomenological type of introspection.

The nature of this type of theorizing may be made clearer by attempting to show how it fits into the schema we have already employed. Figure 2 makes use of the constructs of Lewin, who has been the most articulate of this group of writers so far as the exposition of the formal nature of his theorizing is concerned. Lewin employs the concept of life space to represent the totality of facts which determine the behavior (B) of an individual at a certain moment. The life space includes two groups of constructs, the person (P) and the psychological environment (E). Use is then made of certain concepts from geometry (topology and hodology) and dynamics to represent the existing relationships.[3] By

[3] There is considerable reason to doubt whether Lewin does much more than take over the terms of topology, making little if any use of the postulates (implicit definitions) of this formal system. Koch, after making a very thorough analysis of Lewin's formulations, states that Lewin "finds it expedient to abstract from the postulates (of topology) the properties with which they implicitly endow the constructs, instead of fully stating the postulates" (9, p. 148). In this sense, then, it may be said that Lewin

means of what Lewin calls coördinating definitions these constructs are said to be related to empirical concepts.

Without going into detail, Figure 2 reveals an interesting fact. It is that little, if any, use is made of the S-variables in Lewin's theorizing.[4] The question immediately arises then as to what kinds of laws, if any, does Lewin arrive at. The functional relationship which frequently appears in his writings, $B = f(P, E)$, is obviously not a law of the type that psychologists were said to be interested in, i.e., $R = f(S)$. But if it is not this kind of a law, what kind is it? Some writers have implied that Lewin really does not attain any laws at all. They call attention to the fact that laws are statements of relations between *independently defined variables* and they ask what are the two sets of independent variables in Lewin's formula.

The answer to this question is not easy, and the writer is of the opinion that it has not been met in all instances of field theory. However, an examination of the methods employed by Lewin and his students in determining the structure and properties of their fields reveals that they depend heavily upon the phenomenological introspections of their subjects or themselves. If we now think of these as a kind of verbal response or "perceptual" response, in which the subject tries to describe his own particular way of perceiving the objective situation, we see that Lewin's theory really does provide us with laws mediating between independent variables, i.e., between two different responses of the subject, or, as in some cases, between the experimenter's own perceptual responses and the subjects' subsequent response. Thus Lewin discovers what amount to laws of the following type: $R_1 = f(R_2)$.

Of course, such theorists do not always rely on such phenomenological introspections. Once certain laws of the above type have been

employs very fragmentary parts or sub-systems of topology. As for the formal system of dynamics it remains thus far closeted, to use Koch's happy description, in Lewin's mind. Like so many of these field theorists, Lewin sets up a most attractive program for theory. Taken in conjunction with his interesting experiments the illusion is nicely created that there is some connection between them.

[4] Lewin states that the objective physical and social surroundings "have a relation to the life space similar to that which 'boundary conditions' have to a dynamic system" (15, p. 217). He believes that physicalistic behaviorism has made the mistake of treating such variables as if they were parts of the life space. Attention should be called here to the fact that Koffka concerned himself much more extensively with the objective environmental variables or the geographic environment as he called it. He discussed at some length the relations between the geographic and the behavioral environments—the traditional problem of perception (10).

formulated it is possible to formulate further laws between purely overt behavior items, neither of which are of this introspective, verbal type. There are also instances in which from the pattern of the observed response the theorist makes an inference as to the nature of the hypothetical field; and then by means of his postulates as to what happens in these fields he is able to make certain predictions as to subsequent behavior. An excellent example of the latter is Köhler's theoretical treatment (12) of perceptual problems involving reversible figures and the effects of prolonged inspection in certain types of simple perceptual situations. Thus in the light of perceptual behavior to reversible figures, he formulated the hypothesis that percept processes are associated with fields of electric currents in the nervous system. Then by means of postulates based on knowledge about electrolytical conduction he was able to predict other perceptual behavior.

By and large, however, the field theorist depends heavily upon phenomenological introspection in introducing his theoretical constructs. In order to understand the field of the subject he asks him to describe how he perceives the situation, or he infers it on the basis of his own introspections. With engaging frankness Snygg has made an appeal for the recognition of the important role that phenomenological introspection plays in these theories.[5] Thus he writes in connection with the problem of prediction:

By postulate B the determining locus of action is the behaver's p.f. [phenomenological field]. This is not open to direct observation by an outside observer. The process of prediction therefore involves two steps: 1) the securing of an understanding of the subject's field by inference or reconstruction, 2) the projection of the future field.

The first operation is of the common "Now why did he do that?" or "Under what circumstances would I have done that" character. Much of the topological work of Lewin is of this type and essentially the same procedure was used by Shepard when from the behavior of his rats he inferred the existence of floor cues which he himself was unable to experience (17, p. 413).

That this field approach to the problems of psychology has been fruitful and valuable is amply supported by the experimental contributions it has made, although in the writer's opinion, the theoretical superstructure has played a much less significant role than is sometimes

---

[5] Snygg also admits another obvious characteristic of such theoretical systems which some of its proponents have not always willingly acknowledged. Reference is made here to the fact that such systems are anthropomorphic.

credited to it. Furthermore, the phenomenological approach has its advantages, particularly in the complex field of social behavior of the human adult. It is obviously much easier to gain some notion as to the relevant variables determining such complex behavior by asking the individual to verbalize than it is to employ the procedure of trying to hypothesize them from knowledge of past history. Usually the latter is not available in sufficient completeness to make it even worthwhile to try to theorize as to the nature of such historical laws.[6]

A final point of no little importance is the failure of such field theories to provide us with laws which will enable us to control and manipulate the behavior-determining psychological field. Such laws are obviously a basic prerequisite to successful clinical therapy. While it may be true, as Snygg claims (17), that psychiatrists and teachers find the phenomenological approach most valuable in diagnosing behavior disorders, it is difficult to understand how the response-response laws it provides can be of much use in guiding therapeutic treatment. The latter requires a knowledge of what to do to the individual, what changes in his physical and social environment to arrange, in order to bring about the desired behavior changes. The laws telling us how to proceed in such matters are historical laws and involve as an important component of them objective variables representative of past and present factors in the physical and social environments. Psychiatrists and clinical psychologists who employed a purely phenomenological approach might or might not be successful at diagnosis; it is difficult to see how they could ever prescribe satisfactory reëducative procedures.[7,8]

[6] The situation in the case of animal behavior is somewhat different. Here one usually does have a pretty good record of the past history relevant to the present environmental situation.

[7] Bergmann has summed up this difficulty most succinctly in the form of the following questions:—"But even so, what is the predictive value of the suggestive metaphor 'psychological environment'? Is it not the business of science to ascertain which objective factors in the past and present states of the organism and its environment account for the difference in response, so that we can actually predict it instead of attributing it, merely descriptively and after it has happened, to a difference in the psychological environment?" (1).

[8] Mention should perhaps be made here of the fact that the theoretical constructs (factors) that Spearman (18), Thurstone (20), and other factor analysts arrive at are response derived and hence fall into this class. These men do not, of course, use the phenomenological method, but beginning with response intercorrelations (empirical $R — R$ relations) they arrive at hypothetical factors by various methods of mathematical analysis. Like the phenomenologists their theoretical factors have no tie-up with the S variables.

4. *Theoretical constructs as intervening variables between S and R variables.* In sharp contrast to these response-inferred theories with their emphasis upon the phenomenological approach is the point of view that theoretical constructs in psychology are to be regarded as "intervening variables" which bring into relation with one another the dependent R variables on the one hand and the independent S variables on the other. As Bergmann and Spence (2) have previously pointed out, two psychologists in particular, Hull and Tolman, have advocated, each in his own individual way, this type of psychological theory. In a little known paper Tolman (22) has presented an excellent account of such a theoretical program, while in his new book *Principles of behavior* Hull (7) has demonstrated in actual practice how such intervening variables provide us with a formulation of the basic principles or laws governing simple learning behavior. The following discussion makes no attempt to give a systematic account of this theoretical procedure. Instead we shall merely outline very sketchily its main features and then single out one or two aspects of it for more detailed examination.

According to Hull and Tolman, theoretical constructs, or intervening variables, have to be introduced into psychology either when we do not know all the important variables entering into a set of experimental events, or the precise nature of the interrelating function is not known. Consider, for example, the data obtained from conditioning experiments. These investigations have presented us with a wealth of data showing how the response variable changes or varies with the manipulation of certain other experimental variables. That is to say, various measurable aspects of response are studied as functions of the manipulable environmental variables and the data so obtained are plotted in the form of various curves.

The task of the psychologist here is to discover the precise nature of the interrelations holding within this set of variables. Instead of knowing merely that the response, R, is some function of the variables $X_1, X_2, X_3 \ldots X_n$, he desires to know the precise function. But in such a situation, involving as it does a large number of variables, the function relating the dependent and independent variables is so complicated that we are unable to conceive of it directly. It is necessary, say Hull and Tolman, to proceed by conceiving of it as broken down into successive sets of simpler component functions. These component functions begin by introducing new intervening constructs defined in terms of the independent variables. Further intervening variables are then introduced by stating them as functions of the first set of intervening constructs, until finally the dependent behavior variable is postulated to be a function of one or more of the intervening variables.

Thus Tolman, beginning with the empirical data that the response measure is some function (f_1) of two groups of independent variables (environmental variables and individual difference variables), writes:

In place of the original f_1 function, I have introduced a set of intervening variables, I_a, I_b, I_c, etc., few or many, according to the particular theory. And I have conceived a set of f_2 functions to connect these intervening variables severally to the independent variables on the one hand, and an f_3 function to combine them together and connect them to the final dependent variable on the other (21, p. 9).

It is characteristic of Tolman's theorizing, however, that it never gets beyond the programmatic stage. In his writings Tolman has merely shown how such a theoretical device as the "intervening variable" can provide for the definition and proper utilization within psychology of such mentalistic terms as "demands," "hypotheses," "traits," "discriminanda," etc., but he never actually reaches the point of formulating a specific theory. In the present context this would, of course, require the precise specification of the various functions relating the intervening variables to the independent and dependent experimental variables. Instead of risking guesses on such matters, however, Tolman seems to prefer to ascertain them empirically by a series of what he calls "standard experimental set-ups." He believes the data from these studies will mirror the functions obtaining between the experimental (empirical) and intervening (theoretical) variables.[9]

Quite in contrast to such an approach, Hull has ventured to make guesses as to the precise nature of the functions introducing the intervening variables in his theoretical formulations. Thus he has attempted to formulate the basic laws of simple adaptive behavior (learning) by

[9] Tolman has been accused (and he has usually made no denial) of employing the phenomenological method in his psychology, and, because he has worked with animals, of being guilty of anthropomorphism. The present writer's interpretation is that it is Tolman, the experimentalist, who uses phenomenological introspection; Tolman, the theorist, introduces his intervening variables in terms of objectively defined variables. The difference between Lewin and Tolman on this point is interesting. Lewin, as we have seen, employs the phenomenological method primarily in his theoretical efforts, whereas Tolman uses it chiefly in the formulation of experimental problems.

introducing a number of intervening variables.[10] Beginning with the experimental variables, he has introduced by means of specific mathematical functions such symbolic constructs as stimulus trace (s), habit strength ($_sH_R$), the limit of habit strength (M), excitatory potential ($_sE_R$), inhibitory potential (I_R), effective excitatory potential ($_s\bar{E}_R$), and so on. Ultimately the observable response variable, R, is stated to be some function of the final intervening variable (e.g., $R = f(_s\bar{E}_R)$). Despite the neurophysiological tone of some of the terms that Hull employs to designate these constructs, the mistake should not be made of interpreting them as physiological concepts. Their scientific meaning is given only by the equations introducing them, and in this respect they are strictly comparable to many similar, abstract, mathematical constructs employed by the physicist in his theorizing. The use of neurophysiological terms and such additional statements as Hull sometimes makes as to their possible locus in the nervous system merely serve the purpose of providing experimental hints to persons interested in such matters. It may or may not turn out that they represent actual neurophysiological states or conditions that will some day be measurable by independent neurophysiological procedures.

An example of the specific manner in which Hull introduces his theoretical constructs is shown by the equations which he employs to define the two constructs, habit strength ($_sH_R$) and the limit of habit strength (M). With all experimental variables except the number of reinforced trials (N) and the length of the delay of the goal reinforcement (L) constant, the two equations are:

$$_sH_R = M(\mathrm{I} - e^{-iN})$$
$$M = \mathrm{I00}e^{-kL}.$$

Grice (4) has recently shown how such precisely defined theoretical constructs may be tested. He employed several mazes of different absolute lengths involving a shorter and longer path to the goal and ran different groups of rats on each maze. On the basis of the above two equations the following rational equation was then derived mathematically to describe the rate of learning the mazes:

---

[10] Reference is made here to Hull's latest writings in which the "intervening variable" technique is made more explicit. As Bergmann and Spence (2) have pointed out, Hull's earlier miniature systems (5, 8) really involved the definition of such mediating constructs.

$$\left[N = b \log \left(\frac{e^{-kL} - e^{-kHL}}{e^{-kL} - e^{-kHL} - a} \right) \right].$$

Where N = number of pairs of trials on the two paths to learn the maze.

   L = length of short path to goal.

   H = ratio of long to short path length.

k, a, b = empirical constants.

This rational equation was then shown to fit the experimental data, whereas another equation

$$\left[N = b \log \left(\frac{\log H}{\log H - C} \right) \right]$$

derived from a logarithmic postulate [11] as to the relation of M to L was shown not to be in agreement with the experimental data.

Until constructs are introduced in some such precise fashion as Hull employs one really does not have a scientific theory, for it is only under such conditions that the possibility of verification or refutation exists. Unfortunately, much of what has passed for theory in psychology has been sadly lacking in this respect, a state of affairs which is largely responsible for many of the "theoretical" controversies, and for the low regard in which theory is held in some quarters in psychology. That theory construction has not always been intelligently pursued, however, is no reason for doing without theory. Without the generalizations which theories aim to provide we should never be in a position to predict behavior, for knowledge of particular events does not provide us with a basis for prediction when the situation differs in the least degree. The higher the level of abstraction that can be obtained the greater will be both the understanding and actual control achieved.

IV The Ultra-Positivistic Approach

All the methods of ascertaining the laws of psychology we have discussed so far have agreed, in principle at least, that it is necessary to introduce some type of symbolic construct. It is also apparent that agreement ceases as regards the extent to which the proponents of these different views have insisted on rigorous and objective specification. We turn now to a quite different approach to the same problem

[11] $M = 100 - K \log L.$

—that of the ultra-positivist or empiricist, who tries to eschew all types of theoretical constructs. Usually the writings of such persons are limited to negativistic, critical attacks on all theory. Recently, however, Woodrow has come forward with a constructive proposal as to how general mathematical laws of psychology may be discovered by a method which he believes avoids the necessity of introducing theoretical constructs.

Woodrow's method consists in an attempt to obtain by mathematical curve fitting a general equation describing a wide variety of experimental facts. Thus, after plotting a series of experimental curves of such widely varying situations as learning to abstract, learning to associate numbers and letters, learning a maze, reaction time to different intensities of stimulation, the forgetting of monosyllabic words, brightness and pitch discrimination, the growth of intelligence, etc., Woodrow sought to fit these empirical curves by means of a single general equation. He found that such an equation could be found and that it took the following form:

$$Y = a + \sqrt{p^2 + k^2(\text{I} - f^{X+d})^2}.$$

This equation states a law between two experimental variables, a dependent response variable Y, e.g., errors, successes, latencies, etc., and an independent manipulable variable X, e.g., number of practice periods, intensity of the stimulus, preparatory interval, etc. But it will be noticed further that the law includes more than these two variables. It also involves certain constants or unknowns, termed parameters, the a, p, k, f, and d in the equation. We cannot stop to discuss these parameters in too great detail here. Suffice it to say that the specific shapes of the different empirical curves determine what parameters it is necessary to assume. Two of them, a and b, have no particular psychological significance, they merely express the fact that either one or both variables may have been measured by scales with an arbitrary zero. The parameter, k, is introduced because all his curves exhibit a limit to improvement, no matter how favorable the status given the environmental variable. Another parameter, f, is determined by the rate of approach of the curve to this limit and p, finally, is introduced to take care of the fact that the lower part of the curve sometimes shows positive acceleration.

As Woodrow himself points out, these parameters may be thought of, if one so wishes, as representing hypothetical states or factors within the organism.[12] Woodrow prefers not to do so, for, as he argues, it really makes little difference what the internal referents are since they cannot at present be independently measured anyway. From the point of view of finding a general equation or law that will fit the experimental data the important thing, Woodrow states, is to determine how many parameters are required and the mathematical function of each.

While in general sympathy with Woodrow's mathematical approach and his view that it is unnecessary to specify the factors or complexes of factors inside the organism which determine the values of the parameters, the writer is, nevertheless, of the opinion that such an equation as Woodrow obtains by his analysis is, on the whole, rather barren and sterile. Its defect is not that the factors *within* the subject are not specified, but rather that it fails to give any indication whatever of the conditions or variables even *outside* the subject which determine these parameters. In this respect Woodrow's approach is similar to the field theorists'. We shall have occasion later to point out other resemblances between these two approaches.

This criticism can be made clearer, perhaps, by contrasting the end result of Woodrow's empirical procedure with Hull's rational approach to the same problem. Woodrow's law specifies but a single experimental variable determining the response:

$$Y = f(X_1).$$

Hull's theorizing culminates in a much more comprehensive law. Thus in the case of his theoretical formulation of simple adaptive behavior (learning) his derivation involves the following series of steps:

1. $\boxed{M} = f(T, G)$
2. $\boxed{H} = f(\boxed{M}, T', N)$
3. $\boxed{D} = f(T'')$
4. $\boxed{E} = f(\boxed{D}, \boxed{H})$
5. $\boxed{I} = f(N, W, F)$
6. $\boxed{\bar{E}} = f(\boxed{E}, \boxed{I})$
7. $R = f(\boxed{\bar{E}})$.

[12] Woodrow writes, "Now these parameters may refer to anything whatsoever, conscious, physiological, environmental, psychic, or purely imaginary. Here one is free to follow his predilections, whether for motives, excitatory and inhibitory substances, field forces, states of disequilibrium, inertia of the nervous system, abilities, or what not" (23, p. 4).

Here the squared symbols are intervening variables or hypothetical constructs. The other symbols represent the dependent response measure (R) and the various manipulable, environmental variables $(T, G, T', $ etc.). By substituting in the successive equations, a single equation R as a function of seven environmental variables is obtained.[18]

$$R = f(T, G, T', N, T'', W, F)$$

The latter procedure thus comes much closer to achieving the goal of the scientist, that of discovering all of the experimental variables determining the response measure and the nature of the functional interrelations holding between them. If this is achieved, the parameters become known functions of these experimental variables and thus become experimentally manipulable. Woodrow's formulation, on the other hand, provides us with very little more information than we had when we started.

It is also interesting to note that a strong case can be made out for the position that Woodrow's method is really not a great deal different from those theoretical approaches which infer their constructs from the characteristics of the response. In introducing his parameters Woodrow is, in effect, assuming or postulating some kind of hypothetical factor. Thus, on noticing that some of his curves show an initial period of positive acceleration, Woodrow assumes a factor, p, "whose influence is greatest when the magnitude of the environmental variable is small" (23, p. 7). This factor is inferred, we see, from the characteristics of the response curve and is therefore in a certain sense akin to the hypothetical constructs of the field theorists which, as we have seen, are also inferred from the response characteristics. The important difference is that in arriving at these hypothetical factors Woodrow does not make use of the introspective report associated with a response but rather bases his constructs on the mathematical properties of a curve of successive response measures.

[18] The reader may ask: Why have a series of equations that introduce intervening variables? Why not write the single equation from the beginning and avoid the hypothetical constructs? One obvious reason, of course, is that it is just not possible to conceive of such a complex function all at once. As Tolman says, one can arrive at it only by breaking it down into a series of simpler functions. The reader is referred to a recent article by Hull in which he gives other reasons for using intervening variables with multiple equations rather than a single equation (6).

v Conclusions

In summary, the present paper has stated the task of the psychologist to be that of discovering the general laws of behavior, and has attempted to present a brief and critical outline of five different methods of approaching this task. The conclusions that the writer believes may be drawn from this survey are:

1. That theory is still at a very primitive level in psychology, concerning itself primarily with the discovery of low-order laws rather than the integration of different realms of laws.

2. That there is a variety of different theoretical procedures possible in psychology.

3. That some psychologists substitute, often quite unconsciously, phenomenological introspection and anthropomorphic thinking for theorizing. There is, of course, nothing wrong with such introspection; it has often served as a means of formulating interesting and valuable experiments. In such instances, however, the credit should not be given to a theory.

4. That many theories in psychology have provided us with response-response (R-R) laws rather than stimulus-response (S-R) laws.

5. That the most promising theoretical technique, especially from the point of view of discovering the historical stimulus-response laws, is the so-called "intervening variable" method proposed by Hull and Tolman.

References

1. Bergmann, G. Psychoanalysis and experimental psychology: A review from the standpoint of scientific empiricism. *Mind,* 1943, *52,* 122-140. [Selection No. 23 in this volume.]
2. Bergmann, G. and Spence, K. W. Operationism and theory in psychology. *Psychol. Rev.,* 1941, *48,* 1-14. [Selection No. 3 in this volume.]
3. Carnap, R. Testability and meaning. *Philos. Sci.,* 1936, *3,* 419-471; 1937, *4,* 1-40.
4. Grice, G. R. An experimental study of the gradient of reinforcement in maze learning. *J. exp. Psychol.,* 1942, *30,* 475-489.
5. Hull, C. L. Mind, mechanism and adaptive behavior. *Psychol. Rev.,* 1937, *44,* 1-32.
6. Hull, C. L. The problem of intervening variables in molar behavior theory. *Psychol. Rev.,* 1943, *50,* 273-291. [Selection No. 13 in this volume.]

7. Hull, C. L. *Principles of behavior.* New York: D. Appleton-Century, 1943.

8. Hull, C. L.; Hovland, C. I.; Ross, R. T.; Hall, M.; Perkins, D. T.; and Fitch, F. B. *Mathematico-deductive theory of rote learning.* New Haven: Yale Univ. Press, 1940. [See Selection No. 14 in this volume.]

9. Koch, S. The logical character of the motivation concept. II. *Psychol. Rev.,* 1941, *48,* 127-154.

10. Koffka, K. *Principles of Gestalt psychology.* New York: Harcourt, Brace, 1935. [See Selection No. 24 in this volume.]

11. Köhler, W. *Gestalt psychology.* New York: Liveright, 1929.

12. Köhler, W. *Dynamics in psychology.* New York: Liveright, 1940.

13. Lewin, K. *A dynamic theory of personality.* (Trans. by D. K. Adams and K. E. Zener) New York: McGraw-Hill, 1935.

14. Lewin, K. *Principles of topological psychology.* (Trans. by Fritz and Grace Heider.) New York: McGraw-Hill, 1936.

15. Lewin, K. Field theory and learning. In *Forty-First Year Natl. Soc. Stud. Educ.,* Part II. Bloomington, Ill.: Public School Publishing Co., 1942, 215-242.

16. Pavlov, I. P. *Conditioned reflexes.* (Trans. by F. C. Anrep.) London: Oxford Univ. Press, 1927.

17. Snygg, D. The need for a phenomenological system of psychology. *Psychol. Rev.,* 1941, *48,* 404-424. [See Selection No. 21 in this volume.]

18. Spearman, C. *The abilities of man.* New York: Macmillan, 1927.

19. Spence, K. W. Theoretical interpretations of learning. In *Comparative Psychology,* rev. ed. (F. A. Moss, ed.), New York: Prentice-Hall, 1942, Chap. 11.

20. Thurstone, L. L. *The vectors of mind.* Chicago: Univ. Chicago Press, 1935.

21. Tolman, E. C. The determiners of behavior at a choice point. *Psychol. Rev.,* 1938, *45,* 1-41.

22. Tolman, E. C. Operational behaviorism and current trends in psychology. *Proc. 25th Anniv. Celebr. Inaug. Grad. Stud., Los Angeles:* Univ. of S. Calif. Press, 1936, 89-103. [Selection No. 5 in this volume.]

23. Woodrow, H. The problem of general quantitative laws in psychology. *Psychol. Bull.,* 1942, *39,* 1-27.

5   THE INTERVENING VARIABLE

Edward C. Tolman

I am going to present a brief statement of my own brand of psychology. I shall here call it Operational Behaviorism. And I shall try to show that the principles of such an operational behaviorism will help to illuminate the interrelationships between the types of psychological experiment now actually current.

Before proceeding with the detailed presentation of my system, let me note in an aside that the term "operational" has been chosen with two different meanings in mind. In the first place, I have chosen it to indicate a certain general positivistic attitude now being taken by many modern physicists and philosophers and for which Professor Bridgman (1, 2) has selected this word "operational." In this sense, an operational psychology will be one which seeks to define its concepts in such a manner that they can be stated and tested in terms of concrete repeatable operations by independent observers. In this sense, to quote from S. S. Stevens, "a term or proposition has meaning (denotes something) if, and only if, the criteria of its applicability or truth consist of concrete operations which can be performed." (12, p. 517f. See also 11.) The behaviorism which I am going to present seeks, then, to use only concepts which are capable of such concrete operational verification.

But, in the second place, I have also chosen this designation, "operational," because of what seems to me a second connotation which in connection with the word "behavior" it tends to have. For, behavior as the thing observed also turns out to be essentially an activity whereby the organism in question "operates." In behaving, an organism, as Brunswik (3) puts it, "intends" and more or less successfully "conquers" its environment. It operates on its environment by such intendings and conquerings.[1]

---

[1] See also my own previous analyses of behavior (13, 14).

From E. C. Tolman, Operational behaviorism and current trends in psychology. In *Proc. 25th Anniv. Celebr. Inaug. Grad. Stud.* Los Angeles: Univ. South. Calif. Press, 1936. Reprinted by permission of the author and publisher.

To sum up, then, I will call mine an operational behaviorism because (a) my type of psychology would self-consciously seek to discover the concrete operations which an experimenter, or any observer, has to carry out to test the applicability or nonapplicability in any given instance of a specific psychological concept or proposition; and because (b) the observed behavior itself turns out to be a set of operations performed by the observed organism relative to its own environment. In a word, the activities both of us, the observing and conceptualizing organisms, and of them, the observed and behaving organisms, are all ultimately to be characterized as operations of organisms upon environments.

To return, now, to the specific presentation of my system. The final dependent variable in which, as a psychologist, I am interested is behavior. It is the behavior of organisms, human and subhuman, which I wish to predict and control. As a psychologist I shall not attempt to describe immediate experience. The problem of immediate experience —the problem, that is, of some ultimate statement concerning that initial, as Professor Loewenberg (10) calls it, "pre-analytical" matrix out of which both physics and psychology have developed—is either a problem for the philosophers or it is no problem at all. But, in any case, immediate experience can no longer, I would assert, be conceived as the special province of psychology any more than it is to be conceived as the special province of physics. For psychology, like physics, must now take immediate experience for granted and then proceed to develop maps, rules, and equations for finding one's way about. Physics develops one type of such a map and psychology another, and the two maps are ultimately to be fitted together so as to make complete prediction—complete finding of our way about—possible.

The particular map, the particular subset of predictions, in which psychology is interested concerns the to-be-expected behavior of organisms—the behavior to be expected from other organisms, and the behavior to be expected from ourselves. And in these predictions, mental processes, whether they be those of another or of ourselves, will figure only in the guise of objectively definable *intervening variables*. Or (to borrow a phrase from William James) the sole "cash-value" of mental processes lies, I shall assert, in this their character as a set of intermediating functional processes which interconnect between the initiating causes of behavior, on the one hand, and the final resulting behavior itself, on the other.

Organisms of given heredities, given kinds and amounts of previous training, and given maturities are immersed in environments and are driven by conditions of physiological disequilibrium. And because of these environments and these disequilibria, they behave. Mental processes are but intervening variables between the five independent variables of 1) *environmental stimuli,* 2) *physiological drive,* 3) *heredity,* 4) *previous training,* and 5) *maturity,* on the one hand, and the final dependent variable, *behavior,* on the other.

Let me indicate this situation symbolically. Let S stand for environmental stimulus condition, P for the conditions external and internal whereby physiological drives are defined, H for heredity, T for previous training, and A for age or maturity. We may then write the general equation:

$$B = f_1 (S, P, H, T, A)$$

B is some function f_1 of S, P, H, T, and A. Given this equation, mental processes are concepts which arise when we attempt further to elaborate the nature of this f_1 function. For it is a very complicated function—at least for all cases save those, perhaps, of such very simple behavior as reflexes and tropisms. It is in fact so complicated that we at present seem unable to state it in any single simple statement. We find, rather, that we have to handle it by conceiving it as broken down into successive sets of component functions. These component functions connect the independent variables to logically constructed "intervening variables," and then connect these intervening variables in their turn to one another and to the final dependent behavior. We may symbolize such intervening variables as $I_a, I_b, I_c \ldots I_n$. And, if we do so, we may then write in place of the original single function, $B = f_1 (S, P, H, T, A)$, various sets of component functions of such forms as:

$$I_a = f^a_2 (S, P, H, T, A)$$

$$I_b = f^b_2 (S, P, H, T, A)$$

$$I_c = f^c_2 (S, P, H, T, A)$$

or:

$$I_g = f^g_2 (I_a, I_c \ldots S, P, H, T, A)$$

$$I_h = f^h_2 (I_b, I_c, I_d \ldots S, P, H, T, A)$$

or finally:

$$B = f^x_2 (I_a, I_b, I_c, I_f \ldots H, T, A)$$

It is such intervening I's, whether simply or complicatedly related to the independent variables and to one another, which are all that my operational behaviorism finds in the way of mental processes. These I's are "demands," "discriminanda," "manipulanda," "means-end fields," "traits," and "capacities," and the like. They are objective entities defined in terms of the f_2 functions which connect them to the S's, P's, H's, T's, and A's, on the one hand, and to the final B, on the other.

It is to be pointed out, however, that there is also a second way of trying to conceive and define a set of intervening I's—the physiological way. But when this physiological way is taken, the result is to be called a physiological rather than a psychological operational behaviorism. In such a physiological operationalism the interconnecting I's would be conceived and defined as such and such specific central and peripheral disturbances in the nervous system, as conditioned reflex connections, as anticipatory goal-reactions, as cerebral potential-gradients, as glandular secretions, and the like. Science demands, of course, in the end, the final development of both sorts of behaviorism. And the facts and laws of physiological behaviorism, when obtained, will presumably provide the explanation for the facts and laws of psychological behaviorism. But the psychological facts and laws have also to be gathered and established in their own right. A psychology cannot be explained by a physiology until one has a psychology to explain. Further, it appears to me that it is primarily the job of us psychologists, or at any rate of the "purer" among us, to gather the psychological facts and laws and to leave it to our less pure, physiologically minded brethren to gather the neurological, glandular, and biochemical data which underlie such psychological facts and laws.

Confining myself, then, from here on to psychological operational behaviorism, let me attempt to sketch in the general outlines of the latter. For, as I see it, such a psychological operationalism does no more than give a list of, and attempt to indicate the true functional interrelationship between, the actual types of experiment being done today in psychology.

Psychological operationalism presents three main theses:

1. It asserts a list of intervening I's.
2. It asserts certain laws or functions whereby these I's result from the S's, P's, H's, T's, and A's, and from each other.
3. It asserts certain further laws or functions whereby the final be-

havior B results from combinations of these I's, as well as from S's, P's, H's, T's, and A's.

The following schema indicates my formulation of these three assertions. This schema is, of course, tentative. It will surely need revision before it can be adopted wholeheartedly. I present it, nevertheless, because I believe it to be correct in essence. I believe that even now it is a pretty fair summary of what psychology today is actually, operationally, doing.

The causal sequences run from left to right and are indicated by arrows. The final dependent variable—behavior—is at the extreme right. The initial and independent variables, the S's, P's, H's, T's, and A's, are at the extreme left.

The final dependent behavior has three component aspects. Sometimes it is one and sometimes it is another of these aspects which the given experiment is interested in. No one of these aspects can, of course, be missing, but a given experiment can vary one of them somewhat independently of the other two. They are (a) *direction,* (b) *quantity* or *persistence,* and (c) *efficiency* or *skill.* That is, concretely speaking, a behavior is (a) a doing of one thing, a taking of one direction rather than another: it is speaking certain words rather than other words, sitting in a chair rather than walking about, going into one maze-alley rather than another maze-alley, or the like. And it is (b) a taking of this direction with a certain degree of intensity or persistence as measured concretely in terms of percentage of animals in the given situation who do it, or by the amount of distraction that has to be introduced before it is interrupted, or by some other quantifying technique. And it is (c) the exhibition of a certain degree of efficiency or skill as measured by time, waste motion, or some similar measure. Thus, for example, in a given discrimination problem, using Lashley's technique, the rats (a) jump to one door rather than the other; (b) they do this a certain percentage of times; and (c) they exhibit a certain degree of skill in their actual jumping technique. In different experiments it might be different ones of these three subvariables the causal antecedents of which one is particularly interested in determining.

The initial independent variables, indicated at the left, subdivide into two groups: S's and P's, on the one hand, and H's, T's, and A's, on the other. The former may be characterized as releasing variables. It is these S's and P's which set behavior going. The H's, T's, and A's, on the

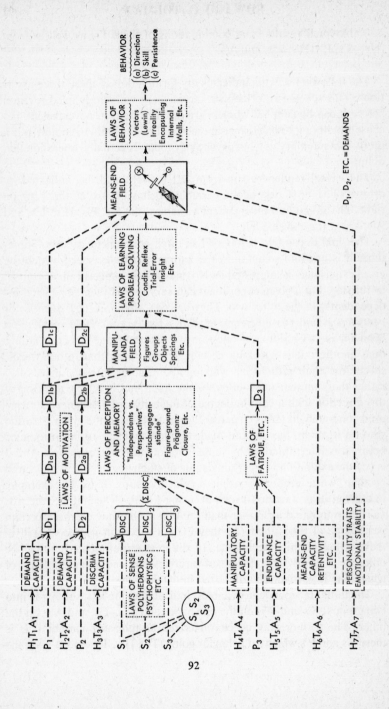

other hand, are to be designated as the governing or guiding variables. Heredity, previous training, and given maturities do not, as such, initiate behavior. But they do govern or guide in a very fundamental way the final character of the behavior which is initiated by given S's and P's. These governing or guiding H's, T's, and A's have been indicated as working together in sub-groups.

There are also two types of intervening variable. These have been indicated as surrounded by solid lines and by dash lines, respectively. Those surrounded by solid lines are to be characterized as mental events, whereas those surrounded by dash lines may be characterized as mental traits or capacities. The traits and capacities are the relatively direct products of the H's, T's, and A's. The events are the products of the S's and P's combined with the traits and capacities.

The functional causal relations are indicated by the arrows with the legends enclosed in dotted lines.

Now, I would insist that the different chapters in modern experimental psychology, as we know them today, are located by such a diagram. That is, each chapter, it seems to me, chooses as its topic some one minor group of the intervening variables, or else the final behavior itself, and then discusses the immediate functional dependencies or laws—the arrows—whereby these variables depend upon various of the preceding variables in the schema.

Thus, for example, the chapter on Motivation is concerned, obviously, with the demands, designated as D_1, D_2, D_3, etc., and the laws or functions whereby these latter depend upon the P's and upon the motivation capacities deriving from H_1, T_1, A_1; H_2, T_2, A_2; and H_5, T_5, A_5.

The chapter on Sensory Psychology concerns the discriminanda, $Disc_1$, $Disc_2$, $Disc_3$, etc., (my name for sensations and images) and the way in which these depend upon the S's and upon sensory capacities.

The chapter on Gestalt Psychology—the Gestalt psychology, that is, of perception and immediate memory—concerns what I have labelled the "manipulanda field" and the laws of Prägnanz, Closure, Good Gestalt, *Zwischengegenstände* (Brunswik) etc., whereby this manipulanda field depends upon the discriminanda, upon the pattern relations among the stimuli (indicated on the diagram by $S_1 \, _{S_3} \, S_2$) and upon manipulation capacities.

The chapter on Problem Solving, Learning, and Reasoning concerns the means-end field and the laws of conditioned reflex, trial and error, and insight, whereby this means-end field results from the manipulanda field, from demands, and from the intellectual and motor capacities deriving from H_6, T_6, A_6.

Further, a chapter which I would call that of Behavior Dynamics concerns the final dependent behavior and the latter's immediate dependence upon the means-end field and upon capacity factors and upon traits, such as emotional stability, deriving from H_7, T_7, A_7. It is the laws of this latter chapter which, as I see it, Professor Lewin (9) has been pioneering with regard to.

Finally, there would be a chapter, or rather many chapters, on *individual differences*. These chapters would concern themselves with the nature of the trait and capacity factors and with the laws of their dependence upon the H's, and T's, and A's. And the question which gives rise to the most disputes would be that as to whether these capacity and trait factors and the H's, T's, and A's which underlie them are relatively many (and specific) or relatively few (and general).

But by this time, I am sure that the critic must be up in arms. How, he will ask, are the intervening variables ever arrived at? All that one has overtly in any experimental setup are, by hypothesis, the left-hand independent variables, on the one hand, and the right-hand dependent behavior, on the other. All that one has actually to operate with are physiological drives (defined in terms of time since last feeding, since last copulation, or the like), environmental stimuli (defined in physical or common sense terms), heredity (defined by breeding charts and the traits of ancestors), and age (defined by number of days and hours since birth, or, if one is being more precise, since insemination), on the one hand, and the finally observed behavior, with its special characteristics of direction, persistence and skill, on the other. Whence, then, come our notions and definitions concerning the intervening variables?

My answer is as follows: In certain carefully chosen, controlled and "standard" experimental setups, one tries to hold all but one, or one small group, of the independent variables constant and studies the functional connection between the variations in this one independent variable, or this one limited group of independent variables, on the one hand, and the correlated variations in some quantitatable feature of the final behavior on the other. For example, one holds all the independent variables but, say, P_1 (time since last feeding) constant. And in doing this, one chooses certain "standard" values for all the other independent variables such as P_2, S_1, S_2, etc. And then, under these conditions, one observes the correlations between the variations in P_1, on the one hand, and the resulting variations in some aspect of the behavior B, on the other.

For example, let us suppose it to be a case of rats, and let us suppose that the feature of the behavior which is in question is the percentage of entrances into the correct alley for groups of rats that have already thoroughly learned the maze. Under such conditions, as we vary P_1 (time since last feeding) we shall obtain some curve such as the following between this B (percentage of entrances into the correct alleys) and P_1.

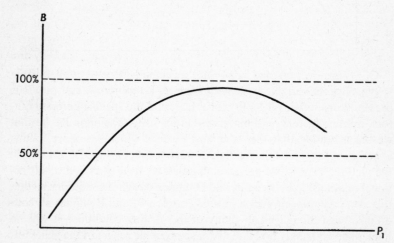

This curve holds, of course, in the first instance only for one given value of H_1, T_1, A_1. We shall assume, however, that the same general form of curve will be obtained whatever the values of H_1, T_1, and A_1 (i.e., of heredity, previous training, and maturity). The effects of these different values of H_1, T_1, and A_1 will, we shall suppose, be simply to give new values to the constants or parameters which determine the height and curvatures of this curve.

We must now, however, make one further assumption. We must suppose that we have chosen the constant "standard" values, which we have given to all the other independent variables, P_2, P_3, S_1, S_2, etc., in such a fashion that this general curve between B and P_1 which we have thus obtained really mirrors directly the functional relation between P_1 and *an intervening variable* D_1 (the demand for the given type of food). In other words, we must assume that we have chosen a setup such that the variations in the selected aspect of the behavior mirror directly those of the desired intervening variable and that we can therefore rescore and relabel our curve as follows:

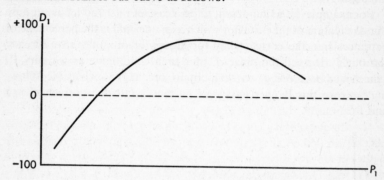

Of course, the obtained behavior does actually depend upon a whole welter of other variables—general stimulus setup, number of previous presentations, other physiological drives, and the specific heredity factors, training factors, and maturity factors, as well as upon P_1. So that we are assuming that the "standard" values which we chose in this experiment for these other variables were such that they did not distort the picture. That is, we are assuming that we have obtained this functional relationship between P_1 and D_1 under standard conditions so that this same relationship will also hold between P_1 and D_1 under all conditions, even though under many of these other conditions it will no longer appear simply and directly in some single aspect of the behavior.

Or, consider the findings of Warden (15) and his co-workers as to the functional relation between P_1 (time since last feeding) and B (number of crossings of the electric grill). Now it is obvious that the interest of such an experiment also depends upon assumptions similar to the above. The first of these assumptions is that the details of the Warden experimental setup (that is, the values given by the experiment to all the other variables: type of obstruction-box chosen; location of the reward object; length of time allowed for crossings; etc.) have all been chosen so that the obtained behavior (number of crossings in 20 minutes) mirrors directly the intervening variable D_1 (demand for the given food). And the second implicit assumption is that the relationship which is thus found between D_1 and P_1 is a characteristic and true relationship—one not limited for its validity to this one type of obstruction apparatus or to the other specific conditions. It is assumed, in short, that the same true relationship, the curve for which we have just drawn hypothetically as the result of the supposed maze experiment, will be found. It is assumed that the Warden obstruction technique is a "standard" experimental setup which uncovers a true, relatively universal relationship between P_1 (hunger) and D_1 (demand for the given food)—a relationship which will also hold for other situations—for other mazes, discrimination boxes, and the like—even though it may not appear simply and directly in any of these other situations. Indeed, it even seems to be assumed by Warden and his co-workers that this relationship thus found between P_1 and D_1, using the obstruction-box technique on rats, is the one which also holds for human beings in general life situations. It is assumed, in short, that this relationship holds not only for different values of the S with the given H_1's, T_1's, and A_1's (rats), but also for quite different values of such H_1's, T_1's, and A_1's (i.e., those of men).

But all such assumptions are ticklish and of very uncertain justification. And yet, however dangerous and open to pitfalls they may be, such types of assumption are, I am convinced, the sort which in psychology we actually do employ today. We do assume intervening variables, and we do try to work forward to them from the independent variables and backward to them from the resulting behavior. We do suppose (in spite of all the complexities) that we can determine in carefully chosen "standard" experimental setups certain relatively unique true functions connecting these intervening variables to specific groups of independent variables. That is, we do assume that when we carefully select our experimental setups, these intervening variables will be betrayed directly in the selected quantified feature of the resulting behavior. And we do suppose that the relationships thus obtained are true and persistent ones which will also obtain in other conditions where the given intervening variables are no longer directly mirrored by any single simple aspect of the behavior.

Turn, now, to another example, the typical discrimination experiment. It is obvious that in this type of experiment we seek to hold all the P's and all the H's, T's, and A's, and all the other S's (than the one type of S that we are specifically investigating), constant. And then we seek to establish a general and universally true relation between the variation in this one type of S and the given resulting type discriminanda (i.e., sense-quality). And we assume that this obtained relation between the values of this type of S and the values of the resulting discriminanda betrays itself in its true form under these standard conditions of such a discrimination experiment. So that we suppose that we thereafter know this relation between this type of S and this type of Disc (between, for example, S, and Disc), even when under other conditions than such a discrimination experiment this relation no longer, as such, appears directly in the final behavior.

So much for suggestions as to what we may call, perhaps, the "first-line" intervening variables—the D's and the Disc's. But it appears, looking at the diagram, that there are also "second-line" and "third-line" and perhaps still further removed intervening variables. These latter are further displaced toward the final behavior and they depend not only upon certain independent variables but also upon combinations of various of the preceding "first-line" or "second-line" intervening variables. Examples of such second- and third-line variables are the manipulanda-field and the means-end field. How do we ever arrive at notions and definitions of these? My answer is that we first assume that we already know the functions which connect the preceding intervening variables to the independent variables. And then we use these preceding intervening variables as independents.

For example, in the study of the manipulanda field we assume that we already know what discriminanda will, under the ideal conditions of a Titchenerian, or a psychophysical, experiment, result from the given sense-stimuli. We also assume that we have average standard individuals with standard capacities. And then we proceed to investigate the laws of the function by which given S's plus their temporal and spatial patterns, plus the manipulanda traits and capacities of the given species produce the manipulanda field. And we assume that this manipulanda field, under these conditions, is betrayed directly by some chosen aspect of the resulting behavior. That is, we devise experiments whereby certain obtained variations in B can be assumed to be direct expressions of "figure-ground," "grouping," or other "gestalt formations," and of whether it is the "projected" or the "independent" size that is intended (14) and the like. In short, we do experiments using sizes, weights, groupings, movements, etc., similar to those of Klüver (6) with monkeys or of Hertz (4, 5) with blue jays or of Wertheimer (16), Köhler (7), Koffka (8), and Brunswik (3) and their co-workers, with human adults.

Again, having thus assumed that we know all the functions which produce the demands, the manipulanda field and the various capacities so that, given the values of the independent variables, we can read off by means of these functions the correlated values of these demands and manipulanda fields, we then proceed to study the laws of learning, conditioned reflex, trial and error, and insight, whereby the manipulanda field plus the demands produce such and such a final means-end field.

And, finally, assuming that we now know the means-end field—assuming, that is, that we know the organism to be responding relative to such and such goals, so and so far off, with such and such obstructions between him and these goals—then we proceed to study the final function connecting the characters of this means-end field with the final behavior. And we discover such laws as those which Lewin (9) has brought to our attention and which he has characterized by such phrases as "resolution of vectors," "going out of the field," "encapsuling oneself," "flight into an irreality plane," "relief of internal tensions," and the like. These are the final types of function which connect behavior to the preceding means-end field and to the personality factors resulting from H_7, T_7, A_7.

In order to make the schema still more real, let me point out, further, just where some of the other chapters of modern psychology would fall.

The chapter on Psychoanalysis would concern itself with P_2 whether this type of P is one or many, and with the question of the heredity and training variables, H_2 and T_2, whereby hierarchies and interactions of the subordinate demands, D_2a, D_2b, etc., are established. It would also concern itself with the building up of special social features in the means-end field and with facts concerning introspectability and non-introspectability arising out of such social features.

The chapter on Motor Skills would concern the manipulation capacities and the laws of their dependence upon heredity differences H_5, on training differences T_5, and upon mere maturation differences A_5.

The chapter on Learning, Reasoning, and all the higher thought processes would be concerned with the development of the means-end field and its dependence upon H_6, T_6, A_6, and upon the manipulanda field.

The chapter on Feeling and Emotion would, I believe, fall in three places. In part it would be a discussion of a peculiar type of discriminandum resulting from interoceptive stimuli. In part it would be a discussion of the laws of motivation whereby the D's derive from the P's. And in part it would be a discussion of certain features of the final behavior dynamics as these are affected by emotional stability and the other personality traits deriving from H_7, T_7, A_7.

And, to repeat once again, the chapter or chapters on individual differences would concern itself with the question of in how far H_1, and H_2, and H_3, etc., up to H_7 are mutually independent of one another. And it would also raise the question as to whether each one of these itself may not really represent a bunch of several or perhaps many independent subvariables.

So much for my attempt to indicate the general operational meaning of the schema. You may, if you will, cavil at its details. But I doubt if you can get away from the general proposition which the schema embodies, namely, that we do in psychology assume intervening variables more or less like the ones I have suggested, and that we do attempt to define these intervening variables by going at them experimentally, i.e., *operationally,* from the two ends.

If you will have none of such a schema, then there are but two alternatives left to you. Either you must return to good old-fashioned introspectionism or you must wait for the appearance of a more refined neurology and physiology. Either you must assume that you know the intervening variables in some immediate direct fashion—not only your own but also of the other fellow and those of the rats who can't tell you about them—or else you must wait until physiology and neurology can give you all the actual neural and physiological interconnections between the independent variables of stimuli, physiological disequilibria, and genes, on the one hand, and final resulting behavior, on the other. But, if you adopt either of these two alternatives, it seems to me that you may as well confess that for the present you must give up psychology altogether.

One last word. Some one is sure to ask: But what about introspection? Is not introspection after all, at least in the case of men, a significant method by which one can get at and define these intervening variables in a direct and really reliable fashion? I doubt it. I believe that introspection is a form of social response—a type of final behavior which would appear at the right on our diagram like any other behavior but one which has very complicated conditions. And I do not believe that this introspection behavior in a standard experimental setup is of a sort to mirror most types of intervening variables any more successfully and truly than do more gross, less social forms of behavior. In fact, it seems to me obvious and already well demonstrated that in most cases introspective behavior is far less successful in such a direct mirroring than are more gross forms of behavior; for these latter are not, as is introspection, subject to distortion by being directed toward an audience. The very essence of introspection lies in the fact that it is a response to audiences—external and internal. And, such being the case, it seems less likely to mirror most types of intervening variable so directly and correctly as do more gross nonsocial forms of behavior.

The above does not, of course, however, preclude the proposition that, where the intervening variable in question is, as in psychoanalysis and in many personality studies, itself some complicated resultant of the social situation, that then such an intervening variable can, and perhaps must, be mirrored by introspection. For example, one of the most significant findings of psychoanalysis is that introspection is impossible or violently distorts in some situations but is valid and adequate in others.

To sum up, then, the validity of introspection is, as I see it, restricted to one special type of investigation—the type of investigation where what we are primarily concerned with are those intervening variables (whatever they may be) which underlie the ability or nonability of being able "to talk about it." But in the other, far greater majority of psychological investigations, this ability or nonability "to talk about" is not important or determinative. And, indeed, when it is called into play, it is apt to lead to decided errors relative to the other types of intervening variable with which, in such cases, we are concerned.

Let me recapitulate:

1. I have tried to present and defend an "operational behaviorism."
2. Such an operational behaviorism comprises two main principles:
   (a) It asserts that the ultimate interest of psychology is solely the prediction and control of behavior.
   (b) It asserts that psychological concepts, i.e., the mental capacities and mental events—may be conceived as objectively defined intervening variables. And it asserts that these intervening variables are to be defined wholly operationally—that is, in terms of the actual experimental operations whereby their presences or absences and their relations to the controlling independent variables and to the final dependent behavior are determined.
3. I have presented a tentative schema for such intervening variables.
4. I have asserted that the different chapters of modern psychology find their natural locations on this schema.

And,

5. I have denied that introspective behavior provides any *sui generis* type

of information concerning the intervening variables. Introspection is just one more behavior which will in some cases (but in other cases most certainly will not) provide a good, standard experimental setup for discovering and studying specific types of intervening variable.

References

1. Bridgman, P. W. The logic of modern physics. New York: Macmillan, 1928.
2. Bridgman, P. W. A physicist's second reaction to Mengenlehre. *Scripta Mathematica,* 1934, *2,* 101-117.
3. Brunswik, E. *Wahrnehmung und Gegenstandswelt-Grunlegung einer Psychologie vom Gegnstand her.* Wien: Deuticke, 1934.
4. Hertz, M. Beobachtungen an gefangenen Rabenvögeln. *Psychol. Forsch.,* 1926, *8,* 336-397.
5. Hertz, M. Weitere Versuche an der Rabenkrahe. *Psychol. Forsch.,* 1928, *10,* 111-141.
6. Klüver, H. *Behavior mechanisms in monkeys.* Chicago: Univ. Chicago Press, 1933.
7. Köhler, W. *Psychologische Probleme.* Berlin: Springer, 1933.
8. Koffka, K. *Principles of Gestalt psychology.* New York: Harcourt, Brace, 1935. [See Selection No. 24 in this volume.]
9. Lewin, K. *A dynamic theory of personality.* (Trans. D. K. Adams and K. E. Zener.) New York: McGraw-Hill, 1935.
10. Loewenberg, J. Pre-analytical and post-analytical data. *J. Philos.,* 1927, *24,* 5-14.
11. Stevens, S. S. The operational basis of psychology. *Amer. J. Psychol.,* 1935, *47,* 323-330.
12. Stevens, S. S. The operational definition of psychological concepts. *Psychol. Rev.,* 1935, *42,* 517-527.
13. Tolman, E. C. *Purposive behavior in animals and man.* New York: Century, 1932. [See Selection No. 29 in this volume.]
14. Tolman, E. C. Psychology vs. immediate experience. *Phil. Sci.,* 1935, 356-380.
15. Warden, C. J. *Animal motivation, experimental studies on the albino rat.* New York: Columbia Univ. Press, 1931.
16. Wertheimer, M. *Diei Abhandlungen zur Gestalttheorie.* Erlangen: Verlag der Philosophischen Akademie, 1925.

6   OPERATIONAL VALIDITY
OF INTERVENING CONSTRUCTS

Kenneth MacCorquodale and Paul E. Meehl

As the thinking of behavior theorists has become more sophisticated and self-conscious, there has been considerable discussion of the value and logical status of so-called "intervening variables." Hull speaks of "symbolic constructs, intervening variables, or hypothetical entities" (3, p. 22) and deals with them in his theoretical discussion as being roughly equivalent notions. At least, his exposition does not distinguish among them explicitly. In his presidential address on behavior at a choice point, Tolman inserts one of Hull's serial conditioning diagrams (8, p. 13) between the independent variables (maintenance schedule, goal object, etc.) and the dependent variable ("behavior ratio") to illustrate his concept of the intervening variable. This would seem to imply that Tolman views his "intervening variables" as of the same character as Hull's. In view of this, it is somewhat surprising to discover that Skinner apparently feels that his formulations have a close affinity to those of Tolman, but are basically dissimilar to those of Hull (7, pp. 436, 437). In advocating a theoretical structure which is "descriptive" and "positivistic," he suggests that the model chosen by Hull (Newtonian mechanics) is not the most suitable model for purposes of behavior theory; and in general is critical of the whole postulate-deductive approach.

Simultaneously with these trends, one can still observe among "tough-minded" psychologists the use of words such as "unobservable" and "hypothetical" in an essentially derogatory manner, and an almost compulsive fear of passing beyond the direct colligation of observable data. "Fictions" and "hypothetical entities" are sometimes introduced into a discussion of theory with a degree of trepidation and apology quite unlike the freedom with which physicists talk about atoms, mesons, fields, and the like. There also seems to be a tendency to treat all hypo-

From K. MacCorquodale and P. E. Meehl, On a distinction between hypothetical constructs and intervening variables, *Psychol. Rev.*, 1948, *55*, 95-107. Pp. 95-96 and 103-107 reprinted by permission of the authors, the *Psychological Review*, and the American Psychological Association.

thetical constructs as on the same footing merely because they are hypothetical; so that we find people arguing that if neutrons are admissible in physics, it must be admissible for us to talk about, e.g., the damming up of libido and its reversion to earlier channels.

The view which theoretical psychologists take toward intervening variables and hypothetical constructs will of course profoundly influence the direction of theoretical thought. Furthermore, what *kinds* of hypothetical constructs we become accustomed to thinking about will have a considerable impact upon theory creation. The present paper aims to present what seems to us a major problem in the conceptualization of intervening variables, without claiming to offer a wholly satisfactory solution. Chiefly, it is our aim here to make a distinction between two subclasses of intervening variables, or, we prefer to say, between "intervening variables" and "hypothetical constructs," which we feel is fundamental but is currently being neglected.

We shall begin with a common-sense distinction, and proceed later to formulations of this distinction which we hope will be more rigorous. Naively, it would seem that there is a difference in logical status between constructs which involve the hypothesization of an *entity, process,* or *event* which is not itself observed, and constructs which do not involve such hypothesization. For example, Skinner's "reflex reserve" is definable in terms of the total available responses without further conditioning, whereas Hull's "afferent neural interaction" involves the notion of processes within the nervous system which presumably occur within the objective physical system and which, under suitable conditions, we might observe directly. To take examples from another science in which we psychologists may have less stake in the distinction, one might contrast the notion of "resistance" in electricity to the notion of "electron." The resistance of a piece of wire is what Carnap has called a *dispositional concept,* and is defined by a special type of implication relation. When we say that the resistance of a wire is such-and-such, we mean that "so-and-so volts will give a current of so-and-so amperes." (For a more precise formulation of this see Carnap, 1, p. 440.) Resistance, in other words, is "operational" in a very direct and primitive sense. The electron, on the other hand, is supposedly an *entity* of some sort. Statements about the electron are, to be sure, supported by means of observational sentences. Nevertheless, it is no longer maintained even by positivists that this set of supporting sentences exhaust the entire *meaning* of the sentences about the electron. Reichenbach, for example, distinguishes *abstracta* from *illata* (from Lat. *infero*). The latter are "inferred things," such as molecules, other people's minds, and so on. They are believed in on the basis of our impressions, but the sentences involving them, even those asserting their existence, are not reducible to sentences about impressions. This is the epistemological form, at rock bottom level, of the distinction we wish to make here.

*   *   *   *   *   *   *   *   *   *

On the basis of these considerations, we are inclined to propose a linguistic convention for psychological theorists which we feel will help to clarify discussion of these matters. We suggest that the phrase "intervening variable" be restricted to the original use implied by Tolman's definition. Such a variable will then be simply a quantity obtained by a specified manipulation of the values of empirical variables; it will involve no hypothesis as to the existence of nonobserved entities or the occurrence of unobserved processes; it will contain, in its complete statement for all purposes of theory and prediction, no words which are not definable either explicitly or by reduction sentences in terms of the empirical variables; and the validity of empirical laws involving only observables will constitute both the necessary and sufficient conditions for the validity of the laws involving these intervening variables. Legitimate instances of such "pure" intervening variables are Skinner's *reserve,* Tolman's *demand,* Hull's *habit strength,* and Lewin's *valence.* These constructs are the behavioral analogue of Carnap's "dispositional concepts" such as solubility, resistance, inflammability, etc. It must be emphasized that the setting up of a definition or reduction for an intervening variable is not a wholly arbitrary and conventional matter. As Carnap has pointed out, it often happens that we give alternative sets of reduction sentences for the same dispositional concept; in these cases there is empirical content in our statement even though it has a form that suggests arbitrariness. The reason for this is that these separate reductions for a given dispositional concept imply that the empirical events are themselves related in a certain way. The notion of amount of electric current can be introduced by several different observations, such as deposition of silver, deflection of a needle, hydrogen separated out of water, and so on. Such a set of reductions has empirical content because the empirical statements together with the reductions must not lead to contradictions. It is a contingent fact, not derivable from definitions alone, that the deposition of silver will give the same answer for "amount of current" as will the deflection of a needle. A similar problem exists in Hull, when he sets up "momentary effective reaction potential" as the last intervening variable in his chain. In the case of striated muscle reactions, it is stated that latency, resistance to extinction, and probability of occurrence of a response are all functions of reaction potential. Neglecting behavior oscillation, which does not occur in the formulation for the second two because they involve many repetitions of the situation, this means that the empirical variables must be perfectly correlated (non-linearly, of course). The only possible source of variation which could attenuate a perfect correlation between probability of occurrence and resistance to extinction would be actual errors of experimental measurement, since there are no sources of uncontrolled variation left within the organism. If we consider average latency instead of momentary latency (which is a function of *momentary* effective reaction potential and hence varies with behavioral oscillation), latency and resistance to extinction should also be perfectly correlated. It remains to be seen whether the fact will support Hull in giving simultaneously several reductions for the notion of reaction potential.

As a second linguistic convention, we propose that the term "hypothetical construct" be used to designate theoretical concepts which do *not* meet the requirements for intervening variables in the strict sense. That is to say, these constructs involve terms which are not wholly reducible to empirical terms; they refer to processes or entities that are not directly observed (although they need not be in principle unobservable); the mathematical expression of them cannot be formed simply by a suitable grouping of terms in a direct empirical equation; and the truth of the empirical laws involved is a necessary but not a sufficient condition for the truth of these conceptions. Examples of such constructs are Guthrie's M.P.S.'s, Hull's r_g's, S_d's, and *afferent neural interaction,* Allport's *biophysical traits,* Murray's *regnancies,* the notion of "anxiety" as used by Mowrer, Miller, and Dollard and others of the Yale-derived group, and most theoretical constructs in psychoanalytic theory. Skinner and Tolman seem to be almost wholly free of hypothetical constructs, although when Skinner invokes such notions as the "strain on the reserve" (7, p. 289) it is difficult to be sure.

We do not wish to seem to legislate usage, so that if the broader use of "intervening variable" has become stuck in psychological discourse, we would propose alternatively a distinction between intervening variables of the "abstractive" and of the "hypothetical" kind. Since our personal preference is for restricting the phrase *intervening variables* to the pure type described by Tolman, we shall follow this convention in the remainder of the present paper.

The validity of intervening variables as we define them cannot be called into question except by an actual denial of the empirical facts. If, for example, Hull's proposed "grand investigation" of the Perin-Williams type should be carried out and the complex hyperspatial surface fitted adequately over a wide range of values (3, p. 181), it would be meaningless to reject the concept of "habit strength" and still admit the empirical findings. For this reason, the only consideration which can be raised with respect to a given proposed intervening variable, when an initial defining or reduction equation is being written for it, is the question of convenience.

In the case of hypothetical constructs, this is not so clear. Science is pursued for many reasons, not the least of which is *n Cognizance*. Since hypothetical constructs assert the existence of entities and the occurrence of events not reducible to the observable, it would seem to some of us that it is the business of a hypothetical construct to be "true." It is possible to advance scientific knowledge by taking a completely "as if" attitude toward such matters, but there are always those whose theoretical-cognitive need dictates that existential propositions should correspond to what is in fact the case. Contemporary philosophy of science, even as represented by those who have traditionally been most cautious about discussing "truth" and most highly motivated to reduce it to the experiential, gives psychologists no right to be dogmatic about the "as if" interpretation of theoretical knowledge (cf. especially Carnap, 2, p. 598, Kaufmann, 4, p. 35, Russell, 6, Introduction and Chapter XXI, and Reichenbach, 5, *passim*). We would find it rather difficult to defend the ingenious conditioning hypotheses developed in Hull's series of brilliant papers (1929-) in the *Psychological Review* on the ground that they merely provide a "convenient shorthand summarization of the facts" or are of value in the "practical manipulation" of the rat's behavior. We suspect that Professor Hull himself was motivated to write these articles because he considered that the hypothetical events represented in his diagrams may have actually *occurred* and that the occurrence of these events represents the underlying truth about the learning phenomena he dealt with. In terms of practical application, much (if not most) of theoretical psychology is of little value. If we exclude the interesting anecdotes of Guthrie, contemporary learning theory is not of much use to school teachers. As a *theoretical* enterprise, it may fairly be demanded of a theory of learning that those elements which are "hypothetical" in the present sense have some probability of being in correspondence with the actual events underlying the behavior phenomena, i.e., that the assertions about hypothetical constructs be true.[1]

Another consideration may be introduced here from the standpoint of future developments in scientific integration. Even those of us who advocate the pursuit of behavioral knowledge on its own level and for its own sake must recognize that some day the "pyramid of the sciences" will presumably catch up with us. For Skinner, this is of no consequence, since his consistent use of intervening variables in the strict sense genuinely frees him from neurophysiology and in fact makes it possible for him to impose certain conditions upon neurophysiological explanations (7, pp. 429-431). Since he hypothesizes nothing about the character of the inner events, no finding about the inner events could prove disturbing to him. At most, he would be able to say that a given discovery of internal processes must not be complete because it cannot come to terms with his (empirical) laws. But for those theorists who do not confine themselves to intervening variables in the strict sense, neurology will some day become relevant. For this reason it is perhaps legitimate, even now, to require of a hypothetical construct that it should not be manifestly unreal in the sense that it assumes inner events that cannot conceivably occur. The "as if" kinds of argument sometimes heard from more sophisticated exponents of psychoanalytic views often seem to ignore this consideration. A concept like *libido* or *censor* or *super-ego* may be introduced initially as though it is to be an intervening variable; or even less, it is treated as a merely conventional designation for a class of observable properties or occurrences. But somewhere in the course of theoretical discussion, we find that these words are being used as hypo-

---

[1] It is perhaps unnecessary to add that in adopting this position we do not mean to defend any form of metaphysical realist thesis. The ultimate "reality" of the world in general is not the issue here; the point is merely that the reality of hypothetical constructs like the atom, from the standpoint of their logical relation to grounds, is not essentially different from that attributed to stones, chairs, other people, and the like. When we say that hypothetical constructs involve the notion of "objective existence" of actual processes and entities within the organism, we mean the same sort of objective existence, defined by the same ordinary criteria, that is meant when we talk about the objective existence of Singapore. The present discussion operates within the common framework of empirical science and common sense and is intended to be metaphysically neutral.

thetical constructs instead. We find that the libido has acquired certain hydraulic properties, or, as in Freud's former view, that the "energy" of libido has been converted into "anxiety." What began as a name for an intervening variable is finally a name for a "something" which has a host of causal properties. These properties are not made explicit initially, but it is clear that the concept is to be used in an explanatory way which requires that the properties exist. Thus, libido may be introduced by an innocuous definition in terms of the "set of sexual needs" or a "general term for basic strivings." But subsequently we find that certain puzzling phenomena are *deduced* ("explained") by means of the various properties of libido, e.g., that it flows, is dammed up, is converted into something else, tends to regress to earlier channels, adheres to things, makes its "energy" available to the ego, and so on. It is naive to object to such formulations simply on the ground that they refer to unobservables, or are "hypothetical," or are not "statistical." None of these objections is a crucial one for any scientific construct, and if such criteria were applied a large and useful amount of modern science would have to be abandoned. The fundamental difficulty with such theories is twofold. First, as has been implied by our remarks, there is the failure explicitly to announce the postulates concerning existential properties, so that these are introduced more or less surreptitiously and *ad hoc* as occasion demands. Secondly, by this device there is subtly achieved a transition from admissible intervening variables to inadmissible hypothetical constructs. These hypothetical constructs, unlike intervening variables, are inadmissible because they require the existence of entities and the occurrence of processes which cannot be seriously believed because of other knowledge.

In the case of libido, for instance, we may use such a term legitimately as a generic name for a class of empirical events or properties, or as an intervening variable. But the allied sciences of anatomy and physiology impose restrictions upon our use of it as a hypothetical construct. Even admitting the immature state of neurophysiology in terms of its relation to complex behavior, it must be clear that the central nervous-system does not in fact contain pipes or tubes with fluid in them, and there are no known properties of nervous tissue to which the hydraulic properties of libido could correspond. Hence, this part of a theory about "inner events" is likely to remain metaphorical. For a genuine intervening variable, there is no metaphor because all is merely short-hand summarization. For hypothetical constructs, there is a surplus meaning that is existential. We would argue that dynamic explanations utilizing hypothetical constructs ought not to be of such a character that they *have* to remain only metaphors.

Of course, this judgment in itself involves a "best guess" about the future. A hypothetical construct which seems inherently metaphorical may involve a set of properties to which hitherto undiscovered characteristics of the nervous system correspond. So long as the propositions about the construct are not stated in the *terms* of the next lower discipline, it is always a possibility that the purely formal or relational content of the construct will find an isomorphism in such characteristics. For scientific theories this is enough, since here, as in physics, the associated mechanical imagery of the theorist is irrelevant. The tentative rejection of libido would then be based upon the belief that no neural process is likely to have the *combination* of formal properties required. Strictly speaking, this is always problematic when the basic science is incomplete.[2]

Summary

1. At present the phrases "intervening variable" and "hypothetical construct" are often used interchangeably, and theoretical discourse often fails to distinguish what we believe are two rather different notions. We suggest that a failure to separate these leads to fundamental confusions. The distinction is between constructs which merely abstract the empirical relationships (Tolman's original intervening variables) and those constructs which are "hypothetical" (i.e., involve the supposition of entities or processes not among the observed).

2. Concepts of the first sort seem to be identifiable by three characteristics. First, the statement of such a concept does not contain any words which are not reducible to the empirical laws. Second, the validity of the empirical laws is both necessary and sufficient for the "correctness" of the statements about the concept. Third, the quantitative expression of the concept can be obtained without mediate inference by suitable groupings of terms in the quantitative empirical laws.

3. Concepts of the second sort do not fulfil any of these three conditions. Their formulation involves words not wholly reducible to the words in the empirical laws; the validity of the empirical laws is not a sufficient condition for the truth of the concept, inasmuch as it contains

[2] We are indebted to Dr. Herbert Feigl for a clarification of this point.

surplus meaning; and the quantitative form of the concept is not obtainable simply by grouping empirical terms and functions.

4. We propose a linguistic convention in the interest of clarity: that the phrase *intervening variable* be restricted to concepts of the first kind, in harmony with Tolman's original definition; and that the phrase *hypothetical construct* be used for those of the second kind.

5. It is suggested that the only rule for proper intervening variables is that of convenience, since they have no factual content surplus to the empirical functions they serve to summarize.

6. In the case of hypothetical constructs, they have a cognitive, factual reference in addition to the empirical data which constitute their support. Hence, they ought to be held to a more stringent requirement in so far as our interests are theoretical. Their actual existence should be compatible with general knowledge and particularly with whatever relevant knowledge exists at the next lower level in the explanatory hierarchy.

References

1. Carnap, R. Testability and meaning, Part IV. *Phil. Sci.,* 1937, *4,* 1-40.
2. Carnap, R. Remarks on induction and truth. *Phil. & phenomenol. res.,* 1946, *6,* 590-602.
3. Hull, C. L. *Principles of behavior.* New York: Appleton-Century, 1943.
4. Kaufmann, F. *Methodology in the social sciences.* London: Oxford Univ. Press, 1944.
5. Reichenbach, H. *Experience and prediction.* Chicago: Univ. of Chicago Press, 1938.
6. Russell, B. *Inquiry into meaning and truth.* New York: Norton, 1940.
7. Skinner, B. F. *Behavior of organisms.* New York: Appleton-Century, 1938.
8. Tolman, E. C. The determiners of behavior at a choice point. *Psychol. Rev.,* 1938, *45,* 1-41.

7   HYPOTHESIS AND CONSTRUCT

Melvin H. Marx

I

The improved scientific sophistication evidenced within recent years by psychological theorists has been largely characterized by an increased sensitivity to the need for operational validity in the formation and use of logical constructs. It has also become increasingly apparent, however, that operational validity, in and of itself, provides no guarantee of effective psychological theory construction. As constructs are made progressively more operational they must by definition be progressively divorced from the hypothetical content which seems to be regarded as a desirable if not essential component by a number of theorists. Within the past year both Tolman (27) and Krech (12), prominent theorists of so-called field-theoretical inclinations, have argued for the inclusion of a definite amount of hypothetical content in logical constructs. It is especially discouraging to find Tolman, whose introduction of the *intervening variable* (25, 26) contributed notably to the establishment of the recent operational trend, now apparently reversing his earlier position and stating that "to use Meehl and MacCorquodale's distinction, I would now abandon what they call pure 'intervening variables' for what they call 'hypothetical constructs,' and insist that hypothetical constructs be parts of a more general hypothesized model or substrate" (27, p. 49).

One may certainly agree with Professor Tolman in his concern for the development of useful models. Nevertheless, it seems to be not only unnecessary but also distinctly dangerous to abandon the operationally defined intervening construct. It is the purpose of this paper, therefore, to attempt a clarification of the problem of the relationship between hypothesis and construct, as these are used in contemporary psychological theory construction. The hypothetical construct and the intervening variable, to continue MacCorquodale and Meehl's (13) terminology, are regarded as lying on a single continuum, each type of

From M. H. Marx, Intervening variable or hypothetical construct? *Psychol. Rev.,* 1951, *58.* Reprinted by permission of the author, the *Psychological Review,* and the American Psychological Association.

construct having a certain useful function in the development of theory but the fully operational type remaining the ultimate theoretical objective. If psychological theories are to be placed on a sound scientific basis, logical constructs of the more distinctly operational type must first supplement and *eventually* replace those of the hypothetical construct type. However, it should be noted that there has probably been a tendency to overlook the value of constructs of the hypothetical type on the part of the more objectively oriented stimulus-response theorists (e.g., Hull, 7, 8; Spence, 21, 22), as well as an opposite tendency to minimize the value of the operational type on the part of the field-theorists. If the wholesale abandonment of operationally valid constructs is not required for the effective use of less operationally defined constructs, neither is the wholesale abandonment of the latter type required for the effective use of the former.

In attempting a clarification of this problem the present paper has a twofold objective: first, to point out the *different* functions of each type of construct, and thereby justify their continued supplementary use; second, to describe a type of intervening variable which gives promise of offering an operationally sound alternative to the hypothetical construct but whose potential usefulness has not thus far been formally recognized.

II

Since the terminological distinction recently proposed by MacCorquodale and Meehl will be followed, a summary of their interpretation of the terms "intervening variable" and "hypothetical construct" will be useful. These authors distinguish between "constructs which merely abstract the empirical relationships (Tolman's original intervening variables) and those constructs which are 'hypothetical' (i.e., involve the supposition of entities or processes not among the observed)" (13, pp. 106-107). They then summarize three characteristics whose presence is typically indicative of the purely abstractive kind of construct— the "intervening variable," as they propose to call it—and whose absence is indicative of the "hypothetical construct." These characteristics are:

First, the statement of such a concept does not contain any words which are not reducible to the empirical laws. Second, the validity of the empirical laws is both necessary and sufficient for the "correctness" of the statements about the concept. Third, the quantitative expression of the concept can be obtained without mediate inference by suitable groupings of terms in the quantitative empirical laws. (13, p. 107.)

In the present discussion a somewhat less detailed differentiation is required between the two terms, although the general tenor of Mac-Corquodale and Meehl's distinction is retained. By intervening variable is meant any intervening construct with a maximum amount of operational validity, or direct empirical reference, and by hypothetical construct is meant any construct with a relatively low degree of operational validity. These two terms, while specifically applicable to behavior problems, may thus be related to a wider methodological framework.

It is also necessary to recognize that a clear-cut distinction can not always be drawn, in actual practice, between these two "types" of constructs. Any such impression, based upon the treatment by MacCorquodale and Meehl or the following discussion, should be quickly discouraged. For the sake of convenience in exposition, however, their essential continuity will not generally be emphasized in the following sections.

III

We may begin our consideration of this problem with a brief examination of the origin and development of logical constructs. A series of stages in this development will be roughly classified and briefly described.

1. *Pre-scientific origins.* From an historical point of view, logical constructs, like scientific problems and hypotheses, originate in the common-sense reflections of men. At a somewhat more sophisticated stage of concept development various refinements may be made which tend to sharpen the dictionary definitions of concepts, and thus gain a certain degree of verbal appeal, but do little to tighten the relations between the concept and the relatively uncontrolled observations which produce it. Such refinements are typically made in philosophy, theology, politics and similar fields. Distinct and dogmatic biases in some of these fields often provide a certain consistency to conceptualizations but scarcely improve their operational validity. Little interest is shown in operational definitions.

2. *Preliminary scientific formulations.* As objective scientific interests arise in a special subject matter area two basically conflicting needs, which may be seen as fundamental to the subsequent conflict between hypothetical content and operational validity in constructs, become apparent. On the one hand, there is the immediate need for a scientific

formulation of problems. Old questions have to be reworded in such a manner that relevant and controlled data can be collected. On the other hand, there is also the increasing pressure for continued operational refinement of the conceptual system that has been taken over, by and large, from the grossly nonoperational systems of the earlier pre-scientific periods. The result is that the pioneering scientist is typically forced to compromise—that is, to brush up his conceptualizations, at least making some gestures in the direction of more operational validity, but actually retaining a certain significant degree of hypothetical content.

a. *General role of hypothetical constructs.* Let us examine more closely the role of the hypothetical construct in the preliminary phases of a new scientific development, such as has been represented within the past few decades by psychology. Of the host of concomitant problems facing the scientist none is more important than the need to ask, as simply and objectively as possible, the kind of straightforward questions which can be given direct empirical answers. Now such questions, it should be apparent, are not easily discovered—not, that is, if they are to have that systematic usefulness that is required of any comprehensive scientific development. In all phases of science such empirical questions must be derived from some kind of prior hypotheses (cf. Cohen and Nagel, 1, ch. 11). In the framing of these hypotheses the scientist must of course use whatever conceptual materials are at hand. In the absence of previous operational refinements he will be forced to rely, in a manner that ought to be explicitly recognized as a temporary expedient, upon such operationally inadequate conceptualizations as we are calling hypothetical constructs. How quickly such constructs can be replaced by more operational ones will, of course, depend upon a number of complex factors, among which may be mentioned the difficulty of the specific subject matter, the ingenuity and scientific skills of the investigators, etc. It is fairly obvious that large differences of this kind have thus far accounted for the appreciable variations in scientific development among the divisions of behavior study.

b. *Problems of semantic usage.* Effective scientific construct formation is complicated by certain unavoidable terminological difficulties. Although these operate at all stages of scientific development they are most apparent, and probably most serious, during the early phases.

It is important to recognize, at the outset, that this semantic problem is actually distinct from the problem of operational validity, although the two are easily and commonly confused in practice. That is, the question of operational validity concerns simply the problem of relating constructs, however they may be named, to the particular empirical data from which they were derived (cf. Pratt, 18; Marx, 14). We are now concerned with the independent problem of choosing names for constructs which, whatever degree of operational validity may be present, will most effectively express their observational basis as well as their theoretical implications to those other persons with whom the scientist wishes to communicate.

An immediate problem is posed, as new constructs are introduced or old ones modified, by the necessity of either 1) using old words, or other symbols, which ordinarily already have acquired a variety of vaguely overlapping meanings, or 2) coining new words or other symbols which may carry relatively unambiguous meaning but are seldom received with much enthusiasm by those outside the immediate systematic framework within which the new concept was developed.[1] In neither case, unfortunately, is there likely to be a long-lasting clarity of meaning achieved, since in spite of the best precautions each reader tends to read into the word, and to a lesser extent perhaps the other types of symbols, his own meanings and biases. This tendency then becomes more difficult to avoid as the term is circulated more widely, perhaps gaining in popularity and thus being increasingly related to other, less carefully defined conceptualizations. The use of isolated letters or mathematical symbols, exemplified by Hull's systematic behavior theory (7, 9), does appear to have the advantage of at least reducing the rate of such popular contamination.

From the standpoint of the subsequent user of the various symbols that represent scientific concepts, a suggestion by Maslow (16) seems to merit serious consideration. He has proposed the formal use of what many of us probably tend to do more or less implicitly and informally —namely, the appending of a subscript, consisting of the original author's name or initial, to indicate the specific meaning that is intended by the use of the particular symbols.

This technique carries the disadvantage of being too awkward for common usage and, more important, of having to contend with the

[1] A modification of these two methods which seems to have certain advantages may also be mentioned. This consists of using familiar words in a new grouping. Examples would be Skinner's *reflex reserve* (20), Hull's *fractional anticipatory goal reaction* (5, 6) and Hovland's *inhibition of reinforcement* (4).

frequent variability that occurs within the usage of particular terms from time to time by the same author. Nevertheless, it has the very important advantage of recognizing not only the great variety of different meanings invariably acquired by common words but also the tendency, if not the privilege, which in actuality writers have of using words in way that suit their own particular purposes. The common failure to appreciate this latter fact is a particularly unfortunate source of confusion. For example, the question, "What *is* perception?" (or "cognition," or "learning," etc.) is a type which is all too frequently found, either formally stated or implied.[2] Or, to use somewhat more sophisticated examples, the questions as to whether "fear" is distinct from "anxiety," "conflict" from "frustration," etc. tend to overlook the simple fact that authors may use these words in such a variety of ways as to make possible practically any answer they may wish. Explicit recognition of this fact and more careful attention, as a result, to the observational determinants of such shifty words would certainly save a considerable amount of the type of discussion and argumentation that helps to keep a large part of psychological theory on the "debating society" level of discourse.

3. *Advanced scientific analysis.* From the point of view of effective theory construction, scientific advance may be considered to be a function, in large part, of the extent to which hypothetical constructs can be transformed into operationally purified intervening variables. In attacking this problem we may first consider the three major outcomes of the use, in preliminary scientific formulations, of those hypothetical constructs with which the scientist undertakes his early theoretical endeavors.

a. *Continuation as hypothetical constructs.* Unfortunately, the most frequent outcome of the use of hypothetical constructs seems to be that they are simply retained as hypothetical constructs, often being modified through a process of more or less extensive verbal reorganization. Thus many of the psychoanalytic constructs have acquired, through a series of primarily verbal accretions, all sorts of alleged explanatory properties, with a progressive widening of the gap between them and

[2] It may be helpful to enumerate some of the more obvious answers to this kind of a question. The concept "perception," for example, may refer to 1) a field of study, 2) a set of more or less specific motor responses, 3) certain physiological processes, 4) a kind of subjective experience, 5) an intervening variable (or hypothetical construct). Which of these is meant must of course be determined if possible from the context.

specific empirical verifications. This process is well described by MacCorquodale and Meehl (13, p. 105 ff.). It is this outcome which is responsible for so much of the dissatisfaction, on the part of many psychologists, with the use of hypothetical constructs. The distinctly negative reactions produced by the more flagrant bad examples of such theorizing tend also to transfer to theory and theory construction in general, as Spence (23) has observed. This unfortunate situation, by no means peculiar to psychology but perhaps for many reasons more prominent there, is the price that must be paid if the more desirable fruits of such activity are to be enjoyed. Probably the only real solution is a continuing pressure on the users of constructs and the developers of theory to improve the operational validity of their formulations.

b. *Suggestion of empirical research.* The most obvious scientific values that derive from the use of hypothetical constructs are those that involve the suggestion of empirical, preferably experimental, research. As mentioned earlier, it is this particular function of the hypothetical construct which both Tolman (27) and Krech (12) have recently emphasized. In this respect exception must be taken to the conclusion of MacCorquodale and Meehl that "hypothetical constructs, unlike intervening variables, are inadmissible because they require the existence of entities and the occurrence of processes which cannot be seriously believed because of other knowledge" (13, p. 106). It is precisely this characteristic of enabling an investigator to go beyond present knowledge and not be tied down to currently orthodox formulations (which may of course later be viewed as wholly inadequate) that helps to justify the usefulness of such hypothetical constructs as guides to experimentation. Köhler's investigation of the figural aftereffect and related perceptual phenomena (10, 11) is an excellent example of this point. The only valid basis on which such hypothetical constructs may be rejected involves their failure to lead to adequate empirical tests.

Although one must recognize the potential fruitfulness of the use of such models as may be generated by means of hypothetical constructs it is necessary to exercise considerable caution with regard to the conclusions which are drawn from empirical results obtained in this way. If the model is regarded only as a tool to be used in suggesting empirical investigation and then discarded, or modified and retained as a useful guide to experimentation, little danger of unjustified theoretical interpretation is likely to be present. More commonly, however, there is a tendency to regard the empirical results obtained as supporting, in some way, the *theoretical* validity of the original model and the particular hypothetical constructs which have been used. Such conclusions can not be legitimately drawn, and, as a matter of fact, should be quickly and vigorously labelled as inadmissible, *unless* in the process of investigation and theoretical reformulation the constructs have acquired a more adequate degree of operational validity (that is, have moved significantly in the direction of true intervening variables).

That some disagreement on this point exists is, I think, fairly obvious. For example, Krech writes as follows: "Because it is assumed that these hypothetical constructs exist, and because of the extrinsic properties that they are assumed to have, the correlations between experimental conditions and results are now seen as *necessary* correlations, as inevitable consequences of the functioning of these hypothetical constructs" (12, p. 75). Now, it is essential to note that if such "postulated actually existing structure" is finally reduced to direct experimental measurement and purely empirical statements it can no longer be regarded, in any useful sense, as a *construct*. And if it continues to be defined indirectly through experimental measurement, and thus remains a construct, any *necessary* correlations of the kind Krech indicates can result only if operational refinement appreciably reduces the original ambiguity of the construct and it thus moves in the direction of the intervening variable.

In clarification of this point it may be helpful to make a gross qualitative distinction between two types of hypothetical constructs: those which postulate the existence of some specific entity or process, the direct empirical identification of which is regarded as a major objection; and those which are deliberately designed to serve only as constructs and thus do not elicit attempts at direct empirical identification. Operational validation of both types is, of course, possible. As noted above, this leads in the case of the first type to purely empirical propositions, and in the case of the second type to the intervening variable kind of construct. It must be recognized, however, that in actual practice the scientific usefulness of the first type does not depend upon its "existence" in a specific empirical sense. An unfortunate amount of confusion seems to have been produced by the somewhat naive expectation that certain hypothetical constructs—for example, the gene—may some day be "seen," in a literal sense, through some sort of direct and specific identification of the entity or process "as it really is." Whether or not this is ever done (and parenthetically it may be observed that most such claims are to be regarded as highly tenuous, at best), it must be said that, from a more realistic point of view, all that need be expected in the way of direct empirical identification is the development of a series of progressively more refined empirical propositions. These typically bear only the slightest resemblance to the originally postulated construct.

The necessity for operational validity in scientific constructs is in no way reduced if the development of a system of formal models is regarded as the primary objective of science, rather than merely as a useful device to direct and unify empirical investigations. For example, Rosenbleuth and Wiener, who adopt the former position, nevertheless also state that "The successive addition of . . . variables leads to gradually more elaborate theoretical models: hence to a hierarchy in these models, from relatively simple, highly abstract ones, to more complex, *more concrete* theoretical structures" (19, p. 319, italics added). It would certainly seem that the only way in which theoretical structures can be made "more concrete" is through coordinating empirical measurements of the kind that characterize operationally valid constructs.

It may be suggested that a large amount of the apparent confusion in psychology on the role of such theoretical structures has been due to the tendency to think in terms of the way in which they have been employed, with eminent success, in the physical sciences. The potential usefulness of theoretical structures of so high a degree of abstraction need not be denied. Nevertheless the most immediate need of psychology would rather plainly seem to be the careful development of a large number of low-level empirical laws, and low-order theories based upon the use of intervening constructs of the more operational type. Higher-order theoretical generalizations may then be built upon a sound empirical framework, in accordance with orthodox scientific procedure (cf. Feigl, 2; Rosenbleuth and Wiener, 19) rather than developed from above, as has too often been attempted in the past and is encouraged by the premature emulation of theoretical models based upon the highly abstract physical pattern.

Support for this point of view is readily adduced from consideration of previous attempts in psychology to construct elaborate theoretical models. With regard to Freudian psychoanalysis, for example, it is instructive to note the generally more favorable reception by academic psychologists of those constructs such as repression and other so-called "dynamisms" which involve relatively close functional relations to empirical operations than those high up in the theoretical superstructure, such as id, ego and super-ego, which bear only remote and tenuous relations to their observational bases. The extent to which any such theoretical superstructures have actually contributed to the development of psychology in a sound scientific direction may be seriously questioned. Their disadvantages are obvious. Broad systematic frameworks certainly serve some useful functions, but in the present state of psychology the most valuable formal models, like the most valuable experiments, seem to be those with definitely restricted objectives.

c. *Transformation into intervening variables.* As has been emphasized throughout the discussion, the ultimate objective of all theoretical construct formation is believed to be the operationally valid, intervening variable type of construct. Although no hard and fast rules can be easily prescribed for this important transformation and no completely black and white distinctions made, a few of the more obvious factors may be mentioned. In general, it is essential that the operationally inclined theorist think in terms of *experimental* procedures as well as theoretical structures. One of the most common characteristics of those theorists who are inclined to rest content with hypothetical constructs is their general tendency to be concerned with verbal distinctions and their general neglect of a critical analysis of the observational bases of their conceptual framework. A second factor which encourages the early transformation of hypothetical constructs into intervening variables is the tendency to set up definite, more or less formal hypotheses. Obviously, the more hypothetical content that can be placed into formal hypotheses the less need there will be for including it in the constructs that are used.[3] Thirdly, the operationally inclined theorist will make a deliberate effort to set up hypotheses which are susceptible to more or less direct *empirical test,* and to work out the implications of the hypotheses that can be so tested. This means that he is more likely to be concerned with specific as well as general problems. The opera-

---

[3] In this respect it is interesting to note that Tolman's major point in favor of use of hypothetical constructs, rather than the intervening variables with "merely operational meaning," is that the latter "really can give us no help unless we can also imbed them in a model from whose attributed properties we can deduce new relationships to be looked for" (27, p. 49). This, of course, is exactly what Hull's systematic behavior theory (7, 9) has attempted to do, largely without the use of hypothetical constructs— although Tolman would probably prefer to use a "model" other than the one Hull has fashioned.

tionally disinclined theorist, on the other hand, often tends to favor hypotheses which are either themselves relatively untestable, or the empirical consequences of which are not easily determined. A further characteristic of such hypotheses may be seen in the fact that it is frequently difficult if not impossible to refute them. Finally, the operationally inclined theorist is generally more interested in the problem of *quantification,* while the operationally disinclined type of theorist is more often content with purely qualitative distinctions.

Before leaving this general problem of modification of constructs it may be suggested that too rapid an attempted transformation into purely operational intervening variables seems to have certain disadvantages. The major risk of such over-expansion is that associated with the premature development of an overly rigid systematic position, especially if there is a concomitant attempt to stifle off continued exploratory efforts at other levels of explanation. The growth of such rigid positions into cult-like systems, with blind acceptance of certain key principles, serves to offset the genuinely sound scientific advances that can result from such concentrated research programs.

IV

Two particular types of intervening variables, each of which seems to have a distinct function in the development of sound scientific theory in psychology, will now be discussed.

a. *The orthodox type of intervening variable.* As ordinarily conceived, the intervening variable is a kind of shorthand expression for the performance of certain specific empirical operations. This type of construct often but not necessarily (cf. Skinner, 20; Tolman, 26) has been given a strong quantitative flavor and placed into a highly mathematical framework (cf. especially Hull, 7, 9). The advantages of such a conceptual tool have been well described in many other papers (e.g., Tolman, 25; Hull, 7 and 8; Spence, 21 and 22; MacCorquodale and Meehl, 13; Marx, 14) and need not be reviewed in detail here. Hull's systematic behavior theory may be considered a good example of the potential value of this use of intervening variables. As even certain of his critics have said (e.g., Hilgard, 3), the development of this type of rigorous scientific system marks a definite objective toward which psychological theories should in the future point.

b. *The E/C type of intervening variable.* I should now like to call attention to a somewhat different use of the intervening variable technique which has been occasionally employed but apparently without formal recognition, and which I think offers considerable promise. Like the orthodox type of intervening variable, this type is a shorthand expression which represents the performance of certain specified empirical operations. Although sharing the generally desirable operational characteristics of the orthodox type it does in addition have the peculiar advantage of contributing to the semantic clarification of psychological language.

In essence, this usage simply provides a particular name—representing the postulated intervening variable—to account for whatever specified behavioral differences are empirically found to result from a specified set of stimulus operations. Since a construct of this kind must generally be a function of a comparison between experimental and control conditions, the term E/C is suggested to mark it off from the orthodox usage. It may best be illustrated by an example from the experimental literature.

In a recent study by Mowrer and Viek (17) hungry rats were given the opportunity to eat moist mash from the end of a small stick offered them through the bars of a shock grid. An electric shock was delivered ten seconds after they had begun to eat, or following an additional ten-second interval if no eating occurred within the first ten seconds. The experimental animals were able to turn off the shock by leaping off the grid, an act which they quickly learned to perform. The control animals were unable to influence the shock directly, but each control animal was given exactly the same duration of shock on every trial as its matched experimental animal. Under these conditions experimental and control animals received identical amounts of electric shock, as objectively measured, but there was an important behavioral difference. The experimental animals ate significantly more frequently and more quickly than the controls. The "sense of helplessness," which is the verbal tag that Mowrer and Viek gave to the assumed psychological function more consistently present in the control than in the experimental animals, may be regarded as a true intervening variable type of construct since it can be tied down, on both the stimulus and the response sides, to empirical measurements.[4]

[4] It should be noted that this is true in spite of any doubts that may be entertained concerning the particular term chosen and the further theoretical implications suggested. In the present case, for example, I have elsewhere (15) questioned Mowrer and Viek's choice of the term "sense of helplessness" on the grounds that their theoretical interpretation of the experiment is not adequately supported.

The semantic advantages of this use of the intervening variable should be apparent. When we speak of any E/C intervening variable we mean—or *should* mean—nothing more than whatever intervening function needs to be assumed in order to account for the experimental-control differences empirically observed. However, in deciding which verbal label to give this intervening variable we may draw upon our own informal observations, or upon some particular theoretical framework. This use of the intervening variable technique thus makes it possible not only to give a purely operational meaning to the constructs used but also to relate them to some prior observations or theoretical system in a way that should help to move these in the direction of a more clear-cut operationism.

There is an obvious semantic danger in this process, however, which needs to be clearly faced. It is most apparent when the names chosen to represent the intervening variables have otherwise acquired a large number of vague and varied meanings. The danger is that such relationships will be emphasized and that subsequent investigation of the basic behavioral functions will be correspondingly diverted. Use of relatively neutral symbols, like letters of the alphabet, may be helpful in discouraging this kind of verbal regression, but these seem to be more readily applied in connection with the orthodox type of intervening variable.

The problem of the generality of intervening variables of the E/C type also needs to be considered. If concepts of a high degree of generality are essential objectives of scientific theory, how can they be obtained through the use of constructs postulated specifically to refer to a particular set of experimental operations?

Two answers to this question may be suggested. In the first place, any particular construct can be given strict, operational meaning through the E/C technique, and can subsequently be broadened to refer to an increasing number of different kinds of experimental situations. Such a broadening of meaning, or generalization, must of course be done with considerable caution. The great advantage of using successive E/C situations, however, is that if anyone cares to question such a generalized construct he may refer directly to the identifying experiments. The degree to which any given construct can be thus generalized will largely depend upon the extent to which the specific empirical situations upon which it is based may be related. In this respect it is useful to recall Stevens' solution for the basic problem of generality in operationism, which may be summarized in his statement that "We combine operations when they satisfy the criteria of a class; and the concept of that class is defined by the operations which determine inclusion within the class" (24, p. 234).

The controlled manipulation of experimental designs upon which successful development of such generalized concepts will depend must be recognized as a difficult but by no means impossible task. Moreover, it is one which psychologists must somehow effectively tackle if they intend to improve the scientific systematization of their theoretical frameworks. As a simple but concrete example of the manner in which related experimentation may in actual practice be performed, mention may be made of a modification of the Mowrer and Viek design, emphasizing a so-called "sense of control," which has recently been used by Marx and Van Spanckeren (15) in a study demonstrating a certain amount of learned "control" of the audiogenic seizure by rats. This construct is definitely of the intervening variable type since it has been given a thoroughly operational meaning, in spite of its subjective sound, in terms of the E/C differences.

Consideration of the relationship between the E/C type of intervening variable and the orthodox type provides us with a clue to a second solution of the problem of generality. E/C intervening variables are considered to be most useful in the exploratory phases of scientific theory construction and experimentation, as a means of spotting new variables, probing for gross functions, etc. As experimental investigation progresses the E/C variables should ultimately be reducible to the more general orthodox type, and in fact should aid greatly in the discovery and delimitation of these in the later stages of systematic theory construction. Translation of such complex variables as "sense of control" into relatively more abstract and general constructs may then be expected to result from their continued experimental analysis. From this point of view the essential continuity of the E/C and the orthodox types of intervening variables is evident.

The other major advantages of the E/C usage of the intervening variable may now be briefly summarized. In the first place, and most importantly, it provides a technique which seems to combine the best features of both the hypothetical construct and the orthodox intervening variable. That is, it offers the experimenter an opportunity to draw upon the suggestions of a theoretical model and yet remain on a strictly operational level of discourse. It thus provides a high degree of freedom of experimental investigation without sacrifice of the methodological rigor that normally accompanies the use of the orthodox intervening variable. This is an especially important characteristic in the present stage of psychological science, with the concomitant needs for more exploratory work and the careful identification of the empirical bases of constructs. Secondly, it permits the formal separation of the hypothetical from the conceptual components of theory construction, and requires that the investigator think more in experimental and less in purely verbal terms. Thirdly, by enabling the empirically minded investigator to indulge, cautiously, in a small amount of construct formation, it encourages the development of a greater amount of theoretical orientation on the part of psychologists whose antipathy to theory and theory construction largely stems from their distrust of hypothetical constructs and accompanying speculation. An increased interest in theory construction by this kind of investigator is regarded as a highly desirable objective.

The successful use of the intervening variable of the E/C type involves several important requirements. It obviously depends, in common with all sound scientific work, upon the experimental validity of the empirical data. It also necessitates a certain amount of ingenuity in the design of the experiment, but once the proper theoretical-experimental attitude is acquired this may be less difficult than it at first appears. It demands that the investigator, once he has performed an experiment and defined his intervening constructs purely in terms of his experimental operations, now continue to apply those particular conceptualizations in an operationally sound manner, as he attempts to relate them to the wider theoretical framework from which they have been derived. This means that, as implied earlier, a clear line needs to be drawn between theoretical implications that are to be directly made upon the basis of the experimental results and those that are merely suggested by them. Finally, it requires that the investigator think in terms of narrow, experimentally manipulable problems—even if they are imbedded in a significantly wider theoretical framework. This is an especially desirable requirement, since it should result in an improved experimental sophistication on the part of those whose speculations too often tend to outstrip their empirical foundations.

In conclusion, it may be noted that there is in this discussion no intention to imply that the E/C usage represents anything more than a refinement and a formalization of currently accepted scientific procedure. However, it is hoped that this technique will encourage that active *experimental* search for new variables and new relationships between variables which is essential for the continued scientific advancement of psychology.

V

In summary, the following conclusions are offered:

1. The hypothetical construct, as defined by MacCorquodale and Meehl (13) and recently justified by Tolman (27) and Krech (12), is to be regarded as in general a temporary expedient in the development of sound psychological theory.

2. Hypothetical constructs are most useful in the early, preliminary phases of scientific work. Their use may have three major outcomes:

a. They may be continued, perhaps in modified form, on a grossly nonoperational level of discourse. This practice can not be scientifically defended.

b. They may lead to important empirical investigations, in which case they serve a useful function in suggesting research. However, the empirical results must not be regarded as constituting evidence in support of the theoretical validity of such conceptual models unless in the process they are given increased operation validity.

c. They may be transformed into operationally valid intervening variables, which are the only kinds of constructs ultimately admissible in sound scientific theory.

3. Two types of intervening variables are currently being used in psychology, each with an important function:

a. The orthodox type of intervening variable is simply a shorthand symbolic expression, often quantitative in character, of a specified set of experimental operations. It is necessary in the relatively advanced stages of theory construction.

b. The E/C type of intervening variable is likewise a verbal expression of a specified set of experimental operations, but is more directly related to the experimental-control differences in the experiment. It offers, through the method of successive approximation, an opportunity to clarify semantic usage in psychological theory construction. Its relatively greater flexibility as a methodological tool makes it especially useful in the exploratory stages of scientific investigation, when theoretical constructs need to be progressively released from their pre-scientific ambiguity. It is thus regarded as an operationally valid alternative to the hypothetical construct.

4. It is strongly recommended that psychological investigators pay more attention to the formal operational requirements of their theory construction, and in particular attempt more explicit use of both types of intervening variables.

References

1. Cohen, M. R. and Nagel, E. *Logic and scientific method*. New York: Harcourt, Brace, 1934.

2. Feigl, H. Operationism and scientific method: rejoinders and second thoughts. *Psychol. Rev.*, 1945, *52*, 284-288.

3. Hilgard, E. R. *Theories of learning*. New York: Appleton-Century-Crofts, 1948.

4. Hovland, C. I. "Inhibition of reinforcement" and phenomena of experimental extinction. *Proc. Nat. Acad. Sci.*, Wash., 1936, *22*, 430-433.

5. Hull, C. L. Knowledge and purpose as habit mechanisms. *Psychol. Rev.*, 1930, *37*, 511-525.

6. Hull, C. L. Goal attraction and directing ideas conceived as habit phenomena. *Psychol. Rev.*, 1931, *38*, 487-506.

7. Hull, C. L. *Principles of behavior*. New York: D. Appleton Century, 1943.

8. Hull, C. L. The problem of intervening variables in molar behavior theory. *Psychol. Rev.*, 1943, *50*, 273-291. [Selection No. 13 in this volume.]

9. Hull, C. L. Behavior postulates and corollaries—1949. *Psychol. Rev.*, 1950, *57*, 173-180.

10. Köhler, W. *Dynamics in psychology*. New York: Liveright, 1940.

11. Köhler, W. and Wallach, H. Figural after-effects, *Proc. Amer. Phil. Soc.*, Phil., 1944, *88*, 269-357. [See Selection No. 25 in this volume.]

12. Krech, D. Notes toward a psychological theory. *J. Personal.*, 1949, *19*, 66-87.

13. MacCorquodale, K. and Meehl, P. E. On a distinction between hypothetical constructs and intervening variables. *Psychol. Rev.*, 1948, *55*, 95-107. [See Selection No. 6 in this volume.]

14. Marx, M. H. The general nature of theory construction. [Selection No. 1 in this volume.]

15. Marx, M. H. and Van Spanckeren, W. J. Control of the audiogenic seizure by the rat. *J. comp. physiol. Psychol.*, 1952, *45*.

16. Maslow, A. H. A suggested improvement in semantic usage. *Psychol. Rev.*, 1945, *52*, 239-240.

17. Mowrer, O. H. and Viek, P. An experimental analogue of fear from a

sense of helplessness. *J. abn. soc. Psychol.,* 1948, *43,* 193-200.

18. Pratt, C. C. *The logic of modern psychology.* New York: Macmillan, 1939.

19. Rosenblueth, A. and Wiener, N. The role of models in science. *Phil. Sci.,* 1945, *12,* 316-321.

20. Skinner, B. F. *The behavior of organisms.* New York: D. Appleton-Century, 1938.

21. Spence, K. W. The nature of theory construction in contemporary psychology. *Psychol. Rev.,* 1944, *51,* 47-68. [Selection No. 4 in this volume.]

22. Spence, K. W. The postulates and methods of "behaviorism." *Psychol. Rev.,* 1948, *55,* 67-78. [Selection No. 11 in this volume.]

23. Spence, K. W. Cognitive versus stimulus-response theories of learning. *Psychol. Rev.,* 1950, *57,* 159-172.

24. Stevens, S. S. Psychology and the science of science. *Psychol. Bull.,* 1939, *36,* 221-263. [Selection No. 2 in this volume.]

25. Tolman, E. C. Operational behaviorism and current trends in psychology. In *Proc. 25th Anniv. Celebr. Inaug. Grad. Stud.* Los Angeles: Univ. South. Calif. Press, 1936. [Selection No. 5 in this volume.]

26. Tolman, E. C. The determiners of behavior at a choice point. *Psychol. Rev.,* 1938, *45,* 1-41.

27. Tolman, E. C. Discussion (from, Interrelationships between perception and personality: a symposium). *J. Personal.,* 1949, *18,* 48-50.

CHAPTER IV

LEVELS OF EXPLANATION

A CERTAIN AMOUNT of the systematic controversy generated within psychology has been said to be the result of a failure to recognize the fact that different points of view will naturally follow from the acceptance of different basic premises and the use of varying theoretical and experimental approaches. Differences in the level of explanation at which various theoretical and systematic endeavors are designed to operate seems to be one of the most important factors in the production of such controversy. The selections in the present chapter deal with this problem of varying levels of explanation and are included in the expectation that a fuller appreciation of the role of such basic differences will result in a reduction of at least some of the more superficial disagreements.

In the first selection Egon Brunswik provides a useful systematic framework that emphasizes the "conceptual focus" of certain of the major systematic positions in psychology, with special reference to their molar-molecular characteristics. The problem of this distinction between molar and molecular is specifically treated in the second selection by Richard A. Littman and Ephraim Rosen, who analyze the various ways in which these terms have been applied. Originally stressed by Tolman (see Selection No. 29), the concept of molar behavior has proven increasingly popular, especially with psychologists of field-theoretical or holistic inclinations, who have thus tended to perpetuate the early Gestalt protest against "atomism" and "elementarism." Although it seems very unlikely that this distinction will be dropped, as Littman and Rosen propose, one may well agree with their concern at the strong emotional overtones which the terms have acquired.

8 THE CONCEPTUAL FOCUS OF SYSTEMS[1]

Egon Brunswik

In the present paper the attempt is made to order systematically some of the conceptual tools which have been used in dealing with psychological topics. In the opinion of the author, a suitable starting point for such a consideration is furnished by a scheme of the following kind (Figure 1).

The drawing represents an organism within its surroundings as described by an observing physicist in terms of measurement and computation. This observer might be able to distinguish different layers within the whole causal texture with reference to the organism. Some of these which became most outstanding in psychological discriminations might be designated by the terms (*c*) remote past, (*b*) the realm of palpable bodies in the actual environment, (*a*) stimulus events located on the retina or on other stimulus surfaces of the organism, (0) intraorganismic events, (*A*) muscular reactions, or behavior in the narrower sense of the word, (*B*) effects of these reactions with regard to the relationship between organism and surroundings, as e.g., the reaching of a goal, and finally (*C*) the more remote consequences and final products of life activities including stabilized mechanical or conceptual tools for further use. For the purpose of further explanation, some of the customary terms not used in this list are included in the chart.

The layers indicated are not supposed to designate singular sequences in time, but rather to furnish a general scheme for cross-sectional classification and coördination of physical events, or features of the physical world, with reference to their causal relationship to an organism. The scheme possesses a certain symmetry, with layers designated by corresponding letters (*a* and *A, b* and *B, c* and *C*) conceptually related to each other.

[1] Paper sent in for the fourth International Congress for the Unity of Science (Cambridge, England, 1938).

From E. Brunswik, The conceptual focus of some psychological systems, *J. unif. Sci.*, 1939, *8*, 36-49. Reprinted by permission of the author and publisher.

Four main types of interest seem to be possible within this system: 1) emphasis upon events belonging to a certain cross-sectional layer and the internal relations of these events among each other, 2) emphasis upon a certain type of causal chains, that is, interest in longitudinal sequences, 3) emphasis upon the external relationships of distant cross-sectional layers among each other, 4) emphasis upon the interrelations of discrete longitudinal patterns among each other.

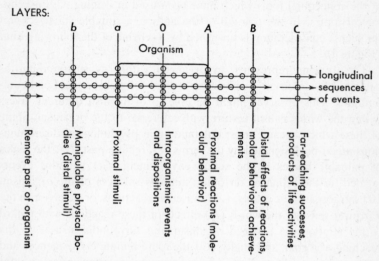

Figure 1   Scheme of the organism in its surroundings

Concepts and laws referring to 1) and 2), that is to single events or to cross-sectional or longitudinal internal relationships, are non-psychological. Roughly speaking, these internal relationships constitute the core of the problems treated in physics proper as far as the left part of the picture and particularly (*b*) is concerned. They constitute the core of the biological sciences in the narrower sense of the word as far as the middle of the picture is concerned, and the "letters" or "Geisteswissenschaften" as far as the right part is concerned. On this latter side those physical features of the world are represented which still reveal the fact that their causal ancestry is partially built up from causal patterns typical to life activities. For example, a mechanical tool made by man would be considered to belong to this group only by virtue of its particular form in connection with a limited number of certain "relevant" properties regardless of all the other traits.

We are now going to attempt to characterize some of the psychological disciplines, or systems, as they grew up historically, in terms of our scheme. In every instance, not the programmatically propounded general frame will be taken as the standard, but rather the conceptual texture of the work actually performed in a sufficiently detailed fashion. This has to be done, since in an arm-chair sense nearly any of the systems might justly consider itself all-inclusive and able to be con-

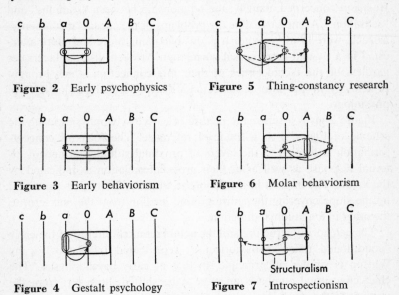

Figure 2   Early psychophysics

Figure 5   Thing-constancy research

Figure 3   Early behaviorism

Figure 6   Molar behaviorism

Figure 4   Gestalt psychology

Figure 7   Introspectionism

siderate in face of every objection without doing violence to its own conceptual framework. In short, we are going to treat systems not in terms of what they could have included but what they did include.

Early experimental psychology still was characterized by the ideology typical of the most paradigmatic nonpsychological sciences. In particular its interests were, as far as the very beginnings are concerned, chiefly longitudinal in the sense characterized above under 2). The first type of experimental research to win importance in psychology was classical psychophysics. Its interest centered around a rather limited fragment of a kind of longitudinal chain, per se. The initial link was defined in terms of what Koffka has named proximal stimulation, that is, stimulation in terms of the causal chains as they just enter the sense organ. The guiding ideal of the psychology of that time was expressed by the wish to know as much as possible about the functional mechanisms of the sense organ and of nervous conduction—in short, about "mediation problems"—and thus to be enabled to pursue the causal chains as closely as possible, in a step-by-step fashion, so to speak. There was, however, as we follow the development from the Johannes Müller to the Fechner era, a noticeable shift of emphasis toward the relationship, per se, of the two end terms of the longitudinal fragment concerned, namely, the relationship between "stimulus" and "sensation." At the same time the problems of the causal "mediations," as such, were losing ground. It is this becoming more and more interested in a by-and-large causal correlation between discrete layers regardless of the technicalities of their interconnection which brought psychology proper into existence as a discipline distinguishable from physiology.

Figure 2 gives a schematic picture of early psychophysics using the scheme of Figure 1 as a frame of reference. The focus of concept-formation is located at the layers of proximal stimulation and of internal response as well as at their gross interrelation as indicated by the arrow. The interest in mediation problems still vital is represented by the slope covering the entire ground leading from the one term to the other in longitudinal direction.

The categorical structure and the actual research interest of the early "conditioned reflex" behaviorism as represented by Pavlov or by Watson is similar, in principle, to that of early psychophysics. The chief conceptual emphasis appears to be shifted, however, from the implicit to the overt response in terms of bodily movements, as such. The interest in mediation problems is centered around the motor rather than the sensory processes, as indicated in Figure 3. In fact, of course, every psychophysics or introspective psychology had to utilize verbal, that is, a particular kind of motor, responses. These responses were supposed to be, however, true representatives of inner states. The aimed-at-focus of concept formation of these disciplines might therefore be considered to lie in the internal life of the individual.

The further development of psychology as an exact science can be characterized as a progressive extension of the range of consideration from the fragmentary or molecular viewpoint to larger units of a "molar" nature. This goes with an increasing emphasis upon gross by-and-large correlations between kinds of events schematically located at a distance from each other, on the one hand, and with a—on the whole—more and more subordinate interest in mediation, per se.

A first important step was Gestalt psychology. Considering the most characteristic core of problems actually treated by Gestalt psychology in the field of perception, the chief difference as compared with traditional psychophysics lies in an extension of the notion of the stimulus to that of a stimulus pattern. The response is treated as a response to the sensory configuration as a whole whereby the laws of dynamic interaction within each of the cross-sectional layers of the sensorium are made the central issue. Gestalt psychology, though totalitarian or molar, is, however, still fragmentary insofar as it is, in its most elaborate parts, a psychology "from the retina inward," so to speak. There is, as in psychophysics, a great deal of interest in mediation problems, as can be seen from the numerous attempts to explain physiologically the facts found. All this is represented schematically in Figure 4.

A further extension of the psychology of perception is given by including into the scope of consideration the manipulable solid bodies, located in the farther environment, and their recognition as the specific determiners of the reaction. The beginnings of this line of interest can be traced back to Helmholtz. This trend, however, did not become conscious of its own character until the last few decades and after the earlier stages of Gestalt psychology already had been completed. In this discipline, the stimulus is not any longer defined in proximal terms but in distal ones. The actual research centers around the question to what extent the perceptual system is able to liberate itself from the disturbing variability of the proximal representation of similar distal stimuli and thus to focus the response upon the latter and not upon the former as the determining event. In other words, the question is how far the organism has established mechanisms which are able to extrapolate, with a sufficiently large chance of success, the causal chains from the retina backward and thus, figuratively speaking, to reach out cognitively into the farther surroundings.

A fairly univocal attachment of a class of reactions to bodily properties, like extension or reflectivity to color, despite changes in the mediating causal pattern is called "thing constancy." We might, then, as well describe these reactions by means of the other term of the external relation in question, or, in short, in terms of their "objects attained." The focus of concept formation is thus shifted away from the organism itself into its farther surroundings, or, more precisely, into a relationship of the organism with layer (b). In other words, the organism is characterized by its ability to achieve something with regard to its environment, not by the intrinsic character of its reactions or by the nature of certain physiological forms of mediation.

In the opinion of the author, there is scarcely another discipline which would reveal as clearly as does constancy research the extent to which the organism is able to render irrelevant the particularities of mediation. Let us take a frequently quoted example. Among the chief constituents of the system of cues which enable the organism to extrapolate the sizes of the surrounding bodies from the retinal stimulus pattern, are the so called "distance-cues," as, for instance, binocular disparity or the perspective distortion of right angles. There are numerous kinds of distance cues. Most of them differ radically from each other as long as we consider intrinsic properties or the physiological mechanisms operated by them. They have in common nothing but a higher or lesser probability of being caused by a certain environmental depth-pattern. And yet they are responded to by the central system of the organism in an identical manner, or, in short, they are "equipotential." It is this feature of organismic reaction and achievement which forces psychology, as it approaches its genuine molar and relational problems, more and more into a focusing upon the end terms of far-reaching relationships. The particular "how" of the mediation processes, on the other hand, necessarily will attract only subordinate interest.

In other words, we do not consider it a matter of choice, whether psychology does focus its concepts on one or on another layer or on a correlation of layers among each other. In looking without preconceptions at nature populated by organisms, gross correlations of higher or lesser degree between kinds of events rather remote from each other in space or time will strike the observer. The network of occurrences participating in such correlations might be conceptually picked out and its constituents labeled as the given foci of life patterns. Psychology has to focus its descriptions on what the organisms have become focussed on, not on events systematically located at the interstices between these foci. Ordo idearum sit idem ac ordo rerum. There has to be a discipline to deal with these foci and their gross correlations, per se. Otherwise there would remain a white spot on the landmap of possible scientific knowledge. By all of its history, it is psychology which is predestined to fill this gap.

In short, molar psychology of achievement is a deliberate "lump" treatment. This feature seems to be the chief obstacle which stands in the way of its acceptance. Correlations between distant layers never hold to an ideal degree. There are always "exceptions" due to the lack of perfection of the cues and means establishing these correlations. In every instance, there is only a higher or lesser degree of probability for the reaching of the usual end. This feature becomes especially clear where we have to do with the so-called instincts. Dealing with instruments of this kind in terms of their achievement leads to an apparent lack of exactitude. It takes a certain courage, a neglect of some of the attitudes sacred to scientific tradition, to give up the safety of molecular correlations, cheap as they are, in favor of the equivocalities or "vaguenesses" of molar correlations. But we have to prefer vagueness focussed upon essentials to security and strict univocality focussed upon nonessentials. This holds especially as long as we are lucky enough to find everything prepared to become strictly physicalistic in our "vaguenesses," quantifying them by the means of correlation statistics and other related mathematical tools.

There always remains a certain self-restriction required in order not to become too curious about the mechanisms causing the "exceptions" and dispersions mentioned, before the task of a bird's-eye-view-inventory of gross correlations had been completed. Of course, there are various ramifications. Looking for exceptions and their causes might, besides being a mere side track, become a corrective measure which enables us to find still more superordinate correlations. These superordinate correlations, however, should be our ultimate aim. Furthermore, concepts and methods referring to mediation problems will have to come back to psychology proper as soon as the precise limitations of the complex achievements in question are subject to closer examination. These problems are out of the scope of psychological consideration only so far as that first phase of research is concerned in which far-reaching gross achievements become discovered and examined in first approximation. On the whole, however, psychology should develop "from above," not "from below." It might proceed to sub-foci of a more and more particular kind and ultimately converge towards and merge with its complementary sciences of a genuinely molecular type.

The schematic representation of constancy research (Figure 5) has to be drawn in the following way: an arrow from a certain type of events in (*b*) to a certain type of events in (0), representing the primary interest; a slope around the group of sub-foci which constitute the "family" of equipotential cue patterns and which circumscribe the extent of variability of the mediational pattern and thus the degree of safeguardedness of the achievement under varying conditions of mediation; and finally a slope around the whole unit of processes involved, including mediation processes. The latter slope has been dotted in order to indicate the subordinate nature of the mediation problems. A further dotted arrow is drawn to connect the event in (0) with an overt response. This is done to indicate that Psychology in Terms of Objects wishes to be, in principle, strictly behavioristic, i.e., refuses to extrapolate without particular controls from the measurable verbal utterances into the field of their internal "meanings."

A picture symmetrical to that of constancy research is yielded by a chief part of the research done within the conceptual frame of molar or purposive behaviorism, as represented by Tolman (Figure 6). The difference is merely a material one, constancy research being concerned with problems of reception and cognition, or the organismic achievement of a backward extrapolation of causal chains, whereas molar behaviorism deals with problems of overt action and its further environmental effects. In molar behaviorism, as contrasted to molecular behaviorism, results are expressed in terms of reaching a certain goal, not in terms of movements made. The comparative irrelevancy of ways and means, that is, their equipotentiality with regard to a certain end, is systematically recognized and attempts are made to prove it experimentally. As it was done for the proximal stimulus cues in the extended psychophysics of perceptual thing constancy, molar behaviorism realizes that the essentials of behavior will become lost in a description focussed on proximal determination. Thus both disciplines are essentially environmentalistic, not mediationalistic or physiologistic.

In both constancy research and molar behaviorism a certain interrelation of longitudinal causal chains is made one of the central issues, namely their equipotentiality within the larger instrument of well-established far-reaching causal couplings. Emphasis is withdrawn, to a certain extent, from a step-by-step determination of these mediating chains of events. Such a restriction is not essential, however, to a molar point of view, as is shown by the type of approach represented by Hull. His general frame of consideration coincides in its most essential features with that of the disciplines mentioned. A still stronger line of interest is focussed, however, on the "family" of mediational patterns, per se. These patterns are analyzed in an essentially associationistic or conditioned reflex fashion, that is in a molecular longitudinal way. In the opinion of the author, the chief objection to such an attitude is a merely practical one, namely, distraction from the gross "first-approximation" treatment of cognitive or behavioral achievement.

The idea of a pure achievement analysis is accomplished, more thoroughly than in any of the other branches mentioned, in the psychology of "tests." At first glance this might seem to be a strictly cross-sectional affair within events in layer (B), these events being correlated among each other statistically. The correlational analysis implies, however, the reference to organisms performing various combinations of achievement. Mediation problems are usually kept entirely outside of consideration.

It might even be said that correlation statistics as a general scientific instrument received a decisive impetus from test psychology (Pearson, Spearman, Thurstone, and others). Starting from rather complex achievements relatively detached from straight sensory or muscular activities, test psychology had the chance to grow up without meeting a resistance comparable to that met by Gestalt psychology or the other molar disciplines mentioned above. The methods developed in test statistics are, therefore, most likely to become paradigmatic to all future molar psychology. As an illustration it might be mentioned that, according to a recent American survey, the term correlation is among the two or three most frequently quoted terms to be found in the textbooks used in this country.

In recent times statistical analysis led to a closer reference to a small number of hypothetical "factors" or basic abilities independent of each other underlying the countless variety of actual performances. This is one of the instances where the stage is set for a genuinely psychological physiological psychology, focussed not on layer (0), as such, or on its interrelations with layers (a) or (A), but on the far-reaching interrelations between (0), on the one hand, and (B)—or (b)—on the other.

A few words only about disciplines like social psychology, genetic psychology, psychoanalysis. They all seem to be focussed primarily on molar interrelations of the organism in its actuality with some complex features of the remote environment, present or past. They fulfill the requirements of a molar psychology as long as they concentrate upon an attempt to segregate abstractively the focal or relevant traits within the patterns they investigate from the actually irrelevant ones.

A certain type of genetic attitude possesses, however, a close resemblance to molecularism. Considering the systematic description of gross achievement or adjustment of the organism to the environment as the primary subject matter of psychology, inquiry about the history of such mechanisms in some cases might easily lose contact with the essential features of the achievemental pattern actually in question. In such instances, asking "why" becomes comparable to the "how" problems of the mediationalistic type. For example, to be concerned primarily as to whether a certain organismic instrument is due to heredity or to learning might occasionally become just another burden for the investigator of that instrument, coördinate with the claim of the physiologically minded criticist whose first concern is to know as much as possible about all the single steps involved in the mechanism in question. Like molecularism, geneticism for its own sake involves the danger of diverting psychology into knowing more and more for the price of knowing it about less and less, or about smaller and smaller fragments of the units which constitute the task of psychology.

In the common language of science, molecular as well as genetic descriptions have often been called "explanations." In contrast to that, molar achievemental analysis is "descriptive" in the most restricted sense of the word. As a deliberate "lump" treatment, it refuses to aim at explanation for its own sake. It is a psychology "in terms of . . . ," a terminological affair, a way of registering and conceptually looking at gross correlations in their straightforward actuality.

Up to this point of our considerations psychology has been treated as if it were built up by means of strictly scientific methods, that is, in principle, as physics was of a certain group of causal correlations. For a large part of psychology this holds true, in principle at least. The events involved are subject to measurement and the interrelations to quantitative treatment. Or, as Lewin would put it, "Aristotelian" concept formation in terms of absolute dichotomies between qualitatively different "principles," as, e.g., the traditional antithesis of "insight" versus "learning," has already been largely substituted by a "Galilean," that is, by more "diagrammatic" forms of thinking in terms of gradual discriminations.

We do not wish, however, to conclude this paper without glancing at some of the forms of psychology which do not or do not fully subscribe to such a methodological ideal.

First of all, there is introspectionism. Common to all introspectionism is the tacit assumption of a strict one to one relationship between verbal utterances and "inner events." Only by virtue of such an attitude is it possible to consider, as is done by introspectionism, words or other events located in layer (A) as valid representatives or "symbols" for inner experiences (0). In all objective psychology verbal utterances are taken not as symbols, but merely as "symptoms" the meaning of which is supposed to be accessible only by means of special correlational investigations. In Figure 7, the substitution mentioned is represented by a parenthesis.

Another kind of substitution is, however, much more fundamental in introspectionism. As emphasized especially by the so-called act-psychologists, e.g., Brentano, the essence of consciousness is characterized by its pointing toward, or aiming at, an object. This relationship has been called intentionality. Though it was said that intentional objects should not be confused with the physical environment, it still can be made clear that introspectionism became infiltrated with a conceptual structure taken to a large extent from the layer of palpable bodies (b). Yet there was no chance of a quantitative treatment on a physicalistic basis, since the relation of (0) to (b)—or to something formally analogous to (b)—had been accepted as univocal without experimentation. Furthermore, this relationship was regarded as a qualitative entity of its own kind entirely incomparable with the causal relationship, to which it is also supposed to be opposite in direction. This relationship was admitted without further control, from a mere inspection of layer (0). This is indicated in Figure 7 by a dashed arrow $0 \to b$ which is also pointing in the opposite direction from the corresponding arrow $b \to 0$ in Figure 5. In philosophy, the problems of "dualism" have to a large extent arisen from confusion and uncritical mutual substitution of the two cross-sectional layers structurally similar to each other. This substitution is comparable to that committed by introspectionism. The fallacies of an uncontrolled substitution of layers by each other have recently been emphasized by Heider.

Introspectionism can be subdivided into two main branches. The one is represented by men like Wundt or Titchener, and also by Mach. It is sometimes called "Structuralism." Its chief feature is to look for basic elements out of which all the complex experiences may "consist" (without questioning whether the grammar of the word "consist" permits such an application). Structuralism coincides in time with the early molecular sensory psychology characterized by its emphasis upon mediational features like proximal stimulation and the structure of the sense receptors. It is obvious that in this general attitude—sometimes characterized as "glorification of the skin"—the mosaic-nature of the events at the sensory surface has been directly carried over to the hypothetical structure of inner events (cf. Figure 7). Thus these came to be understood after the pattern of the sense organ. In structuralism, therefore, not only layers (0) and (A) and layers (0) and (b), but also layers (0) and (a) appear in uncontrolled confusion.

The second branch of introspectionism might be called phenomenalism. It is somewhat related to act psychology, and sometimes the term phenomenology is applied, not quite unmistakably, to it. It is the kind of introspection represented by Gestalt psychology and the Würzburg school of psychology of thinking. There was sufficient sophistication within phenomenalism about the naïve entanglement of structuralism with sensory elementarism, with mediationalism and with functional "explanation." Unbiased "description" of the preanalytically given was aimed at. The structuralist's "consist of" was given up in favor of the phenomenalist's "resembles." Everyday language and even slang was used deliberately. Characteristic examples are the description of the phenomenon of the shadow by Hering as a tiny skin of darkness lying upon the surface of the object, the true color of which shines through the former, or the introduction of the term "Aha-Erlebnis" by Bühler in order to refer to the experience of sudden insight. In this way, phenomenalism grew into a kind of conceptualized and systematized poetry, bringing, in principle, all the various concepts and terms of the common qualitative language into one comprehensive system of resemblances. Since all "qualities" might be regarded as gross reactions of the organism to some features of the environment and thus be systematically located in layer (0), phenomenalism is the strictest expression in existence of an 0-internal system of psychological concept formation.

As a system of mutual resemblances, phenomenalism can be represented by means of a spatial order. The best example for such a quasi-spatial arrangement of qualities, though limited to a certain modality, is the three-dimensional Hering color pyramid. It is built up on an entirely phenomenalistic basis regardless of the physical relationships of colors among each other. Thus it deals with reactions only, not with stimuli. It was the first attempt to deal with psychological problems on a "topological" basis by assigning a certain place in a spatial order to each quality. These qualities could then be determined in terms of basic "dimensions" defined by certain outstanding qualities.

On a somewhat different basis, topological considerations have been recently introduced into psychology by Lewin. In his Topological Psychology, the actual "life space" is represented by a spatial scheme. As is true for phenomenalism, however, not the surroundings defined in terms of physics are taken as a frame of reference, but rather the environment as it is cognitively or functionally responded to by the organism in the particular instance. In a certain way topological psychology is similar to the "Umweltforschung" of Uexküll. It deals, deliberately, not with stimuli or stimulus relationships, but rather with a pattern of reactions to be schematically located in 0, and from 0 dynamically onward until a new equilibrium is reached. Its chief merit is that it furnished an adequate conceptual tool for a description of this organized pattern of "field" intervening between the stimulating surroundings (c, b, a) on the one hand, and the acted-upon surroundings (A, B, C), on the other. Though quasi-spatial and highly generalized, topological psychology is not quantitative and not physicalistic in the usual sense. It enters the picture at a systematic locus symmetrical, or complementary, to the psychology of perception. Psychology of perception deals with the relationship of the world as it "is" for the organism in question, and of the world as it "is" for the observing discursified human being. Only the former is represented in topological psychology.

In conclusion: psychological research today presents itself as a pattern of fragments. These fragments tend to crystallize around the program of a gross correlational analysis in terms of achievement, converging "from above" with the disciplines dealing with molecular problems. Environmentalism seems to take the lead before mediationalism and molecular geneticism (as, e.g., some of the questions of "explanation").

9   THE MOLAR-MOLECULAR DISTINCTION

Richard A. Littman and Ephraim Rosen

Introduction

Psychology has had more propensity than most disciplines to react to concepts as if they were good or bad. Today, for example, it is good to be dynamic, functional, operational, field-theoretical and molar; it is bad to be static, structuralistic, non-operational, atomistic and molecular. The good terms seem to produce a feeling of expansiveness, while the bad ones may be symbolized by a cramped feeling in the face of a confusing multiplicity. Since one can hardly deny the scientist his status as a personality, we may expect the affective components of theory to be with us always. Indeed, some have said that new theories are but a leap from one set of affects to another. But it is also true that the constant reconsideration of affectively charged words is a major technique of scientific advance.

We propose to consider two of the above terms [1] because they represent a rallying point for certain recurrent arguments in systematic psychology. The terms are *molar* and *molecular*. We will attempt to show that the central role they have achieved in psychology has been magnified and distorted by the various ways they have been interpreted. Before reviewing these different usages, a brief glance at their historical setting may prove useful.

A major emphasis in recent methodology is that theories are contingent and that scientific description may take many forms. This view of theories as alternative rather than necessarily contradictory proposals implies that they may be differentiated in terms of the *units of description* they employ. By using these units as criteria of communicability between theories many conflicts have been resolved. Explicit recognition of this approach appeared most clearly in psychology with the publication of Tolman's *Purposive Behavior in Animals and Men* (15).

---

[1] Throughout the paper, *term, concept* and *construct* will be used interchangeably. Our inquiry does not require a more specialized use.

From R. A. Littman and E. Rosen, Molar and molecular, *Psychol. Rev.*, 1950, *57*, 58-65. Reprinted by permission of the authors, the *Psychological Review,* and the American Psychological Association.

The reader need hardly be reminded of the eagerness with which the terms molar and molecular were then adopted. They quickly entered the substance of most psychological theory and only one major protest was heard. Koffka (10) objected to the generosity with which Tolman located the molecular in a systematic hierarchy. For Tolman every level of the hierarchy is equally legitimate, so that, in a sense, molecular and molar are equally important. For Koffka, on the other hand, the levels have a relationship of priority so that the molar is more general and basic.

The general favor with which the distinction was met is quite understandable. Up to that time much research in the applied areas of education, social psychology and personality—not to mention other disciplines such as sociology or anthropology—had been characterized by a certain amount of guilt and defensiveness. Nowhere could one point to the physiological basis of this research, to the real stuff of behavior, as it were. As the applied psychologists hastened to point out, however, consistent and discriminating variables *were* being isolated and defined. While most of the research in learning at this time also lacked organic substantiation, guilt-feelings were avoided by virtue of an historic orthodoxy and a readiness for neurological speculation. This lack of sureness with respect to the necessity for physiological explanations had led to a sharp conflict between two frames of reference, the biological and the psychological. Tolman's efforts to resolve this conflict represented a convergence of many trends: Gestalt psychology; comparative psychology in the persons of Hobhouse, Thorndike, Washburn and Yerkes; the behaviorisms of Watson, A. P. Weiss and Kantor; social psychology and personality study in the related views of McDougall and Freud; and the philosophy of Holt, James and other pragmatists. In a sense Tolman was the final step in establishing the legitimacy of the psychological approach. The unrespectability of much earlier work could be seen, in the light of Tolman's analysis, to have arisen from a disparity between great subtlety with respect to psychological phenomena and a lack of sophistication with respect to operational or investigatory procedures. Accepting the psychological framework of these non-biological theorists,[2] Tolman insisted that such a framework be related to data in a clear-cut, communicable fashion.

---

[2] We are aware that many of the people we have labeled psychologically oriented, e.g., Freud, McDougall, Washburn, were highly trained in the biological sciences, and that they were at all times cognizant of the "animal" nature of their subjects. What we

Another way of looking at Tolman's contribution is to say that he united certain features of positivism and emergentism. The emergentist stressed that organic matter has different levels of functioning which emerge out of the organization of phenomena, and that these *new* levels are real and require their own descriptive devices. Tolman, on the other hand, stressed the *descriptive* aspect of the problem, observing that in addition to the physiological descriptions of organic life, there were possible other descriptions which appeared to be at least as fruitful. Phrased in this way the distinction between levels of functioning becomes neither metaphysical nor existential but methodological. Tolman's approach, then, was to find out what questions could be made systematically meaningful within a purely psychological framework. He argued that a scientific theory has meaning in so far as it is based upon a set of observable events, and that such meanings are a function of the way these events are described—regardless of the kind of event investigated. One way of looking at events, he further suggested, is in terms of whether they can be described as part or total functions. These functions were termed molecular and molar, respectively. The distinction provided a rationale for separating physiology from psychology by labeling physiology as a part process. But Tolman was not too exact in specifying what he meant by part or whole functions and, consequently, the meaning of molar and molecular was left somewhat indefinite and a variety of interpretations arose. It is to these interpretations that we now turn.

We list below seven different meanings which we have arbitrarily named. The first three are propositional; that is, they are explicit definitions of the terms. The remainder are implicit; they have not been formally defined, and operate as programmatic, affective usages in psychological thinking. The reader will note that authors who find the terms molar and molecular useful do not usually specify which of these many meanings is meant. Indeed, most frequently, they intend several of them simultaneously. Univocality is the exception.

---

are emphasizing is that their data and much of their theory were purely behavioral. While all expressed belief in the "dependency" of mind on body, they did not feel guilty about discussing mind; the belief in this dependency gave them permission to emphasize one side of what was for them an equation. Those psychologists who could not calmly accept this equation, and wished to retain the psychological point of view, were the ones who found themselves in the anxious state we have described.

Meanings

1. *Interaction.* Molar has been used to refer to experiments or observational series employing many variables, treating them in interaction with each other. The analysis of variance design would seem to be molar in character. Contrariwise, the classical experiment of one independent, and one dependent, variable in isolation from all others, would appear to be molecular. This type of analysis implies a continuum of molarity-molecularity. Thus the *t* statistic used to evaluate the classical type of experiment is but a special case of the *F* statistic. However, writers who identify molarity with interaction usually mean something other than this statistical tying together of independent entities. They emphasize rather the interdependent nature of the very definitions of these variables, and the necessity of describing events as a matrix of factors. Thus Brunswik, in his *Outline of History of Psychology* (3), distinguishes between molecular and molar as a difference between an approach which is inadequate, fragmentary, over-simplifying, bit-by-bit, atomistic, and microscopic, losing sight of the whole, as contrasted with an approach which is adequate, encompasses the essentials of macroscopic, uses dynamic units ("e.g., of the personality as a whole, of behavior-patterns"), and properly considers coherence and the role and interaction of parts within a context. Brunswik's contrast overlaps some of our later meanings, but his emphasis is on isolated variables vs. comprehensive, interacting variables.

2. *Action-units.* This meaning has become increasingly prominent. A relatively long-time unit is molar, a short-time unit is molecular. The molar unit of description is a behavior episode bounded in time by *initiation* of behavior by a need, and *cessation* of behavior by achievement of a goal (Muenzinger, 13). It is not time-length per se that is emphasized, but rather the meaningfulness of behavioral description in terms of some functional unit. Thus Krech and Crutchfield say,

In the absence of molar units, the description of behavior can be little more than an enumeration of unsystematized bits and pieces of momentary, limited, and unrelated responses. Viewed wholly, in the context of needs and goals, on the other hand, the behavior of the individual can be seen as meaningfully organized. The unity implied in the molar description is not something arbitrarily imposed by the psychologist in viewing the individual as he behaves; the individual is a dynamic unity, a whole person, and it is as such that he takes part in social phenomena (11, p. 31).

It may be noted that this passage reflects Gestalt philosophy as to the nature of the world: molar units are necessary because people *are* molar. The world *is* organized in molar fashion, and the molecular-molar argument is one of content as well as methodology. But not all advocates of such long-time units have tied their conception of behavior to the Gestalt notion of an articulated universe, as have Krech and Crutchfield. Muenzinger advocates these start-end units as the only way of breaking into and handling the fluid, Jamesian stream of events.

3. *Levels*. Psychology is molar, physiology and neurology are molecular. A response is molar, a group of muscle twitches is molecular. Hull (8) explicitly distinguishes between molar and molecular in this way, and we have mentioned Tolman's equation of physiology with part processes. But in the two previous definitions of molar and molecular the physiologist also can be molar. A study of endocrine balance may have many interacting variables, and use long-time units. It seems, then, that it is not physiology that is molecular, but rather physiological explanations of psychological phenomena. Such explanations are obviously reductionistic. The question then becomes, "Is reductionism necessarily molecular?" As judged by some of the above criteria of molarity, a glance at classic physiological explanations of behavior would seem to answer this question positively. The physiological variables used in the past to account for behavior have in the main been simple and momentary—neural bonds, reflexes, twitches, etc. But it would be inapplicable to call isomorphism or Lashley's (12) network theory of brain function molecular; and the future may witness molar attempts at physiological explanation of behavioral phenomena. The theories of Rashevsky (14) and Wiener (17) are illustrative of this possibility.

4. *Construction*. The genotypic is considered to be more molar than the phenotypic or peripheral because it is assumed to possess a greater degree of generality and explanatory power. This usage involves construction of a set of abstract intervening variables considerably removed from peripheral data and presumably accounting for them. A high degree of abstraction is of course possible in dealing with surface variables alone, if by abstraction is meant a rational generalization, verbal or mathematical, which does not merely duplicate or summarize data. But all generalizations are not necessarily molar in the present sense. Hecht's (6) work, and much of Hull's may serve as illustrations of phenotypic, non-molar generalizations though in other respects Hull functions as a molar theorist (e.g., the concept of sH_R); when con-

trasted with the "central layer" abstractions represented by, say, a Thurstone factor, many of the variables of Hecht and Hull would be classified as molecular. In contrast with our first three meanings, the present one is usually an informal coupling rather than a formal definition, for one does not find explicit equation of molar and genotypic in the literature.

5. *Phenomenal.* This usage is in marked contrast with the previous one, for the *phenomenal* criterion equates molarity with treatment of data as given. The emphasis is upon the appearance of the variables and the process by which they are observed. The phenomenal or untutored is molar while the derived or analytic is molecular. Katz's (9) phenomenological varieties of color may be contrasted with the structuralists' description of color sensations.

Lifelike in contrast with artificial is a characteristic often associated with this sense of molar.

Indeed, in this as in our next usages, there is stress on the need for reproducing, by means of scientific procedures, the richness of organismic functioning. There is discontent represented by Goldstein (5) and by Allport (1) with the partialling of life by classical science. The present authors believe that this motivation has been important in generating the first three, more formal definitions. The historical background of the concept of molarity, discussed above, may be viewed as an unfolding of this need for realness. The same motivation plays a part in the *construction* usage: intervening variables are often used as a bridging device for a ready return to lifelike phenomena. There is a great difference, of course, between equating molarity with phenomenal data and equating it with intervening constructs to handle data; yet the motivations of such diverse approaches seem to have a common core.

6. *Urgency.* Here molarity-molecularity has shifted completely from a level of methodological relationships to one of value decisions. If the psychologist's description is believed to be applicable to problems considered significant by society, then it is molar.

Classification according to this category is dependent on belief as to what is important in pure and applied psychology. In so far as psychologists disagree on the relative importance of specific psychological problems, various approaches will be differently classified as molar or molecular. The distinction arose at a time when general psychology was returning to the task of incorporating purposeful behavior into its framework. Present-day concerns with social and clinical problems have reaffirmed the need for such an endeavor.[3]

7. *Holism.* The more consideration there is of the organism as a whole or the unity of the organism, the more molar is the approach. Explicit description of a part of the organism is molecular. Though this criterion seems to stem from Tolman's original contrast of part and whole processes in learning, the distinction has frequently become purely verbal and has been based on the degree of lip-service to wholeness and unity. Indeed, holism as a philosophy antedates Tolman, and many present-day holist philosophers have merely borrowed the term molar from him.

Discussion

We shall consider first the interrelationship of the meanings, and then the contemporary significance of the molar-molecular distinction.

1. Certain problems arise when we attempt to interrelate our seven meanings. One may first examine the question of concurrent use of several meanings. Another passage from Krech and Crutchfield will illustrate the not unusual [4] simultaneity of meanings to be found in the literature:

PROPOSITION I

The proper unit of motivational analysis is molar behavior, which involves needs and goals.

Of first importance in our analysis is the decision as to the units of behavior to be employed. Shall we be concerned with mere simple, segmental activities such as muscle twitches, movements of the limbs, swallowing, sweating, swearing, and the like, or shall we be concerned with total *behavior acts,* such as getting married, voting for a political candidate, participating in a lynching? The former is a "molecular" unit, and the latter a "molar" unit.

[3] The category of urgency brings into focus a paradox. While many of Tolman's principles, usually considered more molar than Hull's, are believed to be applicable to problems of human learning, the latter's have so far found a wider application; for example, in the social-psychological and personality studies of Miller, Dollard, Kluckhohn or Massermann. We are not attempting, however, to evaluate the extent to which Hull's principles have *succeeded* as explanatory concepts in dealing with social and clinical problems. Rather, we are merely noting a current *historical* event.

[4] A number of other authors could have been used as illustrations here, for example, Barker, Wright and Gonick's (2) treatment of molarity. We have selected passages from Krech and Crutchfield because they have verbalized so clearly the significance which molarity has for them. The clarity of their presentation makes it possible to tease out many implications of the problem previously operating on an implicit basis.

The distinguishing features of molar behavior are 1) that it includes all the behavior of the individual occurring at the same time (his needs, emotions, thoughts, perceptions, actions, etc.) and 2) that it consists of relatively discrete, unified episodes with a beginning and an end. . . . The beginning of Mr. Arbuthnot's lunchtime molar, behavior is the onset of feelings of hunger; the end of the episode comes with the completion of eating and the feelings of satiety (11, pp. 30-31).

In the above quotation, molar seems to mean *action units, urgency,* a great number of simultaneous variables (presumably interacting), and *holism* ("*all* the behavior of the individual"). Implicit in such a quotation is the assumption that these four meanings, by an inner logic, are interdependent, standing or falling together. The question is not whether *these* particular meanings are in actuality necessarily inconsistent but whether, as a general rule, the construction of a proposition containing many dimensions of meaning is an advisable procedure. The danger is that if one component of the proposition is negated the entire complex may fall.

Associated with lack of independence in the usage of molar-molecular is a lack of clarity with regard to some basic assumptions: Does molar refer to the *size* or the *qualitative* nature of events? Is molarity methodological, referring to a way of describing, or existential, referring to some thing described? Are its referents internal to psychology, or are they external and inter-systematic? These problems contribute to much of the confusion found in the literature. They highlight the difficulties brought about by multiple meaning. We shall discuss them one at a time.

(A) *Quantity vs. quality.* Many of the usages apparently deal with units of *description,* as illustrated by *holism* which equates molarity with large units. The *construction, phenomenal* and *levels* criteria emphasize the *kind* of unit. *Action-units* seem to require units of a certain kind and also large units. Distinctions between quantity and quality are always dangerous, but there does seem to be a difference between emphasizing the descriptive *inclusiveness* of a unit as contrasted with the *kind* of unit adequate to describe behavior. Which of the two emphases is intended by molar can be clear only if its meaning is specified.

(B) *Methodological vs. existential.* The criteria of molarity often seem to imply that the *subject matter* of psychology is of a special kind, and therefore requires a special manner of description. Behaviorial events *are* molar, so the description, too, must be molar. The criterion of *action-units* often suggests this but even more so does the criterion of *holism.* Though the latter has in the main been unable to specify what units should be chosen, it rejects thoroughly descriptions of part processes; this springs apparently from a conviction that the organism *is* a unitary whole, not merely that it can be *described* as a unitary whole. To the degree that these criteria are existential, they seem to clash with Tolman's original stress on molarity as an instrumental property. The other criteria have in the main retained the original instrumental aspect: It is molar to describe phenomena in a certain way; it is not the content described which is molar or molecular.

The writers feel that existential criteria propose a metaphysical criterion for an empirical procedure. By empirical we mean that events may be described in various ways, one of which is in terms of a distinction between molar and molecular. If desirable this distinction may even be given substantive status. Such a step, however, serves only to define the *locus* of investigation and cannot be considered as a statement about the events that are investigated. Description and ontology should not be confused. In the long run scientific systems appear to be judged by some characteristic such as fruitfulness, rather than by coherence with any given ontology. Perhaps science has tolerated ontologic speculation because it seems to serve the purpose of breaking a mold of thought, a direction habit, so that while the heuristic and propaganda value of theories about the real nature of events is indeed valuable, it appears never to be relevant to any empirical system. Value and ontology act as catalysts, and are presumably social or cultural instruments that define directions rather than specify relations.

(C) *Internal vs. external referents.* The criteria of *levels* and *urgency,* in contrast to the other usages, refer to more than units. They characterize systems, inter-disciplinary relations and applications as molar or molecular in nature. It is not the variable that is molar, but either the hypotheses made, the type of explanation employed, or the use to which the variables can be put.

The criterion of *levels* is unique in contrasting psychology with non-psychological neurology, physiology, etc. While the other usages localize the distinction between molar and molecular within the realm of psychology, the substantive character of neurology and physiology is used to define their molecularity. It is of some significance that this distinction has almost always dealt with interdisciplinary relations in only one direction. That is, there has been little systematic analysis of relations between anthropology, sociology, economics, political science, history and psychology. Often it is implied that these other fields are not to be considered within this framework of classifying behavioral phenomena. Such a position, however, is difficult to maintain, for if the *level*-type of distinction is a substantive one, then any independent research area (defined as a field where investigatory variables may be isolated) demands inclusion within this classification schema. On the other hand, if there exists a characteristic of greater or lesser molarity, the term molecular loses most of its meaning and the substantive distinction loses its heuristic value. Tolman has recognized the problem and offered his solution to it in an interesting review (16).

2. Of what significance are these rather scholastic distinctions for the contemporary scene? Let us re-emphasize the fact that the molar-molecular distinction entered psychology at a time of crisis. Its usefulness in pointing a way out of the schisms that rent the psychology of the time was great. It provided a rationale, a justification for an approach that has borne much fruit and it legitimized new paths of investigation.

With the achievement of this task, however, the role of the molar-molecular distinction has shifted, perhaps to the point of losing its usefulness. Today one seldom finds the question of legitimacy raised with respect to research of a non-physiological nature, the investigation of purposeful behavior, or the consideration of aspects of organismic functioning previously slighted. The frame of reference has changed. The specific contribution made by the distinction has been almost universally accepted so that the multiplicity of meanings we now find may be an index of future unproductiveness. With this multiplicity there has arisen an affective attachment to the terms, *qua* terms, which serves to cloud the problem and dominate fresh approaches. We suggest, therefore, that the terms be abandoned, for it does not seem possible to purge them of their confusing connotations.[5]

Our analysis, therefore, complements those of theorists who have noted a process of convergence in the last twenty years of psychology, a trend toward dissolution of the schools of psychology (Brunswik, 4; Hilgard, 7). Interest in systems has changed to interest in functional relations and systematization. In this shift the distinction between molar and molecular played the vital role of releasing psychology from pre-

---

[5] Dr. Tolman has indicated that he shares this opinion as to the future role of molar and molecular (personal communication).

mature and confining systems. But in so doing it diminished its usefulness and achieved the status of ground rather than figure in current theory.

References

1. Allport, G. W. *Personality: a psychological interpretation.* New York: Holt, 1937.
2. Barker, R. G., Wright, Beatrice A., and Gonick, Mollie R. *Adjustment to physical handicap and illness: a survey of the social psychology of physique and disability.* New York: Social Science Research Council, 1946.
3. Brunswik, E. *Outline of history of psychology.* Mimeographed edition for course given at Univ. of California, no date.
4. Brunswik, E. Points of view. In *Encyclopedia of psychology* (P. L. Harriman, Ed.). New York: Philosophical Library, 1946, 523-537.
5. Goldstein, K. *Human nature: in the light of psychopathology.* Cambridge: Harvard Univ. Press, 1940.
6. Hecht, S. Vision: II. The nature of the photoreceptor process. In C. Murchison (ed.), *A handbook of general experimental psychology.* Worcester: Clark Univ. Press, 1934, 704-828.
7. Hilgard, E. R. *Theories of learning.* New York: Appleton-Century-Crofts, 1948.
8. Hull, C. L. *Principles of behavior.* New York: D. Appleton-Century, 1943.
9. Katz, D. *The world of colors.* London: Kegan, Paul, Trench, Trubner, 1935.
10. Koffka, K. Review of Tolman's *Purposive behavior in animals and men. Psychol. Bull.,* 1933, *30,* 440-451.
11. Krech, D., & Crutchfield, R. S. *Theory and problems of social psychology.* New York: McGraw-Hill, 1948.
12. Lashley, K. S. *Brain mechanisms and intelligence.* Chicago: Univ. Chicago Press, 1929.
13. Muenzinger, K. F. *Psychology: the science of behavior.* New York: Harpers, 1942.
14. Rashevsky, N. *Mathematical biophysics: physicomathematical foundations of biology.* Chicago: Univ. Chicago Press, 1938.
15. Tolman, E. C. *Purposive behavior in animals and men.* New York: D. Appleton-Century, 1932. [See Selection No. 29 in this volume.]
16. Tolman, E. C. Physiology, psychology and sociology. *Psychol. Rev.,* 1938, *45,* 222-241.
17. Wiener, N. *Cybernetics.* New York: Wiley, 1948.

CHAPTER V

THEORETICAL EMPHASES

THIS CHAPTER continues the consideration of the general problem with which Chapter IV was concerned. It offers a combination of two sharply contrasting views as to the nature of the theoretical and methodological emphasis which modern psychology should adopt. In the first selection Gordon W. Allport presents in concise form the major arguments for his insistent demand that scientific orientation in psychology be maintained on a strictly molar and practical level. In direct contrast, Kenneth W. Spence has been equally insistent on the necessity for psychology to utilize rigorous orthodox scientific procedures and to work on as basic a level as possible. The second selection presents his arguments, as applied to modern "behaviorism."

In reading and evaluating these opposed points of view it is necessary for the student to realize that, to a certain extent, Allport and Spence are talking about quite different problems. A clear recognition of this point should help to prevent confusion of the basic issues and allow full scientific recognition and freedom both to those who wish, with Allport, to work on problems of immediate importance, and to those who wish, with Spence, to carry on fundamental research of the more analytic type. However, it is also necessary to realize that in the former no less than the latter case such recognition will depend upon the degree to which sound scientific standards are successfully maintained. Since the two general points of view are each representative of a wide segment of current psychological opinion, and reflect the so-called "fission" that has developed between professional and scientific psychologists, the issues merit a full discussion.

10   THE EMPHASIS ON MOLAR PROBLEMS [1]

Gordon W. Allport

Within the span of remarkably few years, the quantity and quality of investigations in the fields of personality and social psychology have established not only their scientific dignity but likewise their popularity and promise within the psychological profession. The official formation of this large Division within the American Psychological Association is a formal recognition of these facts.

At the same time the significance of this occasion extends beyond the boundaries of the profession. In forming this Division we are, wittingly or unwittingly, stating our readiness to assume a certain responsibility. We are announcing, in effect, that as a group of scientists we believe we have a contribution to make in interpreting and in remedying some of the serious social dislocations of today. For if we did not believe in the potentialities of our science would we thus formally establish it?

The test of our fitness to exist and to prosper, I submit, will be our ability to contribute substantially in the near future to the diagnosis and treatment of the outstanding malady of our time. The malady I refer to is not war, for modern warfare is but a symptom of an underlying morbid condition; it is not the threatening fission of one world into two, ominous as this threat may be; nor is it our apparent inability to control for our safety and profit the transformation of matter into atomic energy, though this crisis too is now upon us. I speak rather of the *underlying* ailment, of the fact that man's moral sense is not able to assimilate his technology.

While technological warfare, technological unemployment, and the atomic age—all by-products of physical science—have overtaken us, mental and moral science have made no corresponding gains in allaying the rivalries and anxieties induced by technology, in devising

---

[1] Address of the Divisional President before the first annual meeting of the Division of Personality and Social Psychology of the American Psychological Association, September 4, 1946.

From G. W. Allport, Scientific models and human morals, *Psychol. Rev.*, 1947, *54*, 182-192. Reprinted by permission of the author, the *Psychological Review*, and the American Psychological Association.

methods of social control, nor in enhancing human coöperation and solidarity. It is, I venture to point out, precisely our own young science, whose formal establishment we are now celebrating, that has failed to keep pace with the needs of the times.

In taking stock of the situation I observe how many of us seem so stupefied by admiration of physical science that we believe psychology in order to succeed need only imitate the models, postulates, methods and language of physical science. If someone points out the present inutility of mechanical models in predicting any but the most peripheral forms of human behavior, we are inclined to reply: Wait a thousand years if necessary and you will see that man is a robot, and that all his mental functions can be synthesized in kind as successfully as we now synthesize table salt, quinine, or a giant calculator. While we righteously scorn what one of us has called "the subjective, anthropomorphic hocus pocus of mentalism" (6), we would consider a colleague emotional and mystical should he dare speak of "the objective mechanomorphic hocus pocus of physicalism."

Let our progress be gradual, we say. By sticking to peripheral, visible operations we may some day be able to approach complex problems of motivation, and then come within hailing distance of the distresses of mankind. We hope that these distresses will keep a thousand years until we are ready to cope with them, and that in the meantime a free science will be permitted to linger along and take its time. But even if such improbable conditions were fulfilled, I question whether we should endorse this counsel of patience or the premises upon which it rests.

The machine model in psychology had its origin not in clinical or social experience, but rather in adulation of the technological success of the physical sciences. Since psychologists, like everyone else, are enmeshed in the prevailing ethos, they too, unless especially on guard, are likely to allow their subservience to technology to outrun their moral sense.

Besides the mechanical model, there are two other currently popular paradigms in psychology that are, in my opinion, only slightly less inept in guiding significant research or theory concerning the foundations of social morality. I refer to the phylogenetic model and to the infant mind. Although both these patterns during the past two generations have brought new insights and correctives into our work, they have not proved adequate to the needs of clinical, personnel, and social psychology.

The Current Appeal to Psychology

Public officials, confronted by post-war dilemmas, are urgently seeking the aid of psychologists. Many of us who have been approached are embarrassed by the scarcity of scientific findings, and even of serviceable concepts and well-formulated problems, that psychology has to offer *of the type that is being sought*. What is asked for is instant help in discovering the sources and conditions of man's moral sense in order that this sense may be enlarged and brought into focus. What is asked for is aid from a science of human relationships whose assistance Franklin D. Roosevelt likewise invoked in his last speech before his death.[2] Yet we may comb the entire file of the *Psychological Abstracts* and find very little that has any bearing upon the improvement of human relationships on an international scale.

Why have we so relatively little to offer? Is it that we are young and need to follow the machine model for a thousand years? Or have we gotten off to a thoroughly bad start through our adoption of root-metaphors that lead away from, rather than toward, the problem at hand? Three generations ago psychology was commonly classified as a "moral science." Though we may not favor the aura of this term, how can we expect anything other than a science *of* moral conduct to discover conditions that will bring the needed counterpoise to technology run wild?

When any one of us undertakes a piece of research he inevitably adopts, according to his preference, one or another of the fundamental models available to psychologists. My thesis is that now if ever we need to test our preferred model for its capacity to yield discoveries that have some sure relevance to moral nature and to social skills.

Expectancy and Intention

If I interpret the matter correctly, American psychology naturally adopted mechanical models because our culture has always been action-oriented and technological. By and large our psychology is a motorized psychology, and is only now widening its concept of action to include the ego-involved participation of the human organism in matters affecting its own destiny (2). The earlier extreme position, represented by

---

[2] "Today we are faced with the preëminent fact that, if civilization is to survive, we must cultivate the science of human relationships—the ability of all peoples, of all kinds, to live together and work together, in the same world, at peace."

E. B. Holt and J. B. Watson, held personality to be essentially a battery of trigger-release mechanisms. This view paid no attention to the sustained directions of striving characteristic of moral behavior, to what in this paper I shall call "intentions."

This trigger-model, still preferred by a few, gave way gradually to a more purposive behaviorism. The concept of "sign-Gestalt expectancy" was introduced by Tolman, and mercifully shortened by Hilgard and Marquis to "expectancy" (9). It is an interesting fact that these authors seem to regard the principle of expectancy as the most purposive of all the essentially mechanical theories derived from the multitudinous experiments on the conditioned reflex (9, p. 101). In other words, some version of the principle of expectancy is as far as many psychologists have come in their conception of the nature of personal and social conduct.

The principle holds that in the presence of certain signs the organism expects a certain goal to appear if it follows the customary behavior route. If the goal is reached, the expectation is confirmed; if not, the organism may vary its behavior (9, p. 88). The principle, while allowing for the importance of attitude, is essentially stimulus-bound. We behave according to the cues we have learned, according to our expectancies.

In order not to complicate my argument I shall leave out of consideration the law of effect, which, it would be easy to show, likewise ascribes behavior wholly to past experience, to learned cues, and to mechanical reinforcements (4). Both principles, so far as I can see, accord nothing to the *un*rewarded, *un*realized, yet persistive, intentions of man's moral nature.

The trouble with these currently fashionable concepts, drawn from the phylogenetic model, is that while they seem to apply aptly enough to animal behavior whence they were derived, they have only a limited or else a remote analogical bearing on the activities of human beings. We may know a person's expectancies and even his past rewards, and yet be singularly unable to predict or control his future behavior, unless at the same time we know also his basic intentions which are by no means a stencilled copy of his previous expectancies and rewards (3).

To take an example, the sign-Gestalten today are such that we may now reasonably expect future trouble with Russia. Does this fact tell in any degree what we can, should, or will do about it? This precise area of conflict is a novel one (as indeed all important situations are). The best predictive basis we have lies in our own national and personal *intentions* regarding Russia. It is our purposes, not our expectancies, that are now the issue.

As if aware of the scantiness of the expectancy principle, Tolman advises us to embrace also a "need-cathexis psychology" (19). But the situation here turns out to be parallel. Need-cathexis psychology—of course I oversimplify—holds essentially that a handful of physiological drives get attached to this, that, or the other object. A man who, in Tolman's pleasing vernacular, is "raised right" meshes his drive into a socially acceptable gear. A man "raised wrong" does not. But what is so striking about human motivation is that so often a desire or aspiration is meshed into no gear. It simply reaches forward hungrily into the future like the tip of a scarlet-runner bean groping for a goal that it does not know about.

The embarrassment of the need-cathexis type of psychology is reflected in the apologetic language it uses when referring to this expansive aspect of human motivation. Accustomed to work with animals or with infants, need-cathexis psychology labels adult human intentions "secondary drives," "derived drives," or "drive conversions." With such depreciating concepts both the mechanical and the phylogenetic psychologists apparently seek to dispose of those morally relevant desires and aspirations that are in fact so different from the drive-impelled excursions of the cozy robot or cozy rodent.[3]

[3] It is instructive to read the perorations of two recent presidential addresses by psychologists, one preferring the machine model, the other the rat model. Though good-humored and witty, both authors candidly acknowledge their own escapist motives. To paraphrase Carlson's quip concerning Cannon's theory of emotions: the authors seem to entertain their models because the models entertain them.

"I believe that robotic thinking helps precision of psychological thought, and will continue to help it until psychophysiology is so far advanced that an image is nothing other than a neural event, and object constancy is obviously just something that happens in the brain. That time is still a long way off, and in the interval I choose to sit cozily with my robot, squeezing his hand and feeling a thrill—a scientist's thrill—when he squeezes mine back again" (6, p. 192).

"And, as a final peroration, let it be noted that rats live in cages; they do not go on binges the night before one has planned an experiment; they do not kill each other off in war; they do not invent engines of destruction, and if they did, they would not be so dumb about controlling such engines; they do not go in for either class conflicts or race conflicts; they avoid politics, economics and papers on psychology. They are marvelous, pure and delightful. And, as soon as I possibly can, I am going to climb back again out on that good old philogenetic limb and sit there, this time right side up and unashamed, wiggling my whiskers at all the dumb, yet at the same time far too complicated, specimens of *homo sapiens,* whom I shall see strutting and fighting and messing things up, down there on the ground below me" (19, p. 166).

My objection to the animal paradigm for personality and for social psychology is not so much that animals lack culture—a fact which Mr. Tolman in his sparkling paper first frankly admits and then amiably represses. My objection is rather that the motivational structure of man and of lower animals seems to be in only a slight degree similar. In this respect as with his evolutionary brain development, "Man," to quote Julian Huxley's conclusion, "stands alone" (12). Animals are demonstrably creatures of stimulus-expectancy and need-cathexis. Man, in all that is distinctive of his species, is a creature of his intentions. We may well doubt that the basic equation for intentional morality, or that for intentional learning, can be written from a study of organisms that lack propositional symbols. To this point I shall return.

While I am disapproving of current models I shall state my final grievance, this time against the rigid ontogenetic stencils that derive from Freudianism. Odd as it may appear, Freud resembles the mechanical and phylogenetic psychologists in wanting his doctrine of motivation anchored to neuro-anatomy. I assume that this is his desire because of his refusal to see anything at all in the coöperative, socialized, affiliative, undertakings of mankind excepting goal-inhibited sexuality. To the sex drive he adds principally the impulses of aggression, destruction, and death. It seems obvious that Freudianism, even though eagerly adopted by many who have found the mechanical and animal models inadequate, offers an equally meagre basis for a serviceable study of man's moral conduct.

The trouble lies chiefly in the excessive emphasis upon infantile experience. We are asked to believe that an individual's character-structure is, in all essentials, determined by the time his last diaper is changed. Even Suttie, who postulates as the foundation of morality an original and embracing instinct of tenderness, affection, and social symbiosis, believes its fate is sealed according to the manner in which the mother handles this affiliative impulse before and after weaning (17). If the chances for peace in the world depend to such a degree upon infant fixations ought we not disband this Division and register as wet nurses to the mewling citizens of tomorrow?

The concept of intention, which I am here opposing to reactivity, expectancy, and infantile fixation, is not immediately congenial to American psychology. Yet its adoption in some form or another, I argue, is necessary. With some malice aforethought I have selected the term *intention*—spiced, as it is, by an aggravating flavor of mentalism—

to signify those aspects of thought and of motivation that play a leading, but now neglected, part in the complex, affiliative, moral conduct of men. I believe it is precisely the "private" worlds of desire, aspiration, and conscience that must be studied if we are to succeed in the task of social engineering.

In using the term intention, however, I am not arguing surreptitiously for phenomenology, though in order to improve our grasp on the subtleties of man's intentions we would do well to emulate the refinement of its descriptive method.[4] Nor am I arguing for a revival of Brentano, though we have neglected unduly the central proposition of Act Psychology: that at every moment man's mind is directed by some intention, be it loving, hating, comparing, understanding, desiring, rejecting, planning, or some similar mental act.

Let us define intention simply as *what the individual is trying to do*. Naïve as this definition may sound it is in reality the product of decades of sophisticated wrestling with the problems of human motivation. In this concept influences as diversified as Brentano, Darwin, Freud, Cannon, and Wertheimer are brought into focus. In essence it no longer draws the sharp distinction, advanced by both Kant and Schopenhauer, between will (or drive) on the one hand, and intellect on the other. The machine, rat, and infant models we have been following (though I am sure they'd be surprised and grieved to know it) preserve this irreconcilable Kantian dichotomy. They side somewhat more, however, with Schopenhauer in regarding the functions of the intellect as wholly instrumental and secondary. Without forgetting for a moment what we have learned about rationalizing and about the untrustworthiness of introspective reports on motives, we may safely declare that the opposing of motive and thought-process has gone much too far. Usually the individual is trying to do something in which his wants and his plans easily coöperate. Instead of being at opposite poles his emotion and his reason canalize into a single endeavor. The direction of his endeavor I designate as the intention, and offer this concept as an improvement upon the one-sided irrationalistic doctrines of drive, need, instinct, and cathexis.

[4] An excellent example is Bertocci's analysis of man's sense of moral obligation (5). He shows that when we study the *ought-consciousness* phenomenologically we discover how entirely different it is from the *must-consciousness*. This discovery leads to a justifiable suspicion that, whatever conscience may be, it does not derive merely from fear of punishment or from social coercion. Too hastily and heedlessly have psychologists accepted Freud's identification of the Super-ego with threat of parental punishment.

In deference to the discoveries of psychoanalysis we readily admit that an individual does not always know precisely what his own intentions are. *Consciously* he may misinterpret the line of his own endeavor. A neurotic frequently does so. In such cases insight is either lacking or partially lacking. But as a rule, the "posture or lay of consciousness" reflects accurately enough that inextricable fusion of driving and planning which we find in the dynamics of mature human conduct.[5]

It is the mark of an intention that it is directed toward the future. Yet it is typical of the models we have followed that they lead to preoccupation with adjustments in the past. While people are living their lives forward, psychologists are busy tracing them backward. The model we need for our investigations of human relationships will escape from our present excessive dependence on geneticism in all its forms (3).

A geneticist, for example one who places great weight on the expectancy-principle, is inclined to define personality as a peculiar set of reaction-tendencies. An intentionist, on the other hand, sees personality as a peculiar set of subjective values. There is a difference. The one learns at best only about moral *accomplishment;* the other gains additional light on moral *potential.*

It may be argued that the models I am presuming to criticize do deal both with "goal reactions" and with "anticipatory goal reactions." Dr. Hull, for example, offers "anticipatory goal reaction" as a "physical mechanism" which he says he regards as equivalent to the concept of "guiding ideas," or what I am calling *intention* (11). The difficulty with "anticipatory goal reaction" as with "expectancy" is that men often have values without having any specific goal in mind. They may have a consistent direction of striving, but their goals are either transient

[5] McDougall specifically objected to the concept of intention on the grounds that conscious intention merely obscures the instinctive motive at work (15, pp. 121 f). He had in mind the indubitable fact that men's verbal reports of their intentions may be rationalizations. But in my use of the term I do not confine intention to reportable purpose. Sometimes the essential direction of an intention is understood well enough by the subject, sometimes not. If the term, as I propose, is taken to mean *both* the understood and non-understood direction of an act I maintain that it can serve as a proper designation for "ultimate motives" and not merely for proximate or rationalized motives.

To my mind it is unnecessary to have recourse to a doctrine of underlying needs or instincts. McDougall, for example, allowed far too little for the ever-changing panorama of man's intentions which, as they evolve from an original genetic equipment, undergo complete change of form and functional significance (1).

or else undefinable. All of a rat's, but only a small bit of human, behavior can be characterized in terms of concrete goals whose attainment will de-tension specific drives. For the most part the course of man's behavior runs according to certain schemata, or in prolonged channels. Only now and then are these channels marked by lights or buoys that represent specific goals.

A simple example may be borrowed from Lecky's analysis of childhood thumbsucking. The following statement distinguishes neatly between expectancy and what I am here calling intention; that is, between behavior regulated by habit and behavior ordered to non-specific schemata.

Certainly the child who sucks his thumb gives the act plenty of exercise and gets enough satisfaction from it to fix it indelibly. Therefore if the habit theory is true, we should be able to predict absolutely that the child will continue to suck his thumb for the rest of his life. But what really happens? Every year millions of children who have industriously sucked their thumbs since birth, and who have successfully resisted every effort to force them to change their behavior, quit the practice spontaneously when they are five or six years old. The reason is that they are beginning at this age to think of themselves as big boys or girls, and they recognize that thumbsucking is inconsistent with the effort to maintain this new idea (13, p. 122 f).

An intention often takes the form of a self-image as in the case of Lecky's reformed thumbsucker. Having adopted a conception of what we want to be we are constrained to make good in the role we have assumed. The specific goals we set for ourselves are almost always subsidiary to our long-range intentions. A good parent, a good neighbor, a good citizen, is not good because his specific goals are acceptable, but because his successive goals are ordered to a dependable and socially desirable set of values. We now know that juvenile delinquency and adult criminality were sadly misconceived so long as they were regarded as a matter of bad habit-formations. For years reformatories have trained habits, but have achieved few reformations. Only a radical shift of outlook and intention remakes a criminal, alcoholic or neurotic character.

The models we have been following lack the long-range orientation which is the essence of morality. Infant and rodent have immediate goals and indulge in anticipatory goal reactions, but have no directive schemata. By contrast, a child in puberty develops a desire to become a successful and respected man of affairs, and acquires this generalized objective long before he knows what concrete goals he has to work for. Thus, customarily, image and intention seem to antedate and to define goal-reactions. The essence of moral behavior is of this sort. It presupposes long-range purposes whose directions precede their specifications.

When President Roosevelt enunciated the Four Freedoms he was speaking of certain common intentions of the human race. An important feature of his historic formulation lies in his assumption that *all* men, in *all* cultures, intend (that is, long for) freedom from want, freedom from fear, freedom of speech and of worship. Note how this assumption contrasts with the prevailing creed of modern social science. Cultural relativity, really a doctrine of stimulus-expectancy, has laid such a heavy hand upon us that we have overlooked the possibility of universal intentions. Yet unless Roosevelt's bold assumption is found justified, we can scarcely hope to find a psychological basis for effective world organization.

In all probability Roosevelt's formulation is psychologically not the best that can be made; nor dare we underestimate the incompatibility of nationalistic intentions and rivalries. What I am saying is that the psychologists' perspective should be equally bold. It is up to us to find out whether there are in fact common purposes that might provide ground for international solidarity. To do so, social psychologists in all lands might well join in a search, through modern instruments of polling, clinical interviewing, child study, and life-histories, for existent moral bases on which international coöperation can be built.

It is conceivable—I think probable—that such research would discover the ruthless pursuit of personal and national power to be a result of the frustration of basically affiliative intentions. In clinical practice we know how often the clamorous manifestations of egotism gain the upper hand when men are denied a proper continuation of the originally friendly and symbiotic relationship with family, friends, and neighbors. It seems probable that every child in every nation, the world over, at a time when he is most plastic, wants security, affection, and an affiliative and comprehending relation to the surrounding world. It is conceivable that the same basic intentions exist in most adults, although thwarting and perversion of this relationship have engendered a vast amount of hatred, emotional instability, and warlike impulse.

Basic research would discover why the taboo on tenderness, on nurturant desires, has grown so excessive that the development of coöperative and affiliative behavior outside one's own family is, at least in our culture, generally disapproved. It would seek to discover under what conditions the impulse to love and to be loved is turned to the impulse to hate and to invite hatred. If it is the child's nature to trust everyone, why is it the nature of national or ethnic groups to distrust nearly everyone? The models we have been following tend to deflect our attention from problems of human affection and the conditions for its development. When a bit of human friendliness is discovered—and it can be discovered only accidentally with models now current—it is likely to be labeled "goal inhibited sexuality," and thus tagged, forgotten. Up to now the sexual activity of rat and man has received incomparably more attention from psychologists than has the coöperative activity of men and nations.

Besides the study of affection and hatred, the possibilities for peace require research into many other strictly human capacities—among them the use of humor, the function of creeds, the processes of communication. For moral development depends on many factors other than root-desires and intentions. But every aspect of moral conduct that one can name depends intricately upon the employment of symbols.

Signs and Symbols

Perhaps the clearest symptom of the present conceptual confusion in our field is the extent to which we confound symbols with signs, or—if one prefers Morris's terminology—symbols with signals.

We know that all animals, as well as men, respond to signals. The principle of expectancy says so, and in this respect is right. A signal is something that exists in the physical world; it is an identifiable stimulus. But even the most behavioristically inclined theorists cannot, and do not, claim that animals can handle propositional symbols—those self-produced signs *of* signs which are man's prized and troublesome possession. An animal, says Thorndike, can "think things," but it cannot "think about things" (18, p. 119). And Yerkes asserts that symbolic processes in chimpanzees are rare and difficult to observe. One may, he says, fairly continue to question their existence, though it may be that signal responses can be regarded in some way as "antecedents of human symbolic processes" (20, p. 189). Surveying relevant investigations and opinions, Cassirer concludes:

In all literature of the subject there does not seem to be a single conclusive proof of the fact that any animal ever made the decisive step from subjective to objective, from affective to propositional, language (7, p. 30).

Cassirer argues, reasonably enough, that the symbolic system creates a wholly new dimension of reality for man. Instead of dealing directly with things themselves or with their visible signals, man deals with their ideational surrogates.[6]

He has so enveloped himself in linguistic forms, in artistic images, in mythical symbols or religious rites, that he cannot see or know anything except by the interposition of this artificial medium (7, p. 25).

Even so behavioristic a writer as Morris admits that the theory of sign-response as developed by himself carries over with difficulty to the human sphere. These are his words:

. . . non-human beings seldom produce the signs which influence their behavior, while human individuals in their language and post-language symbols characteristically do this and to a surprising degree. Here is a basic difference between men and animals, and until behavioral theory develops a semiotic adequate to this difference it will remain what it is today: a careful study of animals and a pious hope for a science of the human person (16, p. 198).

In this passage Morris seems to be saying with fine candor that there is a world of difference between signal and symbol; and that even his own careful system of semiotic fails adequately to bridge the gap. Though I have not actually counted the illustrations in his recent book I have the impression that a majority of them refer to animal responses to signals, and that relatively few deal with human responses to symbols. In any case it is clear that Morris, like many psychologists, is enamored of the phylogenetic model.

I venture to cite another brilliant and candid passage from his book. He writes of the fact that a sign may be *iconic,* that is to say, it may itself resemble the properties of its denotatum. Thus a motion picture is

---

[6] Even in human beings we occasionally encounter a sharp break between symbols and signs. Some of Goldstein's aphasic patients, for example, seem capable of responding to signs but not to symbols, as in the case of the man who could understand the word-signs "Drink it," when a glass full of water was presented to him, but was unable to go through the symbolic motions of drinking it if the glass was empty (8, p. 44).

Without symbols we could not make-believe, dissimulate, or lie; we could not form plans for our future; nor hold those schemata in mind that make possible consistency in moral conduct.

highly iconic; an onomatopoeic word less so; a wholly arbitrary sign not at all iconic. He then goes on to make this highly significant remark:

> One of the dangers of the use of models in science, for instance, arises out of the temptation to ascribe to the subject matter of a theory properties of the model illustrating the theory which are not involved in the theory itself (16, p. 23).

From this warning would it not follow that an adequate theory of symbols can hardly be derived from the animal model in which *signals* alone predominate? How can we expect to understand human symbolism in terms of the phylogenetic type when, as Morris himself asserts, we are tempted to over-extend the properties of our type-model and force them to serve in place of the independent theory that we need to develop?

The Model We Need

To sum up: the designs we have been using in our studies of motivation, of symbol, and hence of the foundations of moral behavior, are not—to borrow Morris's crisp term—sufficiently iconic with our subject matter. Addiction to machines, rats, or infants leads us to overplay those features of human behavior that are peripheral, signal-oriented, or genetic. Correspondingly it causes us to underplay those features that are central, future-oriented, and symbolic.

What sort of a model then do we need? This question opens systematic vistas that lie beyond the scope of this paper. Yet, lest my numerous criticisms indicate a despair that I do not actually feel, I shall mention a few recent signs and portents that signify a newer—and, to my mind—more wholesome outlook.

Most noteworthy is the fact that the war led many psychologists to deal directly with the integrated behavior of GI Joe, of the factory worker, of the civilian. We then learned that the interests of morale, psychotherapy, personnel placement, psychological warfare, could not be pursued successfully by clinging to our threadbare models. Our inadequate root-metaphors went into the ash can for the duration. It is because of this conceptual discard, with its resultant wartime success in the promotion of social engineering, that I have presumed at this time to bring into the open a conflict that many, perhaps most of us, have secretly felt. Must we now resume the tattered stencils that we so recently abandoned with such good effect?

There are various indicators of improvement in theoretical outlook. I have in mind the new and vital conception of the ego that has come into psychotherapy in recent years (3); the discovery and application of psychological principles involved in bringing the worker into a participant relation with his job (2); the discovery and application of procedures leading to successful administration (14). We discern an accelerated movement toward the development of such theories as can have their acid test here and now, not one thousand years hence. These theories neither strain the credulity, nor stretch an inappropriate model some distance beyond its logical breaking point.

We happily find more emphasis than before on the structuring activities of the person, on the importance of centrally initiated motive patterns, on cognitive dynamisms—including ideology, schemata of meaning, frames of reference. We find the contemporaneity of motives stressed, as well as the important functions of self-esteem and ego-involvement. Though symbols are still confused with signals, we are beginning, through content-analysis and interviewing, to study symbols both in their own right, and as the basic ingredients that they are in all complex conduct, including all morally relevant thought and behavior. We have learned, through improved polls and other methods of inquiry, to ascertain the direction of social purpose as it resides in individual minds. From such knowledge it should be possible to fashion a domestic and international social policy that will be sufficiently realistic to succeed.

All these and many more signs indicate the growing dependence of modern theories upon a model that is none the less scientific for being humane. As this design for personality and social psychology gradually becomes better tempered to our subject matter we shall cease borrowing false notes—whether squeaks, squeals, or squalls. We shall read the score of human personality more accurately, and for the benefit of the world audience that waits to listen.

References

1. Allport, G. W. Motivation in personality: Reply to Mr. Bertocci. *Psychol. Rev.,* 1940, *47,* 533-554.
2. Allport, G. W. The psychology of participation. *Psychol. Rev.,* 1945, *53,* 117-132.
3. Allport, G. W. Geneticism *versus* ego-structure in theories of personality. *Brit. J. educ. Psychol.,* 1946, *16,* II, 57-68.

4. Allport, G. W. Effect: a secondary condition of learning. *Psychol. Rev.*, 1946, *54*, 335-347.
5. Bertocci, P. A reinterpretation of moral obligation. *Phil. & phenomenol. Res.*, 1945, *6*, 270-283.
6. Boring, E. G. Mind and mechanism. *Amer. J. Psychol.*, 1946, *54*, 173-192.
7. Cassirer, E., *An essay on man.* New Haven: Yale Univ. Press, 1945.
8. Goldstein, K. *Human nature in the light of psychopathology.* Cambridge, Mass.: Harvard Univ. Press, 1940.
9. Hilgard, E. R. and Marquis, D. G. *Conditioning and learning.* New York: D. Appleton-Century, 1940.
10. Hoslett, S. D. (Ed.). *Human factors in management.* Parkville, Mo.: The Park College Press, 1946.
11. Hull, C. L. Goal attraction and directing ideas conceived as habit phenomena. *Psychol. Rev.*, 1931, *38*, 487-506.
12. Huxley, J. *Man stands alone.* New York: Harpers, 1941.
13. Lecky, P. *Self-consistency: a theory of personality.* New York: The Island Press, 1945.
14. Leighton, A. H. *The governing of men.* Princeton: Univ. Press, 1945.
15. McDougall, W. *Outline of psychology.* New York: Scribners, 1923.
16. Morris, C. W. *Signs, language and behavior.* New York: Prentice-Hall, 1946.
17. Suttie, I. D. *The origins of love and hate.* London: Kegan Paul, 1935.
18. Thorndike, E. L. *Animal intelligence.* New York: Macmillan, 1911.
19. Tolman, E. C. A stimulus-expectancy need-cathexis psychology. *Science*, 1945, *101*, 160-166.
20. Yerkes, R. M. *Chimpanzees: a laboratory colony.* New Haven: Yale Univ. Press, 1943.

11 THE EMPHASIS ON BASIC FUNCTIONS [1]
Kenneth W. Spence

There was a time when the term "behaviorism" in the title of a speech required no further specification. Every psychologist at least knew the referent to be that new brand of psychology, introduced by Watson, which proposed to break with tradition and deny that psychology had anything to do either with a mentalistic entity called consciousness or a method known as introspection. Today the situation is not so simple. The term "behaviorism" may, on the one hand, merely imply a very general point of view which has come to be accepted by almost all psychologists and thus does not point to any particular group or theoretical position. Or, on the other hand, it may refer to any one of several varieties of behaviorism which have been offered as supplementations or modifications of the original formulation of Watson (e.g., molecular behaviorism, molar behaviorism, operational behaviorism, purposive behaviorism, logical behaviorism—to mention only some of the varieties). While these current formulations usually acknowledge some debt to Watson, for various reasons which we cannot stop to discuss they almost invariably take great pains to differentiate themselves from what has come to be known as "Watsonian Behaviorism" or "Watsonianism." In fact, so far as I know, there are no proponents today of the original Watsonian version. Proper care should be taken to note, however, that this statement holds true only for the particular pattern of assumptions that Watson advanced. Many of the basic postulates of his formulation are to be found in the present-day varieties of behaviorism and, what is more important, probably, in the underlying working assumptions of the great majority of present-day American psychologists.

Now that I have taken the precaution to differentiate the behaviorisms

[1] This article was an address given at the Symposium on "The Postulates and Methods of Gestalt Psychology, Behaviorism and Psychoanalysis" given at the Conference on Methods in Philosophy and the Sciences in New York City, November, 1946. Some minor changes have been made in the paper itself and a list of references has been added.

From K. W. Spence, The methods and postulates of "behaviorism," *Psychol. Rev.* 1948, *55,* 67-78. Reprinted by permission of the author, the *Psychological Review,* and the American Psychological Association.

of today from the original version of behaviorism, I should like to call attention to the further interesting fact that with the exception possibly of Tolman very few, if any, current psychologists ever seem to think of themselves, or at least explicitly refer to themselves, as behaviorists. Such labeling, when it occurs, is usually the contribution of psychologists who consider themselves opposed to behaviorism. Undoubtedly, one of the reasons underlying this absence or lack of "old-school-tie" spirit is that a large majority of present-day American psychologists just take for granted many of the behavioristic assumptions and, occupied as they have been with the details of developing and applying their specific research tools, they have had little time or inclination to give much thought to the more general methodological and systematic problems of their science.

Even the more theoretical-minded of the behavioristically-oriented psychologists seem to have been too preoccupied with matters of detail to get around to the consideration of a more general theoretical framework. Instead of attempting to formulate a complete system of psychology, these theorists have been more concerned with the elaboration of relatively specific hypotheses concerning rather limited realms of data—e.g., theories of simple learning phenomena, motivational theories, theories of personality development, etc. As a consequence we find that instead of being built up around the symbol "behaviorism," allegiances tend to become attached to such labels as associationism, conditioning, reinforcement theory, frustration hypothesis, etc. It seems, in other words, that these psychologists have outgrown the stage of schools.

Under these circumstances, I cannot and I shall not undertake to present a fixed set of articles of faith, articulately and self-consciously held by a group of men calling themselves behaviorists. Instead, I shall attempt to formulate a few methodological principles that are, I believe, exemplified in the work of certain contemporary psychologists who would undoubtedly acknowledge a heavy historical debt to that earlier formulation known as the school of behaviorism.

The first problem that I shall discuss has to do with the behavior scientist's conception of the nature of psychological events. In the older, classical psychologies, whether of the structural or act varieties, the point of view taken was that psychology, if it was a natural science, was, to say the least, a somewhat unique one. Instead of being conceived like physics, for example, as concerning itself with events mediated by or occurring in the consciousness or immediate experience of the observing scientist, psychology was said to observe and analyze by a kind of inner sense immediate experience per se. Sensations, emotions, thoughts were regarded as observable aspects of direct experience rather than systematic constructs which, like the physicist's atoms and electrons, were inferred from immediate experience.

Fortunately, the relationship of immediate experience (consciousness) to the data and constructs of science has been considerably clarified in recent years by the writings of several different groups of thinkers. The philosophers of science, particularly the logical positivists (1, 5, 6, 7), philosophically-minded scientists such as Bridgman (3) and, within psychology, such writers as Boring (2), Pratt (15), and Stevens (18) have succeeded, I believe, in making the point that the data of all sciences have the same origin—namely, the immediate experience of an observing person, the scientist himself. That is to say, immediate experience, the initial matrix out of which all sciences develop, is no longer considered a matter of concern for the scientist qua scientist. He simply takes it for granted and then proceeds to his task of describing the events occurring in it and discovering and formulating the nature of the relationships holding among them.

Boring stated this matter very clearly for psychologists in his book of some years ago, *The Physical Dimensions of Consciousness*. He wrote: "Thus the events of physics, as Wundt said, are mediate to experience, which stands in the background as the dator of scientific data, unrealizable as reality except inductively. In the same way psychology must deal with existential reals which are similarly mediate to experience. There is no way of getting at 'direct experience' because experience gives itself up to science indirectly, inferentially, by the experimental method" (2, p. 6).

More recently Pratt, in his *Logic of Modern Psychology* (15), has hammered home this same point with considerable effectiveness. As he points out, the subject matter of psychology is exactly the same in kind as all other sciences; any differentiation among the sciences is merely a matter of convenience, a division of scientific labor resorted to as the amount of detailed knowledge increases beyond the capacity of a single person's grasp.

I think that it is of some historical interest to note in connection with this point that in the first of his articles introducing the behavioristic position, Watson took essentially the same stand. He wrote: "It [psychology] can dispense with consciousness in a psychological sense. The separate observation of 'states of consciousness' is, on this assumption, no more a part of the task of the psychologist than of the physicist. We might call this the return to a nonreflective and naïve use of consciousness. In this sense consciousness may be said to be the instrument or tool with which all scientists work" (21, p. 176).

Acknowledging, then, that the psychologist conceives his task as that of bringing order and meaning into the realm of certain events provided by immediate experience, we now turn to the question of what these particular observed events are. In attempting to answer this question, attention should first be directed to the fact that the sense events in the experience of the observing scientist may depend upon or result from two different classes of conditions, intra-organic and extra-organic, the former exciting the interoceptors and the latter, the exteroceptors. The physical sciences, it should be noted, moreover, deal only with events of an extra-organic origin—i.e., those received through the exteroceptors. The data of classical psychology, on the other hand, were regarded as involving primarily sense events initiated through the interoceptors. These latter were regarded as being stimulated by such internal mental activities as thinking, desiring, emotional reactions, perceiving, etc., and hence were thought of as providing primary data concerning them.

It is apparent, however, that these internally initiated experiences differ rather markedly from the externally aroused ones in the extent to which they are publicly controllable and communicable. At least, if we can judge from the interminable disagreements of the introspective psychologists themselves, this class of experiences does not meet too well the requirements of social verification and acceptance demanded by the scientist. It was in the face of this difficulty that Watson made his suggestion that the psychologist, like all other scientists, should confine himself to those segments of his experience which have their origin in extra-organic conditions. In other words, the events studied by the psychologist, Watson held, should consist in observations of the overt behavior of *other* organisms, other persons than the observing scientist himself, and not in the observation of the scientist's own internal activities.

As everyone knows, however, most behavior scientists have continued more or less to make use of this latter type of material in the form of the objectively recordable verbal reports of their subjects. Indeed, the scientist himself, in certain circumstances, may assume a dual role and serve as both subject and experimenter. In this event his own introspective report is recorded as a linguistic response and becomes a part of the objective data. To some critics of the behavioristic viewpoint, this acceptance of the verbal reports of their subjects as a part of the data has seemed to represent an abandonment of the strict behavioristic position and a return to the conception that psychology studies *experiential* events as well as overt behavior.

Such a contention, it seems to me, fails to note a very important difference in the two positions. The introspectionist, it should be recalled, assumed a strict one-to-one relationship between the verbal responses of his subjects and the inner mental processes. Accordingly, he accepted these introspective reports as *facts* or *data* about the inner mental events which they represented. The behavior scientist takes a very different position. He accepts verbal response as just one more form of behavior and he proposes to use this type of data in exactly the same manner as he does other types of behavior variables. Thus he attempts to discover laws relating verbal responses to environmental events of the past or present, and he seeks to find what relations they have to other types of response variables. He also makes use of them as a basis for making inferences as to certain hypothetical or theoretical constructs which he employs. In contrast, then, to the introspectionist's conception of these verbal reports as mirroring directly inner mental events, i.e., facts, the behaviorist uses them either as data in their own right to be related to other data, or as a base from which to infer theoretical constructs which presumably represent internal or covert activities of their subjects. We shall return later to the use made of such language responses in the theorizing of the behaviorist.

From this all too cursory discussion of the initial data of the behavioristic psychologist, I should like now to turn to a consideration of the nature of the concepts which he employs to record and describe these events. I do not believe it is necessary for me to discuss at any length the position of the behaviorist with respect to the movement known as operationism. The insistence of the early behaviorists on a thoroughgoing operational analysis of the traditional mentalistic concepts was really nothing more than an anticipation of this somewhat overemphasized program. That a body of empirical knowledge cannot be built up without providing for verifiability of the terms in use is simply taken for granted by the behaviorist. Instead, then, of talking about operational definition of psychological concepts, I should like to discuss certain matters related to a second criterion of acceptability of a scientific concept—namely, its *significance*.

One often hears criticisms to the effect that behavioristic concepts are too elementaristic, too atomistic, or that they fail to portray the real essence or true meaning of man's behavior. These latter critics often complain bitterly about the impoverishment of the mind, and of the lack of warmth and glowing particulars in the behaviorist's picture of psychological events. Some of these criticisms merely reflect, of course, a lack of appreciation on the part of some "psychologists" as to the difference between scientific knowledge of an event on the one hand and everyday knowledge, or the kind of knowledge the novelist or poet portrays, on the other. Either by reason of training or because of their basically non-scientific interests, these critics have never really understood the abstract character of the scientific account of any phenomenon. The only reply that can be made to such a critic is to point out that the scientist's interests are quite different from his. There are, of course, other legitimate interpretations of nature and man than the scientific one and each has its right to be pursued. The behavior scientist merely asks that he be given the same opportunity to develop a scientific account of his phenomena that his colleagues in the physical and biological fields have had. If there are aspects of human or animal behavior for which such an account cannot ever be developed, there are not, so far as I know, any means of finding this out without a try. Unfortunately, the attitudes of too many psychologists with regard to this matter are not such as are likely to lead them to the discovery of such knowledge. The difficulty, I fear, is that too many persons whose interests are non-scientific have become psychologists under the mistaken impression that psychology is one of the arts.

As to the criticisms that the behaviorist's concepts are too elementaristic, I must confess to the belief that the term "elementarism" is merely one of those stereotypes, or "rally-round-the-flag" words which the Gestalt psychologist has used in the defense and exposition of his holistic doctrines. However fervently the Gestalt psychologist may claim that he deals only with wholes, with total situations, the fact remains that if he is interested in discovering uniformities or scientific laws he must, of necessity, fractionate or abstract out certain features of the total events he observes. Such uniformities or laws describe ways in which events repeat themselves. Total concrete events, however, are seldom if ever repeated. Only certain features of events are repeated and since this is the case science must always abstract.

The problem here is really one of the size of the "units of description" that the scientist is to employ and this brings us back to the criterion of acceptability of a scientific term which we referred to as *significance*. By the *significance* of a scientific concept is here meant the extent to which a concept or variable aids or enters into the formulation of laws. Significant concepts in science are those which are discovered to have functional relations with other concepts. Unfortunately, there are few if any rules for deciding a priori which concepts will and which ones will not be significant. Whether elementaristic concepts or units of description which, like the Gestaltists, are nearer the "meaningful" common sense level, are to be chosen is entirely a pragmatic matter of which ones are most successful—i.e., which ones lead to the discovery of laws. This can be ascertained only by trying them out.

Attention might also be called here to the further fact that it is entirely conceivable that different sizes or levels of descriptive units may be employed for the same set of events. The physical sciences provide us with numerous instances of this sort of thing and we see examples of it in psychology both in the description of behavior and stimulus events. Thus, employing the terms of Brunswik (4) and Heider (8), we may make use of either a proximal or distal account of the stimulus situation, and behavior may be described either in terms of movements (muscular patterns) or in terms of gross achievements. The particular alternative chosen, molecular or molar, depends upon the interest and purpose of the scientist, the kind of law he expects to find or use. As Hull (11) has pointed out in discussing this matter, some of the seeming disagreements among current psychologists are merely that one prefers to use more molar concepts than another.

Such different descriptions, however, do not necessarily represent fundamental disagreements. If the two systems of concepts should each be successful in leading to the discovery and formulation of laws, it should also be possible to discover coordinating definitions which will reveal the interrelations of the two systems. Or, as Hull (11) suggests, the postulates or primary assumptions of those working at a more molar level may ultimately appear as theorems in a more molecular description.

To sum up, then, the position which the behavior scientist takes with respect to the selection of the descriptive concepts to be employed in his science, recognizes 1) that the *significance* of a concept is to be measured in terms of the extent to which it leads to the formulation of laws about the phenomena; 2) that a scientific law is always, in some greater or less degree, abstract in the sense that it refers only to certain properties of the events or sequence of events it describes and ignores other properties which are irrelevant to the particular momentary purpose; 3) that the method of elementary abstraction or analysis has been highly successful in all fields of science. While the disentanglement of the great complexes of properties and relations (sequences) among psychological events is undoubtedly much more difficult than in the case of physical phenomena, the difference between them need not be regarded as more than one of degree. On the basis of this assumption there would seem to be little reason for abandoning the method of abstraction or analysis.

We have said that the primary aim of the behavior scientist is to bring order and meaning into the particular realm of events he studies. Ordering a set of observable events for the scientist consists in discovering relationships between the events or, as we say, in the finding of empirical laws. The scientist seeks to establish laws relating his concepts or variables because they make possible explanation and prediction.

In the case of such areas of science as physics, the finding of empirical laws has involved chiefly the process of inductive generalization from observation and experimentation. In other words, in physics it has been possible to isolate sufficiently simple systems of observation to arrive at such laws in this manner. The situation in psychology and the other behavior sciences is quite different. Primarily because of the greater complexity of psychological as compared with physical phenomena, the psychologist has either been unable to isolate, experimentally, simple systems, or he has not found satisfactory means of measuring all of the relevant variables in the system under observation. In this circumstance he has resorted to guesses or postulations as to the uncontrolled or as yet unmeasurable factors. As a result of this difference the term "theory" has, as I have pointed out elsewhere (17), come to have a very different connotation in psychology from that which it has in physics. Theories in physics are constructions which serve primarily to integrate or organize into a single deductive system sets of empirical laws which previously were unrelated. The classical example is, of course, the Newtonian integration of the previously unconnected areas of mechanics and astronomy by the gravitational theory. Other well-known examples are the electro-magnetic theory of light and the kinetic theory of gases.

In psychology, on the other hand, theories serve primarily as a device to aid in the formulation of the empirical laws. They consist in guesses as to how the uncontrolled or unknown factors in the system under study are related to the experimentally-known variables. To these hypothetical constructs Tolman (20) has applied the very appropriate term "intervening variable" because they are assumed to intervene between the measurable environmental and organic variables, on the one hand, and the measurable behavior properties on the other.

The manner in which the behavior scientist has used these hypothetical, intervening constructs may be shown by considering the various kinds of laws which the psychologist seeks to discover. Confining ourselves for the moment to laws which do not involve any hypothetical components, we find that the variables studied by the behavioristic psychologist fall into two, or possibly three, main groups:

1. Response variables: measurements of behavior properties.
2. Stimulus variables: measurements of properties of the physical and social environment.
3. Organic variables: measurements of neuroanatomical or neurophysiological properties of the organism.

The different types of empirical relationships or laws in which psychologists have been interested are as follows:

1. $R = f(R)$
2. $R = f(S)$
3. $R = f(O)$
4. $O = f(S)$

Type 1 laws are laws of association of behavior properties. A great deal of use is made of the statistical constant, the coefficient of correlation, in the formulation of these laws and, as is well known, this type of law is investigated extensively in the field of psychological testing.

Type 2 laws may be concerned with the present environment or with past environmental events. Thus in the case of the typical perception experiments, we are interested in the effects of variation of aspects or features of the environmental stimulus on the perceptual or discrimination responses of the subject. Best examples of laws relating behavior to past events in the environment are laws of learning, laws of secondary motivation, etc.

For the most part the present-day behavioristic psychologists tend to concentrate their energies on these two classes of laws and to a very considerable extent they have favored the use of the molar rather than molecular concepts. A few psychologists whose interests have been in mediational problems have concerned themselves with type 3 and type 4 laws. These latter are obviously in the field of neurophysiological psy-

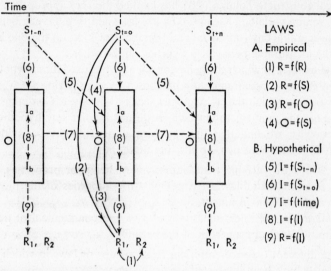

Figure 1   Showing different kinds of laws

chology and have in the main been concerned only with the simplest kinds of behavior phenomena—e.g., sensory responses. Indeed, our inability to develop measures of this class of events (i.e., organic variables) in the case of the more complex behavior phenomena has been one of the factors underlying the substitution of the hypothetical intervening constructs in their place.

Figure 1 continues this analysis of the laws of psychology. In this diagram I have attempted to portray, in addition to the four types of empirical laws which we have been discussing, the new hypothetical or guessed-at types of relationships which are involved in the introduction of the hypothetical intervening constructs. These latter are indicated as I_a and I_b and are represented as *hypothetical state variables* (enclosed within the rectangle). The environment or world situation at three different time intervals is represented by $S_t - n$ (past), $S_t = o$ (present), $S_t + n$ (future). These S's and also the R's represent empirical vari-

ables. I have also represented the class of experimental neurophysiological variables of the first figure by the symbol O, to the left of the
rectangle. The four classes of empirical laws, listed at the right side of
the figure, are represented by the solid curved lines. The guessed-at or
postulated laws relating the hypothetical state variables (I_a, I_b, etc.)
to the various experimental variables are represented by the dotted
lines. Thus No. 5 type of "law" defines or introduces the intervening
variables in terms of past events; No. 6 type relates them to the present
environmental variables and No. 7 to time; No. 8 "laws" present interrelations assumed between these intervening variables, and, finally, the
relations represented by No. 9 relate the intervening variables to
the response variables. That is to say, these dotted lines should be
thought of as representative of different classes of postulated relationships, not the usual notion of an S-R connection.

Those who are acquainted with the theoretical constructs of Hull
(11) will recognize specific examples of these hypothetical laws. Thus
his postulate or definition of the construct habit strength, or $_sH_R$, as a
function of the number of past reinforcements is a good example of
Class No. 5 "law." His assumption of the nature of the manner in which
H and D interact to determine E falls in Class No. 8 and his postulate
as to how the construct of reactive inhibition (I_R) is assumed to change
(disintegrate) with time is an instance of No. 7 type of "law." Incidentally, it will be noted that this last relationship is the only one which is
similar to the so-called dynamic or process laws of physics. This type
of law states or describes the laws governing the changes that occur
within a system in time.

A question concerning these theoretical constructs that invariably
seems to arise is whether they represent some kind of internal, presumably neurophysiological, process or state. The persistence with
which misunderstanding arises on this point is truly surprising. It is
probably to be explained in terms of the difficulty and resistance we
have in shedding old, familiar meanings of words. In this connection it
is not a little amusing to note that whereas Hull is usually accused of
stuffing the organism with mythological brain states, Tolman, whose
theoretical concepts have exactly the same formal structure as those of
Hull—i.e., intervening variables defined in terms of independent environmental events—is often charged with the guilt of dreaming up mentalistic ghosts. The explanation of this situation is readily seen when we
recall the terms employed by these two men to designate their interven-

ing variables. Thus Hull used such words as habit, drive, excitatory potential and inhibitory potential while Tolman named his theoretical constructs, demands, sign-Gestalt-expectations, hypotheses, etc.

The only meanings that these theoretical intervening constructs have *at the present time* is provided by the equations which relate them to the known experimental variables—the environmental measurements on the one hand and the behavior measures on the other. Such equations constitute the definitions of these terms.

The present role of these theoretical constructs we have said is to aid the psychologist in his search for the empirical laws relating behavior to the conditions determining it. In this sense they are a kind of calculational device which helps us to write the complete law describing the interrelations between all of the relevant experimental variables. In a recent article (17) on this problem of theory construction in contemporary psychology I called attention to the point that it is possible in the case of the theoretical formulation of simple learning behavior developed by Hull to substitute in the successive equations introducing the intervening theoretical constructs and obtain a single equation which states the response measure as a function of the several antecedent environmental variables. In this equation the intervening theoretical variables are represented among the parameters of the equation.

While both Tolman and I have emphasized the heuristic value of this type of theoretical construction in the formulation of the complete form of the laws, Hull (12) has called attention to another use which these constructs serve. Such constructs as habit and excitatory potential also provide, he claims, convenient, quantitative representations or indices of the particular complex of experimental variables for which they stand. Thus instead of having to state that the subject has had so many reinforcements in the situation under conditions in which the goal was of such-and-such a magnitude and was delayed for such-and-such a period, it is possible to substitute the calculated value of habit strength.

Finally, there remains the possibility, at least, that these intervening constructs may turn out to have their counterparts somewhere under the skin of the organism. Hull in particular has been quite prone to accept this possibility and has not hesitated to add further statements about these constructs which suggest their possible locus and functioning in the nervous system. His justification, however, has always been that such conjectures provide experimental hints to persons interested in making such coordinations of our knowledge. His main theoretical efforts have been primarily at the molar-behavioral level.

In concluding this discussion of the theoretical framework of the behavioristic psychologist, I should like to emphasize that it is as yet only in a very primitive state of development, a fact which has unfortunately been lost sight of by many of the current critics of this position. The theorist in this field apparently has to choose between attempting to lay down the general theoretical framework of the whole range of behavior phenomena or working out the detailed nature of one small realm of data. Tolman has, for the most part, chosen the former alternative with the consequence that his treatment is characterized by an obvious lack of detailed specification of his theoretical constructs. Hull, on the other hand, has elected to follow the second method. His recent book, *Principles of Behavior,* dealt only with the most *simple* instances of laboratory learning phenomena, classical and instrumental conditioning, and he and his students are now engaged in extending the fundamental laws there discovered to the major phenomena of individual behavior.

So far as theoretical constructs are concerned, it is obvious that the simple behavior phenomena dealt with by Hull and other behavioristic-oriented psychologists have not required (to any great extent) a whole class of hypothetical intervening variables that must ultimately be postulated. Thus the theoretical constructs in Hull's recent book—habit, excitatory and inhibitory potential, drive, etc.—are what might be referred to as *state variables*. Each of these constructs represents a hypothetical condition or state of the organism which is assumed to have resulted from and is defined in terms of the past interactions of the organism and its environment. In contrast the new theoretical constructs referred to above will represent, not states, but hypothetical, non-observable responses, implicit processes, occurring in the individual. Thus, in dealing with the more complex types of animal and human behavior, implicit emotional responses, covert verbal responses and not easily observable receptor-exposure and postural adjustments will have to be postulated in addition to these state variables. As yet only a bare beginning has been made in the use of such theoretical constructs—e.g., anxiety reactions and their secondary reinforcing effects (14), fractional anticipatory goal reactions as the basis of purposive behavior (9, 10).

It is in this realm of theorizing that the verbal reports of human subjects are likely to be of most use to the behavior theorist, for presumably these reports can be made the basis on which to postulate the occurrence of these inferred activities. There are, of course, many pitfalls in the use of such verbal reports and considerable caution needs to be exercised in their use. However, careful control and checking in terms of other, non-verbal responses should provide a means of detecting distortions, both deliberate and otherwise, in this source of data (16).

A discussion of behaviorism, especially when it occurs in conjunction with a symposium which includes Gestalt psychology, requires at least some comment on the distinction often made between field and non-field theories in psychology. The Gestalt psychologists, in particular, have been very fond of this contrast and they have not hesitated to imply that their theoretical structures are similar in some respect to the type of field theory in physics represented by the Maxwell electromagnetic theory and Einstein's gravitational theory. In some instances the further implication has been made that behavioristic theories are a mechanical type of theory and as such are just as outmoded as the mechanistic theories of physics. Now I have often wondered what our theoretical brethren from the field of physics would think of these claims if perchance they were ever to take a serious look at these two groups of theories. Certainly the behavioristic theoretical structure I have been talking about uses neither the mechanical models—i.e., particles with their attracting forces—nor the type of mathematical equations that characterize a mechanical theory. Nor do I believe that there is anything even remotely resembling the field equations of Maxwell and Einstein in the theoretical formulations of the Gestalt psychologists. In the sense, then, in which the theoretical physicist understands the dichotomy, mechanical versus field theory, no such distinction, in my opinion, exists in psychology today.

If, on the other hand, the concept of field refers in psychology essentially to the notion of a system of interdependent variables, with its implication that the behavior of an organism at any moment is a resultant of the totality of relevant variables, then there is not to my knowledge any behavioristic theory today which would not also be a field theory. Furthermore, if we accept the additional notion that it is the pattern of interrelationships between the determining variables that is the crucial factor differentiating psychological field theories from non-field theories, I do not believe that the behavior theories which I have been describing would fail to qualify as field theories. The hypothetical equations which Hull (11) postulates in the introduction of his theoretical constructs provide in precise mathematical form these very patterns of interrelationship. Finally, as to the characteristic of field theory emphasized by Lewin (13) under the principle of contemporaneity—namely, that the behavior at any moment is a function of the situation *at that moment only* and not a function of past or future situations—I find it difficult to believe that any present-day psychologist believes that other conditions than those of the present moment determine the behavior of this moment. Even the psychoanalyst never held, as Lewin sometimes seems to imply, that past events somehow jump through time to determine the present behavior, but, instead, conceived of these past events leaving their effects in the organism and through them determining the behavior of the moment. The behaviorist takes exactly the same view of the matter.

The development of our science has not been helped, in my opinion, by such distinctions as field and non-field theory. A much more useful procedure would be to examine in detail these differing theoretical positions with a view to ascertaining to what extent they differ in the particular variables they believe to be relevant in a particular instance and what differences, if any, exist in their postulation as to the pattern of the interrelationships involved—i.e., in the form of the hypothetical laws they assume. It is my personal belief that if this procedure were followed there would be much less in the way of specific disagreements to settle than is usually thought. I base this prediction not only on the well-known fact that the Gestaltists, psychoanalysts and behaviorists have to a considerable extent been interested in very different realms of psychological phenomena and that hence their theories are not in competition with one another, but also on the fact that very little real theorizing, particularly in the matter of specifying the precise form of the interrelations between the variables, has actually been done. It is most imperative that psychologists attempt to formulate their theories in as precise and articulate a manner as possible, for it is only by means of such theorizing that psychology can hope, finally, to attain full-fledged scientific statehood.

References

1. Bergmann, G. The subject matter of psychology. *Phil. Sci.*, 1940, 7, 415-433.
2. Boring, E. G. *The physical dimensions of consciousness.* New York: Century, 1933.

3. Bridgman, P. W. *The logic of modern physics*. New York: Macmillan, 1928.

4. Brunswik, E. The conceptual focus of some psychological systems. *J. Unified Sci. (Erkenntnis)*, 1939, *8,* 36-49. [Selection No. 8 in this volume.]

5. Carnap, R. Testability and meaning. *Phil. Sci.*, 1936, *3,* 419-471; 1937, *4,* 1-40.

6. Carnap, R. *Philosophy and logical syntax*. London: Kegan Paul, Trench, Trubner, 1935.

7. Feigl, H. Operationism and scientific method. *Psychol. Rev.*, 1945, *52,* 243-246.

8. Heider, F. Environmental determinants in psychological theories. *Psychol. Rev.*, 1939, *46,* 383-410.

9. Hull, C. L. Knowledge and purpose as habit mechanisms. *Psychol. Rev.*, 1930, *37,* 511-525.

10. Hull, C. L. Goal attraction and directing ideas conceived as habit phenomena. *Psychol. Rev.*, 1931, *38,* 487-506.

11. Hull, C. L. *Principles of behavior*. New York: D. Appleton-Century, 1943.

12. Hull, C. L. The problem of intervening variables in molar behavior theory. *Psychol. Rev.*, 1943, *50,* 273-291. [Selection No. 13 in this volume.]

13. Lewin, K. Defining the "field" at a given time. *Psychol. Rev.*, 1943, *50,* 292-310. [Selection No. 19 in this volume.]

14. Mowrer, O. H. A stimulus-response analysis of anxiety and its role as a reinforcing agent. *Psychol Rev.*, 1939, *46,* 553-565. [Selection No. 39 in this volume.]

15. Pratt, C. C. *The logic of modern psychology*. New York: Macmillan, 1939.

16. Skinner, B. F. The operational analysis of psychological terms. *Psychol. Rev.*, 1945, *52,* 270-278.

17. Spence, K. W. The nature of theory construction in contemporary psychology. *Psychol. Rev.*, 1944, *51,* 47-68. [Selection No. 4 in this volume.]

18. Stevens, S. S. The operational definition of psychological concepts. *Psychol. Rev.*, 1935, *42,* 517-527.

19. Tolman, E. C. *Purposive behavior in animals and men*. New York: Century, 1932. [See Selection No. 29 in this volume.]

20. Tolman, E. C. The determiners of behavior at a choice point. *Psychol. Rev.*, 1938, *45,* 1-41.

21. Watson, J. B. Psychology as the behaviorist views it. *Psychol. Rev.*, 1913, *20,* 158-177.

CHAPTER VI

LAWFULNESS IN BEHAVIOR

THE TWO PAPERS paired in this chapter offer directly opposed theses concerning the nature of the "laws" which psychology as a natural science may expect to develop. In accordance with his general theoretical-experimental approach Egon Brunswik argues that psychology should be concerned with molar correlations and must be satisfied with probability functions of a low degree of exactitude (see also Selections No. 8 and 26). The second paper, by Clark L. Hull, was originally presented in the same symposium on psychology and scientific method. Although it is primarily concerned with the problem of intervening variables, in it Hull attempts to answer Brunswik's arguments. He points out that in physical science there are certain limiting conditions which operate to restrict the degree of empirical verification of even the best established physical principles. Physical principles are nevertheless generally accepted as being fundamentally exact. Hull suggests that psychological principles may be equally exact, fundamentally, but that their empirical verification is even more restricted by limiting factors. His entire research program, as a matter of fact, is based upon this assumption. This difference of opinion touches upon a key contemporary issue and should provide interesting material for further discussion.

12   THE PROBABILITY POINT OF VIEW[1]

Egon Brunswik

I

The term "achievement" will be used here as a generic term for the relationships better than chance existing between, and due to, an organism and variables in its physical environment. By physical environment we mean the "geographical" surroundings as well as the stages along the "historic" axis of the organism, that is to say, its past and future. Relatively stable relationships between organism and environment are among the descriptive features of the patterns found in observing life and behavior. Thus the recognition of such functional units need not, and will not, involve us in explanatory problems such as the alternative of mechanism vs. teleology.

Organismic achievement may extend in two main directions: 1) specificity regarding certain stimulus variables as antecedents or causes of reactions, and 2) specificity regarding certain results of organismic reaction. Examples for the former may be taken from the field of perception; for the latter, from the field of overt behavioral effects.

In the establishment of any kind of achievement one may distinguish two phases: 1) the portions of the causal chains within the physical environment, and 2) the portions of the causal chains within the organism. We will discuss the environmental portions first. In each case, variables not located at (that is to say, not defined in terms of) the boundary between organism and environment will be used as examples in order to make explicit the characteristic entanglements within the causal texture of the regions in question. As far as the environment is

[1] This article, and the two following articles by C. L. Hull and K. Lewin, respectively, were addresses given at the Symposium on Psychology and Scientific Method held as part of the Sixth International Congress for the Unity of Science, University of Chicago, September, 1941. [For the articles by Hull and Lewin see Selections No. 13 and 19 in this volume.—Ed.]

Some of the author's remarks in the discussion concerning the papers of Hull and Lewin, as well as some of the replies to criticisms of the present paper, appear as footnotes here. Some minor changes have been made in the paper itself and a list of references has been added.

From E. Brunswik, Organismic achievement and environmental probability, *Psychol. Rev.,* 1943, *50,* 255-272. Reprinted by permission of the author, the *Psychological Review,* and the American Psychological Association.

concerned, one will have to start from the so-called "distal" stimulus- or effect-variables as reference points and study their relationships to the proximal (or boundary-) variables.

On the perception side, an example of a distal variable is the distance of objects. Causal chains determined by distance will, on their way into the organism, exert certain proximal effects, or criteria, upon the sensory surface of the organism. The most important feature of the general relationship between distal and proximal stimulus variables is its lack of univocality.

Firstly, there is ambiguity in the direction from cause to effect. Inventories of possible "cues for third-dimensional distance" have been compiled from the beginnings of psychological inquiry. Current textbooks list something like ten depth criteria, such as binocular parallax, convergence of the eye axes, accommodation, linear and angular perspective, interception of far objects by near objects, atmospheric effects, number of in-between objects, vertical position. The list could be extended considerably further. The necessity for becoming so involved derives from the fact that none of these proximal variables can be considered to be *the* distance cue in the sense of an effect which would be present without exception whenever the distal condition should obtain. Some of the cues will more often, others less often, be present, depending on circumstances, and occasionally all of them may be cut off (so that the fact of a certain distance relationship must remain unrecognized by the organism in question).

Secondly, there also is ambiguity in the reverse direction, that is to say, from effect to cause. A certain proximal stimulus feature, such as binocular parallax, may ordinarily be due to differences in depth, but it could occasionally as well be caused by an artificial setup of two flat pictures in a stereoscope. Or, the characteristic trapezoidal shape of retinal images constituting the depth criterion of perspective may frequently be due to distortion of rectangular objects seen under an angle, i.e., extending into the third dimension; but it may also be due to an actual trapezoidal object in a frontal position with all of its points at the same distance from the eye.

On the environmental portion of the effect side, the relationships between objects and cues are replaced, in a symmetrical fashion, by the relationships between means and ends, or between proximal actions or habits and distal results. Examples showing the ambiguity of these relationships in both causal directions could easily be given in analogous fashion to the ones discussed above for the perception side.

Generally speaking, both the object-cue and the means-end relationship are relations between probable partial causes and probable partial effects. Thereby the entire universe of the living conditions of the organism or species in question might well be taken as a "reference class" defining a "population" of situations. Then there is a good chance that distance as a distal variable will cause distance cues, and that the so-called distance cues have been actually caused by distance, but it will by no means be necessarily so. We use the term "partial" (cause or effect) since the members of the causal chain are in every particular instance determined by a large number of other relevant conditions. Cues as well as means can be ranked into "hierarchies" in accordance with the degree of probability by which they are linked, in both causal directions, to the respective distal variables, and classified accordingly as "good," "misleading," etc. (13).

This brings us to the second point, the contributions of the organism. Survival and its sub-units, which may be defined as the establishment of stable interrelationships with the environment, are possible only if the organism is able to establish compensatory balance in the face of comparative chaos within the physical environment. Ambiguity of cues and means relative to the vitally relevant objects and results must find its counterpart in an ambiguity and flexibility of the proximal-peripheral mediating processes in the organism. This pattern contrasts somewhat with the relatively specific focussing of vital processes upon the central-organismic and the distal-environmental variables. Thus each class of behavioral achievement may be represented, when telescoped into a composite picture covering extended periods of time, by a bundle of light rays passing through a convex lens from one focus to another, with a scattering of the causal chains in the mediating layers. Most objective psychologists who have made efforts to find a formal criterion by which behavior could be delimited from non-behavior have in various forms resorted to something amounting to such a lens analogy. Examples are Tolman's "persistence and docility of activity relative to some end" (12) as a criterion for purposiveness of behavior, Hunter's emphasis upon "vicarious functioning" in defining the subject matter of a behavioristic psychology, Hull's emphasis upon such patterns as the "habit family hierarchy" (6), some considerations put forward by Heider (5), and generally the concept of "equivalence" or of "equipotentiality" of stimuli and of acts.

The point I should like to emphasize especially in this connection is the necessary imperfection, inflicted upon achievements—as relations between classes—by the ambiguity in the causal texture of the environment, which remains apparent as long as single variables, that is, partial causes and partial effects, are considered under otherwise not specifically controlled conditions. Because of this environmental ambiguity, no matter how smoothly the organismic instruments and mechanisms may function, relationships cannot be foolproof, at least as far as those connecting with the vitally relevant more remote distal regions of the environment are concerned. This intrinsic lack of perfection, that is, of univocality, will on the whole be the greater the more wide-spanning the relationships involved are. The only way in which perfection could be secured would be by control over all the remaining conditions which could possibly become relevant in the given case. This, however, is something the reacting organism cannot do for lack of time if not for other more serious reasons—and thus something which the psychologist who wishes to catch and rationally to reconstruct organismic adjustment at large, with all of its faults and fallacies, should also not do. All a finite, sub-divine individual can do when acting is—to use a term of Reichenbach (11)—to make a posit, or wager. The best he can do is to compromise between cues so that his posit approaches the "best bet" on the basis of all the probabilities, or past relative frequencies, of relevant interrelationships lumped together.

One of the comparatively neglected tasks of a molar environmental psychology is to find out the extent to which environmental hierarchies of probabilities of object-cue as well as of means-end relationships do find a counterpart in similar hierarchies of evaluation by the organism. This would mean that the environmental probabilities be first ascertained for all of the cues or means involved, with, say, the "normal" life conditions of the organism taken as the defining reference class. This part of the research would be strictly environmental and preparatory in character and would not involve any reference to organismic reaction.[2] Very little has thus far been done in the direction of such an environmental analysis.

The most conspicuous exception is a certain knowledge we have

[2] In the sense defined in footnote 3, such a statistical analysis of intra-environmental correlations would be termed "psychological ecology" whereas the organism's proper adjustment to such correlations, to be expressed in terms of achievement, would be "ecological psychology."

about the so-called "physiognomic" relationships between certain mental states or abilities in our fellow men, and their external physical characteristics. Such studies have, however, been undertaken primarily because of an interest centering in questions of the expressiveness of human beings viewed as subjects rather than because of an interest in some other subject's social environment and the problems confronting such a subject in his approach to objects of social perception. In effect, however, they have given us some information to be utilized for our purpose. The present writer has selected one of the few ascertained relationships found between ability and physique, namely, the correlation of intelligence with height and with weight. To be sure, these correlations are extremely low, about .15, but this is all to the good, since many of the cues probably in use in perception are of such a low order of validity, including some of the lesser members of what may be called, in analogy to Hull's habit-family-hierarchy, the "cue-family-hierarchy" of the distance criteria listed on page 189. Social perceptual reactions to schematized drawings of human figures as well as to photographs which had been magnified, reduced, and distorted in height and width turned out to be more favorable with respect to apparent intelligence and other apparent personality characteristics in the case of taller and broader body builds (2, 14). There thus may be intuitive responsiveness to social environmental correlations as low as .15 (though other possibilities of an explanation of the reactions, such as, e.g., a psychoanalytic one, would have yet to be tested). Furthermore, there are indications that height and weight contribute only little to the impressions made, when compared with other factors such as the face, etc. Such a finding, if verified, would be in line with what should be expected on the ground of a perceptual compromise principle, since cues of low validity would then have to be given little weight by the organism in establishing the best bet.

The writer is attempting an analysis of the environmental validities of the distance cues, present, absent, and misleading or contradictory, in a set of pictures selected from magazines by a group of subjects and thus probably fairly representative of interesting life situations. The hierarchy thus established in a preliminary way appeared to be on the whole in fair agreement with what can be inferred from results of experimental studies about the subjective weight of distance cues which had been made to conflict artificially in stimulus configurations presented through the stereoscope.

On the whole, only scattered recognition has been given to the fact that object-cue and means-end relationships do not hold with the certainty obtained in the nomothetic study of the so-called laws of nature, but are rather of the character of probability relationships. This deficiency is most clearly reflected in the psychology of learning which has proceeded almost exclusively along a dialectically dichotomized all-or-none pattern of "correct vs. incorrect," "right vs. wrong." Situations in which food can be found always to the right and never to the left, or always behind a black door and never behind a white one, are not representative of the structure of the environment, but are based on an idealized black-white dramatization of the world, somewhat in a Hollywood style. They are thus not sound as experimental devices from the standpoint of a psychology which wishes to learn, above all other things, something about behavior under conditions representative of actual life. In an effort to imitate experimentally the tangled causal texture of the environment more closely than is customary, the writer tested a variety of ambiguous environmental means-end relationships, using rats as subjects (1). The rate of learning (which may be taken as an index of organismic weight given to the means or cue in question) was found to vary with the probability, that is to say, with the combination of relative frequencies, of the intra-environmental relationships tested.

II

I have expanded on this subject to such an extent because I believe that the probability character of the causal (partial cause-and-effect) relationships in the environment calls for a fundamental, all-inclusive shift in our methodological ideology regarding psychology. To be sure, in the field of wide-spanning relationships of a predominantly historic-genetic type, such as of heredity and of individual differences in general, this shift occurred at the time of Galton and his followers who established correlation statistics as a particularly suitable means of quantitatively expressing ambiguous probability relationships. The relationships existing between organism and geographic environment at large will have to be approached in basically the same way. In any wide-spanning correlation, be it of historic or of geographic reference, there are a great many relevant variables and specific control is lacking for all of them except the two (or few) whose relationship is under specific consideration. Such a deliberate neglect of specific control of relevant variables is the most fundamental negative characteristic of the "molar" approach.

Not more than generalized control by which membership is established in a broader class (including care for proper sampling) is exerted over the remaining relevant variables. For example, in comparing parents' intelligence with children's intelligence, not more than the most general features of the upbringing of the children such as health, normality, etc., are taken into consideration, instrumental detail is neglected. The situation is quite similar, though not quite so drastic, when we become interested in how well, in a practical achievement sense, we can estimate distal variables such as distance, or sizes and physical colors of objects, under all the varying circumstances of distance, surroundings, illumination, etc. (perceptual constancies). What the experimentalist is used to calling "isolation of a variable" is in all these cases incomplete to a quite shocking extent. No univocality, no relationship resembling a "law" in the traditional strict sense of the word can be uncovered under such circumstances.

The present paper thus represents an attempt to show that psychology, as long as it wishes to deal with the vitally relevant molar aspects of adjustment and achievement, has to become statistical throughout, instead of being statistical where it seems hopeless to be otherwise, and cherishing the nomothetic ideals of traditional experimental psychology as far as relationships between geographic stimulus variables and response variables are concerned. The price which has to be paid for such a double standard is the limitation of stimulus-response psychology to narrow-spanning problems of artificially isolated proximal or peripheral technicalities of mediation which are not representative of the larger patterns of life.

In particular, the extension of the principles of such an instrument as correlation statistics from individual differences to stimulus-response relationships involves, firstly, that instead of correlating two variables (e.g., different test performances) paired by being drawn from the same sample of individuals characterized in their structure and functioning only as members of a general reference population, one would have to correlate two variables (namely, a set of stimulus values and a set of response values) paired by being drawn from the same sample of situations or tests, characterized merely as belonging to the class, or "population," of living conditions of a particular individual (or category or species). In short, individuals are replaced by situations or tasks (which is to be distinguished from the mere exchange of the role of individuals for tests as in Stephenson's "inverted" correlation technique). The achievement of a single subject, or even of a single subject in a certain particular attitude, could then be represented by a correlation coefficient based on a variety of test situations involving the stimulus variable in question.

To make the analogy complete, one would, secondly, have to insist on representative sampling of situations or tests, just as in the field of individual differences one has to insist on the representative sampling of individuals from a population to ascertain at least some kind of generality for the result. Proper sampling of subjects is thus replaced by proper sampling of objects or objectives. For general adjustment this would mean a randomization of tasks, a sampling of tests carefully drawn from the universe of the requirements a person happens to face in his commerce with the physical or social environment, as the defining class. For adjustment to, or cognitive attainment of, a single stimulus variable, such as distance, one would have to secure perceptual estimates of distance in a set of situations representative of all the situations and conditions in life which require judgment of, or adjustment to, distance. For each subject, this particular type of perceptual achievement could be represented by the correlation coefficient between measured distances and estimated distances. The more molecular pattern of traditional laboratory experimentation could thus be rounded out to include its molar counterpart, that is, an achievement analysis deliberately neglecting the details, even if these details should be relevant in connection with one or the other member of the family of processes mediating this achievement.

An example of the application of the correlation technique to a stimulus-response problem can be found in studies on social perceptual achievement, e.g., when intelligence is to be judged from photographs. Since in typical research of this kind the photographs are not analyzed with respect to their geometric characteristics, the investigation bridges over the mediating layers altogether, in contrast to the purely intra-environmental problems of physiognomics discussed above. It is characteristic of the traditional attitude of psychology that in these studies the sampling problem of social objects has rarely been given due consideration, both regarding sufficient number of social objects as well as the representative character of the sample. And this in spite of the fact that we usually find a sufficient and representative sample of subjects or judges.

On the whole, social perceptual problems have been rooted in the applied disciplines which have not come in too close a contact with the ideology of the "exact" experimental laboratory psychology and thus have been more openminded to statistics from the beginning. As a methodological demonstration rather than with the purpose of fact finding, the present author has recently undertaken a study in perceptual size constancy in which the correlation technique was applied to a traditional academic stimulus-response problem. Proper sampling was attempted, and an effort was made to throw some light upon the traditional mediation problems of proximal stimulation, besides approaching the achievement problem (3). Purposely, one subject only was used. The person was interrupted frequently during her normal daily activities and asked to estimate the size of the object she just happened to be looking at. Measurements of the object-sizes, which were the distal stimulus variable under consideration, and of their distances from the subject, were also taken in each case. These measurements made it possible to compute the relative sizes of the retinal images as well which constituted the most outstanding feature of the mediating proximal stimulus patterns. Estimates of size were found to correlate with object measurements much more closely (between .95 and almost 1.00, depending on method of evaluation) with naive perceptual attitude than with retinal stimulus size (between .2 and .7). This result indicates the selective focussing of the organism's response on the distal rather than the proximal variable. In contrast to most experimental studies this result possesses a certain generality with regard to normal life conditions. It furthermore suggests that focussing of psychology upon the proximal and peripheral layer is not the most fruitful thing to do and may lead to an out-of-focus, sterile type of research.

In short, the notion will have to be revised that, while the psychology of individual differences deals with correlations (at least *de facto*), experimental psychology of the stimulus-response type deals with, or should strive toward, the uncovering of "laws" in the strict sense of the word.

As Mises (9) has pointed out, law finding and the molecular, microscopic approach are inseparably tied together. In a strict sense, the laws of nature have to be formulated as differential equations, yielding a relationship of the variables in question within an infinitesimally small spatio-temporal region. Their customary macroscopic form is the result of a mathematical integration over time or space, an extension which tacitly implies a number of assumptions about the intervening conditions. Such conditions may be controlled in a sufficiently specific manner in an experiment in which either the possibilities of interference are limited (such as in an optical experiment) and can easily be surveyed, or where the span between the independent and the dependent variable is relatively small in space and time. In this sense the laws of nature are not extremely general, but extremely specific.

III

The tie between the nomothetic and the microscopic attitude is reflected not only in traditional experimental psychology, but also in those more recent endeavors which stress law finding in psychology. The two most outstanding of these attempts are represented by Lewin and Hull.

I agree with Lewin when he makes it clear that there is no place for statistics in a strictly nomothetic, or, as he calls it, systematic discipline (8). In fact, not even averages from a large number of cases or repeated observations are in order. Indeed, those psychologists who have accepted the ideology of accumulated observation have already deviated from the strictly nomothetic path. If all the relevant conditions are known, or rather if all disturbing influences are eliminated, only one observation is needed to ascertain a general law once and forever. Lewin calls this the technique of the "pure case" and refers to Galileo's study of falling bodies as an example. In an attempt to apply his principles, Lewin has, however, paid the price of an "encapsulation" of his psychology, at least insofar as theoretical structure is concerned, into what may be called the central layer of the personality. The "field" within which Lewin is able to predict, in the strict sense of the word, is the person in his life space. But the life space is not to be confused with geographic environment of physical stimuli, nor with actually achieved results in the environment. It is post-perceptual, and pre-behavioral. It represents a cross section in time; yet, in spite of its cross-sectional— or, rather, actualistic—character, it is not considered static (as seems to be, for example, Titchener's old structuralism) but rather dynamic since events are defined as starting points for action. Whether or not, and in which way, action is carried out seems, however, a matter of secondary importance to Lewin. Thus no criterion for directedness of action which would be comparable to, say, Tolman's objective criteria for purposiveness of behavior, are explicitly worked out, and predictions can thus in a strict sense of the word not be tested. Furthermore,

Lewin's interest in preparation for action rather than action itself is reflected in his criticism of the use of the concept of achievement, and of the "historic-geographic" conception of psychology in general, as contrasted with the systematic, nomothetic. All this is only another aspect of what has probably led to his rejection of statistical methods. (It is understood, I hope, that I am referring to the fundamental core and texture of Lewin's theoretical work only and not to his practices which represent a healthy synthesis of his theorizing and the established ways of checking on results.)

Encapsulation into the central layer, with dynamics leading out of it, may be the least harmful of all the limitations which possibly could be imposed upon psychology. It may actually mean concentration upon the most essential phase in the entire process of life and of its ramifications. It may be the thing psychology has always been really after throughout its history. And there also is a "dynamic" quality not only in the sense of reaching back to the object (as Brentano and James dreamed of) or forward to the goal (as Lewin undertakes to do) but also in the sense of giving full recognition to cross-sectional interaction within a larger whole, the central system. In his topological psychology, furthermore, Lewin has probably developed the most adequate conceptual tool for dealing with the central layer (which Brentano did not). Yet it is for this methodological perfection that he has paid the price of encapsulation, in that he has furnished but one reference point for all extrinsic dynamics and omitted checks on extra-systemic reference points and thus prevented the actual realization of a truly dynamic outlook.[3]

I should also like to refer to Hull's mathematico-deductive theory of rote learning, as a highly formalized systematic attempt in present-day psychology (7). In spirit, the material used goes back to one of the

[3] In expanding upon his "principle of contemporaneity" (which, by the way, is characteristic of what the present writer has called "encapsulation into the central layer") Professor Lewin made the statement that it was obviously of no interest to the psychologist as a psychologist whether or not a rat in a maze would actually get to the food, or whether or not the experimenter was going to give the food, as long as only the rat would start out on its way (or enter the alley). My reply is, that whether or not the animal is actually going to get to food is exactly what we are interested in. Of course, not a single instance would have to count, but general probabilities of arriving at food and the organism's ability to pick up such general probabilities. In the course of the discussion Lewin suggested that the term "ecology" might be useful in the statistics of the interaction between organism and environment—which, however, Lewin would not want to have included as part of psychology proper.

classics of experimental psychology, namely to Ebbinghaus' studies of mechanical memory and thus to a rather elementaristic body of facts. Again the degree of nomothetic perfection which has been reached (though along a quite different line from that of Lewin) appears to be accompanied by a loss of inclusiveness or broadness of content. It is in concepts like that of the habit-family-hierarchy that Hull has reached the greatest approximation to fundamental structures of life, a fact which is compensated for by the use of a less highly developed systematic apparatus in this latter case.

Somewhat related though much more bound to traditional modes of thought is a large group of psychologists, represented, for example, by Pratt (10), in whose opinion psychology cannot become truly scientific before it has resolved itself into more "basic" disciplines such as physiology. The basic character of physiology is apparently given by the greater chances of dealing with laws in the strict sense, due to a more molecular character in the approach. Yet, as Woodworth (15) has pointed out, we have to realize that psychology is not a "fundamental" discipline in this sense of the word.

What seems to be at the bottom of these tendencies is a certain halo effect regarding the concept of exactitude. The principle of methodological physicalism which defines the unity of the sciences should be understood to postulate intersubjective univocality of observation and of communication, not less, but also not more. This univocality is ascertained by the employment of measurement and of mathematical means of communication including such tools as topology. When Watson became the first great exponent of objectivity in psychology, the ideal of exactitude was pressed considerably beyond the purely methodological aspects of physicalism.

Thus, firstly, a point was made about the mechanistic character of psychology as contrasted with vitalistic notions. However, as Carnap has since emphasized, unity of method does not imply unity of laws (4). Molar behaviorists of the present day, such as Tolman, have thus ceased worrying about the problem of explanatory teleology, for which psychology anyway does not seem to be the competent forum, nor capable of furnishing relevant material.[4]

[4] For this reason, correlations observed between organismic variables and certain results of organismic reaction ("ends") as well as certain proximal or distal stimulus variables (objects) should not be branded as entailing undue teleology. In reply to criticism raised by Professor Hull it might be said that statements about such correlations are "teleological" only in a strictly descriptive and not in the customary explana-

A second, less conceptualized and thus more dangerous, bias is based on the confusion between univocality of observation and communication, on the one hand, and the univocality of prediction. It is the latter which leads to the insistence upon law-finding in psychology. Thus, in addition to the mechanistic bias, we have the nomothetic bias. From the standpoint of methodological physicalism, however, a correlation coefficient is just as exact, that is to say, just as public and palpable in its meaning as a law. And it has, it should be kept in mind, considerably more generality, and thus possibilities of prediction, than has an isolated single event such as those studied, in extreme instances, by historians and geographers. And, in a sense, it has even more generality than the "general" laws of nature which are observed under such meticulously specified conditions.

Another element seems to enter here which may best be characterized by what Lewin (8) has called Aristotelian, as contrasted with Galilean, modes of thought (which, however, he himself has apparently failed to avoid in the instance to be referred to here). According to a certain tradition, sciences fall into two categories, nomothetic, or law finding, and idiographic, or referring to individual events. It seems as if psychology would here and there still maintain an Aristotelian, that is to say, an all-or-none attitude toward this dichotomy; if we cannot have the general law, then let us escape into singularity! In a formal sense, however, imperfect correlations fill in the gap between law and isolated fact. Laws allow prediction with certainty, statistics (correlations) predictions with probability,[5] isolated facts allow no prediction at all (unless reference to laws or correlations is tacitly brought in such as in geography where a certain constancy of the crust of the earth is assumed, or in clinical psychology, where a certain consistency of character is anticipated).

The acceptance of ambiguity of prediction as a legitimate and general feature of psychological results will probably meet with the same resistance which logicians had to face when they proceeded from a dichotomous true-false alternative to multivalued logic, or which empirical scientists had to face when developing out of theological and meta-

---

tory, vitalistic sense. Such terms as "functionalistic" or "focal reference" seem to be suitable to characterize such teleologically neutral references to empirically observed relationships between the organism and foci in its environment.

[5] In discussing this point, Professor Reichenbach referred to statistics as yielding "probability laws." I can see no objection against using the term "law" in such a sense if only the departure from the nomothetic principle is made clear.

physical stages into the positive stage.[6]

Yet, in establishing the methodological unity of science, it will become increasingly important to emphasize thematic differences. Only when diversity of topic and specific method within unity of general method is fully recognized will we be capable of carrying over the full richness of the psychological problems inherited from introspectionism and other preparatory stages into a thoroughly objectified system. Among the primary obstacles to be removed seem to be the confusions surrounding the concept of exactitude, resulting in its over-expansion. There must be recognition of the fact that there can be no truly molar psychology dealing with the physical relationships of the organism with its environment unless it gives up the nomothetic ideal in favor of a thoroughly statistical conception.[7] In turn, the topical unity of psychology within the constitutional hierarchy of the sciences can be established by specifying, in terms of focal variables, width of span, etc., the kinds of probability relationships maintained between the organism and its environment which are to be included within the scope of psychology.

In the end, this may not even mean a permanent renunciation of at least gradual approximation toward univocality of prediction. Techniques such as multiple correlation or analysis of variance, which consist essentially of a combination of correlations, will increasingly make it

[6] Giving up the nomothetic ideal meets with emotional resistance quite comparable to the one encountered when other positions of security and mastery had to be given up in the course of "Copernican revolutions" such as the dominant position of the earth within the universe, of man within the animal kingdom, or of the Ego within the system of human motivation. Thus one of the two major reasons, listed by Jaensch (until his recent death the most prominent figure of officially sanctioned contemporary German psychology) for the rejection of Gestalt psychology is the fact that Gestalt psychologists particularly emphasize ambiguity in perception, which is considered to be a frightening reflection of their own morbid psychic disposition.

[7] It is in the difference in the use of statistics that we discover why psychology is not just simply "physics of the organism in its environment." The difference exists in spite of the recent emphasis upon the statistical nature of some of the most important sections of physics. It lies in the fact that non-univocality is in physics primarily confined to the "microscopic" realm and appears to be eliminated, by the sheer weight of large numbers, as long as we remain within phenomena of a macroscopic order. On the other hand, psychology is thoroughly infiltrated with statistics even in the macroscopic sphere, and in fact the more so the more macroscopic, or "molar," its problems become. It was indeed for the quantitative expression of one of the most wide-spanning types of relationships, that of inheritance, from generation to generation, of physical and mental characteristics, that correlation statistics were first introduced into the sciences of life. The reason for this introduction of statistics is that relationships on the whole tend to become less foolproof the wider the stretch, in terms of spatio-temporal regions, over which they appear to be maintained.

possible to narrow down prediction so that we will, at least in a practical sense, come closer and closer to the traditional scientific ideal, the isolation of variables and the establishment of general cause and effect relationships. If we are not to forget the teachings of Hume and John Stuart Mill, we must realize that there is nothing observed but concomitant variation—of greater or lesser relative frequency—and that all analysis of causal textures rests upon this foundation.[8]

References

1. Brunswik, E. Probability as a determiner of rat behavior. *J. exp. Psychol.*, 1939, *25*, 175-197.
2. Brunswik, E. Perceptual characteristics of schematized human figures. *Psychol. Bull.*, 1939, *36*, 553 (abstr.).
3. Brunswik, E. Size-constancy in life situations. *Psychol. Bull.*, 1941, *38*, 611-612 (abstr.).

[8] In an attempt to show that the relationship of the positions of the three speakers of the meeting was complementary rather than contradictory, the author tried to relate them to well-established disciplines. In visualizing the organism and the organism in its physical (geographical) environment, Lewin's approach seems to be confined to the life center of the organism which may be compared to the study of law and general policy of intra-governmental function in a society. There is indeed lawfulness and consistency within such a system, yet splendid isolation unless contact with other regions is maintained through information, on the one hand, and the executive arm, on the other. Of those external relationships, Hull seems primarily concerned with engineering problems, especially in his attempt to find basic elements such as conditioning to which more complex units could be reduced. Molar behaviorism, in its turn, with its concentration upon vitally relevant if remote historic or geographic variables such as maintenance schedule, time required to reach food, etc., appears in the position of the economist (and hence the term ecological psychology, mentioned above, seems not inappropriate for this kind of approach). An important difference, though one of secondary order, between the type of molar approach represented by Tolman and that proposed by the present writer is that the former seems to put much additional emphasis upon inferences regarding the intra-organismic "intervening variables" (which brings him close to Lewin), e.g., a hunger drive as inferred from maintenance schedule; whereas the latter would tend, at least in principle, to discard for the moment intervening variables wherever they are not directly accessible. By representing an organism's or species' achievement system in terms of attained objects and results, such a psychology would in a sense be *without* the organism (i.e., would neglect all but a few focal details of organismic structure and intra-organismic processes), yet would let us know much *about* the organism (i.e., its relationships to the environment, in both cognition and action). By exerting actual measurement control mostly about stimuli and results, i.e., about historic or geographic variables, and about central variables only where a direct physiological approach is possible, such a psychology would be the direct counterpart to that represented by Lewin. Namely, it would not be post-perceptual and pre-behavioral, but rather perceptual and behavioral. But in the end, it seems that none of the various aspects just discussed can be dispensed with in a completely rounded-out system of psychology.

4. Carnap, R. Logical foundations of the unity of science. *Encycl. Uni. Sci.*, 1938, No. 1, 42-62.

5. Heider, F. Environmental determinants in psychological theories. *Psychol. Rev.*, 1939, *46*, 383-410.

6. Hull, C. L. The concept of the habit family hierarchy and maze learning. *Psychol. Rev.*, 1934, *41*, 33-54, 134-142.

7. Hull, C. L., et al. *Mathematico-deductive theory of rote learning.* New Haven: Yale Univ. Press, 1940. [See Selection No. 14 in this volume.]

8. Lewin, K. *Dynamic theory of personality.* New York: McGraw-Hill, 1935.

9. Mises, R. v. *Probability, statistics and truth.* New York: Macmillan, 1939.

10. Pratt, C. C. *The logic of modern psychology.* New York: Macmillan, 1939.

11. Reichenbach, H. *Experience and prediction.* Chicago: Univ. Chicago Press, 1938.

12. Tolman, E. C. *Purposive behavior in animals and men.* New York: Century, 1932. [See Selection No. 29 in this volume.]

13. Tolman, E. C. and Brunswik, E. The organism and the causal texture of the environment. *Psychol. Rev.*, 1935, *42*, 43-77.

14. Wallace, R. P. Apparent personality traits from photographs varied in bodily proportions. *Psychol. Bull.*, 1941, *38,* 744-745 (abstr.).

15. Woodworth, R. S. Dynamic psychology. In C. Murchison (ed.), *Psychologies of 1925.* Worcester, Mass.: Clark Univ. Press, 1928.

13   THE UNIFORMITY POINT OF VIEW[1]

Clark L. Hull

1 Introduction

There is a striking and significant similarity between the physicalism doctrine of the logical positivists (Vienna Circle) and the approach characteristic of the American behaviorism originating in the work of

[1] Thanks to the kindness of Brunswik, I have had his revised manuscript before me while preparing the revision of the present paper. Owing to the delay in the revision of my paper, it is doubtful whether either Brunswik or Lewin was able to utilize in any way the copies which were sent them immediately on its completion.

From C. L. Hull, The problem of intervening variables in molar behavior theory, *Psychol. Rev.*, 1943, *50,* 273-291. Reprinted by permission of the author, the *Psychological Review,* and the American Psychological Association.

J. B. Watson (13). Intimately related to both of the above movements
are the pragmatism of Peirce, James, and Dewey on the one hand, and
the operationism of Bridgman (4), Boring (1), and Stevens (11), on
the other. These several methodological movements, together with the
pioneering experimental work of Pavlov and the other Russian reflex-
ologists, are, I believe, uniting to produce in America a behavioral
discipline which will be a full-blown natural science; this means it may
be expected to possess not only the basic empirical component of
natural science, but a genuinely scientific theoretical component as
well. It is with the latter that the present paper is primarily concerned.

ii Probability Versus Natural Law
in the Behavior Sciences

Now, scientific theory is concerned with natural laws. These are conceived as being uniform. Do such isolable uniformities exist in the field
of behavior? Of the present panel, Lewin and I believe they do; Brunswik, on the other hand, is convinced that no such uniformities exist,
that the best we may hope for is to find correlations among phenomena
which will always lack appreciably of being 1.00, possibly ranging
mostly between .40 and .60. Since this disagreement concerns whether
something can or cannot be done, it should ultimately be capable of
unambiguous decision. If a set of such laws are actually isolated, the
question will receive an affirmative answer, but if after a very prolonged
effort directed specifically to this task, no such laws are discovered,
there will gradually arise an increasingly formidable presumption that
the answer to the question is negative.

But since the verdict from trial is very laborious and time-consuming,
it is desirable to make as shrewd an estimate of the outcome as possible
from evidence now available, because if the quest appears hopeless, all
of us may as well give it up, as Brunswik seems already to have done.
In this connection Brunswik points to the indisputable fact that under
the complex conditions of life, the behavior of organisms is variable.
This variability, except possibly in the matter of degree, is not peculiar
to the field of behavior. It is easily accounted for without assuming any
lack of uniformity in the supposed laws involved: The outcome of a
dynamic situation depends upon 1) a set of antecedent conditions and
2) one or more rules or laws according to which, given a certain period
of time, these conditions evolve into different conditions or events. It is
evident that such a situation implies some degree of uncertainty of

dynamic outcome, because we always lack absolutely exact knowledge concerning *conditions*. It does *not* necessarily imply that within the causal segment under consideration stable and uniform sequences may not occur which can be formulated into absolutely uniform rules of molar action. Accordingly, the uncertainty or probabilism of the situation may lie entirely in the conditions and not at all in the rules or laws.

This uncertainty may be illustrated by the following example. In the case of falling bodies, the *law* is represented by the form of the equation,

$$s = \tfrac{1}{2}gt^2,$$

and the *conditions* of its operation are represented by the empirical values of *s, g,* and *t,* which must be substituted in the equation if the law is to be verified. In this case the equation is universally believed to be exact, i.e., it is believed that if the measurement of *s* on the one hand and of *g* and *t* on the other were exact, the equation would hold absolutely when applied to objects falling in a vacuum at the earth's geographical pole; in that case the correlation between the right- and the left-hand sides of the equation would be 1.00. But, as a rule, errors of measurement are appreciable, which is to say that it is impossible to know the exact conditions in any given case of a falling body. Therefore, the actual correlation of the values on the respective sides of even the most fully authenticated equations of physics is bound to be something less than 1.00. That this lack of perfect correlation is due to the difficulty of measurement of the conditions rather than to the capriciousness of the alleged law is suggested by the fact that as measurements are improved, repeated, and pooled, the verification of the formula becomes increasingly exact, i.e., the correlation becomes progressively higher. It seems reasonable to suppose that the same situation may exist in the field of behavior.

A second and more serious a priori argument against the probable success of the attempt to isolate true natural science laws in the behavior sciences is that any theory of behavior is at present, and must be for some time to come, a molar theory.[2] This is because neuroanatomy and physiology have not yet developed to a point such that

---

[2] Molar behavior theory is here opposed to the molecular. The latter would presumably deal with the action of the ultimate nerve cell, the protoplasmic molecules making up the neuron or perhaps the atoms constituting the molecule, or even the electrons, protons, neutrons, etc., constituting the atom. Thus the term *molar* as here used corresponds approximately to the term *macroscopic,* or *coarse-grained.*

they yield principles which may be employed as postulates in a system of behavior theory; consequently, both for empirical and theoretical purposes, behavior must be broken up into relatively coarse causal segments, the interior conditions of which cannot be subjected to observation and measurement. It follows from considerations put forward above that even if the action of the ultimate molecular units of the causal segment were absolutely lawful, the molar outcome of the joint action of the numerous internal elements composing a molar causal segment would vary, because the conditions, being unknown, would presumably vary from one molar situation to another. It would follow that molar laws cannot be expected to be absolutely exact. This statement must, I think, be granted.

It would seem, however, that the smaller the molar segment employed, the less will be the uncertainty regarding the conditions and so the smaller will be the role of probabilism in molar dynamic outcomes. By the sagacious pooling of the data obtainable from experimental situations when controlled as well as possible, the net results of the chance variability of the molecular conditions will be largely equalized, and from these there may emerge quantitative laws characteristic of a stable central tendency of the conditions in question.[3] The laws of thermodynamics in gases rest upon exactly this basis; where moderately large samples of gas are involved these laws have a precision which represents a probability of substantially 1.00, something far beyond anything usefully measured by a Pearsonian coefficient of correlation. I conclude, then, that it is not unreasonable to hope for the isolation of both primary and secondary behavioral laws which will hold within a narrow margin of error for averages secured from carefully controlled empirical conditions.[4]

[3] Under the rubric of the oscillation (O) of habit strength below its standard or maximal strength (8, p. 76; 7), there is incorporated in my own theoretical systematization an explicit recognition of a particular phase of this presumptive variability of conditions. This oscillation is tentatively attributed to the random spontaneous firing of the individual nerve cells (7).

[4] I do not at all mean to imply by the above that Brunswik's program of empirical correlation determinations is not without great scientific value. On the contrary, I believe that it is an extremely valuable mode of approach. I do mean, however, that I should expect to derive from molar behavior laws exactly the type of correlations which he finds between the relative potency of the several visual cues in the determination of the verbal responses of his subjects in judging third dimensional distance. Indeed, I am of the opinion that adequate molar laws are even now available which would make this possible; however, such a deduction has not yet been made in rigorous detail, and of course achievements of this kind cannot be claimed with certainty in

III Symbolic Constructs Are Widely Used in Behavior Theory

As Brunswik points out, a second indirect effect of the present molar status of the behavior sciences is the resort to symbolic constructs or intervening variables. This is a widespread and wholly respectable practice, not only in the behavior sciences but in the physical sciences as well. Actually the physical sciences are molar in much the same sense as are the social sciences, and they are similarly forced to piece out by hypothetical entities the region not directly observable. In addition to molecules, atoms and the various hypothetical subatomic entities such as electrons, protons, etc., are for the most part not only unobserved but presumably unobservable.

In this connection it may be of interest to observe that the use of theoretical constructs or intervening variables is practically universal among writers who have seriously attempted the theoretical systematization of behavior. As the first example, let us take a statement by a leading logical positivist, Rudolph Carnap: "At ten o'clock Mr. A was angry" (6, p. 89). Carnap argues that for this statement to have scientific significance, the state of anger must be publicly observable, either directly or indirectly; in this connection he mentions the characteristic behavior which is ordinarily taken as indicating the condition called anger. This behavior, being observable, clearly permits an *indirect* observation of a condition within the body of Mr. A through the conversion, translation, or transformation of the statement about the behavior into a statement about the anger. Thus it becomes apparent that anger, typical of the psychic element in the classical psychology, lies between 1) the antecedent conditions of frustration and what not which precipitated the state, and 2) the observable consequences of the state; i.e., anger is an *unobserved intervening variable*. This dynamic situation is represented conveniently by the diagram of Figure 1, where S represents the antecedent conditions which precipitated the anger, $\dot{R}$ represents the observable response, A represents the anger, f_1 and f_2 represent quantitative functional relationships between S and A and between A and $\dot{R}$ respectively. A circle is drawn around A to indicate

---

advance of performance. If Brunswik is prepared publicly to challenge the possibility of such a derivation, I am prepared to attempt it and publish in this journal the outcome, whatever it turns out to be. My program thus does not oppose that of Brunswik, but merely attempts to supplement it.

that it is a symbolic construct, something not directly observable and measurable.

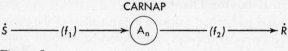

Figure 1

Passing to the more comprehensive statements of Brunswik (2), who is both a logical positivist and a psychologist, we have the situation represented by the diagram of Figure 2, where $\dot{S}$, $\dot{R}$, f_1 and f_2 mean the

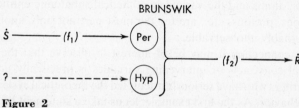

Figure 2

same as in Figure 1, Per represents *perception,* and Hyp, *hypothesis.* Here we find not one intervening variable or construct, but two of them operating jointly. Circles are drawn around Per and Hyp to indicate that they are regarded as symbolic constructs.

A third systematic approach is that of Tolman (12). I have attempted to represent this from the present point of view by the diagram shown in Figure 3, where $\dot{S}$, $\dot{R}$, f_1, f_2, and Hyp mean the same as above, Exp

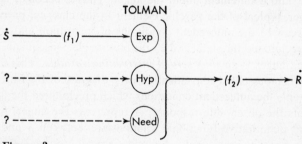

Figure 3

represents *expectation,* and *Need* is unabbreviated. The circles, as above, indicate the symbolic constructs.

A fourth example of the use of symbolic constructs is found in a study by Buxton (5).[5] It may be represented as shown in Figure 4, where $\dot{S}$, f_1, f_2, f_3, Per, Need, and $\dot{R}$ mean the same as above, Cog represents *cognition,* and Force, *psychological force.* It may be noticed

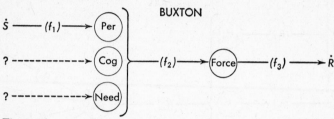

Figure 4

that the Buxton diagram has *two* links in its chain of symbolic constructs, rather than the single link represented in the preceding diagrams.

Finally I may mention my own use of symbolic constructs (7). A considerably abbreviated representation of this is shown in Figure 5,[6] where S, R, G, and N represent the stimulus energy, the response, the nature of the reinforcement, and the number of reinforcements of the original reinforcement or learning situation respectively; $\dot{S}$ represents the evocation or stimulus energy; $\dot{s}$, the afferent neural impulse initiated by the receptor discharge; Need, the number of hours of food privation, for example; D, the state of organic drive resulting from the privation; $_{\dot{S}}E_{\dot{R}}$, excitatory or reaction potential;[7] $\dot{R}$, the reaction itself; $_{\dot{S}}P_{\dot{R}}$, the probability of reaction evocation; $_{st_R}$, the latency of reaction evocation; $_{\dot{S}}A_{\dot{R}}$, the amplitude of reaction evocation; and $_{\dot{S}}n_{\dot{R}}$, the number of unreinforced reaction evocations to extinguish the re-

---

[5] At this point I would have preferred to give a representation of Lewin's (10) of symbolic constructs, but I felt even more uncertain in attempting this than in the case of the representations which were attempted. There seems no doubt, however, that Lewin does employ symbolic constructs both explicitly and on a considerable scale. Perhaps the diagram of Buxton's usage may be considered a rough approximation to that of Lewin, as Buxton in his theorizing seems to have followed Lewin to a considerable degree.

[6] I am indebted to Kenneth W. Spence for the general methodology of representing intervening variables here employed. In this connection see especially page 318 of Spence's Chapter 11, Theoretical interpretations of learning, in *Comparative Psychology* (revised edition), edited by F. A. Moss, New York, Prentice-Hall, Inc., 1942; also see page 11 of Bergmann, G., and Spence, K. W., Operationism and theory in psychology, *Psychol. Rev.,* 1941, *46,* 1-14. [P. 64 of Selection No. 3 in this volume.—Ed.]

[7] It is probable that the construct *reaction potential* ($_{\dot{S}}E_{\dot{R}}$) corresponds rather closely to Buxton's construct called *Force,* and to Lewin's *vector* concept.

action potential to a subthreshold value. As in the preceding figures, circles are drawn around the symbolic constructs.

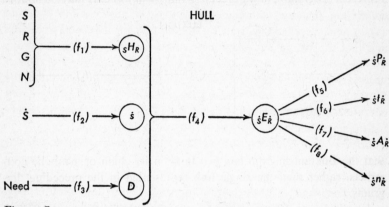

Figure 5

It is quite clear from the above examples that the use of symbolic constructs by behavior theorists is both explicit and general.

IV Requirements for the Satisfactory Use of Symbolic Constructs

It would appear that Brunswik also has considerable pessimism concerning the utility of symbolic constructs in behavior theory, even though he himself in his visual constancy studies seems at certain moments at least to introduce perception as a variable intervening between the physical stimulation of his subjects and their verbal responses. While I would not go so far as to exclude the use of symbolic constructs, I do believe that their use is attended by serious risks which can be avoided only by taking certain definite precautions.

It is quite clear that in the case of all the above diagrams, symbolic constructs can have nothing more than a rather dubious expository utility unless they are anchored to observable and measurable conditions or events on both the antecedent and consequent sides. It follows that some means must be found of determining the value of the intervening variable from the measurement of the antecedent conditions and, knowing this, some means must be found of determining what amount of the consequent observable conditions or event corresponds to the value of the construct.

Specifically, my own system, as represented by the diagram shown in Figure 5, requires that the habit strength ($_SH_{\dot{R}}$), afferent impulse ($\dot{s}$), and drive intensity (D) must each be calculable from their antecedent conditions, that the nature and magnitude of the reaction potential ($_SE_{\dot{R}}$) must be calculable from the values of $_SH_{\dot{R}}$, $\dot{s}$, and D taken jointly, and that the nature and magnitude of the several reaction functions ($_SP_{\dot{R}}$, $_S t_{\dot{R}}$, $_SA_{\dot{R}}$, and $_S n_{\dot{R}}$) must each be calculable from $_SE_{\dot{R}}$. This is necessary because if the values of the constructs are indeterminate, the theory of the relationship between the antecedent and the consequent conditions cannot be verified empirically, and an unverifiable theory has no place in science.

In every case of the proper use of a symbolic construct the calculation must, of course, be performed by means of equations representing the functional relationship in question. In the evolution of my own system considerable effort has been devoted to the derivation of such equations, and numerous tentative ones have been worked out. For example, on the antecedent side (assuming S, R, and G to be practically simultaneous),

[1] $$_SH_{\dot{R}} = w - w(10^{-hN})$$

where w is an increasing function of the nature and amount of the reinforcing agent (G), and h is an empirical constant of the order .03 (7). Next,

[2] $$_SE_{\dot{R}} = f(D) \times f(_SH_{\dot{R}})$$

where $f(D)$ and $f(_SH_{\dot{R}})$ are rather complex increasing functions of drive intensity and habit strength respectively (7).

As an example of the final link in this chain of functional relationships we have,[8]

[3] $$_S n_{\dot{R}} = .66 _SE_{\dot{R}} - 4$$

It is evident that this equational mode of anchoring symbolic constructs to objectively observable and measurable antecedent and con-

---

[8] Tentative equations have now been derived for all of the relationships represented in Figure 5, and the most of the empirical constants involved have been roughly determined. In addition, a number of other functional relationships not represented in the diagram have been worked out in the same tentative manner. It is accordingly possible, given the objective measurable antecedent conditions, S, R, G, H, $\dot{s}$, and D, to calculate the value of the consequent or terminal events, $_SP_{\dot{R}}$, $_S t_{\dot{R}}$, $_SA_{\dot{R}}$, or $_S n_{\dot{R}}$. These are all given in considerable detail in a book now in press (7). However, an immense amount of research must be performed before the relationships in question can be regarded as satisfactorily determined.

sequent conditions or phenomena is necessary, because otherwise their values would be indeterminate and the theory of which they constitute an essential part would be impossible of empirical verification. If left permanently in that state the theory would be reduced to something appreciably worse than nonsense. This seems to be what Brunswik charitably calls the "encapsulation" of symbolic constructs.

v Possibility of Determining Unambiguously the Functional Relationships of Behavior Unobservables to Other Behavioral Values

It is quite clear that the determination of the functional relationship of an unobservable to anything else cannot be carried out merely by the direct fitting of equations to empirical data, because there can be no empirical data on the side of the relationship represented by the construct. This means that the determination must be somewhat indirect and in part trial-and-error. Such procedures are common in the more mature sciences. Suppose, for example, that a person unacquainted with the law of falling bodies,

$$s = \tfrac{1}{2}gt^2,$$

were given the task of determining it directly by empirical methods. He would first let weights fall repeatedly in a vacuum from various heights, and average the falling time associated with the different distances. These means, with the corresponding distances, would make up two parallel columns of numbers. Then he would begin to try out various simple equational forms, to find one in which the substitution of the t-value would yield the corresponding value in the s-column. He would discover by trial that an exact agreement in any given case could be obtained if the value of t were multiplied by some number called a constant, but this coefficient would need to be different for every pair of values and so could not constitute a true solution to the problem. Similarly, it would be found that if one of these coefficients were kept really constant, s could be derived by multiplying the coefficient by various powers of t. But in that case a different exponent would be required for each pair of empirical s and t values, most of the exponents being fractional. Finally, in the search for simplicity, integral exponents might be tried, among which would be 2. This procedure, of course, would require approximately the *same* coefficient for all pairs of values, the coefficient being what appears in the formula as $g/2$. This finding would constitute a solution.[9]

A criticism of such a procedure might be that it is circular, since the value of the number, $g/2$, follows from the assumption that the t should be squared. The reply to this, of course, is that by the procedure outlined neither the $g/2$ nor the t^2 is assumed at first, but that that particular combination of values, i.e., that particular coefficient and that particular exponent in combination, will yield the empirical value of s, and that *no other possible combination will do so*.

In an exactly analogous manner, if a single symbolic construct stands between two observable and measurable conditions ($\acute{S}$ and $\acute{R}$), and it is found by trial that two particular equations, *and those only,* mediate in conjunction with the symbolic construct the precise calculation of $\acute{R}$ from $\acute{S}$, it is submitted that the determination of neither equation may be considered viciously circular. At all events, that is the general method which has been employed in the derivation of the equations given above. The presence of more than one construct (horizontally or vertically, as represented in Figures 1 to 5) considerably complicates the task of working out the equations, but does not change the essential logic.

VI The Scientific Status of Symbolic Constructs When Unambiguously Determined

At this point in the discussion it is easy to imagine a rock-ribbed positivist like my friend Woodrow (14) saying, "If you have a secure equational linkage extending from the antecedent observable conditions through to the consequent observable conditions, why, even though to do so might not be positively pernicious, use several equations where one would do?" It is quite true that in my own equations [1] can be substituted in [2], and [2], thus amplified, can be substituted in [3]; in which case we would have a single equation relating the antecedent conditions directly to the consequent ones, though it would be exceedingly complex. Indeed, if the situation were as simple as this question implies,

---

[9] As a matter of fact, once it is postulated that the equation has the general form of

$$s = at^x$$

the values of both a and x can be calculated by means of simultaneous equations from only two pairs of s and t empirical values. Such calculations, of course, will not reveal the exact values of either s or t, but only rather close approximations, because s and t are themselves only approximations.

there would hardly be any point in the derivation of multiple equations where one would fit the entire situation equally well. It does not seem to me that any single equation would really fit the situation equally well.

In reaching a decision concerning this question, two considerations should be kept in mind. One is that if the antecedent and consequent values have been determined with great precision, only one particular equation will *exactly* satisfy them and that equation would, it is assumed, be no other than the one resulting from the telescoping of the three equations as above suggested. In other words, for the multiple equations to be justified, the single equation giving the best attainable fit to the empirical data would be found in fact to contain within itself in some form or other the mathematical equivalents of the various equations linking the observable and the hypothetical unobservable elements of the situation.

A second and more decisive consideration involved in reaching a decision in this matter is that the occasion of the action of $\dot{S}$, $\dot{R}$, G, and N may be very remote temporally from that of the action of S and the Need. While it is perfectly possible to put into a single equation the values of events which occur at very different times, it is hard to believe that an event such as a stimulation in a remote learning situation can be causally active long after it has ceased to act on the receptors. I fully agree with Lewin that all the factors alleged to be causally influential in the determination of any other event must be in existence at the time of such causal action. I believe that it is some such consideration as this which has led to the universal common-sense use of the concept of habit; in my system $_{\dot{S}}H_{\dot{R}}$ is merely a quantitative representation of the perseverative after-effects of the no-longer-existent compound events represented by $\dot{S}$, $\dot{R}$, G, and N. It follows that the value of $_{\dot{S}}H_{\dot{R}}$ will need to be calculated separately before the influence of $\dot{S}$, $\dot{R}$, G, and N can be combined with that of the reaction-evocation situation represented by S and the Need. It is an obvious convenience to be able to concentrate the influence of four quantitative variables, such as $\dot{S}$, $\dot{R}$, G, and N, into a single numerical value or index. Since this index is not $\dot{S}$ or $\dot{R}$ or G or N, but something distinct from each, convenient symbolic manipulation demands a distinct symbolic representation, i.e., $_{\dot{S}}H_{\dot{R}}$. Semantic exigencies also require the use of a name or term; the universally used word *habit* has been adapted to this use by quantitative redefinition.

In an analogous manner it is hoped that the factors which determine primary drive (such as the number of hours of food or water privation, the intensity of an electric shock, or the number of degrees of temperature below or above the optimum) may each also be convertible into a standard index of motivation (D), presumably by means of a different equation for each type of need. If wholly successful, such a treatment of primary motivation would yield a standard D or drive value in each case which could be *substituted without distinction in the same single equation* [2] *yielding* $_sE_R$ in such a way as to mediate within the limits of errors of measurement the observable behavioral phenomena, $_sP_R$, $_st_R$, etc. If a program like that just outlined should turn out to be successful, it would practically require the use of multiple equations and some of the special signs which we have called symbolic constructs.

It is possible, of course, that animals are so constituted that a program such as has been implicitly outlined in the present paper can never be successfully carried through. Whatever may be our several a priori prejudices in the matter of the probable outcome of such a program, I think we should be able to agree upon two propositions relating to it. One is that if such equations could be found, they would greatly facilitate the theoretical integration of the behavior sciences as well as their practical application to the needs of man. The second proposition is that the only wholly convincing way of demonstrating this possibility is for some person or, preferably, some group of persons, actually to derive the equations in question and show that they do indeed mediate rather precisely the derivation of consequent behavior from the measured complex antecedent conditions as outlined above. Naturally such work will be done by those who hope for its achievement and believe in its possibility; those who do not share these hopes and beliefs will engage in other ventures. In the end, if the equations are derived successfully they will be available for all to use, and both groups should rejoice in the contemplation of the advantages ultimately to accrue. On the other hand, if the quest proves unsuccessful, those engaged in it will have had the thrill of high adventure and the satisfaction of having made a worthy effort.

References

1. Boring, E. G. *The physical dimensions of consciousness.* New York: Century, 1933.
2. Brunswik, E. Psychology as a science of objective relations. *Philos. Sci.,* 1937, *4,* 227-260.

3. Brunswik, E. Organismic achievement and environmental probability. *Psychol. Rev.*, 1943, *50*, 255-272. [Selection No. 12 in this volume.]

4. Bridgman, P. W. *The logic of modern physics.* New York: Macmillan, 1938.

5. Buxton, C. E. Latent learning and the goal gradient hypothesis. *Contr. psychol. Theor.*, 1940, *2*, No. 2.

6. Carnap, R. *Philosophy and logical syntax.* London: Kegan Paul, Trench, Trubner, 1935.

7. Hull, C. L. *Principles of behavior.* New York: D. Appleton-Century, 1943.

8. Hull, C. L.; Hovland, C. I.; Ross, R. T.; Hall, M.; Perkins, D. T. and Fitch, F. B. *Mathematico-deductive theory of rote learning.* New Haven: Yale Univ. Press, 1940.

9. Lewin, K. The conceptual representation and the measurement of psychological forces. *Contr. psychol. Theor.*, 1938, *1*, No. 4.

10. Lewin, K. Defining the 'field at a given time.' *Psychol. Rev.*, 1943, *50*, 292-310. [Selection No. 19 in this volume.]

11. Stevens, S. S. The operational basis of psychology. *Amer. J. Psychol.*, 1935, *47*, 323-330.

12. Tolman, E. C. *Purposive behavior in animals and men.* New York: Century, 1932. [See Selection No. 29 in this volume.]

13. Watson, J. B. *Psychology from the standpoint of a behaviorist.* Philadelphia: Lippincott, 1924 (2nd ed.).

14. Woodrow, H. The problem of general quantitative laws in psychology. *Psychol. Bull.*, 1942, *39*, 1-27.

CHAPTER VII

SPECIAL TECHNIQUES: LOGICO-MATHEMATICAL

WITH THE DEVELOPMENT of psychology as a maturing natural science an increasing number of serious attempts have been made to apply, more or less formally, the well established logical and mathematical techniques utilized in the older sciences. The present chapter includes papers illustrating certain of the more prominent of these recent attempts. In the first selection Clark L. Hull provides a discussion of the applicability of the hypothetico-deductive method in psychology. The paper is the introductory chapter from Mathematico-deductive Theory of Rote Learning, *itself the first example of a thorough-going application of this method to a concrete psychological problem. The second selection is concerned with the development of certain non-quantitative mathematical techniques for representation of psychological problems—a development which has been of much systematic interest in recent years. A clear and simple exposition of the basic field-theoretical approach mainly elaborated and popularized by Kurt Lewin is provided by J. F. Brown, who in this paper helped to introduce the Lewinian methodology to American psychologists. (See also Selections No. 19 and 45 by Lewin.) The paper by Gustav Bergmann and Kenneth W. Spence offers a thorough treatment of the logic underlying psychophysical measurement, with implications for experimentation and theory construction that go well beyond the problems of psychophysics, as ordinarily conceived. In the other selections L. L. Thurstone discusses the role of factor analysis as a mathematical technique in the systematic treatment of psychological problems, and Douglas G. Ellson proposes the application of engineering operations from the field of servo mechanisms to problems of human motor behavior.*

14 THE HYPOTHETICO-DEDUCTIVE METHOD

Clark L. Hull

Introduction

It is quite clear that the beginnings of science evolve from the activities of everyday life. In this humble setting there gradually accumulate a body of observations, on the one hand, and simultaneously a parallel body of ideas or interpretations of these observations, on the other. Thus, even from the very first, scientific development has involved an intimate interaction between observations and ideas. Actually, observations give rise to ideas, and ideas lead to further observations. The orderly arrangement of the observations constitutes the empirical component of science, and the logical systematization of the ideas concerning these observations constitutes the theoretical component. Thus comes about the logico-empirical nature of well-developed sciences.

As observations and related ideas multiply, certain observations demanded by ideas can not be made except under special conditions. The activities involved in the creation of these conditions constitute the substance of experimentation. It is true that occasionally, even in advanced stages of scientific development, an experiment may be performed through mere curiosity as to what will be the outcome. Indeed, when experiments and observations are very simple, ideas may play a minimal rôle in their design and execution. As a general rule, however, theoretical considerations play an increasing rôle in the design of experiments as the complexity of the experiment increases and as the science develops. The rôle of ideas in the conduct of an experiment, as distinguished from its design, is much less prominent.

The more precise scientific experiments are usually carried out in specially constructed laboratories, with the aid of delicate apparatus and elaborate procedures for making exact measurements, for carrying out control experiments, and for the statistical evaluation of results secured. Likewise, the theoretical component of scientific methodology

From C. L. Hull, C. I. Hovland, R. T. Ross, M. Hall, D. T. Perkins, and F. B. Fitch, *Mathematico-deductive Theory of Rote Learning*. New Haven, Conn.: Yale Univ. Press, 1940. Pp. 1-13 reprinted by permission of the authors and publishers.

has its own characteristic procedures and problems. Since the present monograph is designed in part as a study in scientific methodology with special emphasis on the side of systematic theory, it has been thought desirable to include a brief summary of some of the more important aspects of the methodology of theoretical systematization.[1]

Systematic natural-science theory properly consists of three distinguishable portions: 1) a set of definitions of the critical (indispensable) terms employed in the system; 2) a set of postulates concerning presumptive relationships among the natural phenomena represented by the terms; and 3) a hierarchy of interlocking theorems ultimately derived from the postulates by a rigorous logical process. The function of the definitions of critical terms of a natural-science system is to make clear the relationship of these terms (and so of the system as a whole) to the relevant part of nature which the system concerns. The postulates of a theoretical system, if valid, are presumptive natural laws. The hierarchy of theorems, corollaries, etc., make up the bulk of the system. Scientific theorems are "if—then" statements; i.e., they ordinarily state in effect that *if* such and such antecedent conditions exist, *then* such and such consequences will follow. The validity of a scientific theoretical system is dependent upon the extent of the agreement between the theorems, on the one hand, and observations of the natural phenomenon to which they refer, on the other.

Definitions

So far as the mere logic of a scientific system is concerned, the critical terms might perfectly well be replaced by a set of purely arbitrary signs, such as X's, Y's, and Z's. If this were done a person unacquainted with the natural phenomena represented by the signs could deduce the formal theorems of the system but would be completely unable to determine their meaning or whether they agree with known facts. It is only as the critical terms or signs of a system are associated with the phenomena which they represent that it becomes possible to determine either that a given postulate is supposed to be operative in a given natural situation,

[1] The remarks on scientific methodology which follow are intended to be neither complete nor exhaustive, but rather to emphasize a number of points which have appeared to be of special importance in the light of the experience of constructing the present system. Persons wishing a thorough discussion concerning scientific methodology should consult a modern systematic work on logic and scientific method. The following are recommended: John Dewey, *Logic, The Theory of Inquiry* (2); M. R. Cohen and Ernest Nagel, *An Introduction to Logic and Scientific Method* (1).

or that a theorem which results from the operation of certain postulates in a given situation agrees with empirically observed fact. In scientific theory both these conditions are absolutely necessary.

The definitions which are given for purposes of ordinary exposition do not satisfy the more exacting requirements of rigorous systematization. In this connection Dewey remarks,

While all language or symbol-meanings are what they are as parts of a system, it does not follow that they have been determined on the basis of their fitness to be such members of a system; much less on the basis of their membership in a comprehensive system. The system may be simply the language in common use. Its meanings hang together not in virtue of their examined relationship to one another, but because they are current in the same set of group habits and expectations. They hang together because of group activities, group interests, customs and institutions. Scientific language, on the other hand, is subject to a test over and above this criterion. Each meaning that enters into the language is expressly determined in its relation to other members of the language system. In all reasoning or ordered discourse this criterion takes precedence over that instituted by connection with cultural habits. The resulting difference in the two types of language-meanings fundamentally fixes the difference between what is called common sense and what is called science. (2, 49-50.)

In precise definition it is necessary to divide the terms into two groups. Since definition of a term always requires the use of one or more other terms, it follows that in any formal system there must be a number of terms which are not really defined at all. Such concepts are called *undefined notions;* their meanings are merely explained or elucidated in ordinary language. Once an adequate set of such primitive concepts or undefined notions is available, the remaining critical terms employed in the system may presumably be defined with precision.

In the past, ordinary word languages were employed in the definitions associated with deductive systems; this was true of the Greek formulations of geometrical postulates, and of the eight definitions of Newton's *Principia* (10, 1). With care, ordinary words may serve fairly well, and it is probable that in the early stages of the formulation of any natural-science theory it is economical to use this medium. Moreover, there seems no other way in which to elucidate the meaning of the undefined notions wherever the thing represented by the term can not be brought into the physical presence of the reader and directly pointed out. But once the undefined terms or signs have been elucidated, the elaborate methodology of symbolic logic (13, p. 26) is available for effecting elegant and unambiguous definitions.

At this point we meet the interesting problem of the definition of terms representing unobservables; familiar physical concepts of this sort are: *gravity, energy, molecule, atom,* and *electron.* In the present system we have the parallel problem of defining such terms as *stimulus trace, excitatory potential* (E), *inhibitory potential* (I), *reaction threshold* (*l*), and so on. Since in any truly scientific system, all unobservables must be linked to one or more observables by unambiguous logical relationships, it would seem that they should be definable by means of such relationships. An attempt to do this was made in the construction of the present system, but it was abandoned when it was found to involve a restatement of a good share of the postulates of the system in the definition of each term. Possibly it is for this reason that signs representing unobservables are usually placed among the undefined notions. This practice has been followed in the present system.

In this connection it is to be noted that unobservables fall into two distinguishable classes: 1) those which, if conditions were as favorable as they might conceivably be, could really be observed, and 2) those which are inherently unobservable. An example of the former is the class of blood vessels known as capillaries. At the time when Harvey had to postulate such entities in order to complete his theory of the circulation of the blood (6, p. 81) the "anastamosis of veins and arteries" was unobservable because sufficiently powerful microscopes were not available. Here we meet the puzzling problem presented by the hypothetical case in which a theoretically useful postulated entity of the first class turns out to be non-existent in the observational sense when conditions chance to become suitable for such observation. In such an event it would seem reasonable to retain the concept as long as it continues to mediate all other empirically valid theorems; in that case it would pass substantially into the status of the second group of concepts, i.e., it would be regarded as a purely symbolic construct.

It is important to note that a meticulous definition, however perfect from a logical point of view, does not guarantee the scientific validity of the concept defined; this can only be determined by empirical trial. A term to be at all useful ordinarily represents a class or group of phenomena all of which under specified conditions behave according to the same natural principles or laws. If it is discovered empirically that some of the individual phenomena included within a definition behave according to a different set of principles or laws, the concept must either be abandoned or redefined. It thus appears that even definitions must ultimately be validated by observation; they are not subject to the mere whim or arbitrary will of the theorist.

Postulates

At the outset of the consideration of the postulates of a scientific system, it should be observed that there are two distinguishable classes of such assumptions, though as a rule only one of these is discussed as such. The postulates which are usually, and properly, under active discussion in a scientific system are those which purport to be natural laws. Thus Newton, in his *Principia,* presents only three postulates, his three laws of motion (10, p. 13). In the derivation of his theorems, however, he utilizes without specifically listing them a very complex set of mathematical (logical) assumptions. These latter assumptions are examples of the second type of postulates necessarily assumed in the construction of any scientific system. Such logical assumptions are usually not mentioned in the evolution of scientific systems because, for one thing, the sophisticated reader is supposed to be familiar with them.

In works on logic, three criteria are ordinarily given for the postulates of any logical system. They are that the postulates shall be 1) as *few* as possible, 2) *consistent* with each other, and 3) *sufficient* to mediate the deduction, as theorems, of all relevant facts (13). This formulation in relation to a growing science represents an ideal, a goal or state of things to be striven for and to be approximated as closely as possible; it emphatically is not the state of things fully attained during the growth of a system, particularly during the early stages of such growth.[2] It is only in theology and in metaphysics generally that finalistic or closed systems are put forward. Scientific systems develop by a complex trial-and-error process, by an elaborate series of successive approximations.

Because of the growth character of scientific systems, it is impossible to state in advance how many postulates will be required. In case it is later found possible to derive one postulate from a combination of others, the situation is remedied by simply inserting the derived postulate among the theorems, thereby reducing the number of postulates by one. Possibly because it is still in process of rapid development, the number of scientific postulates at the base of even our greatest scientific systematization, mathematical physics, is not precisely known. This has

[2] See Dewey (2). In this work Dewey goes into these problems in convincing detail.

been estimated by W. M. Malisoff as 39.[3] The theoretical system concerning rote learning presented in the present monograph has 18 stated postulates, but further developments now clearly in view will certainly increase this number.

The great reason why inconsistent postulates cannot be tolerated in a scientific theoretical system is that they would lead to different theorems concerning the outcome of the same dynamic situation. Unfortunately, it is not always possible by a mere inspection of a set of postulates to tell in advance whether or not they will permit the generation of conflicting theorems. About the only thing to do in the actual construction of a scientific system is to be always on the alert for such an eventuality. In case such evidence of inconsistency should actually occur, the remedy would be to set up the conditions presupposed in common by the inconsistent theorems, and determine which (if either) of the two alternative theoretical outcomes turns out to agree with observation. The postulate which mediated the theorem shown by this procedure to be false should be discarded, or at least be recast in such a way as to eliminate the false implication.

The principle of sufficiency is the critical consideration in evaluating the postulates of a scientific system. In effect this principle means that the postulates must be sufficient to permit the derivation of theorems which will state the nature of the outcome of all the dynamic situations possible of combination from the conditions implicit in the several postulates as those under which each is operative.

It is even more difficult in the case of the principle of sufficiency than in that of consistency to determine by mere inspection whether or not a postulate set is adequate. Ordinarily this can only be determined by patiently deriving the theorems one by one and observing whether agreement does or does not exist. When a theorem is found to disagree with fact (assuming the logic to be sound) it inevitably means that the postulate set actually involved in its derivation must be revised in some sense until agreement is reached. Among the causes of disagreement between a theorem and observation are: the invalidity of at least one postulate; the action of some principle or principles not yet known and so not included in the postulate set; and the entrance of a factor into the empirical situation which, while definitely postulated, was not recognized as active in the particular situation. In case postulational error is suspected, the suspicion falls more or less over the entire group of pos-

[3] In a private communication, cited with permission of the author.

tulates involved in the derivation of the "sour" theorem. There seems to be no simple formula for determining which, or how many, postulates may be in error, though the intimate knowledge both of the facts and of his system is likely to suggest to the investigator where the trouble lies. The same general rule seems to apply in the case of a suspected new principle. The question of the surreptitious entrance of a principle, recognized by the system, into the empirical dynamic situation (or the failure to be active of a principle which was supposed to be so) while in part a matter to be decided by the sagacity of the experimentalist may itself also turn out to be a matter of the faulty formulation of the conditions under which the relevant postulates operate. In the first case the conditions laid down may be too wide; in the second, too narrow. It is evident, however, that the establishment of the validity of postulates, as sets and individually, is a gradual matter—one of successive approximations and usually one of slow growth.[4]

It is relatively easy, then, to show that *something* about a scientific situation involving theory is invalid. This requires the disagreement of only one of the theorems of a system with an observation, though such disagreement may represent defect in the experiment which led to the observation rather than defect in the system. The establishment of the *validity* of a scientific system is, on the other hand, exceedingly difficult. Indeed, it seems to be quite generally agreed that the establishment of the absolute validity of a postulate set or even of an individual postulate is an impossibility.[5] Though principles are the most important products of scientific effort, apparently the most that can be attained in determining their validity is to build up for them a favorable presumption, or probability, of impressive magnitude.

What is meant by "favorable presumption or probability" may perhaps best be explained by assuming a definitely artificial situation: suppose that by some miracle a scientist should come into the possession of a set of postulates none of which had ever been employed, but which was known to satisfy the logical criterion of yielding large numbers of empirically testable theorems. Suppose, further, that a very large number of such theorems should be deducible by special automatic logical

---

[4] The gradual growth of physical theory, as well as its present inadequacies, is shown by Einstein and Infeld (4), and by Reiche (12). It is evident that as yet no theoretical system has been able to reach perfection, despite a wide range of most impressive achievements.

[5] In this connection consult Dewey (2). Nagel has a very concise treatment of the subject (9, especially p. 60 ff.).

calculation machines, all theorems to be turned over to the scientist at once. Then these theorems would be placed in a box, thoroughly mixed, drawn out one at a time, and compared with empirical fact. Assuming that no failures of agreement occurred for a long time, it would be proper to say that each succeeding agreement would increase the probability that the next drawing from the box would also result in an agreement, just as each successive uninterrupted drawing of white marbles from a large box suspected of containing some black marbles would increase progressively the probability that the next drawing would also yield a white marble. But, just as the probability of drawing a white marble will always lack something of certainty even with the best conceivable score, so the validation of scientific principles must always lack something of being complete. Theoretical "truth" appears in the last analysis to be a matter of greater or less probability. It is consoling to know that this probability frequently becomes very high indeed.

Despite much belief to the contrary, it seems likely that logical (mathematical) principles are essentially the same in their mode of validation; they appear to be merely rules of symbolic manipulation which have been found by trial in a great variety of situations to mediate the deduction of existential sequels verified by observation. Thus logic in science is conceived to be primarily a tool or instrument useful for the derivation of dependable expectations regarding the outcome of dynamic situations. Except for occasional chance successes, it requires sound rules of deduction, as well as sound empirical postulates, to produce sound theorems. By the same token, each observationally confirmed theorem increases the justified confidence in the logical rules which mediated the deduction, as well as in the "empirical" postulates themselves. The rules of logic are more dependable, and consequently less subject to debate, presumably because they have survived a much longer and more exacting period of trial than is the case with most scientific postulates. Probably it is because of the widespread and relatively unquestioned acceptance of the ordinary logical assumptions, and because they come to each individual investigator ready-made, and usually without any appended history, that logical principles are so frequently regarded with a kind of religious awe as a subtle distillation of the human spirit; that they are regarded as never having been, and as never to be, subjected to the usual tests of validity applicable to ordinary scientific principles.[6]

[6] See Dewey (2), especially page 157 ff.

It is probable that all scientific principles must find ultimate validation in this somewhat roundabout and indirect manner, though at first sight it might seem that some postulates (natural laws) can be determined completely by direct experiment. Take, for example, Postulate 13 of the present system, which purports to state the principle of the diminution of inhibitory potential. Ellson (5) has plotted this law to a first approximation from the behavior of albino rats in a situation where the habit of pressing a simple bar to secure food suffered experimental extinction. There emerged from the experiment the general shape of the gradient involved, and a suggestion as to certain constants. Even so, there still remains the problem of the generality of the law: Does it apply to rats in other situations? Does it apply to higher mammals as well as to rats? Even if it should be found to hold for human subjects in conditioned reflex situations, this does not make it certain that it will hold for the "inhibitory potential" supposed to be generated in rote-learning situations. Ultimately the answer to such inevitable questions as to the *generality* even of carefully determined experimental "laws," must be left to systematic trial and error. Many of these may permit relatively direct determination, as in the case of Ellson's experiment, but frequently the law may be operating in such a complex situation that the shape of the gradient, and even its existence, can only be determined very indirectly.[7]

Since it appears probable that everything which exists at all in nature exists in some amount, it would seem that the ultimate form of all scientific postulates should be quantitative. Nevertheless it is a fact that many scientific principles, at least when first stated, are qualitative or, at most, only quasi-quantitative. For example, Pavlov states (11) that with the passage of time following experimental extinction, an extinguished habit will recover its original strength. A step in the direction of quantification would have been to determine experimentally that recovery is more rapid at first than later. Pavlov publishes evidence from which such a statement might have been drawn. Such a formula-

---

[7] The situation here sketched appears in the natural sciences exactly as in the so-called social sciences. The principle that gravity operates according to a gradient such that objects attract each other inversely as the square of the distance separating their centers of gravity, was first detected in relatively simple astronomical situations. But then the question arose as to whether this is true of terrestrial objects. Experiment verified this expectation. Still later the question arose as to whether the law is general enough to hold for unobservable entities such as molecules, atoms, electrons, protons, neutrons, etc. The indirect evidence, which alone is available in these latter situations, seems to point to a negative (12).

tion of the law of spontaneous recovery would correspond rather accurately in stage of development to the formulation of the law of falling bodies previous to the time of Galileo.

The complete quantification of a natural law ordinarily involves three things. The first is a precise statement of one variable as a function of at least one other variable. This normally involves the use of an equation, whose complexity is dependent upon the relationship involved. For example, Ellson found as a first approximation that the law of spontaneous recovery with rats was expressible as a function of time by means of a relatively simple exponential equation (5, p. 357). Secondly, there is ordinarily involved the empirical determination of the values of at least one constant which, while in part a function of the units employed in the measurement of the two variables involved, is also in part dependent upon, and inherent in, the phenomena concerned. Thus we have the simple equation for accelerated motion due to gravity:

$$s = \tfrac{1}{2} g t^2$$

in which g is a constant. In case t is taken in seconds and s in feet, then g is approximately 32.16, depending somewhat upon the place where the determination is made. The corresponding equation tentatively being tried out for the law of spontaneous recovery is:

$$I_n(t) = I_n e^{-dt}$$

in which e is the mathematical constant 2.718 used as the basis of the Napierian logarithms; [8] t is the time in hours since the termination of the extinction; and d is a constant of the type here under discussion. Unfortunately the value of d has not yet been determined empirically. Serious attempts have, however, been made to determine empirically certain other constants involved in the present system, such as F, K, L, and σ_L.

It is inevitable that if genuine measurement is to occur, there must be available a unit of measurement. This presents a peculiarly difficult problem where the entity to be measured is an unobservable. In the present system this problem has been solved in about the same manner that similar problems are solved in the physical sciences. In physics,

---

[8] Any other arbitrary value, such as 10, might here be used quite as well except that mathematicians have a fondness for the value, e (2.718), because of its great advantages in other situations.

energy (an unobservable) is measured *indirectly* by means of the equation,

$$\text{Energy} = \tfrac{1}{2} Mv^2$$

where the values in the right-hand member of the equation are all ultimately measurable in terms of ordinary objective scales such as those employed in the measurement of space and time. In the present system the unobservable "excitatory potential" (E) is measured in units of ΔE, where ΔE is defined as the increment of excitatory potential to the evocation of a particular syllable reaction by one syllable-presentation cycle. Following this, ΔI, L, and σ_L are all determined indirectly in terms of ΔE.

The matter of the mode of presentation of scientific postulates is of great importance. It is clear that the choice in this respect is limited to a certain extent by the available knowledge concerning the postulate. If the law is known only qualitatively it is usually stated in ordinary language. Such purely qualitative postulates may, however, be stated with much greater precision by means of the symbolism developed by symbolic logic. Quasi-quantitative postulates may also be stated in ordinary word language and, alternatively, in terms of symbolic logic, though sometimes a mathematical notation, usually involving $<\,'$s, $>\,'$s, etc., may advantageously be employed. But in the case where a fully developed natural law is involved, the method always to be preferred is a mathematical equation. Even when the substance of the postulates is available in the form of mathematical equations, symbolic logic may be of great value in supplementing the merely mathematical expressions, mainly, perhaps, by aiding in the precise statement of the exact conditions under which the law stated in the postulate is supposed to operate. The present system furnishes illustration of such use of symbolic logic. In the physical sciences these conditions, perhaps because they are so well known, are ordinarily not stated even in words.

Theorems

The theorems,[9] together with their proofs, normally make up the main bulk of any theoretical system. In the discourse of informal exposition there is rarely any attempt at a clear statement of definitions, of postulates, or of the logical steps whereby conclusions are reached. Too

---

[9] The term "theorem" as here used includes all logically proved propositions of whatever nature. It thus includes what are called corollaries in the system later to be presented, as well as what are called theorems proper.

often, indeed, a writer has given very little attention to these critical matters; such a writer when questioned is usually quite unable to say whether his system is based on two or on twenty postulates. When a writer does not himself know what assumptions he has made, the deductions are open to all sorts of fallacies. And while the first draft of a theory might very well be informal in nature, it should later be reworked in some formal manner to facilitate the removal of presumptive fallacies. Unfortunately, for most readers the presentation of formally logical proofs is the most repellent form of exposition. But even if it be thought desirable to employ an informal mode of presentation, the exposition can, for purposes of publication, be translated back into the usual mode. The logical interlude will almost certainly repay the effort involved through enabling the thinker to detect a number of serious fallacies. Such an excursion into logic is likely to prove a wholesome, even if a somewhat disconcerting, exercise.

Probably the simplest and most natural formalization of theory employing the ordinary word language, and available to everyone without special training, is that traditional in geometry (7, 8). This procedure has the great virtue of leading the theorizer at least to attempt definitions of his terms, explicit statements of his postulates, and coherent sequences in the formal steps according to which his theorems are mediated from logically preceding propositions. While actually an extremely imperfect logical medium and by no means a guarantee against serious fallacies, the method employed in geometry is nevertheless an incomparable advance over informal expository discourse. It is especially useful in revealing to the thinker unstated premises which he is tacitly employing without realization.

The technique of symbolic logic appears to be a singularly elegant and precise tool for deriving the implications of postulate sets of the most diverse sorts, particularly where only qualitative or quasi-quantitative postulates are available. While it is true that surprisingly little use has been made of symbolic logic in the construction of dynamic natural-science systems, it would seem that it has great potentialities. The increasing attention being paid by natural-science theorists to symbolic logic augurs well for an increase in the quality of theories to be put forward in the future, especially where they are based for the most part on qualitative postulates.

In science, the worker does the best he is able with what is available; if only qualitative postulates are to be had, he does what he can with them. It is always to be hoped, however, that such postulates will be only a temporary expedient. The great reason why qualitative postulates are so unsatisfactory is that they have so little deductive fertility. In a broad scientific sense they fail on the criterion of sufficiency; it is impossible to derive from them, even with the powerful devices of symbolic logic, more than a small portion of the phenomena which the postulates clearly concern. One of the more important reasons for this relative sterility of qualitative postulates in behavior situations is that very commonly action potentials of opposing sign are operative simultaneously, and the theoretical outcome is dependent upon which of the opposing potentials is dominant. This dominance, obviously, cannot be determined until the amount of each separate potential can be represented by exact symbolism. When the postulates can be written out in equations, or in words which readily generate equations, and especially when, in addition, the constants making up important portions of the equations are known from empirical determination, the rich store of powerful devices which mathematicians have invented at once becomes available. Judging by our experience with the present system, the change from qualitative to quantitative postulates with known constants increases the fertility of the postulate set between ten and fifty times.

Much has been said in the preceding pages about the necessity of an empirical check on the theorems of a scientific system. It is in this connection that theorems primarily concerned with non-observable elements, such as excitatory and inhibitory potentialities, present a serious problem because they can not be subjected to direct empirical test. Indeed, if all of the theorems of a system concerned unobservables, its scientific validity could not be determined at all; such a system would be essentially metaphysical so far as its validation is concerned. However, if theorems concerned primarily with unobservables subsequently aid in the deriving of theorems which concern observables, the difficulty is fully met. Through the observational verification of these latter theorems the empirically untestable theorems, along with the postulates employed in the derivation of both sets of theorems, become subject to indirect verification or refutation and consequently become scientifically legitimate and respectable.[10]

---

[10] The emphasis in the preceding pages on the use of logic in system construction must not be mistaken to imply that this exhausts the role played by logic in science. Actually, hardly a detail even of experimental procedure lacks its logical aspect. An especially illuminating example is seen in the experimental testing of a theorem of a formal scientific system. Such a theorem ordinarily states, at least by implication, that

Is Rigorous Deductive Systematization Possible in the Behavior Sciences?

In the early days of the psychology laboratory it was not uncommon to meet with the view that experiments on the mind were impossible. For the most part, the objections were made by philosophers, the reasons adduced naturally being mainly metaphysical in nature.[11] That question was settled, like most scientific questions, by trial; it is now firmly established that the empirical component of the logico-empirical methodology is generally applicable to the behavior of humans as well as of the lower animals. There still remains the question of whether the logical component of the logico-empirical methodology is also applicable to the behavioral sciences. It is doubtful whether many scientists at present would categorically deny such a possibility. Actually this question, just as that concerning the empirical component, must await the verdict of trial. The present monograph is, in fact, one such trial.

Many persons, while willing to grant the possibility that the sciences of human behavior may ultimately be susceptible to organization in a strict natural-science theoretical system, are inclined to doubt whether the time is yet ripe for the attempt to be made. This raises the question as to what may be expected to mark the proper time to make such an attempt. This question, just as that concerning the empirical methodology, must in the end be settled by trial. In a certain practical sense, one may say the time is ripe for the attempt whenever someone has the impulse to make it. However, the history of science does offer us certain

---

1) if such and such antecedent conditions occur, 2) then such and such consequences will follow. The experimentalist has the task of bringing about these antecedent conditions and these only. This is rarely or never possible; the best that can be done is to eliminate from the antecedent conditions all those which are presumably active or relevant to the expected outcome. In order to make sure that the supposedly inactive conditions really are inactive, control experiments, often of the most intricate nature, must be performed. And when the experimental results are secured, complex statistical procedures must be employed to make reasonably sure that the critical values obtained are not due to mere sampling or chance. In all this, logic plays a vital role. Unfortunately the scope of the present methodological remarks precludes any detailed discussion of these important matters.

[11] For example, Ebbinghaus remarks in the preface to his classical work: "The principal objections which, as a matter of course, rise against the possibility of such a treatment are discussed in detail in the text and in part have been made objects of investigation. I may therefore ask those who are not already convinced a priori of the impossibility of such an attempt to postpone their decision about its practicability." (3)

pertinent suggestions concerning the conditions favorable for such a venture.

While the logical and the empirical naturally develop more or less together, history shows that usually during the early stages of development the empirical phase is dominant. It is much later that the logical, or deductive, aspect of natural science manifests itself in the form of large theoretical systematizations. This, of course, is quite to be expected; since logic cannot work in a vacuum, there must be available a supply of preliminary concepts and tentative principles before it can begin systematization. These initial concepts and principles are yielded automatically (2) by familiarity with the concrete phenomena of the science in question. There is no reason to believe that the science of human behavior will prove to be any exception to this rule of development.

It would seem that in the field of individual (as distinguished from social) human behavior the conditions for the development of systematic theory are definitely favorable. Wundt founded the first psychological laboratory at Leipzig in 1879. Following this beginning, laboratories of psychology sprang up with great rapidity in many different parts of the world. During the sixty-year period which has since elapsed these laboratories have produced an immense volume of meticulous experimental observation. This is particularly true in the field of rote learning, which was initiated fifty-four years ago by the publication of Ebbinghaus's epoch-making monograph, *Über das Gedachtnis*. It would seem that this extended engrossment in the empirical could hardly have failed to shape, at least in a preliminary manner, the more obvious concepts, and to give rise to numerous promising, if tentative, formulations of the more important dynamic relationships existing between such concepts. Such general considerations as the above certainly do not suggest any insuperable obstacles in the way of the application of the complete natural-science methodology to some aspects, at least, of human behavior.

References

1. Cohen, M. R. and Nagel E. *An introduction to logic and scientific method*. New York: Harcourt, Brace, 1934.
2. Dewey, J. *Logic*. New York: Henry Holt, 1938.
3. Ebbinghaus, H. *Memory* (Trans. by H. A. Ruger and C. E. Bussenius). New York: Teachers College, Columbia Univ. Press, 1913.

4. Einstein, A. and Infeld, L. *The evolution of physics*. New York: Simon and Schuster, 1938.

5. Ellson, D. G. Quantitative studies of the interaction of simple habits. I. Recovery from specific and generalized effects of extinction. *J. exp. Psychol.*, 1938, *23*, 339-358.

6. Harvey, W. *Anatomical studies on the motion of the heart* (Trans. by C. D. Leake). Springfield, Ill.: Thomas, 1930 (2nd edition).

7. Hull, C. L. The conflicting psychologies of learning—a way out. *Psychol. Rev.*, 1935, *42*, 491-516.

8. Hull, C. L. Mind, mechanism and adaptive behavior. *Psychol. Rev.*, 1937, *44*, 1-32.

9. Nagel, E. Principles of the theory of probability. *Int. Encycl. unif. Sci.*, *1*, No. 6. Chicago: Univ. of Chicago Press, 1939.

10. Newton, I. *Principia* (Trans. by F. Cajori). Berkeley: Univ. Calif. Press, 1934.

11. Pavlov, I. P. *Conditioned reflexes* (Trans. by G. V. Anrep). London: Oxford Univ. Press, 1927.

12. Reiche, F. *The quantum theory*. New York: E. P. Dutton, 1930.

13. Woodger, J. H. *The axiomatic method in biology*. Cambridge: Cambridge Univ. Press, 1937.

15 TOPOLOGY AND HODOLOGICAL SPACE [1]

J. F. Brown

i Introduction

For the readers of a journal devoted to the application of mathematics to psychological research it is scarcely necessary to spend much time in answering the question, "Why mathematics?" Science may best be defined as that set of postulates regarding experience to which the universal assent of competent observers may be obtained, plus the organization of such postulates into theories for which universal assent

[1] This paper contains in rather abstract form certain arguments of the author's monograph, "The Mathematical Conception Underlying the Theory of Psychological and Social Fields." The monograph has been privately printed in a preliminary form. The whole monograph will be published in the near future.

From J. F. Brown, On the use of mathematics in psychological theory, *Psychometrika*, 1936, *1*, 77-90; 7-15. Pp. 77-90 and 7-14 reprinted by permission of the author and the editors of *Psychometrika*.

is likewise obtainable. Of all the propositions about nature those concerned with mathematics are most readily given universal assent. From this state of affairs the Kantian aphorism that a discipline is as scientific as it contains mathematics is entirely consequent. Kant himself doubted the applicability of mathematics to psychology and so was led to question the possibility of a scientific psychology. Fechner, as is well-known, thought differently and from Fechner's day the application of mathematical procedures has become an increasingly important part of psychological research until today we have a journal devoted to such application alone.

What reputation academic psychology [2] has with the educated layman depends almost entirely on the researches of the line of distinguished men, who following Fechner have attempted to apply the precision which accompanies mathematical thinking alone to psychological problems. Thanks to them, we may determine as much about an individual's intellect in an hour and that probably more accurately, than a teacher's subjective estimate furnishes us in a year. We may decide which of our children are absolutely unsuited for a college or a musical education. From psychological research of a mathematical sort we may often proceed to the decision of important problems of neurophysiology. But despite these many advantages there are good reasons for believing that the application of mathematics has so far helped but little towards making psychology a systematized science. The promises of the early work of Fechner and Binet have not been fulfilled. The question of what, if anything, has been measured and how these measurements are related to psychological theory is still an open one. Thus Thorndike, himself a leader in psychometrical research, writes: "Existing instruments represent enormous improvements over what was available twenty years ago, but three fundamental defects remain. Just what they measure is not known, how far it is proper to add, subtract, multiply, divide and compute ratios with the measures obtained is not known; just what the measures obtained signify concerning the intellect is not known." [3]

A systematized science like modern physics uses mathematics in making measurements as psychology has attempted to do, but an equally

---

[2] As opposed to psychopathology, psychoanalysis, etc.

[3] Thorndike (19). Although this judgment is eight years old, it could well be repeated today. I have gone into my reasons for questioning the systematic value of much psychometrical research in a separate paper (1).

important application of mathematics in physics is to the construction of theories. In any advanced science most of the measurements performed depend on a close integration of theory, law, and experiment. The older views of the scientific method which supposed that measurements lead to laws through the discovery of correlations between sets of measurements on different entities have been shown to be unsound. In actual scientific practice the theory leads to the law and the law to the possibility of measurement more often than measurement leads to laws and hence to theories (1). The psychologist in his attempt at an empiricism, based on what he supposes to be a sound mechanistic methodology, has neglected the possibilities of applying mathematical procedures to the construction of psychological theory. *Psychologists have made wide use of mathematics in measurement, but have scarcely ever used mathematical concepts in theory-building.*[4] The purpose of this paper is to call to the attention of the mathematical psychologist certain mathematical procedures which may be used in the construction of psychological theories. Lack of space prevents the mathematical development of these concepts. The various references, however, should enable the reader to pursue the mathematics of this mode of attack further should he so desire.

Before doing this, two questions must be answered briefly. "Must we have theory in psychology?" and "If so, what must the nature of the theory be?" The first question is to be answered with a strong affirmative. All science is based on theoretical postulates of some sort. Those individuals like the Watsonian Behaviorists who have denied theory the most emphatically have been adherents to a very naïve type of positivistic materialism. They have further implicitly accepted atomistic-mechanism and this theory has frequently dictated to them what the "facts," of which they have made so much, should be (4). The theory is there but it is not properly co-ordinated with the research. Hence, despite the methodological attractiveness of the strictly molecular behavioristic position, the comparative sterility of the results. Individuals like Hull (11) and Tolman (20) have clearly seen the necessity for theory even for the Behaviorists.

Recent methodological research has also shown us the most fruitful type of theory. The theory should be based on what may be called the hypothetico-deductive method, or the method of constructs. In this

---

[4] There are some notable exceptions, of course, like Spearman and Thurstone. It is quite a different approach which will concern us here.

method, hypotheses are devised to account for the descriptive data and from these hypotheses, predictions are made which may be tested in experiment. The constructs used in the hypotheses must be capable of operational definition. They must further lead to theoretical postulates which may be tested in critical experiments. There is so much agreement now amongst methodologists on this point that to argue it further would require space which may better be spent on the development of the constructs themselves.[5]

Arithmetic and algebraic concepts find their chief application to science in measurement. For the building of theories geometry is of greater importance. Consequently, the following sections of this paper will introduce certain geometrical conceptions applicable to psychological theory and give reference to their use in the investigation of concrete problems by the hypothetico-deductive method.

II The Concept of the Psychological Field

In many ways the most important theoretical construct of modern physics is that of the *field*.[6] The idea of psychological fields has been widely but somewhat loosely used by psychologists. It is easy to understand that a construct which has been so fruitful for physical research should be adopted by psychologists at the time when psychology is changing from an Aristotelian to a Galilean science (13). It is to be regretted, however, that many psychologists in using the construct of the psychological field have failed to give it a precise mathematical definition.

The *psychological field* is a *space* construct to which descriptions of psychological behavior may be ordered. Space is a *manifold* in which *positional relationships* may be expressed. In general the manifold may be *continuous* or *discrete,* and position may be defined in terms of *distance* and *direction* as in *Euclidean* space or only in terms of relation as in *topological* space.[7] Geometry, despite the actual derivation of the word, is concerned with all possible logical constructs about space. Since Riemann's great paper (18), spaces may be constructed of any dimensions and properties, provided these are logically consistent. Furthermore, Riemann showed that the properties of a space may be dependent

---

[5] Cf. the papers of Lewin (13, 14), Carnap (6, 7), Brown (2, 3) on this point. The paper of Brown (3) gives considerable attention to the views of other methodologists.

[6] Technical mathematical concepts will be italicized on introduction.

[7] Topology as a branch of geometry will be considered shortly.

on the dynamics of processes within that space. Consequently, metrical or topological fields may be in principle of the same nature as the electromagnetic or gravitational field. This relationship between the properties of physical space and the dynamic processes within it is one of the most important of modern physics. Recent work in psychological theory indicates a similar relationship between the spatial properties of the psychological field and the psychodynamical processes (15). In our definition of the psychological field as a space construct, space must be understood in its post-Riemannian sense. The properties and dimensions of the psychological field will be more precisely defined after a consideration of its general nature.

Every sample of human behavior may be analyzed physically, chemically, biologically, physiologically, psychologically, sociologically, perhaps also ethically. I refill my fountain pen. The physical analysis of such an event would describe the energy exchanges in terms of mechanics (possibly in terms of the changes in atomic structure) which occurred as my hands executed the movements necessary for this act. Chemical analysis would be concerned with the chemical changes attendant upon it. The biologist would treat the activity as a problem in ecological adaptation. The physiologist would concern himself with the changes in the bio-chemistry of my body during the behavior. *To the psychologist the behavior is analyzable as an example of goal-integrated activity*. The sociologist would be concerned with the possible results of the act in the social group to which I belong. The ethicist must decide as to whether I have done right in filling my pen in order to write the lines which you are now reading. Any analysis of the behavior requires *abstraction* of certain of its aspects. To describe the physics of the act the physicist makes use of the construct of the gravitational field; psychologically the act may best be described as occurring in a psychological field. Statements like "the rat is hungry and trying to get the cheese," "I am attempting a clarification of psychological theory," are to be *ordered* to vectors within psychological fields. The psychological field is a *construct* to which all psychological activity, (i.e., behavior) may be ordered. It is spatial in the sense in which space has been defined above.

The idea of psychological field may perhaps be clarified by comparing it with mathematical and physical fields. Mathematical fields are spatial *regions* which may be either scalar or vector fields. A *scalar* field is a region where every point may have an associated set of magni-

tudes. A *vector* field is a region where every point is characterized by
both direction and magnitude. Physical fields, as for instance force
fields, have every point characterized by a vector, which represents
the potential at that point. The points in the psychological field are
associated with both direction and magnitude but these may for the
present only be non-metrically defined. The behavior of an organism
may be said to be *directed towards a goal. The force behind the behavior may be said to have a magnitude.* The magnitude may have an
index-figure assigned to it.[8] Whenever an organism behaves psychologically, it may be said to be behaving in a psychological field. The
goal which it is "trying" to find is to be ordered to a point within this
psychological field. The force which is causing the behavior is to be
ordered to a vector within this psychological field, as is its present
position.

For first analysis a two-dimensional plane suffices as an adequate
construct for all psychological behavior problems. (A one-dimensional
manifold would not be adequate, because we would then have no possibility of ordering behavior which was not in the simple direction
towards or away from the goal.) In the language of data, there is a
rat (a man), which (or who), is trying to get cheese (a solution to
a mathematical problem). In the language of constructs, there is a
vector in the psychological field, activating the rat (man) towards the
goal (cheese or the solution of the problem). Both organism and goal
are to be ordered to positions in the psychological field. The force
(language of constructs), to which the behavior (language of data)
of both is to be ordered, represents a directed magnitude. The value of
this vector depends on its position in the field. It is well known that
when the goal is nearly attained the magnitude of the vector is greater.
From this one can conclude that the co-ordinates to the points in
the psychological field have magnitude. But the magnitude which must
be assigned to position within the psychological field is non-metricized.
*Point-values in the psychological field are not yet metricized in char-
acter, while those in physical fields are metricized.* The direction of
vectors in the psychological field may be defined for certain problems
through the distinctive path between points within the field.[9] Conse-

---

[8] It is necessary to introduce the concepts of both vector and goal at this point.
The exact definition of these will be given later. Since psychological forces are not
measurable in fundamental terms, we speak of index-figures rather than measurements. Cf. below.

[9] Lewin has accomplished this in his recent paper on hodological space (15).

quently the chief methodological difference between the psychological field and the physical field is that direction and magnitude of the point values within the psychological field are not as yet to be given with the same precise definition. When bodies behave physically or psychologically this behavior may be ordered to the construct of the physical or psychological field. The physical and psychological field both represent spatial constructs. Every psychological activity may be ordered, for first approximation, to a two-dimensional plane (a surface), where organism and goal represent certain spatial regions within the surface. The surface must be treated as a topological rather than a metricized field at the present time. It is mathematically possible to create as many additional dimensions to this continuum as are necessary to enable us to treat adequately the psychological descriptions of the language of data.

By *field-structure* we shall mean the variations in precision with the position of points in the psychological field which may be given. Following Lewin (15) we shall call fields *unstructured* where it is impossible to give the position of (i.e., to distinguish) points. A field is said to be *structured* when one can distinguish large regions, but not infinitely small regions within it. When one can distinguish infinitely small regions or points within a field it is said to be *infinitely structured*. The degree of structure refers to topological, i.e., non-metricized, fields. Only metrical fields are infinitely structured. So only in psychological problems where we are concerned with actual physical locomotions of the subject (the rat in the maze, for instance) is the psychological field infinitely structured. We can precisely define goal and initial position. For the chief problems of human psychology (the mathematician solving the problem, for instance) the field may be said to be structured but not infinitely structured. For this reason, except for the simplest problems, like maze running, the space of the psychological field must be treated topologically rather than metrically.

III The Topological Variants in the Structure of the Psychological Field

Topology (analysis situs) is defined by v. Kerékjártó (12) as "that part of geometry, which investigates the properties of figures which remain unchanged under continuous transformation. These are the relationships of connection and position, properties of a qualitative nature." The transformations admitted in topology are arbitrary point-to-point transformations. Topology investigates the non-metrical aspects of space, particularly the possible connections between different spatial regions. It should be quite obvious that there is relationship here to such modern psychological conceptions as Gestalt, configuration, belongingness and membership-character. For psychological purposes one might define topology as the science which investigates the "belongingness" of spatial regions, and their connectivity with other regions.

Like the theory of probability, topology grew up as a mathematical stepchild. Just as Galileo and Laplace amused themselves with the formulation of probability postulates but considered them of little real importance for science, so Leibniz and Euler played with the ideas of topology. Riemann's investigations on the connectivity of surfaces however showed the importance of topology for the theory of functions and since that time, topology has been granted a place as reputable mathematical science.

Poincaré (17) in 1895 first attempted a mathematical foundation for general topology and since then a great many of the ablest geometricians have concerned themselves with its problems.[10] Today there is a great body of proven topological theorems and topology is applied in physical and psychological problems. Furthermore topology has been given a firm mathematical foundation in the theory of abstract sets. The introduction of the theory of abstract sets has been characterized by Fraenkel (8) as creating "a scientific revolution in mathematics, of not less importance than the Copernican system in astronomy, than the Einsteinian relativity theory in physics."

Topology becomes a metricized geometry when direction and magnitude of topological concepts are defined. A circle, an ellipse and any polygon are topologically equal. So are a cube, a sphere and any closed three-dimensional figure. Topology investigates those spatial properties which are independent of metrics. For instance, any closed curve lying in a plane (the topological Jordan curve) has many such properties which have been handled mathematically by topologists. It can be proved that the Jordan curve divides a surface into two regions, of

[10] For the history and general references, cf. v. Kerékjártó (12). For the American psychologist who wishes to orientate himself in this science it is difficult to recommend general texts. Topology has several branches, of which the most important for psychology is surface topology. The brief article of Franklin (9) refers to the chief textbooks and introduces the simpler concepts. The theory of point-sets is presented by Fraenkel (8), who gives adequate references to the works of others. The forthcoming work of Lewin (14) includes a brief topological introduction.

which the curve is the common boundary, that the Jordan curve defines at the most one limited region, that it is impossible to move from the inner limited region to the outer region without crossing the curve.[11] At the present time hundreds of such demonstrations are possible.

Topology is in many ways to be looked on as the basic science of space. With topology geometry becomes truly the science of positional relationships. Since relational thinking tends to structure itself in terms of spatial relationships, topology gives us the mathematics necessary to set up theories about psychological problems, where *fundamental measurement* is impossible at the present time.[12]

We are now ready to introduce the topological concepts applicable to psychological research. Any segment of space represents a *region,* and all spatial configurations (or figures) are regions. A point, a line, a plane, and a solid are regions of respectively 0, 1, 2, and 3 dimensions. Points may be taken as topologically given, or they may be defined as the limiting case where n closed curves are so constructed that each succeeding curve lies within the boundaries of the one preceding it. In the following we will speak of *point-regions* as those segments of space which will be treated mathematically as points. For the first approximation of many problems the individual may be ordered to a point-region in the psychological field. Similarly the goal may be ordered to a point-region, when the goal is clearly definable, i.e., where one can give its exact position relative to the subject. This is by no means always the case for psychological activities. In cases of actual physical locomotion (all sorts of problems of mazes and circuitous routes), the spatial definition of the goal as point is relatively easy. When the goal is the solution of a mathematical problem or the attainment of a social status its definition is more difficult. A *line-region* connecting two points is called a *path.* Psychological activity of all sorts will be ordered to a path and may be said to represent a *locomotion* in the psychological field. Thus a successful running of a maze represents a locomotion along the only path connecting the starting-position with the goal position. One of the chief problems of surface topology is the connectivity of certain points through certain paths and the problem of defining through what regions

[11] Any readers, who are so mathematically naïve as to consider such propositions unnecessary of proof, are reminded of the history of the parallel axiom, which seemed equally self-evident.

[12] In fundamental measurement the arithmetic theorem of addition holds for the numbers involved so scales may be established with equidistant units and a zero point. Cf. Campbell (5).

the path must run in order that the locomotion be attained. Spatial regions are said to be *incident* when it is possible to construct a path from a point in one to a point in the other without crossing any other region. The problem of incidence of regions is of psychological importance for defining the possible locomotions between the individual and the goal. Regions are further characterized as *bounded* and *unbounded, limited* and *unlimited,* and *one-fold, two-fold,* to *n-fold connected.* The properties of such regions will be given in the following lines. These characterizations do *not* pretend to be precise topological definitions as it is necessary to introduce the concept of direction which has no topological meaning. It is believed, however, that for purposes of introduction such an approach will better clarify the concepts as used in actual psychological research. Whether or not a region is limited or bounded and its connectivity may also be determined by pure topological methods.

A region in which a point-region continues locomotion in a given direction indefinitely without return to its initial position is *unlimited.* If the point-region returns eventually to its initial position the region is said to be *limited.* A region in which locomotion of a point-region in a given direction must eventually bring it incident to another region (the boundary) is *bounded.* If the point-region does not eventually become incident to another region, the region is said to be *unbounded.* A region in which any point may be connected to any other point by at least one path, so that the path becomes incident to no other region, is *connected.* A simple or one-fold connected region is one which may be divided into two separate connected regions by any *cut* through the region. Such a cut divides the region into two regions so that every point within the original region belongs to either one or the other of the new regions but not to both. A two-fold connected region requires *under conditions* two such cuts to create two simply connected regions; a three-fold connected region three such cuts, and an *n-fold* connected region *n* such cuts. These concepts may perhaps best be illustrated by reference to Figure 1.

The curve *A* alone represents an unbounded region, i.e., the two-dimensional topological plane. (The curve is broken to indicate the lack of boundary. It is of course necessary to draw it so, because the page itself is bounded.) The contours *B, D, H, L, J,* all define limited, bounded regions, and as contours are topologically all equal. *C* and C_1 represent point-regions, and the lines connecting them are paths between them. All of these paths are topologically equal. *B* is one-fold connected, as one *cut E* may be constructed through the region, dividing it into two simply connected regions B_1 and B_2. *D* is two-fold connected. *D* remains a simply connected region after the construction of the *cut F* through it. In order to create two simply connected regions, the cut, *G,* must also be constructed. All the figures lie in the unbounded, unlimited region *A*. They may be said to be constructed in it. After such constructions have been made the space may be said to be struc-

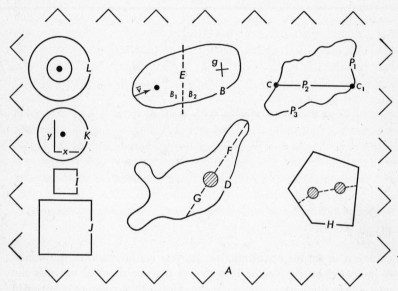

Figure 1

tured. Space is infinitely structured when one can distinguish infinitely small regions within it. Hence *K* may be said to represent a region that is infinitely structured, in that Cartesian co-ordinates may be constructed within it and the *x, y,* values of any point within it may be given. *L* on the other hand is structured, but we may only say that the point lies within both boundaries, i.e., only its topological position may be given. In unstructured space we can say nothing about the *position* of a point. At the present time in psychology the space to which we assign most of our data may be said to be structured but not infinitely structured. (Cf. Lewin, 14, 15.)

The reader is perhaps by this time anxious to see how certain psychological data may be ordered to the topological concepts. The individual is ordered to a point-region in the psychological field. Suppose an individual is on the playing field of one of our modern American athletic stadia, such as the Yale Bowl. If all the exits are blocked the individual's actual physical locomotions occur in a limited, bounded region. The region is furthermore, one-fold connected because a barrier across the field would divide the field into two simply connected regions. (Cf. *B* in Figure 1.) When the individual, either on instruction of the psy-

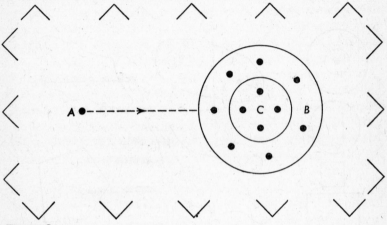

Figure 2

chologist or on his own initiative, moves, his direction of movement is indicated by the vector $\bar{v}$, which is a force directed towards the goal g.[13] In this case if one of the exit doors of the stadium is left open the field becomes unbounded and the individual may leave it.

The example just given is one of actual physical locomotion and the properties of psychological space may be directly ordered to physical space, so that the physical correlates of the subject's locomotion may be given. Although many of the specific problems of animal psychology are to be treated in terms of such a space, the chief problems of human and social psychology require a more developed spatial concept. All behavior is to be ordered to locomotion in the psychological field. The goal may be, as we pointed out above, of the nature of attainment of a certain social status or the solution of a mathematical problem.

---

[13] The vector concept is a non-metricized dynamical concept and will be precisely treated shortly.

An individual, *A*, is a freshman student desirous of becoming a member of a certain fraternity. In this case he is to be ordered to a position in space outside the region to which members of this fraternity belong. The situation topologically is given in Figure 2. *A* represents our student, *B* and *C* together the members of the fraternity. *A* wishes to get into the region *B* and *C*. In order for him to become a full-fledged member *C*, he must go through the pledge region *B*. Psychologically, in terms of the language of data, *A* wants to become a member of the fraternity. We order this situation to a field in which *B* and *C* represent bounded limited regions, where *C* lies within *B*. It is impossible to make the locomotion from *A*'s original position to *C* without first attaining membership-character in the region *B*. In this connection the *boundaries* surrounding both *B* and *C* must be crossed.[14]

A similar situation arises in the case of problem solution. If the individual is trying to solve the Pythagorean theorem, he must, in the language of data, make certain Euclidean constructions in order to arrive at the proof. Topologically the situation is that given in Figure 3.[15] It is necessary to go through regions *B* and *C* to get to the goal *D*.

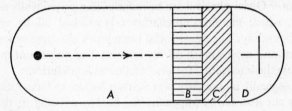

Figure 3

Not all individuals may fulfill this locomotion, and the "ease" with which the barriers are crossed distinguishes a good geometry student from a poor one. An individual is to be located in region *B*, if he has gone so far in the solution of this problem that the first constructions are made.

Regions in the psychological field are marked off by *boundaries*. Boundaries have been topologically defined above. The psychological significance of boundary is that in crossing a boundary the individual's reactions are changed. Our freshman student behaves differently after

[14] The exact definition of boundary and membership-character will be given shortly.
[15] For convenience in drawing we will from now on discard the indication that all our constructions are in the two-dimensional topological plane and simply indicate the field of activity as a bounded region.

he has become a member of the fraternity. Our geometry student's consciousness about the Pythagorean theorem as a problem is differently structured after he sees the first steps in its solution. Sociologically all the members of any organized group are to be ordered to a bounded region. Belonging to the group gives the individual certain psychological characteristics which differentiate him from non-members. Individual point-regions within a bounded-region are said to have *membership-character* within that region. We shall see shortly that the dynamics of the field determine the *variation* in membership-character amongst the individuals. All Catholics have membership-character in the bounded region to which the members of the Catholic Church are ordered, all Unitarians in the bounded region of the Unitarian Church. There is more variation in the Unitarian membership-character than in the Catholic. In other words, a greater latitude of opinion on matters of religious dogma is allowed in the Unitarian Church. *All the individuals within a bounded social region are affected in their behavior through the fact that they have membership-character within this region.* The boundary may be said to be *quasi-physical, quasi-social,* or *quasi-conceptual.*[16] Quasi-physical are boundaries like prison walls and club-buildings, where membership-character is marked off by an actual physical boundary. The quasi-social boundaries are those where social institutions and mores mark off the regions. The quasi-conceptual are those where the intellectual factors function as boundaries.

Psychologically a boundary represents a *barrier* to locomotion. This barrier is not necessarily impenetrable, but, in crossing it, the point-region (individual) becomes ordered to a new social region and his "psychology" is changed. It is convenient to distinguish between two types of psychological barrier, both of which represent topologically bounded social regions. In the following, *group-barriers* will be used to designate the limiting regions of social groups, *inner-barriers* to indicate blockages to locomotions within a given social region. Barriers may be quasi-physical, quasi-social, quasi-conceptual. The mores and social institutions, as well as actual walls and fences are to be ordered to barriers in psychological space.

Figure 4 gives the barrier characterization of the proletariat and bourgeoisie as social groups. P represents the proletariat group barrier,

---

[16] The prefix "quasi" indicates simply derived from physics, from sociology, from logic in these terms. We are interested only in the psychological effects of these physical, sociological and logical entities.

B that of the bourgeoisie. *a, b, c, d, e* all represent inner barriers within these group barriers. The detailed characterization of such barriers may only be given in connection with the non-metricized dynamical concepts now to be introduced.

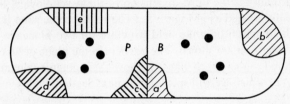

Figure 4

The two-dimensional manifold allows us to treat of all initial positions and goals and consequently to give the topology for any psychological activity considered by itself. It has long been realized by psychologists, however, that there are decided differences in such activities as perceiving, thinking, dreaming and day-dreaming. The differences between such activities necessitate treating problems of individual psychological acts in a three-dimensional manifold. The introduced third dimension has been called the *reality dimension* of

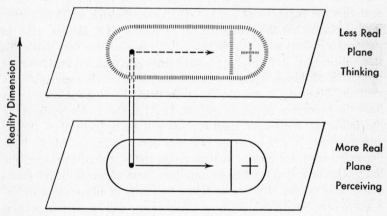

Figure 5

the personality. It is necessary to introduce this third dimension because of the structural differences in activities which may occur practically simultaneously. For normal perception is said to have a higher degree of reality than thinking, and thinking a higher degree of reality than daydreaming. Thinking or even daydreaming may under circumstances, however, have a higher degree of reality than perceiving (16). The same goal may be perceived, thought, or dreamt about. Consequently the degree of reality is the third dimension of the psychological field. It is topologically treated as in Figure 5. (The reality dimension is *continuous*. In the diagram only the field structure for two planes in the continuous dimension are shown. The barriers in the plane of lesser reality are indicated with broken lines to show their greater dynamical permeability, of which we will speak in the next Section.)

IV Non-Metricized Dynamical Variants of the Psychological Field

The topological concepts allow us to assign individuals and goals to certain spatial regions. They allow us to designate what locomotions are possible for an individual and what regions must be traversed in attaining a definite goal. But the topological concepts alone tell us nothing of the actual locomotions performed in psychological activities. So far we have seen that the position of the individual at the start of the psychological activity may be defined in reference to this. Psychological activities may be ordered to *locomotions*. The individual in this sense has the character of a *thing*. The space through which the locomotion occurs has the properties of a *medium*. (Cf. Heider, 10.) In physical problems where the field construct is used, one may make this same distinction. Bodies falling in the earth's gravitational field have the properties of things, while the atmosphere is to be characterized as a medium. Similarly in the electro-static field, the isolated conductors have the properties of things and the field has those of a medium. In the following, individual point-regions will be considered as things, and the fields in which the locomotions occur as media. Media have dynamic properties such as fluidity, permeability, cohesiveness and the like.[17] Our next step must be to introduce these concepts, define them, and give examples of their use. These will only be illustrations; references to exact analyses in terms of a field theory will be given in Section

---

[17] Such dynamic terms have been frequently used by some sociologists and psychologists, usually without precise definition and without the realization that they represent theoretical constructs. It is hoped that the field-theoretical concepts will not be confused with these others.

VI.* Such concepts are only of definite scientific value when they are capable of *operational definition*. In other words, assignment of a certain fluidity to a field is only permissible when it is done on a definite experiential or experimental basis. They may perhaps be useful for speculation, before operational definition is possible. Our language of data is rich in phenomenological descriptions where non-metricized dynamic concepts are used and readily comprehended, and the adoption of them as constructs undoubtedly originates in such phenomenological descriptions. But *scientific meaning* accrues to such concepts only when they may be precisely, i.e., operationally, defined. At the present time we may define these concepts in terms of *experimental* or *statistical indices*. We use the term index purposely to distinguish such numerical assignations from real or fundamental measurement. Experimental indices are gained from actual experiments and have their greatest use in problems of individual psychology. Statistical indices are used chiefly in problems of social psychology and sociology. Thus it is possible to use income-tax returns as an index for the permeability of boundaries separating social classes, or from questionnaire results to obtain indices for the variation of field fluidities amongst social groups.

In the following we shall suggest different operations which may be used in defining each concept. We do *not* wish at this early point in the development of field theory to commit ourselves to too definite procedures in defining our concepts, because, where several indices are available, it may later transpire that one of these has a particular value for a final definition. *In each specific problem where these concepts are used, it is necessary to give them an operational definition*. Unless this is done, the theory may become meaningless.

The non-metricized dynamical concepts which we will use are fluidity, degree of freedom of social locomotion, permeability, tension, and vector. The application of such concepts to psychological fields where the psychological space is quasi-physical, i.e., where initial position and goal may be ordered to infinitely structured space (problems of mazes, circuitous routes, etc.), is quite obvious. For instance the permeability of an electrical grid as a barrier may be assigned an index figure on the basis of strength of electric shock. The strength of a vector towards the goal of a maze may be non-metrically indicated by hours of hunger. For this reason we will deal chiefly with examples of problems where initial position and goal are not so easily defined.

* In original publication.—Ed.

Fluidity. By the degree of fluidity of a medium is meant the ease of locomotion in the medium.[18] Ease of locomotion depends not only on the fluidity of the medium, but also on the distribution of barriers in the medium and on internal psychological factors. It has meaning, however, to speak of the varying fluidity of psychological fields in themselves. For cases of actual physical locomotion it is quite obvious that *ceteris paribus* locomotion by walking across a street is in a more fluid medium than swimming a stream of equal breadth. We speak, however, of the fluidity of psychological fields which have no immediate physical correlate, and of the fluidity of social fields. Phenomenally one "moves about" more easily in daydreaming than in perceiving. Day dreams normally occur in a plane of lesser reality than perception and one is justified in assigning a greater fluidity to fields of lesser reality than to fields of greater reality.[19] Under such conditions fluidity may be operationally defined through the rate of diffuse discharge of tensions in the different fields. The memory for perceived acts and phantasied acts may be used for gaining an index-figure to designate the fluidity. If the tensions in both fields may be considered equal, then perception may be said to occur in a field of less fluidity than phantasy when more perceived acts are remembered than phantasied acts. It goes without saying that such experiments require regular serial variation, control of motivation and the other usual psychological controls.

Likewise social fields may be said to vary in fluidity where fluidity means the ease of social locomotion. One speaks popularly of "stiff" formal parties and compares these with "free" Bohemian ones. The formal party is to be ordered to a field of low fluidity, the Bohemian party is to be ordered to one of high fluidity.

Degree of freedom of social locomotion. By degree of freedom of social locomotion is meant the comparative number of directions in which social locomotion is possible. In a field having a high degree of freedom of social locomotion many locomotions are possible compared with a field having a low degree of such freedom. In general the degree of freedom of social locomotion varies inversely with the number of barriers within the field. The various social classes are to be ordered to fields of varying degrees of freedom of social locomotion. The bourgeoisie is to be ordered to a field of high degree of freedom of social

---

[18] Lewin uses fluidity in a somewhat different sense and believes that only under special conditions may the ease of locomotion be used as a criterion for fluidity.

[19] Cf. the experiments of Brown, of Dembo, and of Mahler, reported in Lewin (16).

locomotion, the petite bourgeoisie to a field of medium degree of freedom, and the proletariat to a field of low degree. Index figures may be
assigned to the degree of freedom of such fields on the basis of economic
and sociological statistics regarding income, consumption, education,
and the like. The various differences in degree of freedom of social
locomotion is indicated in Figure 6. There is a close co-ordination

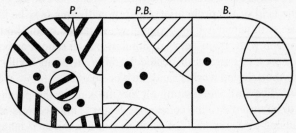

Figure 6

between the number of barriers and their permeability of which we
will next speak.

Permeability. By the degree of permeability of a barrier is meant the
ease with which locomotions are executed through the barrier. Here one
distinguishes between group- and inner-barriers. (Cf. above.)

The group-barrier of the Catholic Church may be said to be less
permeable than that of Protestant denominations. One can join most
Protestant sects by simply going to the meetings, whereas to obtain
membership-character in the Catholic region it is necessary to take
instruction, become baptized, etc. Operationally then we are quite
justified in saying that the barrier permeability of the Catholic Church
region is less than that of the Protestant. Figure 7 gives the dynamical

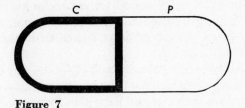

Figure 7

characterization of this situation. Differences in permeability will be
shown by thickness of boundary. Similarly one may speak of differences

in barrier permeability for other groups and define the concept operationally. The boundary separating nations might be assigned an index of permeability on the basis of immigration statistics, that separating class groups within a nation on the basis of income statistics, etc.

Inner-barriers, which represent impediments to locomotion within social field regions, likewise vary in their permeability. The barriers to which laws are ordered are more permeable in the field of the bourgeois than in the field of the proletariat. Operationally this may be indicated by the ease with which bail and council are obtained by the bourgeoisie in comparison with the proletariat. Similarly, such taboos as being late to work represent barriers of decidedly different permeability for the executive, the salaried worker, and the wage earner.

Vectors. The forces activating all locomotions in the psychological field are to be ordered to the concept of vector. These vectors represent forces causing psychological locomotion and are *directed* magnitudes. Their analogies in physical fields are the lines of field force within these fields. Such vectors, which represent forces, are to be indicated by arrows whose direction indicates the direction of the force, whose length represents its magnitude and whose point of application is at the point of the arrow. (Cf. Figure 1.) Vectors are also used to indicate locomotions as in Figures 2, 3, etc. Hence vectors represent the psychological force concepts. We say that the magnitude of vector varies directly with the ease of locomotion through fields and barriers of constant fluidity and permeability.

In all cases of actual physical locomotion vectors may be assigned index figures (though *not* measured) on the basis of hours of hunger, the strength of electric shock which will be suffered in attaining a definite goal, etc. Such procedures are so well known to experimental psychologists that further elucidation of them is unnecessary.

The assignation of "index-figures" for vectors for locomotions other than physical may be accomplished through the operational definition of tension in terms of memory index figures, or in the tendency to resume interrupted acts (16).

In the *social field,* the relative strength of vectors may be operationally defined through attainment or failure to attain membership-character in groups where the social goal lies within definite social regions or statistically through the outbreak of war, revolution or industrial strike.

v Hodological Space

Vectors are directed magnitudes and the problem arises as to the definition of direction in psychological fields. Lewin has recently attempted the mathematical solution of this problem, and has been able to show under what conditions direction of vectors may be defined and what the prerequisites to such definition are. The following lines give only his findings. For the mathematical deductions and proofs the reader must go to his original paper.

For physical locomotions where there is no barrier between the initial position and the goal, the problem of definition of direction raises no particular difficulties. Direction is a binary spatial relationship, which may be defined in Euclidean space by two points and their sequence. Hence the direction from point a to b of a Euclidean plane is given by the straight line joining them. The direction of the vector underlying physical locomotion, where there is no barrier lying in the line between the organism and the goal, is given by the straight line joining the organism and the goal. Hence a child walking towards a piece of candy in a room, is to be ordered to a field as in Figure 8. Such

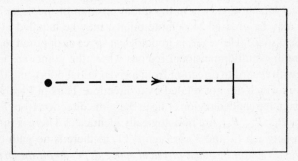

Figure 8

situations, however, are of little psychological interest and as soon as a barrier is imposed, the direction of the vector in quasi-physical space is more difficult of definition. Lewin introduces the concept hodological space (i.e., space of the path), and distinguishes between special and general hodological space. Special hodological space is space in which direction is defined by the initial differential of the distinctive path between two points in the space. By distinctive (ausgezeichnet) path Lewin means one distinguished through some dynamic criterion, such as being the shortest in time, space, energy expenditure, or, under other conditions, longest in time, etc. Consequently, if a barrier is placed between the child and the candy in the above example, the hodological direction is as given in Figure 9. The properties of such a space are immediately dependent on the psychobiological dynamics of the situa-

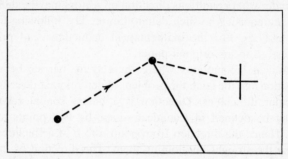

Figure 9

tion, because direction in it is definable only when these factors are taken into consideration. We saw above (Section II), however, that such a procedure is quite allowable in modern geometry. All problems of physical locomotion, where the initial position of the organism and the goal may be ordered to definite points, may be handled in special hodological space. However, in hodological space as opposed to Euclidean, there are multidimensional regions where the points are undifferentiated with regard to direction from a given initial point, and there are point-pairs which are not related by a direction. Thus in Figure 10, all the points in the shaded region A lie in the same direction from P_1. (The directions P_{12}, P_{13}, P_{14}, are hodologically identical.) There is further *no* direction between P_1 and P_2 in Figure 11, as there is no path between them. *The direction in quasi-physical space depends on the properties of the total field.*

When we attempt to define direction for problems where there is no direct correlated physical locomotion (problems in quasi-social and quasi-conceptual space) the difficulties which beset us are even greater. Physical space is usually infinitely structured (durchstruktuiert), while conceptual and social space in general only allow position to be topologically defined, i.e., they are structured, but not infinitely structured.[20] Consequently the paths in *general* hodological space are between topo-

[20] Cf. the distinctions structured, unstructured, infinitely structured, given above.

logical regions rather than between points. *Direction in general hodological space is defined as the step from the initial region to that contiguous region, which lies in the distinctive path to the goal.* In the example given above, of the freshman and the fraternity, the direction towards *C* can be defined through the locomotion *A* to *B*. The *direction* in general

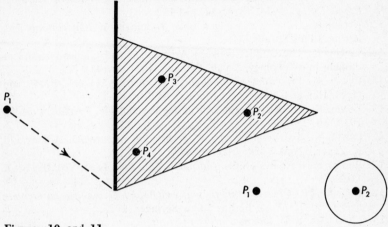

Figures 10 and **11**

hodological space is hence *relative* to the degree of structure of the psychological space. Lewin defines psychological space as a general hodological space. Consequently, the magnitude of our vectors may be defined in terms of an index-figure and its *direction* in terms of hodological space.

References

1. Brown, J. F. A methodological consideration of the problem of psychometrics. *Erkenntnis*, 1934, *4*, 46-61.
2. Brown, J. F. Freud and the scientific method. *Philos. Sci.*, 1934, *1*, 323-337.
3. Brown, J. F. Towards a theory of social dynamics. *J. soc. Psychol.*, 1935, *6*, 182-213.
4. Brown, J. F. and Fedar, D. D. Thorndike's theory of learning as Gestalt psychology. *Psychol. Bull.*, 1934, *31*, 426-437.
5. Campbell, N. R. *Physics: the elements*. Cambridge: Cambridge Univ. Press, 1920.
6. Carnap, R. Die physikalische Sprache als Universalsprache der Wissenschaft. *Erkenntnis*, 1931, *2*, 432-465.

7. Carnap, R. Psychologie in physikalischer Sprache. *Erkenntnis,* 1932, *3,* 107-142.
8. Fraenkel, A. *Einleitung in die Mengenlehre.* Berlin: Julius Springer, 1923.
9. Franklin, P. What is topology? *Philos. Sci.,* 1935, *2,* 39-47.
10. Heider, F. Ding und Medium. *Symposium,* 1926, 109, 110.
11. Hull, C. The concept of the habit family hierarchy and maze learning. *Psychol. Rev.,* 1934, *42,* 35-52, 134-152.
12. Kerékjártó, B. v. Vorlesungen über Topologie. I, *Flachentopologie.* Berlin: Julius Springer, 1923.
13. Lewin, K. The conflict between Aristotelian and Galilean modes of thought in psychology. *J. gen. Psychol.,* 1931, *5,* 141-177.
14. Lewin, K. *Principles of topological psychology.* (Trans. by F. and G. M. Heider.) New York: McGraw-Hill, 1936.
15. Lewin, K. Der Richtungsbegriff in der Psychologie. *Psychol. Forsch.,* 1934, *19,* 250-299.
16. Lewin, K. *A dynamic theory of personality.* (Trans. D. Adams and K. Zener.) New York: McGraw-Hill, 1935.
17. Poincaré, H. Analysis Situs, *Journal de l'Ec. Pol.,* 1895, Vol. II, Part I, 1-121.
18. Riemann, B. *Uber di Hypothesen, welche der Geometrie zu Grunde liegen.* Ed. H. Weyl. Berlin: Julius Springer, 1923.
19. Thorndike, E. L. *The measurement of intelligence.* New York: Teachers College, 1927.
20. Tolman, E. C. and Brunswik, E. The organism and the causal texture of the environment. *Psychol. Rev.,* 1935, *42,* 43-77.

16 PSYCHOPHYSICAL MEASUREMENT

Gustav Bergmann and Kenneth W. Spence

1 Introduction

The aim of this paper is to present a methodological analysis of some of the problems which arise in connection with psychophysical measurement and, incidentally, of certain allied aspects of psychology such as perception and psychological measurement in general. The discussion falls into three main parts. In the first section an attempt is made to

From G. Bergmann and K. W. Spence, The logic of psychophysical measurement, *Psychol. Rev.,* 1944, *51,* 1-24. Reprinted by permission of the authors, the *Psychological Review,* and the American Psychological Association.

indicate the manner in which scientific empiricism, the standpoint from which the present survey was undertaken, approaches these problems. Our exposition of this epistemological point of view must necessarily be restricted to a few very cursory remarks which have an immediate bearing on the problems at hand.[1]

The second section, which deals with physical measurement, cannot pass as a systematic exposition either. Its main purpose, again, has been to call attention to those points concerning physical measurement which must be understood in order to secure an adequate grasp of psychophysical measurement and of psychological measurement in general. Readers who find this second section difficult are referred to the elementary chapters on physical measurement which can be found in several introductory textbooks on logic and scientific method (7, 8, 9, 13). An interesting paper by Nagel (12) is on the intermediate level while the most elaborate analysis of physical measurement so far is due to Campbell (6).[2]

In the third and last part of the paper the particular problems of psychophysical measurement have been re-examined in the light of the points previously elaborated. Also included as a necessary background for this discussion is a sketch of the status of perception as conceived by the behavioristic psychologist.

II The Methodological Frame of Reference

1. Scientific empiricism does not hold to the view, rightly or wrongly associated with Watson's name, that so-called mentalistic or introspectionistic terms such as "sensation," "consciousness," "image," etc., are *necessarily* meaningless or that their referents do not exist. But scientific empiricism does hold that it is the methodological ideal of the sciences of behavior to use such mentalistic terms only after they have been introduced by (*operational*) *definitions from a physicalistic meaning basis*. The meaning of the italicized portion of this statement can probably best be made clear by first giving illustrations of concepts or terms employed in science which meet this criterion. Following this we shall attempt to elucidate further by means of certain simple instances.

---

[1] For a more complete and systematic account of scientific empiricism (logical positivism) the reader is referred to the writings of Carnap, Morris, and others, particularly to the monographs collected in the *International Encyclopedia of Unified Science* (21).

[2] The extent to which the methodological analysis of physical measurement has influenced psychology is best revealed in two papers, an earlier one by McGregor (11) and a recent analysis of mental tests as measuring instruments by Thomas (19).

Familiar examples of satisfactorily defined concepts are "weight," "mass," "electric conductivity," etc., in physics, and "I.Q.," "stimulus trace" (Hull) and "habit strength" (Hull) in psychology. The following paragraph may, for our immediate purpose, pass as an elucidation.

When mentalistic terms are introduced by (operational) definitions from a physicalistic meaning basis, then every statement which contains such terms can be tested by the *scientist's* observations (unquantified) and measurements (quantified) of physical objects. The following are three examples of sentences which express such basic observations and measurements of the scientist: "object A is green," "the pointer of instrument B coincides with the point a of its scale," "the density of object C is 3.57." The first of these statements is, in a certain sense, simpler than the second, because the confirmation of the latter involves the recognition of the instrument B and thus the confirmation of several statements like the first; again, the confirmation of the third presupposes the confirmation of such statements as the first and the second. The theory of physical measurement or, what amounts almost to the same thing, the operational analysis of physics, consists in the reduction in this manner of even the most abstract of its concepts or, as one also says, empirical constructs. Reduction of a concept thus involves indicating the classes of statements as "simple" as our first example, the verification of which is considered a confirmation of the statements in which the concept occurs.

2. Scientific empiricism holds to the position that all sciences, including psychology, deal with the same events, namely, the experiences or perceptions of the scientist himself. The behavior scientist who claims to study such perceptual behavior in his subjects is thus asked to start uncritically from his own perceptions; a piece of advice, the apparent circularity of which has continued to puzzle many of the more philosophically-minded psychologists. To them neither physicalism, a less sophisticated form of empiricism, which dogmatically outlaws all attempts to clarify the puzzle of this circularity by branding them as revivals of the old mind-body metaphysics, nor solipsism, the other, more traditional council of despair, is acceptable. Consequently the philosophical uneasiness thus created appears to find expression in a variety of quasi-metaphysical speculations.

In the schema outlined by the scientific empiricist the experiences of the observing scientist do indeed have a privileged, even unique position. If pressed too far and without the necessary epistemological sophistication, this account of the scientist's position can very easily lead to a metaphysical thesis of the solipsistic type. The fact of the matter is that science is always epistemologically dogmatic. Scientists, *qua* scientists, are usually not interested in such matters beyond receiving the philosopher's assurance that their methodological schema does not allow for any undesirable epistemological inferences. Nevertheless, attention may be called here to the re-examination of the mind-body issue offered by scientific empiricism (2). This re-examination tries, on the one hand, to overcome the dogmatism of *epistemological* physicalism, and on the other, to justify the *methodological* solipsism and physicalism of science. So far as the psychologist is concerned these remarks may be expressed in a somewhat different manner. They are to the effect that the empiricist scientist should realize that his behavior, symbolic or otherwise, does not lie on the same methodological level as the responses of his subjects, and consequently that he should not in reporting the latter use any mentalistic terms which have not been introduced from a physicalistic meaning basis. This latter fact may also be expressed by saying that all his terms should be behavioristically defined.

3. In the terminology now prevailing among empiricists the last point can be stated in the following way: In studying his subjects, including their symbolic responses (object language), the behavior scientist himself uses a different language (pragmatic metalanguage). That linguistic behavior can be utilized in operational definitions, even according to the most rigorous standards, is most generally recognized today. It is important in psychology, however, to distinguish between such utilization of symbolic responses of human *subjects* on the one hand and the use of responses of human *judges* on the other. Let us consider a schematically simplified example. Assume that a scientist calls a behavior fragment of a subject aggressive if 8 out of 10 judges apply this word to the behavior in question. In doing so our scientist has made use of what might be termed the *human yardstick* in the introduction of *his* term "aggressive." The latter lies in the scientist's metalanguage and must, therefore, be carefully distinguished from the judges' term which belongs to the object language. The remarkable statistical refinement which has recently been brought to bear on definitions of this kind has tended to overshadow the rather fundamental methodological difference between concepts introduced with and those introduced without the use of the human yardstick. If the latter are called *strict behavioristic terms,* one would have to say that the scientist of our illustration describes, in

strict behavioristic terms, not the behavior of his subjects, but rather the behavior of the group composed of his subjects *and* of his judges.

Since "behavioristic" has become an honorific label, it might be useful to add that the preceding remarks are not meant as a methodological criticism of correctly defined, but not strict behavioristic terms; they are merely a clarification of their peculiar status. The indispensability of such terms in present day clinical and social psychology is readily conceded. The clinician who applies mentalistic, not strictly introduced, terms to his patients is indeed the limiting case of the schematic situation; in this instance the single judge coincides with the observing scientist. There is, of course, no objection against calling all these procedures behavioristic, but then the word refers to nothing more precise than what is usually called the experimental attitude. And it is only fair to say that the theoretical psychologist as well as the empiricist philosopher are nowadays mainly interested in a behavior science which is behavioristic in the stricter sense (see below, IV 4 and V).

The bearing of these considerations upon some of the quantitative methods most widely used in psychology will become clear in the course of the discussion. And they raise also a question concerning psychophysical measurement proper. Does a human observer who discriminates, in one of the traditional situations, between, say, two pitches, serve as a judge or as a subject? The answer, it will be seen, depends upon which aspects of the psychophysical situation are emphasized.

III Physical Measurement

1. Some properties of and relations between physical objects or events are accessible to further differentiation. The meaning of this statement can only be illustrated. Loudness, hotness, length can be differentiated in this sense; the property "male" ("*X* is a male") and the relation "to-the-left of" ("*A* is to the left of *B*") cannot. Properties of physical objects or events which are amenable to such differentiation we shall call physical *dimensions*. Physical measurement consists in the assignment of numbers to the objects or events of a physical dimension in accordance with certain rules (laws and conventions). The result is a *scale*. The distinction between a physical dimension and any of the scales which have been developed to measure it, pedantic as it might seem, is necessary in order to avoid certain confusions which have arisen. For instance, in discussions on measurement a distinction has sometimes been made between intensive and extensive scales. It will be

shown that intensity and extensity are properties of dimensions and should not be used with reference to scales.

2. A dimension is said to be *intensive* if the following three conditions are fulfilled. *First,* that there exist two physical relations, designated by ">" and "=" respectively, so that the statements "$X > Y$" and "$X = Y$" are both meaningful, X and Y being any two objects or events which have the property that defines the dimension. *Second,* that these statements can be tested by the scientist's observations or *manipulations within the dimension.* The italicized clause will be explained presently (III 4). *Third,* that the two relations fulfill certain axioms, the so-called axioms of order (12, p. 315, 1-6). These axioms are empirical laws, i.e., whether they hold or not for any two physical relations is entirely a question of fact. Two of these axioms, the intuitive meaning of which is obvious, are given here for the purpose of illustration.

[1]   Either $X = Y$, or $X > Y$, or $Y > X$.

[2]   If $X \geq Y$, and $Y \geq Z$, then $X \geq Z$,

where X, Y, Z, are arbitrary objects or events of the dimension.

If these three conditions are fulfilled, then it is (in more than one way) possible to assign to each object or event X of the dimension a number designated by $N(X)$, so that

$$N(X) > N(Y) \quad \text{if and only if} \quad X \geq Y,$$
$$N(X) = N(Y) \quad \text{if and only if} \quad X = Y.$$

Here ">" and "=" are the usual arithmetical symbols. If such a co-ordination has been made then a rank order scale has been constructed for the dimension.

A dimension is called *extensive* if two additional conditions are fulfilled. *Fourth,* that there is a further physical operation within the dimension, designated by "$+$," which is of such a nature that if performed upon any two objects or events of the dimension, it results again in an object or event of the dimension. This latter object or event is designated by "$X + Y$." *Fifth,* this operation, too, is supposed to fulfill certain axioms (12, p. 315, 7-12).[3] Two of them, here given for the purpose of illustration, are

[3]   If $X = X'$ and $Y = Y'$, then $X + Y = X' + Y'$.

[4] $X + Y = Y + X$.

---

[3] It is not the purpose of this paper to examine the formal adequacy, independence, etc., of the set of axioms which Nagel takes over from the mathematician Hoelder.

Furthermore, in an extensive dimension it is always possible to assign the numbers to the objects in such a way that

(A) $N(X \underline{+} Y) = N(X) + N(Y)$.

Again "$=$" and "$+$" are the usual arithmetical symbols and are not to be confused with "$\underline{=}$," "$\underline{>}$," "$\underline{+}$," the names of physical relations and operations. A scale which has this property (A) is called *additive*. That is to say, extensive dimensions and, by the very nature of this definition, only extensive dimensions allow for the construction of additive scales.

Perhaps a simple illustration will show the value of this cumbersome terminology. Length, as is well known, is extensive and its usual scale is additive. If, however, one were to replace the numbers of our ordinary yardsticks by those of which they are the logarithms, the axioms of order and extensity would still be fulfilled, but instead of equation (A) one now has $N(X \underline{+} Y) = N(X).N(Y)$. The ordinary slide rule is another such non-additive length scale. This is one of the reasons why we distinguish between dimensions and scales, between extensity and additivity.

3. One of Campbell's and Nagel's examples (12) will be used to illustrate the next point.[4] The example deals with the density of liquids. This construct is so defined that liquid Y is said to be of greater density than liquid X if X floats on top of Y. (One of our simplifying assumptions is that the two liquids do not mix.) With this definition, density turns out to be an intensive dimension. The physical relation, "$X \underline{>} Y$," reads in this case "Y floats on top of X" and it will be observed that an operation "$\underline{+}$" cannot be found. Let us now attribute numbers, designated by $D(X)$, to this intensive dimension. As we know, this can be done in a great many different ways; the only requirement is that the greater ($\underline{>}$!) density gets the greater ($>$!) number. In actual practice, of course, density is not defined in this way, but as the quotient of weight (W) and volume (V). Let us designate this new "density" of a body X by a lower case symbol: $d(X) = W(X)/V(X)$. If one says that $d(X)$ and $D(X)$ are two different measures of the "same" construct one has reference to the following empirical laws:

$$d(X) > d(Y) \quad \text{if and only if} \quad D(X) > D(Y),$$
$$d(X) = d(Y) \quad \text{if and only if} \quad D(X) = D(Y).$$

[4] It must be borne in mind that all our illustrations are extremely simplified and not descriptions of practical working procedures.

Because of these empirical laws which obtain between the three dimensions, volume, weight, and density (D), one can use $d(X)$ instead of $D(X)$ as a scale of "density." If, in order to scale a dimension, one thus makes use of other dimensions and of the empirical laws obtaining between them and the dimension one wants to scale, then the resulting scale is called a *derived* scale. The usual temperature scale is another familiar instance of a derived scale for an intensive dimension, the extraneous dimension involved being volume, the empirical law used that of thermic expansion. By means of derived scales one can also quantify or "measure" dimensions which are not even intensive in the sense defined above, that is to say, where no physical relations *within the dimension* that fulfill the order axioms can be found.

4. We are now in a better position to elucidate the clause "manipulations (relations) within a dimension" to which attention was called above (III 2). Manipulations within a dimension do not involve utilization of any of the empirical laws which connect it with other dimensions. The manipulations, for instance, by which we compare the lengths of yardsticks and build their operational sum, "$+$," lie entirely within the dimension of length. That is to say, the empirical laws which make length an extensive dimension are the axioms of extensity, if the symbols "$=$," "$>$," "$+$" are read with the appropriate interpretations; e.g., "$X + Y$" reads "Take the stick Y and put one of its ends as close as possible to one end of the stick X, etc." And these laws have no reference to any other dimension.

It should be clear from the above discussion that only in the case of fundamental scales, i.e., those based on operations within the dimension, is inference as to the intensity or extensity of the dimension possible. Derived scales do not allow any such inference. To say the same thing still differently: A dimension is shown to be intensive or extensive respectively, if two or three operations, "$=$," "$>$," "$+$," within the dimension have been found and shown to fulfill the 6 or 12 axioms.

5. Everybody agrees that the customary density scale is preferable to an arbitrary rank order; that it is more convenient to measure time in seconds than by counting the heartbeats of a totem animal, to quote an illustration which Schlick was fond of using in his lectures. What, however, is the correct analysis of this situation? Is it because the one scale measures the *true* density; because any two seconds are *equal* while the intervals of a heartbeat are not? Or, to mention still another expression sometimes ambiguously used in this context, is it the case

that only one of the scales from which we can choose is *valid*? To the confusion surrounding these questions our attention must now be turned.

Consider the law of thermic expansion. Using the customary temperature scale this law can be formulated in the following manner: the volume of any substance is (within certain limits, approximately) a linear function of its temperature: $v_t = v_0(1 + c_X t)$. Let us call "L" this formulation of the law. Assume now that temperature has been scaled by an arbitrary rank order (R), so that, as we know but as the users of the scale do not know, $1R = 0°$ C., $2R = 1°$ C., $3R = 4°$ C., $4R = 17°$ C., etc. Designate, furthermore, by $c(X)_{1,2}$, $c(X)_{1,3}$, $c(X)_{1,4}$, etc., the percentual increase in volume (expansion coefficient) of the substance X between the temperature levels indicated by the indices. Experiments would then lead to the formulation of the following law (L_1): the expansion coefficients of any substance stand in the following relations: $c_{1,3} = 4c_{1,2}$, $c_{1,4} = 17c_{1,2}$, etc.

L_1 is of course the form which L would take if one works with our unusual rank order. One sees that L_1 is mathematically more complicated and less intuitive than L. This observation leads to the very core of the matter under discussion. We choose our scales so that certain empirical laws receive an expression as intuitive and (or) as mathematically simple as possible. It is an inaccurate and misleading way of speaking when such choice of scales is described as an attempt to equalize the unit distances of the scale. If there is a choice as to which law should be selected, then one usually picks that which one considers more "fundamental." But one must realize that "fundamental" is again but a figure of speech; those laws are fundamental which play or which we expect to play a prominent rôle in our ever-changing theoretical structure. If this structure changes or expands, then we frequently also change our scales. In the case of temperature, for instance, the mercury scale has been replaced by the gas scale and the latter, in turn, at least for theoretical purposes, by the entropy scale. Each of these steps marked a progress in the sense that the temperature scale became more directly linked to more and more fundamental laws within an expanding theoretical structure. But it is merely another figure of speech to describe these successive steps as approximations to a true or valid scale of temperature. In itself no scale is more valid than any other. It is hunting the will-o'-the-wisp to believe that such refinement as just described will ever make a scale additive. Additivity, as we have seen, cannot even be defined for nonextensive dimensions.

6. What, in general, is meant by the equality of any two units of a scale or, as one also says, by the equality of differences? An answer to this question has already been partially given in the preceding paragraphs; all that remains is to make it explicit and to supplement it by some concluding remarks. If a derived scale is built by utilizing an empirical law and if the assignment of numbers is made in a manner to give to this or another empirical law a mathematically simple expression, then the *numerical* identity of the differences between two pairs of scale points has *empirical* meaning. Sometimes, as in the case of the mercury scale for temperature or the usual time scale, this meaning is more or less intuitive, sometimes, as in the case of the entropy scale, the simplicity lies on the theoretical level. Always, however, the numerical equality of the differences between two pairs of scale points has exactly that much empirical meaning as has been put into the scale by taking account of empirical laws in attributing the numbers. There is no end to the possible refinements nor to the many quite different ways in which meaning can thus be given to a scale. But again it is very misleading if the search for such refinement, which is the search for empirical laws that could be formulated in any scale, is mistaken for the search for true or valid measurement; or, as happens to be the case in psychophysics, for the search for extensive or additive scales.

In the case of derived scales the empirical laws drawn upon are always of the form "$y = f(x)$," where "y" stands for the derived dimension to be scaled and "x" for one or several extraneous dimensions already scaled. There are, however, other ways to endow a scale and, in particular, the equality of the numerical differences with empirical meaning. This time we shall illustrate by means of the usual hardness scale which, as is well known, is an arbitrary attribution of the numbers 1 to 10 in an intensive dimension. Accordingly, there is no factual meaning in the statement that the hardness differences of two pairs of minerals with the numbers 8, 7; 3, 2, respectively, are equal. But let us now assume that we have ranked, with respect to hardness, all known minerals. Assume, furthermore, that there are altogether 901 of them, and that we rescale hardness so that the softest one gets the number 1, the 101 the number 2, and 201 the number 3, and so on. If such a scale is being used, is our statement about the four minerals (8, 7; 3, 2) still devoid of all factual meaning? Obviously not, for now it means that there are exactly as many minerals the hardness of which lies between those of the first pair as there are minerals the hardness of which lies between the second pair. There is admittedly not much point to this refinement, but the example has at least the virtue of simplicity.

A very common psychological scaling technique can be shown to rest upon exactly the same principles. Assume that a property is, in a statistically stable manner, distributed over a large population and that a percentile scale has been based, in the familiar fashion, upon the area under that curve. The question then arises as to what meaning can be attributed to the numerical equality of score differences, such as, let us say, between 60 and 50, and 25 and 15 respectively. Despite the opinion current among psychologists that this numerical equality does not signify "equality," it does have a well defined empirical meaning, namely this: in any fair sample the number of individuals between 60 and 50 is equal to the number of individuals between 25 and 15. The situation here is, in principle, the same as in our example of hardness. In every such instance some empirical law is used to endow the numerical equality of the differences between scale points with some kind of empirical meaning. In the case of the mercury scale for temperature the law drawn upon is the expansion formula, in the case of the percentile scale it is the (assumed) stability of some statistical distribution, normal or otherwise.

In this connection it might be worthwhile to call attention to the correct analysis of what is often thought of as the equality of sigma units (Z-scores, T-scores, etc.). That a certain concept is normally distributed is a significant empirical law about that concept and for theoretical reasons psychologists are often interested in defining concepts which are thus distributed. However, the translation of raw scores into sigma units amounts, technicalities apart, to nothing but the multiplication with a constant factor. There is no methodological reason for the privileged status which many contemporary psychologists attribute to such units. On this point our analysis is in essential agreement with that of Thomas (19).

Let us close this section by a remark with which the discussion of this point often starts. In extensional dimensions and only *in extensional dimensions, a factual meaning can be given to the equality of the numerical differences without drawing upon any other empirical laws than the axioms of measurement themselves.* The fact is that wherever there is an operation "$+$," there is, in all known instances, also an inverse operation "$-$," so that the two operations stand, loosely speaking, in the same relation as the two arithmetical symbols "$+$" and "$-$." And *if an additive scale is used,* then it is also true that

$$N(X) - N(Y) = N(X') - N(Y') \text{ if and only if}$$

$$X \underset{=}{-} Y \underset{=}{=} X' \underset{=}{-} Y'.$$

The "empirical equation" to the right expresses the empirical meaning of the numerical equality to the left. It is a corollary of the preceding analysis that the phrase "the units of a scale are equal by definition" is, to say the least, not very enlightening.

IV Psychophysical Measurement

1. Psychophysical measurement has traditionally dealt with the quantification of *attributes* (psychological dimensions). The neutral term "quantification" instead of "measurement" has been chosen purposely. *An attribute is not a property of physical events or objects, but is defined by means of the discriminatory responses to such objects or events on the part of observers who are different from the scientist.* Again, the term "observer" has been chosen because of its neutrality; at the present stage of the discussion it should not be identified with either the "subject" or the "judge" of an earlier section (II 3). The customary definitions of attributes are all based upon the verbal discriminations of human observers or, what amounts to the same, upon their motor responses in accordance with verbal instructions. Attributes such as pitch and loudness are thus actually defined by the consistent use of one and the same adjective and its comparative forms. It is important to notice that such responses, even if they are verbal, do not belong to the (pragmatic meta-) language of the scientist, but to the (object) language of the observers. By means of their utterances such as "equally loud" or "louder," the scientist introduces his empirical construct "loudness." To repeat the same thing in a slightly different form, one can also say that the operational basis for the introduction of an attribute includes that of the pertinent physical dimensions and, *in addition,* the observers and the procedures of eliciting their responses.[5] The situation is thus analogous to the one discussed with reference to the social psychologist's term "aggressive," and the observers take, in a certain sense, the place of the judges. But there is also an important difference which must not be overlooked. The ob-

---

[5] Attention should be called to the fact that by means of the conditioning technique attributes for nonarticulate observers can be defined.

servers respond to a physical dimension already scaled by physical measurement, while judges are employed where no working physical scale has yet been found.

These distinctions become particularly important if *numbers* or, rather, to adopt a convenient usage, *numerals* occur in the observer's responses, as in the method of fractionation where the observers are required to bisect or equipartition supraliminal intervals, or to adjust the variable stimulus to "half the given pitch" (17, 18). In using such numerical estimates of observers for the construction of scales one is *not* using numbers in the same sense and in the same way as one does in physical measurement.[6] One only creates confusion if he uses terms like "additivity" or "multiplicativity" in referring to such response scales. Furthermore, confusion is enhanced by the failure to distinguish between additivity of scales and extensionality of dimensions. There shall be occasion to return to this point (IV 5). The distinction between the use of numerical estimates by judges or observers, on the one hand, and the scientist's direct, strictly behaviorisitic use of numbers, on the other, applies of course also to scalings by means of equal appearing intervals outside the field of the so-called sensory discriminations.

2. If one were asked to condense into one sentence a characterization of most of the *nonphysiological* work done in psychophysics, he might venture the following formulation: By laying down the operational procedures (method of limits, constant stimuli, fractionation, etc.), psychophysics first defines the various sensory attributes and then studies the empirical laws that obtain between the responses on the one hand and the dimensions of the physical objects or events, to which these responses are made, on the other. For instance, the procedures of any of the existing methods which lead to the establishment of a j.n.d.-scale contain the (operational) definition of the attribute in question. The *Weber-Fechner curve* thus obtained is one of the empirical laws of psychophysics. And there is of course no a priori reason why, for instance, the curve of "constant-stimuli loudness" should coincide with that of "fractionation loudness."

The adoption of the convenient term "Weber-Fechner curve" re-

---

[6] As the terms are used in his paper, numbers belong to the scientist's meta-language, numerals to the object language used by the subject. This clarification also leads to the correct interpretation of the so-called *ratio scales,* mentioned by Boring (5, p. 52). It might at least be mentioned that an illegitimate fusion between these two ways in which "numbers" occur plays an important rôle in Ramsey's unsuccessful attempt to construct a theory of probability (1). See also the last paragraph of IV 5.

quires two clarifications. *First,* by this curve is meant the *empirical curve* representing the relationship between the quantification of an attribute, based on j.n.d.'s or any other procedure such as fractionation, on the one hand, and the pertinent physical dimensions on the other. Thus neither the logarithmic nor any other form of this empirical relationship is assumed. It would indeed be strange to make any a priori assumptions of this kind. *Second,* and in view of Stevens' results (15), the expression "curve" should be replaced by "polydimensional surface," for as this investigator has shown in some instances, one and the same attribute is, as a matter of fact, a function of several physical dimensions. Pitch, for instance, has been discovered to be a function of both frequency and energy. The classical view of a one-to-one correspondence between physical and psychological dimensions thus turned out to be an oversimplification. The theoretical significance of this finding needs no emphasis. But since this refinement does not affect the present argument and since dealing with surfaces would make our formulations unnecessarily cumbersome, we shall go on speaking about the Weber-Fechner curve.

3. Assume now that by one of the psychophysical methods a Weber-Fechner curve between, let us say, pitch and frequency has been established. If this curve is monotonous, as it actually is, then one can use what we shall refer to hereafter as the *psychological* scale of j.n.d.'s or mels (17) as a scale of the physical dimension frequency. Such a procedure, though not always fruitful, is entirely legitimate and its very possibility throws an interesting light on the nature of psychological scales. As has already been pointed out, such "psychological" measurement can also be considered as a rescaling of physical dimensions by means of observer responses. The Weber-Fechner curve is the mediating empirical law.

It is realized that what is here called a psychological scale is referred to as a psychophysical scale within the traditional field of psychophysics and as a psychological scale only in such instances as the scaling of attitudes, in which no independent physical measurement exists. So far as the instructions to the participating organism and its behavior are concerned, however, there is really no difference between the two cases. Furthermore, both have in common the fact that the experimenter is not interested in the response aspects themselves but rather in the stimulus dimension involved. The difference lies entirely in the circumstance that only in the traditional psychophysical case is there an independent physical scale of the stimulus dimension. In our discussion this difference is expressed by the distinction we make between the two terms "judge" and "observer."

It is also worthwhile noticing in this connection that the empirical content of the Weber-Fechner law consists in the functional connection between the physical dimension and certain response aspects within the chosen procedures such as the number of j.n.d.'s.[7] If one recalls that derived scales are established by means of mediating empirical laws between *two* independently defined *physical* dimensions, then it becomes clear that the scales of traditional psychophysics do not fall into this category. If interest lies in the stimulus aspect then they represent an additional (psychological) scaling of a (physical) dimension already scaled. When the response aspect is emphasized, then we refer to them as scaling an attribute or psychological dimension.

Within the general field of measurement the scales of psychophysics thus constitute a type of their own. Continuing our analysis with a view to describing further operational differences between these scales and physical measurement it is appropriate to elaborate once again the inapplicability to them of the two categories "intensive" and "extensive." Like "derived" these two terms apply only to physical dimensions and not to attributes.

Where indeed are the *scientist's operations upon observer responses* which would justify their use? We must confess to utter inability to think of any operation "$+$," which could be applied to the observers or to any of their responses which have so far been used for the introduction of attributes. Consider the case of loudness and assume even, contrary to fact (16), that the observers' judgments were "twice as loud" if two equal sound emitters, instead of one, are put into action. In this case "$+$" obviously means the simultaneous operation of the two sound emitting devices. What is thus operated upon is the physical dimension, not the attribute or the observer; and this in spite of the occurrence of numerals (ratios) in the observer reports. The same criticism holds true for the relation (operation) "$>$" or intensity, even if one were to use the term "operation" in a sense broad enough to include simply sensory discriminations. The fact would still remain that what falls, in a vague sense, into a serial order are the operations (dis-

[7] Accordingly, the only correct derivation of the Weber-Fechner formula is that which does not make use of differentials. Such a derivation is to be found in Woodworth's textbook (20, p. 435-437).

criminations) of the observer, not those of the scientist, and only upon those of the latter are the original definitions of intensity and extensity based. One could, of course, object that we are dealing with mere matters of definition. To this we would answer, *first,* that these definitions are not arbitrary—they formulate what actually happens in physical measurement; *second,* that the differences of actual procedure, upon which our analysis thus insists, are important matters of fact; and, *third,* that the very grasp of these operational differences has been hampered by the vague use of such terms as "intensive," "extensive," and "additive." It is even fair to say that understanding of the behavioristic frame of reference as a whole has suffered from this state of affairs. As was pointed out before (III 6) the failure to understand what is meant by the equality of units also contributed to the confusion.

4. If our analysis were to stop at this point, the reader would be justified in feeling that it suffers from a physicalistic bias. While it is correct that measurement in psychophysics *can* be considered simply as a regauging of physical dimensions by means of observer reactions, this is by no means the whole story of psychophysics. The psychologist is mainly, and properly so, interested in the *response aspects* of the phenomena. To this phase our attention must now turn, and it will be best to begin with some very general remarks.

Like every other scientist the psychologist is interested in discovering the empirical laws (functional connections) that obtain between the variables of his field. Unlike the physical sciences, however, behavior science at its present stage finds that its variables are divided into groups: on the one hand the so-called response variables (R), and on the other, the group of experimentally manipulated variables (S). The functional relationships the behavior scientist is looking for are typically of the form

$$[5] \qquad\qquad R = f(S).$$

While this is not the place to elaborate such a schema (3, 14), a few further remarks are necessary for the understanding of our last point concerning measurement and psychophysics in general.

(*a*) Neither S nor R is necessarily a single variable. They should rather be considered as representing groups of variables, so that S really stands for $S_1, S_2, \cdots S_n$, and R for $R_1, R_2, \cdots R_m$. The need for the introduction of such groups is particularly likely to arise on the side of the manipulated variables. Indeed, this is the comprehensible content of one of the main theses of the Gestalt writers.

(*b*) Both *S* and *R* are defined operationally by the scientist. The particular purpose of the investigation determines whether one single reflex (actone) or a relatively complex series of acts (action) is to be considered as one response variable and, likewise, which features of the physical environment are to be controlled or manipulated. That is to say, the choice of the descriptive units is entirely a matter of scientific expediency.

(*c*) *S* (stimulus!) always stands for a feature of the physical environment, *R* always for a behavior segment, but the psychologist is, by the nature of his material, forced to consider certain additional variables which fall into one of these two categories only *after they have been subjected to a certain amount of analysis*. These variables, let us call them *state variables*, fall again into different groups, such as motivation (*D*), and training or previous experience (*T*). There are, moreover, the variables representing possible innate individual differences (*I*), which fall neither into the *S* nor into the *R* category. At the present stage of psychological knowledge equation [5] would thus have to be expanded into

[6] $$R = f(S, T, D, I).$$

For our present purposes, however, equation [5] is sufficient, since it is characteristic of sensory discrimination (perception) that the response depends, within very broad limits, only upon clearly defined environmental variables (*S*). This feature could, indeed, be used in a behavioristic definition of what should reasonably be understood by perception. The extensive use of the term "perception," which the Gestalters advocate, makes it a weasel word that covers the whole of psychology only at the price of emptying it of any specific content. Historically speaking, this verbal preference is probably grounded in the intuitionistic philosophical background of the Gestalters.

(*d*) Many, and probably the theoretically most interesting, laws of contemporary psychology undoubtedly are of the forms [5] or [6] in which both stimulus and response variables occur. (The laws of physics would, in this terminology, appear as functional connections between *S*'s only.) But there is also a body of psychological knowledge which consists primarily of response correlations that can be symbolized by either of the two formulæ

[7] $$R_1 = f(R_2), \qquad F(R_1, R_2) = 0.$$

As a matter of fact any correlation between the scores on two different tests is of this type and so is much of our knowledge in the field of personality (correlation of traits). Most of the work of Lewin and his collaborators, if correctly analyzed, turns out to be concerned with $R - R$ laws and, since it lies in the field of human personality, freely uses the human yardstick (II 3). The theorizing of this group is largely a rationalization of these two features (the interest in $R - R$ laws and the use of the human yardstick) which, in themselves, are easily understood consequences of their specific research interests. Historically speaking, these preferences, too, seem to have grown out of the atmosphere which the students of Külpe, Meinong, and in the last analysis, Brentano created at the German universities.[8]

As a matter of historical fact we are often able to discover a response correlation $R_2 = f(R_1)$, when we do not yet know how to ascertain the corresponding stimulus-response relationships

$$[8] \qquad R_1 = f_1(S, \cdots) \quad \text{and} \quad R_2 = f_2(S, \cdots).$$

If, however, $R_1 = f_1(S)$ and $R_2 = f_2(S)$ are both known, then it is always possible to compute the response correlation. In order to do that one has but to solve one of the two equations, say the first one, and then substitute the solution into the second. Symbolically this might be indicated in the following manner:

$$[9] \qquad R_2 = f_2(f_1^{-1}(R_1)).$$

5. The last remarks lead us back to the problem at hand, namely, the response aspects of the scales of psychophysics. Assume that two pitch scales have been constructed by two different procedures, one for instance by the method of constant stimuli, the other by fractionation. As has been said before, there is no a priori reason to expect that any two such scales should stand in a particularly simple relationship.[9] We notice that the relationship between any two such scales is just an instance of the general relationship [9].

Consider now the empirical law, recently confirmed by Stevens and Volkmann (18), that an observer, instructed to "bisect" the interval

---

[8] Boring (5) has recently, with keen cultural sensitiveness, again called attention to these continuities.

[9] It can however be shown that any two scales obtained by the method of constant stimuli and the use of different percentage criteria are distinguished only by a multiplicative factor. This is a simple mathematical consequence of the way the j.n.d.'s are defined in this procedure (10).

between two given pitches P_1 and P_2 by adjusting a third tone so that it is "halfway between P_1 and P_2 in pitch," selects a tone P so that

$$[10] \qquad\qquad P - P_1 = P_2 - P.$$

where P, P_1 and $P_2 (P_2 > P_1)$ are the numbers of a j.n.d. scale. Obviously this law, though it is of the type [7] could be expressed by any scale whatsoever, either in frequencies or by means of still another response scale. It is true, though, that if one uses the j.n.d. scale, the mathematical form of the law takes a particularly simple form. So far the case is completely analogous to that of our earlier example concerning the specific heat of substances (III 5).

Response scales, it is true, offer further advantages in the way of stimulating certain lines of research. In the case under consideration they direct the psychologist's attention towards the relationships between thresholds and supraliminal discriminations. The shape of the functional relationship between a physical and a response scale might also suggest certain lines of physiological research or, to use Boring's (4) happy expression, help the scientist to "tap" the organism at the right place. But such expectations are, of course, purely pragmatic and have no bearing on the methodological analysis of measurement.

Another interesting result of Stevens' experimentation (16) is that what has just been said about pitch does not hold for loudness. In other words, the numbers on a j.n.d. scale for loudness are not proportional to the numbers on a scale constructed by means of the bisection procedure. The point to be made is that it is neither helpful nor enlightening to describe this state of affairs by saying that one can construct an "additive" scale for pitch, while there is no loudness scale which enjoys such mensurational excellence. Such disguise of interesting results as a search for scales cannot possibly be to the advantage of psychophysics. Furthermore, it has the drawback that it tends to blur the really important distinctions of a behavioristic analysis of measurement. In the case under consideration, for instance, the so-called "additivity" of the pitch scale is based on the use of numerals by the observer and this use is not clearly distinguished from the use of numbers by the scientist.

v Summary and Conclusion

The results of the present discussion can be summarized into three points. *First,* it tries to discourage the use of such terms as "intensive," "extensive," and "additive" with reference to scales in psychophysics.

Second, it sets up measurement in psychophysics as a technique in its own right which one cannot without violence subsume under any of the customary classifications of physical measurement. Because of this methodological independence the term "observer," different from both "judge" and "subject," has been consistently used throughout this section. So far as the response aspect of the scales is concerned, however, the observer acts really as a subject, while we have seen (IV 1) that as far as the rescaling aspect goes, his function is similar to that of a judge. *Third,* it points out the awkwardness of the fact that a field of research as significant as psychophysics has been disguised as a search for scales.

A concluding remark might help to forestall misunderstanding. No disparagement of the psychophysical scales is involved in their being set aside from physical measurement. Psychologists should indeed not rush into the use of physical terms if there is nothing else to be gained but a share in the prestige of the physical sciences. Behaviorism today is firmly enough established to make a more discriminating attitude completely compatible with our belief in the ultimate explanatory promise of the physiological level. The most fruitful expression of this belief at the present stage seems to us to emphasize the *theoretical* significance of the $S - R$ as opposed to the $R - R$ type of laws. On the other hand, it is methodologically perfectly conceivable to start the construction of science by measuring length and weight by means of observer-estimates, instead of with yardsticks and balances, provided only that the prescientific common sense level is once epistemologically secured. The actual excellence of physical measurement is entirely a matter of fact.

References

1. Bergmann, G. The logic of probability. *Amer. J. Physics,* 1942, *9,* 263-272.
2. Bergmann, G. An empiricist schema of the psychophysical problem. *Phil. Sci.,* 1942, *9,* 72-91.
3. Bergmann, G. and Spence, K. W. Operationism and theory in psychology. *Psychol. Rev.,* 1941, *48,* 1-14. [Selection No. 3 in this volume.]
4. Boring, E. G. A psychological function is the relation of successive differentiations of events in the organism. *Psychol. Rev.,* 1937, *44,* 445-461.
5. Boring, E. G. *Sensation and perception in the history of experimental psychology.* New York: Harcourt, Brace, 1942.
6. Campbell, N. R. *Physics: the elements.* Cambridge: Cambridge Univ. Press, 1920.

7. Campbell, N. R. *What is science?* London: Methuen, 1921.
8. Carnap, R. *Physikalische Begriffsbildung.* Karlsruhe: B. Braun, 1926.
9. Cohen, M. R. and Nagel, E. *An introduction to logic and scientific method.* New York: Harcourt, Brace, 1934.
10. Egan, J. P. The measurement of sensory dimensions. Unpublished Master's Thesis, State Univ. Iowa, 1940.
11. McGregor, D. Scientific measurement and psychology. *Psychol. Rev.,* 1935, *42,* 246-266.
12. Nagel, E. Measurement. *Erkenntnis,* 1930, *2,* 313-333.
13. Ramsperger, A. G. *Philosophies of science.* New York: Crofts, 1942.
14. Spence, K. W. Theoretical interpretations of learning. In F. A. Moss (ed.), *Comparative Psychology.* New York: Prentice-Hall, 1942 (rev. ed.).
15. Stevens, S. S. Volume and intensity of tones. *Amer. J. Psychol.,* 1934, *46,* 397-408.
16. Stevens, S. S. A scale for the measurement of a psychological magnitude: loudness. *Psychol. Rev.,* 1936, *43,* 405-416.
17. Stevens, S. S.; Volkmann, J. and Newman, E. B. A scale for the measurement of the psychological magnitude pitch. *J. acoust. Soc. Amer.,* 1937, *8,* 185-190.
18. Stevens, S. S. and Volkmann, J. The relation of pitch to frequency: a revised scale. *Amer. J. Psychol.,* 1940, *53,* 329-353.
19. Thomas, L. G. Mental tests as instruments of science. *Psychol. Monogr.,* 1942, *54,* No. 3.
20. Woodworth, R. S. *Experimental psychology.* New York: Holt, 1938.
21. *Int. Encycl. Unif. Sci.* (eds. O. Neurath, R. Carnap, C. W. Morris), Chicago: Univ. of Chicago Press, 1938–.

17 FACTOR ANALYSIS [1]

L. L. Thurstone

Factor analysis originated in an epoch-making paper by Spearman in 1904. Spearman probably saw important implications in that paper but it seems doubtful whether he could have realized at that time the super-

[1] Presidential address, American Psychological Association, Division on Evaluation and Measurement, Detroit, September 9, 1947.

From L. L. Thurstone, Psychological implications of factor analysis, *Amer. Psychol.,* 1948, *3,* 402-408. Pp. 402-406 reprinted by permission of the author, the *American Psychologist,* and the American Psychological Association.

structure that was to be built on his first observations on what he called hierarchy. For a quarter of a century the journals were full of controversy about Spearman's single-factor theory of intelligence. His hypothesis and his uni-dimensional methods were extended to the n-dimensional case in 1930. In the last seventeen years, multiple-factor analysis has seen a very fast development so that even in this short period there have been published several thousand papers on multiple-factor theory and experimental results.

Our purpose here is to review some psychological implications of multiple-factor analysis and to make only incidental reference to the factorial methods as such. It is time that we take stock more frequently of how the factorial methods are affecting psychological concepts, and how these in turn affect the development of appropriate factorial methods. It should be emphasized that factor analysis is a scientific method that must be adjusted to each problem. It is not merely a statistical method, and it is not a routine that can be applied fruitfully to every correlation table in sight.

In the light of a good deal of experience with the factorial methods, we should be able to give students a few practical suggestions. In the Psychometric Laboratory at Chicago, we spend more time in designing the experimental tests for a factor study than on all of the computational work, including the correlations, the factoring, and the analysis of the structure. If we have several hypotheses about postulated factors, we design and invent new tests which may be crucially differentiating between the several hypotheses. This is entirely a psychological job with no computing. It calls for as much psychological insight as we can gather among students and instructors. Frequently we find that we have guessed wrong, but occasionally the results are strikingly encouraging. I mention this aspect of factorial work in the hope of counteracting the rather general impression that factor analysis is all concerned with algebra and statistics. These should be our servants in the investigation of psychological ideas. If we have no psychological ideas, we are not likely to discover anything interesting because even if the factorial results are clear and clean, the interpretation must be as subjective as in any other scientific work.

Another hint for the student is that he usually tries to accomplish something too ambitious in his first factorial studies but that is also typical in the formulation of other thesis subjects. A factorial study is more likely to give convincing findings if it covers a restricted domain with only enough measures of known factorial composition to serve as a linkage between the factors that are already known and the factors that we hope to discover or isolate.

Most of the factorial studies that have been done so far have been concerned with the cognitive domain. Previous work had discovered a number of group factors such as the verbal, the numerical, and the visual. These were more clearly revealed by the more powerful multiple-factor methods. The further breakdown of the cognitive intellective functions into primary factors has revealed that the cognitive field represents a large number of functional unities or factors. We no longer speak of "the" verbal factor as if it were unitary. At least three verbal factors are known and several additional verbal factors are clearly indicated. One of these verbal factors has been denoted V and it represents facility in understanding verbal material. Another verbal factor has been denoted Word Fluency W and it represents facility in finding words to represent restricted context. A third verbal factor F represents ideational fluency with words. There is indication that a naming factor exists which is independent of the three that have been mentioned. In some forms of aphasia we seem to be dealing with patients who have one or more of these verbal factors intact while they are lacking in other verbal factors. Without understanding the differences between the several distinct verbal factors, one is at a loss to understand why the patient can do certain verbal tests while he fails on other verbal tests. This field should be experimentally investigated more intensively in the light of factorial results.

The ability to memorize has been found to be a primary factor that is independent of other cognitive functions. Incidental memory seems to be an ability that is distinct from the ability to memorize intentionally. There is good indication that auditory memory is not the same ability as visual memory.

One of the most important of the primary abilities is that of visualizing space which has been denoted the Space factor S. It is involved in all thinking about solid objects and flat objects in space.

The perceptual functions have been broken down into a number of distinct primary factors. Among the most interesting are those which represent facility in perceptual closure in which there are very large individual differences. Perceptual closure has been found in a battery of visual tests and also in a battery of twenty-eight auditory tests that were specially designed for factorial analysis. It is a curious circumstance that we do not yet know whether the closure factor in visual material is the same as the closure factor in auditory material. In order to solve that problem, it will be necessary to include both visual and auditory tests of closure in the same factorial analysis. It will then be interesting to ascertain whether perceptual closure is a primary factor that transcends the visual and auditory modalities. If so, then closure is a central factor that may be of considerable importance in the human intellect. On the other hand, it may be found that closure is represented by two or more factors that are specific for each modality. An extensive study of perceptual abilities has recently been carried out by Harold P. Bechtoldt.

It is not our purpose here to summarize all of the primary factors that have been identified but only to describe the general nature of these findings.

When we consider the increasing number of distinct functional unities into which the field of cognition is being divided, we find that it is necessary to revise very fundamentally our notions about general intelligence. Factorial results make it imperative that we describe each individual in terms of a profile of mental abilities instead of by a single index such as the I.Q.

With further progress in this field we shall have a profile for each person with a very large number of columns. It is our present belief that if we knew the twenty most important primary factors we should be able to undertake educational and vocational counseling with more confidence than at present. Even in the present state of knowledge with about ten of these factors identified, we certainly can do much better in appraising the intellective assets of a person than by the older methods by which each person was described in terms of a single I.Q.

Factorial work raises interesting questions about the general intellective factor of Spearman. According to his hypothesis, general intelligence is mediated by a central intellective factor which he denoted "g." This hypothesis has been the subject of much controversy in the last forty years. When the multiple-factor methods began to isolate quite a number of primary factors in the cognitive domain, it looked at first as if the Spearman single-factor hypothesis would have to be discarded but that does not seem to be necessary. It was found that the primary factors of cognition were positively correlated. For adults, most of these correlations are under + .30. When the positive correlations between the primary factors are examined factorially, there appear second-order factors, and the most conspicuous of these second-order factors agrees well with Spearman's hypothesis. Here we have a clue to an interpretation that may unify the early work of Spearman and the later work with multiple-factor analysis. The interpretation that seems plausible at this time is that the primary factors represent different kinds of mental facilities such as several kinds of memory, several kinds of perceptual closure, several visualizing factors, and several verbal factors. These primary abilities may be regarded as media for the expression of intellect and people differ markedly in the effectiveness with which they can express themselves in these different media. The second-order factors may represent parameters that are more central in character and more universal in the sense that they are not determined by the efficiency of each modality or imagery type. The first-order primary factors may be regarded as separate organs, in a general sense, while the second-order or general factors represent parameters which influence the activities of the several organs or primary factors. The general factors may then be expected to have no particular locus whereas some of the primary factors may eventually be rather definitely localized.

This attempt to unify Spearman's work with the later multiple-factor work seems to be plausible in terms of the findings of recent factorial studies but it should not be taken very literally. We can make only a tentative sketch of the underlying order at this early stage of knowledge of the organization of human intellect. If Spearman's general intellective factor is the same as the second-order inductive factor, then we can now determine that general factor uniquely. That is something which Spearman was never able to do. I have spoken of second-order factors in the plural. The reason is that we seldom find a single second-order general factor which would be indicated by Spearman's original hypothesis. Such complications are to be expected with the development of any science and it should not be interpreted as a discredit to Spearman's early work on which all of us have built.

In introducing our speculation about the relation of Spearman's general intellective factor "g" to later multiple-factor studies, we have noted that the primary factors are positively correlated. This also introduces a conflict between our statistical habits and psychological judgment. Some students of factorial theory bring to this subject their statistical habits and they sometimes insist that factors must be uncorrelated in order to be meaningful and useful. This is a curious situation. We deal all the time with meaningful measures that are correlated such as height and weight, but when we turn to the mental abilities, we are told that we must force them to be uncorrelated. Scientific judgment dictates that we report the correlations between primary factors as they are actually found, irrespective of statistical convenience. The correlated abilities are represented in factor analysis by oblique reference axes. That is not so convenient as a coordinate system in which all of the axes are at right angles.

Psychological studies of aptitudes frequently refer to such categories as mechanical aptitude, artistic aptitude, and musical aptitude. We shall describe briefly a current study of mechanical aptitude as an illustration of the psychological aspects of factorial analysis. It is rather common to hear mechanical aptitude referred to as if it were a single entity but it is our hypothesis that mechanical aptitude is a complex of abilities rather than a single unitary trait. It also seems plausible that we are dealing here with a rather restricted number of abilities. It is our job now to try to discover how many important abilities are involved in the complex known as mechanical aptitude and what those abilities are. Further, we make the hypothesis that mechanical aptitude is mostly in the head. It is not uncommon to hear this type of talent described as if it were in the finger tips, even associated with a certain amount of stupidity and a willingness to get one's hands dirty. In fact, it is rather common in the public schools to send the verbally slow learners into technical schools with the idea that if a boy is sufficiently stupid, he may become a good machinist. This is one of the educational blunders of our generation. It is our hypothesis that when a mechanic inspects a piece of machinery that is misbehaving, and when he diagnoses what is wrong with it, he is using his head and only incidentally his hands. Musical talent is also a complex that is not confined to finger dexterity. The psychological problem in the current study is to discover, if possible, what cognitive primary functions are involved in mechanical aptitude. If we could solve that problem, we might make a contribution of importance to education as well as to industry.

In the current study of this problem, we have made some tentative hypotheses which are in turn represented by differentiating tests that were specially designed for the purpose. One hypothesis which will almost certainly be sustained, as it has been in previous studies of this problem, is that mechanical aptitude consists in some large part of the space factor S, namely, the ability to think about objects in two-dimensional and in three-dimensional space. There are tremendous individual differences in this ability to visualize space, and in an educated audience we could find a fairly large proportion of individuals who, although otherwise gifted, are very poor in this ability. The tests by which this factor has been identified all involve the visualizing of objects that are stationary. In dealing with mechanical problems, one must be able to think of objects in motion. Their relative motions have definite restrictions that are studied in a separate discipline known as kinematics. We might therefore add another psychological hypothesis, namely, that there exist one or more abilities that are revealed in the ability to think about solid objects in motion as distinguished from thinking about them when they stay still. Another hypothesis about this group of aptitudes is that the ability to remember visual form has some part in mechanical aptitude. Still another hypothesis is that the perception of fine detail is involved. Perhaps one of the most fruitful hypotheses is that mechanical aptitude involves non-verbal reasoning.

When a list of hypotheses has been assembled, the next step is to invent a set of experimental tests which shall be crucially differentiating among the hypotheses. When that has been done, the tests are prepared and tried out for suitable time limits and performance instructions. Then they are given to several hundred individuals who are known to differ widely in mechanical aptitude. There is no need to represent the general population. In fact, it is wasteful to assemble a group of experimental subjects so as to represent the general middle range. It is better to include extremes of all available types in the experimental group. It will generally be found that all this work requires more time than the computational work that follows.

Similar studies should be undertaken in the fields of artistic aptitude and of musical aptitude in the hope of determining the dimensionalities of these fields. It has been our experience that no domain is completely determined in a single factor study because every study raises more psychological problems than it answers, but this is the natural course of science.

When a factorial analysis has been completed, one is tempted to try to interpret all of the common variance in terms of common factors, but it usually happens that some of the factors are indeterminate while some of them are clear and easily interpreted. It should be pointed out that a factorial study can make a major scientific contribution to our understanding of mind, even if it does not attempt to identify all of the common factors clearly. An important contribution can be made even if only one new factor is isolated and psychologically described even if all of the rest of the variance remains an unknown muddle. Such results depend on the structure that happens to be found in the factorial battery that is assembled to represent a domain, and every factor study is in this sense a gamble.

The inheritance of mental abilities has been investigated on 150 pairs of identical and fraternal twins. They were given forty psychological tests, including both group tests and individual performance tests. It was found that the identical twins were more nearly alike than the fraternal twins. Their differences were especially marked in the visualizing factors. It was found that spelling ability was one of the most conspicuous in differentiating the identical from the fraternal twins. The ability to learn spelling seems to be quite independent of most other abilities and it should be investigated to determine its relations to the primary factors.

One of the most important implications of factorial work is the breakdown of the line of demarcation between intellect and temperament. It is becoming increasingly evident that these two domains are not so completely separated as they have frequently been assumed to be. For example, the primary factors that identify perceptual closure are certainly cognitive in character and yet they seem to be definitely related to temperamental characteristics as well. In this connection the recent work of Dr. John G. Lynn is of special interest. He gave some tests of primary mental abilities to psychiatric patients and he noted in particular those patients who were relatively much better gifted in the space factor than in the verbal factors. He noted also the opposite extreme, namely, those patients who were much better gifted in the verbal factors than in the space factor. He found interesting differences in the symptoms of these two groups of patients. For example, he found that among the patients who were much higher in the space factor than in the verbal factors, there were no hallucinations. This field calls for very intensive study so that we may know more definitely the relations between the emotional symptoms and the relative strengths of the cognitive primary factors. Other studies of normal subjects have shown indication of temperamental differences between those who excel in the visualizing factors and those who excel in the verbal factors.

Factorial work is customarily based on experimental populations of several hundred subjects and the primary factors are isolated, ordinarily, on populations of normal subjects. I should like to suggest a parallel form of experimentation that should give results consistent with the factorial experiments. It is well known that among feeble-minded subjects we find occasionally conspicuous cases in which one or more abilities remain intact and even of superior quality while the subject is otherwise so poorly endowed mentally that he must have institutional care. I believe that significant studies could be made of single subjects in order to clarify our understanding of the primary mental abilities. For example, a single patient might be found who excels on a few similar tests while he fails hopelessly on the rest of them. Now, the investigator should alter slightly the several tests which the patient can do in order to determine just what characteristics must be retained in order for the patient to be able to do the task and just what characteristics of the test are associated with his failures. The investigator would have to try a large number of slight variations in the tests in order to be able to draw a sort of psychological map, as it were, to show just what the patient can do and what it is that he fails to do. If it can be assumed that one or a few of the abilities are intact in the patient, then we might be able to determine from the successive performances of a single patient just what each primary factor involved. The results should then be verified factorially by a study of normal subjects. I am calling attention to this type of inquiry in order to show again the intimate relations between factorial experiments and psychological hypotheses. We must not regard factor analysis merely as a toy for the statisticians to play with. It is a scientific method that should be useful in testing hypotheses in experimental, clinical, and social psychology.

18 OPERATIONAL ANALYSIS [1,2]

Douglas G. Ellson

1 The Source of the Problem

A considerable amount of research on the effects of the characteristics of the task on motor behavior was performed during the recent war and interest in this field has persisted in many psychological laboratories. Most of this work should be classed as applied psychological research. It was stimulated largely by requests for data from engineers and designers of military, aviation, and other types of complex equipment which require highly skilled human operators. Very few of their questions concerning details of motor behavior could be answered on the basis of research performed prior to 1940, but a considerable body of data has accumulated since, most of it not yet published in the general literature. The wartime research was chiefly designed to obtain immediate answers to specific problems in the design of equipment. It included the determination of the effects of such variables as size, shape, and location of control knobs; friction, damping, and inertia of controls; operating radii of controls; and gear ratios upon the accuracy and speed of control movements. Post-war research has been concerned with similar variables, but it has utilized laboratory apparatus which provided better control of conditions than was possible with the modified service equipment chiefly used during the war.

As might be expected in a relatively new area, most of this research

[1] The possibility and potential value of applying operational analysis and related methods used in the study of servo systems to human motor behavior was originally suggested to the writer by personnel of the Armament Laboratory, Air Materiel Command.

A major purpose of this paper is to provide a general theoretical introduction to a series of experiments soon to be reported from the Aviation Psychology Project, Indiana University. This work is being performed under Contract with Psychology Branch, Aero Medical Laboratory, Engineering Division, Air Materiel Command.

[2] I wish to express my appreciation for the cooperation of Dr. Gilbarg who made this article possible by clarifying my ideas concerning the mathematical aspects of operational analysis, and who wrote the appendix presenting the basic equations.

From D. G. Ellson, The application of operational analysis to human motor behavior, *Psychol. Rev.*, 1949, 56, 9-17. Reprinted by permission of the author, the *Psychological Review*, and the American Psychological Association.

has been exploratory. The effects of stimulus variables (in this case, existing or conceivable design characteristics of machines) upon response characteristics (accuracy, speed, frequency, latency of movements, etc.) were investigated sometimes systematically, sometimes on the basis of more or less inspired hunches. In some cases data obtained in different experimental situations are supplemental; in other cases there is little indication of what factors determine apparently contradictory results. One investigation may indicate that increasing the radius of a crank produces greater accuracy in tracking. Another investigation indicates the reverse, but the differences in the two situations which may reconcile these two results are not apparent. When such contradictions exist, it is obviously impossible to predict the effect of a given variable in a new situation. A theoretical formulation is needed which will integrate the available data and indicate what variables are significant, but, so far, psychologists have not produced such a theory. Learning theory is too broad to be useful in this case since it has been concerned primarily with factors which determine the occurrence or nonoccurrence of a response and has not been extended to the details of response form which are important for the design of mechanical equipment.

II The Method of Operational Analysis

Although an adequate psychological theory has not been suggested, there is available a well worked out method of analyzing the characteristics of physical transmission systems which may be applicable to certain aspects of human motor behavior. This method, operational analysis, is widely used by engineers to predict the response of mechanical follow-up systems and electrical networks which are too complex to allow the computation of the performance of the whole from performances of individual components. In this and other ways this method represents a direct parallel in engineering of the behavioral approach in psychology. Its basic measurements are made on the input and output of a transmission system which correspond to the stimulus and response in a psychological organism. The relationships between input and output are the basic functions, and they may be investigated without reference to intervening mechanisms.

A simple example of a transmission system whose response to complex inputs may be predicted by means of operational analysis is a pendulum suspended from a support which can be moved horizontally.

Movement of the support provides an input; movement of the bob is the output. For a particular pendulum the movements of the bob resulting from movements of the support of any complexity can be predicted with great accuracy on the basis of a relatively simple set of measurements. These consist of a determination of the output—the amplitude of the output oscillations and their phase shift (usually lag behind the input)—when the input is a series of sine form movements of a wide range of frequencies. The basic principles involved in predicting the pendulum movements can be utilized successfully in predicting the response characteristics of such varied mechanical and electrical transmission systems as levers, vacuum tubes, amplifying networks and complex servo or booster systems such as those used to move control surfaces in airplanes and to compute gun leads.

Fundamentally the principles of operational analysis are simple. The basic problem, as illustrated in the pendulum example, is the prediction of the response of a transmission system to a given, usually complex, input. The prediction is made by adding the outputs which the system produces in response to all of the components of the given input. The procedure involved may be represented as follows:

$$\text{Input}_1 \longrightarrow \text{Output}_1$$
$$\text{Input}_2 \longrightarrow \text{Output}_2$$
$$\cdot$$
$$\cdot$$
$$\cdot$$
$$\text{Input}_n \longrightarrow \text{Output}_n$$
$$\text{Input}_x \longrightarrow \text{Output}_x$$

When (complex) $\text{Input}_x = \text{Input}_1 + \text{Input}_2 + \cdots \text{Input}_n$

Then: $\quad \text{Output}_x = \text{Output}_1 + \text{Output}_2 + \cdots \text{Output}_n$

The conditions which must be satisfied in order to apply operational analysis are:

Condition 1. In any given application or experimental test, the components of the complex input must be known.

Condition 2. The outputs of the transmission system produced separately by the simple inputs included as components of a complex input must be known.

Condition 3. The transmission system must be "linear." A linear system is defined as one in which the outputs produced by simple inputs are additive when these inputs are added as components of a complex input.

For purposes of operational analysis complex inputs are usually broken down into either step function components (illustrated in Figure 1) or sine wave components.

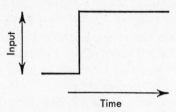

Figure 1 Diagrammatic presentation of a step-function input

It is possible mathematically to construct a single-dimension input of any complexity by adding (or integrating) either step functions or sine waves of suitable amplitude and time or phase relationship. Although it is possible to analyze inputs into other types of components, the step function and sine wave breakdown are more generally used since the mathematical procedures for handling them have been most completely developed. The term *frequency analysis* is applied to the type of operational analysis based on sine wave components. It is a highly developed analytical method used most widely with electrical circuits where the transmitted inputs are chiefly cyclical. Analysis by means of step function inputs may be more convenient experimentally when the complex inputs involved are slower or nonrepetitive as in DC circuits and in certain mechanical transmission systems. However, the basic conditions listed above must be satisfied in order to apply operational analysis with any type of input breakdown.

The first condition, knowledge of the components of the complex input, is required in making specific predictions of outputs either for practical purposes or for making tests of linearity. In an input synthesized for experimental purposes the components will ordinarily be known. In other cases it may be necessary to determine the components of a given input by means of mathematical analysis.

To satisfy condition two, it is necessary to provide inputs which are the components to be used in the analysis and to measure the resulting output when each input is presented separately. For frequency analysis these components are sine waves of a single frequency. Theoretically the response to all possible frequencies must be determined, but in practice it is necessary to use only a limited range of frequencies. If the resulting output is in sine wave form, the output characteristics measured are 1) output amplitude as a percentage of input amplitude, and 2) phase shift (usually a lag behind the input). For step function (transient) analysis a single step function is introduced into the input, and the output is measured as a function of time following the introduction of the step.

To satisfy the third condition, linearity of the transmission system, it must be shown that the output produced by superimposing two or more component inputs is equal to the sum of the outputs obtained with each component separately. This implies the experimental verification of the unqualified hypothesis that outputs are additive, and as such, absolute proof could not be obtained from any finite set of experiments. Furthermore, all transmission systems are linear only within limits. Consequently, the question becomes: within what limits and under what conditions is the system linear? Again, this question can be answered specifically only for inputs and other conditions which are tested experimentally. In practice, this means that linearity or its limits will be determined in a finite number of experiments sufficient to satisfy the requirements of the experimenter.

A simple test of linearity under obviously limited conditions is to double the input to a system, or to multiply it by a constant. In a linear system this will result in doubling the output or multiplying it by the given constant. More general tests of linearity will include (a) the determination of the input-output functions for a step-function input or for a wide range of single frequencies as required by condition one, (b) the presentation of a variety of complex inputs, and (c) a comparison of the resulting outputs with those predicted from the appropriate input components. For frequency analysis, a wave analyzer may be used to determine the components of the output and it may also be used to analyze the input if the complex input is not synthesized from controlled components.

III Uses of Operational Analysis in Human Engineering

Operational analysis is essentially a method of analyzing input-output functions of transmission systems designed to make possible the prediction of outputs when the input is known. One of its simplest applications is indicated in the pendulum example given above; the characteristics of the response to complex inputs is computed on the basis of empirical determinations of the response to a limited series of single-frequency sine form inputs. Similarly, the fidelity with which a radio amplifier system will reproduce the human voice can be determined by measuring its response to a sampling of single frequencies in the range of frequencies included in speech. It may be found that a certain band of frequencies is amplified relatively more than others, producing an unbalanced tone or emphasizing high frequency static. This may be corrected by adding a second transmission system in the input or output circuit—a second amplifier or a filter which counteracts the defects of the first amplifier by reducing the amplitude with which the overemphasized frequencies are transmitted.

If the response of a human "transmission system" is linear as defined above, then operational analysis may be utilized in order to design certain machines which are controlled by human operators. When a man operates a gunsight or controls the movements of an airplane or automobile, he may be considered as one transmission system component of a larger system which includes both the machine and its operator. If he over-responds or under-responds to certain frequency components of the input (the movement of the target or the path he is attempting to follow), this distortion may appear in his output (the movements by which he controls the machine).

As tracking errors or deviations from the path he is attempting to follow, these errors may have other effects. In operating the machine component of the total man-machine transmission system, the output of the man serves as input to the machine. If input frequencies distorted by the human operator are matched by similar distortions of the same frequencies by the machine he operates, then his tracking or control errors will be magnified. This condition has occurred in the operation of certain experimental computing sights: the operator's tracking errors were magnified by a factor of three or more in the output of the system. This was presumably due to a matching of the frequency characteristics of the machine and its human operators such that a phenomenon similar to resonance occurred. It is obviously desirable for designers of such machines to know the frequency characteristics of potential human operators. If these characteristics can be determined, it may not only be possible to avoid amplifying human errors, but the machine may be designed so as to "filter out" much of this error.

The example given above utilizes frequency analysis. There are many other applications of operational analysis in which a knowledge of the input-output functions of human transmission systems can be potentially used to stabilize the performance of a mechanism composed of a machine and its human operator (1).

IV Applicability of Operational Analysis to Human Motor Behavior

Operational analysis applied to human motor behavior has two aspects. As a method for predicting certain characteristics of the performance of human operators of machines, it is potentially a powerful tool in human engineering. As a set of assumptions concerning the relationships between certain stimulus and response characteristics, it is a limited psychological theory which must be verified experimentally. Fundamentally the difference is small. Both the practical and theoretical value of the application of operational analysis to human behavior depend on the agreement of its predictions with observed data.

The type of motor performance to which operational analysis is most obviously applicable is tracking or pursuit responses, either direct or compensatory. In this situation there is a specific stimulus or input and a specific response or output, both of which may be measured in terms of characteristics which are adapted to operational analysis. Since a human being, qualitatively at least, is considerably different from any existing machine or electrical circuit, there are many factors which must be considered in determining whether the attempt to apply operational analysis is worthwhile. The first reaction of many psychologists to the suggestion that operational analysis may be applicable at all to human behavior would be to expect failure. Human behavior, in general, appears extremely variable and the determination of stable relationships between a response and the characteristics of any single stimulus has been difficult. In operational analysis the characteristics of the response are predicted from the characteristics of a very limited part of the total situation which may be affecting the organism at the time. However, it is possible that in certain laboratory and practical situations tracking behavior may be sufficiently well isolated by means of instructions and training that distracting factors may be ignored. This question can be answered only on the basis of experimental evidence. There are experiments in several laboratories at various stages of completion but not yet published which indicate a very high degree of constancy in tracking performance. Consequently, it seems desirable to attempt to apply operational analysis to this limited type of behavior.

The first step in applying operational analysis to any transmission system is to determine whether the system is linear or the limits of its linearity. The general procedures for doing this are indicated above. They are the same whether the system is an electronic amplifier or a human being operating a steering wheel. Since the human being is obviously far more complex than any transmission system to which operational analysis has previously been applied, it will be necessary to test linearity for many variations of the complex input and in many different situations. The first question, of course, is whether the human being is linear in *any* situation. Although little research has been done which is specifically applicable to this question, there are many general observations which indicate that a human being has some characteristics of a linear system. Time-and-motion engineers, for example, use as a working hypothesis the assumption that within certain fairly wide limits the time required for a movement is constant regardless of its extent. We know from general observation and some experimental evidence that a human being can adjust his rate of movement in a pursuit task to match the rate of stimulus movement within fairly wide limits. Errors are variable rather than constant. In both of these examples multiplication of the input amplitude has the effect of multiplying the output by the same factors, indicating that in a general way the requirements for a linear system are satisfied.

Taylor, Walker and Householder (2) performed an experiment in which they presented subjects with step-function target displacements of varying amplitudes. This experiment represents one of the simplest tests of linearity which may be performed with any transmission system.

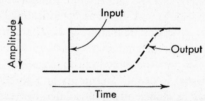

Figure 2 Response to a single step-function input

It uses the step-function as the basic input unit for operational analysis. The task is a direct pursuit problem in which the subject manipulates a stylus to follow a point which moves in one dimension. The response to an instantaneous movement of the point is shown schematically in Figure 2. A period of no response (reaction time) is followed by a movement, roughly sine form, with an amplitude approximately equal to the input movement.

Taylor and his co-workers report that "the data indicate an approximately linear increase in rate of correction with increase in magnitude of displacement," which indicates that under these conditions at least the human subjects act as linear systems. This is true since a step-function of large amplitude is in effect a "complex" input produced by adding step-functions of smaller amplitude. According to Taylor's statement, the addition of inputs results in a comparable addition of outputs as shown in Figure 3.

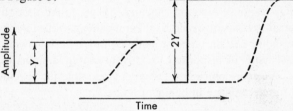

Figure 3 Change in response resulting from doubling the input amplitude

Tests of linearity under different conditions may be made by means of other complex inputs such as those shown in Figure 4.

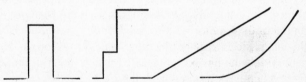

Figure 4 Complex inputs analyzable into step-function components

Experimental tests of linearity using complex inputs such as those shown in Figure 4 are in progress at Indiana University. Preliminary results indicate close agreement with the requirements of linearity.

If a human being acts as a linear system, it is quite possible that he may be a *different* linear system in different situations. This would mean that in a given situation, such as that presented in tracking by means of a hand wheel, his response to simple input components may be different from his response to the same simple input components in another situation, such as tracking by means of a lever, but that the output components obtained in each situation are additive in that situation. Another possibility is that the human transmission system, even though it may be linear, has different characteristics as a function of practice.

This is almost certainly the case, but at present we do not know whether the processes of learning involve a change in the way in which response components are combined or a change in the components themselves. If a definite answer to this practical problem can be obtained, it will be of considerable importance for a theory of motor learning.

Operational analysis will also be concerned with individual differences. The problem here is somewhat similar to one introduced by learning. Are the differences between individuals due to their being different non-linear systems, that is, systems which combine response components differently, or are they systems which combine different stimulus-response functions linearly? If it is found that all individuals are linear systems, it would be theoretically possible to construct selection tests for certain types of complex motor behavior on the basis of measurements of response to relatively simple stimulus input components. The score on such a test might resemble the specifications now given for electronic amplifiers.

v Summary

Recent development in military, aviation, and industrial equipment design has produced a need for specific information concerning characteristics of the motor behavior of the human operators of these machines. A considerable amount of research has been performed recently on the form of motor responses as a function of those characteristics of the task which are determined by design of machines. To date, no conceptual scheme has been presented which integrates the many isolated facts which have resulted from these experiments.

This paper calls attention to a method, *operational analysis,* which has been developed by mathematicians and engineers for the analysis of input-output relationships of electrical and mechanical transmission systems. This method, which permits the prediction of the response to complex inputs on the basis of a limited number of determinations of the response to simple input components is potentially applicable to certain aspects of human motor behavior. From a psychological point of view, the operational analysis method provides a ready-made, limited psychological theory which may be verified experimentally. The method is a direct parallel of the stimulus-response approach in psychology, which is concerned with the relationships between stimuli and responses rather than with intervening physiological mechanisms. Essentially it assumes that the motor response to complex changes in a stimulus input may be predicted from the addition or integration of responses of simpler components of this input. If this assumption is verified, aside from its value in application, it will provide a means for examining the nature of learning and individual differences in motor behavior.

References

1. MacColl, L. A. *Fundamental theory of servomechanisms.* New York: Van Nostrand, 1945.
2. Taylor, F. V.; Walker, R. Y. and Householder, A. S. Some aspects of eye-hand coordination in a simplified tracking situation. *Amer. Psychol.,* 1946, *1*, 282-283 (Abstr.).

Appendix

By David Gilbarg

The method of operational and frequency analysis described in the body of this report is based on certain mathematical facts which are roughly summarized as follows: If the response of a linear system to certain "elementary" stimuli or inputs is known, the response to any input, however complex, can be predicted. The purpose of this Appendix is to formulate these mathematical facts in a form in which they can be used for actual calculation.

Let a system, such as the human operator, transform an input function, $f(t)$, into the output, $g(t)$. For the purpose of brevity we shall state this symbolically in operational notation, $T(f(t)) = g(t)$, where T is the "operator" which transforms $f(t)$ into $g(t)$. The system is called *linear* if, for arbitrary inputs $f_1(t)$ and $f_2(t)$ and constants a, b,

[1] $$T(af_1 + bf_2) = aT(f_1) + bT(f_2) = ag_1 + bg_2$$

where $g_1(t)$, $g_2(t)$ are the outputs corresponding to $f_1(t)$, $f_2(t)$. We shall demand, in addition, of the linear system, that if $f(t, w)$ is a family of inputs depending on the parameter w (e.g., a family of sine waves, $\sin wt$, of different frequencies), then,

[2] $$T\left(\int_{w_1}^{w_2} a(w) f(t,w)dw\right) = \int_{w_1}^{w_2} a(w) T(f(t,w))dw = \int_{w_1}^{w_2} a(w)g(t,w)dw,$$

where $$T(f(t,w)) = g(t,w).$$

The two classes of "elementary" inputs most frequently used in analyzing linear systems are 1) the sine waves and 2) the step-functions. The analysis based on these two classes is discussed here.

Let $F(t)$ be an arbitrary input function. If $F(t)$ satisfies certain general mathematical conditions, it is possible to express it as an integral sum of sines and cosines by means of the Fourier integral theorem [3] as follows:

Let

$$a(w) = \frac{1}{\pi} \int_{-\infty}^{+\infty} F(x) \sin wx \, dx,$$

$$b(w) = \frac{1}{\pi} \int_{-\infty}^{+\infty} F(x) \cos wx \, dx;$$

then,

[3] $$F(t) = \int_0^\infty (a(w) \sin wt + b(w) \cos wt) dw.$$

It follows from the linearity of the operator, as expressed in equation [2], that

[4] $$T(F(t)) = \int_0^\infty (a(w) T(\sin wt) + b(w) T(\cos wt)) dw.$$

Thus, if the responses $T(\sin wt)$, $T(\cos wt)$ are known for every value of w, the output $T(F(t))$ can be calculated by means of this equation.

If $F(t)$ happens to be a periodic function of period τ, then the above method of the Fourier integral simplifies to analysis in terms of harmonic components. We have, in this case,[4]

[5] $$F(t) = a_0 + \sum_{n=1}^\infty \left(a_n \sin \frac{2\pi nt}{\tau} + b_n \cos \frac{2\pi nt}{\tau} \right),$$

$$a_n = \frac{2}{\tau} \int_{-\tau}^{+\tau} F(x) \sin \frac{2\pi nx}{\tau} \, dx,$$

$$b_n = \frac{2}{\tau} \int_{-\tau}^{+\tau} F(x) \cos \frac{2\pi nx}{\tau} \, dx; \qquad n = 1, 2, \cdots,$$

$$a_0 = \frac{1}{\tau} \int_{-\tau}^{+\tau} F(x) dx,$$

[3] See, for example, R. Courant, *Differential and integral calculus,* New York: Blackie & Son, 1937, Vol. 2, p. 318 ff.

[4] See, for example, R. Courant, *Differential and integral calculus,* New York: Blackie & Son, 1937, Vol. 1, p. 437 ff.

and the response to $F(t)$ is

$$[6] \quad T(F(t)) = T(a_0) + \sum_{n=1}^{\infty} \left(a_n T \left(\sin \frac{2\pi nt}{\tau} \right) + b_n T \left(\cos \frac{2\pi nt}{\tau} \right) \right).$$

Hence, if the outputs to all harmonics are known, the response to $F(t)$ can be calculated by means of this sum.

If the basis of the analysis is to be the response to step-functions, the procedure is as follows: Let $u(t)$ represent the unit step-function,

$$u(t) = 0, t < 0$$
$$= 1, t \geq 0.$$

Let $A(t) = T(u(t))$ be the response to the unit step input. It will be assumed that, if the step input is applied at $t = \tau$, the response is simply displaced by the amount τ, i.e., $T(u(t - \tau)) = A(t - \tau)$. Now consider any input function $F(t)$, then the response of the linear system is given by [5]

$$[7] \qquad T(F)(t)) = F(0)A(t) + \int_0^t \frac{dF(\tau)}{d\tau} A(t - \tau)d\tau.$$

Thus, if the response to the unit step function is known, the right hand side can be calculated for any input $F(t)$, and the output determined.

The formulas [3], [6], and [7] are the means of predicting the response of a linear system to any input, [3] and [6] using the response to sine waves as basis, and [7] the response to a step-function. The two methods are equivalent when they are both valid.

[5] See, for example, T. von Kármán and N. A. Biot, *Mathematical methods in engineering*, New York: McGraw-Hill, 1940, p. 403.

CHAPTER VIII

SPECIAL TECHNIQUES: FIELD-THEORETICAL

IN THIS CHAPTER consideration is given to three types of "field theory" which have been influential within recent years. In the first selection Kurt Lewin presents his interpretation of field theory, with special reference to the problem of temporal relations. Lewin's general systematic position represents a definite modification of the orthodox Gestalt system with which he was associated while at the University of Berlin. There he directed a series of very ingenious studies mainly during the late 1920's and laid the basis for the highly influential work that he subsequently did in this country, the culmination of which has been the important group dynamics movement. For further discussions of Lewinian field theory see the Selections by Spence (No. 4), Brunswik (No. 12), Brown (No. 15), and Lewin (No. 45). The second paper is by J. R. Kantor and provides a general presentation of his "interbehavioral" orientation, which may be considered a kind of behaviorism as well as a kind of field theory (although it is probable that such classifications would not be made by Kantor himself). In the final selection Donald Snygg offers a combination of phenomenology and field theory which has received considerable attention within recent years, especially within the clinical and applied areas of psychology.

19 THE NATURE OF FIELD THEORY [1]

Kurt Lewin

1 Field Theory and the Phase Space

The history of acceptance of new theories frequently shows the following steps: At first the new idea is treated as pure nonsense, not worth looking at. Then comes a time when a multitude of contradictory objections are raised, such as: the new theory is too fancy, or merely a new terminology; it is not fruitful, or simply wrong. Finally a state is reached when everyone seems to claim that he had always followed this theory. This usually marks the last state before general acceptance.

The increasing trend toward field theory in psychology is apparent in recent variations of psychoanalysis (Kardiner, Horney) and also within the theory of the conditioned reflex. This trend makes the clarification of the meaning of field theory only the more important, because, I am afraid, those psychologists who, like myself, have been in favor of field theory for many years have not been very successful in making the essence of this theory clear. The only excuse I know of is that this matter is not very simple. Physics and philosophy do not seem to have done much analytical work about the meaning of field theory that could be helpful to the psychologist. In addition, methods like field theory can really be understood and mastered only in the same way as methods in a handcraft, namely, by learning them through practice.

Hilgard and Marquis (7), in a recent publication, quote from a letter of Clark Hull the following sentence: "As I see it, the moment one expresses in any very general manner the various potentialities of behavior as dependent upon the simultaneous status of one or more variables, he has the substance of what is currently called field theory."

[1] This is the third paper given at a Symposium on Psychology and Scientific Method held as part of the Sixth International Congress for the Unity of Science, University of Chicago, September, 1941. The first paper is by Egon Brunswik and the second by C. L. Hull. [Selections No. 12 and 13 in this volume.—Ed.]

From K. Lewin, Defining the 'field at a given time,' *Psychol. Rev.,* 1943, *50,* 292-310. Reprinted by permission of the *Psychological Review* and the American Psychological Association.

It is correct that field theory emphasizes the importance of the fact that any event is a resultant of a multitude of factors. The recognition of the necessity of a fair representation of this multitude of interdependent factors is a step in the direction toward field theory. However, this does not suffice. Field theory is something more specific.

To use an illustration: Success in a certain sport may depend upon a combination of muscular strength, velocity of movement, ability to make quick decisions, and precise perception of direction and distance. A change in any one of these five variables might alter the result to a certain degree. One can represent these variables as five dimensions of a diagram. The resultant of any possible constellation of these factors for the amount of success can be marked as a point in the diagram. The totality of these points then is a diagrammatic representation of this dependence, in other words, of an empirical law.

Physics frequently makes use of such representation of a multitude of factors influencing an event. To each of certain properties, such as temperature, pressure, time, spacial position, one dimension is coordinated. Such a representation in physics is called "phase space." Such a phase space may have twenty dimensions if twenty factors have to be considered. A phase space is something definitely different from that three-dimensional "physical space" within which physical objects are moving. In the same way the psychological space, the life space or psychological field, in which psychological locomotion or structural changes take place, is something different from those diagrams where dimensions mean merely gradations of properties.

In discussing these questions with a leading theoretical physicist, we agreed that the recognition of a multitude of factors as determining an event, and even their representation as a phase space, does not presuppose field theory. In psychology, Thurstone's factor analysis deals with such relations of various factors. Any character profile recognizes the multitude of factors. Field theorists and non-field theorists can both avail themselves of these useful devices, but not everybody who uses them is therefore a field theorist.

What is field theory? Is it a kind of very general theory? If one proceeds in physics from a special law or theory (such as the law of the free-falling body) to more general theories (such as the Newtonian laws) or still more general theories (such as the equations of Maxwell), one does *not* finally come to field theory. In other words, field theory can hardly be called a theory in the usual sense.

This fact becomes still more apparent when we consider the relation between the correctness or incorrectness of a theory and its character as a field theory. A special theory in physics or psychology may be a field theory, but nevertheless wrong. On the other hand, a description of what Hans Feigl calls an "empirical theory on the lowest level" may be correct without being field theory (although I do not believe that a theory on the higher levels of constructs can be correct in psychology without being field theory).

Field theory, therefore, can hardly be called correct or incorrect in the same way as a theory in the usual sense of the term. *Field theory is probably best characterized as a method:* namely, a method *of analyzing causal relations and of building scientific constructs*. This method of analyzing causal relations can be expressed in the form of certain general statements about the "nature" of the conditions of change. To what degree such a statement has an "analytical" (logical, a priori) and to what degree it has an "empirical" character do not need to be discussed here.

II The Principle of Contemporaneity and the Effect of Past and Future

One of the basic statements of psychological field theory can be formulated as follows: Any behavior or any other change in a psychological field depends only upon the psychological field *at that time*.

This principle has been stressed by the field theorists from the beginning. It has been frequently misunderstood and interpreted to mean that field theorists are not interested in historical problems or in the effect of previous experiences. Nothing can be more mistaken. In fact, field theorists are most interested in developmental and historical problems and have certainly done their share to enlarge the temporal scope of the psychological experiment from that of the classical reaction-time experiment, which lasts only a few seconds, to experimental situations, which contain a systematically created history through hours or weeks.

If a clarification of the field theoretical principle of contemporaneity could be achieved, it would, I feel, be most helpful for an understanding among the various schools in psychology.

The meaning of this far-reaching principle can be expressed rather easily by referring to its application in classical physics.

A change at the point x in the physical world is customarily characterized as dx/dt; that is to say, as a differential change in the position of x during a differential time-period dt. Field theory states that the change dx/dt at the time t depends only on the situation S^t at the time t (Figure 1, p. 305).

[1]
$$\frac{dx}{dt} = F(S^t)$$

It does not depend, in addition, on past or future situations. In other words, the formula [1] is correct, but not the formula [1a].

[1a] $dx = F(S^t) + F^1(S^{t-1}) + \cdots + F^2(S^{t+1}) + \cdots$

Of course, there are cases in physics where one can state the relation between a change and a past situation S^{t-n} (where $t - n$ is a time not immediately preceding t; $|t-n| > dt$). In other words, there are occasions where it is technically possible to write:

[2]
$$\frac{dx}{dt} = F(S^{t-n})$$

However, that is possible only if it is known how the later situation S^t depends on the previous situation S^{t-n}; in other words, if the function F in the equation

[3]
$$S^t = F(S^{t-n})$$

is known. Such knowledge presupposes usually (a) that both situations are "closed systems" which are genidentic (11); (b) that the laws are known which deal with the change of all points of the previous situation S^{t-n} and also the laws dealing with the changes in the situations between the previous situation S^{t-n} and the later situation S.

The meaning of linking a change to a past situation by formula [2] might be clarified best by pointing out that it is possible in a similar way to link a present change to a future situation S^{t+n} and to write:

[2a]
$$\frac{dx}{dt} = F(S^{t+n})$$

This is possible whenever we have to deal with a "closed system" during the time-period t until $t + n$, and if the laws of the on-going changes during this period are known.

The possibility of writing this functional equation does not mean that the future situation S^{t+1} is conceived of as a "condition" of the present change dx/dt. In fact, the same dx/dt would occur if the closed system would be destroyed before the time $(t + n)$. In other words, the change dx/dt depends on the situation (S^t) at that time only (in line with formula [1]). The technical possibility of expressing this change mathematically as a function of a future or a past time does not change this fact.[2]

The equivalent to dx/dt in physics is the concept "behavior" in psychology, if we understand the term behavior to cover any change in the psychological field. The field theoretical principle of contemporaneity in psychology then means that the behavior b at the time t is a function of the situation S at the time t only (S is meant to include both the person and his psychological environment),

[4] $$b^t = F(S^t)$$

and not, in addition, a function of past or future situations S^{t-n} or S^{t+n} (Figure 2). Again, it is possible to relate the behavior b indirectly to either a past situation (S^{t-n}) or a future situation (S^{t+n}); but again, this can be done only if these situations are closed systems, and if changes in the intermediate periods can be accounted for by known laws. It seems that psychologists are increasingly aware of the importance of this formula.

III How to Determine the Properties of a Field at a Given Time

If one has to derive behavior from the situation at that time, a way has to be found to *determine* the character of the "situation at a given time." This determination implies a number of questions which are, I think, interesting both psychologically and philosophically.

To determine the properties of a present situation or—to use a medical terminology—to make a diagnosis, one can follow two different procedures: One may base one's statement on conclusions from history (*anamneses*), or one may use diagnostic *tests of the present*.

To use a simple example: I wish to know whether the floor of the attic is sufficiently strong to carry a certain weight. I might try to gain this knowledge by finding out what material was used when the house was built ten years ago. As I get reliable reports that good material has been used, and that the architect was a dependable man, I might conclude that the load probably would be safe. If I can find the original blueprints, I might be able to do some exact figuring and feel still more safe.

---

[2] Frequently an occurrence is said to be caused by the "preceding conditions." This term seems to have been misunderstood by psychologists to refer to a distant past situation (S^{t-n}), although it should refer to the present situation, or at least to the "immediately preceding situation" (S^{t-dt}). We will come back to this question.

Of course, there is always a chance that the workmen have actually not followed the blueprints, or that insects have weakened the woodwork, or that some rebuilding has been done during the last ten years. Therefore, I might decide to avoid these uncertain conclusions from past data and to determine the present strength of the floor by testing its strength now. Such a diagnostic test will not yield data which are absolutely certain; how reliable they are depends upon the quality of the available test and the carefulness of testing. However, the value of a present test is, from the point of view of methodology, superior to that of an *anamneses*. An *anamneses* includes logically two steps: namely, the testing of certain properties in the past (of the quality, size, and structure of the woodwork) and the proof that nothing unknown has interfered in the meantime; in other words, that we have to deal with a "closed system." Even if a system is left untouched by the outside, inner changes occur. Therefore, in addition, the laws governing these inner changes have to be known (see above) if the properties of a situation are to be determined through an *anamneses*.

Medicine, engineering, physics, biology are accustomed to use both methods, an inquiry into the past and a test of the present. But they prefer the latter whenever possible.[3]

Psychology has used diagnosis by *anamneses* rather excessively, particularly in classical psychoanalysis and other clinical approaches to problems of personality. Psychology of perception and psychology of memory have been relatively free from the historical type of diagnosis. Experimental psychology, on the whole, has shown a progressive trend toward testing the present situation.

The method of determining the properties of a situation (S^t) by testing them at that time t avoids the uncertainties of historical conclusions. It does not follow, however, that this method eliminates considerations of time-periods altogether. A "situation at a given time" actually does not refer to a moment without time extension, but to a certain time-period. This fact is of great theoretical and methodological

---

[3] There are cases where a historical procedure is preferable. For instance, the hunger of a rat can probably be better determined by the duration of starvation than by a physiological or psychological test of the hunger at the time t. This conclusion from the past to the present can be made, however, only during periods and in settings where a "closed system" (no interference from outside) can be enforced; e.g., for animals which during this period do the same amount of work, which have been on a known diet, etc. The difficulties of this type of control have led Skinner (19) to link the problem of drive strength to properties of present consumption.

importance for psychology.

It may be helpful to go back for a moment to the procedure in physics. If the vertical lines in Figure 1 represent the so-called physical "world-lines," a "situation" means a cut through these lines at a given time t. A description of such a situation has to include 1) the relative position of the parts of the field at that time; 2) the direction and the

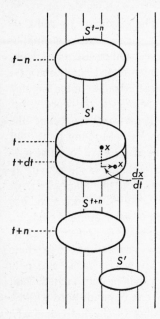

Figure 1 S during $t - n$ until $t + n$ is a "closed system"; but S is not genidentic with S'. dx/dt indicates the velocity of x.

velocity of the changes going on at that time. The first task is fulfilled by ascribing certain scalar values to the different entities; the second, by ascribing certain vectors to them. The second task contains a difficulty which I would like to discuss.

To describe the direction and velocity of a change going on at a given moment, it is necessary to refer to a certain period of events. Ideally, a time-differential should suffice for such determination. Actually, one has to observe a macroscopic time-interval or at least the position at the beginning and at the end of such interval to determine that time-differential. In the simplest case the velocity at a given time is assumed to equal the average velocity during that macroscopic time-interval. I will not attempt to follow up the details of this procedure in physics. If sufficient laws are known, certain indirect methods like those based on the Doppler effect permit different procedures.

However, it remains a basic fact that the adequate description of a situation at a moment is impossible without observation of a certain time-period. This observation has to be interpreted (according to the "most plausible" assumption and our knowledge of the physical laws) in a way which permits its transformation into a statement of the "state of affairs at the time t."

In psychology a similar problem exists. The person at a given time may be in the midst of saying "a." Actually such a statement implies already that a certain time-interval is observed. Otherwise, only a certain position of mouth and body could be recorded. Usually the psychologist will not be satisfied with such a characterization of the ongoing process. He likes to know whether this "a" belongs to the word "can" or "apple" or to what word it does belong. If the word was "can," the psychologist wants to know whether the person was going to say: "I cannot come back" or "I can stand on my head if I have to." The psychologist even likes to know whether the sentence is spoken to an intimate friend as a part of a conversation about personal plans for the future or whether this sentence is part of a political address and has the meaning of an attempt to retreat from an untenable political position.

In other words, an adequate psychological description of the character and the direction of an ongoing process can and has to be done on various microscopic and macroscopic levels. To each "size of a unit of behavior" a different "size of situation" can be coordinated. That the individual in our example is saying "a" can be made sure without taking into account much of the surrounding of the individual. To characterize the sentence as a part of a political retreat, much more of the surrounding has to be considered.

Without altering the principle of contemporaneity as one of the basic propositions of field theory, we have to realize that to determine the psychological direction and velocity of behavior (i.e., what is usually called the "meaning" of the psychological event), we have to take into account in psychology as in physics a certain time-period. The length of this period depends in psychology upon the scope of the situation. As a rule, the more macroscopic the situation is which has to be described the longer is the period which has to be observed to determine the direction and velocity of behavior at a given time (Figure 2).

In other words, we are dealing in psychology with "situational units" which have to be conceived of as having an extension in regard to their field dimensions and their time dimensions. If I am not mistaken, the problem of time-space-quanta, which is so important for modern quantum theory in physics (17), is methodologically parallel (al-

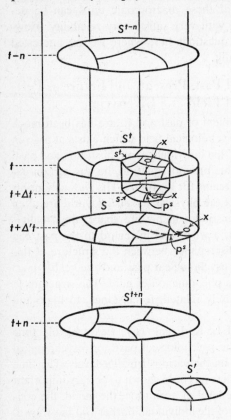

Figure 2 S during $t - n$ until $t + n$ is a "closed system"; but S is not genidentic with S'. $s^{t, t + \triangle t}$ is a small time-field-unit which extends over a relatively small area and includes the relatively small time-period t until $t + \triangle t$. $S^{t, t + \triangle' t}$ is a larger time-field-unit covering a larger area and including the longer period t until $t + \triangle' t$. p^s and p^S indicate the change in position of x during the small and large time unit.

though, of course, on a more advanced level) to the problem of "time-field-units" in psychology.

The concept of situations of different scope has proved to be very helpful in solving a number of otherwise rather puzzling problems. Tolman (20), Muenzinger (16), and Floyd Allport (1), have stressed that a psychological description has to include the macroscopic as well as the microscopic events. Barker, Dembo, and Lewin (2) distinguish and treat mathematically three sizes of units of processes and corresponding sizes of situations. They have handled certain problems of measuring the strength of frustration during extended periods by referring to overlapping situations in regard to two different sizes of time-field units. Lippitt and White (15), in their study of social atmosphere, distinguish still larger periods of events. They have shown that the beginning and end of these macroscopic units can be determined rather precisely and with very satisfactory reliability. However, I will not discuss these questions here where we are interested in methodological problems only.

IV The Psychological Past, Present, and Future as Parts of a Psychological Field at a Given Time

The clarification of the problem of past and future has been much delayed by the fact that the psychological field which exists at a given time contains also the views of that individual about his future and past. The individual sees not only his present situation; he has certain expectations, wishes, fears, daydreams for his future. His views about his own past and that of the rest of the physical and social world are often incorrect, but nevertheless constitute, in his life space, the "reality-level" of the past. In addition, a wish-level in regard to the past can frequently be observed. The discrepancy between the structure of this wish- or irreality-level of the psychological past and the reality-level plays an important role for the phenomenon of guilt. The structure of the psychological future is closely related, for instance, to hope and planning (2).

Following a terminology of L. K. Frank (6), we speak of "time perspective" which includes the psychological past and psychological future on the reality-level and on the various irreality-levels. The time perspective existing at a given time has been shown to be very important for many problems such as the level of aspiration, the mood, the constructiveness, and the initiative of the individual. Farber (4) has shown, for instance, that the amount of suffering of a prisoner depends more on his expectation in regard to his release, which may be five years ahead, than on the pleasantness or unpleasantness of his present occupation.

It is important to realize that the psychological past and the psychological future are simultaneous parts of the psychological field existing at a given time t. The time perspective is continually changing. According to field theory, any type of behavior depends upon the total field, including the time perspective at that time, but not, in addition, upon any past or future field and its time perspectives.

It may be illustrative to consider briefly from this field theoretical point of view the methodological problems connected with one of the basic concepts of the conditioned reflex theory, namely, the concept of "extinction." An individual has experienced that after a certain stimulus, let us say the ringing of a bell, food will appear. Being hungry, the individual eats. After a number of such experiences, the individual will show certain preparatory actions for eating as soon as the eating bell rings. The individual is then said to be "conditioned." Now, the situation is secretly changed by the experimenter and the eating bell is not followed by food. After a while the individual catches on and does not show the preparatory action for food when the bell rings. This process is called "extinction."

"Habits" of a person at a given time can and have to be treated as parts of the present field. Whether they should be represented partly as cognitive structure or resistance to change of cognitive structure, partly as a building up or fixation of valences (13), or whether they have to be conceptualized in other ways is not a problem here. Habits of action (18, 14), as well as of thinking, are dealt with in field theoretical research. They are closely related to problems of ideology (9) and expectation.

As Tolman (20), Hilgard and Marquis (7), and others have correctly pointed out, conditioning as well as extinction are both related to changes in the reality-level of the psychological future. Field theorists have to distinguish in regard to conditioning and extinction two types of problems. The one type deals with such a question as how expectation is affected by perception on the one hand, and memory on the other. What changes in the perceived structure of the psychological present lead to a change in the structure of the psychological future, and what are the laws governing the interdependence of these two parts of the psychological field? The studies on level of aspiration have provided some knowledge about the factors which influence the structure of the future reality-level. Korsch-Escalona (10) has made a step toward a mathematical treatment of the effect of the future reality-level on the forces which govern present behavior. Study of the level of aspiration has also given us considerable insight into the effect of the psychological past (namely of previous success or failure) on the psychological future. This question is obviously closely related to extinction.

The methodological position of these types of problems is clear: They deal with the interdependence of various parts of the psychological field existing at a given time t. In other words, they are legitimate field theoretical questions of the type $b^t = F(S^t)$.

The second type of questions, treated in the theory of conditioned reflex, tries to relate a later situation S^4 (for instance, during extinction) to a previous situation S^1 during learning or to a number of similar or different previous situations $S^1, S^2, S^3, \cdots$: it relates behavior to the number of repetitions. In other words, these questions have the form $b^t = F(S^{t-n})$ or $b^t = F(S^{t-n}, S^{t-m}, \cdots)$. Here field theory demands a more critical and more analytical type of thinking. One should distinguish at least two types of problems:

(a) How the perceived psychological situation will look at the time S^4 depends obviously upon whether or not the experimenter will provide food and on similar external physical or social conditions. Everybody will agree, I suppose, that these factors cannot possibly be derived from the psychological field of the individual at the previous time, even if all the psychological laws were known. These factors are alien to psychology.

(b) There remain, however, legitimate psychological questions in this second type of problem. We can keep the boundary conditions of a life space constant or change them in a known way during a certain period and investigate what would happen under those conditions. These problems lie definitely within the domain of psychology. An example is the problem of restructurization of memory traces. We know that these processes depend on the state of the individual during the total period S^{t-n} until S^t (Figure 2) and are different, for instance, during sleep and while being awake. Doubtless the experiments on conditioned reflex have given us a wealth of material in regard to this type of problem. They will have to be treated finally in the way which we discussed in the beginning, namely, as a sequence of relations between a situation S^t and the immediately following situation S^{t+dt}.

On the whole, I think the psychological trend is definitely going in this direction. For instance, the goal gradient theory has been formulated originally as a relation between behavior and past situations. Straight, analytical thinking demands that such a statement should be broken up into several propositions (12), one of which has to do with the intensity of goal striving as a function of the distance between individual and goal. This is identical with a statement about certain force fields and is probably correct. A second proposition implied in the goal gradient theory links the present behavior to the past situation S^{t-n}. The specific form is, to my mind, unsatisfactory. But even if it should be correct, it should be treated as an independent theory. Hull's formulation of a "Gradient of Reinforcement Hypothesis" is a step in this direction.

v Psychological Ecology

As an elaboration of our considerations, I would like to discuss some aspects of Brunswik's treatment of the role of statistics (3). I do not expect ever to live down the misunderstandings created by my attack on some ways in which statistics have been used in psychology. I have been always aware that quantitative measurement demands statistics (see Hull's answer to Brunswik [8]). That statement holds also for "pure cases"; i.e., situations where it is possible to link theory and observable facts in a definite way. Since psychology is increasingly abandoning the inadequate objectives of statistics, further discussion might have little pragmatic value.

However, Brunswik has brought into the open new and important aspects, and I feel that their clarification may be helpful for psychological methodology in general.

Within the realm of facts existing at a given time one can distinguish three areas in which changes are or might be of interest to psychology:

1. The "life space"; i.e., the person and the psychological environment as it exists for him. We usually have this field in mind if we refer to needs, motivation, mood, goals, anxiety, ideals.

2. A multitude of processes in the physical or social world, which do not affect the life space of the individual at that time.

3. A "boundary zone" of the life space: certain parts of the physical or social world do affect the state of the life space at that time. The process of perception, for instance, is intimately linked with this boundary zone because what is perceived is partly determined by the physical "stimuli"; i.e., that part of the physical world which affects the sensory organs at that time. Another process located in the boundary zone is the "execution" of an action.

Brunswik states correctly (3, p. 266): "The 'field' within which Lewin is able to predict, in the strict sense of the word, is the person in his life space." Then he proceeds, "But the life space is not to be confused with geographic environment of physical stimuli, nor with actually achieved results in the environment. It is post-perceptual, and pre-behavioral." This statement is partly incorrect, namely, insofar as perception and behavior, to my mind, are legitimate problems of psychology. This view is a necessary consequence of the field theoretical approach according to which the boundary conditions of a field are essential characteristics of that field. For instance, processes of perception which should be related to the boundary zone depend partly on the state of the inner part of the psychological field; i.e., upon the character of the person, his motivation, his cognitive structure, his way of perceiving, etc., partly on the "stimulus distribution" on the retina or other receptors as enforced by physical processes outside the organism. For the same reasons, the problems of physical or social action are legitimate parts of psychology proper.

Brunswik, however, is correct in assuming that I do not consider as a part of the psychological field at a given time those sections of the physical or social world which do not affect the life space of the person at that time. The food that lies behind doors at the end of a maze so that neither smell nor sight can reach it is not a part of the life space of the animal. In case the individual knows that food lies there this *knowledge,* of course, has to be represented in his life space, because this knowledge affects behavior. It is also necessary to take into account the subjective probability with which the individual views the present or future state of affairs because the degree of certainty of expectation also influences his behavior.

The principle of representing within the life space all that affects behavior at that time, but nothing else, prevents the inclusion of physical food which is not perceived. This food cannot possibly influence his behavior at that time under the conditions mentioned. Indeed, the individual will start his journey if he thinks the food is there even if it is actually not there, and he will not move toward the food which actually is at the end of the maze if he doesn't know it is there.

In the past this principle has not always been adhered to in animal psychology but it seems to me so obvious that I had assumed all psychologists agreed on this point. Statements which could be interpreted otherwise I had regarded as loose terminology rather than an expression of differences of opinion until I listened to Brunswik's paper. The discussion following this paper seems to have brought out the issue still more clearly and it will be appropriate, I hope, to refer to this discussion.

According to Brunswik, it is possible to think in terms of laws rather than mere statistical rules if one limits the psychological field in the way described. However, he claims that for this gain one has to pay "the price of an encapsulation" into a realm of problems which actually leaves out the most dynamic aspects of psychology. He wishes to include in the psychological field those parts of the physical and sociological world which, to my mind, have to be excluded. These parts, he states, have to be studied in a statistical way, and the probability of the occurrence of events calculated.

To my mind, the main issue is what the term "probability" refers to. Does Brunswik want to study the ideas of the driver of a car about the probability of being killed or does he want to study the accident statistics which tell the "objective probability" of such an event? If an individual sits in a room trusting that the ceiling will not come down, should only his "subjective probability" be taken into account for predicting behavior or should we also consider the "objective probability" of the ceiling's coming down as determined by the engineers? To my mind only the first has to be taken into account, but to my inquiry, Brunswik answered that he meant also the latter.

I can see why psychology should be interested even in those areas of the physical and social world which are not part of the life space or which do not affect its boundary zone at present. If one wishes to safeguard a child's education during the next years, if one wishes to predict in what situation an individual will find himself as a result of a certain action, one will have to calculate this future. Obviously, such forecast has to be based partly on statistical considerations about non-psychological data.

Theoretically, we can characterize this task as discovering what part of the physical or social world will determine during a given period the "boundary zone" of the life space. This task is worth the interest of the psychologists. I would suggest calling it "psychological ecology."

Some problems of the "life history" of an individual have their places here. The boundary conditions of the life space during long- as well as short-time periods depend partly on the action of the individual himself. To this degree they should be linked to the psychological dynamics of the life space. The rest of the calculation has to be done, however, with other than psychological means.

The essence of explaining or predicting any change in a certain area is the linkage of that change with the conditions of the field at that time. This basic principle makes the subjective probability of an event a part of the life space of that individual. But it excludes the objective probability of alien factors that cannot be derived from the life space.

References

1. Allport, F. H. Methods in the study of collective action phenomena. *J. soc. Psychol.*, SPSSI Bulletin, 1942, *15*, 165-185.

2. Barker, R. G.; Dembo, Tamara and Lewin, K. Frustration and regression; Studies in topological and vector psychology II. *Univ. Ia. Stud. Child Welf.*, 1941, *18*, 1-314.

3. Brunswik, E. Organismic achievement and environmental probability. *Psychol. Rev.*, 1943, *50*, 255-272. [Selection No. 12 in this volume.]

4. Farber, M. L. Imprisonment as a psychological situation. Unpublished Ph.D. Thesis, State Univ. Iowa, 1940.

5. Festinger, L. A theoretical interpretation of shifts in level of aspiration. *Psychol. Rev.*, 1942, *49*, 235-250.

6. Frank, L. K. Time perspectives. *J. soc. Phil.*, 1939, *4*, 293-312.

7. Hilgard, E. R. and Marquis, D. G. *Conditioning and learning.* New York: D. Appleton-Century, 1940.

8. Hull, C. L. The problem of intervening variables in molar behavior theory. *Psychol. Rev.*, 1943, *50*, 273-291. [Selection No. 13 in this volume.]

9. Kalhorn, J. Ideological differences among rural children. Unpublished Master's Thesis, State Univ. Iowa, 1941.

10. Korsch-Escalona, S. The effect of success and failure upon the level of aspiration and behavior in manic-depressive psychoses. *In* Lewin, K., Lippitt, R., and Korsch-Escalona, S., Studies in topological and vector psychology I. *Univ. Ia. Stud. Child Welf.*, 1939, *16*, No. 3, 199-303.

11. Lewin, K. Der *Begriff der Genese in Physik, Biologie und Entwicklungsgeschichte.* [The concept of genesis in physics, biology and theory of evolution.] Berlin: Julius Springer, 1922.

12. Lewin, K. The conceptual representation and the measurement of psychological forces. *Contr. psychol. Theor.*, 1938, *1*, No. 4.

13. Lewin, K. Field theory and learning. In *41st Yearb. Nat. Soc. Stud. of Educ.*, Part II, 1942.

14. Lewin, K. The relative effectiveness of a lecture method and a method of group decision for changing food habits. Committee on Food Habits, National Research Council, 1942.

15. Lippitt, R. An experimental study of the effect of democratic and authoritarian group atmospheres. *Univ. Ia. Stud. Child Welf.*, 1940, *16*, No. 3, 44-195.

16. Muenzinger, K. F. *Psychology: the science of behavior.* Denver: World Press, 1939.

17. Reichenbach, H. *From Copernicus to Einstein.* New York: Alliance Book Corp., New York Philosophical Library, 1942.

18. Schwarz, G. IV. Über Ruckfalligkeit bei Umge wohnung. I, II. [On relapses in re-learning.] *Psychol. Forsch.*, 1927, *9*, 86-158; 1933, *18*, 143-190.

19. Skinner, B. F. *The behavior of organisms.* New York: D. Appleton-Century, 1938.
20. Tolman, E. C. *Purposive behavior in animals and men.* New York: Century, 1932. [See Selection No. 29 in this volume.]

20 INTERBEHAVIORAL PSYCHOLOGY

J. R. Kantor

When the writer first planned the present work [1] some two decades ago, his intention was to indicate how psychology could approximate the status of a natural science. The basic need at that time seemed to be 1) the isolation and accurate investigation of distinctly psychological phenomena with 2) an appreciable freedom from the general cultural and specific traditions which had always hampered psychological progress. This need the writer regarded as satisfied by the organismic (interbehavioral) hypothesis.

A glance over the past twenty years reveals a gratifying development of psychology toward its natural science goal. Recent changes in the attitudes and interests of psychologists and the accumulation of many important facts make possible a gradual, if slow, departure from traditional dualism and an approach toward an organismic or interbehavioral [2] psychological position.

[1] This article was originally prepared as a preface for a projected reissue of my *Principles of Psychology* which have been out of print for some years. Because of the present unsettled condition of the learned world it seems hardly likely that this reissue will be feasible for some time to come. Accordingly, I am modifying the material of the preface into article form with the purpose of indicating some sharpening of construction and refinement of exposition which I should like to introduce into the Principles.

[2] Since the original publication of this work, the term *organismic,* which I used to characterize its viewpoint, has been employed to mark a position not in accord with mine. In consequence, though I do not for this reason altogether abandon the term, which I first introduced into psychology in an article on emotions in 1921 (4), I am very partial toward the term *interbehavioral* to distinguish the hypothesis of the present treatise.

From J. R. Kantor, Preface to interbehavioral psychology, *Psychol. Rec.,* 1942, *5,* 173-193. Pp. 173-181 reprinted by permission of the author and the Principia Press.

Scientific achievement is directly proportional to the scientist's departure from problems concerning general existence or reality and his approach toward an investigation of specific happenings. This principle applies to psychology equally with all the other sciences. Accordingly, psychologists may turn squarely away from the opinion held by the father of experimental psychology (8) that "psychology is an empirical science which deals not with a limited group of specific contents of experience, but with the immediate contents of all experience"—and instead occupy themselves exclusively with the investigation of the activities of organisms. This change of attitude is reflected in the increasing shift of interest away from sensation studies to those of conditioning and learning. Historically considered, sensation problems arose out of the psychologist's concern with the psychic structure of the universe, whereas learning problems indicate an interest in the way psychological organisms interbehave with their surroundings. Now there is no reason why studies on color, sound, and other quality discrimination should not be conducted by observing the interbehavior of organisms with things. But even when psychologists and physiologists shift toward this view, their hypotheses and interpretations plainly indicate that in this type of work venerable traditions still hold sway.

The tremendous number of experiments on animal conditioning, the intensive interest in learning, and the accurate record of child development all reveal a laudable scientific faith in specific psychological events. This faith is still better indicated by the employment of exact quantitative techniques for ascertaining the functional relations between animal behavior and topography, temperature, light, mechanical and chemical conditions, etc.

We do not mean to imply that these assiduous pursuits are all free from entangling assumptions. Unfortunately most interpretations of the findings on animal conditioning and learning are still influenced by traditional views concerning the primacy of the cerebral and other physiological factors. As a consequence, physiological findings—for example, correlations of the intensities of excitatory agents with excitation processes—are substituted for perceiving events which are entirely different in character. Despite the validity of such physiological data there is the serious danger here of unwittingly adopting the view that an accumulation of physiological facts will organize themselves into a significant psychological structure.

Again there is the belief that it is better to obtain quantitative data of whatever sort rather than find out all one can concerning an important event (1, 2, 3). Psychologists perhaps more than other scientists frequently forget that it is easier to make measurements than to know exactly what one is measuring. Our point, then, is not that the investigation of the behavior of organisms necessarily results in an adequate science, but rather that the momentum of data properly controlled can be directed toward such an end. For this reason we deem it still desirable to stress the interbehavioral hypothesis.

Interbehavioral Psychology and Current Science

Interbehavioral psychology, we believe, is in full accord with the present reorientation of science. This reorientation increasingly insists upon specificity of observation and interpretation, and emphasizes the place of the observer in an investigation. These newer scientific trends are well illustrated by 1) relativity theory, which teaches that observations and measurements depend upon a particular space-time reference frame instead of general absolute coordinates, 2) quantum mechanics, which allows for, if not based upon, the complementarity of phenomena, such that light under certain circumstances must be treated as a stream of corpuscles and under others as a train of waves, 3) the indeterminacy principle, which instructs us that the methods, instruments, and results of an investigation are inevitably bound up with the factors comprising a given event, so that in a given case only one or two factors— say, velocity or position—can be known, and 4) the Kant-Bridgman discrimination against meaningless questions, the consequence of which is that only such problems are considered valid as can be solved by observation and experiment—in short, concrete operations of the scientist. To these must be added 5) an equally cogent consideration— namely, scientific success is a definite function of the freedom from conventional bias with which the scientist approaches his field of operation (7). The last point does not, of course, imply that facts force themselves upon us independently of our hypotheses, instruments, and techniques, but rather that in specific situations we must ascertain whether we derive our results on the basis of conventional scientific prejudices or from our operations upon the crude data that set our problems for us. For example, when we test two individuals who consistently differ widely in their scores, are we discovering innate psychic powers or variations in brain structure or function, or are we obtaining an indication of a large number of functional relationships between an organism and all sorts of interacting conditions? Freedom from scientific bias means freedom to choose between as many available alternatives as possible.

Since interbehavioral psychology is committed to the principle that the subject matter of psychology is the interbehavior of organisms and objects under specific developmental and immediate conditions, it is directly in line with current scientific trends.[3] Interbehavioral psychology assumes that psychological science consists of the interbehavior of the investigator with the interbehavior of the observed organisms and their stimulational objects. Above all, such a view avoids all sorts of forces and powers assumed to bring about certain conditions. Described happenings are not only regarded as functional relationships of the components of a situation, but also depend upon the instruments and operations of the investigator.

Postulates for Psychological Science

Current scientific reorientation demands that all investigation and systematization be based upon definite and deliberate postulates. The following set of postulates which definitely formulate the interbehavioral principles contained in the present work are designed to summarize the main problems peculiar to present day psychological science.

1. *Psychology is homogeneous with other sciences.*

All sciences constitute investigative enterprises for the purpose of ascertaining the nature of specific events. Such events as come to the notice of scientists are reducible to things, their behavior, conditions and relations as these are analyzed out of the complex events. It is assumed that nature comprises an intricate manifold of events—fields in which things (particles, waves, organisms, etc.) operate in certain ways and change under certain specific conditions. Each science including psychology isolates some phase of this manifold for its special object of study. The data and methods of psychology are therefore homogeneous with those of all other sciences. Since scientific investigations and

---

[3] As the writer has indicated in the former Preface (5, p. xvi) it is this notion of the interbehavior of factors in a situation or system that differentiates the Galilean—that is, the modern scientific departure—from the Aristotelian doctrine of internal causes or principles.

techniques vary with the kind of subject matter operated upon, so psychological techniques of observation are in part similar to and in part different from those of other specific sciences. It is assumed here that all sciences are coordinate, none being more basic than any other. Whatever hierarchy of sciences one may set up can only be based upon quantity of achievement. All are natural and each is as fundamental as any other.

2. *Psychology is a relatively independent science.*

Although the fact that all sciences draw upon the same manifold of things and events implies that there is an interrelationship between all sciences, it is still true that they may be relatively independent of each other. Psychology having its own subject matter and accumulation of facts and principles cannot therefore borrow abstractions from any other science as its data. Whatever similarities there may be between psychology, physics, and biology result from a similarity in objects dealt with and techniques of study. Psychology, then, does not require any specific neural or general biological guarantee for the reality of its data.

3. *Psychology is interrelated with the social as well as biological and physical sciences.*

Since all sciences operate in a common field of natural phenomena it is inevitable that their data should overlap. Especially is this the case with psychology which studies events involving all sorts of physical, chemical and biological conditions. While the cooperation of the psychologist with the physicist and biologist in solving problems involving the responses of organisms to stimuli has always been recognized, the importance of social or cultural conditions influencing the origin and operation of psychological interbehavior remains still to be adequately appreciated.

The import of this postulate may be readily discerned by glancing at the prevailing present day ideas of psychologists with reference, for example, to the process of perception. In this field of psychological work there is an admirable orientation in and use of data from physics and biology. The result, however, is not so salutary. Descriptions of visual interbehavior with objects, for instance, certainly are reduced to effects of radiation on organic parts without regard to the actual character and properties of things.

In perceiving a common red brick psychologists assume that the individual is a neurobiological mechanism, whereas the brick is simply an absorber and reflector of light rays. Actually, the scientific constructions in psychology must be made against a background of cultural development and present circumstances of the individual and the object. How a brick is perceived, what it means to the individual, how he reacts to it, are functions of cultural as well as organic and physico-chemical events. So far as the brick is concerned it is just as much a factor in a cultural system as in a system of chemistry and physics. While the chemist and physicist may neglect its cultural properties, the psychologist can not do so.

It is not satisfactory justification to say that the neglect of the cultural features of events 1) brings psychological descriptions to the abstract and analytic level and 2) articulates psychology with physics and biology. In the first place, this view implies that constructions are ends in themselves and not simply tools for the orientation of the scientist to events. Again, there is the implication that psychological events need to be reduced to the events of other sciences. This latter point does not allow for the autonomy and worth of psychological events. And finally there is erroneously implied that the processes followed by physics and biology to obtain valid constructions are not available to students of cultural events.

4. *Crude data and constructions are continuous.*

Since all science consists of the development of descriptive and interpretative constructions, there must be a continuity between such constructions and the original events constituting the crude or preanalytic data. This means essentially that all constructions must be made upon the basis of investigative contacts of the scientist with the events which originally stimulate the interest in and work upon the problem. Thus, while constructions are different from the original data and are influenced by the instruments and hypotheses of the investigator, they are neither arbitrary nor simply impositions upon the events through the influence of traditions.

In describing or interpreting an event the worker cannot incorporate in his construction any factor not derived from an original operation upon data. For example, when a psychologist observes an organism discriminate a red from a green square, he cannot regard the color quality as a psychic or neural middle term between the stimulation—regarded as operation of light rays—and the response—considered as the operation of muscular processes. Such constructions are clearly influenced by historical traditions rather than by the investigative operations of science.

This postulate is designed to emphasize further that constructions should not only be derived from and made applicable to original events, but also that whenever it is necessary to build upon prior constructions such building must be carefully controlled. What is decidedly to be avoided is confusing the fact that the scientist constructs abstractions, descriptions, laws, etc., concerning events with the belief that the events themselves are constructs. True it is that interbehavior with events is conditioned by various prior interbehaviors, so that the events are approached with varying degrees of prior endowment, but this is no obstructing bar to carrying on investigations of the prepatinated events. An excellent psychological illustration of what must be guarded against is building psychological constructions out of prior biological (muscle action) and physical (energy) constructions as though these were pre-analytic investigative events.

5. *Interbehavior is the essential datum of psychology.*

The specific events which psychology investigates consist of the interactions of organisms with objects, events or other organisms and their specific qualities, properties, and relations. These interbehaviors, whether movements toward or away from things, manipulations of all sorts, speaking of them, or reflecting upon them are all concrete actions based upon observable events and in no sense manifestations of any occult powers or forces. Furthermore, none of the objects or their properties are psychic creations or projections of organisms or individuals. When the individual imagines or invents something, this also is an interbehavior—an interbehavior in this instance with substitute stimulus objects. Similarly, when the individual interbehaves with an object not on the basis of its natural properties, but on the basis of attributed properties, as in social psychological situations, we have a definite interbehaviorial situation. In other words, we have stimulus and response functions in a specific locus or field. When in any given instance we are unable to observe the details of the interbehavior, we can only assume, as in the case of every other science, that this incapacity is owing to nothing more than the intricacy of the phenomena or the ineffectiveness of our techniques.

6. *Psychological interbehavior comprises unique details.*

While all natural phenomena consist of interbehavior of various sorts, the specific details of such interbehavior vary considerably. Physical as compared with psychological interbehavior is commutative. The contacts of two physical objects (billiard ball impacts) can be described as a mathematically equivalent interchange of energies. In more complicated phenomena such as hysteresis in a magnetic field a similar interrelation obtains. Although the inductive behavior of a piece of iron varies on the basis of its previous history, so that, on the one hand, when it is completely unmagnetized it requires a higher magnetizing field strength to induce a given magnetization than if it had been previously magnetized, and, on the other, requires a coercive field strength in addition to the reversal of the original field to reduce its magnetic intensity to zero, the energy used up in alternately magnetizing and demagnetizing the iron is equivalent to the quantity of heat that appears in it. The whole phenomenon can after all be interpreted as the comparatively simple molecular rearrangement of the substances.

Because the biological organism is itself a complex of interrelated members with many energy interchanges of all sorts, the way an organism interacts with an object varies greatly from that of the interbehavior of two physical objects. The biological organism responds to a stimulus. The organismic system can store up energy and expend it in larger quantities and in forms which vary both from the stored up energy and the energy expended upon it. Again, since every organism is constructed on a complex plan of relatively variable and invariable structures, its movements and other performances are not only extremely intricate, but also significant from the standpoint of its environment. Hence an $E = E$ formula can hardly represent biological phenomena.

Since biological interbehavior is definitely conditioned by the structural organization of the individual the biological responses of organisms are specific and constant and may be described as physiological functions of anatomical structures. All the essentially biological events constitute changes for the maintenance of the individual throughout the variations and changes in its environment. Such responses may be symbolized by R←S which indicates that the organism is not inert, but sensitive to its surroundings and can be put into action by their stimulating influences.

Psychological organisms are at the same time biological organisms and physical objects. Hence their behavior comprises both physiological and physical processes. But while it is true that physical and physiological events participate in every psychological event, psychological interbehavior is not limited by the former. Naturally there is wide variation between psychological events. While the activities of the simpler organisms closely approach biological action, the interbehavior of human organisms is not strictly determined by the individual's biological organization or the natural properties of objects. Although all normal human organisms from a psychological standpoint are biologically equivalent, their activities vary widely according to their specific cultures. Psychological interbehavior may be symbolized as R$\longleftrightarrow$S to indicate that it is definitely spontaneous on the basis of previous interactions. Such interbehavior is explorative, manipulative, and orientative leading to the complex discriminating, knowing, liking, and choosing performances of human organisms.

7. *Psychological science is correlated with organismic biology.*

By contrast with the classical view that psychological (psychic) phenomena are processes correlated with particular organs (localization of function, etc.), interbehavioral psychology assumes that only the activities of the total organism participate in psychological events. Specifically this means that no organ is primary or in control of any other organ. Interbehavioral psychology does not attribute any greater importance to any one structure, whether it be a cerebral or glandular organ or a biological system, than to any other.

8. *Psychological phenomena are ontogenetic.*

A unique characteristic of specific psychological events is that they originate in the lifetime of particular individuals. Psychological phenomena evolve during the course of the interbehavior of the organism with specific stimulus objects. The particular ways in which individuals and their stimulus objects operate in given events depend upon the way they have previously interacted under definite conditions or auspices. This evolution of mentality may be regarded as a third stage following upon the organism's phylogenetic and ontogenetic biological developments (6).

References

1. Carr, H. A. The quest for constants. *Psychol. Rev.*, 1933, *40*, 514-532.
2. Carr, H. A. The search for certainty. *Psychol. Rev.*, 1937, *44*, 274-296.
3. Johnson, H. M. Some follies of "emancipated" psychology. *Psychol. Rev.*, 1932, *39*, 293-323.
4. Kantor, J. R. An attempt toward a naturalistic description of emotions. *Psychol. Rev.*, 1921, *28*, I and II, 19-42; 120-140.

5. Kantor, J. R. *Principles of psychology.* New York: Knopf, 1924 (Vol. I) and 1926 (Vol. II).
6. Kantor, J. R. The evolution of mind. *Psychol. Rev.,* 1935, *42,* 455-465.
7. Kantor, J. R. The operational principle in the physical and psychological sciences. *Psychol. Rec.,* 1938, *2,* 1-32.
8. Wundt, W. *Outlines of psychology.* Leipzig: Engelmann, 1907.

21   THE PHENOMENOLOGICAL FIELD

Donald Snygg

II * Inadequacy of the Objective Approach for Prediction of Human Behavior

Of the two possible points of view it is probable that most psychologists would prefer to use the objective approach because of its record of success in the physical sciences. It does not appear, however, that any observational approach is adequate at the present time to furnish the required principles for prediction. Whatever their possibilities for the future, attempted objective systems have up to now shared the defects of mixed systems by leaning heavily upon hypothetical loci of action or by requiring an unwieldy number of independent causal principles.

As viewed by outside observers, the behavior of living organisms varies even when the environment remains unchanged. This variability has been explained in the past by postulating mind as an unseen determiner of behavior. It is more frequently explained at present by assigning the same determining function to hypothetical changes in the organism, usually in the nervous system. If instruments can be invented which will make organic states more accessible to observation, the latter concept may prove to be a very fruitful one; but up to the present time both concepts have functioned almost exclusively as explanatory concepts, being relatively useless for prediction. Accurate prediction is possible only when the causal entities are open to inspection.

* Section I not reprinted here.—Ed.

From D. Snygg, The need for a phenomenological system of psychology, *Psychol. Rev.,* 1941, *48,* 404-424. Pp. 409-415 reprinted by permission of the author, the *Psychological Review,* and the American Psychological Association.

A tempting alternative to the use of unexplored causal fields is that adopted by the early behaviorists who attempted to refrain completely from causal inferences and to restrict themselves to data which could be objectively observed. Because of the notorious variability of animal behavior under objectively identical conditions such attempts to discover purely descriptive laws have not, however, been very successful. A common and necessary assumption of the objective way of search has been that the apparent irresponsibility of living organisms to physical causation is due to the gross character of the units studied. Further analysis, it is hoped, will show the parts of the organism functioning in ways predictable by an adequate physics. By withdrawing from the study of organismic behavior into the study of part behavior, of reflexes, or of S–R bonds, it is possible to maintain the concept of lawful causation of events and at the same time maintain the objective approach. This procedure, however, involves an indefinite multiplication of causal processes, with attendant confusion in prediction. Since it is possible to investigate the relation between an animal's behavior and any feature of a situation which can be experienced by the experimenter, present day objectivists are embarrassed by a plethora of causal factors. Buel(2) has reviewed eighty-three factors which have been found to affect the pathway chosen by a white rat approaching a point of bifurcation in a maze. He points out that the list is not exhaustive and the eighty-third factor is "chance." The hopelessness of using such a large number of independent principles as bases for accurate prediction is obvious.

The situation, then, is this: From the objective point of view, behavior which is not pertinent to the situation as viewed by the experimenter is random, indeterminate, fortuitous. To accept this indeterminism, however, as final would involve the abandonment of all hope for accurate prediction. Any science which hopes to predict must postulate lawfulness. Lawfulness in an objective system, however, can be maintained only by postulating additional causal agents unseen by the experimenter, as mind, past experience, instincts, or organic change. As long as these entities remain inaccessible to the experimenter they can be endowed with any necessary characteristics and are ideally suited to function as explanatory concepts. But, conversely, as long as these agents remain inaccessible the systems of which they are parts will have vital gaps in their causal fields with consequent inaccuracy in prediction. Since the unseen agents are usually invoked to explain individual variations in behavior, objective systems are apt to restrict themselves in practice to the prediction of normative behavior, concerning themselves chiefly with the establishment of norms and coefficients of correlation. This knowledge of what "most people," "the average individual," or "the typical three-year-old" is most likely to do in a given situation "other things being equal" is of little value, however, to the applied worker, the clinical psychologist, or the classroom teacher who must predict and control the specific behavior of particular individuals. If the analysis of this paper is correct, the accurate prediction of such specific individual behavior, from an objective point of view, will have to wait until one of the explanatory agents, most probably the physical organism, is laid open to observation by methods and instruments not yet devised.

Pending the perfection of these devices, it appears desirable that an attempt be made to explore the possibilities of the alternative point of view, that of the behaving organism. The remainder of this paper is devoted to a discussion of a phenomenological system that has been used with some success in predicting previously unobserved behavior (6, 7, 8). The discussion is restricted roughly to the field of learning, which is the most crucial to the problem of prediction.

The reader will bear in mind that the "facts" of such a system will necessarily conflict with those derived from the objective point of view and that the validity of any frame of reference must be judged, not by the degree to which its facts correspond to the facts derived from other approaches, but by its usefulness in prediction.

III The Characteristics of a Phenomenological System

1. *The basic postulates*. Assuming that the task of psychology is the prediction and control of behavior, a phenomenological system must rest upon three basic assumptions [1] and three principles.

A. All behavior is lawful. This is a necessary assumption of any system, since chance behavior would be unpredictable.

B. Behavior is completely determined by and pertinent to the phenomenological field of the behaving organism. By phenomenological field, hereafter abbreviated to p.f., is meant the universe, including himself, as experienced by the behaver at the moment.

C. There is some relationship between the phenomenological fields of different individuals. This is a necessary assumption, since control is impossible if one individual is unable to affect another's field. The

---

[1] The first assumption is common to all scientific systems, the second and third are matters of direct observation but impossible of proof.

locus of the relationship, usually presumed to be an underlying reality, is not open to observation.

D. Greater precision of behavior (learning) is concomitant with greater differentiation of the phenomenological field. Another characteristic of p.f's. is that they are fluid and shifting; their phenomena are continually reshaped and given new meanings by the character of the total configuration. Memories, for example, are strongly affected in this way (1). Maier (3) found that the crucial act of solutions was forgotten as soon as the solution was made; and Wees and Line (9) found that school children, in the act of reading a story, distorted its details in ways that made it more meaningful and pertinent to their own experiences. Since behavior is part of the field, taking part in the field's interaction, principle E is in some ways a restatement of the second postulate B.

E. The characteristics of the parts of the phenomenological field are determined by the character of the field itself. More specifically, the direction and degree of differentiation are determined by the phenomenological needs of the behaver.[2] The reader may find, for example, that in reading this paper he has been particularly aware of the points which substantiate his own views. The fundamental need in a phenomenological system appears to be the preservation of the organization and integrity of the p.f. and especially of that part of the field which is the phenomenal self, whence our tendency to remain unaware of, or to reject with emotion, data inconsistent with our own beliefs.[3]

F. Differentiation takes time. It follows from this principle that the way to accelerate learning is to arrange the situation so that the required differentiations are either more obvious or are unnecessary. For instance, in a black Warden multiple-U maze of the LRRRLLRLLR pattern which had been learned by a group of white rats in a median

---

[2] Both D and E invalidate introspection by the learner as a means of reconstructing his own field. Much of the field is too vague and undifferentiated (D) to be verbalized; and the need to observe and report may considerably alter the character of the field (E) and the nature of the problem.

[3] This recognition that the self we are trying to preserve is the phenomenal self, that is to say, is our own picture of ourselves, explains the need which various schools have described as drives for self-esteem, self-respect, security, status, superiority, power, or complacency. When self-preservation is thus referred to the phenomenal self, it is adequate for the explanation of suicide and martyrdom. These two forms of behavior have always been a source of difficulty from a systematic point of view. Objective systems have been forced to ignore them, along with other un-normal behavior, and mixed systems can include them only by postulation of independent motives conflicting with self-preservation, such as Menninger's death wish (4).

of 29 trials, the application of white paint to the critical 2, 5, 7, 8, and 10 sections, where changes in procedure were necessary, enabled an experimental group to learn the maze in a median of 12 trials (7). When the differentiation of individual sections from one another was made completely unnecessary by painting the blind alleys white and the correct pathway black, or vice versa, the median number of trials required for learning was lowered to 7 (6).

2. *The problem of prediction.* By postulate B the determining locus of action is the behaver's p.f. This is not open to direct observation by any outside observer. The process of prediction therefore involves two steps: 1) the securing of an understanding of the subject's field by inference or reconstruction, 2) the projection of the future field.

The first operation is of the common "Now why did he do that?" or "Under what circumstances would I have done that?" character. Much of the topological work of Lewin is of this type and essentially the same procedure was used by Shepard (5) when from the behavior of his rats he inferred the existence of floor cues which he himself was unable to experience. The teacher who hears his pupil report that 3×0 is 3 and infers that his reasoning is "Zero is nothing so it does nothing to the three" has taken this step. The operation acquires its validity in this system by the postulate (B) that behavior is completely determined by the p.f., whence it follows that variations in behavior are always indicative of concurrent variations in the field. The complete operation of prediction imposes two important conditions. To reconstruct an individual's field from his behavior it is necessary to have some idea what fields are like, and to project the future field it is necessary to understand how fields change.

3. *The nature of the field.* The p.f. is simply the world of naive, immediate experience in which each individual lives, the everyday situation of self and surroundings which the unsophisticated person takes to be real. Studies on the nature of this field indicate that all parts of the field are not equally distinct. The field consists of figure and ground, or focus and margin; there are not two definite, static levels, but one level may shade into the other so that the figure may be large and relatively indistinct or small and highly differentiated. Experience in any sense field can be figure. Pain, fatigue, or the disturbed organic states involved in emotion may emerge so sharply as the focus of the field, with all the rest of the field fading into the homogeneity of ground, that the individual will lose touch with his surroundings and become uncon-

scious. Since by postulate B behavior is completely determined by the p.f., a highly detailed and differentiated field will include definite and precise behavior, while, as anyone who has tried to find a snap switch in a strange room in the dark will agree, behavior in a vague and undifferentiated field is vague and confused. This leads to principle D.

4. *How fields change.* Principle D of our system identified differentiation with learning; principle E made the determinants of differentiation somewhat explicit. Differentiation may be defined as knowing a difference, the basic act of knowledge. It is the manifestation of the continuous process by which the integrity and organization of the field are maintained. "When an individual, rat or human, is confronted with a task . . . the general procedure is determined by his initial perception of the nature of the problem; it is a gross response to a relatively undifferentiated situation. Should the first procedure, the response to the gross situation, prove inadequate the task is differentiated perceptually into segments each of which is solved by simple procedures" (7).

Although he is aware that his own field may be affected (E) by his desire to maintain the predictive advantages of having only one process in the system, the writer feels that differentiation may be safely assumed to be the only process of change in the p.f. The emergence of a new entity or character into figure implies the lapse of other characters into ground. Both are necessary for the existence of a difference and are not two independent processes but complementary aspects of the same process, which might be called "change." Since, however, it is the newly emerged figure, the focus of the behaver's field, which is the most directly potent in determining behavior, it seems more practical to emphasize the more effective aspect of the process and call it "differentiation" or "individuation" rather than the nonvaluative "change."

References

1. Bartlett, F. C. *Remembering.* New York: Macmillan, 1932.
2. Buel, J. Differential errors in animal mazes. *Psychol. Bull.,* 1935, *32,* 67-99.
3. Maier, N. R. F. The behavior mechanisms concerned with problem solving. *Psychol. Rev.,* 1940, *47,* 43-58.
4. Menninger, K. A. *Man against himself.* New York: Harcourt, Brace, 1938.
5. Shepard, J. F. More about the floor cue. *Psychol. Bull.,* 1935, *32,* 696 (abstr.).

6. Snygg, D. The relative difficulty of mechanically equivalent tasks: II. Animal learning. *J. genet. Psychol.*, 1935, *47*, 321-336.

7. Snygg, D. Maze learning as perception. *J. genet. Psychol.*, 1936, *49*, 231-239.

8. Snygg, D. Mazes in which rats take the longer path to food. *J. Psychol.*, 1936, *1*, 153-166.

9. Wees, W. R. and Line, W. The influence of the form of a presentation upon reproduction: the principle of determination. *Brit. J. Psychol.* (Gen. Section), 1937, *28*, 167-189.

CHAPTER IX

SPECIAL TECHNIQUES: PSYCHOANALYTIC

THIS CHAPTER is concerned with certain methodological questions raised in connection with psychoanalytic theorizing. Although academic psychologists have been quick to criticize what they have considered to be certain flagrantly unscientific features of much psychoanalytic theorizing they have also come to recognize, in increasing numbers, the fruitfulness of psychoanalytic techniques, properly applied. It is also being increasingly realized that one of the most important tasks ahead of psychology is the careful working through of the many hypotheses proposed by the psychoanalysts on the basis of clinical insights. A necessary prerequisite for this process of scientific validation is the methodological relating of psychoanalytic to more orthodox scientific procedures. The first selection marks a step in this direction in providing a scientific orientation for psychoanalytic theorizing, from a friendly but critical point of view. It is by an active contemporary psychoanalyst, Ernst Kris, who represents the recent trend within psychoanalysis towards rapprochement with academic scientific psychology. For further concrete evidence of this trend the selections of Chapter XII, and Selections No. 42 and 47, may be consulted. The second selection is by the philosopher of science, Gustav Bergmann, who traces some of the methodological relationships between psychoanalysis and experimental psychology, primarily from the point of view of stimulus-response learning theory, in an attempt to demonstrate their fundamental compatibility.

22   PSYCHOANALYTIC PROPOSITIONS [1]

Ernst Kris

The word *psychoanalysis* will be used in the context of this paper to designate a body of hypotheses. I shall speak of *the psychoanalytic movement* in order to designate a social force, consisting mainly of the association of individuals who believe in the truth of these propositions, and who wish to propagate their acceptance, sometimes, especially early in this century, in an attitude of opposition to current social values. I shall speak of *psychoanalytic therapy* in order to designate a therapeutic technique, and of *psychoanalytic observation* in referring to the investigatory value of the *psychoanalytic interview:* the regular and frequent association of subject and observer, patient and therapist, over long stretches of time and under special rules of procedure.

Psychoanalytic hypotheses are derived from this interview situation, which is, at the same time, the most important testing ground for their validity. This leads to the crucial question of how reliable this observational method is in which the observer fulfills a threefold function: he records the behavior of his subject, he judges his own reactions to this behavior, which are part of the record, and he acts in order to produce changes in his subject. The lack of precision that results from such triple involvement of the observer is a cause for discomfort to the scientist. But there also are other grounds for discomfort: some lie in the development of psychoanalysis, and others are connected with the subject matter with which the propositions deal.

Psychoanalysis has developed outside institutionalized science and has been carried forward almost exclusively by the psychoanalytic movement. For over forty years professional associations of psychoanalysts have provided the necessary facilities for all those who have

[1] In the course of this paper I have liberally drawn on ideas and formulations that emerged in discussions with H. Hartmann, and with him and R. Loewenstein. Only a part of these discussions has as yet been published, jointly.

From E. Kris, The nature of psychoanalytic propositions and their validation. In S. Hook and M. R. Konvitz (eds.), *Freedom and Experience, Essays Presented to Horace Kallen.* Ithaca, N. Y.: Cornell University Press, 1947. Reprinted by permission of the author, the editors and the publisher.

wished to study psychoanalysis and its applications; mainly they have provided facilities for the training of psychiatrists in the handling of psychoanalytic therapy. Even at the present time, when psychoanalytic propositions are permeating various psychological systems and are forming the hard core of psychiatry, psychoanalysis is taught at but few medical schools and only in exceptional cases in other departments of American universities. It seems that some of the—admittedly more superficial—difficulties with which many scientists are faced in their first contact with psychoanalysis have to do with this state of affairs. There is, for instance, a lack of trained clarifiers, who might properly co-ordinate the various propositions with each other or try to eliminate the inequities of language in psychoanalysis. As examples of such inequities one may mention that definitions of terms are sometimes unsatisfactory, that even their translation from German into English is not always fortunate; that in psychoanalytic writings metaphors tend to obscure the meaning of statements; and that such usages are ingrained by the fact that a generation of scientists adopted what now seems understandable as the peculiarity and privilege of one genius (28).

No other large body of hypotheses in recent science reveals to a similar extent the influence of one investigator. This has a number of consequences of varying significance. In the present context we refer to one of these consequences only: terminology and constructs of psychoanalysis reflect ideas and connotations dominant in Freud's formative years, i.e., in the 1870's and 1880's. Many interacting influences have to be considered: the humanist tradition in European education of the period, the concepts of "classical" neurology, the impact of twenty years of experiments and clinical work in the physicalist physiology of the school of Helmholtz and Du Bois-Reymond (5) and finally the influence of evolutionism, both Darwinian and Lamarckian. It has been argued that since some of the concepts of psychoanalysis are derived from overaged connotations, for instance, from the mechanistic psychology of Herbart and his followers (10), psychoanalysis itself is either in general overaged or, more specifically, limited to the viewpoints which originally suggested the terms used. The argument is clearly fallacious (24). The concepts borrowed from other sciences gained a new meaning in the new context: if in psychoanalysis reference is made to "associations"—mainly to the "free associations" of the subject—this has little to do with the traditional associationism of the nineteenth century. On the contrary, it seems that, historically speaking, the method of free associations has suggested some of the early criticism of the older association theories. Or, to use an even more significant example, Freud borrowed the term regression from brain pathology, but Freud's and not the neurological meaning of the term has found entrance in modern psychopathology and psychology. While it seems possible that the reverberations of overaged connotations attached to some of the psychoanalytic terms and constructs might act as a factor delaying their understanding or impeding communication, this origin does not affect their function. And in the present context we are interested in this function. How well do the constructs of psychoanalysis permit the establishment of a systematic set of propositions that review present knowledge, and how well do they function in suggesting "new" propositions that can be empirically tested—empirically tested in spite of the great number of independent variables? [2]

The subject matter of psychoanalysis was new within science when Freud started on his investigation; it is new and bewildering even today. That subject matter is human behavior viewed as conflict. Before Freud it had been the exclusive province of intuitive insight, religious, poetic, or philosophic: these had created the various patterns of "the image of man" around which philosophy and the arts of Eurasian civilization have centered throughout the ages. And rapid changes of that image were under way in the outgoing nineteenth century, in the age of Darwin, Nietzsche, Dostoievsky. The relation of psychoanalysis to this world of thought has not yet been satisfactorily investigated, a study that will clearly be one of the major assignments of a future biographer of Freud. Suffice it to say here that a distinction between tangible influences of contemporary intellectual movements on Freud's thought and between "mere" similarities of his approaches to that of others working in other fields cannot always be made. However, the coincidences are often astonishing—no less astonishing and unexplored than the rapidly spreading influence that Freud's thought has exercised on the intellectual life of the twentieth century. To give only one example: The method of free association, one of the main avenues of exploration in psychoanalytic observation, has so clearly influenced literary fashions of the twentieth century that one has been inclined to assume that the "stream

---

[2] Cf. in this connection K. W. Spence's (49) somewhat extreme views on the relation between independent variables and constructs: "Theories come into play whenever we do not know all variables entering into a set of experimental events or the interrelation between them."

of consciousness," as a medium of poetic expression, was derived from it. And yet that very medium was used in France in 1887 in Edouard Dujardin's novel *Les Lauriers sont coupés* (31), several years before Freud ever applied the method of free association in his explorations. There is no evidence that Freud ever read Dujardin's novel, and there hardly need be any. Both Freud's approach and some of the literary currents of the second half of the nineteenth century are part of a general trend in the history of ideas, that tended ever increasingly to pay tribute to the manifestations of psychopathology. The quest for the first relevant traces of this interest within science leads to the French psychiatrists of the nineteenth century, who stimulated Freud's interest in the new field (38).

Freud's first reaction to that field was similar to that through which many students of later generations including our own have passed and are passing. When, at the age of thirty, he first had contact with the study of neurosis, he reacted by a partial withdrawal. After his return from Paris, where he had studied with Charcot in 1886, and from Nancy, where he had worked with Bernheim in 1888, he renewed his interest in physiology and brain pathology. His studies on aphasia (14), one of the first attempts at a functional approach in neurology—functional as contrasted to traditional localizationism—were written in these years of retreat; Freud's interest and publication in the field of neurology continued until the end of his fourth decade.[3] When, at the age of almost forty, he published his first psychoanalytic case histories, he confessed to a feeling of *discomfort*. He who had been trained in the school of experimental sciences was writing what read like a novel. Not personal preference, he said, but the subject matter forced such presentation on him (15). We may add that one particular property of the subject matter was responsible: the property that led to the discovery of the importance of the individual's past in relation to society, to primary and secondary groups—the clinician's role as life historian and social historian—drove him toward the novelist.

Psychoanalytic constructs and assumptions are designed to cope with this difficulty and to make the scientific study of human conflict possible. In the present context it suffices briefly to characterize some of these constructs. The first step in the formation of Freud's theories led to an application of the dynamic concepts of Herbartian psychology to the study of conflict in general, in all areas of human behavior, but espe-

[3] For a bibliography see Freud (16).

cially to the already familiar problems of the stages of awareness, i.e., to the then current ideas concerning conscious and unconscious mental processes. Consequently, "unconscious" became a dynamic attribute, instead of a merely descriptive one; and a special term, "preconscious," was introduced to designate processes that are only descriptively unconscious. The dynamic concepts are supplemented by assumptions dealing with the nature of psychic energy and its somatic source in basic drives and needs; and by specific assumptions that deal with the general principles regulating the functioning of the psychic apparatus in its relation to discharge of tension and its postponement. All these assumptions are characterized by their relation to physiology. Contrary to the tradition of German psychology and psychopathology of the late nineteenth century, Freud kept at a safe distance from making too close a link between psychological and physiological assumptions. He borrowed this approach from French psychiatrists: "The clinical observation of the French [psychiatrists]," he writes in 1892, in his introduction to the German translation of Charcot's *Leçons du mardi,* "gains undoubtedly in independence, since it relegates physiological viewpoints into a second plane . . . not by omission, but by an intentional exclusion, that it considered to serve a purpose." Freud himself never loses sight of this second plane. When after many tentative formulations he developed his structural model of the psychic apparatus, in his assumptions regarding the development of the psychic organizations during ontogenesis, the Id, the Ego, and the Superego, he defined these organizations as physiologists define organs, i.e., he defined them by their functions (28). While neither Freud nor the majority of later workers in the field find it advisable to establish strict correlations between these functions and certain parts of the nervous system, such lack of correlation is considered provisional. Freud explicitly assumed that the time would come when psychological constructs would be replaced by physiological or biochemical constructs.[4]

The constructs of psychoanalysis here briefly characterized have in the course of forty years been repeatedly revised. Sometimes so radically that older propositions were—silently—superseded by newer ones. As

[4] Cf. *Beyond the Pleasure Principle* (18, p. 79): "The shortcomings of our description would probably disappear if for the psychological terms we could *already now* substitute physiological or chemical ones." The words "already now" are omitted from the quoted translation by an error of the translator. The German text has in the corresponding passage the words *"schon jetzt."* For a similar later statement of Freud's, see *New Introductory Lectures* (19), p. 198.

a consequence, the student who wishes to familiarize himself with the system of propositions has to study its history. No fully satisfactory comprehensive statement on the system itself is known to me. This is one of the reasons why random quotations from psychoanalytic writings are of particularly dubious value. A young American scholar has recently pointed to the fact that much confusion about what is believed to be a psychoanalytic proposition is due to the exclusive acquaintance with one or the other phase in the development of hypotheses as embodied in Freud's writings (31). This state of affairs is symptomatic of the social setting in which psychoanalysis is developing; the interest of psychiatrists who alone have access to the full set of observational data can hardly be expected to center on problems of semantic and systematic clarification, at a time when the rapid advance of clinical insight attracts their attention. A time lag exists between their insight and their theoretical formulations and even between clinical experience and published case histories; the clinical tradition, at the present time, is richer and both more concrete and more precise than the psychoanalytic literature tends to reveal. Since the evidence on which the handling of psychoanalytic therapy rests is on the whole convincing to those who apply it, the need for systematic clarification presents itself mostly when controversial issues arise among those who work with this therapy.

There are obviously many reasons why such controversies have been frequent since, early in the century, Freud gained his first collaborators; and there are obviously many reasons why they should have taken the specific form of "splits" of what we here call the psychoanalytic movement. One of these reasons, however, is directly relevant in the context of the present paper: it is the elusive nature of the subject matter (52). The fact that there are many psychoanalytic propositions that have not yet been verified by procedures used in science seems to explain why controversies tend on the whole to be less fruitful and less centered on essential issues than they otherwise might be. Whatever the incentives to controversy, unverified propositions are readily taken as training ground by those polemically inclined.

Not all propositions currently included in psychoanalysis can be made subject to verification. To mention only two examples: The large set of propositions which accounts for human behavior in using phylogenetic assumptions frequently implies another purely biological proposition, the inheritance of acquired characteristics; and so long as there is no reason to consider this proposition verified by biologists, it seems appropriate to exclude psychoanalytic propositions based on it. Similarly, Freud's assumption of a drive toward death ("death instinct") as a propensity of living matter should not be used in establishing empirical propositions, so long as the implied biological assumption has not been tested—the assumption, namely, that living matter tends toward extinction even when chemical self-intoxication is eliminated. Psychoanalysis as a science cannot, I believe, directly deal with these propositions; moreover, their value for the formulation of other empirical propositions can be seriously questioned.[5] Their place in Freud's thinking, however, and their immensely stimulating effect is a matter of great concern to those interested in the history of ideas.

In turning to the problem of validation of psychoanalytic propositions, I shall distinguish validation provided by psychoanalytic observation from other "objective methods" (48) of verification. In discussing the latter, I shall distinguish experimental procedures from observational evidence.

The validation of psychoanalytic propositions through psychoanalytic observation can in this context only briefly be characterized; any attempt to do so must start with the exclusion of what one might expect to be the most convincing test: the success of psychoanalytic therapy. This therapy operates with a number of agents. In many cases it remains to some extent doubtful which of these agents has produced the desired change; even if the probability is great that one particular agent can be made responsible, evidence is as a rule difficult to establish. However, this limitation does not seriously restrict our discussion since, apart from the question of the effectiveness of psychoanalytic therapy, the psychoanalytic interview provides a setting of experimental character through its rules of procedure; it covers an area and makes data accessible that are otherwise not observable under conditions of comparably relative precision.[6] Not only does the total course of the association between observer and subject provide an experimental setting and permit the testing of long range predictions; each interview provides potentially a number of opportunities for the testing of forecasts. Each one of the manifold reactions of the subject to the interventions of the observer can be described as a reaction to a deliberately introduced change in the situation between observer and subject. The reactions of acknowledgment to any interpretation given, for instance, that of sud-

---

[5] For one example, see Hartmann and Kris (27, pp. 21 ff.).

[6] For a full discussion, see Hartmann (24) and Hermann (30).

den insight combined with the production of confirmatory detail or substitute reactions of a variety of kinds, frequently—but not always—permit confirmation or falsification of the hypotheses on which the given intervention was based. It seems appropriate to discuss the simplest example of such confirmatory evidence: the interpretation has removed obstacles to recall; the forgotten memory can take its place within awareness. It is naturally not assumed that in such cases the interpretation "produced" recall; rather the situation existing previous to the interpretation, the one which "suggested" the interpretation, must be described as one of incomplete recall (and, therefore, as in some measure similar to the situation in which the memory trace was laid down). Interpretation, therefore, acts here as a help in completion. Incomplete recall had announced itself by a variety of signs in the individual's behavior. The subject may have acted in relation to an actual rival as he once acted toward a sibling, and the interpretation of the observer merely translated the nonverbalized into verbalized response, unconscious repetition into conscious recollection. The similarity of the situations to which we here refer need exist only in the meaning of the situation to the subject, for instance, in the dynamic structure of the constellation in his life, as this constellation may have been modified by previous interview situations. The frequency of such experiences during analytic observation is in part due to the rules of procedure. They are designed to bring about the experience of similarity of present and past. Thus in many instances the personal relation to the observer is experienced as "similar" to the relation to one or another member of the subject's primary group—we here refer to rules concerning the relative anonymity and passivity of the observer during the interview situation. In saying that the subject exhibits behavior similar to earlier behavior patterns, behavior that would, as it were, be appropriate in another context, we refer to a large number of behavioral details, actions in life as well as during the interview, dreams, and verbalizations that follow the process of free association. In order to eliminate a number of problems concerning the reliability of confirmations of reconstructions by recall of the subject, it seems appropriate to mention that in a considerable number of instances in which interpretation was used to reconstruct the past, or, as one might say, to "predict the past" (27), objective verification of the reconstruction was possible. Inquiries in the environment of the subject and for recollections of members of his family brought confirmations of astonishing details. Thus Marie Bonaparte (7) reported a case in which confirmation was obtained for a reconstructed experience that occurred in the second year of life; the reconstruction was largely based on one dream. At least one subject, the psychologist E. Frenkel-Brunswik, has published an account from her own experience under psychoanalytic observation. From her behavior, and from associations about her two sisters, the analyst had interpreted what he called a "Cordelia motive." He suggested to her that she was displaying in her life the role of Cordelia, the youngest daughter of King Lear. To her answer that she had read most of Shakespeare's dramas but not *King Lear,* the analyst replied that Cordelia was the best and most generous daughter of King Lear, who nevertheless preferred his other two daughters because of their flattering attitudes. Such an interpretation was at that time refused by the author rather emotionally. Later it was received somewhat more favorably. But she was still very surprised when much later she discovered, in looking through old notes, that at the age of about fifteen she had copied the entire role of Cordelia. Thus she must at that age have been very much concerned with the fate of Cordelia, with whom she probably had identified, later repressing not only this identification but also all other memory of the play.

The confirmation of reconstructions by objective evidence played a considerable part in the early history of psychoanalysis, at a time when Freud was constantly experimenting with new propositions. From as yet unpublished notes it appears that he felt considerably encouraged as to the validity of his theories on dream interpretations when the interpretation of one of his own dreams led to the reconstruction of an experience in his third year of life, which was subsequently confirmed by a recollection of his mother.

But even without the support of objective confirmation psychoanalytic observation has in many instances been able to decide between alternative propositions. Thus the hypothesis that there was a regular or extremely frequent occurrence of actual seduction by adults in the childhood of individuals who later in life develop hysterical symptoms, or a regular or frequent correlation between the severity of the birth experience to incidence of neurosis in the adult, was falsified by this procedure.

A survey of the body of psychoanalytic propositions reveals, however, that in other instances psychoanalytic observation does not provide criteria for verification. Observers using the same proposition claim different results; and even when they submit their data to each other, no decision can be reached. The number of variables and the fact that no repetition of the experimental procedure under comparable conditions is feasible, limit in these cases the possibility of decision. This is, for instance, true of propositions suggested by M. Klein (36) and S. Isaacs (33), concerning earliest reactions of the infant to deprivation.[7] They claim, for instance, that in earliest infancy, at the age of a few months, the child reacts with self-punitive tendencies to the extraordinarily intense destructive impulses that it feels against an environment imposing even slight and unavoidable frustrations. I select this instance since it is typical of a large number of other propositions that are indispensable in psychoanalysis: they deal with reactions of the child during the preverbal stage or during the earliest stages of development of its verbal faculties; propositions which will tend to remain controversial unless verified by objective methods. It should be added that they are not the only propositions of which it is true that a decision cannot be reached. Briefly, if we speak of verification of psychoanalytic propositions by objective methods, we do so not in order to make psychoanalytic propositions "respectable" in science, or in order to establish unity in the field of psychology, but because sooner or later the ever more precise empirical test becomes an essential element in the development of any system of scientific propositions. In the development of psychoanalysis this moment seems to have arrived.

Validation of psychoanalysis by experimental procedure has been the preoccupation of individuals and groups of writers over many years, in certain areas (relation of dream formation to percepts, symbolism in dreams) for over thirty years. The interest in this approach is so rapidly growing that recent bibliographies, though incomplete (47, 48), enumerate several hundred contributions, and "experimental psychoanalysis" has come to be considered "a field of its own." The importance of this trend in experimental psychology can hardly be overestimated. The walls that a generation ago separated the psychological laboratory from "life" have been pierced; the relevance of the problems investigated has increased; experimental work is gradually moving from a concern with peripheral factors determining human behavior to the central problems, on which man's existence depends. That movement is—naturally—slow, but it is effective. And from the experimental

---

[7] See Wälder (51) and Glover (20) for a discussion of these theories and methodological questions.

setup there leads a way to test-situations and test-procedures and their ever wider application in techniques of welfare and social control.

Through this trend in experimental psychology the isolation of psychoanalysis from other systems and approaches in psychology has been considerably reduced. Furthermore, a number of psychoanalytic propositions have gained wide recognition and are moving rapidly into the area of common-sense psychology. This corresponds to a regular sequence: the greater familiarity with some psychoanalytic propositions leads to their becoming part of "what one always knew."

Before discussing the significance of these experiments for the verification of psychoanalytic propositions it seems appropriate to introduce a distinction applicable to the most frequently tested and most relevant psychoanalytic proposition (27). Psychoanalysis describes processes of conflict solution in their time sequence. It seems, therefore, necessary to organize psychoanalytic propositions according to two viewpoints: according to whether or not they deal with dynamic or genetic (ontogenetic) interrelations. "Dynamic propositions are concerned with the interaction of forces and the conflicts within the individual and with their reaction to the external world at any given time or during brief time spans. Genetic propositions describe how any condition under observation has grown out of an individual's past extended through his total life span. If we take as examples of dynamic propositions defense against danger and reaction to frustration, genetic propositions state how defense and reaction come into being and are used in an individual's life." A survey of the vast number of experiments dealing with reactions to frustration indicates that they frequently test only dynamic propositions. They are concerned "with the field conditions as they exist here and now" and view the subject "who is a product of his past experiences as a static part of the field conditions" (45).[8] Thus Dollard and his collaborators (9) have ably dealt with the proposition that frustrations sometimes lead to aggression; Barker, Dembo, and Lewin (1) with that asserting that frustration sometimes results in primitivization of behavior, in what Freud called ego-regression. Both investigations have convincingly verified psychoanalytic propositions. However, these propositions are of a general kind, and the question arises under what condition an individual will react to frustration either with aggression or with regression or with another

[8] For a more detailed discussion of this point and a critical discussion of K. Lewin's position, see Hartmann and Kris (27).

mechanism of defense. Dynamic propositions alone cannot answer the question. An example may illustrate the reasons: Lewin and his collaborators investigated the reaction of children when suddenly deprived, but still in view, of highly desirable toys. Let us transfer this laboratory situation into life: "When children visit department stores with their mothers, they are in an almost equally tantalizing situation. What will their reaction then be? It will depend on what meaning the 'You can't have it' and the 'It is too expensive' gains for the child, by the way in which the mother puts it to him. This depends on a variety of factors: on the child's relation to the mother; on the mother's own relation to similar present and past experiences; and how, in the child's own previous development, tolerance for deprivation in general and for certain specific deprivations has developed" (27).

This comparison is not meant as a criticism of the laboratory technique; it is only an attempt to characterize the limitations of the predictions that can be based on experiment. Lewin and his collaborators can naturally not generalize "to what kind of frustration and under what circumstances a child will respond with regression" instead of with a different mechanism. However, when the data available cover the individual's past, when both dynamic and genetic propositions are applied, such forecast frequently becomes possible. Thus, in order to prognosticate the child's behavior in the department store, data on both the mother and the child's past experience are essential, detailed data that hardly ever are assembled outside of psychoanalytic observation.

Other experimental approaches have been singularly successful in studying genetic propositions. The experimenter can view life as a series of learning processes (4, 42). The outstanding example of an experimental setup of this kind is J. McV. Hunt's article on "The Effect of Infant Feeding Frustration upon Adult Hoarding in the Albino Rat" (32). He found that the experience of frustration in infancy modifies adult behavior under two conditions: first, that the frustration be experienced at a certain early point during the maturational sequence, and second, that the adult animal be exposed to frustration experiences. The behavior of the satiated animal cannot be said to have been modified; nor will the behavior of the adult animal exposed to frustration be modified if the infantile frustration was experienced at a late period of maturation. This experiment reproduces not only the general proposition that under certain conditions frustration modifies subsequent behavior but also the specific interrelation between experience and predisposition, which is part of all genetic propositions in psycho-analysis. Any experience, it is contended, will become effective only if the child meets it at a given moment of his development.[9]

The value of experiments such as those of Hunt's and of a limited number of similar ones by O. H. Mowrer (41) and D. M. Levy (39) is self-evident: they have succeeded in demonstrating experimentally the validity of genetic propositions of psychoanalysis in an incontrovertible manner.

Whatever gratification one feels at such results is somewhat reduced by the fact that the proposition verified is a good deal removed from the area in which, from the point of view of psychoanalysis, verification of propositions is most urgently needed. To remain in the province covered by Hunt's experiment, we would wish to know what constitutes frustration to the human child, when does what kind of experience act how on what kind of children in what kind of environment—variables in whose effects psychoanalysis is equally interested and whose inter-relations are tentatively covered by psychoanalytic propositions, which, as a rule, cannot be verified by experimental procedure.

The use of animal experiments reaches its limit when propositions are so specific that they apply to one species only, to the human animal. The limit of experiments with humans rests on the fact that the laboratory cannot as a rule reproduce dangers or basic needs with which the genetic propositions of psychoanalysis deal.

A number of authors have contested this point and have claimed that the difference between quasi needs and "true needs" can be neglected; the study of human motivation can, they suggest, be exclusively based upon investigations of behavior determined by quasi needs. Lewin (40), who has advanced this view, argues that tensions of low and high intensity are only quantitatively and not qualitatively different; that the fact of this quantitative difference cannot affect the laws in question. Henle (29), who has more recently elaborated on Lewin's views, argues that experiments in a variety of fields have proved that Lewin's contentions are correct. None of these experiments seem entirely convincing; but one of Henle's examples encourages a more detailed discussion. Henle claims that Freud's analysis of the psychopathological phenomena of everyday life, of slips of the tongue, and parapraxes have

---

[9] In speaking here of development instead of maturation, we refer to a definition: we ascribe to maturation processes relatively independent of environment; to development those highly dependent on environment (27).

shown that in an area where tensions of low intensity operate, phenomena come into being that clearly follow the same principles as the symptom formation in neurotic behavior, i.e., phenomena of great intensity.

Henle's argument is misleading. Not only is it worth remembering that not all essential propositions concerning the formation of the neurotic symptom apply to parapraxes (the theory of symptom formation was known to Freud when he hit upon the explanation of parapraxes, and it is doubtful whether a reversal of the sequence could have led to equally satisfactory results); but also the assumptions that the conflicts that lead to parapraxes are necessarily or typically of low intensity is entirely unwarranted. Evidence to the contrary is rather suggestive. But I should like to introduce a different kind of argument. Assuming that even in some cases the intensity of the conflict that leads to parapraxes be low, the nature of the conflicts remains significant. The conflict is of the same kind as the conflict that leads to symptom formation in neurosis; it may involve libidinal and aggressive impulses, love, hate, guilt, and anxiety, and the part played by the three psychic organizations may be in details comparable to that observable in symptom formation.

The quasi needs of the laboratory investigations are of a different kind. There is no doubt that, as Zeigarnik (54) and a host of experimenters since the publication of her paper have shown, the need to complete an uncompleted task exists. But that need is of a very specific kind; [10] seen from the point of view of the psychoanalyst, it is a complex desire in which, however, two elements, that of avoiding failure, or that of feeling unsatisfied because one has not complied with a task, seem to predominate—impulses in which the Ego and the Superego are predominantly involved; as a rule no Id impulses are either frustrated or gratified. Consequently, the conflict that arises when the impulse to complete is frustrated can hardly be compared to conflicts that may arise when the impulse to complete an action with aggressive or libidinal connotation is impeded. In these cases the impediment, whether external or internal, is frequently experienced as a threat and

[10] Hartmann (25) repeated Zeigarnik's experiments with obsessional neurotic subjects and found that contrary to Zeigarnik's expectations based on experiments with normal subjects, they did not *prefer* incomplete to completed tasks. . . . The need to repeat . . . that predominates in the clinical picture of the majority of obsessional subjects overrides the need to complete the uncompleted. The specific impulses of the obsessional neurotic "modify the structure of the quasi-needs."

the individual frequently reacts with anxiety. The difference in the situations here referred to, which Lewin described as one of mere quantitative character, can be demonstrated in terms of physiological reactions: the bodily changes (Cannon) attending anxiety states are different in kind and not in degree from other and lower tension states in the organism; their closest relative is the state of rage. Considerations of this kind must be taken into account in discussing the relation of quasi needs of the laboratory to the true needs of life, and when evaluating the bearing of certain types of experiments.

It should here be added that experimental approaches to the study of "true" conflict situations have repeatedly been attempted. They were initiated by H. A. Murray (43) who, in his paper on "The Effect of Fear upon Estimates of the Maliciousness of Other Personalities," clearly demonstrated the working of projection. Murray's method has been elaborated by others (cf. 23), and experimentation in this area is rapidly developing. The preliminary reports of various wartime setups for the selection of specialized personnel, where subjects were exposed to considerable strain, seems to indicate that the "paper and pencil" experiments are finding rivals in controlled observation of individuals exposed to real or almost real threat situations.[11]

And yet it seems doubtful whether any experimental method will ever be able to rival the confirmation of psychoanalytic hypotheses concerning human reaction to danger that can be obtained by carefully controlled data of observation. To quote a recent example (37): the fantastic prediction that bombing of civilians in the Second World War would produce mass neuroses was made by those who were unaware of psychoanalytic propositions. The result of bombing surveys, however, confirmed the latter; they state that an individual's reaction to objective danger in a clearly structured situation—under adequate leadership and morale—will depend on the state of inner tension of the individual. All surveys on reaction to bombing in England (53) have shown that pathological reaction was maximized with one group of citizens, the adolescents, i.e., with those whose level of adjustment is for biological reasons least stable and in whose life conflict is supreme. Some surveys (cf. 8) have been interpreted (37) as showing that a

---

[11] At the present time only incomplete evidence as to the experimental procedure used is available. Cf. Bion (6), and *Fortune Magazine*, March, 1946, where a cursory description of the various tests applied by Murray in the selection of personnel for the Office of Strategic Services is given.

similar peak of the curve existed for the age groups 3–5, in which another set of psychoanalytic propositions locates a high propensity to anxiety. Verifications of this kind seem particularly significant since they are based on data selected for other purposes.

The limitations of the laboratory to quasi needs (and quasi dangers) seriously restrict the area of propositions that can be experimentally verified. In fact, up to the present, experimental approaches have been more successful in dealing with propositions concerning substitution [12] than they have been with propositions concerning repression (45, 27). The child represses an experience because the remembrance would entail conflicts of "too great intensity" in the presence of what to the child are vital threats. Situations of this type can hardly be reproduced by the experimenter, but they can be successfully studied by trained observers of behavior, who live in close contact with the child. The ideal of an intense study of the child by a team of participant observers of many skills is as yet unfulfilled, partly for organizational reasons. The communication between "academic" and "psychoanalytic" studies of child development is very incomplete. Quotation marks are used to indicate the spurious character of a division according to which one group of observers would be mainly interested in maturational aspects, the other, the psychoanalytic observer, in the "emotional" or "social" aspect of the child's life,[13] a division of interests which is bound to reduce the value of both sets of findings. In fact, observation has been most meaningful when it covers many areas at the same time and tends to illustrate how all sides of the child's personality are interdependent. The observations by A. Freud and D. Burlingham in a wartime nursery in London may be quoted as outstanding examples (12, 13). Similarly, the investigations of R. Spitz (50) on hospitalism have produced quantified data demonstrating how lack of stimulation by mother or mother-substitute may seriously and under certain conditions irreversibly affect the total development of the infant. In both these investigations the plan to verify psychoanalytic propositions has led far afield: the investigators have not only been able to decide between alternative hypotheses but, what is even more essential, to suggest new ones. The requirements of scientific procedure would suggest that observation of

[12] As an example, see, for instance, Henle's experiments (29).

[13] As an example of such a division, I refer to the data on the development of the child's views on morality by Piaget (44) and similar sets of data produced by psychoanalysis. Cf. de Saussure (46).

this kind should not be limited to random groups but to representative samples, that it should be conducted over long periods of time, and that studies of child development should be extended and should form the substance of systematic studies in life histories.

Data cannot be restricted to any one cultural or subcultural area. The study of the "nursery" as a matrix of civilization has gained considerable impact from the fieldwork of anthropologists who followed the lead of the genetic propositions of psychoanalysis (Bateson, Erikson, Mead, and others) or used these propositions in their interpretation of anthropological data on child-rearing (21, 22; 34, 35). While advance in this area has been rapid, one other possible field of elucidation has been neglected: the study of identical twins, which would permit access to factors of heredity.[14]

In speaking of validation of psychoanalytic hypotheses by psychoanalytic observation, experimental procedure, and systematic observation, I may have unwittingly conveyed the impression that psychoanalysis is a complete system of propositions, or one near completion. Both impressions would be equally misleading. While psychoanalysis covers a wide area, the closer one investigates the interrelation of propositions, the more "the gaps" hit one's eye; the more does it become evident that however suggestive is the sketch at which one looks, a sketch it is, richer in some parts, more general and painted with a broader brush in others.

Psychoanalysis is not static. Out of psychoanalytic observation a stream of new propositions constantly emerges; the increased number of workers, the changing conditions of observation, such as those of

---

[14] According to Freud's observation (17) three peculiarities, orderliness, parsimony, and obstinacy (or the opposites of all or one of them), tend to form a character triad, i.e., they frequently occur together. A further empirical finding of Freud's indicates that in the life of individuals who show that triad of characteristics, excretory function obtained accentuated importance in childhood. He furthermore assumes that under equal environmental conditions during childhood only certain constitutionally predisposed individuals are likely to develop the indicated triads. In studying the character traits of adult identical twins Hartmann (26) found confirmation for a part of Freud's propositions. He investigated ten pairs of identical twins and found that if in one of the twins one of the three character traits forming the triads of anal eroticism was of importance, in the other the same or another trait of the triads regularly predominates, either in its positive or in its negative form. The three character traits are, therefore, para-variable, i.e., they substitute for each other. No analysis of overt behavior of the twins could have established a meaningful relationship between the disorderliness of the one and the obstinacy of the other. Only the genetic proposition of Freud, which considers the triads of traits as reaction-formations to experiences in the anal phase of libidinal development, made the relationship meaningful.

wartime, advances in neighboring fields, but most of all an ever more careful evaluation of the data obtained by psychoanalytic observation are all reflected in psychoanalysis. Hence the quest for verification refers to "old" and "new" propositions alike.

It cannot be a static process; it must be dynamic and continuous. Finally I would venture the forecast that the gradual amalgamation of psychoanalysis with other sciences, mainly with psychology and psychiatry, will find its expression in the institutions of higher learning. The psychoanalytic movement will yield its function to institutionalized science—for better or worse; there are advantages and serious dangers implied in this development. The tradition of courageous exploration that lives on in psychoanalysis may well be lost in this transformation.

References

1. Barker, R.; Dembo, Tamara and Lewin, K. Frustration and aggression, an experiment with young children. *Univ. Ia. Stud. Child Welf.*, 1941, *18*.

2. Bateson, G. Cultural determinants of personality. In J. McV. Hunt (Ed.), *Personality and behavior disorders*, Vol. II. New York: Ronald Press, 1944.

3. Bateson, G. and Mead, Margaret. *Balinese character, a photographic analysis.* New York: N. Y. Acad. Sci., 1942.

4. Bergmann, G. Psychoanalysis and experimental psychology. A review from the standpoint of scientific empiricism. *Mind,* 1943, *52,* 122-140. [Selection No. 23 in this volume.]

5. Bernfeld, S. Freud's earliest theories and the school of Helmholtz. *Psychoanal. Quart.,* 1944, *13,* 341-362.

6. Bion, W. R. The leaderless group project. *Bulletin of the Menninger Clinic,* 1946, *10,* 77-81.

7. Bonaparte, Marie. Notes on the analytical discovery of a primal scene. *Psychoanal. Stud. Child,* 1945, *1,* 119-125.

8. Burt, C. *Under fives in total war.* London: Brit. Psychol. Assoc., 1941.

9. Dollard, J.; Doob, L. W.; Miller, N. E.; Mowrer, O. H.; and Sears, R. R. *Frustration and aggression.* New Haven: Yale Univ. Press, 1939.

10. Dorer, M. *Die Historischen Grundlagen der Psychoanalyse.* Leipzig: Meiner, 1932.

11. Erikson, E. H. Childhood and tradition in two American Indian tribes. *Psychoanal. Stud. Child,* 1945, *1,* 319-350.

12. Freud, Anna and Burlingham, Dorothy T. *War and children.* New York: Medical War Books, International Univ. Press, 1943.

13. Freud, Anna and Burlingham, Dorothy T. *Infants without families.* New York: Medical War Books, International Univ. Press, 1944.

14. Freud, S. *Zur Auffassung der Aphasien, eine kritische Studie,* 1891.
15. Freud, S. and Breuer, J. Studies in hysteria. *Nerv. Ment. Disease Monogr.,* New York, 1947.
16. Freud, S. Inhaltsangabe der wissenschaftlichen Arbeiten des Privatdozenten Dr. Sıgmund Freud (1877-1897). *Int. Z. Psychoanal., Imago,* 1940, *25.*
17. Freud, S. Character and anal erotism. *Collected papers,* Vol. II. London: Hogarth, 1924.
18. Freud, S. *Beyond the pleasure principle.* London: Hogarth, 1922.
19. Freud, S. New introductory lectures. In *Autobiography* (Trans. by J. Strachy). New York: Norton, 1935.
20. Glover, E. Examination of the Klein system of child psychology. *Psychoanal. Stud. Child,* 1945, *1,* 75-118.
21. Gorer, G. Themes in Japanese culture. *Trans. N. Y. Acad. Sci.,* 1943, *5,* 106-124.
22. Gorer, G. *Japanese character structure and propaganda.* Mimeographed memorandum, Committee on Intercultural Relations, New York, 1942.
23. Harrower, M. and Grinker, R. R. The stress tolerance test. Preliminary experiments with a new projective technique utilizing both meaningful and meaningless stimuli. *Psychosom. Med.,* 1946, *8,* 3-15.
24. Hartmann, H. *Grundlagen der Psychoanalyse.* Leipzig: 1927.
25. Hartmann, H. Ein Experimenteller Beitrag zur Psychologie der Zwangsneurose. (Ueber das Behalten erledigter und unerledigter Handlungen.) *Jahrbücher für Psychiatrie und Neurologie,* 1934, *50.*
26. Hartmann, H. Psychiatrische Zwillingsprobleme. *Jahrbücher für Psychiatrie und Neurologie,* 1934, *51.*
27. Hartmann, H. and Kris, E. The genetic approach in psychoanalysis. *Psychoanal. Stud. Child,* 1945, *1,* 11-30.
28. Hartmann, H.; Kris, E. and Loewenstein, R. Some comments on the formation of psychic structure. *Psychoanal. Stud. Child,* 1946, *2.*
29. Henle, Mary. The experimental investigation of the dynamic and structural determinants of substitution. *Contr. psychol. Theor.* 1942, *2,* No. 3.
30. Hermann, I. Die Psychoanalyse als Methode. *Imago,* Leipzig, 1934, *1.*
31. Hoffman, F. J. *Freudianism and the literary mind.* Baton Rouge: Louisiana State Univ. Press, 1945.
32. Hunt, J. McV. The effect of infant feeding frustration upon adult hoarding in the albino rat. *J. abn. soc. Psychol.,* 1941, *36,* 338-360.
33. Isaacs, Susan. *The psychological aspects of child development.* London: Evans, 1935.
34. Kardiner, A. *The individual and his society.* New York: Columbia Univ. Press, 1939.

35. Kardiner, A. *Psychological frontiers of society*. New York: Columbia Univ. Press, 1945.

36. Klein, Melanie. *Psychoanalysis of children*. London: Hogarth, 1932.

37. Kris, E. Danger and morale. *Amer. J. Orthopsychiatry*, 1944, *14*, 147-156.

38. Kris, E. Review of Hoffman, *Freudianism and the literary mind*. *Psychoanal. Quart.*, 1946, *15*, 226-234.

39. Levy, D. M. Experiments on the sucking reflex and social behavior of dogs. *Amer. J. Orthopsychiatry*, 1934, *4*, 203-224.

40. Lewin, K. The conceptual representation and the measurement of psychological forces. *Contr. psychol. Theor.*, 1938, *1*, No. 4.

41. Mowrer, O. H. An experimental analogue of "regression" with incidental observations on "reaction-formation." *J. abn. soc. Psychol.*, 1940, *35*, 56-87.

42. Mowrer, O. H. and Kluckhohn, C. Dynamic theory of personality. In J. McV. Hunt (Ed.), *Personality and behavior disorders*, Vol. I. New York: Ronald Press, 1944.

43. Murray, H. A. The effect of fear upon estimates of the maliciousness of other personalities. *J. soc. Psychol.*, 1933, *4*, 310-329.

44. Piaget, J. *The moral judgment of the child*. New York: Harcourt, Brace, 1932.

45. Rapaport, D. Freudian mechanisms and frustration-experiments. *Psychoanal. Quart.*, 1942, *11*, 503-511.

46. Saussure, R. de. Ueber genetische Psychologie und Psychoanalyse. *Imago, 20*.

47. Sears, R. R. Survey of objective studies of psychoanalytic concepts. *Soc. Sci. Res. Council Bull.*, 1943, No. 51.

48. Sears, R. R. Experimental analyses of psychoanalytic phenomena. In J. McV. Hunt (Ed.), *Personality and behavior disorders*, Vol. I, New York: Ronald Press, 1944.

49. Spence, K. W. Theoretical interpretations of learning. In F. A. Moss (Ed.), *Comparative psychology*. New York: Prentice-Hall, 1942 (rev. ed.).

50. Spitz, R. Hospitalism. An inquiry into the genesis of psychiatric conditions in early childhood. *Psychoanal. Stud. Child*, 1945, *1*, 53-74.

51. Wälder, R. The problem of the genesis of psychical conflict in earliest infancy. *Int. J. Psychoanal.*, 1937, *18*, 406-473.

52. Wälder, R. Present trends in psychoanalytic theory and practice. *Bulletin of the Menninger Clinic*, 1944, *8*, 9-17.

53. Wolf, Katherine M. Evacuation of children in wartime. A survey of the literature with a bibliography. *Psychoanal. Stud. Child*, 1945, *1*, 389-404.

54. Zeigarnik, Bluma. Ueber das Behalten von erledigten und unerledigten Handlungen. *Psychol. Forsch.*, 1927, *9*, 1-85.

23   PSYCHOANALYSIS AND EXPERIMENTAL PSYCHOLOGY

Gustav Bergmann

This paper proposes to discuss from a purely methodological angle, with occasional references to the history of ideas, the relationship between psychoanalysis and what is usually called experimental or academic psychology. "Methodology" is here understood in that very general sense which is almost synonymous with the current expression "philosophy of science." Accordingly, the writer is neither an experimentalist nor a psychoanalyst, but a philosopher interested in the foundations of behaviour science; his epistemological frame of reference is that of Logical Positivism (Scientific Empiricism). The discussion, therefore, moves on a level of generality which, it is hoped, will justify its appearance in a philosophical magazine. But it must also be said that if terms like "mechanistic" and "deterministic" have been used with the clear-cut meaning that they have in science, this should not be interpreted as a rejection of their more subtle epistemological analysis which the empiricist *qua* philosopher is also bound to perform. The point is that, from the standpoint of Scientific Empiricism, those finer distinctions are almost completely irrelevant to the methodological schema of contemporary behaviour science. If they are urged upon the scientist, this is usually done in order to make him subservient to some metaphysical residue.

I

Psychoanalysis was and still is, for better or worse, not only a scientific approach, but also a cultural phenomenon of broader scope and rather deep impact. In this respect it is comparable to Marxism and Darwinism. These, too, in their times transcended the limits of their respective fields, and, partly as symptoms, partly as causal factors, played a very conspicuous rôle in the formation and transformation of our ideological structure. Small wonder, therefore, that men of letters

From G. Bergmann, Psychoanalysis and experimental psychology: a review from the standpoint of scientific empiricism, *Mind,* 1943, *52,* 122-140. Reprinted by permission of the author and publishers.

and philosophers paid so much attention to psychoanalysis. From the scientist's viewpoint this attention has not always been very helpful; it has rather added to the confusion by emotionalizing and reading immediate cultural significance into scientific issues which, if at all, are only of indirect cultural impact. Let it be added, by way of clarification, that the kind of philosophy which most eagerly rallies around or chooses to combat such movements has little to do with that very theoretical, entirely analytical, and entirely non-evaluative criticism of the sciences and of knowledge in general in which modern empiricism sees its main task. Thus I shall say very little about those broader implications of psychoanalysis or, to use Freud's own and very appropriate term, of the psychoanalytic movement; nor shall I say anything about the merits of psychoanalysis as a therapeutic method, but, instead, proceed to characterize some of its more fundamental theoretical aspects.

Within the broad and, as far as precise knowledge goes, still rather loose framework of the history of ideas, the rise and structure of psychoanalysis seems to have been contingent upon and continuous with three main factors. These three factors, very different though not causally independent from each other, are: *first,* the group culture out of which it grew; *second,* those elements in the nineteenth-century thought-pattern which are frequently referred to as Darwinism; and *third,* and finally, certain trends in German metaphysical and literary philosophy which are best epitomized by such names as Schopenhauer and Nietzsche. Since the Viennese background is of merely anecdotal interest, I shall not say more about it.

Freud himself, in his autobiography, has acknowledged the influence of Darwinism upon his thought. What I mean by Darwinism or, as I shall also call it, functionalism, is the repeated drawing upon the functional or adjustment aspect of acquired responses. The term "functionalism" is therefore used here in the specific sense in which it applies to a later American school of psychology. This group of psychologists, probably also under the cultural impact of Darwinism, mistook adjustment value for an explanatory concept, whatever this latter term "explanatory concept" might mean. For it is never the concepts which are explanatory, but only the laws and theories which are formulated in terms of these concepts. By laws I mean nothing but the regularities or correlations arrived at and generalized from observation, and by theory, roughly speaking, a logically integrated body of such laws. What the word "logical" here refers to looks reassuringly like a textbook of mathematics. This again by way of clarification and in contradistinction to certain types of traditional philosophy.

The Darwinistic background is, I believe, responsible for one of the greatest virtues as well as for one of the most serious limitations of psychoanalysis. The virtue I see in the hypothesis that the prime motivators, such as hunger, thirst, pain-avoidance and sex, are the driving power, the source of energy behind the whole infinitely complex pattern of socio-psychological behaviour. It is only fair to say that psychoanalysis has pioneered by advancing this hypothesis on culturally tabooed grounds, but it is also true that this basic naturalistic assumption, as one might also call it, is nowadays not only common ground but commonplace for all behaviour sciences. And, what is more important, today it is also realized that expressions such as "driving power" or "source of energy," which have just been used, are, at best, loose and suggestive metaphors, not in themselves blue-prints of a scientific theory. That psychoanalysts are not always too clear on this point just goes to show that they, too, form no exception from the familiar sociological phenomenon that the erstwhile pioneers end up as stalwarts. I am here, of course, referring to the confusion which surrounds such terms as "instinct," "drive," and "libido" in the psychoanalytical literature and, worst of all, to the completely wild and irresponsible speculations of Ferenczi's bioanalysis. So the objection on this score would be, not that psychoanalysts are too naturalistic, but rather that they sometimes do not do a good job of being naturalistic. On the other hand, I am deeply suspicious of the adverse criticism which comes from those nicifiers who object to psychoanalysis because of its being what they call a *drive psychology*. By this they mean that psychoanalysis bases its explanatory attempts upon the prime motivators; what they ignore, or want us to overlook, is that in this respect, psychoanalysis and contemporary experimental psychology do exactly the same thing. There is criticism and criticism. Writers like Miss Horney, as most clearly revealed by her criticism of the James-Lange theory on introspectionistic (!) grounds, are really the guardians of the good old spiritualistic tradition in philosophy, or, as psychoanalysts would phrase it, they are the carriers of the cultural resistance. I always feel like reminding those ladies and gentlemen that painting a picture is still painting a picture, in spite of the genetic connection which psychoanalysts claim to have discovered between these and other culturally less highly evaluated phenomena and activities. The values, after all, are not called into question if their occurrence is scientifically explained, and for the rest, one does not crusade for the place of variables in an explanatory schema. So there seems to be something wrong with the criticism from the right. The criticism from the left, as one might call it, comes from experimental psychology and from those students of scientific empiricism who are interested in the methodology of the behaviour sciences. This type of criticism heartily endorses the naturalistic assumption of psychoanalysis; all it urges is to make the whole approach more and more concrete, less and less elusive and ambiguous; what it wants to promote is the integration of psychoanalysis, in a less sectarian and more democratic fashion, into the whole of our scientific knowledge. But to repeat again, the tough-minded naturalism which, historically speaking, psychoanalysis owes to its Darwinian background is, from this standpoint, one of its greatest virtues.

The disadvantage inherited from the Darwinian outlook I see in the propensity to teleological thinking and in the tendency to take teleological patterns for scientific explanation. To be more explicit on this crucial point: the observation that a certain type of response has survival value, or, more specifically as psychoanalysts express it, can be *understood* in the psychic economy of their patients, might help to focus a problem, but does not yet constitute a scientific explanation. Such explanations are to be sought in terms of the mechanisms by which the habit in question is acquired, not in terms of the so-called aims which it serves. To put the same thing differently in order to avoid misunderstanding: to be sure, the behaviour of organisms shows the most marked teleological or purposive features, but every scientific account of them in teleological terms is necessarily very superficial, really a description rather than an explanation, a subjective account rather than an objective prediction. The task or, at least, the ideal and methodological standard of any science remains always to derive those teleological features within the frame of a causal mechanism. Therefore, again, the stricture against psychoanalysis which could be made from the left is not that it is too mechanistic, but rather that, because of its immersion into functionalistic thought habits, it is not always mechanistic enough. The word "mechanistic" is used in the very unphilosophical and very unemotional sense in which it is almost synonymous with "scientific." This time, too, I am rather confident that I express the general attitude of experimental psychology and again, I am afraid, I shall find myself in disagreement with writers like Miss Horney and the Gestalters.

Two further clarifications are best inserted at this point. The one is a criticism of psychoanalysis, the other a criticism of the nicifiers. Let us begin with the latter.

It is almost needless to say that all modern science is thoroughly deterministic. What remains after this high-sounding word has been deflated is, *first,* that a science which is not able to predict from an appropriate set of data the future course of all its variables has not yet solved its task, and, *second,* that there is no reason in heaven or on earth why this aim should be in principle unattainable to the behaviour sciences. Quite to the contrary, though we do not have too much to show in the behaviour field so far, still the whole frame of reference of both contemporary science and empiricism points strongly towards such a determinism, this in spite of certain much misunderstood developments in theoretical physics. Incidentally, one might add that whatever sense there is in the old metaphysical puzzle of the freedom of the will is completely safeguarded within the framework of such a scientific determinism, though the fear that such might not be the case provides one of the most powerful motives for all sorts of nicifiers, psychoanalytical or otherwise. What then is the meaning of the criticism that psychoanalysis is guilty of an entirely unjustifiable and destructive biological determinism? One must remember that only with this qualification as "biological" has the objection any meaning, for without it the term "deterministic," like "mechanistic," means almost the same as "scientific." As far as I understand them, people who raise this kind of objection usually mean that psychoanalysis does not pay enough attention to the causal factors which are located in the organism's physical and social environment, and too much attention to allegedly hereditary and the so-called biological factors, which latter term is used for the prime motivators. Thus formulated the objection undoubtedly makes sense, and I am in no position to evaluate it. Only, it appears that this is not a methodological question about, but a pragmatic question within science itself as to the actual success of hypotheses which attribute, loosely speaking, different weights to the various sets of variables. As to the actual position of the psychoanalysts on this question, I am under the impression that our knowledge about the rôle of hereditary factors in personality development is still very rudimentary and that psychoanalysts, on the whole, have been rather careful not to commit themselves in either direction. As far as the environmental factors are concerned, psychoanalysis has, through the importance which it attributes to the family history and to such culturally conditioned processes as sublimation, taken account of them on the very groundfloor of its structure. How inadequate this structure may be is a different question, but it certainly cannot be said that psychoanalysis has failed to provide for these factors within its systematic structure. There is, however, another aspect of this criticism which deals with the historical character of psychoanalysis. To this crucial point I shall return later.

Let me now turn to the last in this string of general remarks collected under the heading of Darwinism. This, as I have indicated before, is a stricture and not a defence of psychoanalysis. A direct comparison with so-called evolutionary theory will prove useful. In the generation of our parents Darwinism was often descried as a bold, all too bold theory, not sufficiently substantiated by facts and uncritically embraced for ulterior purposes by the radicals. As it presents itself to the modern methodologist, the situation shows, ironically enough, just the opposite picture. One can hardly think of a scientific fact better and more impressively documented than the phylogenetic hierarchy, established as it is by the threefold evidence of embryology, comparative anatomy, and paleobiology. As to the facts, nothing or next to nothing is left to be desired. On the other hand, it seems that there is as yet hardly any theory at all. For the observation that the species best fitted to a certain environment will ultimately replace other less fortunate ones is either a pseudo-teleological truism or a tautology. This just illustrates the point which was made before concerning the superficiality of teleological accounts. The real problem is to discover the biological mechanisms or, as Freud would call them, chemisms which regulate the transformation of species. A well-integrated body of such empirical laws, together with the data concerning the physical environment, would yield a causal account of the actual course the development of life has taken. This and only this would deserve the name of a *theory* of evolution, and for such a theory, as we know, experimental biology as yet has hardly laid the groundwork.

The analogy to psychoanalysis is obvious. Psychoanalysis, too, has discovered or rather, against the resistance of cultural taboos, forced our attention towards an impressive array of indisputable facts, but it has, to my mind, achieved relatively little in the way of a satisfactory, verifiable theory. The facts I have in mind are those of so-called infantile sexuality, the dream symbolism, and the decisive causal rôle which sexual factors, in the broad analytic sense of the term, play in the etiology of the psychoneuroses, in the formation of the normal personality, and in such group phenomena as the arts and folkways. These are, in a loose way of speaking, facts which nowadays baffle only the old ladies, the literati, and the Gestalters among the scientists. As far as theory is concerned, however, I find nothing except one rather sketchy law which could be formulated in this way: An individual's personality mechanisms, that is, certain not too well-defined general response patterns, have something to do with his experiences and behaviour in certain crucial periods and/or with respect to certain crucial situations. Far be it from me to belittle the achievement which is represented even by this hypothesis and whatever elaboration it has been given, for it is probably the only step which has so far been made beyond the mere correlation of traits in this very difficult field of personality. But on the other hand, it seems absurd to consider such an ingenious vision, almost entirely devoid of any articulate causal determination, as the ultimate achievement, to be scholastically elaborated, not as just one of the starting-points of a theory of personality to be developed.

I shall not take the time to say more than a few words about the last of the three background factors, those speculative trends for which Schopenhauer and Nietzsche were chosen as significant representatives. These influences are most clearly noticeable in writings such as Freud's "Beyond the Pleasure Principle" and the theorizing or, as I should prefer to call it, the speculations about the so-called death instinct. As far as I can see, there is hardly any empirical content in this type of psychoanalytical literature and it takes much broad-mindedness and goodwill even to interpret these utterances as confused suggestions for alternative formulations of whatever theory there is. Here, I believe, the psychoanalysts have become the victims of their own metaphors and what lives on in the empty verbal shell is the ghost of a certain type of German metaphysics. It is fair to say, though, that Freud in his autobiography disavows any such influences. But does not psychoanalysis itself insist that what a man or a group recognizes as the motive or goal of his behaviour does not necessarily coincide with what the behaviour scientist calls its cause? Here again, by the way, we make use of an insight which was genuinely revolutionary at the time of Freud and Pareto and which is just common sense and almost commonplace in contemporary behaviour science.

II

After this general stage-setting, I shall devote the rest of the paper to the elaboration of a thesis which has already been indicated. This, approximately, is what it says: The basic ideas and the systematic structure of psychoanalysis and of contemporary experimental psychology are not, as it sometimes appears, in conflict with each other. Quite to the contrary, it is more accurate to say that these two approaches are, in their basic features, almost identical and, in a certain sense, namely with respect to the phenomena they study, complementary. Obviously, the one and only field which psychoanalysis is interested in is that which, in more academic terms, would be called *personality*. Experimental psychology, on the other hand, at least that part of it which is theoretically most significant, can well be said to centre around the so-called laws of learning. What is thus rationalized into a pseudo-opposition turns out, as it so often happens, to be a mere difference of interest. In the case of psychoanalysis versus experimental psychology, this apparent opposition is re-enforced, not only by certain institutional factors, but also by the circumstance that the field of personality research is not yet, and possibly never will be, amenable to the exact laboratory methods in which the experimentalists very justifiably set their greatest pride. But I see by now that the last few sentences, in order not to be misunderstood, require a good deal of explaining. So let us start on a new string of explanations and qualifications.

The statement that the psychology of learning is theoretically the most significant experimental field must not be taken as a disparagement of the work done in physiological psychology and in perception psychology in particular. What it asserts is only that perception psychology, if divorced from physiological psychology, is hardly of any theoretical interest at all, and that the *reductive* research of physiological psychology is, as yet, of little help in the study of molar behaviour. "Reduction," in this context, refers to an explanation of molar behaviour by physiology; "molar," as here used, covers a range wide enough to comprehend both the behaviour of the white rat in the learning maze and the symptoms of the psychoneurotic. Presently we shall see that within the behaviour field which, as a whole, is molar from the reductionist's point of view, the two phenomena just mentioned, animal maze learning and personality formation, lie far enough apart and are probably so related that they again can be opposed to each other as molecular (or microscopic) and molar (or macroscopic) respectively. These remarks should also elucidate our usage of the expression "behaviour science." It excludes, quite arbitrarily and for merely practical reasons, physiology and all kinds of reductive research.

A similarly qualifying remark is needed to explain the attribution of the personality field to psychoanalysis or, more correctly speaking, to clinical psychology of the psychiatric type. Again this involves no disparagement of the careful work, usually classified as experimental, which has been done in such fields as intelligence and the correlation of personality traits, normal or abnormal, with each other and with environmental variables. The point is rather, first, that *some* of this work, valuable as it is as a collection of data, as a statistical stabilization and often as a wholesome correction of our pre-scientific insights, does not hold the promise of theoretical significance; second, that *nowhere* in this field has the necessity of a comprehensive theory, of a causal mechanism, been as clearly recognized as in psychoanalysis. It becomes necessary here to make a qualification within a qualification to the effect that so far this relative excellence of psychoanalytic theorizing has expressed itself not so much in the level of achievement or in the stringency of verification, but only in the underlying assumptions and in the systematic conceptions of the analytic approach. As to actual, reliable achievement experimental psychology seems far more advanced. On the other hand, it is fair to recognize that the tremendous difficulty of the task which psychoanalysis set out to accomplish has at least something to do with this undeniable difference.

Even after these qualifications have been made, the repeated use of the expression "significance" calls for justification, for the term is evaluative, at least in the sense that it involves an appraisal as to the future course of science. "Significant" has been used synonymously with "instrumental" for the construction of a factually adequate, genuinely causal theory. Such significance must not be confused with immediate social or therapeutic significance, though on the other hand we have of course good reason to believe that every theoretical progress will ultimately redound into increased social and therapeutic control. Any discrepancy between clinical and theoretical psychology which is construed by means of the ambiguity inherent in the term "significance" is only a rationalized and often emotionalized difference of emphasis and interest. Clearly the outcome of a maze learning experiment is completely devoid of any significance in the latter, non-theoretical sense.

On the other hand, it is at least conceivable that carefully worked out relationships between intelligence scores and environmental factors, in spite of their overwhelming social import, are not very interesting to the theorist. To explain this: it is at least conceivable that, within the systematic framework of a fully developed science of psychology, those intelligence correlations will find their place as rather remote and complex corollaries of basic laws which have first been abstracted from the just mentioned rat experiments, while, on the other hand, the intelligence correlations themselves will not have yielded any such "theoretically significant" suggestions. Whatever bias was contained in the earlier formulation can now at least be very succinctly formulated: what has just been called a conceivable course of science is the course that science is most likely to take. This bias is apparently shared by the majority of the experimentalists, and, again, they find themselves in substantial agreement with the empirical core of psychoanalysis. To put the whole issue into a nutshell: the central idea of the psychoanalytic theory can very well be stated as an application of the laws of learning to the field of personality. To the elucidations and qualifications which such an *aperçu* requires we must now turn our attention.

A quick glance at physics will yield interesing cues concerning the way in which both the psychology of learning and modern empiricism formulate the task of behaviour science. Physics has now in all its branches reached the level of achievement first exemplified by Newton's theory of planetary motion. In this case, if the relative positions, velocities, and masses of the member planets at any moment are known to the physicist, he can, by application of his laws, compute or, as we also say, predict the positions and velocities at any earlier or later time point; he controls the process. The extent to which contemporary behaviour science falls short of this ideal is best elucidated in the following manner: *first,* we do not possess as yet such *process laws* of a closed system comprehending the organism and its environment; we must concentrate upon the organism as a system which interacts with its environment. The ingoing ones of these effects, issuing from the objective physical environment, are called stimuli, the outgoing ones responses. *Second,* because of this lack of functional equations describing the temporal unfolding of a closed system, we must rely upon the more primitive analysis in terms of cause and effect: in order to obtain lawfulness, we must watch for the regularities which exhibit themselves in the succession of isolated temporal cross-sections of the behaviour stream. Any such cross-section could also be referred to as a *state of the organism,* and each such state is at least partially characterized by its stimulus and/or response aspects. The qualification "at least partially" is of the essence of the argument, for, if we restrict our attention to the stimulus and response aspects of, for instance, two successive temporal cross-sections or states, attempts to find lawful connections will fail. To put the same thing positively: as is well known, most of the responses we are interested in depend not only upon the features of the objective environment to which they are made, but also upon the organism's training and its drive state. The neglect of these additional variables undoubtedly vitiates a certain kind of early psychological theory known as associationism. Again a word of warning is needed. The word "associationism" is now also used to refer to the stimulus-response technique of defining the variables of the problem. Clearly such a *technique* is not a *theory,* but rather, as we have seen, the methodologically correct way of formulating what all experimentalists and clinicians, no matter whether or not they call themselves S—R theorists, do. Attempts to discredit this technique by an emotive use of the ambiguous term "associationism" or, still more colourfully, "mechanistic and elementaristic associationism," clearly stem from and appeal to anti-naturalistic residues. Again psychoanalysis and experimental psychology are on the same side of the fence. In itself, reference to the two variable groups just mentioned as the organism's knowledge, perceptual or otherwise, and as its desires, conscious or unconscious, is of course not objectionable; objectionable is only the methodological confusion which slips in under the cover of the introspectionistic terms. The main offenders in this respect are not, as their fanciful terminology might lead one to expect, the psychoanalysts, but, because of their grounding in intuitionistic metaphysics, the Gestalters. What, on the other hand, keeps the experimentalists and the clinicians from committing the anthropomorphic fallacy is not so much an explicit epistemology, but rather their respective Watsonian and Darwinian backgrounds. The starting point of the confusion is this: different organisms, or, for that matter, one and the same organism at different points in his life history, respond differently to one and the same physical environment. Hence, so the argument runs, the psychological environments, not to be confused with the physical ones, were different in each case and upon them the psychologist is therefore bound to concentrate his attention. Be it granted that the psychological environments were different; be it also granted that in the case of an articulate subject we could find out *some* times *some* things about his psychological environment if we could interview him before he acts. It will be noted that the point against which I am arguing has just been stretched to the utmost, for, strictly speaking, the verbal report mentioned belongs to the overt behaviour to be predicted. But even so, what is the predictive value of the suggestive metaphor "psychological environment"? Is it not the business of science to ascertain which objective factors in the past and present states of the organism and of its environment account for the difference in response, so that we can actually predict it instead of attributing it, merely descriptively and after it has happened, to a difference in the psychological environment? As in the case of teleological thinking, the animistic metaphor is mistaken for the answer to the question which it puts. It should not be necessary, though it might be wise, to stress at this point that the methodologically correct use of verbal reports, as data, and of introspectionistic terms, in the scientist's account of them, is not impugned. Even as much as to expect that they could be dispensed with in the field of human personality is mere utopia to-day, though a utopia whose methodological possibility can help us to clarify our ideas. One should realize that the denial of this possibility leads ultimately either to dualism or to Aristotelianism, possibly in one of its modernized emergentist forms. The particular problems connected with man's consciousness or, what for all scientific purposes amounts to the same, his symbolic responses, will be treated later. First, some remarks to complete this sketch of the experimentalist's schema are in order.

In the field of animal behaviour, where, for the obvious reason of relative simplicity, the greatest advances have been made in recent years, very successful definitions of the non-environmental variables have been achieved in such terms as food, water, sex deprivation periods, and number and temporal spacing of trials. Certain objective phases of the so-called consummatory or goal states, such as eating or the cessation of a nocuous stimulus, also play an important part. Reenforcement theorists believe that these latter states are even indispensable if learning is to take place. This is not the place to formulate, by means of these *terms,* the most recent hypotheses as to the *laws* of learning, but two of the most important aspects of this body of interrelated hypotheses shall at least be mentioned. They are the well-known principles of conditioning and of generalization. The first states that under certain conditions, most important among which is probably temporal contiguity, a stimulus situation comes to arouse a part of a response not appropriate to itself but only to the succeeding goal situation. Pavlov's salivating dogs come here readily to mind. Significant is, furthermore, the fact that, according to present conceptions, states of the organism such as these anticipatory salivations fulfil a steering and organizing function in that chaining of responses of which all learning consists. The principle of generalization states, roughly speaking, that of two objectively similar stimulus situations each will, to a degree depending upon the degree of their similarity, elicit the response originally acquired toward the other.

It is also noteworthy that the laws of learning are *historical* laws in the sense that at the present state of knowledge one cannot, as in the Newtonian case, predict the future course of events from any amount of data collected at the time point where the process to be predicted starts, but that one is forced to utilize additional information concerning the past life-history of the organism. It will help to throw light on this point as well as upon some earlier remarks if one points out that only with the actual achievement of the physiological reduction are historical laws likely to disappear from the theoretical core of the behaviour sciences. This also shows that the methodological distinction between historical and non-historical or systematic laws, important as it is, is not a distinction of principle in the sense that the occurrence of historical laws constitutes an a priori characteristic of certain subject matters. But it seems undeniable that their essentially historical character is one of the most significant features psychoanalysis and present-day psychology of learning have in common. A last remark should further elucidate the point and forestall certain objections. If a rat enters the maze with a number of marks on his back which have been made there as a record of the numbers of trials through which he has been put, the *present* reading of these marks still amounts to the utilizing of historical information. Likewise, if the psychoanalytic patient now recalls and reports certain events of his life history, he, too, conveys historical information, though this fact is somewhat obscured by the additional circumstance that his recalling and telling it now is not so external to the ongoing process as the application and the reading of the colour marks in the case of the rat. All one has to do to justify this analysis is to point at the significance, both therapeutic and theoretical, which psychoanalysts attribute to the emergence of the actual historical truth during the course of a cure. In the last sentence the term "historical" has been used in its customary connotation, not with the specific meaning in which it occurs in the rest of this paragraph.

III

At this point of the discussion it should be obvious that I have not dodged my promise to talk about psychoanalysis and, under the sway of my behaviouristic prejudices, extolled the virtues of the white rat instead. As far as it is possible in such a brief survey, I even believe I have proved my point that the same basic ideas and the same frame of reference underlie both psychoanalysis and the experimental psychology of learning. In the phenomena of conditioning, for instance, and in the learning of more complex appetitive or escape (avoidance) behaviour with respect to beneficial or nocuous stimuli one recognizes the mechanisms to which psychoanalysts refer as the pleasure and the reality principle. Likewise, all those kinds of behaviour which, in a different terminology, are referred to as anxiety are based upon the general anticipatory responses to nocuous stimulations. Mechanisms like that of generalization contain at least the possibility of producing such personality mechanisms as displacement and projection. It will be noticed that the term "mechanism" is here used in a rather vague and indiscriminate manner. The elimination of this ambiguity will be one of our last points. Let us first notice that already that halo of vagueness which surrounds such terms as "drive," "instinct," and "libido" in the psychoanalytic literature has disappeared. What remains is this: which consummatory states represent satisfiers or soothers for which hunger states belongs, within the limits of a non-physiological behaviour science, to the basic laws which must be experimentally ascertained. This is one of the three points at which psychology is supported by its so-called biological basis; all the rest is learning and therefore, though in a historical manner, environmental. Clearly, the term "instinct" has no place in such a structure. If at all, experimentalists use it only to refer to certain very elementary unlearned stimulus-response connections like the lid reflex or the patellar response. These instincts or reflexes are the second point of contact where behaviour science, factually though not methodologically, rests upon its biological understructure. For, though this elementary outfit is decisive for the fate of the organism, it is evident that it constitutes the kind of material which psychology treats as data (basic laws). It provides the basis upon which psychology erects its explanatory structure. The explanation of this basis devolves, in turn, upon the biological sciences in the narrower sense of the term. The third point of contact is provided by those individual constants, hereditary and/or constitutional, which make for individual differences not reducible to environmental factors. Incidentally, the last few remarks indicate, in a rough manner, what there is left of a hierarchical structure within the methodologically unified system of the sciences.

Lest the last paragraph be misunderstood as too sweeping an attack on the so-called libido theory, let me attempt a crude but plain formulation of what appears to be the empirical core of this part of the psychoanalytic theory. It will turn out to be the so-called theory of psychosexual personality development. The idea is that there are several pairs of hunger and goal states, corresponding to each other like thirst and drinking, which have the following properties: 1) the intensity of these hunger states varies, according to some biologically given maturation curves, during the organism's life span; 2) these hungers are so interrelated that, under certain conditions, goal states corresponding to one of them reduce the others (substitution); 3) all the hungers of this group and only these hungers, unlike sleep, food, water hunger, etc., are highly plastic in the sense that by some kind of generalization-like mechanism they can be brought to accept secondary satisfiers (sublimation).

The possibility of sublimation clearly depends upon culture or, to say the same thing differently, upon the possibility of the symbolic response. By mentioning it we have therefore reached the stage where language and, with it, consciousness have to be taken into account. From this point on, little concrete information can be expected from the contemporary psychology of learning; at this juncture psychoanalysis takes over. This is, we recall, the respect in which psychoanalysis and the psychology of learning have been called complementary to each other. The situation is, however, not so simple as that, for in making this step we undoubtedly cross, in a certain sense, the borderline of reliable knowledge and shall have to be content with an as yet much lesser degree of articulateness and precision. Such a state of relative scientific ignorance is typically the one in which the philosophical methodologist can be of some modest use; for the philosopher with his prevailing interest in broad outlines will be naturally most eager to stress the discoverable structural identities and continuities. In the case at hand he will, of course, stress the stimulus-response view of language. In doing so he draws, historically speaking, upon the ingenious anticipatory vision first developed by G. H. Mead and that brand of social behaviourism that originates with him. Pragmatism, particularly as represented by Mead and Peirce, is, on the other hand, also one of the historical roots of Scientific Empiricism. To observe such interrelations between the new philosophy and the new anthropology, in Kant's broad sense of the latter term, is certainly significant to the historian of ideas and, to the student of either field, very encouraging.

The verbal symbol, vocal or subvocal, and/or the mental image is, according to this view, a particular kind of intermediate response. That means that it originally occurs in a relatively long chain of stimuli and responses which begins, in presence of a primary hunger, with the external stimulus and ends with an overt response. Thus it lies, even in its most complex form, on a continuum with the anticipatory salivation of Pavlov's dogs. The difference in complexity, however, is no doubt tremendous and has many aspects. First, these symbolic states or symbols, as we shall shortly call them, seem to be particularly apt to establish horizontal connections between widely different stimulus-response chains. What this pictorial expression tries to convey is this: imagine, vertically diagrammed, two different stimulus-response chains already established. Assume that the one leads ultimately to an overt appetitive act, the other to an overt avoidance response; assume, furthermore, that one and the same symbol or similar symbols (generalization!) occur in both chains. This is sometimes sufficient to extinguish or, as one also says, to inhibit the appetitive response. Under different conditions the appetitive chain will at least be modified by elements of the avoidance chain under consideration. The "many track" variability of such processes is further increased by the apparent ease of the mechanisms which establish associative connections of all kinds between the symbols. Second, to mention only one more feature, the external presentation of the symbolic stimulus alone, through speech or other symbolic devices, becomes very often sufficient to start in the organism one of those sequences of responses which follow it in one of the chains belonging to the habit pattern the individual has already acquired. The stimulus aspect of such an occurrence is just another complex case of learning; as to its motivational aspects, one can at least imagine that the cross connections just mentioned make it relatively easy to tap at least one of the just active hungers. Thus a new connection might become established and leave its trace upon the habit pattern or personality of the subject. At this point another feature should at least be mentioned which, according to Mead, operates in the communicative, culture-forming function of language. The war cry of the attacking animal "means" to him attack, while to his victim it "means" flight. Less metaphorically expressed, the response chains called out in both organisms are different. A symbol, however, if occurring with and verbalized or otherwise expressed by a member of a cultural community, is apt to start what one might call, with considerable looseness, the same response chain in any of his fellows. The limits of this sameness coincide roughly with what in other contexts is referred to as the emotive limitations of communication.

Clearly, these few remarks are but a philosopher's map of scientific No Man's Land; even to consider them as the sketch of a learning theory of personality and of the higher processes would be inexcusable wishful thinking. But they can serve as an expository device and furnish the background for further elucidation of the relationship between the two approaches, psychoanalysis and the experimental psychology of learning. If there is any anticipatory truth at all in this speculative map, then the relationship in question is that between two corresponding molar and molecular levels, as these terms have been used in an earlier paragraph of this paper. It is convenient to begin with a clarification of the term "mechanism." So far it has been used ambiguously to denote, on the one hand, regular stimulus-response sequences, both innate (reflexes) and acquired, and, on the other hand, the laws of learning which regulate their acquisition. This ambiguity is harmless; to point it out is sufficient to avoid confusion. More pertinent to our purpose is the fact that psychoanalysts and experimentalists, if they both speak about mechanisms, speak about lawfulness on two different levels. Again an analogy from physics should help. At a certain stage in the kinetic theory of matter thermodynamic laws, like the formula of Boyle and Charles, are considered as consequences of the laws of Newtonian mechanics which operate, behind the surface, between the numerous particles of the substance. Certain statistical assumptions provide the very elaborate deductive connection between this micromechanism of Newtonian mechanics and the macromechanism of the gas laws. The illustration is meant to clarify the meaning of our terms. The point to be made can be stated in the following manner: the experimental psychology of learning studies the micromechanisms of which the so-called personality mechanisms of psychoanalysis are the very complex macro-result. The mediating theory, comparable to the statistical assumptions and their elaboration by Maxwell and Boltzmann, is so far missing. This decisive fact should not become obliterated by certain similarities between the respective mechanisms which find their verbal expression in the use of such terms as "inhibition" in both fields. Possibly these similarities are all very superficial; possibly, but not probably or improbably, for not even a hypothesis can be offered at the present stage of our knowledge. If one were in a position to do that or if this reduction were actually achieved, psychoanalysts, when asked for the explanation of a personality trait would not, instead of an answer, give that endless enumeration of possibilities which is so exasperating to the scientific mind. This shows that the methodological unification here attempted does not invite any rash optimism. Quite to the contrary, while it helps to eliminate pseudo-arguments, it also brings to the fore the difficulty of the task ahead. The main root of this difficulty lies, no doubt, in the tremendous complexity of the symbolic apparatus which mediates between man's prime motivators and his overt responses.

Let us, in conclusion, test the plausibility of this schema by inquiring what light it sheds upon the metaphorical terminology of the psychoanalysts. Within the limits of a broad, structural allocation one finds the *Id* rather satisfactorily represented by the prime motivators and those response habits which have been partially extinguished by the learning process. *Ego* and *Superego* are somewhat cruder conceptions. What they represent, personalized and endowed with some driving power of its own, is apparently the difference between the total pattern of the responses as they would occur before, and as they actually do occur after, the development of the symbolic apparatus during the learning process. *Conscious* are, by definition, those intermediate states of the organism which contain the actual occurrence of a verbal symbol and/or image. "Intermediate" is always understood as referring to a response which stands, in an acquired chain, somewhere between the external stimulus and the overt response. The additional complication that vocalized verbal responses acquire culturally the value of overt non-verbal responses is here neglected. But even so it seems plausible that the symbolic responses are located relatively near the end of their chains and that the reaction is therefore less easily stopped short of overt expression if the process has once reached the conscious stage. Repression, that is, the stopping of an initiated response sequence before it reaches that stage, becomes thus plausible as the result of association with strongly negative states; it also becomes plausible that anxiety, the general anticipatory response to such states, is aroused whenever strongly inhibited response sequences are about to reach consciousness. It is significant in this context and has been pointed out by C. L. Hull that the first training of the libidinal hungers takes place in that period of life history where the child's symbolic apparatus is still entirely missing or relatively rudimentary. So it seems indeed that we acquire much of our personality traits, like the rat its maze habits, through unconscious learning.

PART TWO

Theory Foundations

CHAPTER X

PERCEPTION

THREE of the most significant contemporary positions in the field of perception are represented in this chapter. The first selection is from Kurt Koffka's Principles of Gestalt Psychology, *which is probably the most ambitious attempt yet made to achieve a thoroughly comprehensive Gestalt system of psychology. The excerpt presents the orthodox Gestalt interpretation of visual perception, concluding with the rejection of previous explanatory efforts and the acceptance of an explanation in terms of primary organizational factors. The brief excerpt from the monograph by Wolfgang Köhler and Hans Wallach provides some background for their experimental investigation of the figural after-effect, which has been perhaps the most fruitful outcome thus far of the Gestalt theory of isomorphism. The final selection offers a summary of the influential "thing constancy" research which Egon Brunswik has actively developed (see also Selections No. 8 and 12 for other presentations of this point of view). This work is of interest not only in its own right but also because Brunswik has succeeded in shaping a general systematic position in which so central a role is played by perception.*

24   THE GESTALT INTERPRETATION OF PERCEPTION

Kurt Koffka

The First Answer

Why, then, do things look as they do? We shall systematically take up various answers that may be given to this question, although they have been implicitly refuted in our previous discussion. A first answer would be: things look as they look because they are what they are.

Although this answer seems banal, it is not only utterly inadequate, but in many cases literally wrong. Let us single out a few aspects of behavioural things and compare them with the real ones. The pen with which I am writing is a unit in my behavioural environment and so is the real pen in the geographical. So far, so good. But if our proposition were true, to be a real unit would be a necessary and sufficient condition for a thing to be also a behavioural unit. But it is easy to show that it is neither necessary nor sufficient. If it were a necessary condition, it would mean: to every unit in my behavioural field there corresponds a unit in the geographical environment; for if behavioural units could exist without corresponding geographical ones, then the existence of the latter would no longer be necessary for the existence of the former. Nothing, however, is easier to point out than behavioural units to which no geographical units corre-

Fig. 1

spond. Look at Figure 1. In your behavioural field it is a unit, a cross; in reality, in the geographical environment, there is no cross, there are just eleven dots in a certain geometrical arrangement, but there is no connection between them that could make them a unit. This is, of course, true of all pictures, equally true of the stellar constellations like Charles's Wain, a case which Köhler has chosen as an illustration of this point.

If the visible existence of real units were the *sufficient* condition for the appearance of a behavioural unit it would mean that whenever our eyes were directed on a physical unit we should perceive a behavioural one. But this is not true either. Certainly, in most cases, this correspondence exists, but there are exceptions. As a matter of fact, it is possible to interfere with the real units in such a way that they will no longer look like units, an effect which we try to produce when we want to conceal certain well-known objects. If a gun is covered with paint in such a way that one part of it will "fuse" with the bole of a tree, another with the leaves, a third with the ground, then the beholder will no longer see a unit, the gun, but a multiplicity of much less important objects. Camouflage was an art well developed during the war, when even big ships were destroyed as real units in the behavioural world of the scouting enemy. Thus existence of a real unity is neither the necessary nor the sufficient cause of behavioural unity.

If we choose size as the aspect in which we should find correspondence we see at once that no direct relation between real and apparent size can exist, for the moon looks large on the horizon and small on the zenith.

And even for the aspect of motion it is easy to prove that the existence, within the field of vision, of real motion is neither a necessary nor a sufficient condition for the perception of motion. It is not a necessary condition, for we can see motion when no real motion occurs, as on the cinematographic screen, but neither is it sufficient, for apart from the fact that too slow and too fast real motions produce no perception of motion, there are many cases where the apparently moving object is really at rest, as the moon that seems to float through the clouds.

We forbear discussing other aspects because our material is sufficient to prove the first answer to our question wrong. That things are what they are does not explain why they look as they look.

Consequences implied in the first answer. Before we discuss another answer to our question we may for a moment consider what it would mean if the first answer were right. If things looked as they do because they are what they are, then the relation between the behavioural and the geographical environment would be simple indeed. Then for all practical purposes we could substitute the latter for the former. Conversely, since we know that the answer is wrong, we must guard against this confusion, which is not as easily avoided as one might think. To show how a disregard of our warning has influenced psychological theory, we will formulate our conclusion in still another manner. If things looked as they do because they are what they are, then perception would not contain in its very make-up a cognitive problem. Perception would, barring certain unusual conditions, be cognitive of the geographical environment. A cognitive problem might arise in the field of generalized thought, but as long as we remained in the field of direct perception we ought to be face to face with objective reality. The proposition, included in many philosophical systems, that the senses cannot lie, is a special form of this more general idea. To be sure, the existence of special cases where perception was deceptive was generally admitted. But these cases were treated as exceptions to the general rule, and for this reason the so-called geometric optical illusions received so much attention in the development of psychology. And when one reads the older literature on the subject, and some of the recent too, one will find explanations of this kind: if of two equal lines, one looks longer than the other, then we must look for special conditions which mislead our *judgment* about the relative length of these lines. Remove these distracting circumstances and the judgment will be correct; the normal state of affairs, in which the behavioural world corresponds to the geographical one, will be re-established. That is to say, illusory perceptions were not accorded the same rank as non-illusory ones; they presented a special problem, whereas the normal appearance presented no problem at all. This distinction between two kinds of perception, normal and illusory, disappears as a psychological distinction as soon as one becomes thoroughly aware of the fallacy which it implies, much as it may remain as an epistemological distinction. For each thing we have to ask the same question, "Why does it look as it does?" whether it looks "right" or "wrong."

Two meanings of the term stimulus. These last considerations ought to have shown that our refutation of the first answer is not so banal as might have been thought. At the start it might well have been argued, How can the first answer be right, when the geographical things are not in direct contact with the organism? When I see a table, this table qua table does not affect my senses at all; they are affected by processes which have their origin in the sun or an artificial source of light, and which are only modified by the table before they excite the rods and cones in our retinae. Therefore, these processes, the light waves, and not the geographical objects, are the direct causes of our perceptions, and consequently we cannot expect a very close relationship between behavioural and geographical things. For the light waves do not depend only upon the things qua things, but also upon the nature of the source of light (which only in the case of self-luminous bodies belongs to them as their own property) and on the position of the things with regard to our own bodies. This last relation is regulated by the laws of perspective, the first by laws of light absorption and reflection. But perspective, light absorption, and reflection remain outside our organisms. The retinae receive a pattern of excitations, and it can make no difference to the retinae how these excitations have been produced. If, without a table and even without light (for instance, by electrical stimulation of the rods and cones), we could produce the same pattern of excitation with the same curvature of the lenses which is ordinarily produced on our retinae when we fixate a table, then the person on whose retinae these excitations were produced should and would see a table. This leads us to introduce a new terminological distinction. The causes of the excitations of our sense organs are called stimuli. We see now that this word has two different meanings which must be clearly distinguished from each other: on the one hand the table in the geographical environment can be called a stimulus for our perception of a table; on the other hand the excitations to which the light rays coming from the table give rise are called the stimuli for our perception. Let us call the first the *distant* stimulus, the second the *proximal* stimuli. Then we can say that our question why things look as they do must find its answer not in terms of the distant, but of the proximal, stimuli. By a neglect of this difference real problems have been overlooked, and explanations proffered which are no explanations at all. We shall see this presently in detail, but we can point out here how the confusion of distant and proximal stimuli can have such a fatal effect on psychological theory. The danger of this confusion lies in the fact that for each distant stimulus there exists a practically infinite number of proximal stimuli; thus, the "same stimulus" in the distant sense may not be the same stimulus in the proximal sense; as a matter of fact it very seldom is. Thus the sameness of the former conceals a difference of the latter, and all arguments based on identical stimulation are spurious if they refer to identity of the distant stimulus only.

The Second Answer

The introduction of our term proximal stimulus has, however, given us a clue to the second answer to our question: things look as they do because the proximal stimuli are what they are. Now in its broadest interpretation this proposition is certainly true, but the interpretation usually given to it is distinctly limited and therefore false. In the widest interpretation our proposition means no more than this: any change in the proximal stimulation will, provided it be not too small, produce *some* change in the look of things, but *what kind* of change in the behavioural world will follow upon a change in the proximal stimulation cannot be derived from our proposition; whereas in the narrower interpretation the proposition also contains implicitly a statement about the kind of this change. Two objects project retinal images of different size on our retinae and appear to be at the same distance. Then the one which corresponds to the larger retinal image will look larger. We see two adjacent surfaces at an equal distance in front of us, the one looks a lighter, the other a darker, grey; then the retinal image corresponding to the former will contain more light than that of the latter. From these examples two conclusions might be drawn: the larger the retinal image, the larger the perceived object, and the greater the intensity of the image the more white will the object look; consequently when I change the stimulus corresponding to one object by making it smaller, the object should look smaller too, and if I reduce the intensity of stimulation the object should look blacker. These conclusions which have been actually accepted as axioms of sense psychology will seem very plausible. But neither do they follow from our examples, nor are they true. They do not follow from our examples because they only take in a part of the conditions of these examples and they are continually contradicted by the facts. Look at a white surface and then reduce the illumination of this surface; for a long time the surface will remain white, and only when you have reduced your illumination to a very low point will it become greyish. As a matter of fact a surface which still looks white under a low illumination may send much less light into our eyes than a black surface in good illumination. Disregard for the moment such plausible explanations as that when the light is decreased the pupil dilates so as to allow more of the incoming light to fall on our retinae, and that simultaneously the sensitivity of our retinae increases so as to make the effect of light greater. As we shall see later, both these factors, which are admittedly real, have been ruled out as sufficient explanations of our effect, so for simplicity's sake we neglect them altogether in our present discussion. Have we then shown that a change in the stimulus, in our case a diminution of light, has no effect at all on the look of things? If we had, we should have contradicted our general interpretation of the proposition: things look as they do because the proximal stimuli are what they are, an interpretation which we have accepted. But we have shown no such thing; we have only shown that the particular effect which would follow from the narrower interpretation of our proposition has failed to materialize. But there is an effect notwithstanding. For when the illumination is reduced, we become aware of a *darkening* of the *room*. Comparing this case with our former example we see that a change in the intensity of the retinal image may have at least two different effects: it may make the particular object look whiter or blacker, or it may make the whole room appear brighter or darker.

And the same is true of our other example. Look at the moon, particularly when it is at the horizon, and compare its size with that of a shilling held at arm's length. You will find the moon looking very much larger, whereas the retinal image of the shilling is larger than that of the moon. At the same time you see the moon at a much greater distance. Therefore decrease in size of a retinal image may either produce a shrinking or a receding of the corresponding object in the behavioural environment.

Two old experiments confirm this conclusion. In both, the observer looks monocularly at a screen with a circular hole in it. At some distance behind the screen there is a well-illuminated homogeneous white wall part of which is visible through the hole. In the first experiment (3) a taut vertical black thread between the screen and the wall passes through the centre of the circle exposed by the hole. This thread is attached to stands which can be moved backwards and forwards in a sagittal line from the observer in such a way that the thread, whatever its distance from the hole, divides the circle into equal halves, the stands being invisible behind the screen. A movement of the thread has then no other effect than an increase or decrease of the width of its retinal image, apart from a possible blurring due to insufficient accommodation. Under these conditions the observer sees, as a rule, a sagittal motion of a thread with *constant* thickness, and not an increase or decrease of the thickness of an immovable thread. In the second experiment there is no thread at all, and the room is totally dark so that the light circular hole is the only visible object in it. The variable is this time the opening of the hole itself which is made by an iris diaphragm which can be opened or closed. The retinal conditions are still simpler than in the first case, the retinal area on which the light falls increasing or decreasing. Accompanying these retinal changes the observers see either a forward or backward movement of the light circle, or its expansion or contraction, or finally a joint effect in which expansion and approach, contraction and recession, are combined.

We can now present our argument in a more generalized form. If the answer, things look as they do because the proximal stimuli are what they are, were true in the narrower sense, two propositions should hold. 1) Changes in the proximal stimulation unaccompanied by changes of the distant stimulus-object should produce corresponding changes in the *looks* of the behavioural object, and 2) any change in the distant object which produces no effect in the proximal stimulation should leave the looks of the behavioural object unchanged.

That 1) is not true follows from the example we have discussed. A white surface continues to look white, a black one black even when the proximal stimulation to which they give rise varies over a very wide range; my pencil looks no bigger when I hold it in my hand than when it is at the other end of my desk, when its retinal image may be less than half the size of the image of the pencil in my hand; the seat of a chair looks rectangular, although its retinal image will be rectangular in a negligibly small number of occasions only. In other words the behavioural things are conservative; they do not change with every change of the proximal stimulation by which they are produced. The constancy of real things is to a great extent preserved in the constancy of the *phenomenal* things despite variations in their proximal stimuli.

*   *   *   *   *   *   *   *   *   *

We can summarize our discussion in this way: if "meaning" as employed by the interpretation theory has any assignable meaning, then it is neither the necessary nor the sufficient condition of discrepancies between the pattern of the proximal local stimuli and the perceived objects—not necessary because these discrepancies appear under conditions where we can exclude meaning, not sufficient because they fail to appear where meaning is clearly present. Thus the interpretation theory and the constancy hypothesis with which it is inextricably connected have to disappear from our system for good.

Constancy Hypothesis and Traditional Physiological Theory

Local stimulation. In the beginning of this discussion we have claimed that the interpretation hypothesis is closely bound up with the traditional physiological hypotheses about brain processes. We can now make this claim more explicit. The interpretation hypothesis was demanded by the constancy hypothesis which we shall now formulate in a somewhat different manner. Recalling the arguments on which it was based we see that it correlated behavioural characteristics not with the total proximal stimulation but only with such parts of it as corresponded to the distant stimulus objects under discussion. In other words, it derived the characteristics of behavioural objects from the properties of *local* stimulations. In its consistent form the constancy hypothesis treats of sensations, each aroused by the local stimulation of one retinal point. Thus the constancy hypothesis maintains that the result of a local stimulation is constant, provided that the physiological condition of the stimulated receptor is constant (e.g., adaptation). This implies that all locally stimulated excitations run their course without regard to other excitations, in full accord with the traditional physiological hypotheses. When now we see that the constancy hypothesis has to be abandoned we know already what has to take its place, for we have demonstrated in our second chapter that physiological processes must be considered as processes in extension. But that means that no local stimulation can determine the corresponding excitation by itself, as the constancy hypothesis implied, but only in connection with the totality of stimulation. The form of the process in extension must depend upon the whole extended mosaic of stimulation, and all its parts become what they are as a result of the organization of the extended process. Only when we know the kind of organization in which a local process occurs can we predict what it will be like, and therefore the same change in local stimulation can produce different changes in the behavioural world according to the total organization which is produced by the total stimulation. Thus we can say: only when the total conditions are such that two visible objects will appear in *one* frontal vertical plane will the one whose retinal image is larger also look larger. The abandonment of the constancy hypothesis does not mean that we put in its place an arbitrary connection between proximal stimulation and the looks of things. All we intend to do is to replace laws of local correspondence, laws of machine effects, by laws of a much more comprehensive correspondence between the total perceptual field and the total stimulation, and we shall, in the search for these laws, find at least indications of some more specific constancies, though never one of the type expressed by the constancy hypothesis.

The experience error. There is one last aspect of the constancy hypothesis which must be specially emphasized, although we have discussed it already. Strictly speaking, the constancy hypothesis should refer to points only. In reality it has been used much less precisely; as a rule the local stimulus considered was the proximal stimulus coming from a definite distant stimulus object, the table, the thread in Wundt's experiments and so forth. But this looser use of the hypothesis implies a serious logical fallacy. Because the distant object is a thing by itself, the assumption is tacitly made that the retinal image corresponding to it is also. But as we have seen this assumption is by no means true. The stimuli at two adjacent points on the retinae contain nothing qua stimuli that will make the two corresponding points in behavioural space belong to two different objects or to one and the same object. If an object in the behavioural field is a thing by itself, it must be an integrated whole separated or segregated from the rest of the field. The stimuli as a pure mosaic possess neither this integration nor this segregation. And therefore we saw that it is as misleading to speak of pictures of outside things being on our retinae as on a photographic plate. If we speak of pictures or images as stimuli we mistake the result of organization for the cause of organization, a mistake that is being committed again and again. Köhler has called it the experience error (2). I have formulated the actual state of affairs by saying: we see, not stimuli—a phrase often used—but on account of, because of, stimuli (1, p. 163).

The True Answer

The refutation of the two answers given explicitly or implicitly to our question has led us to the true answer. Things look as they do because of the field organization to which the proximal stimulus distribution gives rise. This answer is final and can be so only because it contains the whole problem of organization itself. Thus our answer, instead of closing a chapter in psychology, has opened one, a fact of which anyone who is acquainted with the psychological literature must be aware. It means that we have to study the laws of organization.

References

1. Koffka, K. *Psychologie der Wahrnehmung.* VIIIth Int. Congr. of Psychol., Groningen, Proceedings and Papers, 1926, 159-165.
2. Köhler, W. *Gestalt psychology.* New York: Liveright, 1929.
3. Wundt, W. *Grundzuge der physiologischen Psychologie,* 5. Aufl. 3 vols. Leipzig, 1903.

25   THE FIGURAL AFTER-EFFECT

Wolfgang Köhler and Hans Wallach

The concept of figural after-effects is just emerging from its formative stage. About ten years ago remarkable instances of such effects were discovered by J. J. Gibson. But his observations referred to quite particular figural conditions. Unfortunately an investigation of reversible figures with which we were occupied at the time, and which dealt with certain other effects of prolonged inspection, seemed equally restricted in scope. Thus it happened that for years the close relationship between Gibson's experiments and our own work was not realized. In our present report we hope to give the concept of figural after-effects a clearer connotation so that in the future such effects will be more easily recognized.

Gibson reported his first discovery in 1933 (2). His subjects observed that during prolonged inspection slightly curved lines gradually became less curved. When afterwards straight lines were shown in the location and orientation of the curves, such straight lines appeared curved in the opposite direction. Their distortion could be measured. The effect was again measured by Bales and Follansbee (1), who also added some new observations. Gibson himself, however, did not restrict his experiments to the case of visual curves. He asked blind-folded subjects to move their fingers along a convexly curved edge and to repeat this movement for several minutes. They reported that the curve gradually appeared less convex. Afterwards a straight edge felt definitely concave. In vision he found that not only curves gave clear after-effects but also lines which were bent at the middle into an obtuse angle. When the apex of the angle had been fixated for some time, straight lines of the same location and orientation appeared bent in the opposite direction.[1] A further phenomenon was observed and measured by Gibson (2, 3, 5), M. D. Vernon (8), and Gibson and Radner (4). When their observers

---

[1] Gibson (4, p. 562) mentions that this effect was first observed by F. H. Verhoeff (7).

From W. Köhler and H. Wallach, Figural after-effects: an investigation of visual processes, *Proc. Amer. Phil. Soc.*, Philad., 1944, *88*, 269-357. Pp. 269-270 reprinted by permission of the authors and the American Philosophical Society.

inspected a straight line which was moderately tilted with regard to the vertical or the horizontal, afterwards the objective vertical or horizontal appeared tilted in the opposite direction. Moreover, when the position of the vertical (horizontal) was thus altered the horizontal (vertical) tended to turn in the same direction.

Apart from these basic observations the authors, particularly Gibson himself, reported further facts which served to clarify the nature of such after-effects. In the *first* place it was found by Gibson that the after-effects were fairly closely restricted to the locus of the inspection figure. Here the term locus is to be understood in reference to the visual sector of the nervous system, because an effect which was caused by inspection of a figure in one place would show on an appropriate test object elsewhere as soon as the eyes were turned into the right position relative to this object. *Secondly,* however, Gibson observed that when only one eye was used during the inspection period an after-effect of somewhat smaller amount could clearly be observed in the corresponding part of the other eye's field. *Thirdly,* long inspection times, although desirable for certain purposes, proved not to be necessary for noticeable after-effects. When Gibson and Radner measured the "tilted line" effect after varying periods of inspection they found that it was unmistakably present after five seconds, and about maximal as early as one or two minutes later. With such inspection times the curve of the development tended to become parallel to the abscissa. Particularly impressive is the *fourth* observation. Once a strong figural after-effect had been obtained it often persisted for many minutes. As a matter of fact, with one of Gibson's subjects the after-effect did not disappear within twenty-four hours when by a proper device the inspection of vertical curves had been continued for several days. But, *fifthly,* individual differences as to the amount of the after-effects were quite conspicuous, although only Bales and Follansbee found them entirely absent in some subjects.

We agree with most factual statements made by Gibson and by the authors who continued his work. But we do not believe that Gibson's interpretation of his data is correct. He assumes that it is deviation of inspection objects from "norms," like straight lines in general and verticals or horizontals in particular, which leads to figural after-effects. Actually, figural after-effects are not restricted to such special instances. It will soon be seen that, as a matter of principle, inspection of any specific entity in a visual field can cause figural after-effects. Gibson's discoveries will therefore have to be re-interpreted within the larger body of facts which is now at our disposal.

The existence of figural after-effects in a more general sense was first inferred from the behavior of reversible figures. Some data concerning the spontaneous reversals of such figures under conditions of prolonged inspection have been given elsewhere (6, pp. 67 ff.). Here we will repeat merely that the speed of those reversals tends to increase as fixation is continued, that then the figures will still be unstable after rest periods of several minutes, and that for this reason their instability can be enhanced in a sequence of separate inspection periods. This fact of summation or accumulation suggests that prolonged presence of a figure in a given location tends to operate against further presence of this figure in the same place. It may be concluded that the presence of a figure in the visual field is associated with a specific figure process in the visual sector of the brain, and that this process gradually alters the medium in which it occurs. In a reversible figure a redistribution of the figure process seems to occur when that change has reached a certain level.

It follows from these assumptions that a figure which has become unstable in its original location must again appear more stable when it is shown in a new position. Such a recovery can actually be demonstrated.

Quite apart from any reference to Gibson's discoveries, our assumptions contained certain implications which were not restricted to reversible figures. However, we did not at once realize that our interpretation involved *two* hypotheses, and that only one of them was concerned with reversible figures. According to the first hypothesis a specific figure process occurs whenever a figure appears in the visual field. And this process tends to block its own way if the figure remains for some time in the same location. The second hypothesis states that in reversible figures the figure-ground relationship will suddenly be reversed when the figure process has altered the medium beyond a critical degree. Obviously, only the second hypothesis refers to reversible figures. In the first hypothesis such particular patterns play no part. This assumption must therefore apply to all figures without exception. In other words, continued presence of *any* figure in a given location must change conditions for subsequent figure processes in the same region of the field.

References

1. Bales, J. F. and Follansbee, G. L. The after-effect of the perception of curved lines. *J. exp. Psychol.*, 1935, *18*, 499-503.
2. Gibson, J. J. Adaptation, after-effect, and contrast in the perception of curved lines. *J. exp. Psychol.*, 1933, *16*, 1-31.
3. Gibson, J. J. Vertical and horizontal orientation in visual perception. *Psychol. Bull.*, 1934, *31*, 739 (Abst.).
4. Gibson, J. J. and Radner, M. Adaptation, after-effect, and contrast in the perception of tilted lines. I. Quantitative studies. *J. exp. Psychol.*, 1937, *20*, 453-467.
5. Gibson, J. J. Adaptation, after-effect, and contrast in the perception of tilted lines. II. Simultaneous contrast and the areal restriction of the after-effect. *J. exp. Psychol.*, 1937, *20*, 553-569.
6. Köhler, W. *Dynamics in psychology*. New York: Liveright, 1940.
7. Verhoeff, F. H. A theory of binocular perspective. *Amer. J. Physiol. Opt.*, 1925, *6*, 436.
8. Vernon, M. D. The perception of inclined lines. *Brit. J. Psychol.*, 1934, *25*, 186-196.

26   THE PSYCHOLOGY OF OBJECTIVE RELATIONS

Egon Brunswik

In a physical description of the environment of an organism, concepts such as the following are used: sizes of bodies, sizes of the projections of such bodies on a photographic plate or on the retina; actual shapes of body surfaces and the projected shapes of such surfaces; weights, densities, kinetic energies of moving bodies; areas; volumes; number of items; and so on. All such entities may be designated "objects" (Gegenstände) using this term to apply to single object-characters, per se. And such "objects" are defined in terms of purely physical and objective processes of measurement and computation.

The use and therefore the knowledge of certain of these "objects" is biologically very important for the organism. Such objects will deter-

From E. Brunswik, Psychology in terms of objects. In *Proc. 25th Anniv. Celebr. Inaug. Grad. Stud.* Los Angeles: Univ. South. Calif. Press, 1936. Reprinted by permission of the author and the publisher.

mine directly the usefulness of any given body as a means to reaching a final goal. This is true, for example, for the actual sizes of manipulable bodies. Other kinds of objects, on the other hand, will have less immediate biological importance. Thus, any projective size (the size of the area on the retina of the eye, stimulated by any given body) will have relatively little immediate significance since this may be caused either by a large body far away or by a small body near at hand. Obviously, the actual nature of distant objects can not be learned from the projective size.

The task of the perceiving organism is, then, to keep its reactions free of the variations of projective stimulus-size. This can be done by combining the projective size of an object with distance-cues into single, unified wholes, or "sign-gestalten" as Tolman might call them. According to Bühler's "duplicity principle" no "thing-constancy" can be established without such a twofold stimulus-basis.

In this way, the higher organisms succeed in establishing a constant relationship between their reactions and the physical properties of manipulable bodies far from the retina. The mediating stimulus properties vanish from explicit representation, i.e., become bridged over. Thus, for example, the size of a given body may be represented in the eye either by a large retinal image combined with a cue for a short distance, or by a small retinal image combined with a cue for a long distance. In both cases the perceptual reaction will be about the same and will correspond to the constant objective size of the body, while the decided variations in the retinal values will scarcely be noticed. Another way of stating this same fact would be to say that whereas the kind of object called "body-size" is actually "attained" in perception, the type of mediating object called "projective-size" is not attained. This is true since these varying retinal sizes are, as such, not responded to except in the retina.

Size-constancy is only approximate, an ideal size-constancy hardly ever being realized. Extensive experimentation has shown that bodies of a given size usually persist in looking a little larger when near at hand than when at a distance, due to their larger projective values. But the influence of this effect of projective-size is only slight, for the apparent size does not increase as the object is brought closer in anything like the same degree as does the size of the retinal image. By means of a simple ratio it is possible to express the degree of interference of projective-sizes with the perception of body-sizes in generalized quantitative terms. Thus, for example, in a given situation we might obtain, roughly speaking, a 95 per cent body-size constancy, with a 5 per cent influence of projective-size, per se. The real object of perception, then, or that which is actually attained, may be said to be a compromise-object between body-size and projective-size.

Perception is led to combine the different viewpoints of body-size and of projective-size, per se, in its effort to obtain a quick survey of the biologically important facts in the environment; for, perception is forced to rely upon the indirect efforts of the distant objects and to use these latter as cues. Thus, for example, binocular disparity may yield a good cue for distance. But even this type of cue is not altogether unambiguous. Binocular disparity may in some cases be caused not by real depth but by two flat pictures in a stereoscope and it will then mislead perception. The perceptual system may thus in the end be led to respond to these and similar failures by a kind of distrust of all kinds of cues, so that all cues for depth distances will come to be taken not quite seriously. Therefore, in establishing size-constancy, a slight influence will be allowed to projective-size, per se, instead of a full admission of distance cues. And the acceptance of this influence will be correct in that it will correspond to an actual slight objective probability that a large retinal image may be caused by a really large object at various distances rather than by a really small object at the same distances. The perceptual re-action may thus be said to be governed by a set of more or less general-ized implicit "hypotheses" (as behavioristically defined by Tolman and Krechevsky) concerning the relationship between the stimulus cues and the distant means-objects. These will have different degrees of emphasis or "subjective" certainty, and will interact accordingly. The final actual perceptual reaction will then turn out to be a kind of compromise be-tween these, and will tend to achieve for the organism a relatively high amount of probable success.

All behaviour can be described in terms of hypotheses concerning different kinds of cue-means and means-goal relationships, where these hypotheses differ among themselves in degrees of "subjective" certainty. Furthermore, as seen from the standpoint of the observing psychologist, such hypotheses will also differ in the degree of objective correctness or stupidity, their narrowness or their overgeneralization. And percep-tion, especially, proves to consist of a relatively primitive and stereo-typed system of hypotheses. The perception-system proves, in short, to function in a way not very dissimilar from that of such an animal as the white rat.

In a set of special experimental studies, it has been found that perception-constancy increases in children, reaching its maximum when they are between 10 and 15 years of age, and decreasing in the educated adult, if the latter are not specifically trained in perception. It would seem that high perceptual success is needed *less* as sophisticated discoursive knowledge increases. It has also been found experimentally that the degree of perceptual attainment can be increased by special exercise and that perception even can be conditioned to new and arbitrary cues. Further, the degrees of perceptual attainment, relative to different kinds of objects, have also been investigated experimentally. For example, a very high degree of form-constancy with variations of accompanying size has been found. Again, areas in varying forms have been found to exhibit a high degree of perceptual constancy. They are only affected slightly by the different lengths and proportions of the separate sides or by the total length of the periphery. On the other hand, such physically distinct factors as volume, surface-area, and height of tridimensional bodies interfere with one another much more and tend to form one single complex impression of *magnitude*. Further, the apparent number of elements in a group has been found to be influenced by the size, the distribution and even the value of the elements. Similar compromises have been obtained from experiments on the perception of weight, density, kinetic energy, and speed.

It must be emphasized that the type of experiments just indicated do not require in principle any use of qualitative introspection. By an analysis of the objective environmental situations leading to equal reactions, the kind of objects picked out of the environmental causal texture by perception can be stated in objective quantitative terms. We may call this procedure the "method of equal reactions." Constancy-research is thus objective not only in measuring the results but also in the method of obtaining such results.

By simultaneously varying the objects and situations to be compared in many different ways, constancy-research has developed an advantage over the simpler types of discrimination experiment as carried out in traditional psychophysics. The psychophysical experiments did not make possible any clear-cut and non-introspective decisions concerning the *kinds* of objects really determining the perceptual reaction; i.e., body-size versus projective-size, or weight versus density, etc. Constancy-experiments, on the contrary, can be called a complex, "multipolar" or "multidimensional" psychophysics, inasmuch as it is able to determine in an objective fashion the relative influence of such alternatives.

It has been found to hold as a rather general rule for the outcome of constancy-experiments, that biologically significant kinds of objects are attainable to a relatively high degree, even though their stimulus-mediation is a very complex and varying one. Relatively unimportant objects, on the other hand, are much less accurately responded to as such, even when they belong to the mediating data and are represented on the stimulus-surface in a very unambiguous fashion (as, for example, in the case of projective size).

All of the above facts concerning the functioning of the organism in perception suggest a general way of consideration which would seem to be the one most profitable for psychology. Thus, both for reception and for action, it turns out that the special manner in which anything is mediated (or done) is not especially essential or significant. One and the same means-object may be represented at different times by very different stimulus configurations. And one and the same goals may be reached equally well by very different kinds of movements and means-object manipulations. The focal-points of life occurrences, i.e., means-objects and final goal-effects, lie, respectively, relatively far away in time and space, backward (in cognition), or forward (in action). They are removed from the actual stimulus conditions and the actual body movements, so that the really significant question always is: What are the kinds of such objects and final goal-effects which the organism is able to attain independently of all the varying circumstances with a relatively large degree of accuracy and probability; achieving them by perception, on the one hand, and by action, on the other? In short, questions of "what" are much more important in psychology than questions of "how." And thus to seek to describe the abilities and performance of an organism by giving an inventory of the kinds of objects attained by it, may be called a "Psychology in Terms of Objects" (Psychologie vom Gegenstand her). In principle, this viewpoint need not have any concern with the organism's actual sensory, nervous, or motor conditions—i.e., with mere mediation problems, as studied in traditional behaviorism, psychophysics, and physiological psychology. For, all behavior can, in last essence, be described in a purely objective and quantitative fashion merely by indicating its success in establishing far-reaching couplings between types of means-objects available in the environment and types of final biological goal-effects. Constant relationships of this type seem to me to be the primary subject matter of psychology; they are focused on certain biologically important types of object relatively independently of the varying causal patterns of mediation. Such a psychology will combine the treatment of complex and genuinely psychological problems with exactness and objectivity of methods and of conceptual representation.

CHAPTER XI

LEARNING

NO CONCEPT has played a more central role in the development of recent systematic behavior theories than has that of learning. This is especially true of the various behavioristic, or "neo-behavioristic," systems. It is exemplified, in the present chapter, by the extent to which the various theorists have come to identify their views on learning with their general behavior systems. The first selection is from a paper on the law of effect by its chief proponent, Edward L. Thorndike, whose connectionistic theories and experiments have had a remarkably persistent influence on American psychological thinking since the beginning of the century. The selection by Clark L. Hull is the first important paper which he published on learning theory. It served to introduce the series of brilliantly conceived theoretical interpretations of conditioning which he wrote during the 1930's. The general position has been called "neo-behaviorism" since it represents a refinement of the broad fundamental principles laid down by Watson. Building upon the early learning theories of Pavlov and Thorndike, Hull has consistently attempted to apply rigorous mathematical and logical techniques to basic behavioral problems (see Selections No. 13 and 14). His reference has continued to be to learning principles derived from relatively simple conditioning studies, mainly performed with rats. No matter what one may think of the particular details of his systematically formalized behavior theory, its profound influence on contemporary psychological theory and experimentation can not be denied. The paper reprinted here presents his general systematic approach, based upon the two key concepts of reinforcement *and* inhibition, *and suggests his continuing concern with problems of biological adaptation. For a more up-to-date source his* Principles of Behavior *or other more recent publications must of course be consulted (see Selection No. 13 for a summary of his more formal recent system, and also Selections No. 3, 4, and 11).*

The introductory chapter from Edward C. Tolman's Purposive Behavior in Animals and Men *is reproduced as Selection No. 29. It summarizes his arguments in support of his purposive behaviorism, which is a unique attempt to integrate the behavioristic and the Gestalt (or field-theoretical) approaches to behavior problems. Historically, it served to popularize his important distinction between molar and molecular as descriptive terms (see also Selection No. 9). Tolman's intention to remain within a strictly objective behavioristic framework, in spite of the inclusion of other points of view in his system, is evident in his other paper reprinted in this volume (Selection No. 5). Edwin R. Guthrie's contiguity theory of conditioning as the prototype of all learning is presented in the fourth selection. Although this paper was the first important presentation of his learning system, no major modification has been subsequently made. The fifth selection is from an early paper by B. F. Skinner, and indicates the rationale of his closely knit behavior system. Methodologically, as a pure descriptive positivist, Skinner stands at the opposite pole from Hull, who has emphasized the highly formal use of theory. The final selection is an excerpt from one of K. S. Lashley's experimental reports. It summarizes his general position on the problem of stimulus equivalence, with which he has been actively concerned over a period of years.*

27 CONNECTIONISM

Edward L. Thorndike

One of the objections to the hypothesis that a satisfying after-effect of a mental connection works back upon it to strengthen it is that nobody has shown how this action does or could occur. It is the purpose of this article to show how a mechanism which is as possible physiologically as any of the mechanisms proposed to account for facilitation, inhibition, fatigue, strengthening by repetition or other forms of modification, could enable such an after-effect to cause such a strengthening. I shall also report certain facts and hypotheses concerning the work which this mechanism has to do and the way in which it seems to do it. These are of value regardless of the correctness of my identification of the mechanism itself.

For convenience we may use symbols as follows:

N = the neurones of an animal.

B = the rest of the animal's body.

C = any activity, state, or condition of N.

S = any situation or state of affairs external to N considered as a cause of some C.

R = any response or state of affairs external to N, considered as a result of some C.

By a satisfying state of affairs or satisfier is meant one which the animal does nothing to avoid, often doing things which maintain or renew it. By an annoying state of affairs is meant one which the animal does nothing to preserve, often doing things which put an end to it.

A satisfier exerts an influence that strengthens any modifiable C upon which this influence impinges. Not knowing what Cs are made of, or how a strong C differs from a weaker form of the same C, one must speak in figures and analogies. The influence may thus be thought of as like an addition of current or potential, or a decrease of resistance, or an intimacy of connection, or a continuance for a longer time.

The Cs upon which it impinges most will be among those which

From E. L. Thorndike, A theory of the action of the after-effects of a connection upon it, *Psychol. Rev.*, 1933, *40*, 434-439. Reprinted by permission of the *Psychological Review* and the American Psychological Association.

have recently been active or will shortly be active. That is, the action of a satisfier is conditioned by its place in the succession of *C*s.

The *C*s upon which it impinges will be preferentially those situated in the part or feature or pattern or system or organization of *N* in which the satisfier occurs. When an animal that runs about seeking food attains it, the strengthening will be more likely to influence the *C*s concerned with its locomotion, its hunger, and its ideas about food and eating, than those concerned with contemporaneous casual scratchings of an itching ear, or stray thoughts about Shakespeare's sonnets or Brahms' symphonies.

More narrowly the influence will impinge preferentially upon the *C* (or *C*s) to which the satisfier "belongs" as a part of a more or less unitary group of *C*s, or larger *C*. In the animal just mentioned, the satisfier will strengthen the *C* between reaching the doorway to the food-box and going in, more than the *C* between reaching that doorway and pausing to inspect it. The excess strengthening will be far more than the slight difference in time can account for. If, in an exercise in completing a word, say oc · re, by supplying a missing letter, a person tries first *a*, then *e*, then *i*, then *o*, and then *h*, being rewarded by "Right" for the last, and then at once proceeds to look at the next word, the satisfier will strengthen the *C* with *h* enormously more than the next preceding or following *C*, far more than the removal by one step and a second or so could account for.

Its influence will not, however, pick out the "right" or "essential" or "useful" *C* by any mystical or logical potency. It is, on the contrary, as natural in its action as a falling stone, a ray of light, a line of force, a discharge of buckshot, a stream of water, or a hormone in the blood. It will strengthen not only the *C* which is the most preferred according to the principles stated above, but also to some extent *C*s which are wrong, irrelevant, or useless, provided they are close enough to the satisfier in the succession of *C*s.

One naturally asks first whether the action of a satisfier may be by stimulating the general circulation and thus causing the *C*s which happen to be in a state of excitement at or near the time of occurrence of the satisfier to be preferentially strengthened by some metabolic process. The facts seem to deny this possibility. The strengthening influence of a satisfier is probably in the form of a reaction of the neurones themselves. It is too rapid to be via an increase or decrease in the general circulation, or by the liberation of a hormone. When a series $S \rightarrow R \rightarrow$ Reward or

Punishment, $S \rightarrow R \rightarrow$ Reward or Punishment, $S \rightarrow R \rightarrow$ Reward or Punishment is run at the rate of 3 seconds per unit, the action of each satisfier is localized at and around its point of application in the series with almost perfect clearness. And this is approximately true with rates of 1½ seconds or even 1 second per unit. Moreover, remoteness in steps seems (though the data are not yet adequate) very much more important than remoteness in time in restricting its application.

This unknown reaction of neurones which is aroused by the satisfier and which strengthens connections upon which it impinges I have called the "Yes" reaction, or O. K. reaction, or confirming reaction. Though its intimate histological basis and physiological nature are no better known than those of facilitation, inhibition, fatigue, strengthening by repetition, or any other forces causing temporary or permanent modifications in N, certain facts about it are known in addition to those already stated concerning its causes and results.

The confirming reaction is independent of sensory pleasures. A pain may set it in action, as Tolman, Hall, and Bretnall have recently demonstrated in a striking experiment (1). The confirming reaction, though far from logical or inerrant, is highly selective. It may pick out and act upon the words one is saying, leaving uninfluenced one's posture and gross bodily movements and all that one is seeing.

The confirming reaction seems often to issue from some overhead control in N, the neural basis of some want or "drive" or purpose or then active self of the animal. This overhead control may be rather narrow and specific, as when a swallow of liquid satisfies thirst, and the satisfaction confirms the C which caused the swallowing, and makes the animal continue or repeat that C. This may happen while the main flow of his purposes concerns the work he is doing or the game he is playing or the book he is reading. It may be very broad and general, as when the purpose is to do well and win a game or to pass the time pleasantly, and is satisfied by any one of many movements in response to some play of one's adversary or by attentiveness to any one of many sights and sounds. It may be stimulated to send forth its confirming reaction by a rich sensory satisfier, such as freedom, food, and companionship for an animal escaping from a cage, or by a purely symbolic satisfier, such as the announcement of "Right" in an experiment in learning. If what the overhead control wants is the announcement of "Right," that is what will most surely lead it to make the confirming reaction.

As suggested by the preceding paragraph, several wants or purposes or controls may be operative at the same time or in close alternation.

Arrangements may be made whereby certain events acquire power to cause the confirming reaction in the absence of anything that would ordinarily be called an overhead control. The reward or satisfier may then exert the confirming reaction directly upon the C.

If a $S \rightarrow R$ connection has a satisfying after-effect which causes some control in the N to send forth a confirming reaction, and if the S continues, the confirming reaction tends to cause a continuance or continued repetition of the R then and there, and often with more vigor and shorter latency. If the situation has vanished, the strengthening of the C can only manifest itself when S recurs, which may be in a few seconds or only after months. There will then be an increased probability of repetition over what there would have been if no confirming reaction had affected the C in question. In either case the strengthening causes the repetition, not the repetition the strengthening.

The potency of a confirming reaction may bear little relation to the intensity of the satisfier. A "want" or "purpose" or "self" may be as well satisfied, and so issue as full and adequate a confirming reaction, by a moderate reward as by one much larger. There seems to be an upper point beyond which increases in a reward add only excitement. Toward the low end there is a range where the reward fails more and more frequently to arouse an adequate confirming reaction. There seems to be a point below which a confirming reaction is not evoked. A state of affairs below this degree of satisfyingness is satisfying to the extent of being tolerated, and nothing is done to abolish or evade it, or to replace the C which caused it by some other C; but also nothing is done to strengthen the C and continue it longer than it would otherwise have been continued, or to repeat it in the future more frequently than it would otherwise have been repeated.

At the other end of this neutral zone begin states of affairs which are annoying to the animal and stimulate him to do whatever his repertory provides as responses to the annoyance in question. His repertory does not provide a general destructive or weakening reaction which is comparable and opposite to the confirming reaction, and which subtracts from the C upon which it acts. Any apparent subtraction is due to the increased strength of competing tendencies. The annoyer does not then and there destroy or weaken the connection of which it is the after-effect, but only causes the animal to make a different response to the S in question.

I do not think that this tendency to do something different in response to an S, the first response to which has resulted in an annoying state of affairs, is a unitary tendency applicable to any C, and replacing it indifferently by any other C than it. The confirming reaction set in action by a satisfier, has, if my observations are correct and adequate, no comparable altering reaction set in action by an annoyer. The reactions in the latter case seem specialized and closely dependent on what the annoyer is and what state the N is in.

Whether or not this is so, an annoying after-effect of a certain $S \rightarrow R$ has very different possibilities *according as the S remains or vanishes*. If it vanishes, the annoyer can do nothing, because it cannot change the response to an S which is not there. So, in multiple-choice learning in which each S vanishes as soon as it is responded to, punishments have zero influence upon learning and punished connections may do more harm to learning by occurring than they do good by being punished. If the S remains and the response to it is changed, the animal may benefit from the fact of changing, and from the occurrence and the after-effects of the $S \rightarrow R_2$ which has replaced $S \rightarrow R_1$.

What sort of force acting through what sort of process or mechanism can be and do what the confirming reaction is and does? The answer which seems to me to fit all or nearly all the facts is that the force and mechanism of the confirming reaction are the force and mechanism of reinforcement, applied to a connection.

All explanations of reinforcement agree that one part of N can exert a force to intensify activities elsewhere in N, and that processes or mechanisms exist whereby this force can be directed or attracted to one activity rather than promiscuously; and that is all that is required to explain the fundamental physiology of the confirming reaction. It is distinguished from other sorts of reinforcement by the fact that satisfaction sets the force in action and that the force acts on the connection which was just active in intimate functional association with the production of the satisfier, or on its near neighbors.[1]

---

[1] The differences between the present theory of the action of after-effects upon connections and that suggested by the writer twenty years ago should perhaps be mentioned. The older theory, though possibly true so far as it went, paid insufficient attention to the positive reinforcement of a connection as contrasted with the mere leaving it undisturbed. It also was inadequate to explain the spread or scatter phenomenon whereby unrewarded or punished connections are strengthened if they are in close enough proximity to a rewarded connection.

References

1. Tolman, E. C.; Hall, C. S. and Bretnall, E. P. A disproof of the law of effect and a substitution of the laws of emphasis, motivation, and disruption. *J. exp. Psychol.*, 1932, *15*, 601-614.

28   NEO-BEHAVIORISM

Clark L. Hull

Introduction

The experimental evidence now available shows quite clearly that the conditioned reflex is a two-phase phenomenon. One phase is obviously primary and the other is definitely secondary. Viewed physiologically, the primary phase is positive or excitatory in its nature; the secondary phase is negative or inhibitory. Functionally regarded, the primary phase appears to be a tentative trial, or first-approximation aspect of an adaptive process, while the secondary phase is the selective, corrective, or precision-insuring aspect. These two phases of the conditioned reflex, operating jointly, thus stand revealed as an automatic trial-and-error mechanism which mediates, blindly but beautifully, the adjustment of the organism to a complex environment.

The primary or excitatory phase of the conditioned reflex is the one which is best known and which has been employed most extensively as an explanatory principle. The knowledge of certain aspects of it, indeed, is as old as associationism itself. A much more comprehensive view of the process has recently been exploited to considerable advantage by H. L. Hollingworth under the name of *redintegration*. As applied to the conditioned reflex, this term represents the fact that all elements of a stimulus complex playing upon the sensorium of an organism at or near the time that a response is evoked, tend themselves independently and indiscriminately to acquire the capacity to evoke substantially the same response. For our present purposes the indiscriminateness of the tendency is particularly to be noted.

From C. L. Hull, A functional interpretation of the conditioned reflex, *Psychol. Rev.*, 1929, *36*, 498-511. Reprinted by permission of the author, the *Psychological Review*, and the American Psychological Association.

But the redintegrative aspect is only one of at least four which are discernible in the primary phase of the conditioned reflex. A second significant tendency is an almost total lack of responsiveness to the patterning of the stimulus complex. A third is a remarkable lack of specificity of the conditioned reactions as regards the conditioned stimuli which may evoke them; the reflexologists call this *irradiation*. A fourth characteristic of great significance is the curious tendency, where the conditioned stimulus precedes the unconditioned one in the conditioning process, for the reaction to be attracted forward toward the former. Under certain circumstances the reaction (after a number of reenforcements) may begin a considerable interval before the delivery of the unconditioned stimulus. In the case of certain defense reactions this may even result in the organism not receiving the nocuous unconditioned stimulus at all.

The secondary or inhibitory phase of the conditioned reflex appears to be less widely appreciated. For the most part this phase is not open to ordinary observation, only becoming manifest as the result of ingenious experimental procedures. Corresponding to the four aspects of the excitatory phase, each to each, we find here four parallel inhibitory aspects. They are: 1) inhibition from experimental extinction, 2) conditioned inhibition, 3) differential inhibition, and 4) inhibition of delay. In this connection it is to be noted that a given inhibitory tendency can only be developed on the basis of a corresponding excitatory tendency which must previously have been established.

We may now proceed to the consideration of the biological function performed by the several phases of the conditioned reflex process.

Redintegration and Experimental Extinction

Of what biological utility is the redintegrative tendency? It clearly results in the multiplication of the stimulus complexes which are capable of evoking particular reactions. With certain limitations, these conditioned stimulus complexes become equivalent to, i.e., substitutable for, the corresponding native or unconditioned stimuli. But just how does this substitution tendency result in augmenting the survival chances of the organism? It is quite clear, for example, that for any and every stimulus complex to have the capacity to evoke any and every response would not be good biological economy. Such an arrangement could lead to nothing but a wild and unadaptive chaos of behavior. No doubt many psychologists and biologists with a vitalistic leaning will urge that, if the process be really blind and automatic as assumed, we should expect exactly such a chaos. The problem deserves serious consideration.

The solution of the problem is seen perhaps most readily in the conditioning of defense reactions. The unconditioned stimuli for such reactions are ordinarily genuine injuries. With such unconditioned stimuli the organism will rarely or never make an unnecessary defense reaction for the reason that a defense will always be needed. Such certainty could hardly be attained with any other type of stimulus. This is a characteristic example of biological conservatism. The trouble with this particular type of arrangement is that, in order for the defense reaction to take place, the organism must always receive an injury. This is bad biological economy. Clearly a corrective accessory mechanism is needed. This exists in the substitution-of-stimulus tendency characteristic of redintegration.

Now the nature of nocuous stimuli practically limits them to such as involve actual contact with the organism before being effective. But if, as will usually be the case, the nocuous stimulus is of such a nature as also to stimulate a distance receptor like the eye, this latter stimulus is likely to get conditioned to the defense reaction. Here we have a means whereby effective defense behavior may be evoked without always being preceded by an injury. The retinal image of the threatening object when at a moderate distance will be sufficiently like that which is received when it is close enough to deliver the injurious stimulus, to evoke the defense reaction (withdrawal, flight) early enough for the organism to escape the injury altogether. Indeed it may very well be that the frequency among primitive conditioned reflexes of the substitution of distance receptors for contact receptors is due to this combination of circumstances.

Granting the tremendous biological advantage of occasionally being able to substitute certain stimulus complexes for certain others we still are pursued by the threat of a behavior chaos. There remains, in short, the difficulty presented by the indiscriminateness of the redintegrative tendency. Quite irrelevant stimulus elements will almost certainly find their way into every stimulus complex. By the principle of redintegration alone these irrelevant ones must get conditioned exactly as do the relevant. Why does not this produce the blind chaos of behavior previously suggested?

The answer is found in the corrective principle of experimental extinction. Stimulus elements which are not biologically relevant will not accompany a given unconditioned stimulus with any regularity, whereas the truly significant elements must do so. The latter, of course, will develop ordinary conditioned reflexes. The former, also, will tend to do so during their first accidental reinforcements or occasional short unbroken sequences of reinforcements. In so far as this accidental reinforcement takes place there may be realized a genuine unadaptiveness of behavior. Presumably this mechanism is responsible for a certain amount of human and other animal error.

Fortunately complete functional conditioning usually does not take place until after repeated combined stimulations. Except for very unusual runs of chance coincidences of stimuli, the irrelevant stimulus would appear one or more times *unaccompanied* by the unconditioned stimulus before the accidentally initiated redintegrative tendency should have risen above the functioning threshold. Such failures of reinforcement at once produce a tendency to experimental extinction. In this connection it must be remembered that experimental extinction is not a mere passive failure to strengthen an excitatory tendency according to the so-called "law of use." Instead it is a very potent tendency to repress existent excitatory tendencies, particularly the one from which it has taken its origin (1). Since chance alone will ordinarily present the irrelevant stimulus without reinforcement much more frequently than with it, the resulting inhibitory tendency will very soon become much more potent than the positive redintegrative tendency. Even if by some chance the false conditioned tendency should have gotten above the reaction threshold, the combination of circumstances just referred to would very soon convert it into a permanently inhibited and impotent state.

Patterned Stimuli and Conditioned Inhibition

After observing the utter indiscriminateness of the primary phase of the conditioned reflex as to the components of the stimulus complex which it tends to endow with action-evoking powers, we should not be greatly surprised to find a similar obtuseness as regards sensitivity to the particular combination or patterning of such complexes. Extensive experiments show, as a matter of fact, that the primary conditioning tendency leaves the components of the conditioned stimulus in an essentially unorganized state as regards the evocation of response. It is true that, if only a part of the original stimulus complex be presented, the intensity and promptness of the response will be reduced. This, how-ever, is an addition-subtraction type of reaction rather than a sensitivity to organization or pattern. Barring accidental variability in the potency of the several components of the conditioned stimulus, this reduction in the magnitude of the response closely parallels the reduction in the number of the conditioned stimulus elements. With the same reserva-tion, it may be said that one combination of stimulus elements from an original conditioned stimulus complex, will evoke the same response (both qualitative and quantitative) as any other combination having the same number of elements. Similarly, if two distinct stimuli which have been independently conditioned to a given response be presented together, the intensity of the resulting response is likely to approach closely the arithmetical sum of the responses to the two stimuli if pre-sented separately. It is accordingly clear that, except for characteristic differences in potency, the individual components of a primarily con-ditioned stimulus complex are completely interchangeable and appear to have little or no functional individuality. Under such circumstances there is naturally no differential sensitivity to any particular combina-tion or pattern of stimulus components.

Now it is evident to ordinary observation that the simple addition-subtraction relationship obtaining among the components of a condi-tioned stimulus in the primary phase of the conditioning process, is a fairly adequate first approximation for many life situations. Indeed, if the vertebrate organism were to be dependent upon but a *single* stimu-lus mechanism, it is doubtful whether any other conceivable one would be more conducive to successful environmental adjustment and sur-vival. In the long run, where fewer signs of danger appear, the less danger there is likely to be. Similarly, where two signs of danger appear, both of which independently are tolerably reliable, the organism is pragmatically justified by the law of chance alone in making unusually prompt and vigorous defense reactions. The same may be assumed to hold for positive reactions such as those involved in food getting.

Even so, innumerable life situations arise where the simple addition or subtraction of the potencies of the several components of a stimulus complex is not adequate. In many situations a particular combination or pattern of stimulus components (either simultaneous or temporally extended) is the very essence of the stimulus. To change a single minute component of certain stimuli will completely change the nature of the appropriate response. A telegram is an example of such a patterned stimulus complex. If a single letter in it be changed, the reaction of the receiver may be made either one of joy or of despair.

Numerous experimental examples of differential sensitivity to the patterning of stimuli are found in the conditioned reflex literature. We reproduce from Pavlov one involving a temporal pattern:

The following is an experiment by Dr. Ivanov Smolensky. The positive conditioned alimentary stimulus was made up of a hissing sound (H), a high tone (hT), a low tone (lT), and the sound of a buzzer (B), applied in that order, namely H–hT–lT–B. The inhibitory stimulus was made up with the order of the two middle components reversed, namely H–lT–hT–B.

Time	Conditioned Stimulus	Secretion of Saliva in Drops During 30 Seconds	Remarks
3:10 P.M.	H–hT–lT–B	4	Reinforced
3:17 P.M.	H–lT–hT–B	0	Not reinforced
3:27 P.M.	H–hT–lT–B	3	Reinforced
3:32 P.M.	H–hT–lT–B	4	"
3:38 P.M.	H–lT–hT–B	0	Not reinforced
3:46 P.M.	H–hT–lT–B	2	Reinforced

The formation of these inhibitory reflexes usually required a great deal of time; although a relative differentiation could sometimes be observed quite early, absolute differentiation was obtained in extreme cases only after more than one hundred repetitions without reinforcement (1, pp. 146-147).

How is this obvious inadequacy of the primary phase of the conditioned reflex met? As in the case of the primary redintegrative tendency, a corrective appears in the corresponding inhibitory phase, i.e., in experimental extinction. This was implied in the example just cited.

A special case of this is known in the literature as *conditioned inhibition*. This is of particular interest because it reveals in some detail one of the simplest mechanisms by which sensitivity to the patterning of a stimulus is mediated. Again we choose an example from Pavlov (1, p. 68).

A positive conditioned stimulus is firmly established in a dog by means of the usual repetitions with reinforcement. A new stimulus is now occasionally added, and whenever the combination is applied, it is never accompanied by the unconditioned stimulus. In this way the combination is gradually rendered ineffective, so that the conditioned stimulus when applied in combination with the additional stimulus loses its positive effect, although when applied singly and with constant reinforcement it retains its full powers.

Irradiation and Differential Inhibition

One of the most clearly marked of the primary tendencies of the conditioning process is that of spontaneous generalization. When a conditioned reflex has been set up in the usual manner, it is found that many other stimuli of a somewhat similar nature will also evoke the response. This is particularly common where a pseudo-conditioned stimulus operates through the same sensory analyzer as the true conditioned stimulus. Under certain circumstances this vicarious spreading of the conditioned tendency may extend even into entirely different sense fields such as from the skin to the senses of the eye and the ear. This primitive tendency to generalization is known among the reflexologists as *irradiation*.

It is evident upon only a little reflection that irradiation is a tendency of enormous importance. Indeed it is hard to conceive how any organism requiring very complex learned adjustments could survive without it. It is a commonplace observation in the animal world that stimuli varying within a rather wide range may require substantially the same reaction. Take, for example, a simple command. Physical analysis of sound shows that the particular stimulus complex constituting a vowel sound such as ä is largely different as spoken by a man and a woman, and even as spoken by the same person at different pitches or different persons of the same sex at the same pitch. Similar variability is found among all sorts of other stimuli which, for most purposes, are considered the same. Indeed it is doubtful whether, in a strict sense, a given stimulus is ever exactly repeated. It follows that if the conditioning process were to be based upon a principle of strictly exact repetitions of the conditioned stimulus, even within the differentiating limits of the analyzer, rarely or never would a sufficient number of such identical repetitions accumulate to raise the conditioning tendency above the functioning threshold. But even if by some miracle of chance a conditioned reflex should get set up under such conditions, of what biological value would it be? Without the principle of irradiation, it could never function except on the rare chance that the organism should encounter the particular shade of the stimulus upon which the conditioned reflex tendency was originally based. All of the innumerable other shades of variability of the stimulus biologically requiring the reaction could be of no adaptive value to the organism. To be so, each possible shade of the stimulus would need to be separately conditioned. But since the number of such differences would be indefinitely great, the organism might well consume the better part of its life in perfecting the conditioning process of a single response. It is very clear that irradiation is an indispensable principle of learned adjustment.

There is, however, a decided disadvantage in the unlimited tendency to irradiation. If irradiation were extended to its logical limit, it would ultimately bring about a state in which any stimulus whatever would tend to evoke, with little or no distinction, every conditioned response possessed by the organism. This would indeed produce an unadaptive behavior chaos. But, just as we have observed in the two preceding aspects of the primary phase of the conditioning process, an inhibitory tendency enters to save the biological situation. In this third case the corrective tendency is known as *differential inhibition.*

Let us suppose that a conditioned alimentary reflex has been set up to a bell of a certain pitch. Our knowledge of the irradiation tendency makes it quite safe to assume that another bell of a pitch and quality measurably different from the first will also evoke the response. We will assume that the second bell is not a biologically relevant stimulus. In this case it will not, when presented, receive reinforcement. This in turn (assuming an adequately discriminative analyzer mechanism) will gradually develop an inhibition for the pseudo-conditioned stimulus. Meanwhile the true bell will be steadily reinforced which will preserve the biologically valuable conditioned tendency intact. Thus the two tendencies, working jointly, bring about a most excellent adaptation which neither alone could conceivably effect.

The Anticipatory Tendency and Inhibition of Delay

Pavlov describes an experiment (1, p. 40) in which a dog was given a tactile stimulus continuously for one minute, after which there was a pause of one minute, whereupon some dilute acid was introduced into the dog's mouth. Such an introduction of acid is always followed after a brief interval by a flow of saliva—an unconditioned reflex. Pavlov seems not to have interested himself in the phenomenon here emphasized, so that the detailed timing of the process is not given in his report. It is plain, however, that at the beginning of the experiment the flow of saliva could not have taken place until some seconds *after the termination* of the one-minute pause. After the procedure described above had been repeated a number of times, a significant change takes place. The saliva begins to appear during the one-minute pause, i.e., *preceding* the introduction of the acid. The first time there was only half of a drop, presumably appearing just at the close of the period. Ten minutes later, ten drops appear during the pause. Since each drop requires some time for secretion, the first of these drops must have preceded the acid by a considerable part of the one-minute pause. A later repetition yielded fourteen drops during the pause, the first drop of which presumably preceded the introduction of the acid by a still longer interval. This experiment illustrates very nicely a most interesting and significant aspect of the excitatory phase of the conditioned reflex. It is the tendency of the reaction to creep forward in time toward the conditioned stimulus in such a way as to lessen the interval originally separating the two and to make the reaction antedate the presentation of the unconditioned stimulus.

We can now ask what may be the survival value of this anticipatory characteristic of the conditioned reflex. The writer ventures a fairly confident prediction that this primitive mechanism will be found intimately connected with the "short circuiting" so essential a part of the more complex forms of learning. By *short circuiting* is here meant the tendency of a significant or critical reaction in a learning behavior sequence, to move forward in the series in such a way as to antedate (and thus eliminate) useless and irrelevant behavior segments formerly preceding it. But quite apart from this possibility, the shortening of the time interval between the conditioned stimulus and its response has a most obvious and immediate biological significance. As usual this is most easily seen in the case of defense reactions, particularly those involving withdrawal and flight. If the conditioned defense reaction were to preserve unchanged its temporal distance from the conditioned stimulus, the organism would (assuming the conditioned stimulus to be related in a constant temporal manner to the unconditioned stimulus) encounter the injurious stimulus on every occasion. It would thus in no wise profit by the conditioning of the defense reaction, say, to a distance receptor. This would obviously be very bad biological economy. Clearly, for a defense reaction to be wholly successful, it should result in a complete escape from injury. The only way this can be effected is to have the flight reaction antedate the possibility of the impact of the nocuous stimulus. This the basic anticipatory tendency of the conditioned reflex brings about.

But not all reactions are defensive in this sense. Certain behavior acts, such as the various delayed reactions, require for their success in mediating biological adjustment that the period of latency or delay, instead of being reduced to a minimum, shall be separate from the stimulus by a quite definite and fairly prolonged period. This *inhibition of delay,* as it is called, has been studied experimentally by the reflex-ologists. By special techniques they have been able in dogs to condition periods of delay up to thirty minutes, with considerable precision. These experiments yield convincing evidence that the delay results from an inhibition which represses what would otherwise be an overt tendency for the reaction to follow the conditioned stimulus at once. The follow-ing report taken from Pavlov describes one of the more illuminating of these experiments (1, p. 41):

The animal can be given food regularly every thirtieth minute, but with the addition, say, of the sound of a metronome a few seconds before the food. The animal is thus stimulated at regular intervals of thirty minutes by a combination of two stimuli, one of which is the time factor and the other the beats of the metronome. Further, if the sound is now applied, not at the thirtieth minute after the preceding feeding, but, say, at the fifth or eighth minute, it entirely fails to produce any alimentary conditioned reflex. If it is applied slightly later, it produces some effect; applied at the twelfth minute the effect is greater; at the twenty-fifth minute greater still. At the thirtieth minute the reaction is of course complete. If the sound is never combined with food except when applied at the full interval, in time it ceases to have any effect even at the twenty-ninth minute and will only produce a reaction at the thirtieth minute—but then a full reaction.

Once more, then, we observe the primary excitatory phase and the secondary inhibitory phase of the conditioned reflex combining in a kind of trial-and-error process to bring about a type of biological adapta-tion which neither tendency could possibly produce alone.[1] The tenta-tive or trial process is mediated by the excitatory phase; the selective or corrective process is effected by the inhibitory phase—at bottom, experimental extinction brought about automatically by failure of re-inforcement.

The Dilemma of the Conditioned Defense Reaction

In connection with that aspect of the conditioned reflex last con-sidered, a curious and rather sharp distinction appears between positive

[1] While undoubtedly related, this process is not to be confused with the trial-and-error of ordinary learning such as of the maze. The author hopes in a later paper to elaborate this distinction.

reactions such as those involved in the taking of food, and defense reactions such as involve withdrawal or flight. In the case of an alimentary reaction, a successful response would ordinarily be followed each time by the consumption of food. This means, of course, that the conditioned tendency is continuously reinforced, which will keep it up to full strength. In this respect the case of the defense reaction is quite otherwise. As pointed out above, for a defense reaction to be wholly successful, it should take place so early that the organism will completely escape injury, i.e., the impact of the nocuous (unconditioned) stimulus. But in case the unconditioned stimulus fails to impinge upon the organism, there will be no reinforcement of the conditioned tendency which means (one would expect) that experimental extinction will set in at once. This will rapidly render the conditioned reflex impotent which, in turn, will expose the organism to the original injury. This will initiate a second cycle substantially like the first which will be followed by another and another indefinitely, a series of successful escapes always alternating with a series of injuries. From a biological point of view, the picture emerging from the above theoretical considerations is decidedly not an attractive one.

The sharpness of the conflict here invites speculation as to how the problem is met by nature. One possibility which suggests itself is that the greater potency of the defense reaction tendencies may make them less subject to the weakening tendencies of experimental extinction. Another possibility is that the tendency to experimental extinction may be more or less in abeyance where defense reactions are concerned. But as soon as the principle of experimental extinction becomes inoperative, the organism is exposed to the dangers resulting from accidentally conditioned irrelevant stimuli (p. 402). There is thus presented a kind of biological dilemma apparently not at all the product of misplaced ingenuity on the part of the theorist. If experimental extinction operates fully the organism seems doomed to suffer the injury of the nocuous stimulus periodically in order to renew the strength of its conditioned defense reactions. If, on the other hand, experimental extinction does not operate, the organism seems doomed to dissipate much of its energy reacting defensively to irrelevant stimuli.

It is suggested on the basis of mere casual observation that what might be called a kind of organic compromise may be operating in this curious situation. It may be that experimental extinction becomes progressively in abeyance as the gravity of the injury increases. Thus slight injuries would suffer considerably from experimental extinction and would consequently require more frequent nocuous reinforcement. Reactions to grave injuries would be affected relatively little by experimental extinction but for this reason would be very prone to become attached to irrelevant stimuli. This last, indeed, may account for the prevalence of phobias which appear, at least superficially, to be more or less accidental conditionings of irrelevant stimuli to strong emotional reactions. On the other hand very mild punishment is very likely to require frequent repetition. The problem presents a fascinating field for experimental investigation.

References

1. Pavlov, I. P., *Conditioned reflexes* (Trans. by G. V. Anrep). London: Oxford Univ. Press, 1927.

29   MOLAR AND PURPOSIVE BEHAVIORISM[1]

Edward C. Tolman

1 Mentalism vs. Behaviorism

The mentalist is one who assumes that "minds" are essentially streams of "inner happenings." Human beings, he says, "look within" and observe such "inner happenings." And although sub-human organisms cannot thus "look within," or at any rate cannot report the results of any such lookings within, the mentalist supposes that they also have "inner happenings." The task of the animal psychologist is conceived by the mentalist as that of inferring such "inner happenings" from outer behavior; animal psychology is reduced by him to a series of arguments by analogy.

Contrast, now, the thesis of behaviorism. For the behaviorist, "mental processes" are to be identified and defined in terms of the behaviors to which they lead. "Mental processes" are, for the behaviorist, naught but

---

[1] Much of the argument of the present chapter has already appeared in the following articles: (31, 32, 33).

Reprinted by permission of author and publisher from E. C. Tolman, *Purposive Behavior in Animals and Men*. New York: The Century Co., 1932.

inferred determinants of behavior, which ultimately are deducible from behavior. Behavior and these inferred determinants are both objectively defined types of entity. There is about them, the behaviorist would declare, nothing private or "inside." Organisms, human and sub-human, are biological entities immersed in environments. To these environments they must, by virtue of their physiological needs, adjust. Their "mental processes" are functionally defined aspects determining their adjustments. For the behaviorist all things are open and above-board; for him, animal psychology plays into the hands of human psychology.[2]

II Behaviorisms and Behaviorisms

The general position adopted in this essay will be that of behaviorism, but it will be a behaviorism of a rather special variety, for there are behaviorisms and behaviorisms. Watson, the arch-behaviorist, proposed one brand. But others, particularly Holt, Perry, Singer, de Laguna, Hunter, Weiss, Lashley, and Frost, have since all offered other rather different varieties.[3] No complete analysis and comparison of all these can be attempted. We shall here present merely certain distinctive features as a way of introducing what is to be our own variety.

III Watson: The Molecular Definition

Watson, in most places, seems to describe behavior in terms of simple stimulus-response connections. And these stimuli and these responses he also seems to conceive in relatively immediate physical and physiological terms. Thus, in the first complete statement of his doctrine, he wrote:

We use the term *stimulus* in psychology as it is used in physiology. Only in psychology we have to extend somewhat the usage of the term. In the

[2] It is obvious that we have oversimplified the views of both "mentalist" and "behaviorist." One ought no doubt to eschew any attempt to envisage progress as a too simple contest between "movements" (cf. 1). But the temptation is too great.

[3] W. McDougall (14, p. 277) declares that he was the first to define psychology as the study of behavior. He says: "As long ago as 1905 I began my attempt to remedy this state of affairs [i.e., the inadequacies of an 'Idea' psychology] by proposing to define psychology as the positive science of conduct, using the word 'positive' to distinguish it from ethics, the normative science of conduct." Cf. also, his *Psychology, the Study of Behavior* (11), "We may then define psychology as the positive science of the behavior of living things." But the credit or discredit for the raising of this definition of psychology to an *ism* must certainly be given to Watson (34, 35). For the best analysis and bibliography of the different varieties of behaviorism extant to 1923, see A. A. Roback, *Behaviorism and Psychology* (26, pp. 231-242).

psychological laboratory, when we are dealing with relatively simple factors, such as the effect of ether waves of different lengths, the effect of sound waves, etc., and are attempting to isolate their effects upon the adjustment of men, we speak of stimuli. On the other hand, when factors leading to reactions are more complex, as, for example, in the social world, we speak of *situations*. A situation is, of course, upon final analysis, resolvable into a complex group of stimuli. As examples of stimuli we may name such things as rays of light of different wave lengths; sound waves differing in amplitude, length, phase, and combination; gaseous particles given off in such small diameters that they affect the membrane of the nose; solutions which contain particles of matter of such size that the taste buds are thrown into action; solid objects which affect the skin and mucous membrane; radiant stimuli which call out temperature response; noxious stimuli, such as cutting, pricking, and those injuring tissue generally. Finally, movements of the muscles and activity in the glands themselves serve as stimuli by acting upon the afferent nerve endings in the moving muscles. . . .

In a similar way we employ in psychology the physiological term "response," but again we must slightly extend its use. The movements which result from a tap on the patellar tendon, or from stroking the soles of the feet are "simple" responses which are studied both in physiology and in medicine. In psychology our study, too, is sometimes concerned with simple responses of these types, but more often with several complex responses taking place simultaneously (36, pp. 10 ff.).

It must be noted, however, that along with this definition of behavior in terms of the strict physical and physiological *muscle-twitches* which make it up, Watson was apt to slip in a different and somewhat conflicting notion. Thus, for example, at the end of the quotation just cited he went on to say:

In the latter case [that is, when in psychology our study is with several complex responses taking place simultaneously] we sometimes use the popular term "act" or adjustment, meaning by that that the whole group of responses is integrated in such a way (instinct or habit) that the individual does something which we have a name for, that is, "takes food," "builds a house," "swims," "writes a letter," "talks" (36, pp. 11 f.).

Now these "integrated responses" have, perhaps, qualities different from those of the physiological elements which make them up. Indeed, Watson himself seems to suggest such a possibility when he remarks in a footnote to his chapter on "Emotions":

It is perfectly possible for a student of behavior entirely ignorant of the sympathetic nervous system and of the glands and smooth muscles, or even of the central nervous system as a whole, to write a thoroughly comprehensive and accurate study of the emotions—the types, their interrelations with habits, their rôle, etc. (36, p. 195; p. 225 for 1929 ed.).

This last statement seems, however, rather to contradict the preceding ones. For, if, as he in those preceding citations contended, the study of behavior concerns nothing "but stimuli as the physicist defines them," and "muscle contraction and gland secretion as the physiologist describes them," it certainly would *not* be possible for a "student of behavior entirely ignorant of the sympathetic nervous system and of the glands and smooth muscles, or even of the central nervous system as a whole, to write a thoroughly comprehensive and accurate study of the emotions."

Again, in his most recent pronouncement (37), we find Watson making statements such as the following:

Some psychologists seem to have the notion that the behaviorist is interested only in the recording of minute muscular responses. Nothing could be further from the truth. Let me emphasize again that the behaviorist is primarily interested in the behavior of the whole man. From morning to night he watches him perform his daily round of duties. If it is brick-laying, he would like to measure the number of bricks he can lay under different conditions, how long he can go without dropping from fatigue, how long it takes him to learn his trade, whether we can improve his efficiency or get him to do the same amount of work in a less period of time. In other words, the response the behaviorist is interested in is the common-sense answer to the question "what is he doing and why is he doing it?" Surely with this as a general statement, no one can distort the behaviorist's platform to such an extent that it can be claimed that the behaviorist is merely a muscle physiologist (37, p. 15).*

These statements emphasize the whole response as contrasted with the physiological elements of such whole responses. In short, our conclusion must be that Watson has in reality dallied with two different notions of behavior, though he himself has not clearly seen how different they are. On the one hand, he has defined behavior in terms of its strict underlying physical and physiological details, i.e., in terms of receptor-process, conductor-process, and effector-process per se. We shall designate this as the *molecular* definition of behavior. And, on the other hand, he has come to recognize, albeit perhaps but dimly, that behavior, as such, is more than and different from the sum of its physiological parts. Behavior, as such, is an "emergent" phenomenon

* Copyright by W. W. Norton and Company, Inc. By permission of the publishers.—Ed.

that has descriptive and defining properties of its own.[4] And we shall designate this latter as the *molar* definition of behavior.[5]

IV The Molar Definition

It is this second, or molar, conception of behavior that is to be defended in the present treatise. It will be contended by us (if not by Watson) that "behavior-acts," though no doubt in complete one-to-one correspondence with the underlying molecular facts of physics and physiology, have, as "molar" wholes, certain emergent properties of their own. And it is these, the molar properties of behavior-acts, which are of prime interest to us as psychologists. Further, these molar properties of behavior-acts cannot in the present state of our knowledge, i.e., prior to the working-out of many empirical correlations between behavior and its physiological correlates, be known even inferentially from a mere knowledge of the underlying, molecular, facts of physics and physiology. For, just as the properties of a beaker of water are not, prior to experience, in any way envisageable from the properties of individual water molecules, so neither are the properties of a "behavior-act" deducible directly from the properties of the underlying physical and physiological processes which make it up. Behavior as such cannot, at any rate at present, be deduced from a mere enumeration of the muscle twitches, the mere motions *qua* motions, which make it up. It must as yet be studied first hand and for its own sake.

An act *qua* "behavior" has distinctive properties all its own. These are to be identified and described irrespective of whatever muscular, glandular, or neural processes underlie them. These new properties, thus distinctive of molar behavior, are presumably strictly correlated

[4] For a very clear summary of the various different notions of "emergence" which are now becoming so popular among philosophers see W. McDougall, *Modern Materialism and Emergent Evolution* (15). It should be emphasized, however, that in here designating behavior as having "emergent" properties we are using the term in a descriptive sense only. We are not here aligning ourselves with any philosophical interpretation as to the ultimate philosophical status of such emergents.

"Emergent" behavior phenomena are correlated with physiological phenomena of muscle and gland and sense organ. But descriptively they are different from the latter. Whether they are or are not ultimately in some metaphysical sense completely reducible to the latter we are not here attempting to say. .

[5] The distinction of molar and molecular behaviorism originates with C. D. Broad (2, pp. 616 f.), and was suggested to us by Dr. D. C. Williams (40). Broad intends primarily to distinguish behaviorism which appeals only to *some* gross observable activity, from behaviorism which must appeal to hypothetical processes among the molecules of the brain and nervous system.

with, and, if you will, dependent upon, physiological motions. But descriptively and per se they are other than those motions.

A rat running a maze; a cat getting out of a puzzle box; a man driving home to dinner; a child hiding from a stranger; a woman doing her washing or gossiping over the telephone; a pupil marking a mental-test sheet; a psychologist reciting a list of nonsense syllables; my friend and I telling one another our thoughts and feelings—*these are behaviors* (qua *molar*). And it must be noted that in mentioning no one of them have we referred to, or, we blush to confess it, for the most part even known, what were the exact muscles and glands, sensory nerves, and motor nerves involved. For these responses somehow had other sufficiently identifying properties of their own.

v Other Proponents of a Molar Definition

It must be noted now further that this molar notion of behavior—this notion that behavior presents characterizable and defining properties of its own, which are other than the properties of the underlying physics and physiology—has been defended by other theorists than ourselves. In particular, acknowledgment must be made to Holt, de Laguna, Weiss, and Kantor.

Holt:

The often too materialistically-minded biologist is so fearful of meeting a certain bogy, the "psyche," that he hastens to analyse every case of behavior into its component reflexes without venturing first to observe it as a whole (4, p. 78).

The phenomena evinced by the integrated organism are no longer merely the excitation of nerve or the twitching of muscle, nor yet the play merely of reflexes touched off by stimuli. These are all present and essential to the phenomena in question, but they are merely components now, for they have been integrated. And this integration of reflex arcs, with all that they involve, into a state of systematic interdependence has produced something that is not merely reflex action. The biological sciences have long recognized this new and further thing, and called it "behavior" (4, p. 155).[6]

De Laguna:

The total response initiated by the distance receptor and reinforced by the contact stimulus (e.g., reaching out toward, pecking at, and swallowing) forms a functional unit. The act is a *whole* and is stimulated or inhibited as

[6] The present chapter, as well as most of the subsequent ones, was written before the appearance of Holt's most recent book, *Animal Drive and the Learning Process* (5).

a whole . . . Where behavior is more complex, we still find a similar relationship (10, pp. 169 f.).

The functioning of the group [of sensory cells] as a whole, since it is a *functioning,* and not merely a "chemical discharge" is not in any sense a resultant of the functioning of the separate cells which compose it (9, p. 630).

Weiss:

The investigation of the internal neural conditions form part of the behaviorist's programme, of course, but the inability to trace the ramifications of any given nervous excitation through the nervous system is no more a restriction on the study of effective stimuli and reactions in the educational, industrial or social phases of life, than is the physicist's inability to determine just what is going on in the electrolyte of a battery while a current is passing, a limitation that makes research in electricity impossible (38, p. 634; cf. also 39, esp. chapter VI).

Kantor:

Psychologists are attempting to express facts more and more in terms of the complete organism rather than in specific parts (brain, etc.) or isolated functions (neural) (6, p. 429).

Briefly, psychological organisms, as differentiated from biological organisms, may be considered as a sum of reactions plus their various integrations (7, p. 3).

vi The Descriptive Properties of Behavior as Molar

Granting, then, that behavior *qua* behavior has descriptive properties of its own, we must next ask just what, in more detail, these identifying properties are.

The first item in answer to this question is to be found in the fact that behavior, which is behavior in our sense, always seems to have the character of getting-to or getting-from a specific goal-object, or goal-situation.[7] The complete identification of any single behavior-act requires, that is, a reference first to some particular goal-object or objects which that act is getting to, or, it may be, getting from, or both. Thus, for example, the rat's behavior of "running the maze" has as its first and perhaps most important identifying feature the fact that it is a get-

[7] For convenience we shall throughout use the terms *goal* and *end* to cover situations being got away from, as well as for situations being arrived at, i.e., for *termini a quo* as well as for *termini ad quem.*

ting to food. Similarly, the behavior of Thorndike's kitten in opening the puzzle box would have as its first identifying feature the fact that it is a getting away from the confinement of the box, or, if you will, a getting to the freedom outside. Or, again, the behavior of the psychologist reciting nonsense syllables in the laboratory has as its first descriptive feature the fact that it is a getting to (shall we say) "an offer from another university." Or, finally, the gossiping remarks of my friend and myself have as their first identifying feature a set of gettings to such and such mutual readinesses for further behaviors.

As the second descriptive feature of a behavior-act we note the further fact that such a getting to or from is characterized not only by the character of the goal-object and this persistence to or from it, but also by the fact that it always involves a specific pattern of commerce-, intercourse-, engagement-, communion-with such and such intervening means-objects, as the way to get thus to or from.[8]

For example, the rat's running is a getting to food which expresses itself in terms of a specific pattern of running, and of running in some alleys rather than in others. Similarly the behavior of Thorndike's kitten is not merely a getting from the confinement of the box but it is also the exhibition of a specific pattern of biting, chewing, and clawing such and such features of the box. Or, again, the man's behavior is not merely that of getting from his office to his be-wife-ed and be-pantry-ed home; it is also the doing so by means of such and such a specific pattern of commerce with the means-objects—automobile, roads, etc. Or, finally, the psychologist's behavior is not merely that of getting to an offer from another university; but also it is characterized in that it expresses itself as a specific pattern of means-activities or means-object commerces, viz., those of reading aloud and reciting nonsense syllables; of recording the results of these, and a lot of other bosh besides, in a *Protokoll,* and later in a typed manuscript, etc.

As the third descriptive feature of behavior-acts we find that, in the service of such gettings to and from specific goal-objects by means of commerces with such and such means-objects, behavior-acts are to be characterized, also, in terms of a *selectively greater readiness* for *short* (i.e., easy) means activities as against *long* ones. Thus, for example,

---

[8] These terms, *commerce-, intercourse-, engagement-, communion-with,* are attempts at describing a peculiar sort of mutual interchange between a behavior-act and the environment which we here have in mind. But for convenience we shall hereafter use for the most part the single term *commerce-with.*

if a rat is presented with two alternative spatial means-object routes to a given goal-object, one longer and one shorter, he will within limits select the shorter. And so in similar fashion for temporally and gravitationally shorter means-object routes. And what thus holds for rats will hold, no doubt, in similar and even more distinctive fashion for still higher animals and for man. But this is equivalent to saying that this selectiveness towards means-objects and means-routes is relative to the means-end "direction" and "distance" of the goal-object. The animal when presented with alternatives always comes sooner or later to select those only which finally get him to, or from, the given demanded, or to-be-avoided, goal-object or situation and which get him there by the shorter commerce-with routes.

To sum up, the complete descriptive identification of any behavior-act per se requires descriptive statements relative to (a) the goal-object or objects, being got to or from; (b) the specific pattern of commerces with means-objects involved in this getting to or from; and (c) the facts exhibited relative to the selective identification of routes and means-objects as involving short (easy) commerces with means-objects for thus getting to or from.

vii Purposive and Cognitive Determinants

But surely any "tough-minded" reader will by now be up in arms. For it is clear that thus to identify behaviors in terms of goal-objects, and patterns of commerces with means-objects as selected short ways to get to or from the goal-objects, is to imply something perilously like purposes and cognitions. And this surely will be offensive to any hard-headed, well-brought-up psychologist of the present day.

And yet, there seems to be no other way out. Behavior as behavior, that is, as molar, *is* purposive and *is* cognitive. These purposes and cognitions are of its immediate descriptive warp and woof. It, no doubt, is strictly and completely dependent upon an underlying manifold of physics and chemistry, but initially and as a matter of first identification, behavior as behavior reeks of purpose and of cognition. And such purposes and such cognitions are just as evident, as we shall see later, if this behavior be that of a rat as if it be that of a human being.[9]

---

[9] McDougall, in his lecture entitled "Men or Robots" (14), divided all behaviorists into "Strict Behaviorists," "Near Behaviorists," and "Purposive Behaviorists." He classed the present writer and Professor R. B. Perry in the last group. It is then to Professor McDougall that we owe the title "Purposive Behavior," while it is primarily to Professor

Finally, however, it must nonetheless be emphasized that purposes and cognitions which are thus immediately, immanently,[10] in behavior are wholly objective as to definition. They are defined by characters and relationships which we observe out there in the behavior. We, the observers, watch the behavior of the rat, the cat, or the man, and note its character as a getting to such and such by means of such and such a selected pattern of commerces-with. It is we, the independent neutral observers, who note these perfectly objective characters as immanent in the behavior and have happened to choose the terms *purpose* and *cognition* as generic names for such characters.

VIII The Objective Definition of Behavior Purposes

Let us consider these immediate dynamic characters which we call purpose and cognition in more detail; we begin with purpose. By way of illustration, take the case of Thorndike's cat. The cat's purpose of getting to the outside, by bursting through the confinement of the box, is simply our name for a quite objective character of his behavior. It is our name for a determinant of the cat's behavior which, it will now appear, is defined in the last analysis by certain facts of learning. Thorndike's description of the actual behavior reads:

When put into the box the cat would show evident signs of discomfort and of an impulse to escape from confinement. It tries to squeeze through any opening; it claws and bites at the bars of wire; it thrusts its paws out through any opening and claws at everything it reaches; it continues its efforts when it strikes anything loose and shaky; it may claw at things within the box . . . The vigor with which it struggles is extraordinary. For eight or ten minutes it will claw and bite and squeeze incessantly. . . . And gradually all the other non-successful impulses will be stamped out and the particular impulse leading to the successful act will be stamped in by the resulting pleasure, until, after many trials, the cat will, when put in the box, immediately claw the button or loop in a definite way (29, p. 35 f.).

Perry (see below) that we are indebted for the original notions both of the immediate purposiveness and of the immediate cognitiveness of behavior.

Finally, it is to be noted that purposiveness and cognitiveness seem to go together, so that if we conceive behavior as purposive we *pari passu* conceive it also as cognitive. This complementary character of purpose and cognition has likewise been emphasized by McDougall (15, Chapter III); and by Perry, who also points out in some detail that "there is no purpose without cognition" (23). And that "all forms of purposive behavior depend on beliefs for the issue" (22; see also 24).

[10] The term *immanent* is used by us in a purely colorless sense to mean merely directly in behavior.

We note two significant features in this description: (a) the fact of the behaving organism's readiness to persist through trial and error, and (b) the fact of his tendency on successive occasions to select sooner and sooner the act which gets him out easily and quickly—i.e., the fact of *docility*.[11] And it is these two correlative features which, we shall now declare, define that immediate character which we call the cat's purpose to get to the freedom outside. The doctrine we here contend for is, in short, that wherever a response shows docility relative to some end—wherever a response is ready (a) to break out into trial and error and (b) to select gradually, or suddenly, the more efficient of such trials and errors with respect to getting to that end—such a response expresses and defines something which, for convenience, we name as a purpose. Wherever such a set of facts appears (and where save in the simplest and most rigid tropisms and reflexes does it not?), there we have objectively manifested and defined that which is conveniently called a purpose.

The first clear recognition and pronouncement of this fact that the docility of behavior is an objective definition of something appropriately to be called its purposiveness, we owe to Perry. In an article published in 1918 he wrote:

If the kitten should be excited to effort by the mere appearance of a button in a vertical position; if these efforts should continue until a way was hit upon to turn it horizontally; and if the random efforts should then be replaced by a stable propensity to perform the successful act, then we could say that the kitten was *trying to turn the button.* . . . [i.e., purposing the turning of the button] In order that an organism may be said to act in a certain way because of [by virtue of purposing] a certain result, it is necessary that acts, proving themselves to have a certain result, should derive a tendency to occur from this fact; and that other acts, proving not to have the result, should derive from that fact a tendency to be excluded. It is necessary that acts of the eligible type and of the ineligible type should occur *tentatively,* and then take on a stable or dispositional character according to the result (20, p. 13 f.).[12]

Finally, it must be noted that McDougall has also sponsored a seemingly similar doctrine. For he, like Perry (and ourselves), finds that

[11] Webster defines *docility* as (a) teachableness, docileness; (b) willingness to be taught or trained; submissiveness, tractableness. We use it throughout in the sense of "teachableness."

[12] This emphasis upon the docility of behavior as the definition of its purposiveness (and also of its cognitiveness) has been expanded by Perry in other places, to wit: (18, 19, 21, 22, 23, 24, and 25).

behavior, as such, has distinctive properties of its own, and these distinctive properties he cites as six:

1) a certain spontaneity of movement; 2) the persistence of activity independently of the continuance of the impression which may have initiated it; 3) variation of direction of persistent movements; 4) [the] coming to an end of the animal's movements as soon as they have brought about a particular kind of change in its situation; 5) preparation for the new situation toward the production of which the action contributes; 6) some degree of improvement in the effectiveness of behavior, when it is repeated by the animal under similar circumstances (12, Chapter II, pp. 44-46; see also 13).

And the first five of these, he says, indicate purpose. McDougall's doctrine also seems, therefore, at least superficially, very similar to ours.

It must be noted, however, that he does not particularly emphasize the sixth character, "some degree of improvement"—i.e., the "docility" of behavior which, as we see it, following Perry, is the crown and significance of the other five.[13]

And one further difference must also be emphasized. For whereas, for Professor Perry and for us, purpose is a purely objectively defined variable, which is defined by the facts of trial and error and of resultant docility; for Professor McDougall, purpose seems to be an introspectively defined subjective "somewhat," which is a something other, and more than, the manner in which it appears in behavior; it is a "psychic," "mentalistic" somewhat, behind such objective appearances, and to be known in the last analysis through introspection only. This difference

[13] In this connection it may be remarked parenthetically that we formerly tended to side with McDougall (30; also 32). That is, we then tended to hold that purpose might be said to inhere in mere trial and error and in mere persistence-until, irrespective of whether or not these tended to produce resultant learning. This seems to us now, however, an error. We have come to accept Professor Perry's *dictum* as to the need of *docility* for a true definition of purpose. It is only because there is implied in the category of trial and error and of persistence-until the further category of a resultant docility that trial and error and persistence-until have the meaning they do. Mere variability of response which involved no resultant selection among the "tries" would not be one's ordinary notion of "trial and error." Nor would mere keeping-on-ness seem a real "persistence-until." It is only when such variations and such persistences have implicit within them the further character of a resultant selection of the more efficient of the tries (i.e., *docility*) that they have their usual significance and are to be said to define purpose.

It should be noted that Singer also seems to hold much the same notion as that presented here of behavior as such and of purpose as one of its most fundamental characters. He says, to cite at random: "The history of my body's behavior reveals a purpose running through its various acts, a purpose quite like that which characterizes my neighbor, my dog, the moth which flutters by me" (27, p. 59). See also (28).

between our point of view and McDougall's is fundamental and implies a *bouleversement complet*.[14]

IX The Objective Definition of Behavior Cognitions

Consider, now, the fact of cognition. The docility feature of behavior also objectively defines, we shall declare, certain immediate, immanent characters for which the generic name *cognitions* or *cognition-processes* is appropriate. More specifically, our contention will be that the characteristic patterns of preferred routes and of commerces-with which identify any given behavior-act can be shown to be docile relative to, and may *pari passu* be said cognitively to assert: (a) the character of a goal-object, (b) this goal-object's initial "position" (i.e., direction and distance) relative to actual and possible means-objects, and (c) the characters of the specifically presented means-object as capable of supporting such and such commerces-with. For, if any one of these environmental entities does not prove to be so and so, the given behavior-act will break down and show disruption. It will be followed by subsequent alteration. It is, then, such contingencies in the continuance of any given behavior-act upon environmental characters actually proving to be so and so, which define that act's cognitive aspects.

The fact of these cognitive aspects is readily illustrated in the case of a rat's behavior in the maze. After a rat has once learned a given maze his behavior is a very specific dashing through it. But the continued release upon successive occasions of this same very specific dashing can easily be shown, experimentally, to be contingent upon the environmental facts *actually proving to be so and so*. It is contingent upon the food at the goal-box actually proving to have such and such a character. It is also contingent upon such and such alleys actually proving to be the best and shortest way to that food. And, finally, this dashing is contingent upon these alleys actually being shaped the way they are. For, if any of these environmental facts be unexpectedly changed, i.e., no longer prove to be so and so, this given behavior, this given dashing, will break down. It will exhibit disruption. Its continuing to go off as it does constitutes, then, the objective expression of a set of immediate contingencies. Its continuing to go off as it does asserts that the environmental features have those characters for which such behavior does not

---

[14] This was written before the appearance of McDougall's chapter entitled "The Hormic Psychology" in *Psychologies of 1930* (16). In this latter place McDougall seems to deny any necessary connection between his doctrine of purpose and an animism.

break down. And it is such contingencies (assertions) for which the generic name cognitions seems appropriate.

x The Organism as a Whole

The above doctrine that behavior is docile and, as thus docile, purposive and cognitive, also means, it should now be pointed out, that behavior is always an affair of the organism as a whole and not of individual sensory and motor segments going off *in situ,* exclusively and by themselves. For such docilities, as we have illustrated, mean shifts and selections and substitutions among motor responses and among sensory activities often widely distributed throughout the parts of the organism. The readiness to persist can involve wide shifts from one sensory and motor segment to another. Behavior as a type of commerce with the environment can take place only in a whole organism. It does not take place in specific sensory and motor segments, which are insulated and each by itself.

Indeed, this fact that behavior is an adjustment of the whole organism and not a response of isolated sensory and motor segments, going off, each in lonely isolation, can readily be demonstrated for organisms even lower in the scale than rats. Thus, for example, the behavior of crayfish in a simple T-maze led Gilhousen to conclude:

No definite evidence was found to substantiate *any* doctrine of learning that would conceive it, even in the case of these relatively low animals, as primarily a reënforcement or inhibition of a particular reaction to a given stimulus. As has been illustrated . . . in the analysis of runs, the learning was characterized by continuously *differing* reactions to the maze situation. Intact crayfish which performed in a superior manner did so, *not by reacting invariably to the same specific cues with some invariable reaction,* but, as far as could be observed, by *reacting in properly modified ways to different cues on different trials* (3; final italics ours).

In this connection, it must be noted that certain behaviorists have tended to take this fact that behavior is of the whole organism as *the* fundamentally distinctive feature of behavior, as molar. For example, Perry, to whom we owe the original emphasis upon the docility of behavior, often tends to emphasize as the one distinctive thing about behavior the fact that it is of the *whole* organism. He writes:

Psychology [i.e., behaviorism] deals with the grosser facts of organic behavior, and particularly with those external and internal adjustments by which the organism acts as a unit, while physiology deals with the more elementary constituent processes, such as metabolism or the nervous impulse. But in so far as psychology divides the organism it approaches physiology, and in so far as physiology integrates the organism it approaches psychology (21, p. 85).

He says further:

The central feature of this conception of human behavior is that general state of the organism which has been termed a determining tendency. The organism as a whole is for a time preoccupied with a certain task which absorbs its energy and appropriates its mechanisms (21, p. 97).

And again:

In proportion as the organism is unified and functions as a whole its behavior is incapable of being translated into simple reactions correlated severally with external events (21, p. 102).

Weiss and de Laguna also emphasize this same point (39, p. 46; 10, esp. Chapter VI).

It may be noted finally, however, that from the point of view here presented the fact that behavior is of the whole organism seems to be derivative rather than primary. It is a mere corollary of the more fundamental fact that behavior *qua* behavior, as molar, is docile and that successful docility requires mutual interconnections between all the parts of an organism.

xi The Initiating Causes and the Three Varieties of Behavior Determinant

We have sought to show that immanent in any behavior there are certain immediate "in-lying" purposes and cognitions. These are functionally defined variables which are the last step in the causal equation determining behavior. They are to be discovered and defined by appropriate experimental devices. They are objective and it is we, the outside observers, who discover—or, if you will, infer or invent—them as immanent in, and determining, behavior. They are the last and most immediate causes of behavior. We call them, therefore, the "immanent determinants."

But these immanent determinants, it must now briefly be pointed out, are, in their turn, caused by environmental stimuli and initiating physiological states. Such environmental stimuli and such organic states we designate as the ultimate or "initiating causes" of behavior. The immanent determinants intermediate in the causal equation between the initiating causes and the final resultant behavior.

Further, however, it must now also be made clear that beside the intermediating immanent determinants there are really two other classes of behavior-determinants intervening between stimuli (and the initiating physiological states) and behavior. They are to be designated as "capacities" and "behavior-adjustments." Such capacities and behavior-adjustments will be discussed at length in various later portions of the book. For the present it must suffice to draw attention to the fact of them and to suggest a few preliminary characterizations.

First, as to capacities. It is fairly evident in these days of mental tests and the insistence upon individual and genetic differences that the nature of the finally aroused immanent determinants will themselves on any given occasion be dependent not only upon the characters of the initiating causes—stimuli and physiological states—occurring on that occasion, but also upon the capacities of the individual organism or species of organism in question. Stimuli and initiating states work through capacities to produce the immanent purposive and cognitive determinants and thus the final resulting behavior.

Second, as to behavior-adjustments. It must also be noted that in certain special types of situation it will appear that the immanent purposes and cognitions eventually allowed to function may depend for their characters upon a preliminary arousal in the organism of something to be called behavior-adjustments. Behavior-adjustments constitute our behavioristic substitute for, or definition of, what the mentalists would call conscious awareness and ideas. They are unique organic events which may on certain occasions occur in an organism as a substitute, or surrogate, for actual behavior. And they function to produce some sort of modifications or improvements in what were the organisms's initially aroused immanent determinants, such that his final behavior, corresponding to these new modified immanent determinants, is different from what it otherwise would have been.

To sum up. The first initiating causes of behavior are environmental stimuli and initiating physiological states. These operate on or through the behavior-determinants. The behavior-determinants are, it appears further, subdivisible into three classes: (a) immediately "in-lying" objectively defined purposes and cognitions—i.e., the "immanent determinants"; (b) the purposive and cognitive "capacities" of the given individual or species, which mediate the specific immanent determinants as a result of the given stimuli and the given initiating states; (c) "behavior-adjustments," which, under certain special conditions, are produced by the immanent determinants in place of actual overt behavior and which serve to act back upon such immanent determinants, to remould and "correct" the latter and thus finally to produce a new and different overt behavior from that which would otherwise have occurred.

xii Recapitulation

Behavior, as such, is a molar phenomenon as contrasted with the molecular phenomena which constitute its underlying physiology. And, as a molar phenomenon, behavior's immediate descriptive properties appear to be those of: getting to or from goal-objects by selecting certain means-object-routes as against others and by exhibiting specific patterns of commerces with these selected means-objects. But these descriptions in terms of gettings to or from, selections of routes and patterns of commerces-with imply and define immediate, immanent purpose and cognition aspects in the behavior. These two aspects of behavior are, however, but objectively and functionally defined entities. They are implicit in the facts of behavior docility. They are defined neither in the last analysis, nor in the first instance, by introspection. They are envisaged as readily in the behavior-acts of the cat and of the rat as in the more refined speech reactions of man. Such purposes and cognitions, such docility, are, obviously, functions of the organism as a whole.[15] Lastly, it has also been pointed out that there are two other classes of behavior-determinants in addition to the immanent determinants, viz., capacities and behavior-adjustments. These also intervene in the equation between stimuli and initiating physiological states on the one side and behavior on the other.

References

1. Boring, E. G. Psychology for eclectics. *Psychologies of 1930*. Worcester, Mass.: Clark Univ. Press, 1930, 115-127.
2. Broad, C. D. *The mind and its place in nature*. (2nd impression). New York: Harcourt, Brace, 1929.
3. Gilhousen, H. C. The use of vision and of the antennae in the learning of crayfish. *Univ. Calif. Public. Physiol.*, 1929, *7*, 73-89.
4. Holt, E. B. *The Freudian wish*. New York: Holt, 1915.

[15] It should be noted that both Koffka (8) and Mead (17) have suggested the term *conduct* for much the same thing, it would seem, that we here designate as behavior *qua* behavior, that is, behavior as a molar phenomenon.

5. Holt, E. B. *Animal drive and the learning process.* New York: Holt, 1931.

6. Kantor, J. R. The evolution of psychological textbooks since 1912. *Psychol. Bull.,* 1922, *19,* 429-442.

7. Kantor, J. R. *Principles of Psychology,* Vol. I. New York: Knopf, 1924.

8. Koffka, K. *The growth of the mind.* New York: Harcourt, Brace, 1928 (rev. ed.).

9. Laguna, Grace A. de. Sensation and perception. *J. Philos., Psychol. Sci. Meth.,* 1916, *13,* 533-547; 617-630.

10. Laguna, Grace A. de. *Speech, its function and development.* New Haven: Yale Univ. Press, 1927.

11. McDougall, W. *Psychology, the study of behavior.* New York: Holt, 1912.

12. McDougall, W. *Outline of psychology.* New York: Scribners, 1923.

13. McDougall, W. Purposive or mechanical psychology. *Psychol. Rev.,* 1923, *30,* 273-288.

14. McDougall, W. Men or robots? I and II, *Psychologies of 1925.* Worcester, Mass.: Clark Univ. Press, 1926, 273-305.

15. McDougall, W. *Modern materialism and emergent evolution.* New York: Van Nostrand, 1929.

16. McDougall, W. The hormic psychology. *Psychologies of 1930.* Worcester, Mass.: Clark Univ. Press, 1930, 3-36.

17. Mead, G. H. A behavioristic account of the significant symbol. *J. Philos.,* 1922, *19,* 157-163.

18. Perry, R. B. Purpose as systematic unity. *Monist,* 1917, *27,* 352-375.

19. Perry, R. B. Purpose as tendency and adaptation. *Philos. Rev.,* 1917, *26,* 477-495.

20. Perry, R. B. Docility and purposiveness. *Psychol. Rev.,* 1918, *25,* 1-21.

21. Perry, R. B. A behavioristic view of purpose. *J. Philos.,* 1921, *18,* 85-105.

22. Perry, R. B. The independent variability of purpose and belief. *J. Philos.,* 1921, *18,* 169-180.

23. Perry, R. B. The cognitive interest and its refinements. *J. Philos.,* 1921, *18,* 365-375.

24. Perry, R. B. The appeal to reason. *Philos. Rev.,* 1921, *30,* 131-169.

25. Perry, R. B. *General theory of value.* New York: Longmans Green, 1926.

26. Roback, A. A. *Behaviorism and psychology.* Cambridge, Mass.: Sci-art, 1923.

27. Singer, E. A. *Mind as behavior and studies in empirical idealism.* Columbus, O.: Adams, 1924.

28. Singer, E. A. On the conscious mind. *J. Philos.,* 1929, *26,* 561-575.

29. Thorndike, E. L. *Animal intelligence.* New York: Macmillan, 1911.

30. Tolman, E. C. Instinct and purpose. *Psychol. Rev.,* 1920, *27,* 217-233.

31. Tolman, E. C. A new formula for behaviorism. *Psychol. Rev.*, 1922, *29*, 44-53.
32. Tolman, E. C. Behaviorism and purpose. *J. Philos.*, 1925, *22*, 35-41.
33. Tolman, E. C. A behavioristic theory of ideas. *Psychol. Rev.*, 1926, *33*, 352-369.
34. Watson, J. B. Psychology as a behaviorist views it. *Psychol. Rev.*, 1913, *20*, 158-177.
35. Watson, J. B. Image and affection in behavior. *J. Philos., Psychol., sci. Meth.*, 1913, *10*, 421-428.
36. Watson, J. B. *Psychology from the standpoint of a behaviorist.* Philadelphia: Lippincott, 1919.
37. Watson, J. B. *Behaviorism.* New York: Norton, 1930 (rev. ed.).
38. Weiss, A. P. The relation between physiological psychology and behavior psychology. *J. Philos., Psychol., sci. Meth.*, 1919, *16*, 626-634.
39. Weiss, A. P. *A theoretical basis of human behavior.* Columbus, O.: Adams, 1925.
40. Williams, D. C. A metaphysical interpretation of behaviorism. Harvard Ph.D. Thesis, 1928.

30   CONTIGUITY THEORY

Edwin R. Guthrie

Is there a single formula which can be made to include all or most of the established generalizations concerning the nature of learning? If there is such a formula it will in all probability be some form of the ancient principle of association by contiguity in time, which has been a part of all theories of memory and learning since before Aristotle, and has retained its essential character in spite of a variety of names, such as "conditioning," "associative memory," "redintegration." The remainder of this paper will consider the possibility that the facts of learning may possibly all be cited as instances of simple conditioning.

In order to examine its possibilities, the principle of conditioning may be stated in a simple form: *Stimuli acting at a given instant tend to acquire some effectiveness toward the eliciting of concurrent responses, and this effectiveness tends to last indefinitely.*

The phrase "tend to acquire" is used instead of "acquire" because we

From E. R. Guthrie, Conditioning as a principle of learning, *Psychol. Rev.*, 1930, *37*, 412-428. Pp. 415-427 reprinted by permission of the author, the *Psychological Review,* and the American Psychological Association.

have no assurance that this acquisition always occurs. It is the contention of this paper that this acquisition, when it does occur, is the fundamental mode of learning. The presumptive changes which make this re-routing of impulses lasting are the physiological basis of learning.

The principle is deliberately formulated to apply only to the momentary event. It is assumed that the phenomenon occurs during that small fraction of a second occupied by the conduction of an impulse through a center.

One more remark needs to be made concerning the language of the principle. The word "stimuli" need not be taken in the sense of elementary stimuli to the individual receptor cells. It seems quite probable that patterns of such elementary stimuli may act as functional units and be subject to conditioning as units, that the elementary stimulus group *ABCD* may as a group excite a group of pathways *P,* while another stimulus group, *AEFG,* excites pathway *Q.* Conditioning redirection at remote association areas would affect these stimulus groups as functional units and not as elements. The stimulus *A* would be a conditioner of one response element through *P* and a conditioner of another, possibly an antagonistic element through the pathway *Q.*

The notion that such stimulus patterns might act as functional units *is not to be confused with the suggestion of the Gestalt psychologists that the patterns might act as functional units without reference to the receptors excited.* That is a very different matter.

We may now undertake an examination of the facts of learning in the light of this formulation of the ancient principle of association or conditioning. This amounts to an attempt to describe all of the forms of learning mentioned in the beginning as instances of the first, namely, simple, simultaneous conditioning. *This does not at all mean that learning is described in terms of conditioned reflexes.* This phrase assumes a fixed unit of behavior which is organized in stereotyped form. It tends to obscure the fact that the behavior of an intelligent organism at any instant is a resultant of the total stimulus situation including internal stimuli. Reflexes and responses are never twice alike, because the total stimulus situation is never repeated. We may, at the outset, distinguish a theory of learning in terms of *conditioning* from a theory of learning in terms of *conditioned reflexes.* We have made no assumptions concerning the elementary acts which comprise behavior.

II

The characteristics of learning mentioned at the beginning of the paper were: 1. Conditioning; 2. Inhibitory conditioning; 3. Remote conditioning; 4. Improvement by practice; 5. Forgetting; 6. Temporary extinction; 7. Emotional reinforcement; 8. Irradiation; 9. Response to pattern as such; 10. Insight. We may attack these in order.

1. *Conditioning.* This is, of course, the principle itself, and hence needs no reduction. Our inquiry concerns the possibility of reducing the other facts of learning to instances of this. We may then begin with the second.

2. *Inhibitory Conditioning.* The circumstances under which a stimulus combination which has previously elicited a response will lose the power to evoke that response may be briefly stated. If the stimulus combination occurs, and the response is prevented by any means, the stimulus combination loses its power to elicit the response and, if the situation is repeated, will acquire a positive inhibiting effect on its former response. The response may have been prevented by inhibition from incompatible responses which prevail because the conditioning combination is weakened. Inhibitory conditioning is essentially the conditioning of inhibiting responses, and behaves like other conditioning in that it shows the effects of practice, is subject to forgetting, and so on.

3. *Remote Conditioning.* In Pavlov's experiments a new stimulus is presented several seconds or minutes before an unconditioned stimulus, and then acquires the power to elicit the response unsupported, with a latent period corresponding to the interval used in the experiment. Pavlov's explanation attributes this delay to mysterious latencies in the nervous system. He supposes the impulse to be somehow "held up" in the cortex. This assumption is quite unnecessary. Like Bechterev, Pavlov tends to forget that his experimental animals have sense organs which are stimulated by their own movements. When the bell rings the dog responds by "listening," which is a series of movements, postural changes, turning of the head, pricking of the ears, and the like. When the salivary glands begin to secrete, the accompanying stimuli are not furnished by the bell but by these responses to the bell. The direct response to the bell is probably over in a small fraction of a second. After that the dog is responding to his first response to the bell. Just as when we answer the telephone we are, strictly speaking, answering the telephone only for an instant. After that we are answering ourselves,

answering our start to answer the bell.

Such an explanation would account for a number of features of the "delayed" and the "trace" reflex. These are subject to inhibition or sudden release by new stimuli. What these new stimuli probably do is to alter the regular series of movements which comprise listening and the gradual recovery from listening. Delayed and trace reflexes are probably not direct conditioning at all. The true conditioning of saliva flow is on a stimulus pattern which follows the bell and is a consequence of the bell.

The apparent separation in time of a conditioning stimulus and its response is then quite possibly an illusion, and the assumption that responses to stimuli are either immediate or else do not occur at all is quite in accord with Pavlov's facts.

In delayed and trace reflexes the conditioning stimulus precedes the unconditioned. Pavlov states that no conditioning occurs if the stimulus to be made a conditioner follows the unconditioned stimulus. In a University of Washington experiment soon to be published something strongly resembling such "backward" conditioning was found with human subjects. The results of experiments on backward association suggest this also. This form of remote conditioning may also be in reality based upon simultaneous conditioning. No acts are instantaneous. Contracted muscles, through their own sense organs, tend to maintain their contraction. A new stimulus which follows the stimulus for a particular act may easily be simultaneous with the proprioceptive stimulation involved in the act itself, and hence become a conditioner of the act.

4. *The Effects of Practice*. Improvement as the result of practice is a familiar fact. The increased certainty of successful performance which results on repeated practice has led numerous psychologists to the notion that the attachment of a conditioning stimulus to its response is somehow increased by repetition of the sequence, which is a very different matter. Improvement demands more *detachment* of stimuli *from* responses than *attachment* of stimuli *to* responses. In order to improve in a performance the awkward, embarrassing, misdirected movements must be eliminated and replaced by movements which lead to a successful outcome. At the end of training the individual must be doing something quite different from what he was doing at the beginning of training.

The assumption that a stimulus-response sequence is made more certain by repetition has been embodied in a number of "laws of exercise" or "laws of frequency." It is quite possible, however, that the assumption is a mistaken one.

Pavlov's results in experiments in conditioning seem at first glance to indicate unambiguously that a conditioning stimulus is "established" by its repetition with a stimulus combination which elicits salivary flow, and to indicate that the "strength" or certainty and lasting quality of its establishment is a function of the number of occasions on which the two stimuli have been paired.

These experiments may be given a quite different interpretation. Conditioning, so far as elementary conditioning stimuli are concerned, may be an all-or-nothing affair, analogous to the setting of a switch, and not analogous to the wearing of a path, which has been a favorite simile. The increased certainty of response following on a given stimulus situation may involve an increase in the number of conditioners, rather than an increased "strength" of individual conditioners. In Pavlov's experiment, for instance, the bell signal results in extensive movements of orientation and postural adjustment, each movement causing appropriate stimulation to proprioceptors and exteroceptors. These movements are not identical each time the bell is struck because they depend in part on initial posture as well as on the bell. Repetition of the bell may enlist an increasing number of postural and other reflexes as conditioners of saliva flow, and hence gradually increase the certainty that salivary secretion will follow the bell.

It is entirely possible that if Pavlov could have controlled all stimuli instead of a very few, conditioning would be definitely established with one trial instead of fifty or more. The writer suggests that it is quite plausible that the more nearly such a complete control is established, the more nearly certain will be the result of the bell as a conditioner. Pavlov's whole method and experience suggest this.

The "strengthening" of a stimulus-response connection with repetition may very possibly be the result of the enlistment of increasing numbers of stimuli as conditioners, and not the result of the "strengthening" of individual connections.

5. *Forgetting.* The conception of forgetting presented in the textbooks has been that the effects of learning tend to be dissipated by some sort of physiological change at synapses which is a function of time. The form of the forgetting curve, though it differs for different sorts of material, indicates that forgetting is comparatively rapid when

practice is discontinued and that the rate regularly diminishes.

There are some signs of a shift of opinion toward an explanation of forgetting in terms of conditioning. Hunter, in his article on learning in the recent volume of "The fundamentals of experimental psychology," quotes with approval the statement of Jenkins and Dallenbach in an article on "Obliviscence during sleep and waking" that "the results of our study as a whole indicate that forgetting is not so much a matter of decay of old impressions and associations as it is a matter of interference, inhibition, or obliteration of the old by the new."

The evidence that forgetting is to be explained in terms of new conditioning is of several kinds. Forgetting is radically affected by intervening activities. If the intervening situations are materially different from the practice situations forgetting is less evident than when a certain amount of similarity holds of the situations. Probably the stimuli which are repeated while new responses prevail lose their conditioning effect on their previous responses and become conditioners of the new responses, and consequently inhibitors of the original ones. Furthermore, forgetting during a period of sleep is less than forgetting during a period of waking activity. This seems to be readily explained in the same terms. The stimuli which had become conditioners of certain responses are not repeated during sleep, and have no chance to be alienated from their attachment to these responses. During a period of waking, multitudes of stimuli from postural adjustments, movements, or from exteroceptive sources, which had been made conditioners of the activities in question, are components of new situations and become conditioners of new responses. If we accept evidence from outside the laboratory we may quote those instances of vivid and detailed memories conserved for many years, which would, incidentally, have depended on one conditioning occasion rather than a practice series. The occasion for the restoration of such memories is probably an unusually complete restoration of situation, usually aided by such an absence of present distraction and inhibition as is found when we are on the border of sleep. Marcel Proust has described a common experience in which a memory evoked while lying in bed with closed eyes has persisted until a change in posture dissipated it completely. Association *may* occur after one connection, and *may* last indefinitely.

If forgetting is to be explained as new conditioning which replaces the old, how is the form of the curve of forgetting to be explained? Is it not entirely possible that the increased uncertainty of a conditioned response to a stimulus situation is due to the progressive alienation of conditioners from their response, an alienation explained by their acquisition of new allegiances? The curves of forgetting may owe their shapes to the cumulative effect of this alienation. Since the bulk of the conditioners are probably proprioceptive, the result of the organism's own movements, the activities following on a given case of conditioning would alienate whole regiments of conditioners at the start and a decreasing number as time elapsed, because there would be a decreasing number to eliminate.

This statistical decrease in conditioners with time which is described by the forgetting curve would resemble, to use a frivolous illustration, the decreased expenditures of a certain artist whose method of protecting himself from starvation was to change the proceeds of his rare sales into dimes and broadcast these about his large and disordered studio. The following day dimes were retrieved easily in numbers. As time went on more and more search was required, though he seldom reached such a pass that an afternoon's search would not yield a dime.

These last faithful dimes resemble the last faithful conditioners which are indicated by the failure of forgetting curves to reach the zero point. The fact that some forgetting occurs during sleep may be due to the fact that some activity occurs during sleep, and hence some chance for the alienation of stimuli.

This conception of forgetting explains forgetting entirely in terms of new conditioning. It is, of course, not denied that there may be physiological changes like those in senility which do result in the deterioration of memory, but the normal occasion of forgetting is the alienation of cues following the occurrence of these cues at times when their conditioned responses are excluded by the general situation.

6. *Temporary Extinction.* Pavlov's temporary extinction and Dunlap's Beta law are also conceivable as instances of the general principle of conditioning. They might be described as forced forgetting.

When an established conditioner is repeated without the unconditioned stimulus, why should it quickly lose its conditioning power? Pavlov connects this loss with the brevity of the interval between applications. On his own showing this is not the determining factor. It is rather the *number of times the unsupported stimulus is repeated* that determines the extinction. Pavlov conceals this from himself by recording the results in terms of elapsed time from the start of the experiment. With short intervals, less elapsed time is required to extinguish, but in the case of both long and short intervals the number of applications is approximately the same.

If temporary extinction depends upon the number of times the conditioner is applied without support from the unconditioned stimulus, it is possible to explain temporary extinction in terms of the general principle of conditioning.

It should be noted, in the first place, that this temporary extinction or tendency to disappear with repetition is not an absolute generalization as it stands. It represents an exception to the rule of frequency. Sometimes one of these effects occurs, and sometimes the other. Obviously, in those cases in which temporary extinction prevails a special condition must have held. This special condition is probably what Pavlov asserts, the withdrawal of the unconditioned stimulus. It is the unconditioned stimulus that represents the most powerful determiner of the response. With the unconditioned stimulus withdrawn only occasional combinations of conditioners elicit the response, for it should be remembered that the animal is, in spite of sound-proof room and uniform lighting, in constant motion and subject to a continuously changing pattern of stimulation. At times there are more conditioners present, and at other times fewer. When the response fails, or is diminished because relatively few conditioners are present, these and other stimuli present become inhibitors, or, what is the same thing, conditioners of other responses.

There remains to be explained the reëstablishment of the conditioned response after a lapse of time. We have a hint toward this explanation in the fact that a sudden extraneous and unusual stimulus may cause the conditioned response to recover its original strength and certainty. It is possible that the inhibiting stimuli in this case include the somewhat specific details of posture and environment which hold during the process of extinction. A sudden interruption disorganizes posture and orientation, removes many recently conditioned inhibitors, and allows the original posture and conditioners to prevail again. The reflex is restored much as a baulky horse is startled out of his baulking, or a man who has built up an obstinate attitude may be shaken out of it by a sudden change in situation.

7: *Emotional Reinforcement and Dynamogenesis.* Explanation of the facilitating effect of exciting emotion on learning cannot be complete until a satisfactory physiology of the emotions has appeared. In the meantime attention may be called to the fact that exciting emotion involves general muscular tonus, and may possibly consist very largely in such increase in general tension. The physiologists have described many types of muscle-to-muscle reflexes which are excited by muscular contraction, the stretching of a muscle, or resistance to the contraction of a muscle. Intense stimulation of one receptor field resulting in the contraction of a limited number of muscles results in the contraction of other muscle groups through such muscle-to-muscle reflexes. States of general tension may be built up by the "reverberation" of impulses in this fashion.

The origin of such states of general tension probably lies in intense stimulation of some receptor field, or in obstacles to free movement. In such states of general tension the acts which "go through" are more energetic and complete. They involve the stimulation of many proprioceptor systems which would be undisturbed by action not so energetic.

The increased stimulation would give opportunity for increased conditioners, especially since the excitement itself is subject to conditioned revival.

In what has been called "dynamogenesis" we have possibly two ways in which the irrelevant stimuli may facilitate learning. The new stimuli may serve to increase general tonus through the "reverberation" which has been described above and so serve to make action more vigorous and complete; and they may also, through the tendency to deflection which constitutes conditioning, serve to reinforce directly the prevailing responses.

8. *Irradiation*. What Pavlov describes as irradiation, namely, the acquisition of conditioning effect by neighboring receptors which were not stimulated in training, may well be the result of simple conditioning, instead of the result of a direct spread of an entirely speculative condition with an inexplicable delay to neighboring portions of the projection areas of the cortex. It has already been suggested that the bell signal is not the direct conditioner in any of Pavlov's experiments, especially when it is learned that by "simultaneous" presentation he usually means sounding the bell some two seconds before the food is presented. In two seconds many things may have happened. In direct response to the bell the dog "listens." The act of listening may be much the same whether the signal is a bell or a whistle of another pitch. Since the real conditioners of the salivary flow are the movements of listening, and not the bell, the whistle may result in salivary flow.

To a touch on the flank the dog responds by shifting his posture.

This shift furnishes the conditioners of the glandular response. To a touch on a nearby point the response is a shift in posture involving much the same muscle groups as in the first case. To a touch on a more distant point the response will be different. The decreasing effect of stimulation of more remote areas may be the consequence of the decreasing likeness of the postural adjustment.

If we accept this much, Pavlov's experiments suggest the reason why "irradiation" decreases with practice, since it is explained that with practice there is an increasing tendency for listening movements or defensive postural adjustments to disappear and give place to the eating movements and the eating posture.

One feature of these experiments as reported in "Conditioned reflexes" remains unexplained. This is the statement that corresponding points on the two sides of the dog have exactly equal effect. Being unable to explain this, the writer may be forgiven for expressing some scepticism concerning the facts, which seem to have no analogue in human behavior.

9. *Patterns*. That we do respond to patterns as such is not open to question. And this would seem to involve the complete breakdown of any theory of conditioning such as is being presented, for at varying distances the actual receptors and afferent paths activated by a visual pattern must be quite distinct. The fact, indeed, cannot be questioned, though it should be noted that it is not a general or uniform occurrence. The child who has learned to read the raised letters on his blocks will not ordinarily recognize the letters when he sits on them. The effectiveness of patterns applies only within very limited fields.

Is it not entirely possible that the method by which we come to recognize a face at different distances as that of one and the same person is essentially the same method by which we come to recognize the rear aspect of this same person as his own back? In this case of recognition there is no question of similar patterns, for the back of his head resembles his face less than his face resembles the faces of others. If we maintain an attitude, or repeat a response to an object while that object is the occasion of shifting stimulation and of new stimulus patterns the maintained response may be conditioned on the new stimuli. Our response to a person at different distances is the same, with differences appropriate to the distance. Why may we not attribute this sameness and this difference to the sameness and the differences originally present in the stimuli furnished by our original behavior in his presence?

If we accept conditioning as an explanation for responding appropriately to a person on hearing his footstep, which offers a stimulation pattern quite different from the visual pattern to which we previously responded, why should we consider it mysterious that the appropriate response could be called out by the stimulation of a quite different group of visual receptors? The fact that they have the same pattern is irrelevant.

The Gestalt psychologists assert not only that we respond in similar ways to similar patterns, which we undoubtedly do, but also that we do this *without any opportunity for conditioning,* which the writer does not at all believe. In the case of the hen which performed its trick using the eye which had been blindfolded during learning it is entirely possible that the cues for the proper movement were not primarily visual, but were furnished by movements connected with vision before the experiment was begun. Animals and man both have movements of skeletal muscles congenitally associated with vision. These movements may be in part identical for stimulation of either retina. If the act is conditioned on these movements, it might be elicited from either eye, without regard to which eye entered into practice.

10. *Insight.* Concerning insight as described by the Gestalt psychologists the writer has much the same opinion as concerning response to patterns. The facts which are reported are not to be questioned and are typical of the behavior of the higher animals. An important part of the report has, however, been omitted. If the behavior described as insight is asserted to occur without previous learning, the essential part of the experiment would be the control of previous learning, and in the experiments the histories of insight are conspicuously lacking. No new category of facts concerning learning has been shown to be offered by the behavior described as insight.

In the writer's experience, insight in animals and in man is the result of accumulated habit. It was not a strange coincidence that the most ingenious person ever at work in the local laboratory has been a practical engineer for many years. When this member of the staff solved with little hesitation problems which had baffled the writer, there was a choice of explanations. It could be said that one man had insight and the other none, which seemed the poorer explanation; or it could be pointed out that one man had had previous training and the other none, an explanation much more charitable.

31 DESCRIPTIVE BEHAVIORISM

B. F. Skinner

VI *

We may summarize this much of the argument in the following way. A reflex is defined as an observed correlation of two events, a stimulus and a response. A survey of the history discloses no other characteristic upon which a definition can legitimately be based. The physiological investigation does not question the correlative nature of the reflex, for its data and its concepts deal essentially with the conditions of a correlation; but heterogeneous instances of correlations which would be embraced by the definition, read literally, are excluded by the physiological refinements of usage. It now remains for us to deal more specifically with the reflex in the description of behavior. What is the description of behavior, and how does the reflex, as a correlation, enter into it? Here (the reader may again be warned) we shall be concerned not so much with the validity or the adequacy of the concept as with its nature and the method peculiar to it.

Lacking some arbitrary distinction, the term behavior must include the total activity of the organism—the functioning of all its parts. Obviously, its proper application is much less general, but it is difficult to reach any clear distinction. The definition of the subject matter of any science, however, is determined largely by the interest of the scientist, and this will be our safest rule here. We are interested primarily in the movement of an organism in some frame of reference. We are interested in any internal change which has an observable and significant effect upon this movement. In special cases we are directly interested in glandular activity, but this will usually concern us only secondarily in its effect upon movement. The unity and internal consistency of this subject matter is historical: we are interested, that is to say, in what the organism *does*.

* Section ɪ through ᴠ not reprinted here.—Ed.

From B. F. Skinner, The concept of the reflex in the description of behavior, *J. gen. Psychol.*, 1931, *5*, 427-458. Pp. 445-454 reprinted by permission of the author and the Journal Press.

But the description of behavior, if it is to be either scientific or satisfying, must go further. As a scientific discipline, it must describe the event not only for itself but in its relation to other events; and, in point of satisfaction, it must *explain*. These are essentially identical activities. In the brief survey at the beginning of this paper it was occasionally necessary to regard the stimulus as a newly discovered cause of movement for which various conceptual causes had previously been designed. In this way we represented a real aspect of the history of the reflex. But we may now take that more humble view of explanation and causation which seems to have been first suggested by Mach and is now a common characteristic of scientific thought, wherein, in a word, explanation is reduced to description and the notion of the function substituted for that of causation. The full description of an event is taken to include a description of its functional relationship with antecedent events. In the description of behavior we are interested in the relationships within a regressive series of events extending from the behavior itself to those energy changes at the periphery which we designate as stimuli. We stop here in the regression only because further steps are beyond the field of behavior. The two end events, the behavior and the stimulus, have, moreover, a particular importance, because they alone are directly observable in an intact organism, and because they limit the series. With the relationship of these two end terms the description of behavior is chiefly concerned.

The reflex is important in the description of behavior because it is by definition a statement of the *necessity* of this relationship. The demonstration of the necessity is ultimately a matter of observation: a given response is observed invariably to follow a given stimulus, or exceptions to this rule may be independently described. In its extension to total behavior the principle generalizes the statement of the necessity observed in a particular reflex, the form of the expression remaining essentially the same. That is to say, the hypothesis that "the behavior of an organism is an exact, if involved, function of the forces acting upon the organism" states the correlation of a stimulus and a response, both of which remain wholly undifferentiated. It is, in this sense, the broadest possible statement of a reflex, but it is not an observed correlation and is therefore a hypothesis only.

It is, nevertheless, solely the fault of our method that we cannot deal directly with this single correlation between behavior as a whole and all the forces acting upon the organism stated in the hypothesis. Quantitative statements of both stimulus and response and a statistical demonstration of the correlation are theoretically possible but would be wholly unmanageable. We are led, for lack of a better approach, to investigate the correlation of parts of the stimulus with parts of the response. For the sake of a greater facility (and in this case the very possibility) of description, we turn to analysis.

Originally, the use of analysis was quite accidental and unrecognized, but it has, nevertheless, always been necessary. The early observations were possible only after it had been achieved in some form or other. This is not difficult to understand if we remember that the correlation that we call a reflex rests ultimately upon observation. In an intact newt, to return to Hall's experiment, it would have been very nearly impossible to observe a correlation between the movement of the tail and the application of a probing needle, because the movement of the tail was also correlated with other stimuli and the action of the probing needle with other movements. *In the isolated tail,* however, one kind of movement followed a given stimulus and was absent in the absence of the stimulus. The correlation was obvious and therefore observed.

Marshall Hall and his few predecessors divided the behavior of an organism into parts by the expedient method of dividing the organism. This became, in general, the method of reflex physiology, although, for obvious reasons, the division of the nervous system supplanted the division of the whole organism. The best-known group of reflexes to be studied in surgical isolation are those surviving in the body of the organism after section of the cord just below the bulb. This is the "spinal" preparation, which has been the basis for the greater part of the physiological investigation, notably that of Sherrington. Other common reflex systems are the decerebrate, in which the medulla and the cerebellum remain intact, and the various mid-brain and thalamic preparations, as, for example, those of Magnus. A further extension of the method involves the surgical or physiological exclusion of end-organs, as by extirpation or anaesthetization (for example, of the labyrinth), or by section of afferent nerves. The common object of these procedures is to permit the investigation of a particular response in relation to a controlled variable, independent of other variables also related to that response.

But the same result may be obtained in another way. The experiment may be so designed that the undesired variables do not vary. The distinction between the two methods will appear in the following example from the work of Magnus (1). Certain postural effects in a mid-brain animal are correlated partly with the position of the labyrinths relative to the earth and partly with the condition of flexion or extension of the muscles of the neck. The correlation between the posture and the state of the neck muscles can be studied alone if the labyrinths are cocainized or extirpated. But Magnus was also able to obtain the isolation by designing his experiments in such a way that the position of the labyrinths relative to the earth did not change. Perhaps the best examples of this method, however, are to be found in the work of Pavlov (2). Here the organism is intact and the very active receptors of the head segments fully functional. By controlling light, sound, odor, and other conditions in the experimental chamber, it is possible to observe in isolation the correlation between a given response and a selected stimulus. Placing an animal in a dark room, that is to say, is equivalent for purposes of isolation to blinding it, to sectioning the optic tracts, or to destroying the visual projection areas in the cortex, and has the great advantage over these surgical methods of being relatively free from unknown artifacts.

The practical merits of both these methods are obvious; but we are concerned with a broader aspect of analysis. For the physiologist, the isolation of a reflex is a preliminary matter of method and is relatively insignificant. In the description of behavior it is of first importance. How legitimate, then, is the process of analysis, and what is the nature of its product?

Let us deal entirely with the flexion reflex in the spinal dog, as a familiar and convenient example. We have already analyzed, of course, when we have once named, so that we must go back for a moment to the behavior as a whole. Without regard to its correlation with stimulating forces, behavior, as we have seen, is simply part of the total functioning of the organism. The problem of analysis at this level is common to physiology and anatomy. We shall not need to solve it, but shall assume that for purposes of description the body of an organism may be divided into parts (that we may speak, for example, of a leg), and that the functioning of a particular part may be described in isolation (that we may speak, for example, of the flexion of a leg). Moreover, we shall assume that the forces acting upon the organism may be analyzed and described in the manner common to the physical sciences. Our own problem lies beyond these assumptions.

In the flexion reflex our first experimental datum is the nearly simultaneous occurrence of the flexion of a leg and, let us say, the electrical stimulation of the skin of the foot. If we measure both events very carefully and repeat the stimulation, we obtain a second flexion which closely resembles the first, and we find that we may corroborate the observation, within limits, as often as we like. We call the observed correlation a reflex and, for convenience of reference, give it a special name, the flexion reflex.

The question then arises: *what is the flexion reflex?* If we try to answer by describing in detail a stimulus and a response, we meet embarrassing difficulties. We find that the exact degree and direction of flexion may vary with many factors. We find, for example, that it was very important for our original measurements that the torso of the animal had a particular position, that the contralateral leg was, say, unsupported, and so on. But we cannot specify these incidental conditions in our description without destroying its generality. Thereupon we shall probably resort to surgical methods. Theoretically, at least, we may pare down the structures underlying the flexion reflex until the collateral variables are no longer effective. But we can never be sure that the reflex that we have thus carved out of the behavior of the organism would not have been grossly otherwise if our operative procedure had been different. We are not sure, that is to say, that what turns up at the end of our process of isolation is the flexion reflex. There is another method open to us. In the flexion reflex we are dealing essentially with a group of correlations showing many characteristics in common. They involve the same effectors acting roughly in the same way and stimuli which resemble each other at least in their gross anatomical reference. We may, therefore, if we wish, *construct* a flexion reflex by a statistical treatment of many of these separate correlations. We may, in other words, determine and state a correlation between the characteristics common to all our observed responses and the characteristics common to all our observed stimuli, and we may name this construct the flexion reflex. But the resulting description of this statistical entity will likewise depend upon our choice of observations and upon our method of analysis.

We have been proceeding, of course, upon an unnecessary assumption, namely, that there *is* a flexion reflex, which exists independently of our observations, and which our observations approximate. Such an assumption is wholly gratuitous, but it is remarkably insistent. It arises in part from the nature of the reflex. If we remain at the level of our observations, we must recognize a reflex as a correlation. But the immediate uncritical reaction to a definition on that basis is that a correlation, in point of satisfaction, is not enough. There is an urge toward solidification, clearly evident throughout the history. We turn instantly to the reflex arc for material support. Although our knowledge of the critical part of the arc is, as we have seen, derived wholly from the observation of a correlation, we much prefer to regard the characteristics of the correlation as properties of the synapse than to retain them simply as characteristics of a correlation. Under the same pressure, then, but with less justification, we are led to assume that there are isolated reflexes concealed in the behavior of an organism, which by proper investigatory methods we may discover, and in the description of behavior to state the corollary of this proposition, namely, that behavior is the sum or the integration of these units.

Here we are touching upon the subject of a widespread current controversy, but we may, by virtue of what we have already said, dispose of the matter briefly. Let us phrase two typical questions. Is a reflex a unitary mechanism? Is behavior a sum of such mechanisms? Then, if by reflex we mean a hypothetical entity which exists apart from our observations but which our observations are assumed to approach, the questions are academic and need not detain us; if, on the other hand, we define a reflex as a given observed correlation or as a statistical treatment of observed correlations, the questions are meaningless, for they ignore the process of analysis implied in the definition. A reflex, that is to say, has no scientific meaning apart from its definition in terms of such experimental operations as we have examined, and, so defined it cannot be the subject of questions of this sort.

There is a certain practical advantage, it is true, in regarding a reflex as a unitary mechanism—an advantage, as Mach might have said, that may have given rise to the practice. It is only when we misconstrue a purely practical device and take it to be an integral part of our definition that the possibility of theoretical misunderstanding arises. Our sample questions deal necessarily with the reflex defined in terms that we have seen to be well beyond any observational justification. As Poincaré has said of a similar issue, *"ces questions ne sont pas seulement insolubles, elles sont illusoires et depourvues de sens"* (3, p. 192). A common mistake in the present case has been to suppose that, because an answer is lacking, the principle of the reflex is somehow impeached. As we have repeatedly noted, the validity of the reflex as a scientific concept is not here in question. The reflex remains, as it has always been, an observed correlation of stimulus and response.

VII

It remains for us to consider how a reflex as a correlation is dealt with experimentally. The first step, as we have seen, is the isolation of a response and the identification of its correlated stimulus. In practice, the demonstration of the correlation is usually left at an elementary level. It is based upon the appearance of the two events together and their failure to appear separately. As an experimental datum of this sort, a reflex may be given the expression

[1] $$R = f(S)$$

where R is a response and S a stimulus. Theoretically, the exact nature of the function is determinable, although for any present purpose corresponding values of S and R are obtainable by observation only. Choosing convenient measures of both stimulus and response, we may vary the strength of S and observe variations in the strength of R. This is common practice, although very little has been done toward determining how a given R varies with its corresponding S. One characteristic of the relationship is the threshold: for values below a given value of S, $R = 0$. There are also temporal aspects of the function, which have been investigated under the headings of latency and after-discharge.

Threshold, latency, after-discharge, and the order of variation of S and R are thus descriptions of the correlation that we call a reflex. They may be investigated with only one elicitation of the reflex or, at most, with a single set of corresponding values of S and R. There is a second field of investigation, however, which is concerned with variations in any aspect of a correlation, as they may appear in the comparison of successive elicitations. If, for example, we select a value of S and repeat the elicitation of the reflex at a given rate, we shall observe a progressive decrease in the value of R. Or, again, if the interval between two successive elicitations be made brief enough, the second R may be of greatly reduced magnitude or wholly lacking. Here are significant variations in the value of the terms in Equation [1]. They do not challenge the necessity of the relationship expressed therein (as they might well do if they were less orderly), but they do require that, in the description of a reflex, account be taken of *third variables*. We may indicate the required change by rewriting our equation as

[2] $$R = f(S, A)$$

where A is a variable designed to account for any given observed change in the value of R.

As it appears in such an experiment, A is properly either time or the number of elicitations at a given rate. The inference is commonly made that it represents a factor of another sort, which varies with time or the number of elicitations in the same way. In the first example noted above the phenomenon has been called reflex fatigue, which is regarded as a synaptic change—as the exhaustion of a substance or state, or as an increase in resistance, according to one's preference in synaptic theory. But in the description of behavior, where we are only secondarily interested in these physiological inferences, reflex fatigue is nothing more than an orderly change in some measured aspect of a given correlation. A law describing the course of that change, where the independent variable is time or the number of elicitations or some other condition of the experiment, is peculiarly a law of behavior. It may become a law of the synapse, by virtue of certain physiological inferences, but it has by that time passed beyond the scope of the description of behavior.

Nevertheless, if we are to follow current usage, a definition of reflex fatigue as an observed variation in *one* aspect of a correlation is too narrow, for we know from observation that, when such a change has taken place, the other aspects of the correlation have also changed. If we have observed, for example, a change in the ratio of a particular R and S, we may expect to find all other ratios, as well as the threshold, latency, and after-discharge of the reflex, likewise changed. It is usual, therefore, to regard the particular change that we chance to observe as a sample of a greater process. Occasionally, where a change in one aspect of a correlation is alone important (as in summation, which is chiefly a matter of threshold), the characteristic may possibly be defined in terms of a single change. But such a characteristic as reflex fatigue, or the refractory phase, or facilitation, is by intention a description of a group of concurrent changes.

If we are to speak in terms of these group changes, it is almost necessary to have a term describing the *state* of a correlation at any given time with respect to all its aspects. The physiologist, of course, may use the synapse for this purpose. When he has once described reflex fatigue as the exhaustion of a synaptic substance, for example, he may attribute a change in *any* aspect of a correlation to that exhaustion. Although he may observe and measure at one time a change in after-discharge and at another a change in the magnitude of R, he may reasonably consider himself to be dealing with the same process in both cases. Fortunately, there is also a term serving the same purpose at the level of behavior. If, in a given reflex, the threshold is low, the latency short, the after-discharge prolonged, and the ratio R/S large, the reflex is ordinarily said to be strong. If, on the other hand, the threshold is high, the latency long, the after-discharge short, and the ratio R/S small, the reflex is said to be weak. An attribute of *strength* is imputed to the reflex. The strength of the response, of course, is not meant; a weak response may indicate a strong reflex, if it be elicitable with a very weak stimulus.

"Reflex strength" expresses in a very general way the state of a given correlation at a given time in respect of many of its characteristics. It is a useful term, for it permits us to deal with reflex fatigue, for example, as a *change in reflex strength,* without stopping to specify the particular changes that compose it. Nevertheless, its usefulness does not extend beyond this qualitative level. The concept is subject to a major objection, which holds as well for the parallel use of the synaptic state. We do not know, since it has never been determined, whether the changes that compose such a characteristic as reflex fatigue all proceed at the same rate. If the threshold, let us say, and the magnitude of R do not vary in precisely the same way, we are not justified in taking either as a measure of a supposed common variable, nor, indeed, in continuing to regard reflex fatigue as a unitary process.

The study of the reflex, then, leads to the formulation of two kinds of law. The first are laws describing correlations of stimulus and response. A reflex, as we have defined it, is itself a law, and of this sort. It has a considerable generality in spite of the specificity of its terms, but it must be supplemented by other laws describing the exact conditions of a correlation. Secondly, there are laws describing changes in any aspect of these primary relationships as functions of third variables, where the third variable in any given case is a condition of the experiment. These secondary laws may be dealt with in groups, according as they involve the same experimental third variable, and they may be spoken of, for convenience, as describing changes in reflex strength. In the behavior of intact organisms the apparent variability of specific stimulus-response relationships emphasizes the importance of laws of the second sort. Conditioning, "emotion," and "drive," so far as they concern behavior, are essentially to be regarded as changes in reflex strength, and their quantitative investigation may be expected to lead to the determination of laws describing the course of such changes, i.e., to laws of the second sort.

It is difficult to discover any aspect of the behavior of organisms that may not be described with a law of one or the other of these forms. From the point of view of scientific method, at least, the description of behavior is adequately embraced by the principle of the reflex.

References

1. Magnus, R. *Körperstellung. Experimentell-physiologische Untersuchungen über die einzelnen bei der Körperstellung in Tätigkeit tretenden Reflexe, über ihr Zusammenwirken und ihre Störungen.* Berlin: Springer, 1924.
2. Pavlov, I. P. *Conditioned reflexes* (Trans. by G. V. Anrep). London: Oxford Univ. Press, 1927.
3. Poincaré, H. *La science et l'hypothesé.* Paris: Flammarion, 1903.

32   THE PROBLEM OF STIMULUS EQUIVALENCE

K. S. Lashley

VII * Theoretical Considerations

The discrimination experiment presents the animals with a definite situation, then with another having different characteristics, and ultimately establishes a different reaction to each situation. What is the basis for this differential reaction? For a stimulus-response psychology the one situation is associated with approach, the other with withdrawal: $S_a \rightarrow R_a : S_w \rightarrow R_w$: all simple and neat. Unfortunately this formula does not include the essential feature of discrimination, the fact

* Sections I through VI not reprinted here.—Ed.

From K. S. Lashley, The mechanism of vision: XV. Preliminary studies of the rat's capacity for detail vision, *J. gen. Psychol.*, 1938, *18*, 123-193. Pp. 183-187 reprinted by permission of the author and the Journal Press.

that the efficacy of each stimulus is dependent upon the character of the other; $S_a = FS_w$. The moment we examine the concept of stimulus critically, the inadequacy of such general formulations becomes apparent.

The Nature of the Adequate Stimulus. Analysis of the differential response reveals the following facts concerning the character of the effective stimulus:

1. The positive or negative reaction is determined by some fraction of the total visual situation. In every case the total situation may be broken down into an effective part, the figure, and an indifferent part, the ground.

2. The effective fraction of each situation is always some character which differentiates the negative from the positive stimulus. The animal trained to the larger of two circles chooses the larger of other figures, but not a circle from other forms of equal area.

3. The differentiating characters are always abstractions of general relationships subsisting between figures and cannot be described in terms of any concrete objective elements of the stimulating situations.

4. In isolating these characters the animal itself is an important factor, since in identical situations no two animals may react on the basis of the same properties.

These conclusions, which are amply supported by the experimental evidence, show that the description of discrimination as a mere combination of a positive and a negative reaction misses the essential features of the process, which are the isolation of figure, the discovery of differences, and the generalizing character of the response. These are prior to and not a result of the training.

The Fractioning of the Visual Field. Physically, visual stimulation of the rat consists of the excitation of some 28 millions of structurally independent rhabdomes with various intensities of light. The light rays reaching the individual rhabdomes are the elements of the stimulus. Any functional relations of pattern or form must be determined by the interaction of impulses from the rhabdomes at some central level. Studies of figure-ground relations show that there are certain general principles of organization applicable to the isolation not only of familiar but of new figures. The general effectiveness of continuity of figure, contrast, or conformation to a regular geometrical arrangement in determining the structure of figure cannot be accounted for in terms of trial-and-error learning except by the postulation of some capacity for generalization which begs the question at issue between nativistic and habit-system theories. The experiments of Turner (10), Lashley and Russell (5), and Hebb (1, 2, 3) and the data on the congenitally blind with restored vision (8) all point to the conclusion that the isolation of figure occurs at the first moment of visual stimulation. The fractioning of the visual field into coherent units must then be recognized as an immediate product of organic structure and an indicator of the character of the integrative mechanism.

The Generalization of Attributes. In equivalence tests the properties of the figure may be varied through a wide range, so as to destroy any physical identity with the training figure without destroying the reaction (6). This does not mean, as Pavlov (7) has asserted, that "at first only the most general features of the situation act and only later, gradually, under the influence of special conditions, a further analysis takes place and the more special components of the stimuli begin to act." There is evidence that on the first presentation of a figure the animal may be stimulated by any or all of the special components to which he will ever react. If an animal is trained on horizontal vs. vertical striations, next on triangle and circle, and is then given critical trials with the figures superimposed on the striations, the latter are likely to dominate his reactions. But if both grounds are striated horizontally or both vertically, his reactions are determined by the triangle and circle. We cannot assume that in one case he is stimulated by the striations and not in the other, but must conclude that the reaction is selective among effective stimuli. In the transfer from a solid figure to an outline of the same, the animal's time for jumping may be increased from half a second to five minutes, yet he finally jumps with 100 per cent accuracy. It is not failure to see the difference which leads to transfer, but the identification of the common characteristic of the two otherwise diverse situations. Differentiation of the conditioned reflex is not the development of differential sensitivity to the stimulus, as Pavlov implies, but the definition for the animal of the properties to which he must react. We must recognize that any discrimination of a difference is prior to the association of that difference with a new reaction.

Identical Elements or Abstract Relations. For many years the doctrine has been urged upon psychologists that a recognition of identical existential elements in different situations is the most primitive and simple of reactions and therefore to be preferred among alternative explanations of similarity. During the controversies concerning the value of formal discipline the theory of transfer of training through the presence of identical elements reached the height of its vogue and won a practical victory, even though its proponents finally admitted that identity after all is not identity and elements are relations.

The assumption that reaction to identical elements is physiologically a simple process is a consequence of the connectionist or telephone theory of integration. If cerebral integration occurs by the interaction of dynamic fields (4), then reaction to abstract relations should be the most immediate and direct form of response, whereas the recognition of the identity of existential elements should require the combined recognition of all of the common properties of the situations. It is time that we realize that the doctrine of transfer through identical elements has no greater a priori claim to explanatory value or simplicity than has any relational or organismal theory.

Equivalence tests show that so long as the abstract property which differentiates the positive figure from the negative is preserved, differential reaction persists. No physical identity of stimuli is necessary for transfer nor is there any evidence that even in successive identifications of the same figure, physical identity is the determining factor.

The Limits of Abstraction. The relational properties which form the basis of the rat's reactions seem to be quite limited in number and to be chiefly those arising from the relation of the figure to the animal's orientation in space. Relative distance is quickly learned, relative number not at all; direction far more easily than specific pattern. What determines this limitation of the rat's capacity in comparison with the cat, monkey, or man? Is it past experience or structural organization? Is the predilection to see certain relations a result of the rat's mode of life, or is the mode of life determined by such limitation of capacity? Questions of this kind are of fundamental importance for understanding the evolution of behavior. There is no decisive evidence upon which an answer can be based, but both comparative and clinical material is consistent with the view that the relational framework within which generalization occurs is determined by innate structural or physiological organization.

I must take sharp issue with the view of Smith (9) that such speculations concerning constitutional determiners of activity do not further our knowledge of behavior. They do not, of course, provide any immediate explanation but they do formulate a definite problem which offers a meaningful alternative to a theory of redintegration, such as he proposes, and which is capable of solution by experimental means.

Perhaps the most significant result of this study is the indication that the development of ability for generalization or abstraction does not present a few well marked and easily defined steps, such as a capacity to abstract relations, a capacity to generalize form, or a capacity for education of relations, but rather that material and process cannot be sharply separated. The education of a size relationship differs in difficulty according to the figures used and differs also from education of a number relation. The processes involved may have only logical, not physiological similarity. Once we recognize this, stop trying to fit the animal's behavior into a few a priori logical categories, and turn to detailed analysis of relational behavior and of the conditions limiting abstraction and generalization the way is opened for an adequate account of the evolution of intelligence.

References

1. Hebb, D. O. Innate organization of visual activity: I. Perception of figures by rats reared in total darkness. *J. genet. Psychol.*, 1937, *51*, 101-126.

2. Hebb, D. O. Innate organization of visual activity: II. Discrimination of size and brightness by rats reared in total darkness. *J. comp. Psychol.*, 1937, *24*, 277-299.

3. Hebb, D. O. Studies of organization of behavior: I. Behavior of the rat in a field orientation. *J. comp. Psychol.*, 1938, *25*, 333-352.

4. Köhler, W. The problem of form in perception. *Brit. J. Psychol.*, 1924, *14*, 262-268.

5. Lashley, K. S. and Russell, J. T. The mechanism of vision: XI. A preliminary test of innate organization. *J. genet. Psychol.*, 1934, *45*, 136-144.

6. McKinney, F. Identical sensory elements versus functional equivalents in visual transfer reactions. *J. genet. Psychol.*, 1932, *41*, 483-489.

7. Pavlov, I. P. The reply of a physiologist to psychologists. *Psychol. Rev.*, 1932, *39*, 91-127.

8. Senden, M. v. *Raum- und Gestaltauffassung bei operierten Blindgeborenen vor und nach der Operation.* Leipzig: Barth, 1932.

9. Smith, K. U. Visual discrimination in the cat: III. The relative effect of paired and unpaired stimuli in the discriminative behavior of the cat. *J. genet. Psychol.*, 1936, *48*, 29-57.

10. Turner, W. D. The development of perception: I. Visual direction; the first eidoscopic orientations of the albino rat. *J. genet. Psychol.*, 1935, *47*, 121-140.

CHAPTER XII

PSYCHODYNAMICS

THE INTEGRATION of the fields of emotion and motivation under the rubric psychodynamics, *with particular emphasis on frustration and anxiety, has been one of the outstanding developments of recent years. In the present chapter several of the major systematic formulations in this field are considered. The first selection is from* The Problem of Anxiety, *one of Sigmund Freud's most influential works, and represents his later views on the key concept of anxiety. The chapter here reproduced is specifically concerned with the relationship between anxiety and symptom formation and concludes with the frank admission of the lack of any unifying principle in explanation of neurosis. The tremendous systematic influence of Freud's contributions may nevertheless be seen in the fact that each of the following formulations represents, in one way or another, a modification of his theories. Two more recent psychoanalytic contributions, by Franz Alexander and Karen Horney, are next presented. Alexander's summary of the systematic principles underlying the recent important work in the field of psychosomatic medicine is especially authoritative in view of his position as head of the Chicago Psychoanalytic Institute and active director of one of the best integrated psychosomatic research programs. Horney's theory of neurotic conflict is offered in the next selection. She has been generally regarded as one of the leaders of the group of neo-analysts who have attempted to substitute a basic social orientation for the orthodox Freudian biological, or instinctual, foundation. In the fourth selection Saul Rosenzweig presents his classification of types of reaction to frustration. This interpretation was directly stimulated by Freudian theories but has been of particular interest in its own right. The selection from A. H. Maslow gives his interpretation of the theory of*

453

threat, which has also gained considerable independent recognition beyond its essentially psychoanalytic derivation. The well-known frustration-aggression hypothesis of the so-called Yale group is described in the next selection, from a paper prepared chiefly by Neal E. Miller. This fruitful hypothesis has been extremely influential in clinical as well as strictly theoretical activities. As another active exponent of the application of basic learning principles to clinical problems, O. H. Mowrer, also of the early Yale group at the Institute of Human Relations, has likewise been generally prominent in both fields within recent years. The selection presents his highly influential stimulus-response analysis of anxiety, an interpretation which has been of considerable experimental fruitfulness and has been basic to much of his own ingenious animal experimentation. The final selection is taken from N. R. F. Maier's recent book, Frustration, *which gathers together the main results of a decade of experimentation on abnormal phenomena with animal subjects. The excerpt reprinted gives his special theory of frustration-instigated behavior, which holds, in essence, that such behavior is not subject to the same basic principles as is normally motivated behavior. This dichotomy is in direct opposition to the views of the various stimulus-response theorists (Miller and Mowrer, for example), and the disagreement has already stimulated experimental as well as purely theoretical inquiry.*

33 THE FREUDIAN THEORY OF ANXIETY

Sigmund Freud

The Relation between Symptom and Anxiety

It now remains to deal with the relationship between symptom formation and the development of anxiety. Two opinions about this seem to be prevalent. One of them terms the anxiety itself a symptom of the neurosis, the other conceives of a far more intimate connection between the two. According to this latter view, all symptom formation would be brought about solely in order to avoid anxiety; the symptoms bind the psychic energy which otherwise would be discharged as anxiety, so that anxiety would be the fundamental phenomenon and the central problem of neurosis.

The at least partial justification of this second position can be supplied by means of certain striking examples. If an agoraphobic who has been accompanied whenever he went out on the street is left alone there, he produces an attack of anxiety; if a compulsion neurotic is prevented from washing his hands after touching something, he becomes a prey to almost insupportable anxiety. It is clear, therefore, that the stipulation of being accompanied and the compulsion to wash has as their purpose, and also their result, the averting of an outbreak of anxiety. In this sense, every inhibition also that the ego imposes on itself can be termed a symptom.

Since we have reduced the development of anxiety to a response to situations of danger, we shall prefer to say that the symptoms are created in order to remove or rescue the ego from the situation of danger. If symptom formation is prevented, then the danger actually makes its appearance—that is to say, a situation analogous to birth comes about, a situation in which the ego finds itself helpless against the ever-increasing strength of the instinctual demand in question; in other words, we have present the first and earliest of the determinants of anxiety. For our point of view the relationships between anxiety and symptom prove to be less close than was supposed, the result of our

From S. Freud, *The Problem of Anxiety*. (Trans. by H. A. Bunker.) New York: Psychoanalytic Quarterly Press, and W. W. Norton and Co., 1936. Pp. 85-92 reprinted by permission of the *Psychoanalytic Quarterly*.

having interposed between the two the factor of the danger situation. We can also say, in supplement to this, that the development of anxiety induces symptom formation—nay more, it is a *sine qua non* thereof, for if the ego did not forcibly arouse the pleasure-pain mechanism through the development of anxiety, it would not acquire the power to put a stop to the danger-threatening process elaborated in the id. At the same time there is an obvious tendency on the part of the ego to restrict the development of anxiety to a minimum, to employ anxiety only as a signal, for otherwise there would merely be experienced somewhere else the unpleasure threatened by the instinctual process—a result which would not accord with the purpose of the pleasure principle, although often enough coming about, it is true, in the neuroses.

Symptom formation thus has the actual result of putting an end to the danger situation. It has two aspects: one of them, which remains concealed from us, causes in the id that alteration by means of which the ego is preserved from danger; the other, visible to us, reveals what it has created in place of the instinctual process thus modified, namely, substitute formation.

We should express ourselves more accurately, however, if we ascribe to the process of defense what we have just said of symptom formation, and used the term symptom formation itself as synonymous with substitute formation. It then seems evident that the defensive process is analogous to flight, by means of which the ego avoids a danger threatening from without, and that it represents, indeed, an attempt at flight from an instinctual danger. The considerations which weigh against this comparison will themselves prove illuminating. In the first place, the objection might be raised that object loss (loss of the object's love) and the threat of castration are just as much dangers threatening from without as is for example a ravening beast, and are therefore not instinctual dangers. Yet the case is not at all the same. The wolf would probably attack us, regardless of how we behaved towards it; but the beloved person would not withdraw his love, we should not be threatened with castration, if we did not cherish within ourselves certain feelings and desires. Thus it is these instinctual impulses which become the precondition of the external danger, its *conditio sine qua non,* and thereby themselves a source of danger; and we can now combat the external danger by measures taken against dangers from within. In the animal phobias the danger seems still to be perceived entirely as an external one, just as in the symptom also it undergoes an external displacement. In compulsion neurosis the danger is to a far greater degree internalized; that part of the fear of the super-ego which may be called social anxiety still represents an internal substitute for an external danger, while the other part, fear of conscience, is entirely endopsychic.

A second objection would be to the effect that in the attempt to escape from a threatening external danger all that we do, in fact, is to increase the distance in space between us and that which threatens. We do not put ourselves in an attitude of defense against the danger, we do not try to change anything in the danger itself, as would be the case if we attacked the wolf with a club or shot at it with a gun. But the defensive process seems to go beyond what would correspond merely to an attempt at flight; it actually interferes with the threatening instinctual process, suppresses it somehow, deflects it from its aim, and thereby renders it harmless. This objection appears to be a very cogent one, and one we shall have to take into account. We believe it may well be that there are defensive processes which can with justice be compared to an attempt at flight, while in the case of others the ego offers resistance of a far more active kind, undertaking vigorous counteractive measures. But it is possible that the comparison of defense with flight is rendered untenable by the fact that the ego and the instinctual drive in the id are in fact parts of the same organization, and do not have, as the wolf and the child do, a separate existence from each other; so that every form of behavior on the part of the ego must have a modifying influence upon the instinctual process.

Through the study of the situations which occasion anxiety we have had to envisage with what might be called rational idealization the behavior of the ego in defense. Every danger situation corresponds to a given period of life or stage of development of the psyche, to which it appears appropriate. In early infancy the organism is not really equipped to cope psychically with large amounts of excitation reaching it from without or within. At a certain period of life it is in actual fact to the individual's greatest interest that the persons upon whom he is dependent shall not withdraw their tender care. When the boy perceives the powerful father as his rival for the mother and becomes aware of his aggressive tendencies against his father and his sexual desires towards his mother, he is quite right in being afraid of him; and the fear of being punished by him may, when reënforced phylogenetically, be expressed as fear of castration. On his becoming a social being, fear of the superego, conscience, becomes a necessity, omission of this step the source of severe conflicts and dangers. But at this point a new problem enters.

Let us for the moment try the experiment of substituting for the affect of anxiety some other affect, for example that of grief. We consider it entirely normal that a little girl should weep bitterly at the age of four if her doll is broken, at the age of six if her teacher reprimands her, at the age of sixteen if her sweetheart neglects her, at the age of twenty-five, perhaps, if she buries her child. Each of these grief-occasioning situations has its proper time and vanishes with its passing; but the later and more definite ones remain operative throughout life. We should be rather surprised, in fact, if this girl, after she had become a wife and mother, should weep over some knickknack getting broken. Yet this is how neurotics behave. Although in their mental apparatus there have long since developed all the agencies necessary for dealing with a wide range of stimuli, although they are mature enough to be able to gratify the greater part of their needs themselves, although they knew perfectly well that castration is no longer practised as a punishment, they nevertheless behave as though the old danger situation still existed, they remain under the spell of all the old causes of anxiety.

The answer to all this will prove somewhat prolix, for it will have in the first place to sift the actual facts of the case. In a large number of instances the old causes of anxiety have in reality become inoperative, but only after having first brought neurotic reactions into existence. The morbid fear of being alone, of the dark, and of strangers, on the part of the smallest children, which is almost to be labelled normal, disappears for the most part at a somewhat later age; such fears are "outgrown," as we say of many other disturbances of childhood. The phobias of animals so frequently met with share this same fate; many of the conversion hysterias of childhood are not carried over into later life. In the latency period the practice of ceremonials is of extremely frequent occurrence, yet only a very small percentage of these cases later develop a full-blown compulsion neurosis. The neuroses of children, so far at least as concerns upper-class urban children of the white race, are regularly occurring episodes in development, although too little attention is still paid to them. In not a single adult neurotic do the indications of a childhood neurosis fail of occurrence, while on the other hand by no means all children who show them become neurotic subsequently. Therefore in the course of growing up the anxiety-determinants which once existed must have been relinquished, the situations originally endowed with danger have lost their significance. To this must be added that certain of these danger situations survive into a later period of life by means of a modification, in keeping with that later period, of the character of what gives rise to anxiety. Thus, for example, castration anxiety persists in the guise of syphilophobia, after it has been learned that castration is no longer customary as a punishment for giving the sexual appetites free rein but that serious diseases threaten instinctual freedom instead. Certain other of the things that occasion anxiety are destined not to disappear at all, but are to accompany the human being throughout life, such as, for example, the fear of the superego. The neurotic is then distinguished from the normal person in that his response to these dangers is disproportionately increased. Yet against the return of the original traumatic anxiety situation even maturity offers after all no adequate protection; there may exist for every one a limit beyond which his psyche fails in the attempt to cope with the demands which the excitation in question makes upon him.

These minor reservations cannot possibly be taken as militating against the fact which we have been discussing: the fact, namely, that in their response to danger so many people remain infantile, continuing to react with anxiety to situations which should have long ceased to evoke it; to dispute this would be to deny the very fact of neurosis, for it is exactly such persons whom we call neurotics. But how does this situation come about? Why are not all neuroses merely episodes in the individual's development which become a closed chapter when the next stage of development is reached? Whence comes the element of permanency in these reactions to danger? Whence springs the preference over all other affects which the affect of anxiety seems to enjoy in alone evoking reactions which we distinguish from others as abnormal and which in their inexpediency obstruct the stream of life? In other words, we find ourselves abruptly confronted once again by the oft-repeated riddle: What is the source of neurosis, what is its ultimate, its specific, underlying principle? After decades of analytic effort this problem rises up before us, as untouched as at the beginning.

34   PRINCIPLES OF PSYCHOSOMATIC RESEARCH [1]

Franz Alexander

Although psychosomatic research is of recent origin, it deals with one of the oldest, if not *the* oldest, problems of scientific thought—with the mind-body problem. This may explain the heavy load of traditional concepts and assumptions which hamper its development. At first I shall take up the concept of *psychogenesis* in general, then that of *hysterical conversion* in particular, and finally the question of the *specificity* of emotional factors involved in somatic dysfunctions.

1. *Psychogenesis.* The question of psychogenesis is linked up with the ancient dichotomy: psyche versus soma. When the Journal of Psychosomatic Medicine was started, our editorial staff felt that in the first issue some clear statement should be made about this confusing philosophical issue to discourage authors from writing endless discussions on this point. I quote from this introductory statement of the editors:

> Emphasis is put on the thesis that there is no logical distinction between "mind and body," mental and physical. It is assumed that the complex neurophysiology of mood, instinct and intellect differs from other physiology in degree of complexity, but not in quality. Hence again divisions of medical disciplines into physiology, neurology, internal medicine, psychiatry and psychology may be convenient for academic administration, but biologically and philosophically these divisions have no validity. It takes for granted that psychic and somatic phenomena take place in the same biological system and are probably two aspects of the same process, that psychological phenomena should be studied in their psychological causality with intrinsically psychological methods and physiological phenomena in their physical causality with the methods of physics and chemistry (1).

In spite of this statement, we still receive manuscripts in which the authors involve themselves in a hopeless struggle with this age-worn

[1] Paper presented at the Conference on Psychiatry, held at Ann Arbor, Michigan, October 22-24, 1942, under the auspices of the University of Michigan and the McGregor Fund.

From F. Alexander, Fundamental concepts of psychosomatic research: psychogenesis, conversion, specificity, *Psychosom. Med.*, 1943, *5*, 205-210. Reprinted by permission of the author and the Williams and Wilkins Co.

problem. For example, an author gives an excellent description of the effect of psychological factors upon some clinical condition, then becomes apologetic and tries to dodge the whole issue of psychogenesis by saying that one should not speak of psychogenesis but of the coexistence of certain psychological factors with certain physical symptoms.

It is important that the question of psychogenesis should be clarified, stating explicitly what is meant by it. First let us examine an example. In the case of emotionally caused elevation of the blood pressure, psychogenesis does not mean that the contraction of the blood vessels is effected by some non-somatic mechanism. Rage consists in physiological processes which take place somewhere in the central nervous system. The physiological effect of rage consists of a chain of events— among them the elevation of blood pressure—in which every link can be described at least theoretically in physiological terms. The distinctive feature of psychogenic factors such as emotions or ideas and fantasies is that they *can* be studied also psychologically through introspection or by verbal communication from those in whom these physiological processes take place. An automobile climbing a hill has no sensation of effort, tiredness, or of a goal to reach. In contrast to a man-built machine the organism climbing a mountain has an awareness of certain of its internal physiological processes in the form of effort, tiredness, discouragement, renewed effort, and so on. Moreover, man in contrast to the animal organisms is able to convey these internal sensations to others by verbal communication. Verbal communication is therefore one of the most potent instruments of psychology and consequently also of psychosomatic research. When we speak of psychogenesis we refer to physiological processes consisting of central excitations in the nervous system which can be studied by psychological methods because they are perceived subjectively in the form of emotions, ideas, or wishes. Psychosomatic research deals with such processes in which certain links in the causal chain of events lend themselves, at the present state of our knowledge, more readily to a study by psychological methods than by physiological methods since the detailed investigation of emotions as brain processes is not far enough advanced. My expectation is, however, that even when the physiological basis of psychological phenomena will be better known we will not be able to dispense with their psychological study. It is hardly conceivable that the different moves of two chess players can ever be more clearly understood in biochemical or neuro-physiological than in psychological and logical terms.

2. *Conversion.* The concept of hysterical conversion too is closely related to the philosophical question of mind and body. The expression itself carries the connotation that a psychological process is transmuted into a bodily manifestation. Freud formulated the concept of conversion in the following way: "In hysteria the unbearable idea is rendered innocuous by the quantity of excitation attached to it being transmuted into some bodily form of expression, a process for which I should like to propose the name of conversion" (20). Essentially an hysterical conversion symptom is nothing but an unusual innervation; it does not differ in principle from any other voluntary innervation or from such expressive movements as speech, laughter, or weeping. When we want to hit someone our arms are brought into movement; when we speak our ideas are converted into movements of the laryngeal muscles and of the lips and tongue. In laughter or weeping also, an emotion finds bodily expression. It was unfortunate that Freud spoke, referring to hysterical conversion, of a "mysterious leap" from the psychic to the physiologic (19). In a conversion symptom like hysterical contracture, the "leap from the psychic into the somatic" is not more mysterious than in any of the common motor innervations, such as voluntary movements or expressive movements, as laughter or weeping. The meaning of conversion symptom was originally very definite: a conversion symptom was a symbolic substitute for an unbearable emotion. It was assumed that the symptom relieved, at least to some degree, the tension produced by the repression of the unbearable emotion. It was considered a kind of physical abreaction or equivalent of an unconscious emotional tension. From the beginning Freud insisted that the repressed emotion ultimately can be always retraced to a sexual tension. Ferenczi made this even more explicit by postulating that a physical conversion symptom is always a kind of genitalization of that part of the body (15). I shall not enter into the discussion of the validity of the exclusively sexual origin of conversion symptoms at the present moment.

Repeated attempts have been made to extend the original concept of hysterical conversion to all forms of psychogenic disturbances of the body, even to those of the visceral vegetative organs. It was claimed that the essence of psychogenic disturbances is always the same. A repressed emotional tension finds expression through bodily channels. Whether it takes place in vegetative organs controlled by the autonomic nervous system or in the voluntary neuro-muscular and sensory perceptive systems is a secondary matter. According to this concept emotional hypertension is the conversion of repressed rage or some other emotion into a physical symptom—the elevation of blood pressure. The adherents to this concept even went so far as to say that a peptic ulcer might be considered a conversion symptom. Some repressed emotion, let us say some biting fantasies, find somatic expression in tissue changes of the stomach. In previous writings I have tried to demonstrate the grave error inherent in such superficial generalizations (2, 3, 7). I pointed out that the original concept of hysterical conversion is still an excellent and valid one if it is restricted to those phenomena on which it was originally based by Freud. At the same time I introduced the concept of another form of psychogenic process which is observed in vegetative disturbances such as emotional hypertension or in psychogenic organic conditions such as peptic ulcers. Since these publications I have arrived at still more precise formulations which I should like to present on this occasion.

I still uphold my original suggestion that we restrict hysterical conversion phenomena to symptoms of the voluntary neuro-muscular and the sensory perceptive systems and differentiate them from psychogenic symptoms which occur in vegetative organ systems, the functions of which are under the control of the autonomic nervous system. The rationale of this distinction is about as follows: Hysterical conversion symptoms are substitute expressions—abreactions—or emotional tensions which cannot find adequate outlet through full-fledged motor behavior. For example, sexual excitation, which normally is gratified by intercourse, if repressed may find expression in some other motor innervation such as convulsions imitating the muscular movements of intercourse. Or, anger which cannot find expression through yelling, shouting, accusing, hitting, might lead to conversion symptoms in organs which are used for the legitimate expression of rage—the larynx or the extremities in the form of hysterical aphasia or paralysis. As Freud originally stressed it, these substitutive innervations never bring full relief; they are only attempts at relief; the symptoms express at the same time both the repressed emotion and its rejection. Just because they do not relieve the tension fully we have a pathological condition. The important issue, however, is that the emotional tension is at least partially relieved by the symptom itself. We deal with a different psychodynamic and physiological situation in the field of vegetative neuroses although there are some similarities to the conversion symptoms. Here the somatic symptoms are not substitute expressions of repressed emotions but they are normal physiological accompaniments of the symptom. For example, the emotional states of rage and fear are connected with a physiological syndrome consisting of such diversified vegetative processes as the stimulation of the adrenal system, mobilization of sugar, elevation of the blood pressure, changes in the distribution of blood which is squeezed out from the splanchnic area into the muscles, to the lungs and the brain. These physiological processes are normal corollaries of rage and fear; they do not relieve suppressed rage but they accompany rage. They are the adjustment of the organism to definite tasks which it has to face in a dangerous situation, to fight or to flee. They are a utilitarian preparation and adaptation of the internal vegetative processes to a specific type of behavior which is requested from the organism. The elevated blood pressure or mobilization of sugar does not relieve the anger in the least; these symptoms do not appear in place of the emotional tension; they simply accompany the emotion of rage; they are an inseparable part of the total phenomenon which we call rage. They are the systemic reaction of the body to rage. The chronicity of an emotional tension alone is what makes such a condition morbid. The non-neurotic individual is able to get rid of his rage by some legitimate expression. Some psychoneurotics can drain off the suppressed hostile feelings in compulsion symptoms. The hypertensive patient's pathology consists in the fact that he is under a constant or frequent, not repressed, but unexpressed, emotional tension which is not drained either by psychoneurotic symptoms or by legitimate expression such as verbal or physical combat. He has not the relief that the angry man has of beating up his adversary or at least telling him what he has on his mind. The difference between conversion symptom and vegetative neurosis is now obvious. A conversion symptom is a symbolic expression of a well-defined emotional content—an attempt at relief. It is expressed by the voluntary neuro-muscular or sensory perceptive systems whose original function is to express and relieve emotional tension. A vegetative neurosis like emotional hypertension is not an attempt to express an emotion but is the physiological accompaniment of constant or periodically recurring emotional states.

The same conditions described in emotional hypertension can be applied readily to all other vegetative systems. Similarly a gastric neurosis consisting of a chronic disturbance of the secretory and motor functions of the stomach is not the expression or drainage of an emotional tension but the physiological accompaniment of it. These patients want to be loved, to be taken care of, a wish to which they cannot give legitimate expression because of a neurotically exaggerated sense of shame or guilt; therefore they are under constant influence of these emotional tensions. The wish to be loved is deeply associated with the wish to be fed since the nursing situation is the first one in which the child enjoys parental love and care. Because of early emotional associations the chronic longing to be loved and taken care of is apt to stimulate the stomach functions. The stomach symptoms are the physiological corollaries of the passive state of expectation of receiving food. The disturbance of the secretory and motor functions of the stomach is not the substitute expression of an emotion but the physiological counterpart of an emotion, namely, of the desire to be taken care of. The wish to be taken care of may be repressed and transformed into the wish to be nursed. This is not a conversion, however, but the substitution of one desire for another. Corresponding to this wish to be nursed are certain vegetative innervations which are not substitutes for the wish to be nursed but are the inseparable physiological sequelae. If the desire to be taken care of is satisfied for example through sanitorium treatment, the constant pressure of this wish may cease and with it the stomach symptoms may fully disappear. Neurotic stomach symptoms, however, are not conversions of a repressed longing for love into stomach symptoms; they do not appear in place of the emotions, but are the physiological concomitants of a chronic or periodic emotional tension. Bulimia, in contradistinction to a stomach neurosis, may be considered as a conversion symptom. Here the wish to be loved, to be given things or to take things is drained, that is to say satisfied, at least to some extent by incorporating food. Eating becomes both a satisfaction and a symbolic substitute for being loved or being impregnated or for a biting aggressive attack. It fulfills all the requirements of a conversion symptom. Asthma also has components of a hysterical conversion symptom since it can serve as the direct expression and partial substitute for a suppressed emotion such as the wish to cry. Breathing—although an automatic function—is also under the control of voluntary innervations. Acid secretion of the stomach, however, is not. Breathing is used in such expressive functions as speech and crying; stomach secretion may be a concomitant of an emotional state but is never used for its symbolic expression as is speech or crying. Possibly there are mixed conditions in which both types of mechanism coexist. The psychodynamic background of most psychogenic skin disturbances is still very unclear, but it appears that in the skin both conversion mechanisms and vegetative neurotic symptoms may occur. The skin is partially a sensory perceptive but also a vegetative organ. Blushing is obviously a conversion symptom. On the other hand it is probable that the physiological mechanism in psychogenic urticaria follows the pattern of vegetative neuroses. Psychosomatic disturbances involving sphyncter functions both under autonomic and voluntary control, such as constipation, diarrhea, pollakuria, urine retention, etc., represent a combination of hysterical conversion symptoms and vegetative neuroses.

Finally, peptic ulcer is neither a conversion symptom nor a vegetative neurosis. In some cases it is the somatic end result of a long-standing neurotic stomach dysfunction but in itself has nothing whatever directly to do with any emotion. It is not the symbolic expression of a wish or a self-punishment. It is a secondary physiological end-effect of a long-standing dysfunction. It is an organic disturbance which in many cases is the end result of a psychogenic functional disturbance, a vegetative neurosis of the stomach.

To summarize: it seems advisable to differentiate between hysterical conversion and vegetative neurosis. Their similarities are rather superficial: both conditions are psychogenic, that is to say, they are caused ultimately by a chronic repressed or at least unrelieved emotional tension. The mechanisms involved, however, are fundamentally different both psychodynamically and physiologically. The hysterical conversion symptom is an attempt to relieve an emotional tension in a symbolic way; it is a symbolic expression of a definite emotional content. This mechanism is restricted to the voluntary neuro-muscular or sensory perceptive systems whose function is to express and relieve emotions. A vegetative neurosis consists of a psychogenic dysfunction of a vegetative organ which is not under control of the voluntary neuro-muscular system. The vegetative symptom is not a substitute expression of the emotion, but its normal physiological concomitant. We assume that corresponding to every emotional state there is a certain distribution of vegetative innervations. When we have to fight or undergo physical exertion the vegetative organs of digestion are relaxed whereas the muscular system and the lungs are in a state of preparation. The emotional attitude accompanying and preceding food intake and digestion again is accompanied by a different distribution of vegetative tonus. In this instance the visceral organs become hyperemic whereas the skeletal muscle tonus decreases and the concomitant drowsiness is the indication of a transitory anemia of the cortex. If these emotional states are chronically sustained the corresponding vegetative innervations also become chronic. The circulatory system of the hypertensive behaves as if this person were ready to attack somebody at any moment. On the other hand, when the stomach neurotic breaks down under an excessive load of responsibility he recoils from his habitual overactivity and assumes the vegetative mood of the state that accompanies digestion, to which his alimentary tract reacts with a continuous hyperactivity. This recoiling from exaggerated outward activity and strain we may call "vegetative retreat." It is a counter-coup phenomenon, a kind of exhaustion following sustained effort. According to all indications an outward directed active aggressive state is connected with a sustained excess of tonus of the sympathetic-adrenal system from which the individual when exhausted may retreat into the opposite attitude in which the tonus of the vagal-insular system is increased. This increased tonus of the parasympathetic system possibly connected with a simultaneous relaxation of sympathetic-adrenal tonus is what I denote by the expression "vegetative retreat." This may assume different forms consisting in some hyperactivity of visceral organs resulting from parasympathetic excitation such as hypersecretion and hypermotility of the stomach, diarrhea, or psychogenic hyperinsulinism (psychogenic hypoglycemia).[2] Possibly the condition described by Gowers as vagal attacks which he considered as related to the epileptic seizure is the most extreme example of a vegetative retreat (21).

3. *Specificity*. This brings us to the last crucial problem of psychosomatic research, the question of specificity, which I shall only briefly touch upon on this occasion. According to one school of thought there is no specific correlation; any emotional tension may influence any vegetative system. The choice of the symptoms may depend upon the history of the patient and on his constitution; if he has a weak stomach,

---

[2] In a number of patients with a so-called psychogenetic fatigue, Sidney A. Portis suggested that a possible physiological mechanism involved was that of hyper-insulinism. This resulted from a temporary or prolonged parasympathetic stimulation. Daily physiological doses of atropine by mouth brought about a cessation of the fatigue symptom. See Sidney A. Portis and Irving H. Zitman, "A mechanism of fatigue in neuropsychiatric patients," J. A. M. A., Vol. 121, 1943.

he has a stomach upset when he gets angry; if he has a labile vaso-motor system he might become a hypertensive under the influence of aggressions. Perhaps an early respiratory infection has made his lungs suspectible; then he will react to every emotional upset with an asthma attack. The other heuristic assumption, which has guided our investigative work in the Chicago Psychoanalytic Institute, is that the physiological responses to different emotional tensions are varied; that consequently vegetative dysfunctions result from specific emotional constellations. As I have emphasized, we know from human and animal experiment that different emotional states have their specific vegetative tonus. The vegetative syndrome which corresponds to rage and fear is definitely different from that of passive relaxation during digestion; a state of impatience or of tense attentiveness has bodily concomitants in vegetative and skeletal innervations different from those in a paralyzing state of panic. The vegetative concomitants of various emotional states are as different from each other as laughter from weeping—the physical expression of merriment from that of sorrow. It is therefore to be expected that just as the nature of the chronic unrelieved emotional state varies, so also will the corresponding vegetative disturbance vary. The results of current investigations are all in favor of the theory of specificity (4-7, 9-11, 13-14, 16-18, 22-32, 34).[3] Gastric neurotic symptoms have a different psychology from those of emotional diarrhea or constipation; cardiac cases differ in their emotional background from asthmatics. The emotional component in functional glycosuria has its own peculiarities and there is good evidence that the emotional factor in glaucoma has again its specific features. This emotional specificity can only be ascertained, of course, by careful, minute observation for which the best method available is the prolonged interview technique of psychoanalysis. However, briefer but careful psychiatric anamnestic studies conducted by well-trained observers often reveal the specific personality factors involved in different types of cases. To what extent constitutional factors influence the picture, and to what extent a pre-existing organic pathology or sensitivity are responsible are questions to be decided by further careful clinical studies.

[3] For a more complete literature concerning specific emotional factors, I refer to Dr. H. F. Dunbar's book, *Emotions and Bodily Changes* (12) and different reviews published in the *Journal of Psychosomatic Medicine* (8, 33, 35, 36). See also Weiss and English, *Psychosomatic Medicine*, Saunders Co., 1943.

Summary

1. An attempt is made to clarify the concept of psychogenesis.

2. The fundamental psychological and physiological differences between *conversion symptoms, vegetative neuroses,* and *psychogenic organic disease* are elaborated.

3. The problem of specificity of emotional factors in different vegetative neuroses is discussed. Evidence for the specificity of emotional factors is offered.

References

1. Introductory Statement. *Psychosom. Med.,* 1939, *1,* 1.
2. Alexander, F. Functional disturbances of psychogenic nature. *J. A. M. A.,* 1933, *100,* 469-473.
3. Alexander, F. Critical discussion of the extension of the theory of conversion hysteria to the field of organic diseases. In *Medical value of psychoanalysis.* New York: Norton, 1936 (2nd ed.).
4. Alexander, F. Emotional factors in essential hypertension. *Psychosom. Med.,* 1939, *1,* 173-179.
5. Alexander, F. Psychoanalytic study of a case of essential hypertension. *Psychosom. Med.,* 1939, *1,* 139-152.
6. Alexander, F. Gastrointestinal neuroses. In Portis, S. A. (ed.), *Diseases of the Digestive System.* Philadelphia: Lea & Febiger, 1941.
7. Alexander, F., and Co-workers. The influence of psychologic factors upon gastrointestinal disturbances: a symposium. *Psychoanal. Quart.,* 1934, *3,* 501-538.
8. Brush, A. Louise. Recent literature relative to the psychiatric aspects of gastrointestinal disorders. *Psychosom. Med.,* 1939, *1,* 423-428.
9. Daniels, G. E. Psychiatric aspects of ulcerative colitis. *New Engl. J. M.,* 1942, *226,* 178-184.
10. Deutsch, F. Emotional factors in asthma and other allergic conditions. Paper read before the Assoc. Med. Social Workers, Febr., 1938.
11. Dunbar, H. Flanders. Psychoanalytic notes relating to syndromes of asthma and hayfever. *Psychoanal. Quart.,* 1938, *7,* 25-68.
12. Dunbar, H. Flanders. *Emotions and bodily changes.* New York: Columbia Univ. Press, 1938 (2nd ed.).
13. Dunbar, H. Flanders. Character and symptom formation. *Psychoanal. Quart.,* 1939, *8,* 18-47.
14. Dunbar, H. Flanders, Wolfe, T., and Rioch, Janet McK. The psychic component of the disease process in cardiac, diabetic and fracture patients. *Am. J. Psychiat.,* 1936, *93,* 649-679.
15. Ferenczi, S. The phenomena of hysterical materialization. In *Further contributions to the theory and technique of psychoanalysis.* London: Hogarth Press, 1926.

16. French, T. M. Psychogenic factors in asthma. *Am. J. Psychiat.*, 1939, *96*, 87-101.

17. French, T. M. Physiology of behavior and choice of neurosis. *Psychoanal. Quart.*, 1941, *10*, 561-572.

18. French, T. M., Alexander, F., and Co-workers. Psychogenic factors in bronchial asthma. Part I. *Psychosom. Med. Monogr.*, 1941, *1*, No. 4. Part II. *Psychosom. Med. Monogr.* 1941, *2*, No. 1 and 2. National Research Council, Washington.

19. Freud, S. *A general introduction to psychoanalysis.* New York: Boni & Liveright, 1920.

20. Freud, S. The defence neuro-psychosis (1894). In *Collected Papers,* Vol. 1. London: Hogarth Press, 1924.

21. Gowers, W. Vagal and vaso-vagal attacks. In *The borderland of epilepsy.* Philadelphia: Blakiston, 1907.

22. Hill, L. B. Psychoanalytic observations on essential hypertension. *Psychoanal. Rev.*, 1935, *22*, 60-64.

23. Menninger, K. A., and Menninger, W. C. Psychoanalytic observation in cardiac disorders. *Am. Heart J.*, 1936, *11*, 10-21.

24. Miller, M. L. Bloodpressure findings in relation to inhibited aggression in psychotics. *Psychosom. Med.*, 1939, *1*, 162-172.

25. Miller, M. L. A psychological study of a case of eczema and a case of neurodermatitis. *Psychosom. Med.*, 1942, *4*, 82-93.

26. Miller, M. L. and McLean, Helen V. The status of the emotions in palpitation and extrasystoles with a note on the effort syndrome. *Psychoanal. Quart.*, 1941, *10*, 545-560.

27. Mittelman, B., Wolf, H. G., and Scharf, Margaret. Emotions and gastroduodenal functions. Experimental studies on patients with gastritis, duodenitis and peptic ulcer. *Psychosom. Med.*, 1942, *4*, 5-61.

28. Saul, L. J. A note on the psychogenesis of organic symptoms. *Psychoanal. Quart.*, 1935, *4*, 476-483.

29. Saul, L. J. Psychogenic factors in the etiology of the common cold and related symptoms. *Int. J. Psychoanal.*, 1938, *19*, 451-470.

30. Saul, L. J. Hostility in cases of essential hypertension. *Psychosom. Med.*, 1939, *1*, 153-161.

31. Saul, L. J. Some observations on the relations of emotions and allergy. *Psychosom. Med.*, 1941, *3*, 66-71.

32. Saul, L. J. and Bernstein, C. The emotional settings of some attacks of urticaria. *Psychosom. Med.*, 1941, *3*, 349-369.

33. Stokes, J. H., and Berman, H. Psychosomatic correlations in allergic conditions: a review of problems and literature. *Psychosom. Med.*, 1940, *2*, 438-458.

34. Van der Heide, C. A study of mechanisms in two cases of peptic ulcer. *Psychosom. Med.*, 1940, *2*, 398-410.

35. Weiss, E. Recent advances in pathogenesis and treatment of hyper-

tension. A review. *Psychosom. Med.,* 1939, *1,* 180-198.

36. White, B. V., Cobb, S. and Jones, C. M. Mucous colitis. A psychological medical study of 60 cases. *Psychosom. Med. Monogr.* 1939, *1,* No. 1, National Research Council, Washington.

35 SOCIAL THEORY OF NEUROTIC CONFLICT

Karen Horney

Whatever the starting point and however tortuous the road, we must finally arrive at a disturbance of personality as the source of psychic illness. The same can be said of this as of almost any other psychological discovery: it is really a rediscovery. Poets and philosophers of all times have known that it is never the serene, well-balanced person who falls victim to psychic disorders, but the one torn by inner conflicts. In modern terms, every neurosis, no matter what the symptomatic picture, is a character neurosis. Hence our endeavor in theory and therapy must be directed toward a better understanding of the neurotic character structure.

Actually, Freud's great pioneering work increasingly converged on this concept—though his genetic approach did not allow him to arrive at its explicit formulation. But others who have continued and developed Freud's work—notably Franz Alexander, Otto Rank, Wilhelm Reich, and Harald Schultz-Hencke—have defined it more clearly. None of them, however, is agreed as to the precise nature and dynamics of this character structure.

My own starting point was a different one. Freud's postulations in regard to feminine psychology set me thinking about the role of cultural factors. Their influence on our ideas of what constitutes masculinity or femininity was obvious, and it became just as obvious to me that Freud had arrived at certain erroneous conclusions because he failed to take them into account. My interest in this subject grew over the course of fifteen years. It was furthered in part by association with Erich Fromm who, through his profound knowledge of both sociology and psychoanalysis, made me more aware of the significance of social factors over and above their circumscribed application to feminine psychology. And my impressions were confirmed when I came to the United States in 1932. I saw then that the attitudes and the neuroses of persons in this country differed in many ways from those I had observed in European countries, and that only the difference in civilizations could account for this. My conclusions finally found their expression in *The Neurotic Personality of Our Time*. The main contention here was that neuroses are brought about by cultural factors—which more specifically meant that neuroses are generated by disturbances in human relationships.

In the years before I wrote *The Neurotic Personality* I pursued another line of research that followed logically from the earlier hypothesis. It revolved around the question as to what the driving forces are in neurosis. Freud had been the first to point out that these were compulsive drives. He regarded these drives as instinctual in nature, aimed at satisfaction and intolerant of frustration. Consequently he believed that they were not confined to neuroses per se but operated in all human beings. If, however, neuroses were an outgrowth of disturbed human relationships, this postulation could not possibly be valid. The concepts I arrived at on this score were, briefly, these. Compulsive drives are specifically neurotic; they are born of feelings of isolation, helplessness, fear and hostility, and represent ways of coping with the world despite these feelings; they aim primarily not at satisfaction but at safety; their compulsive character is due to the anxiety lurking behind them. Two of these drives—neurotic cravings for affection and for power—stood out at first in clear relief and were presented in detail in *The Neurotic Personality*.

Though retaining what I considered the fundamentals of Freud's teachings, I realized by that time that my search for a better understanding had led me in directions that were at variance with Freud. If so many factors that Freud regarded as instinctual were culturally determined, if so much that Freud considered libidinal was a neurotic need for affection, provoked by anxiety and aimed at feeling safe with others, then the libido theory was no longer tenable. Childhood experiences remained important, but the influence they exerted on our lives appeared in a new light. Other theoretical differences inevitably followed. Hence it became necessary to formulate in my own mind where I stood in reference to Freud. The result of this clarification was *New Ways in Psychoanalysis*.

In the meantime my search for the driving forces in neurosis continued. I called the compulsive drives neurotic trends and described ten of them in my next book. By then I, too, had arrived at the point of recognizing that the neurotic character structure was of central significance. I regarded it at that time as a kind of macrocosm formed by many microcosms interacting upon one another. In the nucleus of each microcosm was a neurotic trend. This theory of neurosis had a practical application. If psychoanalysis did not primarily involve relating our present difficulties to our past experiences but depended rather upon understanding the interplay of forces in our existing personality, then recognizing and changing ourselves with little or even no expert help was entirely feasible. In the face of a widespread need for psychotherapy and a scarcity of available aid, self-analysis seemed to offer the hope of filling a vital need. Since the major part of the book dealt with the possibilities, limitations, and ways of analyzing ourselves, I called it *Self-Analysis*.

I was, however, not entirely satisfied with my presentation of individual trends. The trends themselves were accurately described; but I was haunted by the feeling that in a simple enumeration they appeared in a too isolated fashion. I could see that a neurotic need for affection, compulsive modesty, and the need for a "partner" belonged together. What I failed to see was that together they represented a basic attitude toward others and the self, and a particular philosophy of life. These trends are the nuclei of what I have now drawn together as a "moving toward people." I saw, too, that a compulsive craving for power and prestige and neurotic ambition had something in common. They constitute roughly the factors involved in what I shall call "moving against people." But the need for admiration and the perfectionist drives, though they had all the earmarks of neurotic trends and influenced the neurotic's relation with others, seemed primarily to concern his relations with himself. Also, the need for exploitation seemed to be less basic than either the need for affection or for power; it appeared less comprehensive than these, as if it were not a separate entity but had been taken out of some larger whole.

My questionings have since proved justified. In the years following, my focus of interest shifted to the role of conflicts in neurosis. I had said in *The Neurotic Personality* that a neurosis came about through the collision of divergent neurotic trends. In *Self-Analysis* I had said that neurotic trends not only reinforced each other but also created conflicts.

Nevertheless conflicts had remained a side issue. Freud had been increasingly aware of the significance of inner conflicts; he saw them, however, as a battle between repressed and repressing forces. The conflicts I began to see were of a different kind. They operated between contradictory sets of neurotic trends, and though they originally concerned contradictory attitudes toward others, in time they encompassed contradictory attitudes toward the self, contradictory qualities and contradictory sets of values.

A crescendo of observation opened my eyes to the significance of such conflicts. What first struck me most forcibly was the blindness of patients toward obvious contradictions within themselves. When I pointed these out they became elusive and seemed to lose interest. After repeated experiences of this kind I realized that the elusiveness expressed a profound aversion to tackling these contradictions. Finally, panic reactions in response to a sudden recognition of a conflict showed me I was working with dynamite. Patients had good reason to shy away from these conflicts: they dreaded their power to tear them to pieces.

Then I began to recognize the amazing amount of energy and intelligence that was invested in more or less desperate efforts to "solve" the conflicts or, more precisely, to deny their existence and create an artificial harmony. I saw the four major attempts at solution in about the order in which they are presented in this book. The initial attempt was to eclipse part of the conflict and raise its opposite to predominance. The second was to "move away from" people. The function of neurotic detachment now appeared in a new light. Detachment was part of the basic conflict—that is, one of the original conflicting attitudes toward others; but it also represented an attempt at solution, since maintaining an emotional distance between the self and others set the conflict out of operation. The third attempt was very different in kind. Instead of moving away from others, the neurotic moved away from himself. His whole actual self became somewhat unreal to him and he created in its place an idealized image of himself in which the conflicting parts were so transfigured that they no longer appeared as conflicts but as various aspects of a rich personality. This concept helped to clarify many neurotic problems which hitherto were beyond the reach of our understanding and hence of our therapy. It also put two of the neurotic trends which had previously resisted integration into their proper setting. The need for perfection now appeared as an endeavor to measure up to this idealized image; the craving for admiration could be seen as the patient's need to have outside affirmation that he really was his idealized image. And the farther the image was removed from reality the more insatiable this latter need would logically be. Of all the attempts at solution the idealized image is probably the most important by reason of its far-reaching effect on the whole personality. But in turn it generates a new inner rift, and hence calls for further patchwork. The fourth attempt at solution seeks primarily to do away with this rift, though it helps as well to spirit away all other conflicts. Through what I call externalization, inner processes are experienced as going on outside the self. If the idealized image means taking a step away from the actual self, externalization represents a still more radical divorce. It again creates new conflicts, or rather greatly augments the original conflict—that between the self and the outside world.

I have called these the four major attempts at solution, partly because they seem to operate regularly in all neuroses—though in varying degree—and partly because they bring about incisive changes in the personality. But they are by no means the only ones. Others of less general significance include such strategies as arbitrary rightness, whose main function is to quell all inner doubts; rigid self-control, which holds together a torn individual by sheer will power; and cynicism, which, in disparaging all values, eliminates conflicts in regard to ideals.

Meanwhile the consequences of all these unresolved conflicts were gradually becoming clearer to me. I saw the manifold fears that were generated, the waste of energy, the inevitable impairment of moral integrity, the deep hopelessness that resulted from feeling inextricably entangled.

It was only after I had grasped the significance of neurotic hopelessness that the meaning of sadistic trends finally came into view. These, I now understand, represented an attempt at restitution through vicarious living, entered upon by a person who despaired of ever being himself. And the all-consuming passion which can so often be observed in sadistic pursuits grew out of such a person's insatiable need for vindictive triumph. It became clear to me then that the need for destructive exploitation was in fact no separate neurotic trend but only a never-failing expression of that more comprehensive whole which for lack of a better term we call sadism.

Thus a theory of neurosis evolved, whose dynamic center is a basic conflict between the attitudes of "moving toward," "moving against," and "moving away from" people. Because of his fear of being split apart on the one hand and the necessity to function as a unity on the other, the neurotic makes desperate attempts at solution. While he can succeed this way in creating a kind of artificial equilibrium, new conflicts are constantly generated and further remedies are continually required to blot them out. Every step in this struggle for unity makes the neurotic more hostile, more helpless, more fearful, more alienated from himself and others, with the result that the difficulties responsible for the conflicts become more acute and their real resolution less and less attainable. He finally becomes hopeless and may try to find a kind of restitution in sadistic pursuits, which in turn have the effect of increasing his hopelessness and creating new conflicts.

This, then, is a fairly dismal picture of neurotic development and its resulting character structure. Why do I nonetheless call my theory a constructive one? In the first place it does away with the unrealistic optimism that maintains we can "cure" neuroses by absurdly simple means. But it involves no equally unrealistic pessimism. I call it constructive because it allows us for the first time to tackle and resolve neurotic hopelessness. I call it constructive most of all because in spite of its recognition of the severity of neurotic entanglements, it permits not only a tempering of the underlying conflicts but their actual resolution, and so enables us to work toward a real integration of personality. Neurotic conflicts cannot be resolved by rational decision. The neurotic's attempts at solution are not only futile but harmful. But these conflicts *can* be resolved by changing the conditions within the personality that brought them into being. Every piece of analytical work well done changes these conditions in that it makes a person less helpless, less fearful, less hostile, and less alienated from himself and others.

Freud's pessimism as regards neuroses and their treatment arose from the depths of his disbelief in human goodness and human growth. Man, he postulated, is doomed to suffer or to destroy. The instincts which drive him can only be controlled, or at best "sublimated." My own belief is that man has the capacity as well as the desire to develop his potentialities and become a decent human being, and that these deteriorate if his relationship to others and hence to himself is, and continues to be, disturbed. I believe that man can change and go on changing as long as he lives. And this belief has grown with deeper understanding.

36 TYPES OF REACTION TO FRUSTRATION

Saul Rosenzweig

This paper represents a short excursion in the armchair. We take our place there in the hope of discovering a classification of *apperceptive types of conscious reaction to frustration* that will serve as the basis for further, possibly experimental, research.

If the attempt is made to describe the typical modes of conscious reaction to frustration, one possible result is that summarized in the accompanying table.

APPERCEPTIVE TYPES OF CONSCIOUS REACTION TO FRUSTRATION

	Extrapunitive	*Intropunitive*	*Impunitive*
Emotions	Anger and indignation	Humiliation and guilt	Embarrassment and shame
Judgments	Blames others: "You played me dirty. I'll get you for that."	Blames self: "How could I have done a thing like that! I'll never forgive myself."	Condones: "It couldn't be helped. Let bygones be bygones."

In the "extrapunitive" type of conscious reaction to frustration, the individual experiences anger and indignation against others, whom he holds blameworthy. For example, the extrapunitive reaction to being snubbed by a friend would be to regard him as an ill-bred, perhaps ungrateful, person, whatever the objective evidence might be.

In the "intropunitive" type of reaction, the individual experiences humiliation and guilt, for he holds himself blameworthy. For example, the intropunitive reaction to being snubbed by a friend would be to regard oneself as an inferior person, unworthy of the other's attention, whatever the objective evidence might be.

In the "impunitive" type of reaction, the individual experiences embarrassment and shame, and is more interested in condonement than

From S. Rosenzweig, Types of reaction to frustration: a heuristic classification, *J. abn. soc. Psychol.*, 1934, *29*, 298-300. Reprinted by permission of the author, the *Journal of abnormal and social Psychology,* and the American Psychological Association.

in blame. For example, the impunitive reaction to being snubbed would be to connive at or gloss over the incident as if it were the result of a mere oversight, whatever the objective evidence might be.

The expression "whatever the objective evidence might be" indicates the apperceptive character of our types. We are concerned not with what is objectively present by way of responsibility in the experience of frustration, but rather with what the individual who is frustrated chooses to emphasize or even read into the situation in accordance with his personal traits and needs. In so far as the situation is objectively evaluated, without any degree of apperceptive distortion, our types are inapplicable.

To avoid misunderstanding, at least two further points should be noted.

1) The present classification applies, in the first instance, not to individuals but to mechanisms. It describes types of reaction, not of reacting persons. While we may assume with relative safety that the majority of normal individuals have a consistently characteristic way of responding to frustration, whether it be extrapunitive, intropunitive or impunitive, we must of course allow that no individual reacts in his characteristic way without exception. Moreover, it is easily possible that a person should consistently respond in some one of the above three ways in one sort of situation and should consistently follow one of the other two in another sort of situation.

2) The above is a description of the *conscious,* not of the *unconscious,* processes involved in reacting to frustration. The relations of the two—by way of compensation and the like—constitute a fundamental problem that is just beginning to be solved.

In elaboration of the present schema several additional statements may be made.

1) The above account omits to consider genetic and dynamic factors. We may remedy this to some extent if we avail ourselves of the psychoanalytic classification of needs into aggressive and erotic. We may then speculate that the extrapunitive and intropunitive types are both aggressive in character, the aggression being outwardly directed in the former case, inwardly in the latter. The impunitive type of reaction, on the other hand, may be conceived to draw its energy from erotic sources; it would then not be thought of as intermediate to the other two but as contrasted with them.

2) It seems likely that each of our types of reaction would have a

special relation to memory. One might expect that both the extrapunitive and the intropunitive reactions would entail remembering the
occasion of frustration, in the former case, as if in anticipation of
revenge, in the latter, as if in preparation for nursing the wounds to
one's pride and "eating one's own heart out." It is as if the aggressive
impulses were being preserved to be expressed later, in the former case,
against outer objects, in the latter, against the subject's own self. The
impunitive type of reaction, on the other hand, might be expected to
entail a conscious forgetting of the occasion of frustration, as if in order
to reconcile one's self—and others—to the disagreeable situation. The
impunitive reaction might thus be summed up in the expression "For-
give and forget," whereas the other two types would involve neither
forgiving nor forgetting.

It goes without saying that extensive investigation is necessary before
the above notions can be correctly evaluated or satisfactorily completed.

37   THE THEORY OF THREAT[1]

A. H. Maslow

It is easy in the discussion of frustration to fall into the error of seg-
menting the human being. That is to say, there is still a tendency to
speak of the mouth or stomach being frustrated, or of a need being
frustrated. We must keep in mind constantly the truism that only a
whole human being is frustrated, never a part of a human being.

With this in mind, an important distinction becomes apparent,
namely the difference between deprivation and threat to the personality.
The usual definitions of frustration are in terms simply of not getting
what one desires, of interference with a wish, or with a gratification.
Such a definition fails to make the distinction between a deprivation
which is unimportant to the organism (easily substituted for, with few

[1] Prepared for the 1940 meeting of the Eastern Psychological Association in the Symposium on Effects of Frustration.

From A. H. Maslow, Deprivation, threat and frustration, *Psychol. Rev.*, 1941,
48, 364-366. Reprinted by permission of the author, the *Psychological Review,*
and the American Psychological Association.

serious after-effects), and, on the other hand, a deprivation which is at the same time, a threat to the personality, that is, to the life goals of the individual, to his defensive system, to his self-esteem or to his feeling of security. It is our contention that only a threatening deprivation has the multitude of effects (usually undesirable) which are commonly attributed to frustration in general.

A goal object may have two meanings for the individual. First it has its intrinsic meaning, and secondly, it may have also a secondary, symbolic value. Thus a certain child deprived of an ice-cream cone which he wanted may have lost simply an ice-cream cone. A second child, however, deprived of an ice-cream cone, may have lost not only a sensory gratification, but may also feel deprived of the love of his mother because she refused to buy it for him. For the second boy the ice-cream cone not only has an intrinsic value, but may also be the carrier of psychological values. Being deprived merely of ice-cream *qua* ice-cream probably means very little for a healthy individual, and it is questionable whether it should even be called by the same name, i.e., frustration, which characterizes other more threatening deprivations. It is only when a goal object represents love, prestige, respect, or achievement that being deprived of it will have the bad effects ordinarily attributed to frustration in general.

It is possible to demonstrate very clearly this twofold meaning of an object in certain groups of animals and in certain situations. For instance, it has been shown that when two monkeys are in a dominance-subordination relationship a piece of food is 1) an appeaser of hunger and also 2) a symbol of dominance status. Thus if the subordinate animal attempts to pick up food, he will at once be attacked by the dominant animal. If, however, he can deprive the food of its symbolic dominance value, then his dominator allows him to eat it. This he can do very easily by a gesture of obeisance, i.e., presentation as he approaches the food; this is as if to say, "I want this food only to still hunger, I do not want to challenge your dominance. I readily concede your dominance." In the same way we may take a criticism from a friend in two different ways. Ordinarily the average person will respond by feeling attacked and threatened (which is fair enough because so frequently criticism is an attack). He therefore bristles and becomes angry in response. But if he is assured that this criticism is not an attack or a rejection of himself, he will then not only listen to the criticism, but possibly even be grateful for it. Thus, if he has already had thousands of proofs that his friend loves him and respects him, the criticism represents only criticism; it does not also represent an attack or threat.

Neglect of this distinction has created a great deal of unnecessary turmoil in psychoanalytic circles. An ever-recurring question is: Does sexual deprivation inevitably give rise to all or any of the many effects of frustration, e.g., aggression, sublimation, etc.? It is now well known that many cases are found in which celibacy has no psychopathological effects. In many other cases, however, it has many bad effects. What factor determines which shall be the result? Clinical work with non-neurotic people gives the clear answer that sexual deprivation becomes pathogenic in a severe sense only when it is felt by the individual to represent rejection by the opposite sex, inferiority, lack of worth, lack of respect, or isolation. Sexual deprivation can be borne with relative ease by individuals for whom it has no such implications. (Of course, there will probably be what Rosenzweig calls need-persistive reactions, but these are not necessarily pathological.)

The unavoidable deprivations in childhood are also ordinarily thought of as frustrating. Weaning, elimination control, learning to walk, in fact every new level of adjustment, is conceived to be achieved by forceable pushing of the child. Here, too, the differentiation between mere deprivation and threat to the personality enjoins caution upon us. Observations of children who are completely assured of the love and respect of their parents have shown that deprivations can sometimes be borne with astonishing ease. There are few frustration effects if these deprivations are not conceived by the child to be threatening to his fundamental personality, to his main life goals, or needs.

From this point of view, it follows that the phenomenon of threatening frustration is closely allied to other threat situations much more than it is to mere deprivation. The classic effects of frustration are also found frequently to be a consequence of other types of threat—traumatization, conflict, rejection, severe illness, actual physical threat, imminence of death, humiliation, isolation, or loss of prestige.

This leads us to our final hypothesis, that perhaps frustration as a single concept is less useful than the two concepts which cross-cut it, 1) deprivation, and 2) threat to the personality. Deprivation implies much less than is ordinarily implied by the concept of frustration; threat implies much more.

38   THE FRUSTRATION-AGGRESSION HYPOTHESIS [1]

Neal E. Miller

The frustration-aggression hypothesis is an attempt to state a relationship believed to be important in many different fields of research. It is intended to suggest to the student of human nature that when he sees aggression he should turn a suspicious eye on possibilities that the organism or group is confronted with frustration; and that when he views interference with individual or group habits, he should be on the look-out for, among other things, aggression. This hypothesis is induced from common-sense observation, from clinical case histories, from a few experimental investigations, from sociological studies and from the results of anthropological field work. The systematic formulation of this hypothesis enables one to call sharp attention to certain common characteristics in a number of observations from all of these historically distinct fields of knowledge and thus to take one modest first step toward the unification of these fields.

A number of tentative statements about the frustration-aggression hypothesis have recently been made by us in a book (1). Unfortunately one of these statements, which was conspicuous because it appeared on the first page, was unclear and misleading as has been objectively demonstrated by the behavior of reviewers and other readers. In order to avoid any further confusion it seems advisable to rephrase this statement, changing it to one which conveys a truer impression of the authors' ideas. The objectionable phrase is the last half of the proposition: "that the occurrence of aggression always presupposes the existence of frustration and, contrariwise, that the existence of frustration always leads to some form of aggression."

The first half of this statement, the assertion that the occurrence of

[1] This article is a revision of a paper read at the Symposium on Effects of Frustration at the meeting of the Eastern Psychological Association at Atlantic City, April 5, 1940.

From N. E. Miller (with the collaboration of R. R. Sears, O. H. Mowrer, L. W. Doob, and J. Dollard), The frustration-aggression hypothesis, *Psychol. Rev.*, 1941, *48*, 337-342. Reprinted by permission of the author, the *Psychological Review*, and the American Psychological Association.

aggression always presupposes frustration, is in our opinion defensible and useful as a first approximation, or working hypothesis. The second half of the statement, namely, the assertion "that the existence of frustration always leads to some form of aggression" is unfortunate from two points of view. In the first place it suggests, though it by no means logically demands, that frustration has no consequences other than aggression. This suggestion seems to have been strong enough to override statements appearing later in the text which specifically rule out any such implication (1).[2] A second objection to the assertion in question is that it fails to distinguish between instigation to aggression and the actual occurrence of aggression. Thus it omits the possibility that other responses may be dominant and inhibit the occurrence of acts of aggression. In this respect it is *inconsistent* with later portions of the exposition which make a distinction between the instigation to a response and the actual presence of that response and state that punishment can inhibit the occurrence of acts of aggression (1).[3]

Both of these unfortunate aspects of the former statement may be avoided by the following rephrasing: Frustration produces instigations to a number of different types of response, one of which is an instigation to some form of aggression.

This rephrasing of the hypothesis states the assumption that was actually used throughout the main body of the text. Instigation to aggression may occupy any one of a number of positions in the hierarchy of instigations aroused by a specific situation which is frustrating. If the instigation to aggression is the strongest member of this hierarchy, then acts of aggression will be the first response to occur. If the instigations to other responses incompatible with aggression are stronger than the instigation to aggression, then these other responses will occur at first and prevent, at least temporarily, the occurrence of acts of aggression. This opens up two further possibilities. If these other responses lead to a reduction in the instigation to the originally frustrated response, then the strength of the instigation to aggression is also reduced so that acts of aggression may not occur at all in the situation in question. If, on the other hand, the first responses do not lead to a

[2] Pp. 8-9, 19, 58, 101-102.

[3] Pp. 32-38; also 27, 39-50, 75-87, 111, 166. In this later exposition a distinction is made not only between instigation to aggression and acts of aggression but also between conspicuous acts of overt aggression and inconspicuous acts of non-overt aggression. It is assumed that the former are more apt to be culturally inhibited by strong punishments than the latter.

reduction in the original instigation, then the instigations to them will tend to become weakened through extinction so that the next most dominant responses, which may or may not be aggression, will tend to occur. From this analysis it follows that the more successive responses of non-aggression are extinguished by continued frustration, the greater is the probability that the instigation to aggression eventually will become dominant so that some response of aggression actually will occur. Whether or not the successive extinction of responses of non-aggression must inevitably lead to the dominance of the instigation to aggression depends, as was clearly stated in later pages of the book, upon quantitative assumptions beyond the scope of our present knowledge (1, p. 40.)[4]

Frustration produces instigation to aggression but this is not the only type of instigation that it may produce. Responses incompatible with aggression may, if sufficiently instigated, prevent the actual occurrence of acts of aggression. In our society punishment of acts of aggression is a frequent source of instigation to acts incompatible with aggression.

When the occurrence of acts of aggression is prevented by more strongly instigated incompatible responses, how is the existence of instigation to aggression to be determined? If only the more direct and overt acts of aggression have been inhibited, as is apt to be the case because such acts are the most likely to be punished, then the instigation to aggression may be detected by observing either indirect or less overt acts of aggression. If even such acts of aggression are inhibited, then a different procedure must be employed. Two such procedures are at least theoretically possible. One is to reduce the competing instigations, such as fear of punishment, and observe whether or not acts of aggression then occur. The other is to confront the subject with an additional frustration which previous experiments have demonstrated would by itself be too weak to arouse an instigation strong enough to override the competing responses inhibiting the aggression in question. If the instigation from this additional frustration now results in an act of aggression, then it must have gained its strength to do so by summating with an already present but inhibited instigation to aggression. The presence of the originally inhibited instigation to aggression would be demonstrated by the effects of such summation. Thus the fact that an instigation may be inhibited does not eliminate all possibility of experimentally demonstrating its presence.

[4] The notions used here are similar to those employed by Professor Hull in describing trial-and-error learning (2).

At this point two important and related qualifications of the hypothesis may be repeated for emphasis though they have already been stated in the book. It is not certain how early in the infancy of the individual the frustration-aggression hypothesis is applicable, and no assumptions are made as to whether the frustration-aggression relationship is of innate or of learned origin.

Now that an attempt has been made to clarify and to qualify the hypothesis, four of the chief lines of investigation which it suggests may be briefly considered.[5]

1. An attempt may be made to apply the hypothesis to the integration and elucidation of clinical and social data. Here the fact that certain forms of aggression are spectacularly dangerous to society and to the individual is relevant. This means that acute personality conflicts are apt to arise from the problem of handling aggression and that the problem of aggression is apt to play an important rôle in shaping certain great social institutions such as the in-group as an organization against the out-group.

2. An attempt may be made to formulate more exactly the laws determining the different ways in which instigation to aggression will be expressed under specified circumstances. Some of the problems in this field are suggested by the phenomena of displacement of the object of aggression, change in the form of aggression, and catharsis of aggression.

3. An attempt may be made to secure more information concerning the other consequences which frustration may produce in addition to the instigation to aggression. Such an attempt would lead into studies of rational thought and problem solution as suggested in the classical work of John Dewey, and into studies of experimental extinction, trial-and-error learning, substitute response and regression.[6] Work along this line of investigation may deal either with the clinical and social significance of these other consequences of frustration or with the discovery of the laws governing them.

4. An attempt may be made to improve or to reformulate the basic

[5] Both of the first two of these chief lines of investigation have been developed at length in *Frustration and Aggression*. No attempt was made here to elaborate upon either the third or the fourth. Thus that first effort does not purport to be a complete systematization of all principles within a single field, but, rather, an exploratory attempt to apply a strictly limited number of principles to several different fields (1, pp. 18, 26).

[6] These problems are discussed in more detail by Dr. Sears in the next paper of this series, "Non-aggressive responses to frustration" (3).

frustration-aggression hypothesis itself. The determination of the laws which allow one to predict exactly under which circumstances instigation to aggression may be expected to occupy the dominant, the second, the third, or some other position in the hierarchy of instigations aroused by a frustrating situation is a most important problem of this type. Another problem is the reduction of the frustration-aggression hypothesis to more fundamental principles and the more accurate restatement of the hypothesis in terms of these more basic principles. One of the steps in this direction would be to scrutinize any exceptions to the hypothesis as now formulated. Another step would involve a careful study of the early stages of the socialization of the individual in an attempt to analyze the interlocking rôles of three factors: first, innate physiological reaction patterns; second, learning mechanisms; and third, the structure of the social maze which poses the learning dilemmas and contains the rewards and punishments. An empirical and theoretical analysis along these lines might lead to a fundamental reformulation giving a closer approximation of the socially and scientifically useful truths imperfectly expressed in the present frustration-aggression hypothesis.

References

1. Dollard, J.; Doob, L. W.; Miller, N. E.; Mowrer, O. H.; and Sears, R. R. *Frustration and aggression.* New Haven: Yale Univ. Press, 1939.
2. Hull, C. L. Simple trial-and-error learning—an empirical investigation. *J. comp. Psychol.,* 1939, *27,* 233-258.
3. Sears, R. R. Non-aggressive responses to frustration. *Psychol. Rev.,* 1941, *48,* 343-346.

39   STIMULUS-RESPONSE THEORY OF ANXIETY [1]

O. H. Mowrer

Within recent decades an important change has taken place in the scientific view of anxiety (fear),[2] its genesis, and its psychological significance. Writing in 1890, William James (5) stoutly supported the then current supposition that anxiety was an *instinctive* ("idiopathic") reaction to certain objects or situations, which might or might not represent real danger. To the extent that the instinctively given, predetermined objects of anxiety were indeed dangerous, anxiety reactions had biological utility and could be accounted for as an evolutionary product of the struggle for existence. On the other hand, there were, James assumed, also anxiety reactions that were altogether senseless and which, conjecturally, came about through Nature's imperfect wisdom. But in all cases, an anxiety reaction was regarded as phylogenetically fixed and unlearned. The fact that children may show no fear of a given type of object, e.g., live frogs, during the first year of life but may later manifest such a reaction, James attributed to the "ripening" of the fear-of-live-frogs instinct; and the fact that such fears, once they have "ripened," may also disappear he explained on the assumption that all instincts, after putting in an appearance and, as it were, placing themselves at the individual's disposal, tend to undergo a kind of obliviscence or decay unless taken advantage of and made "habitual."

Some years later John B. Watson (11) demonstrated experimentally that, contrary to the Jamesian view, most human fears are specifically relatable to and dependent upon individual experience. Starting with the reaction of infants to loud sounds or loss of physical support, which

---

[1] This paper, in substantially its present form, was presented before the Monday Night Group of the Institute of Human Relations, Yale University, March 13, 1939.

[2] Psychoanalytic writers sometimes differentiate between anxiety and fear on the grounds that fear has a consciously perceived object and anxiety does not. Although this distinction may be useful for some purposes, these two terms will be used in the present paper as strictly synonymous.

From O. H. Mowrer, A stimulus-response theory of anxiety and its role as a reinforcing agent, *Psychol. Rev.,* 1939, *46,* 553-565. Reprinted by permission of the author, the *Psychological Review,* and the American Psychological Association.

he refused to call "instinctive" but did not hesitate to regard as "unlearned" or "reflexive," Watson was able to show, by means of Pavlov's conditioning technique, that an indefinitely wide range of other stimuli, if associated with this reaction, could be made to acquire the capacity to elicit unmistakably fearful behavior. This was an important discovery, but it appears to have involved a basic fallacy. Watson overlooked the fact that "loud sounds" are intrinsically *painful,* and he also overlooked the fact that "loss of physical support," although not painful in its own right, is almost certain to be followed by some form of stimulation (incident to the stopping of the body's fall) that is painful. The so-called fearful reaction to loss of support—if not confused with an actual pain reaction—is, therefore, in all probability itself a learned (conditioned) reaction, which means that, according to Watson's observations, human infants show no innate *fear* responses whatever, merely innate *pain* responses.

Freud seems to have seen the problem in this light from the outset and accordingly posited that *all* anxiety (fear) reactions are probably learned; [3] his hypothesis, when recast in stimulus-response terminology, runs as follows. A so-called "traumatic" ("painful") stimulus (arising either from external injury, of whatever kind, or from severe organic need) impinges upon the organism and produces a more or less violent defence (striving) reaction. Furthermore, such a stimulus-response sequence is usually preceded or accompanied by originally "indifferent" stimuli which, however, after one or more temporally contiguous associations with the traumatic stimulus, begin to be perceived as "danger signals," i.e., acquire the capacity to elicit an "anxiety" reaction. This latter reaction, which may or may not be grossly observable, has two outstanding characteristics: (i) it creates or, perhaps more accurately, consists of a state of heightened tension (or "attention") and a more or less specific readiness for (expectation of) the impending traumatic stimulus; and (ii), by virtue of the fact that such a state of tension is itself a form of discomfort, it adaptively motivates the organism to escape from the danger situation, thereby lessening the intensity of the tension (anxiety) and also probably decreasing the chances of encountering the traumatic stimulus. In short, *anxiety (fear) is the*

---

[3] Freud (3) has explicitly acknowledged the possibility of anxiety occurring, especially in birds and other wild animals, as an instinctive reaction; but he takes the position that in human beings, instinctive anxiety (not to be confused with "instinctual" anxiety, i.e., fear of the intensity of one's own organic impulses) is probably nonexistent or is at least inconsequential.

conditioned form of the pain reaction, which has the highly useful function of motivating and reinforcing behavior that tends to avoid or prevent the recurrence of the pain-producing (unconditioned) stimulus.

In the mentalistic terminology that he characteristically employs, Freud (3) has formulated this view of anxiety formation and its adaptational significance as follows:

Now it is an important advance in self-protection when this traumatic situation of helplessness [discomfort] is not merely awaited but is foreseen, anticipated. Let us call the situation in which resides the cause of this anticipation the danger situation; it is in this latter that the signal of anxiety is given. What this means is: I anticipate that a situation of helplessness [discomfort] will come about, or the present situation reminds me of one of the traumatic experiences which I have previously undergone. Hence I will anticipate this trauma; I will act as if it were already present as long as there is still time to avert it. Anxiety, therefore, is the expectation of the trauma on the one hand, and on the other, an attenuated repetition of it (pp. 149-150).

Affective [anxiety] states are incorporated into the life of the psyche as precipitates of primal traumatic experiences, and are evoked in similar situations like memory symbols (p. 23). Anxiety is undeniably related to expectation; one feels anxiety *lest* something occur (pp. 146-147).

According to views expressed elsewhere by Freud, expectation and anxiety lie along a continuum, with the former merging into the latter at the point at which it becomes uncomfortably intense, i.e., begins to take on motivational properties in its own right. The preparatory, expectant character of anxiety is likely, however, to be obscured by the fact that danger situations sometimes arise and pass so quickly that they are over before the anxiety reaction—involving, as it does, not only an augmentation of neuro-muscular readiness and tension but also a general mobilization of the physical energies needed to sustain strenuous action—has had an opportunity to occur. The result is that in situations in which danger is so highly transitory, as, for example, in near-accidents in motor traffic, anxiety is commonly experienced, somewhat paradoxically, *after* the danger is past and therefore gives the appearance of being indeed a useless, wasted reaction (cf. James). It must not be overlooked, however, that situations of this kind are more or less anomalous. The fact that in a given situation the element of danger disappears before flight, for which the anxiety-preparedness is most appropriate, has had time to occur, does not, of course, mean that anxiety-preparedness in the face of danger is not in general a very adaptive reaction.[4]

As early as 1903, Pavlov (10) expressed a point of view that bears a striking resemblance to the position taken by Freud in this connection. He said: "The importance of the remote signs (signals) of objects can be easily recognized in the movement reaction of the animal. By means of distant and even accidental characteristics of objects the animal seeks his food, avoids enemies, etc." (p. 52). Again, a quarter of a century later, Pavlov (9) wrote as follows:

It is pretty evident that under natural conditions the normal animal must respond not only to stimuli which themselves bring immediate benefit or harm, but also to other physical or chemical agencies—waves of sound, light, and the like—which in themselves only *signal* the approach of these stimuli; though it is not the sight and sound of the beast of prey which is in itself harmful to the smaller animal, but its teeth and claws (p. 14).

Although both Pavlov and Freud thus clearly recognize the biological utility of anticipatory reactions to danger signals, there is, however, an important difference in their viewpoints. Pavlov emphasizes the mechanism of simple stimulus substitution (conditioning). According to his hypothesis, a danger signal (the conditioned stimulus) comes to elicit essentially the *same* "movement reaction" that has previously been produced by actual trauma (the unconditioned stimulus). It is true that the blink of the eyelids to a threatening visual stimulus is not greatly unlike the reaction made to direct corneal irritation. A dog may learn to flex its leg in response to a formerly neutral stimulus so as to simulate the flexion produced by an electric shock administered to its paw. And a small child may for a time make very much the same type of withdrawal reactions to the sight of a flame that it makes to actual contact with it. However, any attempt to establish this pattern of stimulus substitution as the prototype of all learning places severe restrictions on the limits of adaptive behavior: it implies that the only reactions that can become attached to formerly unrelated stimuli (i.e., can be learned) are those which already occur more or less reflexly to some other type of stimulation.

According to the conception of anxiety proposed by Freud, on the other hand, a danger signal may come to produce any of an infinite variety of reactions that are wholly unlike the reaction that occurs to

[4] Cf. the discussion of the "startle pattern" by Landis and Hunt (6).

the actual trauma of which the signal is premonitory. Freud assumes that the first and most immediate response to a danger signal is not a complete, overt reaction, as Pavlov implies, but an implicit state of tension and augmented preparedness for action,[5] which he calls "anxiety." This state of affairs, being itself a source of discomfort, may then motivate innumerable random acts, from which will be selected and fixated (by the law of effect) the behavior that most effectively reduces the anxiety. Anxiety is thus to be regarded as a motivating and reinforcing (fixating) agent, similar to hunger, thirst, sex, temperature deviations, and the many other forms of discomfort that harass living organisms, which is, however, presumably distinctive in that it is derived from (based upon anticipation of) these other, more basic forms of discomfort.[6]

By and large, behavior that reduces anxiety also operates to lessen the danger that it presages. An antelope that scents a panther is likely not only to feel less uneasy (anxious) if it moves out of the range of the odor of the panther but is also likely to be in fact somewhat safer. A primitive village that is threatened by marauding men or beasts sleeps better after it has surrounded itself with a deep moat or a sturdy stockade. And a modern mother is made emotionally more comfortable after her child has been properly vaccinated against a dreaded disease. This capacity to be made uncomfortable by the mere prospect of traumatic experiences, in advance of their actual occurrence (or recurrence), and to be motivated thereby to take realistic precautions against them, is unquestionably a tremendously important and useful psychological mechanism, and the fact that the forward-looking, anxiety-arousing propensity of the human mind is more highly developed than it is in lower animals probably accounts for many of man's unique accomplishments. But it also accounts for some of his most conspicuous failures.

The ostrich has become a proverbial object of contempt and a symbol of stupidity because of its alleged tendency, when frightened, to put its head in the sand, thereby calming its emotional agitation but not in the slightest degree altering the danger situation in its objective aspects. Such relevant scientific inquiry as has been carried out indicates, however, that infra-human organisms are ordinarily more realistic

[5] Cf. the revised theory of conditioning proposed by Culler (2).

[6] Freud has never explicitly formulated this view in precisely these words, but it is clearly implied in various of his writings.

in this respect than are human beings. For example, if a dog learns to avoid an electric shock by lifting its foreleg in response to a tone, it will give up this response entirely when it discovers that the tone is no longer followed by shock if the response is not made. Human beings, on the other hand, are notoriously prone to engage in all manner of magical, superstitious, and propitiatory acts, which undoubtedly relieve dread and uncertainty (at least temporarily) but which have a highly questionable value in controlling real events.[7] The remarkable persistence of such practices may be due, at least in part, to the fact that they are followed relatively promptly by anxiety-reduction, whereas their experienced futility at the reality level may come many hours or days or even months later.[8] The persistence of certain forms of "unrealistic" anxiety-reinforced behavior may also be due to the fact that in most societies there seem always to be some individuals who are able and ready to derive an easy living by fostering beliefs on the part of others in "unrealistic" dangers. For the common man protection against such "dangers" consists of whatever type of behavior the bogey-makers choose to say is "safe" (and which furthers their own interests).

Yet other forms of "unrealistic" anxiety-reinforced behavior are to be observed in the symptomatic acts of the psychoneuroses. According to Freud, anxiety is in fact "the fundamental phenomenon and the central problem of neurosis" (3, p. 111). He further says:

> Since we have reduced the development of anxiety to a response to situations of danger, we shall prefer to say that the symptoms are created in order to remove or rescue the ego from the situation of danger. . . . We can also say, in supplement to this, that the development of anxiety induces symptom formation—nay more, it is a *sine qua non* thereof, for if the ego did not forcibly arouse the pleasure-pain mechanism through the development of anxiety, it would not acquire the power to put a stop to the danger-threatening process elaborated in the id (3, pp. 112-113).

Willoughby (12), in a scholarly, well-documented paper, has previously stressed the similarity of magical rites (including religion) and neurotic symptoms and has shown that both types of behavior spring from the common propensity of human beings to deal with their anxie-

---

[7] Under some circumstances, e.g., when warriors are preparing for battle, malevolent incantations or similar anxiety-reducing magical procedures may, of course, be objectively efficacious, not, to be sure, in the supposed magical way, but in that they alter human conduct in crucial life situations (i.e., make the warriors bolder and better fighters).

[8] Cf. Hull's concept of the "goal gradient" (4).

ties unrealistically, i.e., by means which diminish emotional discomfort but do not adaptively alter external realities. This excellent study has, in the present writer's opinion, only one important weakness: it takes as its point of departure what Freud has called his "first theory" of anxiety formation (1894), which he subsequently abandoned for the one outlined above. In brief, Freud's earlier supposition was that anxiety arose whenever a strong organic drive or impulse was prevented from discharging through its accustomed motor outlets. According to this view, inhibition was the primary state, anxiety the resultant. In all his more recent writings, on the other hand, Freud takes the position, here also adopted, that anxiety (as a reaction to a "danger signal") is primal and that inhibition of anxiety-arousing, danger-producing impulses,[9] is a consequence (3). Reaction mechanisms (magic, symptoms, etc.) that contribute to this end tend, for reasons already given, to be reinforced and perpetuated. Willoughby's analysis is not of necessity predicated upon Freud's original view of anxiety formation and would seem to gain rather than lose cogency if based instead upon his more recent formulations.

Magical and neurotic practices constitute a very perplexing and challenging problem from the point of view of traditional psychological theory; but, as Allport (1) has recently pointed out, so also do many other types of human activity that are commonly regarded as both rational and normal. Allport rightly stresses the inadequacies of the conditioned-reflex concept as a comprehensive explanation of learning and personality development in general. He also justly criticizes the view that all human conduct is to be accounted for in terms of trial-and-error striving to eliminate immediately felt organic needs. The plain fact is that much of modern man's most energetic behavior occurs when

[9] One of Freud's most fundamental discoveries, basic to the understanding of reaction-formation, repression, projection, and other neurotic mechanisms, is that organic impulses, even though they are not consciously experienced and identified, may function as "danger signals" and thereby evoke anxiety. This relatively simple yet frequently misapprehended finding (Freud has himself contributed to the confusion by sometimes speaking as if anxiety *is* the "danger signal," instead of a *reaction* to it) can be readily translated into Pavlovian terminology by saying that an organic need, or drive, which has in the past led to overt behavior that was severely punished will tend upon its recurrence, even at low intensities, to elicit a conditioned pain (anxiety) reaction. Yet, as will be shown in a later paper on the so-called "experimental neurosis," Pavlov and his followers have largely ignored this possibility of internal, as well as external, stimuli acquiring "signal" value, i.e., becoming "conditioned," and have consequently made apparent mysteries of some laboratory observations which, when viewed more broadly, seem completely intelligible.

his organic needs are ostensibly well satisfied. In an attempt to account for this state of affairs, without, on the other hand, falling back on a forthright mentalistic type of approach, Allport elaborates the view, previously advanced by Woodworth, that habits themselves have an on-going character, independent of the motivation that originally brought them into being, and that this type of habit-momentum constitutes a form of self-sustained motivation. Allport calls this the principle of "functional autonomy" and relies heavily upon it in developing his system of the "psychology of personality."

In the estimation of the present writer, "functional autonomy" is on a par with "perpetual motion." Its author clearly perceives an important psychological problem, but it seems unlikely that his is a scientifically tenable solution to it. The position here taken is that human beings (and also other living organs to varying degrees) can be motivated either by organic pressures (needs) that are currently present and felt *or* by the mere anticipation of such pressures and that those habits tend to be acquired and perpetuated (reinforced) which effect a reduction in *either* of these two types of motivation. This view rests upon and is but an extended application of the well-founded law of effect and involves no assumptions that are not empirically verifiable. It has the further advantage that it is consistent with common-sense impressions and practices and at the same time serves as a useful integrational device at the scientific level.

The present analysis of anxiety (anticipation, expectancy) and its role in shaping both "adaptive" and "mal-adaptive" behavior in human beings is also consistent with the growing tendency to eliminate the distinction between learning through "punishment" and learning through "reward." The earlier view was that so-called punishment "stamped out" habits and that reward "stamped" them in. This distinction now appears to have been spurious and to have depended upon a selectivity of emphasis or interest (7). If an individual is motivated by an internal discomfort or need (produced by his own metabolic processes), and if another individual provides the means of eliminating it, and if, in the process, the first individual acquires new behavior, this is called learning through "reward." But if a second individual supplies the need (by inflicting or threatening to inflict some form of discomfort), and if the affected individual supplies the means of eliminating this discomfort (by flight, inactivity, propitiation, compliance, or the like), and if, in the process, this individual acquires new behavior, then this is called learning through "punishment." The truth of the matter seems to be that all learning presupposes (i) an increase of motivation (striving) and (ii) a decrease of motivation (success) and that the essential features of the process are much the same, regardless of the specific source of motivation or of the particular circumstances of its elimination.[10]

There is, however, one practical consideration to be taken into account. Although learning through "punishment" does not seem to differ basically from learning through "reward," inter-personal relationships are likely to be affected very differently in the two cases. If the method of "reward" is employed, inter-personal relationships are likely to be made more "positive" (i.e., approach tendencies will be strengthened); whereas, if the method of "punishment" is employed, inter-personal relationships are likely to be made more "negative" (i.e., avoidance tendencies will be strengthened). From a purely social point of view, it is therefore preferable to employ the method of "reward," whenever this is possible; but "punishment" may have to be resorted to if no *organic* needs are present to be "rewarded" or if means of rewarding them are not available. Punishment (or the threat of punishment, i.e., anxiety) is particularly convenient in that it can be produced instantly; but this advantage is accompanied by disadvantages which cannot be safely disregarded (8).

Even the practical basis for distinguishing between learning through reward and through punishment just suggested becomes tenuous when one considers the type of situation in which one person withholds from another an expected reward. This, in one sense, is a form of "punishment," and yet its effectiveness is based upon the principle of "reward." This complicated state of affairs seems especially likely to arise in the parent-child relationship and has implications that have been but slightly explored in stimulus-response terms.

[10] According to this point of view, old habits are eliminated, not by being "stamped out" or extracted, as it were, "by the roots," but by the functional superimposition of new, more powerful, antagonistic habits (7). Anxiety may thus be said to exercise an "inhibitory" effect (see foregoing discussion of Freud's "first theory" of anxiety) upon established behavior trends mainly through its motivation and reinforcement of opposing behavior trends. In this way emphasis falls primarily upon the positive, habit-forming consequences of anxiety and only secondarily and indirectly upon its negative, inhibitory functions.

Summary

In contrast to the older view, which held that anxiety (fear) was an instinctive reaction to phylogenetically predetermined objects or situations, the position here taken is that anxiety is a learned response, occurring to "signals" (conditioned stimuli) that are premonitory of (i.e., have in the past been followed by) situations of injury or pain (unconditioned stimuli). Anxiety is thus basically anticipatory in nature and has great biological utility in that it adaptively motivates living organisms to deal with (prepare for or flee from) traumatic events in advance of their actual occurrence, thereby diminishing their harmful effects. However, experienced anxiety does not always vary in direct proportion to the objective danger in a given situation, with the result that living organisms, and human beings in particular, show tendencies to behave "irrationally," i.e., to have anxiety in situations that are not dangerous or to have no anxiety in situations that are dangerous. Such a "disproportionality of affect" may come about for a variety of reasons, and the analysis of these reasons throws light upon such diverse phenomena as magic, superstition, social exploitation, and the psychoneuroses.

Moreover, by positing anxiety as a kind of connecting link between complete well-being and active organic discomfort or injury, it is possible to reconcile the fact that much, perhaps most, of the day-to-day behavior of civilized human beings is not prompted by simultaneously active organic drives and the fact that the law of effect (principle of learning through motivation-reduction) is apparently one of the best-established of psychological principles. This is accomplished by assuming (i) that anxiety, i.e., mere anticipation of actual organic need or injury, may effectively motivate human beings and (ii) that reduction of anxiety may serve powerfully to reinforce behavior that brings about such a state of "relief" or "security." Anxiety, although derived from more basic forms of motivation, is thus regarded as functioning in an essentially parallel manner as far as its role as an activating and reinforcing agent is concerned. This analysis is consistent with the common-sense view in such matters and does not conflict with any known empirical fact. Finally, it has the advantage of being open to objective investigation and of giving rise to a host of problems that have scarcely been touched experimentally (8).

References

1. Allport, G. W. *Personality*. New York: Henry Holt, 1937.
2. Culler, E. A. Recent advances in some concepts of conditioning. *Psychol. Rev.*, 1938, *45,* 134-153.
3. Freud, S. *The problem of anxiety*. New York: Norton, 1936.
4. Hull, C. L. The goal gradient hypothesis and maze learning. *Psychol. Rev.*, 1932, *39,* 25-43.
5. James, W. *Principles of psychology,* Vol. II. New York: Henry Holt, 1890.
6. Landis, C. and Hunt, W. A. *The startle pattern*. New York: Farrar & Rinehart, 1939.
7. Mowrer, O. H. Preparatory set (expectancy)—a determinant in motivation and learning. *Psychol. Rev.*, 1938, *45,* 61-91.
8. Mowrer, O. H. Preparatory set (expectancy)—some methods of measurement. *Psychol. Monogr.*, 1940, *52,* No. 2.
9. Pavlov, I. P. *Conditioned reflexes*. (Trans. by Anrep). London: Oxford Univ. Press, 1927.
10. Pavlov, I. P. *Lectures on conditioned reflexes*. (Trans. by Gantt.) New York: International Publishers, 1938.
11. Watson, J. B. Experimental studies on the growth of the emotions. *Psychologies of 1925,* Worcester, Mass.: Clark Univ. Press, 1928, 37-51.
12. Willoughby, R. R. Magic and cognate phenomena: an hypothesis. In *A Handbook of Social Psychology*. Worcester, Mass.: Clark Univ. Press, 1935, 461-519.

40 THEORY OF FRUSTRATION-INSTIGATED BEHAVIOR

Norman R. F. Maier

The Postulation of Two Behavior Mechanisms Simplifies Theory

The purpose of the discussion in the preceding pages has been to establish the view that abnormal behavior fixations produced under frustration are different in kind from behaviors produced through motivated

Reprinted from *Frustration: the Study of Behavior Without a Goal,* by N. R. F. Maier. Copyright 1949. Courtesy of McGraw-Hill Book Co., New York. Pp. 157-162.

learning. Experimental evidence supporting this qualitative distinction was presented, and it was argued that the basic assumption which postulates that all behavior is influenced by motivation is inconsistent with these experimental facts. To account for the basically different behaviors, two different psychological processes or mechanisms were postulated, one of which was called *the frustration process* and the other *the motivation process*. With different processes controlling behavior, it follows that each will have its distinct laws and that failure to differentiate between them will give the appearance of irregularity and inconsistency.

In the light of this postulation an examination of other experimental studies of frustration was then made to determine whether or not these findings were consistent with the theory of frustration developed in animal studies. It was found that the characteristics of aggression and regression readily lent themselves to this reinterpretation and that certain difficulties were circumvented at the same time.

Let us examine some difficulties encountered and the assumptions that must be made when this distinction is not accepted. When motivation is postulated to be a factor in all behavior, one has the problem of demonstrating that in all aggressive and regressive responses there is a desire to solve problems and at the same time one must explain why these responses often appear unadaptive. In order to deal with this problem it has been postulated that a number of needs, both conscious and unconscious, often operate and that when these are known they explain why the individual sometimes seems to behave in a contradictory or unadaptive manner.

Thus it has been stated that the enuretic child expresses his unconscious hostility for his mother, and the behavior is his way of striking at her and doing her injury. That he does not succeed in removing his frustration merely shows that in satisfying one desire he sacrifices the satisfaction of others.

The postulation that a problem is solved by frustration-induced behavior is implicitly made when it is stated that aggression represents a means for (*a*) protecting oneself, (*b*) obtaining satisfaction from a hostile world, (*c*) destroying the source of pain, or (*d*) overcoming an obstacle. When aggressive responses fail to accomplish any of the postulated desires and instead accomplish additional frustration, it still is necessary to explain why the unadaptive aggressive responses occur.

To explain unadaptive aggressive responses for which no needs can

be found the principles of learning have been utilized. By assuming that aggression is a learned response one may state that the organism tends to resort to aggressive responses that have produced satisfaction on previous occasions. However, the postulation of learning introduces a new problem, that of explaining why aggression occurs without learning and why persistent aggression is not altered by repeated failure.

That regressive behavior likewise is regarded as motivation determined is reflected by definitions which state that regression represents (*a*) a return to a formerly secure state, and (*b*) a way of escaping from a difficult or frustrating problem. Since regressive behaviors seldom overcome obstacles or correct the source of frustration, there is little evidence to support the contention that this type of behavior is a problem-solving process. Thus regressive behavior is less satisfactorily explained by motivation and learning concepts than is aggression, but both types of behavior readily lend themselves to classification under the frustration process. As a matter of fact they actually enrich the concept that frustration-instigated behavior is different from motivation-induced behavior.

An examination of the literature on experimental neuroses and experimentally induced convulsions likewise fails to support the view that such behavior has a basis in learning and motivation. Instead, the findings seem in many ways to be inconsistent with learning and motivation principles. If, however, this experimental evidence is classified as frustration-instigated behavior and not regarded as controlled by motivation, the behavior characteristics observed seem to be consistent with other findings on frustration.

Behavior under Frustration and Motivation Contrasted

When we assemble all the behavior properties associated with frustration and consider them to be descriptive of the frustration process, we find that they are quite different from those found in motivated problem solving and learning. At present a number of basic differences can be described.

1. A problem situation produces stereotyped behavior in the frustrated individual, whereas it produces variable behavior in the motivated individual.

2. Responses produced under frustration, in so far as they show fixation, are rigid and stereotyped to a degree that exceeds responses produced by rewarded learning. Thus the motivated individual is

characterized by plasticity and the frustrated individual by rigidity.

3. Responses produced during frustration (such as abnormal fixations) are not responsive to alteration by punishment although reward-learned responses can be altered by punishment.

4. Punishment may serve as a frustrating agent and when this occurs a learned response may be replaced by a characteristic frustrated response.

5. Frustration-induced responses seem to be an end in themselves. They are not influenced by consequences except in so far as the consequences may alter the state of frustration, whereas motivated responses are a means to an end.

6. The method of guidance is highly effective for altering frustration-produced responses but it has no great value for replacing reward-learned responses.

7. Frustration-instigated responses are compulsive in nature whereas responses appearing in motivation situations are choice reactions.

8. The degree of frustration can be relieved by the expression of responses, regardless of whether or not the response is adaptive, whereas responses expressed by a motivated individual are satisfying only when the responses are adaptive.

9. Frustration-instigated responses are either nonconstructive or destructive in nature whereas motivated responses are constructive.

10. The response expressed during frustration is influenced to a great extent by its availability to the organism, whereas the response expressed in the state of motivation is influenced more by anticipated consequences than by availability.

11. Learning takes place under motivation and permits an increase in the number of differentiations the organism can make, whereas frustration leads to dedifferentiation (regression) and in some cases to convulsive or mass behavior.

12. The trait of resignation that may appear in frustration contrasts with the zest shown in states of motivation.

The number of contrasting features present in motivated and frustrated behavior offers great difficulty if one attempts to reduce them to the same basic principles. If the characteristics of each are assembled into two separate groups, however, consistency between the characteristics of each group can be obtained. These two groupings of behavior characteristics thus furnish the basis for a description of the two types of behavior mechanisms.

Basic Characteristics of Frustration-instigated Behavior

The frustration process produces behavior that is purely an end in itself and not a means to an end. The behavior thus elicited is not an expression of a preference since it is not influenced by what it accomplishes. In this sense the behavior is compulsive in nature, and the type of behavior that is selected in frustration is a matter of its availability at the time as well as of a number of other factors not yet clearly understood. This type of behavior is altered most readily by a reduction in the state of frustration. When this is not possible, frustration-instigated behavior may be directed along different channels by the introduction or removal of barriers and other forms of restraints or by various forms of guidance. By means of such techniques the pattern of available responses is altered. Thus aggression induced by economic hardship may be directed away from government offices and toward food stores or racial groups. Restraints of various kinds may be produced by our culture and may train people not to strike at certain objects, but at the same time, certain other responses may be facilitated by suggestion and cultural backgrounds. Through training and education some responses may obtain a lower availability than other responses. In such cases the frustrated responses are channelized differently but not eliminated. Thus a first step in therapy would be reducing the state of frustration by directing destructive responses along socially harmless channels.

CHAPTER XIII

PERSONALITY

THIS CHAPTER presents the theoretical views of certain of the most prominent workers in the field of personality. The first selection is from an early but fundamental paper by Gordon W. Allport. It gives the basic formulation of his "trait" theory, which has constituted the core of Allport's highly influential emphasis on personality as the integrating concept in psychology. Henry A. Murray's development of the concept of personal "thema," exemplified in his Thematic Apperception Test, is summarized in the second selection. Directly influenced by psycho-analytic thinking, this work has been significant in promoting the trend towards interpretation of personality organization in terms of historical and motivational factors. Carl R. Rogers' discussion of the systematic basis for his development of the non-directive, or client-centered, type of psychotherapy emphasizes its important implications for personality theory. The final selection indicates the systematic position developed by Gardner Murphy. The excerpt from his recent Personality *suggests his eclectic but highly integrative approach to the problems of person-ality.*

41   THE PERSONALITY TRAIT [1]

Gordon W. Allport

At the heart of all investigation of personality lies the puzzling problem of the nature of the unit or element which is the carrier of the distinctive behavior of a man. *Reflex* and *habits* are too specific in reference, and connote constancy rather than consistency in behavior; *attitudes* are ill-defined, and as employed by various writers refer to determining tendencies that range in inclusiveness from the *Aufgabe* to the *Weltanschauung; dispositions* and *tendencies* are even less definitive. But *traits,* although appropriated by all manner of writers for all manner of purposes, may still be salvaged, I think, and limited in their reference to a certain definite conception of a generalized response-unit in which resides the distinctive quality of behavior that reflects personality. Foes as well as friends of the doctrine of traits will gain from a more consistent use of the term.

The doctrine itself has never been explicitly stated. It is my purpose with the aid of eight criteria to define *trait,* and to state the logic and some of the evidence for the admission of this concept to good standing in psychology.

1. A trait has more than nominal existence.

A trait may be said to have the same kind of existence that a habit of a complex order has. Habits of a complex, or higher, order have long been accepted as household facts in psychology. There is no reason to believe that the mechanism which produces such habits (integration, *Gestaltung,* or whatever it may be) stops short of producing the more generalized habits which are here called traits of personality.

2. A trait is more generalized than a habit.

Within a personality there are, of course, many independent habits;

[1] Read at the Ninth International Congress of Psychology, New Haven, 1929.

From G. W. Allport, What is a trait of personality? *J. abn. soc. Psychol.,* 1931, *25,* 368-372. Reprinted by permission of the author, the *Journal of abnormal and social psychology,* and the American Psychological Association.

but there is also so much integration, organization, and coherence among habits that we have no choice but to recognize great systems of interdependent habits. If the habit of brushing one's teeth can be shown, statistically or genetically, to be unrelated to the habit of dominating a tradesman, there can be no question of a common trait involving both these habits; but if the habit of dominating a tradesman can be shown, statistically or genetically, to be related to the habit of bluffing one's way past guards, there is the presumption that a common trait of personality exists which includes these two habits. Traits may conceivably embrace anywhere from two habits to a legion of habits. In this way, there may be said to be major, widely extensified traits, and minor, less generalized traits in a given personality.

3. A trait is dynamic, or at least determinative.

It is not the stimulus that is the crucial determinant in behavior that expresses personality; it is the trait itself that is decisive. Once formed a trait seems to have the capacity of directing responses to stimuli into characteristic channels. This emphasis upon the dynamic nature of traits, ascribing to them a capacity for guiding the specific response, is variously recognized by many writers. The principle is nothing more than that which has been subscribed to in various connections by Woodworth, Prince, Sherrington, Coghill, Kurt Lewin, Troland, Lloyd Morgan, Thurstone, Bentley, Stern, and others. From this general point of view traits might be called "derived drives" or "derived motives." Whatever they are called they may be regarded as playing a motivating role in each act, thus endowing the separate adjustments of the individual to specific stimuli with that *adverbial* quality that is the very essence of personality.

Some psychologists may balk at the doctrine of the absorption of driving power into the integrated mechanism of traits. If so, it is equally possible, without violence to the other criteria of this paper, to accept the view that a trait is a generalized neural set which is activated ecphorically or redintegratively. But it seems to me that this second doctrine is only slightly less dynamic than the first. The difference is simply one between trait considered as a drive aroused through the operation of a specific stimulus, and trait conceived as powerfully directive when an effective stimulus arouses the organism to action.

4. The existence of a trait may be established empirically or statistically.

In order to know that a person has a *habit* it is necessary to have evidence of repeated reactions of a constant type. Similarly in order to know that an individual has a trait it is necessary to have evidence of repeated reactions which, though not necessarily constant in type, seem none the less to be consistently a function of the same underlying determinant. If this evidence is gathered casually by mere observation of the subject or through the reading of a case-history or biography, it may be called empirical evidence.

More exactly, of course, the existence of a trait may be established with the aid of statistical techniques that determine the degree of coherence among the separate responses. Although this employment of statistical aid is highly desirable, it is not necessary to wait for such evidence before speaking of traits, any more than it would be necessary to refrain from speaking of the habit of biting fingernails until the exact frequency of the occurrence is known. Statistical methods are at present better suited to intellective than to conative functions, and it is with the latter that we are chiefly concerned in our studies of personality.

5. Traits are only relatively independent of each other.

The investigator desires, of course, to discover what the fundamental traits of personality are, that is to say, what broad trends in behavior do exist independently of one another. Actually with the test methods and correlational procedures in use, completely independent variation is seldom found. In one study expansion correlated with extroversion to the extent of $+.39$, ascendance with conservatism, $+.22$, and humor with insight, $+.83$, and so on. This overlap may be due to several factors, the most obvious being the tendency of the organism to react in an integrated fashion, so that when concrete acts are observed or tested they reflect not only the trait under examination, but also simultaneously other traits; several traits may thus converge into a final common path. It seems safe, therefore, to predict that traits can never be completely isolated for study, since they never show more than a relative independence of one another.

In the instance just cited, it is doubtful whether humor and insight (provided their close relationship is verified in subsequent studies) represent distinct traits. In the future perhaps it may be possible to agree upon a certain magnitude of correlation below which it will be acceptable to speak of *separate* traits, and above which *one* trait only will be recognized. If one trait only is indicated it will presumably represent a broadly generalized disposition. For example, if humor and insight cannot be established as independent traits, it will be necessary to recognize a more inclusive trait, and name it perhaps "sense of proportion."

6. A trait of personality, psychologically considered, is not the same as moral quality.

A trait of personality may or may not coincide with some well-defined, conventional, social concept. Extroversion, ascendance, social participation, and insight are free from preconceived moral significance, largely because each is a word newly coined or adapted to fit a psychological discovery. It would be ideal if we could in this way find our traits first and then name them. But honesty, loyalty, neatness, and tact, though encrusted with social significance, *may* likewise represent true traits of personality. The danger is that in devising scales for their measurement we may be bound by the conventional meanings, and thus be led away from the precise integration as it exists in a given individual. Where possible it would be well for us to find our traits first, and then seek devaluated terms with which to characterize our discoveries.

7. Acts, and even habits, that are inconsistent with a trait are not proof of the non-existence of the trait.

The objection most often considered fatal to the doctrine of traits has been illustrated as follows: "An individual may be habitually neat with respect to his person, and characteristically slovenly in his handwriting or the care of his desk."

In the first place this observation fails to state that there are cases frequently met where a constant level of neatness is maintained in all of a person's acts, giving unmistakable empirical evidence that the trait of neatness is, in some people at least, thoroughly and permanently integrated. All people must not be expected to show the same degree of integration in respect to a given trait. *What is a major trait in one personality may be a minor trait, or even non-existent in another personality.*

In the second place, we must concede that there may be opposed integrations, i.e., contradictory traits, in a single personality. The same individual may have a trait *both* of neatness *and* of carelessness, of ascendance *and* submission, although frequently of unequal strength.

In the third place there are in every personality instances of acts that are unrelated to existent traits, the product of the stimulus and of the attitude of the moment. Even the characteristically neat person may become careless in his haste to catch a train.

But to say that not all of a person's acts reflect some higher integration, is not to say that no such higher integrations exist.

8. A trait may be viewed either in the light of the personality which contains it, or in the light of its distribution in the population at large.

Each trait has both its unique and its universal aspect. In its unique aspect, the trait takes its significance entirely from the role it plays in the personality as a whole. In its universal aspect, the trait is arbitrarily isolated for study, and a comparison is made between individuals in respect to it. From this second point of view traits merely extend the familiar field of the psychology of individual differences.

There may be relatively few traits, a few hundred perhaps, that are universal enough to be scaled in the population at large; whereas there may be in a single personality a thousand traits distinguishable to a discerning observer. For this reason, after a scientific schedule of universal traits is compiled, there will still be the field of *artistic* endeavor for psychologists in apprehending correctly the subtle and unique traits peculiar to one personality alone, and in discovering the *pattern* which obtains *between* these traits in the same personality.

42 PERSONALITY THEMA

Henry A. Murray

Event and Thema

Psychologists have always agreed that conscious experience should be analyzed into separable variables (components, attributes, or relations). But, it is only now that some are becoming convinced not only that each of the selected variables must be considered to have an objective aspect, but also that one or more of these variables may at any time be unconscious—that is, it may determine a conscious experience or a course

From H. A. Murray, Basic concepts for a psychology of personality, *J. gen. Psychol.*, 1936, *15*, 241-268. Pp. 255-264 reprinted by permission of the author and the Journal Press.

of action without the subject's being aware of it. Gestalt psychologists have taught us, furthermore, that our variables are not dependent entities. They are mutually dependent parts of configurated wholes, which the psychologist abstracts by analysis, and later mentally re-synthesizes in order to arrive at an imaginative representation of the original totality. Though one should not exaggerate the unity of regnancies, it is best to begin by assuming that each of them is an ordered whole. We must remember that, if there were no organization, there would be no organism.

To accord with the philosophy of organism as developed by White-head (6), a regnancy, I believe, should be regarded as a single, complex temporal gestalt, a "drop of experience," to use William James's phrase, which consumes, let us say, a small fraction of a second. It is one kind of "actual entity"; for a psychologist the most "real thing." Unfortunately, we are unable to observe, subjectively or objectively, the manifestations of a single regnancy. Just as perception is unable to distinguish what the new cameras reveal—for instance, the separate flashes of a single bolt of lightning—so is introspection, because of its limited span and speed of discrete awareness, unable to grasp a single regnant moment and hold it for analysis. From numberless, successive regnancies one apprehends only fragments and much of this is immediately forgotten. Consequently, one cannot deal directly with the ultimate organic units.

It seems, however, that, since successive acts, as well as successive moments of subjective experience, frequently manifest an obvious degree of functional coordination, successive regnancies must be bound together into larger temporal wholes; and, if this is true, these may be selected as our fundamental psychological units. We have only to decide upon the best criterion for distinguishing separate, single, temporal wholes. But, before attempting to do this, we should ask ourselves: what is it that organizes a single regnancy or a succession of regnancies?

The expression "functional organization" is used when significant effects are economically achieved by the harmonious coordination of a number of different parts. In the simplest case several mutually dependent processes contribute to the achievement of a single result. This is not to be taken as a manifestation of conscious purpose, but as a manifestation of a tendency towards temporary end states. It is similar to the phenomena described by the Second Law of Thermodynamics.

Thus, since organization always involves a directional tendency, that is to say, a tendency to achieve certain effects, and, since it is this tendency which unifies diversities of function, a succession of regnancies may be taken as a single temporal gestalt when the same tendency recurs in (or perseverates through) each of them. According to the terminology which we have adopted, the regnant directional tendency is the immediate result of a *need*—a *need* being defined as a regnant tension which is evoked by the perception (conscious or unconscious) of a certain kind of internal state or external situation. The tension tends to persist and to incite effective activity until an internal state or external situation (opposite in kind to the one which stimulated it) has been arrived at. Thus, as long as a single need persists, successive regnancies will be more or less unified. Even when nothing is achieved—due to the organism's ineptitude—there is, at least, a perseveration of directional effort. The exposition of the concept of need must be postponed, but enough has been said about it, I think, to suggest the following proposition: since the organization of successive regnancies into one society is due to the operation of a single need, the two limits of such a society—a distinct, temporal gestalt—are established by the arousing and stilling, respectively, of that need. Thus, other things being equal, degree of regnant integration is a function of the intensity and protensity of an uncontested need. Since, according to our formulation, effective activity is the direct outcome of a need, we may regard the latter as the underlying, motivating force of the organism. A *mode* (action pattern)—a subordinate concept—is the means whereby a need is stilled (equilibrium is restored, the organism is "satisfied"). It is important to distinguish between these two, since approximately similar effects (need-satisfactions) are achieved by different modes, and approximately similar modes may lead to different effects.

A primary (somagenic) need is the direct resultant of the internal perception (conscious or unconscious) of a specific bodily state. This state may be aroused spontaneously, that is, it may be the product of a succession of physiological events, or it may—during its *ready* period —be excited by the (external) perception of appropriate incentives. In most cases we should start with the internally evoked need rather than with the external stimulus, since 1) self-generated activity is the primary "givenness" of all living organisms, 2) a need may be internally generated in the absence of external objects—the organism may search for food, 3) the selective perception of some rather than other external incentives is due to the operation of a particular need, and 4) even an unconditioned external incentive does not evoke specific regnant tension unless the need in question is in a state of readiness—a replete organism does not respond to food. Since we know, however, that the organism usually has many potential needs in readiness, which one of these is stimulated will be decided by what incentives are present in the environment. Furthermore, the characterization of the incentive which arouses or is sought by the need serves as a further characterization of the need itself. Finally, we know that the frequency, the characteristic intensity and protensity, as well as the integration of recurrent needs may be temporarily or permanently modified by manipulating the environment. Consequently, the discovery of possible stimulus-response patterns is a matter of prime importance.

The special task of the student of motivation, then, becomes the discovery of all the separable variables (components, attributes, and dimensions) which may combine to determine the trend of behavior as well as those which may combine to determine the specific modes employed. As Lewin puts it: "The *cause* of the events is the *relationship between the parts of the situation as dynamical facts,* and a complete characterization of these dynamical facts would be a complete analysis" (2). It may be suggested that this is the major problem of general psychology.

To accord with these considerations the fundamental dynamic unit might be said to consist of a single stimulus-response pattern. Unfortunately this convenient terminology does not suit us, since the term "stimulus" usually stands for a single excitation, and "response" for a single reflexive contraction. In our dynamic unit the stimulus is not to be understood as a single sense-impression, structured or unstructured. For, just as we have argued that the fundamental response is not the immediate specific act, *qua* act, but the trend of activity as manifested by the succession of subsidiary effects achieved by many different acts, so also do we argue that stimuli usually appear objectively as an ordered succession of related impressions, that is, as a stimulus-gestalt which may be taken as-a-whole. The successive single stimuli are organized as a totality either because they "mean" the same thing or because they represent different aspects of the same thing—they may be words, for instance, spoken by an object, words which manifest a single, persisting attitude—or because they represent harbingers, agency objects, or pathways prospective of certain consequences if approached, manipulated, avoided, or otherwise responded to. For such a stimulus-gestalt we shall employ the term press.[1]

Thus, instead of using the phrase "stimulus-response pattern" we shall refer to a "press-need (p-n) pattern." [2] The stimulus-response pattern is adequate for reflexes (fixed relations), but when, as is usually the case, it is a matter of complex behavior, we must use the p-n formula. As a rule, a p-n occurrence may be analyzed into numberless subsidiary stimulus-response connections, but what is important to note is that the latter will usually differ according to the nature of the press-need relations, a fact which proves the subsidiary dependence of the former.

Thus, the limits of a temporal gestalt are usually set by the duration of the press-need combination rather than by the duration of the need alone. A succession of regnancies which forms a temporal gestalt of this kind—a complex series of processes coordinated and limited by the endurance of the combination of a single press (dynamically related series of perceptions) and a single need (regnant directional tension)— will be called an *event*. Since the perceptions of the subject usually correspond to the perceptions of the investigator, and since the activity of exopsychic needs is usually manifested by a particular trend of overt action, the word *event* may be conveniently, though loosely, used to designate an objective occurrence or episode—for instance a single subject-object interaction. An event, then, is any actual, concrete occurrence which has a simple p-n structure. Since there are many possible presses and many needs, there are an even greater number of press-need combinations (kinds of events). The term which has been selected to designate the particular press-need combination is *thema*—*thema* being defined as the dynamical (p-n) structure of an event. A *thema* also includes a reference to the outcome of the subject-object interaction, expressed in terms of degrees of satisfaction or dissatisfaction (success or failure) for the subject. Thus, a person's life may be dynamically formulated as a succession of more or less interrelated *themas* —some of them recurrent and typical, others occasional and critical.

---

[1] As a plural form we select "press" (rather than "presses").

[2] A need may be either exopsychic—directly achieving physical or social effects in the environment—or endopsychic—achieving internal psychical effects (such as creating imaginal or verbal reconstructions of emotional experience, solving intellectual problems, arriving at judgments of value, constructing conceptual schemes, resisting temptation, developing will power, and so forth). In the present discussion, however, I have limited myself to the consideration of exopsychic needs, and I shall continue to do so.

When nothing is known of the press, or the press is merely the usual environment, the *thema* will consist merely of the subject's initiating need. When, on the other hand, only the press is known or the press is of sole importance—something happens, or an object does something and the subject merely experiences it or adapts himself to it—the *thema* is constituted by the press alone. In representing an event the symbol "p" is used as a prefix before the word which characterizes the environmental press (incitement or reaction), but no symbol is attached to the word which characterizes the subject's need (initiation or response). In events which involve two human beings the press may be appropriately described in terms of the object's action (manifest need). Thus: Robbery → pPunishment → Atonement th signifies that the subject stole something, was punished by the object, and then, later, atoned for his act. Events which are merely phantasied or dreamt are differentiated by enclosing the *thema* within square brackets and putting the abbreviation "ph" before them: ph [pPursuit (Monster) → Flight → pCapture]. It is a great mistake to suppose that one can arrive at a satisfactory understanding of personality by limiting oneself to the observation of overt behavior. Inner states are facts of experience and as much a part of personality as overt actions. Our own procedure is to make a distinction between *latent* and *manifest* aspects of personality.

The press is named in terms of its common *signification*—its usual, socially-accepted (objective) meaning. In this context "meaning" refers to the "bearing" of the press upon the enjoyable existence of most subjects. The meaning which the subject gives the press is indicated by his response. It may be a special, private (subjective) meaning. If, in any instance, it is necessary to represent the strength of a press or the force of a need, this may be done by the use of a number [from 0 (zero) to 5 (five) scale] placed after the term, thus: pDanger 2, or Aggression 4, and so forth.

Analysis and Classification of Events

If personology is ever to become a systematic discipline, it must begin with an analytical description and classification of its subject matter. If, as we have suggested, psychological events form the subject matter of personology, then it is these which must be analyzed and classified. This is a methodological step which other sciences—chemistry, zoology, and botany—have had to take, and there is no reason to believe that personology can avoid it. If this opinion is correct, we must analytically describe events and then mentally separate those which are dissimilar and aggregate those which are similar. Each aggregate will manifest a uniformity—a uniformity which must then be defined and named. This will form the basis of a classification.

Each event may be analyzed (described) in a variety of ways. It depends upon what kinds of attributes, or variables, are shown to be significant. The mode of analysis which we have suggested—by which an event is differentiated in terms of a particular press-need combination—may be termed *thematical*. What could be called a *structural* analysis would distinguish and measure such general variables as re- activity (speed of response), tempo (rate of functioning), intensity (force of response), protensity (endurance of response), conjunctivity (coordination of response), and so forth. Together with "emotionality" these are considered by some psychologists to be variables of *tem- perament* (F. H. Allport, Bloor, and others). McDougall, on the other hand, calls them variables of *temper*. There are other modes of analysis, some of which will have to be simultaneously employed in order to obtain an adequate representation of a personality, but this is a matter which falls outside the compass of present considerations.

The Order of Personological Variables

It will be noted that a dynamical analysis yields variables of a high order—a kind of press and a kind of need, each of which is necessarily a rather ill-defined, complex, abstract entity. For in an actual event the press is the product of innumerable, nameless low-order variables, and the need is objectified by action patterns which may be analyzed into countless contributing modes. A concrete press, for instance, might be the sudden encountering in the wilderness of a grizzly bear facing the subject a few feet away—the subject being on foot and without a gun. This might be designated "pDanger (Wild Animal)." If the en- counter were less sudden, if it occurred near a convenient retreat, if the bear were tame or a cub or a black bear or chained or in a cage or a long distance away or looking in the opposite direction, if the man were armed or in an automobile, the press might be different. It might no longer be "pDanger." Likewise, the response to pDanger might be the need for Security, but what one would actually observe would be a man climbing a tree—an action which could be analyzed into a vast number of extensions, flexions, rotations, abductions, and adductions of both limbs.

It is the business of general psychology to study these low-order variables. They are important determining factors, but they do not fall within the domain of personology.[3] If personology stopped to analyze every event into its molecular parts, it would never get on with its proper business—the representation of personality as-a-whole. It is a general principle in science that the subject matter of each discipline demands concepts which are directly applicable to its own level of complexity. The concrete phenomena should be immediately illumined by the variables employed. Any amount of analysis is permissible, but it must be shown how the low-order entities thus disclosed were combined to form the high-order entities originally distinguished. In applying this principle to the matter at hand, we should say that the personologist has to deal with the reception in the regnancy of a pattern of afferent processes originating in a press and the excitation there of a pattern of efferent processes to form a trend, each pattern taken as a single variable. It is the psychophysicist or psychophysiologist who busies himself with the details of sensory and motor processes. The variables of the personologist are complex products of numberless determinants, which is one of the many reasons why they can never be more than inaccurate generalities.

The Representation of Personality

If the *thematical* mode of analysis can be made efficient and the most important *themas* are defined and named, it may be feasible abstractly to represent a person's life in terms of successive *themas*. This abstract biography, or *psychograph,* would resemble a musical score. It would show what differentiations and developments occurred with age and also what *themas* were most frequently repeated during any particular period. Presumably such a graph would have a recognizable time-structure. For just as each event is organized within itself, so also are successive events organized in respect to each other—at least to some extent.

These considerations suggest—as Whitehead (5) has pointed out—that there are three possible meanings for the notion of a particular

[3] General Psychology attempts to discover the changes in the group (or majority) response which occur when the environment is systematically modified, whereas Differential Psychology (McDougall's term), or Personology (our term), takes note of the differences between individual responses to the same environment. It must be obvious that the two points of view are complementary to one another.

personality: 1) the configuration of the regnancies during one event in a subject's life—the most concrete meaning, 2) the historic route of such configurations from birth to death, and 3) the most commonly repeated configurations during any period of his existence. These may be named: momentary personality, life-time personality, and common personality, respectively. The latter, which is the most abstract, is the one which psychologists usually have in mind when they use the term "personality."

A psychograph of a life-time personality may be greatly abbreviated by omitting the *themas* which recur in the everyday experience of all people. This procedure would be in accord with definitions of personality based upon idiosyncrasy: Personality "consists in those attributes which differentiate it from other individuals" (3), is that "combination of behaviour forms in the individual . . . which distinguish that individual from others of a group" (7), is "the organized system, the functioning whole or unity, of habits, dispositions and sentiments that mark off any one member of a group as being different from any other member of the same group" (4).

As important as the recognition of simple and complex *themas* is the recognition of the change of *themas* and the change of thematic relations with age. This involves a *developmental analysis,* which calls for a separate set of variables.

Common experience and research have shown that many of the press in a person's life are not merely thrust upon him. They are searched for or selected. Dominant needs drive him towards certain situations and away from others. There is, in other words, a phantasy, plan, or purpose determining his activity which includes imaginal representations (conscious or unconscious) of the desired or undesired objects. Thus, an inner tension is usually combined with a temporal gestalt of images. Together they constitute what may be called a need-integrate. Since a need-integrate is a phantasied, wished-for event, it may be analyzed thematically. Thus, we may say that a person is motivated (consciously or unconsciously) by one or more need-*themas*. With these considerations in mind, a much briefer formulation of a personality may be arrived at if it is found that certain simple or complex *themas* recur frequently and that these may be explained by assuming the activity of an underlying need-*thema*. A widely and persistently determining need-*thema* of this kind may be called a *unity-thema.* A *unity-thema* is usually found to be the repetition of or a reaction formation to some infantile experience—usually an excessive gratification, frustration, deprivation, or trauma.

It is often illuminating to portray the life of a subject in terms of his interactions with objects of special interest. A single meeting, or a series of recurring associations between a subject and a particular object (a thing, an animal, a human being, or an institution), may be called a *relational*. Since an enduring relational may be represented as a sequence of constituent *themas,* relationals are convenient foci for the organization of thematical material.

This, in brief, is our tentatively adopted procedure for the analysis and representation of the dynamical constitution of a human being. To those who complain that there are hundreds of distinguishable *themas,* and to describe them all would be a Herculean task, our answer would be that until the task is performed the science of personology will be adrift.

References

1. Allport, G. W. and Vernon, P. E. The field of personality. *Psychol. Bull.,* 1930, *27,* 677-730.
2. Lewin, K. Vectors, cognitive processes, and Mr. Tolman's criticism. *J. gen. Psychol.,* 1933, *8,* 318-345.
3. Ritter, W. E. Individual and person. *Amer. J. Sociol.,* 1929, *35,* 271-274.
4. Schoen, M. *Human nature.* New York: Harper, 1930.
5. Whitehead, A. N. *Symbolism, its meaning and effect.* New York: Macmillan, 1927.
6. Whitehead, A. N. *Process and reality.* New York: Macmillan, 1929.
7. Yoakum, C. S. The definition of personality. *Rep. Brit. Assoc. Adv. Sci.,* 1924, *92,* 442 (Abst.).

43   PERSONALITY ORGANIZATION

Carl R. Rogers

If we attempt to describe in more conventional psychological terms the nature of the process which culminates in an altered organization and integration of self in the process of therapy it might run as follows. The individual is continually endeavoring to meet his needs by reacting to the field of experience as he perceives it, and to do that more efficiently by differentiating elements of the field and reintegrating them into new patterns. Reorganization of the field may involve the reorganization of the self as well as of other parts of the field. The self, however, resists reorganization and change. In everyday life individual adjustment by means of reorganization of the field exclusive of the self is more common and is less threatening to the individual. Consequently, the individual's first mode of adjustment is the reorganization of that part of the field which does not include the self.

Client-centered therapy is different from other life situations inasmuch as the therapist tends to remove from the individual's immediate world all those aspects of the field which the individual can reorganize except the self. The therapist, by reacting to the client's feelings and attitudes rather than to the objects of his feelings and attitudes, assists the client in bringing from background into focus his own self, making it easier than ever before for the client to perceive and react to the self. By offering only understanding and no trace of evaluation, the therapist removes himself as an object of attitudes, becoming only an alternate expression of the client's self. The therapist by providing a consistent atmosphere of permissiveness and understanding removes whatever threat existed to prevent all perceptions of the self from emerging into figure. Hence in this situation all the ways in which the self has been experienced can be viewed openly, and organized into a complex unity.

It is then this complete absence of any factor which would attack the concept of self, and second, the assistance in focusing upon the perception of self, which seems to permit a more differentiated view of self and finally the reorganization of self.

From C. R. Rogers, Some observations on the organization of personality, *Amer. Psychol.,* 1947, *2,* 358-368. Pp. 366-368 reprinted by permission of the author, the *American Psychologist,* and the American Psychological Association.

Relationship to Current Psychological Thinking

Up to this point, these remarks have been presented as clinical observations and tentative hypotheses, quite apart from any relationship to past or present thinking in the field of psychology. This has been intentional. It is felt that it is the function of the clinician to try to observe, with an open-minded attitude, the complexity of material which comes to him, to report his observations, and in the light of this to formulate hypotheses and problems which both the clinic and the laboratory may utilize as a basis for study and research.

Yet, though these are clinical observations and hypotheses, they have, as has doubtless been recognized, a relationship to some of the currents of theoretical and laboratory thinking in psychology. Some of the observations about the self bear a relationship to the thinking of G. H. Mead (7) about the "I" and the "me." The outcome of therapy might be described in Mead's terms as the increasing awareness of the "I," and the organization of the "me's" by the "I." The importance which has been given in this paper to the self as an organizer of experience and to some extent as an architect of self, bears a relationship to the thinking of Allport (1) and others concerning the increased place which we must give to the integrative function of the ego. In the stress which has been given to the present field of experience as the determinant of behavior, the relationship to Gestalt psychology, and to the work of Lewin (6) and his students is obvious. The theories of Angyal (2) find some parallel in our observations. His view that the self represents only a small part of the biological organism which has reached symbolic elaboration, and that it often attempts the direction of the organism on the basis of unreliable and insufficient information, seems to be particularly related to the observations we have made. Lecky's posthumous book (4), small in size but large in the significance of its contribution, has brought a new light on the way in which the self operates, and the principle of consistency by which new experience is included in or excluded from the self. Much of his thinking runs parallel to our observations. Snygg and Combs (9) have recently attempted a more radical and more complete emphasis upon the internal world of perception as the basis for all psychology, a statement which has helped to formulate a theory in which our observations fit.

It is not only from the realm of theory but also from the experimental laboratory that one finds confirmation of the line of thinking which has been proposed. Tolman (10) has stressed the need of thinking as a rat if fruitful experimental work is to be done. The work of Snygg (8) indicates that rat behavior may be better predicted by inferring the rat's field of perception than by viewing him as an object. Krech (Krechevsky, 3) showed in a brilliant study some years ago that rat learning can only be understood if we realize that the rat is consistently acting upon one hypothesis after another. Leeper (5) has summarized the evidence from a number of experimental investigations, showing that animal behavior cannot be explained by simple S-R mechanisms, but only by recognizing that complex internal processes of perceptual organization intervene between the stimulus and the behavioral response. Thus there are parallel streams of clinical observation, theoretical thinking, and laboratory experiment, which all point up the fact that for an effective psychology we need a much more complete understanding of the private world of the individual, and need to learn ways of entering and studying that world from within.

Implications

It would be misleading however if I left you with the impression that the hypotheses I have formulated in this paper, or those springing from the parallel psychological studies I have mentioned, are simply extensions of the main stream of psychological thinking, additional bricks in the edifice of psychological thought. We have discovered with some surprise that our clinical observations, and the tentative hypotheses which seem to grow out of them, raise disturbing questions which appear to cast doubt on the very foundations of many of our psychological endeavors, particularly in the fields of clinical psychology and personality study. To clarify what is meant, I should like to restate in more logical order the formulations I have given, and to leave with you certain questions and problems which each one seems to raise.

If we take first the tentative proposition that the specific determinant of behavior is the perceptual field of the individual, would this not lead, if regarded as a working hypothesis, to a radically different approach in clinical psychology and personality research? It would seem to mean that instead of elaborate case histories full of information about the person as an object, we would endeavor to develop ways of seeing his situation, his past, and himself, as these objects appear to him. We would try to see with him, rather than to evaluate him. It might mean the minimizing of the elaborate psychometric procedures by which we have endeavored to measure or value the individual from our own frame of reference. It might mean the minimizing or discarding of all the vast series of labels which we have painstakingly built up over the years. Paranoid, preschizophrenic, compulsive, constricted—terms such as these might become irrelevant because they are all based in thinking which takes an external frame of reference. They are not the ways in which the individual experiences himself. If we consistently studied each individual from the internal frame of reference of that individual, from within his own perceptual field, it seems probable that we should find generalizations which could be made, and principles which were operative, but we may be very sure that they would be of a different order from these externally based judgments *about* individuals.

Let us look at another of the suggested propositions. If we took seriously the hypothesis that integration and adjustment are internal conditions related to the degree of acceptance or nonacceptance of all perceptions, and the degree of organization of these perceptions into one consistent system, this would decidedly affect our clinical procedures. It would seem to imply the abandonment of the notion that adjustment is dependent upon the pleasantness or unpleasantness of the environment, and would demand concentration upon those processes which bring about self-integration within the person. It would mean a minimizing or an abandoning of those clinical procedures which utilize the alteration of environmental forces as a method of treatment. It would rely instead upon the fact that the person who is internally unified has the greatest likelihood of meeting environmental problems constructively, either as an individual or in cooperation with others.

If we take the remaining proposition that the self, under proper conditions, is capable of reorganizing, to some extent, its own perceptual field, and of thus altering behavior, this too seems to raise disturbing questions. Following the path of this hypothesis would appear to mean a shift in emphasis in psychology from focusing upon the fixity of personality attributes and psychological abilities, to the alterability of these same characteristics. It would concentrate attention upon process rather than upon fixed status. Whereas psychology has, in personality study, been concerned primarily with the measurement of the fixed qualities of the individual, and with his past in order to explain his present, the hypothesis here suggested would seem to concern itself much more with the personal world of the present in order to understand the future, and in predicting that future would be concerned with the principles by which personality and behavior are altered, as well as the extent to which they remain fixed.

Thus we find that a clinical approach, client-centered therapy, has led us to try to adopt the client's perceptual field as the basis for genuine understanding. In trying to enter this internal world of perception, not by introspection, but by observation and direct inference, we find ourselves in a new vantage point for understanding personality dynamics, a vantage point which opens up some disturbing vistas. We find that behavior seems to be better understood as a reaction to this reality-as-perceived. We discover that the way in which the person sees himself, and the perceptions he dares not take as belonging to himself, seem to have an important relationship to the inner peace which constitutes adjustment. We discover within the person, under certain conditions, a capacity for the restructuring and the reorganization of self, and consequently the reorganization of behavior, which has profound social implications. We see these observations, and the theoretical formulations which they inspire, as a fruitful new approach for study and research in various fields of psychology.

References

1. Allport, G. W. The ego in contemporary psychology. *Psychol. Rev.,* 1943, *50,* 451-478.
2. Angyal, A. *Foundations for a science of personality.* New York: Commonwealth Fund, 1941.
3. Krechevsky, I. Hypotheses in rats. *Psychol. Rev.,* 1932, *39,* 516-532.
4. Lecky, P. *Self-Consistency: A theory of personality.* New York: Island Press, 1945.
5. Leeper, R. The experimental psychologists as reluctant dragons. Paper presented at APA meeting, September 1946.
6. Lewin, K. *A dynamic theory of personality.* New York: McGraw-Hill, 1935.
7. Mead, G. H. *Mind, self, and society.* Chicago: Univ. Chicago Press, 1934.
8. Snygg, D. Mazes in which rats take the longer path to food. *J. Psychol.,* 1936, *1,* 153-166.
9. Snygg, D. and Combs, A. W., *Individual behavior: a new frame of reference for psychology.* New York: Harper, 1949.
10. Tolman, E. C. The determiners of behavior at a choice point. *Psychol. Rev.,* 1938, *45,* 1-41.

44 APPROACHES TO PERSONALITY

Gardner Murphy

Three Levels of Complexity

At least three levels of complexity must be considered when confronting personality problems. Personality may be conceived, first, as an object or an event in a larger context—a dot on a chart, a billiard ball on a table. It is identifiable, strictly localized in time-space, and homogeneous. Its internal structure need not be considered. This view is useful in many sociological and some psychological problems, especially those of a statistical character. For example, just as we may compare large dots with small dots, or red balls with white, we may compare adults with children, men with women, Chinese with Japanese.

At a second level of complexity, personality may be likened to a chrysalis. It is again identifiable and strictly bounded, but it has internal structure. It is no longer homogeneous; it is organized. One chrysalis differs from another not only in size, weight, and color, as in the first-level analysis, but in the character of its constituent parts and of their interrelations. This second level requires patient and penetrating consideration of the nature of the internal structure from one such chrysalis to another, and of problems of types, or classes of organization. This approach is currently being used more and more, with great improvement in prediction and control.

At the third level of analysis, however, the chrysalis is an unsatisfactory model. It is encapsulated and it stays put. When you find one in the woods you may wonder whether there is still life in it. Something may have snuffed out its capacity to yield a butterfly. This something indicates that encapsulated though it was, it was not really self-contained. It could live only as long as a delicate relation obtained between its own structure and the outer structure of its habitat. The inner structure was supported and partly guided in its development by a field of external relations.[1]

[1] Greek philosophy made use of the three methods of interpretation suggested here; they are too obvious to have been overlooked by such analytical minds as Democritus, Plato, and Aristotle, to whom, in the order named, the three present approaches could quite properly be ascribed.

From G. Murphy, *Personality*. New York: Harper and Brothers, 1947. Pp. 3-7 reprinted by permission of the author and publishers.

If this is true even of a chrysalis, it is much more compellingly true of the butterfly or the mouse or the man. Here there is even less encapsulation. The world of atmosphere, food, light, gravitation flows into the defenseless organism. The organism exists because outer changes and inner adjustments are nicely attuned, because in the broad sense of the evolutionist the organism evolved only so far as it maintained itself in intimate unity with the environment at each stage of its development —literally as a node in a physical field, defined, limited, governed by the field relations. The organism has *a practical boundary* for some purposes—for example, the skin and mucous membranes. From other standpoints, however, the skin makes by no means an absolute barrier. The air we breathe is "within us" not when it passes valve-like barriers, but by degrees as it passes through nostrils, bronchi, the red blood cells and, with chemical reshuffling, back through veins and breath to the windowpane or to the people around us. To find a sharp barrier between self and non-self is a nice metaphysical task. If this is true of the simplest facts of biological existence, it is hard to see how people can be considered solely from the point of view of internal structure, of the personality that lies within the skin. If biology is right in considering the organism not as an encapsulated unit but as a node, an organizing point in a field, there is a level of analysis at which the man-world relation, the organism-environment field, may be studied.

Such a view may, if we wish, be called a *field* view, if we note that fields studied by biology are in a state of perpetual *redefinition*. Inner and outer structures are unstable; indeed, in the chemistry of nutrition and respiration there are structures which are neither outer nor inner, but lie in a zone where the two flow together or apart, moment by moment. The perpetually resulting changes mean that the time dimension is as essential to biology as it is to physics. The word "field" may remind us of the surveyor, and the maps used to portray a field are, after all, just maps; but world and self flow into one another. The boundary is often vague or non-existent, but the flow is always *directed* to some extent by the relations between the outer and inner structures.

No single word is likely to serve perfectly for this conception. The word "field" will perhaps serve if we expressly state that it is used as it is in physics; an electromagnetic field, for example, permits no strict demarcation of a boundary and may change continually as a result of varying currents.

All three conceptions of personality just indicated will need to be used. In discussing the simplest relations of age to behavior, the first will often suffice. In discussing the interaction of conflicting motives, the second will often be adequate; at least, it will suffice when we are gathering data about events within the organism (strictly, within the skin). When the thing we recognize as personality in our daily doings confronts us, we shall find ourselves pushing forward to the third level of analysis, knowing that in doing so we are abandoning simplicity, courting trouble, and raising far more questions than we can solve.

It has become accepted doctrine that we must attempt to study the whole man. Actually we cannot study even a whole tree or a whole guinea pig. But it is a whole tree and a whole guinea pig that have survived and evolved, and we must make the attempt. When it comes to studying the whole man, we are confronted by three ways in which he refuses to cooperate. First, his traits do not seem intelligible in their own right; they express something complicated going on inside. This is what has driven us from the first level to the second, namely, the study of inner structure. Second, some of the phases of this inner structure are hidden, pocketed off, oriented with respect to some long-past situation which man had to confront; the students of conditioning and of psychoanalysis tell us we need to reconstruct the man historically after the manner of the archeologist. Often there is only a fragment, and the reconstruction fails or is incomplete. Third, the man is reacting to something in the present that we do not understand. We have, if you like, the response but not the stimulating situation, and we are driven into an arduous and often futile search for what the environmental structure means to him, so that the field relations will be clear.

But let us suppose that we succeed at all three levels. We discover events relating to the whole man as he is and as he changes. Since whole personalities in their interrelations make a society, we have, if our logic is sound, made a first approach to a theory of interpersonal relations, a theory of society. Man is a creature that responds to other men in as full a sense as he responds to oxygen or gravity; he is as fully anthropotropic as geotropic. Man as man is in some degree social; the inner-outer structure which is the product of a particular organism-culture inter-action gives at the same time the first law of cultural reaction, the key to the cultural nexus itself. If all the man and all of the culture—its geographic, economic, institutional patterns—are held in view at once, personality study becomes a biosocial, not only a biological investigation. In these terms, the social is simply the biological pattern that embraces interorganism events.

But man is not only one with his immediate physical environment in the sense that he is enmeshed within it, and in the same sense enmeshed within his social environment. He is part of a still larger context, as an aspect not only of a community but of a cosmos. This is the cosmos which has, as one of its limitless propensities, the propensity of producing man. Man is the kind of creature that can love not only his fellow man, but the trees and rocks, sands and oceans of his Mother Earth, and the sun and stars beyond. Because, as man has wondered at the beauty of the world and striven with tubes and numbers to fathom it all, personality is actualized not only through his being drawn to other men but through his being drawn, as artist, to patterns of color and tone or, as scientist, to schemata in time and space. Such patterns are sought, seized, appropriated, lived for. Personality is social, but it is more. It is a drop of the cosmos, and its surface tensions bespeak only a fragile and indefinite barrier that marks a region of relative structuring, relative independence. This structuring and independence can exist only because they are relative, that is, because of the confluence of the self and the nonself. As the musician melts into and identifies with his beloved instrument, the Hopi Indian on the rim melts into his Grand Canyon.

CHAPTER XIV

SOCIAL INTERACTION

THREE of the most important theoretical formulations in the field of social psychology are represented in this chapter. The first selection by Kurt Lewin presents his basic field-theoretical approach to problems of social interaction, utilizing the problem of adolescence as a social phenomenon. It is this theoretical position which developed into the currently significant group dynamics movement, headed by Lewin until his recent death. For further discussion of Lewinian field theory Selections No. 4, 12, 15 and 19 should be consulted. The second selection, from Neal E. Miller and John Dollard's Social Learning and Imitation, *provides a sample of their application of orthodox stimulus-response learning theory to problems of social behavior. The concept of basic personality structure, as developed primarily by Abram Kardiner in his attempt to apply psychoanalytic techniques to anthropological problems, is described in the final selection. This work represents the currently important tendency towards an integration of social psychology with anthropology and psychiatry.*

45 FIELD THEORY IN SOCIAL PSYCHOLOGY

Kurt Lewin

The sociologists, I suppose, have reason to be satisfied with the recent trends in psychology. Traditionally, most psychologists seem to have felt more or less obliged to emphasize the biological character of the individual, to believe in the reality of physical and physiological processes, but to be rather suspicious of social categories and to regard as mystic those who claimed that social facts were as real as physical ones.

Recently, however, a growing number of psychologists seem to have abandoned this view. They seem to be persuaded that social facts are equally or even more important for psychology than the so-called "physiological facts." These psychologists recognize that the child from his first day of life is objectively a part of a social setting and would die within a few days if he were to be withdrawn from it. Also, the so-called "subjective" psychological world of the individual, his life-space, is influenced in a much earlier stage by social facts and social relations than anyone would have expected a few decades ago. Already, at a few months, the child seems to react to another person's smile and voice in a rather specific way. It is probably safe to say that the child is able to perceive and to distinguish the friendliness and unfriendliness of another person at an earlier age than he is able to distinguish the pattern of physical lines in a countenance which expresses these social attitudes.

Beginning with this early age, the child's behavior is molded in every respect by his social situation. Of course, his morale, his religion, and his political values are determined by his being a part of, and reacting to, the society in which he lives. If one considers the findings of cultural anthropology and of experimental psychology, one can, I think, establish evidence that social influences enter every action of the individual, even actions which seem to have nothing to do with society.

Human behavior is either a directed action or an emotional expression. Experimental psychology has shown that the formation of goals depends directly upon the laws which govern the level of aspiration,

From K. Lewin, Field theory and experiment in social psychology: concepts and methods, *Amer. J. Soc.*, 1939, *44*, 868-896. Pp. 868-884 reprinted by permission of the University of Chicago Press.

particularly upon the effect which success or failure has in raising and lowering the level of aspiration (3, 5, 7). These experiments make it evident that the level of aspiration is greatly influenced by such social facts as the presence or absence of other persons or by the competitive or noncompetitive character of the situation. It has been shown, too, that the goal-setting depends upon certain ideal goals, upon what the sociologists call the "ideology" of the person. Cultural anthropology proves that these ideologies vary extremely among different cultures. As to the emotional expression, experiments have shown that, for instance, the emotional reaction to failure can be changed to a great extent by appropriate praise or change in social atmosphere (3, 8). This substantiates the general thesis that the management of tension (4) by the individual depends upon his particular social and cultural setting.

From this it should be apparent that experimental psychology is instrumental in helping the sociologists to realize their most ardent dream: the demonstration of the fundamental, direct, and widespread effect of social facts on behavior.

There is a growing number of psychologists who emphasize the "historical," social side of psychological facts; and even the hard-boiled believers in a stimulus-reaction psychology show a peculiar interest in getting as much of, and as close to, social facts as they can. I believe there is no longer any need for the traditional opposition between psychologists and sociologists in this basic issue.

I

Unfortunately, this insight into the social dependency of behavior does not end the problem for the psychologist. His problems rather begin here. For the sociologist, too, they should begin here. Psychology, including social psychology, cannot possibly be satisfied with any "generalities" (however correct they may be). It has to judge scientific concepts and theories largely by their ability or inability to handle problems of dynamic interdependence and to handle them in a manner sufficiently specific to attack the concrete tasks of the laboratory or the clinic.

Of course, for hundreds of years the belief was prevalent that personality, will, and emotion were not subject to strict laws and that they could not be studied experimentally. A similar view is traditionally strong in sociology. In the long run, however, *dira necessitas* is bound to be stronger in both sociology and psychology than those metaphysical

prejudices, and sociology seems to be ready now for im
away from these prejudices. Psychology as a science mig
be somewhat more advanced technically and conceptuall
some of its areas. However, on the whole, and particularly
social psychology, it, too, is facing the task of developin
approach which offers specific conceptual tools for solving the concrete
problems of a vast and diversified area.

Social psychology indicates, probably better than any other part of
psychology and of sociology, what is needed. Its progress depends upon
an overcoming of certain major difficulties, which include at least the
following:

a) The integrating of vast areas of very divergent facts and aspects: the
   development of a scientific language (concepts) which is able to treat
   cultural, historical, sociological, psychological, and physical facts on
   a common ground.
b) The treating of these facts on the basis of their interdependence.
c) The handling of both historical and systematical problems.
d) The handling of problems related to groups as well as to individuals.
e) The handling of all "sizes" of objects or patterns (social psychology has
   to include problems of a nation and its situation, as well as of a play
   group of three children and their momentary struggle).
f) Problems of "atmosphere" (such as friendliness, pressure, etc.).
g) Experimental social psychology will have to find a way to bring the
   large-size patterns into a framework small enough for the technical
   possibilities of experimentation.

The variety of facts which social psychology has to treat might really
seem frightening to even a bold scientific mind. They include "values"
(such as religious and moral values), "ideologies" (such as conservatism or communism), "the style of living and thinking," and other
so-called "cultural" facts. They include sociological problems, i.e.,
problems of group and group structure, their degree of hierarchy and
type of organization; or such problems as the difference between a rural
and an urban community, their rigidity or fluidity, degree of differentiation, etc. They also include so-called "psychological" problems, such as
the intelligence of a person, his goals and fears, and his personality.
They include such "physiological" facts as the person's being healthy
or sick, strong or weak, the color of his hair and of his complexion.
They include, finally, such "physical" facts as the size of the physical
area in which the person or a group is located.

FIELD THEORY IN SOCIAL PSYCHOLOGY

It is utterly fruitless and merely a negative scientific treatment to put these facts into classificatory pigeonholes, however accurately built and fitted they may be. It is widely accepted today that we need positive means of bringing these various types of facts together in such a way that one can treat them on one level without sacrificing the recognition of their specific characteristics. The problem of adolescence which we will discuss as an example shows, I think, particularly clearly that a way must be found to treat bodily changes, shift of ideology, and group-belongingness within one realm of scientific language, in a single realm of discourse of concepts. The question is "How can that be done?"

Behaviorism has tried to answer this question by interpreting every-thing as a conditioned reflex. One of the main reasons for the appeal of such approach is the same as that which lies behind the popular appeal of the "unity of science" idea: namely, it appeared to put every prob-lem on a "physiological" basis (although in fact it did not), and in this way it seemed to promise integration of the divergent facts on one level.

Today most research workers in sociology and social psychology will agree that the program of describing and explaining sociopsychological processes by concepts and laws of physics or physiology might at best be something to talk about as a distant possibility for a speculative philosopher. But such a way would definitely not be a realistic research program for attacking the sociopsychological problems of today. On the other hand, to elaborate on the "fundamental differences" beween phys-ics, sociology, and psychology and to rest satisfied with such distinctions is no help either.

To discuss these problems adequately would involve a more thorough treatment of certain questions of comparative theory of science than is possible here. As far as I can see the solution lies in the direction (a) that a science should be considered a realm of problems rather than a realm of material; (b) that the different realms of problems might necessitate different universes of discourse of constructs and laws (such as those of physics, aesthetics, psychology, and sociology); and (c) that any one of them refers more or less to the same universe of material.

For any practical purpose of research—and that, after all, is what counts—sciences like sociology or psychology should feel fully free to use those types of constructs which they think most adequate for han-dling their problems; and they should attempt to find the integration we have discussed on their own level. They should not feel obliged to use constructs of another science merely out of philosophical reasons (e.g., because some philosophies or popular metaphysics apply "true reality" to physical entities only). On the other hand, feeling confident in their own right, those sciences do not need to be afraid of using methods or concepts (e.g., mathematical concepts) which might or might not have similarities with those of other sciences.

The field-theoretical approach is intended to be a practical vehicle of research. As is true with any tool, its characteristics can be understood fully only by the use of it in actual research. Therefore, instead of stating general methodological principles *in abstractum,* I prefer to discuss the problem of adolescence and the definition of a social group as an illustration. Our purpose in discussing them is not the proving of certain facts or theories (which might or might not be fully correct) but to survey certain major aspects of the field-theoretical approach. In discussing these examples I will therefore, from time to time, point to similar aspects in other problems. A forthcoming article by Mr. Lippitt (12) offers a more detailed example of actual research.

II

We have chosen the problem of adolescence because the changes in behavior which are supposed to be characteristic for this period seem, at first sight, to give excellent backing to a biological view in sociology. Obviously, adolescence has something to do with sexual hormones and with certain periods of bodily growth. The more recent treatments of the problem of adolescence, however, seem to emphasize its social aspect. They point particularly to the fact that the behavior typical for this age is rather different in different societies (2, 14). Considerable argumentation has been advanced for and against both views.

However, in regard to the problem of adolescence, as in relation to other social and psychological problems, it does not help much to argue whether adolescence is a biological or psychological effect. It does not help very much either to try to describe, on a statistical basis, to what degree this problem is biological or psychological in nature. Even if an answer could be found, it would be of as little value as, for instance, the determining of the degree to which heredity and environment affect intelligence. We still would not have gained any insight into the way in which bodily and social factors are working together and against each other, integrating the concrete behavior of the adolescent. It would seem to be more fruitful to start with an analysis of the setting in a concrete case. This case should be chosen not so much according to the frequency of occurrence as according to the amount of insight it offers into a constellation which is typical at least for a part of the setting in question.

In regard to the problem of adolescence, it might be helpful to refer first to cases which show the so-called "typical" difficulties of adolescent behavior. A field-theoretical analysis of such a situation should give some hints as to what conditions would increase or decrease these symptoms.

The period of adolescence can be said to be a period of transition. It seems to imply, at least under certain circumstances, a more rapid or deeper shift than the period before. After the rather important changes around the age of three years, often a more stable situation has arisen. Maybe minor crises have come up; but particularly in cases where the adolescence is characterized by special disturbances, a relatively quiet or stable time might have preceded it. If one tries to characterize the nature of the transition, one can point to several aspects.

a) One can view adolescence as a change in group-belongingness. The individual has been considered by himself and by others as a child. Now he does not wish to be treated as such. He is ready to separate himself from things childish and to try seriously to enter adult life in manners and in outlook on occupation, as on life in general. Any change in belongingness from one group to another is of great importance for the behavior of the person; the more central for the person this belonging is, the more important is the change. A shift in group-belongingness is a "social locomotion." That means it changes the position of the person concerned.

It is a simple fact, but still not sufficiently recognized in psychology and sociology, that the behavior of a person depends above all upon his momentary position. Often, the world looks very different before and after an event which changes the region in which a person is located. That is the reason why, for instance, a *fait accompli* is so feared in politics. A change in position, for instance, the locomotion from one group to another, changes not only the momentary surroundings of a person but more or less the total setting: what has been a neighboring region, easily accessible from the previous position, might now be farther away or no longer accessible at all. On the other hand, different regions are now neighbors, and new ones may be accessible. The shift into the group of the adults, for instance, makes possible certain activities which previously were forbidden but which are now socially permitted. The individual might attend certain parties, have access to certain activities. On the other hand, certain taboos exist for the adults that do not exist for the child (Figure 1, *a* and *b*).

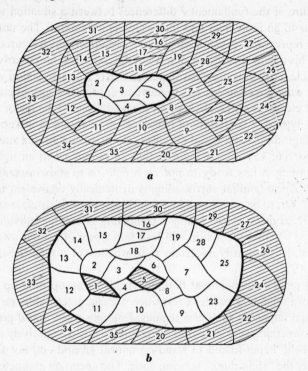

Figure 1 Comparison of the *space of free movement* of child and adult. The actual activity regions are represented. The accessible regions are blank; the inaccessible shaded. (**a**) The space of free movement of the *child* includes the regions *1–6* representing activities such as getting into the movies at children's rates, belonging to a boy's club, etc. The regions *7–35* are not accessible, representing activities such as driving a car, writing checks for purchases, political activities, performance of adults' occupations, etc. (**b**) The *adult* space of free movement is considerably wider, although it too is bounded by regions of activities inaccessible to the adult, such as shooting his enemy or entering activities beyond his social or intellectual capacity (represented by regions including *29–35*). Some of the regions accessible to the child are not accessible to the adult, for instance, getting into the movies at children's rates, or doing things socially taboo for an adult which are permitted to the child (represented by regions *1* and *5*).

b) The change from the group of children to that of the adults is a shift to a more or less unknown position. Psychologically, it is equivalent to entering an unknown region, comparable to coming into a new town. Experiments in the field of learning, for example, give some kind of picture of the fundamental differences between a situation which is familiar to an individual and that which is unfamiliar. The unfamiliar can be represented psychologically as a cognitively unstructured region (9). This means that that region is not differentiated into clearly distinguishable parts. It is not clear therefore where a certain action will lead and in what direction one has to move to approach a certain goal. This lack of clearness of the direction in the field is one of the major reasons for the typical "uncertainty of behavior" to be found in unknown surroundings. Studies on social pressure and on ascendant and submissive behavior (6, 15) clearly indicate that an individual in an unfamiliar surrounding is less ready to put up a fight or to show ascendant behavior. An unfamiliar surrounding is dynamically equivalent to a soft ground. Or, to be more specific, the lack of a cognitively clear structure is likely to make every action a conflicting one. The individual, not knowing whether the action will lead him closer or farther away from his goal, is necessarily uncertain as to whether or not he should carry it out (9).

The child's development naturally leads to an opening up of new unknown regions. Periods of transition are characterized by more than the usual impact of such new regions. Entering a new social group can mean something very similar to being thrown into a cognitively unstructured field, being forced to stand on unfirm ground and not knowing whether the "right thing" is being done. The uncertain character of the adolescent's behavior and his conflicts can partly be explained by the lack of cognitive clarity concerning the adult's world which he is going to enter (Figure 2). It clearly follows that this uncertainty is greater the more the individual has previously been kept out of the adult world and has been kept in the dark about it.

c) One region particularly close and important to the individual is his own body. Psychologically one's own body can be treated in some respects in the same way as one's environment. Generally the individual "knows" his body sufficiently. That means he knows what he can expect from it and how it will react under given circumstances. The time of sexual maturity brings with it changes which make the individual sometimes disturbed by his own body. More or less strange and new body

experiences arise and make this part of the life-space which is so close
and vital to the individual strange and unknown. In this case the change
does not mean merely the usual uncertainties of a new and strange
environment; but, in addition, a region which previously appeared to
be well known and reliable becomes now unknown and unreliable. This

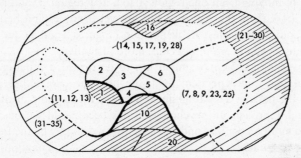

Figure 2 The *space of free movement* of the *adolescent* as it appears to him.
The space of free movement is greatly increased, including many regions which
previously have not been accessible to the child, for instance, freedom to smoke,
returning home late, driving a car (regions *7–9, 11–13, . . .*). Certain regions
accessible to the adult are clearly not accessible to the adolescent, such as
voting (represented by regions *10* and *16*). Certain regions accessible to the
child have already become inaccessible, such as getting into the movies at children's rates, or behaving on too childish a level (region *1*). The boundaries of
these newly acquired portions of the space of free movement are only vaguely
determined and in themselves generally less clearly and sharply differentiated
than for an adult. In such cases the life-space of the adolescent seems to be
full of possibilities and at the same time of uncertainties.

change necessarily shakes the belief of the individual in the stability of
the ground on which he stands and perhaps even in the stability of the
world at large. Since the region of the body happens to be very important and central for anyone, this doubting might be rather fundamental.
It might lead, on the one hand, to increased uncertainty of behavior
and to conflicts; on the other, to the aggressiveness of some of the
adolescent reactions.

Such explanation would be in line, e.g., with the findings of L. B.
Murphy (13) that insecure situations lead both to highly aggressive
and highly sensitive behavior. The disastrous effect which the breakdown of a previously firm ground might have is dramatically illustrated
by foster-children, who discover at a late age the true facts concerning
their parentage. The trauma of such a collapse of a social ground some-

times permanently destroys their belief in the world.

d) The "radicalism" which makes some adolescents flock to extreme "left" or "right" political parties and be extreme in many judgments has to deal also with a second factor. A period of radical change is naturally a period of greater plasticity. The very fact that a person is in the state of moving from one region *A* to a new region *B*, and is therefore cut loose from the region *A* but not yet firmly established in the region *B*, puts him in a less stable position (Figures 2 and 4) and makes him, as any object in *statu nascendi*, more formative.

The psychological environment has to be regarded functionally as a part of one interdependent field, the life-space, the other part of which is the person. This fundamental fact is the keynote of the field-theoretical approach. In psychology it has become, in various forms, more and more recognized and can be expressed simply by the formula: Behavior = Function of person and environment = Function of life-space ($Be = F[P, E] = F[L\,Sp]$) (1, 11). The instability of the psychologic environment leads, in some respects, therefore, to greater instability of the person. "Being established" means having a well-defined position and definite relations to the many regions of a highly differentiated life-space: under such circumstances any major change means a great number of steps and a shift of interrelation. In an unestablished, new situation the field is not very much differentiated, and whatever differentiation has occurred is not very firm. The shift of position of the individual from one region to another, which in the less differentiated field might be merely one step (Figure 2), would have to be considered a major change (equivalent to many steps) in a more differentiated field (Figure 1, *b*). Similarly, what in reality is a not very great and easily made shift in cognitive structure of the ideological field of the adolescent, which contains relatively few regions, appears to be a radical shift to the adult, with his highly differentiated cognitive field. The difference in cognitive differentiation is probably one of the reasons why adolescents easily go to extremes.

e) The widening of the life-space into unknown regions concerns not only geographical surroundings (interest in traveling, hiking, etc.) and social surroundings (more inclusive social groups like political or occupational ones) but also the time dimension of the life-space. Persons of all ages are influenced by the manner in which they see the future, that is, by their expectations, fears, and hopes. The scope of time ahead which influences present behavior, and is therefore to be regarded as a part of the present life-space, increases during development. This change in time perspective is one of the most fundamental facts of development. Adolescence seems to be a period of particularly deep change in respect to time perspective.

The change can be partly described as a shift in scope. Instead of days, weeks, or months, now years ahead are considered in certain goals. Even more important is the way in which these future events influence present behavior. The ideas of a child of six or eight in regard to his occupation as an adult are not likely to be based on sufficient knowledge of the factors which might help or interfere with the realization of these ideas. They might be based on relatively narrow but definite expectations or might have a dream or playlike character. In other words, "ideal goals" and "real goals" for the distant future are not much distinguished, and this future has more the fluid character of the level of irreality.

In adolescence a definite differentiation in regard to the time perspective is likely to occur. Within those parts of the life-space which represent the future, levels of reality and irreality are gradually being differentiated. That which is dreamed of or wished for (level of irreality in the future) becomes separated from what is expected (level of reality in the future). Vague ideas have to be replaced by more or less definite decisions in regard to preparation for future occupation. In other words, one has to "plan": to structure the time perspective (5) in a way which is in line both with one's own ideal goals or values and with those realities which must be taken into account for a realistic structuring of the plane of expectation (Figure 3, *a* and *b*).

This task is characteristic for all kinds of planning. The situation of the adolescent in this respect is particular only in that he has to form the time perspective in regard to a field which is especially great and unknown. What he learns from books and adult council about what an individual might accomplish is full of contradiction: the adults praise the hero who has realized what seemed to be impossible, and at the same time preach the moral of "standing with both feet on the ground."

In another respect the adolescent finds the adults (the group he is to enter) full of contradiction. A variety of conflicting religious, political, and occupational values is obviously powerful within that group. A child may fail to bring to adolescence a well-established framework of values, or he may have thrown the values of his childhood away. In either case the structure of his adolescent time perspective will be un-

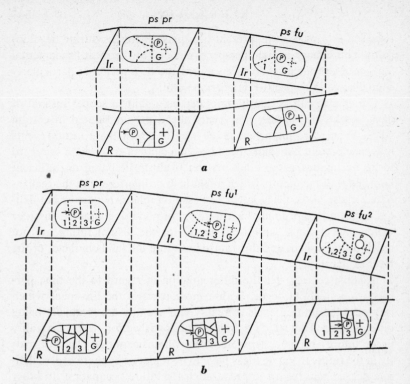

Figure 3 *Time perspective* of child and adult. The diagram represents the life-space of an individual *P* as it exists at a certain time. At that time the person sees himself in a certain situation at present and expects certain situations in his immediate or later future (represented as "psychological time" *ps pr* = psychological present, *ps fu¹* = immediate psychological future, *ps fu²* = later psychological future). Probably each of these situations includes a reality level (*R*) equivalent to what the person really expects to come true, and an irreality level (*Ir*), corresponding to what he might dream, hope for, or fear (for instance, on the irreality level the person, *P*, sees himself closer to the goal than he expects to be at that time). Mathematically the reality—irreality dimension and the past-present future dimension makes the life-space existing at a given moment a manifold which has at least four dimensions (to represent change of life-space would mean a fifth one). (It is, of course, impossible mathematically to represent in a diagram a continuous four-dimensional manifold adequately, but we trust that this discontinuous representation will suffice.)

(**a**) Live-space of a *child*. (**b**) Life-space of an *adult*. 1) The adult life-space shows a greater degree of differentiation in the dimension reality—irreality for a given psychological time, for instance, for the psychological present. 2) The time perspective of the adult influencing his present behavior generally covers a larger time span and is more differentiated in regard to time sequence.

(*Continued on opposite page.*)

stable and undetermined, owing to the uncertainty of not only what can be done (which we have discussed previously) but also what should be done. The uncertain character of the ideals and values keeps the adolescent in a state of conflict and tension which is the greater the more central these problems are. The wish to structure these fields in a definite way (and in this manner to solve the conflict) seems to be one of the reasons behind the readiness of the adolescent to follow anyone who offers a definite pattern of values.

f) The transition from childhood to adulthood may be a rather sudden shift (for instance, in some of the primitive societies), or it may occur gradually in a setting where children and adults are not sharply separated groups. In case of the so-called "adolescence difficulties," however, a third state of affairs is often prevalent: children and adults constitute clearly defined groups; the adolescent does not wish to belong any longer to the children's group and, at the same time, knows that he is not really accepted in the adult group. In this case he has a position similar to what is called in sociology the "marginal man."

The marginal man is a person who stands on the boundary (Figure 4, *b*) between two groups, *A* and *B*. He does not belong to either of them, or at least he is not certain about his belongingness. Not infrequently this situation occurs for members of an underprivileged minority group, particularly for the more privileged members within this group. There is a strong tendency for the members of the underprivileged minority group to cut loose and to try to enter the majority group (10). In case the person is partly successful in establishing relationships with the privileged group without being fully accepted, he becomes a marginal man, belonging to both groups but not fully to either of them. The fact of being located in a social "no man's land" can be observed in very different types of minority groups—for instance, racial groups or the hard-of-hearing, which is a marginal group between the deaf and the normal group.

Characteristic symptoms of behavior of the marginal man are emo-

---

3) The adult is generally more able to distinguish between wishes and realistic expectation. That is true particularly for the future; the structure of the reality level of his life-space in the psychological future is less directly dependent upon the irreality level (although for the *distant* future this influence might be not much less than for a child). For instance, the position in which the person, *P*, sees himself on the future reality level is for the child probably more similar to that on the irreality level than for the adult.

tional instability and sensitivity. They tend to unbalanced behavior, either to boisterousness or shyness, exhibiting too much tension, and a frequent shift between extremes of contradictory behavior. The marginal man shows a typical aversion to the less privileged members of his

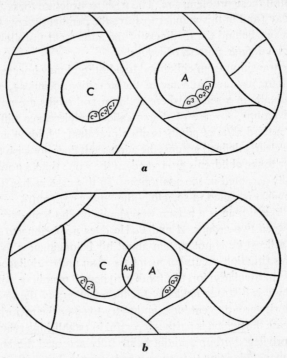

a

b

Figure 4 The adolescent as a *marginal man*. (a) During *childhood* and *adulthood* the "adults" (A) and "children" (C) are viewed as relatively separated groups, the individual child (c^1, c^2) and the individual adult (a^1, a^2) being sure of their belonging to their respective groups. (b) The *adolescent* belonging to a group (Ad), which can be viewed as an overlapping region of the children's (C) and the adults' (A) group, belonging to both of them, or as standing between them, not belonging to either one.

own group. This can be noted in the hostile attitude of some subgroups of the Negroes or other races against members of their own race, and the hard-of-hearing against the deaf.

To some extent behavior symptomatic for the marginal man can be found in the adolescent. He too is oversensitive, easily shifted from one extreme to the other, and particularly sensitive to the shortcomings of his younger fellows. Indeed, his position is sociologically the same as that of the marginal man: he does not wish to belong any longer to a group which is, after all, less privileged than the group of adults, but at the same time he knows that he is not fully accepted by the adults. The similarities between the position of the members of the underprivileged minority and the adolescent and between their behavior seems to me so great that one might characterize the behavior of the marginal members of the minority group as that of permanent adolescence.

We might sum up our discussion of the adolescent in the following manner:

a) The basic fact concerning the general situation of the adolescent can be represented as the position of a person during locomotion from one region to another. This includes (i) the widening of the life-space (geographically, socially, and in time perspective [Figures 1, 2, and 3]) and (ii) the cognitively unstructured character of the new situation (Figure 2).

b) Somewhat more specifically, the adolescent has a social position "between" the adult and the child, similar to a marginal member of an underprivileged minority group (Figure 4, *b*).

c) There are still more specific factors involved in adolescence, such as the new experiences with one's own body, which can be represented as the baffling change of a central region of the established life-space.

From this representation one can derive conceptually:

I. The adolescent's shyness, sensitivity, and aggressiveness, owing to unclearness and instability of ground (follows from *a*, *b*, and *c*).

II. A more or less permanent conflict between the various attitudes, values, ideologies, and styles of living (follows from *b*).

III. Emotional tension resulting from these conflicts (follows from *a, b,* and *c*).

IV. Readiness to take extreme attitudes and actions and to shift his position radically (follows from *a, b,* and *c*).

V. The "adolescent behavior" should appear only if the structure and dynamic of the field is such as represented by *a, b,* and *c*. The degree and particular type of behavior should depend upon the degree of realization of this structure and upon the strength of the conflicting forces. Above all, the degree of difference and of separation between adults and children which is characteristic for a particular culture is important; also, the extent to which the particular adolescent finds himself in the position of a marginal man. According to field theory, actual behavior depends upon every part of the field. It follows that the degree of instability of the adolescent should be greatly influenced also by such factors as general stability or instability of the particular individual.

References

1. Brown, J. F. *Psychology and the social order.* New York: McGraw-Hill, 1936.
2. Cole, Luella. *Psychology of adolescence.* New York: Farrar & Rinehart, 1936.
3. Fajans, Sara. Erfolg, Ausdauer und Aktivität beim Säuglings und Kleinkind: Untersuchung zur Handlungs- und Affektpsychologie XIII (Success, perseverance and activity in the infant and young child: Studies in the psychology of action and emotion XIII). Ed. Kurt Lewin. *Psychol. Forsch.,* 1933,*17,* 268-305.
4. Frank, L. K. The management of tensions. *Amer. J. Sociol.,* 1928, *33,* 705-736.
5. Frank, L. K. Time perspective. *J. soc. Philos.,* 1939, *4,* 293-312.
6. Jack, Lois M. An experimental study of ascendant behavior in preschool children, in Lois M. Jack, Elizabeth M. Manwell, Ida G. Mengert, and others. Behavior in the preschool child. *Univ. Ia. Stud. Child Welf.,* 1934, *9,* No. 3.
7. Jones, H. E., Conrad, H. S., and Blanchard, M. B. Environmental handicap in mental test performance. *Univ. Calif. Public. Psychol.,* 1932, *5,* No. 3.
8. Keister, Mary E. The behavior of young children in failure: An experimental attempt to discover and to modify undesirable responses of preschool children to failure. *Univ. Ia. Stud. Child Welf.,* 1937, *14,* No. 4.
9. Lewin, K. The conceptual representation and measurement of psychological forces. *Contr. psychol. Theor.,* 1938, *1,* No. 4.
10. Lewin, K. Bringing up the child. *Menorah J.,* 1940, *28,* 29-45.
11. Lewin, K. *Principles of topological psychology.* New York: McGraw-Hill, 1936.
12. Lippitt, R. Field theory and experiment in social psychology. *Amer. J. Soc.,* 1939, *45,* 26-49.
13. Murphy, Lois B. *Social behavior and child personality: An exploratory study of some roots of sympathy.* New York: Columbia Univ. Press, 1937.
14. Reuter, E. B. The sociology of adolescence. *Amer. J. Sociol.,* 1937, *43,* 414-427.
15. Wiehe, F. Die Grenzen des Ichs. Reported from the manuscript in Kurt Lewin, *A dynamic theory of personality.* New York: McGraw-Hill, 1935, 261-264.

46 STIMULUS-RESPONSE THEORY IN SOCIAL PSYCHOLOGY

Neal E. Miller and John Dollard

A Pattern Case of Imitation

Imitative behavior has attracted the attention of humanists and social psychologists for centuries. The small child sits in father's chair, scuttles around in his carpet slippers, or wants her hair done up like mother's. "Copy-cat" is a well-known reproach to the socially aspiring. Explanations of imitative behavior have varied from time to time, but each serious attempt has leaned heavily upon a particular psychological theory. The analysis proposed here is no exception. It rests upon a psychology which may be called, in brief, a reinforcement theory of social learning. It derives from the work of Pavlov (3), Thorndike (4, 5, 6), and Watson (7), although it should not be confused with the detailed position of any one of these writers. Its best current statement and synthesis have been made by Hull (2). The basic position has already been outlined. The present object is to see its relevance in a restatement of the nature of imitative behavior.

Common speech has already directed attention to imitative acts. Language, being a folk creation, would not be expected to provide a very exact discrimination of the forms of action which it lumps under the general term "imitation." It is, indeed, this inclusiveness of common speech which poses the scientific problem and demands that the scientist make further and more exact distinctions. The authors have decided to use three phrases to indicate the sub-mechanisms which seem to account for all or most of the cases for which the term "imitation" is ordinarily used. These mechanisms are: *same* behavior; *matched-dependent* behavior; and *copying*. The authors agree with Faris (1) that no single sub-mechanism will adequately account for all cases of imitation, but disagree with him in that they hold that the three sub-mechanisms, derived from a single general learning theory, suffice to account for all cases.

From N. E. Miller and J. Dollard, *Social Learning and Imitation*. New Haven, Conn.: Yale Univ. Press, 1941. Pp. 91-97 reprinted by permission of the authors and publishers.

Same behavior does not require the detailed analysis which will be given to the other two types of imitation. The characteristic fact is that two people perform the same act in response to independent stimulation by the same cue, each having learned by himself to make the response. Two persons, for instance, may take the same bus because each reads the card indicating its destination. Similarly, the crowd at a football game resolves itself into an ordered unit, each group of individuals presenting their tickets at the proper gate, each independently discriminating the letters above the proper doors and making similar adaptive responses. *Same* behavior may be learned with or without imitative aids.

Copying also will be mentioned only briefly at this point. In the characteristic case, one person learns to model his behavior on that of another. It is crucial that the copier know when his behavior is the same; the essential learning in copying centers around this knowledge. The copier must have criteria for the sameness and difference of the acts he performs. He must be aware that his copy falls within the band of tolerance as a match for the model act. Training to copy often begins with an external critic who rewards similarity and punishes dissimilarity; in the end the copier must be able to respond independently to the cues of sameness and difference.

The third mechanism, that of matched-dependent behavior, will be discussed in detail in the present chapter. It is extremely important in social life. It tends to occur whenever one person is older, shrewder, or more skilled than another. Younger people match behavior with, and are dependent upon, older people. Stupid children must, perforce, follow their more intelligent associates. Householders prepare for an ice storm when their scientists (meteorologists) give the sign. Social climbers must follow their status superiors through an intricate routine of watching and imitating. Learners of a foreign language must learn the appropriate situations in which to use certain words by following those who already speak the foreign tongue. The study of socialization in children offers innumerable examples where children match behavior with their elders and are dependent on them for cues as to when to do so. It will be useful and perhaps interesting to discuss one full-bodied example of such dependence matching as it was recorded by a gifted child observer. Such examples force us to fit theory to the actualities of social life. Since imaginary examples often lead to imaginary solutions, the authors have insisted that every example presented have an actual location in space and time and that they be able to give names and circumstances in further elaboration if necessary.

The following case is instructive just because the imitative behavior was maladaptive. Two boys—Jim, aged six, and Bobby, aged three—were playing a game with their father in the living room of their house. The father explained that he would hide two pieces of candy while the children were out of the room. When he gave the signal, they were to return and look for the sweets. When each child found his piece of candy, he could eat it. The father put one piece of candy under a pillow on the davenport and the other beside the radio cabinet. The older child came into the room, followed by his younger brother. The older boy, Jim, looked in the fireplace. The younger brother, Bobby, followed and looked there also. Jim looked inside the piano bench; so also did Bobby. Then Jim looked under the pillow on the davenport and found his piece of candy. Thereupon he stopped looking. Bobby was now helpless. He went again and looked under the pillow where his older brother had found his candy, but of course had no success. Finally, Bobby's candy was produced and given to him.

On a succeeding trial of the same game, exactly the same thing happened. The younger child would look only in the places already examined by his older brother. He could not respond to place cues by looking for himself.

This behavior, comical when it occurred, is nevertheless worthy of attention. It could not have been acquired in previous situations of the identical kind since this occasion was the first when the game was played. Perhaps it was acquired in other but, in some respects, similar situations. A search of the life histories of the children proved that the latter was the correct surmise. The younger child had been rewarded for matching behavior with the older in a large number of situations which had cue elements in common with that of the game. It appears, therefore, that the tendency to match had generalized in this case from other similar cues to the cues of the new game. Out of the many rewarded examples of dependence matching discovered as the "background" for the game, one is selected for exposition. It is not advanced as proof of our theory. Such proof can come only from the better controlled conditions and the more exact communication of the experiments to be subsequently reported. The example, however, is intimately related to the structure of the experiments which follow. It shows, pattern perfect, the crucial elements in one type of imitative behavior.

A Case of Matched-Dependent Behavior. The same two children, each a year younger, were playing in their bedroom, which was adjacent to the family kitchen. The kitchen opened upon a back stairway. It was six o'clock in the evening, the hour when father usually returned home, bearing candy for the two children. While playing in the bedroom, Jim heard a footfall on the stairs; it was the familiar sound of father's return. The younger child, however, had not identified this critical cue. Jim ran to the kitchen to be on hand when father came in the back door. Bobby happened on this occasion to be running in the direction of the kitchen and behind Jim. On many other occasions, probably many hundreds, he had not happened to run when Jim did. He had, for instance, remained sitting, continued playing with his toys, run to the window instead of the door, and the like; but on this occasion, he was running behind his brother. Upon reaching the kitchen, Jim got his candy and Bobby his.

On subsequent nights with similar conditions, the younger child ran more frequently at the mere sight of his older brother running. When he ran, he received candy. Eventually, the behavior, under pressure of continued reward, became highly stabilized, and the younger child would run when the older ran, not only in this situation but in many others where time and place stimuli were different. He had learned in this one respect to *imitate* his older brother, but he had not learned to run at the sound of his father's footfall.

Apparently, learning in this and other similar situations, in which responding imitatively was rewarded, generalized to the game and was the source of the maladaptive imitation observed there. Since imitation was not rewarded in the game, we should expect a discrimination eventually to be established; the younger child should learn not to imitate in such a situation.

Analysis of the Behavior of the Imitator Child. Bobby's behavior can be analyzed in the form of a learning paradigm, as follows:

IMITATOR

Drive – – – – – – – – – Appetite for candy

Cue – – – – – – – – – – Leg-twinkle of brother

Response – – – – – – – – Running

Reward – – – – – – – – Eating candy

Analysis of Leader's Behavior. The leader's problem is slightly different; his behavior parses out as follows:

LEADER

Drive   – – – – – – – – Appetite for candy

Cue   – – – – – – – – – Father's footfall

Response   – – – – – – – Running

Reward   – – – – – – – Eating candy

The leader in this case is reacting to the stable environmental cue provided by culture, i.e., the father's footfall on the stair, but otherwise his problem is identical with that of the imitator, or follower. Jim had obviously completed his learning of the connection between footfall and the running response before Bobby had commenced his. It might be added that it is not essential in every analysis of this type of imitation to know all of the factors operating to determine the leader's act. It is enough actually to be sure that he is following a cue which the imitator cannot discriminate.

Complete Paradigm of Matched-Dependent Behavior. The relationship between the acts of leader and imitator can be put together into one diagram as follows:

	LEADER	IMITATOR
Drive	Appetite for candy	Appetite for candy
Cue	Father's footfall	Leg-twinkle of leader
		dependent ⟶
Response	Running ⌐ – – – – matched – – Running	
Reward	Eating candy	Eating candy

It will be noted above that the responses are *matched,* thus fulfilling one important condition of imitative behavior. It is further clear that the response of the imitator is elicited by cues from the act of the leader. His behavior is therefore *dependent* on that of the leader. Simple, or simple-minded, as an analysis so detailed of an incident so humble may seem, it represents, nevertheless, a large class of cases of social behavior which is called imitative. Such cases are frequently encountered when the history of the act is not known, and therefore the observer cannot be certain that the imitative act was learned. Every case ought at least to be examined to see whether the variables called for by the learning hypothesis are not in fact present.

In order to emphasize the crucial rôle of learning principles in the behavior of the imitator child above, one can look at the elements of the paradigm from another standpoint. If Bobby had had no drive—that is, if he had not been hungry for candy—it would have been impossible for reinforcement to occur, and the connection between the response and the cue of the leg-twinkle would not have been fixed. If he had been unable to perceive his brother's cue—if, say, he had been blind—it would have been impossible for the learning to occur. If he had been unable to make the response of running—if, for instance, he had been kept in the room by a barrier which only his brother could leap—it would have been impossible to learn the imitative response. If he had not been rewarded on the occasions when he did follow his brother, he could not have learned to imitate. This example should indicate, therefore, that imitative acts of this type follow the laws of learning. What is crucial about them is that the cue from the leader's behavior is often more stable than other cues provided by the environment. If the leader child is, for instance, responding to the cue of the hands of a clock, he can make his response more regularly and discriminatingly than can the imitator child, who must depend on the cue of the leader's action. If, for example, the leader is gone for the day, the imitator child will be unable to make his response at all.

In social life, individuals are constantly being placed in situations analogous to the one above. The young, the stupid, the subordinate, and the unskilled must depend on the older, the brighter, the superordinate, and the skilled to read cues which they cannot themselves discriminate. They can respond only in the wake of those better instructed. Society, as will be shown, is so organized that the situation diagrammed above occurs over and over again. Imitative responses are not confined to childhood. They can and do appear at any time along the life line where the situation calls for them. They can be outgrown and abandoned when the need for them disappears; or they can be a permanent feature of the life of every individual, as in the case of dependence upon the skill of the political leader, the scientist, or the expert craftsman.

References

1. Faris, E. *The nature of human nature.* New York: McGraw-Hill, 1937.
2. Hull, C. L. *Principles of behavior.* New York: D. Appleton-Century, 1943.
3. Pavlov, I. P. *Conditioned reflexes.* (Trans. by Anrep.) London: Oxford Univ. Press, 1927.
4. Thorndike, E. L. *Animal intelligence.* New York: Macmillan, 1911.
5. Thorndike, E. L. *Educational psychology.* New York: Columbia Univ., Bureau Public., Teachers College, 1914.
6. Thorndike, E. L. *Human nature and the social order.* New York: Macmillan, 1940.
7. Watson, J. B. *Psychology from the standpoint of a behaviorist.* Chicago: Lippincott, 1919.

47 THE BASIC PERSONALITY STRUCTURE

Abram Kardiner

The processes of adaptation in man have been treated in various ways. The biologist limits the meaning of the term to those autoplastic changes in bodily structure which take place presumably to accommodate the organism to its physical environment. On this basis he can describe certain long-term phases of human adjustment, but he has to treat his subject with bold strokes and in relation to long periods of time. Morphological criteria cannot be used to describe the adaptive maneuvers of man covering short periods of time. Morphological adaptation in our species seems to have become almost stabilized, in spite of a long series of minor variations which now form the basis for the concept of race. Moreover, such adaptations record only the response of man to his external physical environment. What has become more important in the thinking of the past century is the adaptation of man to his human environment, the behavioral adjustments which he has had to make to the conditions imposed by social living.

While the morphological adjustments of our species could be studied

Reprinted from Ralph Linton, editor, *The Science of Man in the World Crisis.* Copyright 1945 by Columbia University Press. Pp. 107-112.

and described in the familiar terms of biology, new techniques had to be devised for the description of behavioral and psychological adjustments. The concept which showed the greatest usefulness and viability in this connection was that of culture. This concept was purely descriptive, but it furnished a definite way of identifying at least the end products of the processes of adaptation and hence laid a basis for the comparison of various types of adaptive maneuvers.

The culture concept was first used with relation to the culture trait, an item of behavior common to the members of a particular society. Such a culture trait was presumably isolated and idiosyncratic. Later, the sociologists developed the concept of institutions—configurations of functionally interrelated culture traits, which are the dynamic units within culture. Although comparative studies of the forms of the institutions within various cultures could now be made, no significant conclusions concerning the relations of institutions within the same culture were possible without the aid of new techniques. Up to now only one technique has been able to yield decisive results in the interpretation of the variations in institutional combinations—and this technique is a psychological one. This psychological technique has shown itself capable of investigating the minutiae of those adaptive processes which cover short spans of time and represent reactions to both the natural and the human environment.

Preliminary attempts to establish relationships between institutions within the same culture had to draw heavily upon our knowledge of psychopathology. From this contact there emerged the concept of the psychological culture pattern (1). However, early attempts based on too close analogies between society and the individual did not furnish a basis for a dynamic concept of society. The culture pattern merely gave recognition to the fact that personality and institutions were always to be found in some persistent relationship. It remained a difficult technical problem to demonstrate this relationship in an empirically verifiable manner without merely referring in a descriptive way to certain pathological configurations of frequent occurrence in individuals.

The study of "primitive" societies offered the best opportunity for the working out of such a technique. It could be legitimately anticipated that "primitive" societies would prove simpler in structure than our own and that the psychological constellations there found would be more consistent and more naïve in character. By far the most difficult problem was that of selecting a psychological technique suited to this particular assignment. Neither the classical psychologies, behaviorism, nor Gestalt psychology had made more than sporadic attempts to apply themselves to this problem. Psychoanalysis seemed the technique best suited to the task; yet Freud himself, in spite of his application of psychoanalysis to sociology, did not develop an empirically verifiable technique. On the whole, his efforts were dedicated to the verification in primitive society of those constellations found in modern man. This endeavor was consistent with the evolutionary hypothesis regarding the development of society and culture which was in vogue at the end of the nineteenth century. Among the most valuable suggestions made by Freud was that of an analogy between the practices of primitive people and neurotic symptoms. Some rather unproductive hypotheses resulted from the pursuit of this analogy to too great lengths; nevertheless, the study of the origin of neurotic symptoms in the individual laid a basis for the understanding of the minimal adaptive tools of man. Thus, even though the neurotic symptom is a special case, the principles upon which symptom formation are based cannot be very different from those involved in the development of any of the habitual modes of behavior which we identify in the character of the individual.

The integration of the two techniques, anthropological and psychological, was later facilitated by the abandonment of the evolutionary hypothesis exploited by the early anthropologists. For this was substituted the concept of cultures as functional wholes and the study of primitive societies as entities, a point of view of which Malinowski was the earliest exponent. All that was gained by the application of the concept of psychological culture pattern to primitive societies was the impression that institutions within a society were in large measure consistent with each other and that this consistency could be described in terms of analogies with entities found in psychopathology. This was a definite gain, but it was not a technique.

The most obvious approach to the problem of devising a definite technique was to utilize the known fact that cultures are transmitted within a society from generation to generation. It was natural, therefore, to attempt to develop such a technique with the aid of learning-theory formulations. However, what we know about acculturation and diffusion indicates that there is a limit to the sort of culture content which can be transmitted by direct learning processes. Though no one can deny the role of direct learning in culture transmission, qualified of course by the age of the individual who is exposed to culture change, there seems to be a high degree of selection in the acceptance of elements from any culture by individuals reared in another. Moreover, if learning process alone could account for the transmission of culture, it is difficult to see how culture change without borrowing from other cultures could ever take place. The point is that learning processes do not account for the integrative character of the human mind in so far as the emotional relationships of the individual to his environment are concerned. There is another factor at work, a factor upon which psychoanalytic technique can throw much light. In addition to direct learning processes, the individual builds up a highly complicated series of integrative systems which are not a result of direct learning. The concept of basic personality structure was established on the basis of a recognition of these factors.

The purely descriptive use of very similar concepts is an exceedingly old one. One can easily find it, by implication, in the writings of Herodotus and Caesar. Both of these authors recognize that the various peoples they described not only had unique customs and practices but were also unique in temperament, disposition, and character. Caesar took this factor into account and used it to the advantage of Rome in his dealings with the various barbarian tribes. However, the recognition that there are different basic personality structures for different societies really takes us no farther than did the concept of psychological culture pattern. It can acquire an operational significance only when the formation of this basic personality structure can be tracked down to identifiable causes and if significant generalizations can be made concerning the relation between the formation of basic personality structure and the individual's specific potentialities for adaptation.

The realization that the concept of basic personality structure was a dynamic instrument of sociological research was not an a priori judgment. It was a conclusion reached after two cultures described by Linton—the Tanala and the Marquesan—had been analyzed with the objective of correlating personality with institutions. In the analysis of these two cultures the potentialities of psychoanalytic principles were first shown. The analyses began with the study of the integrational systems formed in the child by the direct experiences during the process of growth. In other words, the approach was a genetic one. It followed two standards: 1) that integrative processes were at work, and 2) that the end results of these integrative processes could be identified. A technique which follows this line is, however, bound to have limitations. The first limitation is that, if the investigator is a citizen of Western society, and if he is moreover a psychopathologist, he will usually be able to identify only those end products which have significance in the neurotic and psychotic disturbances in his own society. But it must be recognized that, simultaneously, other end products were formed which we in our society could not possibly identify. Notwithstanding these limitations, some significant results were obtained in the first few attempts. The first correlation to be observed was that, in any given culture, religious systems were replicas of the experiences of the child with parental disciplines. It was noted that the concept of deity was universal, but that the technique for soliciting divine aid varied according to the specific experiences of the child and the particular life goals defined by the society. In one culture this technique for solicitation was merely to demonstrate endurance; in another it was to punish oneself in order to be reinstated in the good graces of the deity, a position that had been lost by some transgression clearly defined in the actual life practices sanctioned by the community. These variations in the technique of soliciting divine aid pointed, therefore, to different influences which shaped the personality in each specific culture.

From this first correlation several important conclusions could be drawn. The first of these was that certain culturally established techniques of child treatment had the effect of shaping basic attitudes toward parents and that these attitudes enjoyed a permanent existence in the mental equipment of the individual. The institutions from which the growing child received the experience responsible for the production of these basic constellations were, therefore, called primary institutions. The religious ideologies and methods of solicitation were, for the most part, consistent with these basic constellations and had presumably been derived from them by a process known as projection. In other words, primary institutions laid the basis for the projective system which was subsequently reflected in the development of other institutions. Institutions developed as a result of the projective systems were, therefore, called secondary institutions. If this correlation proved to be correct, it followed that between the primary experiences and the end results, identifiable through their projective manifestations, there stood this entity which could now be called the basic personality structure. Primary institutions were responsible for the basic personality structure which, in turn, was responsible for the secondary institutions.

It must be emphasized that the important feature of this concept is not its name—although a good many investigators have since attempted variations in the name without any effort to modify or criticize the technique by which it was derived. This name stands for a special technique. Its importance depends upon the fact that it is possible to demonstrate that certain practices are significant for the individual during his period of growth and that the constellations thus formed remain as a continuity in the personality. This technique is an achievement of psychodynamics.

References

1. Benedict, Ruth. *Patterns of Culture*. New York: Houghton Mifflin, 1934.

SUGGESTED FURTHER READINGS

The following selected references in no sense constitute a comprehensive bibliography but are intended simply as an aid in facilitating search of the literature. For convenience they are arranged under the chapter headings of the book. Those for Part One are mainly organized around problems, those for Part Two largely restricted to other publications of the individual theorists. Recent modifications of basic theoretical positions may be found in certain of the references for Part Two. The selections for a given chapter are ones which as a rule do not appear in the separate lists of references at the end of each of the selections for that chapter. For this reason a number of important references are not included here but will be found in the individual reference lists, which should also be consulted. Page numbers for the more extensive of these are given in brackets immediately under the chapter headings.

General Sources

Boring, E. G. *A history of experimental psychology.* New York: Appleton-Century-Crofts, 1950 (rev. ed.).

Brunswik, E. Points of view. In P. L. Harriman (ed.), *Encyclopedia of psychology.* New York: Philosophical Library, 1946.

Cohen, M. R. and Nagel, E. *An introduction to logic and scientific method.* New York: Harcourt, Brace, 1934.

Dennis, W. (ed.), *Readings in the history of psychology.* New York: Appleton-Century-Crofts, 1948.

Griffith, C. R. *Principles of systematic psychology.* Urbana, Ill.: Univ. Illinois Press, 1943.

Hilgard, E. R. *Theories of learning.* New York: Appleton-Century-Crofts, 1948.

Murphy, G. *Historical introduction to modern psychology.* New York: Harcourt, Brace, 1949 (rev. ed.).

Pratt, C. C. *The logic of modern psychology.* New York: Macmillan, 1939.

Woodworth, R. S. *Contemporary schools of psychology.* New York: Ronald, 1948 (rev. ed.).

Chapter I. Introduction—General Nature of Theory Construction

[Selection reference list on p. 19.]

Cantril, H.; Ames, A., Jr.; Hastorf, A. H.; and Ittelson, W. H. Psychology and scientific research. I, II, III. *Science,* 1949, *110,* 461-464, 491-497, 517-522.

Geldard, F. A. "Explanatory principles" in psychology. *Psychol. Rev.,* 1939, *46,* 411-424.

Guthrie, E. R. On the nature of psychological explanations. *Psychol. Rev.,* 1933, *40,* 124-137.

Guthrie, E. R. Psychological principles and scientific truth. In *Proc. 25th Anniv. Celebr. Inaug. Grad. Stud.* Univ. South. Calif., 1936, 104-115.

Hospers, J. On explanation. *J. Philos.,* 1946, *43,* 337-356.

Johnson, H. M. Pre-experimental assumptions as determiners of experimental results. *Psychol. Rev.,* 1940, *47,* 338-346.

Miller, D. L. The meaning of explanation. *Psychol. Rev.,* 1946, *53,* 241-246.

Nock, S. A. Sound and symbol. *Phil. Sci.,* 1941, *8,* 352-370.

Chapter II. Operationism and Logical Positivism

[Selection reference lists on pp. 51-54, 65-66.]

Bergmann, G. An empiricist schema of the psychophysical problem. *Phil. Sci.,* 1942, *9,* 72-91.

Bergmann, G. Remarks concerning the epistemology of scientific empiricism. *Phil. Sci.,* 1942, *9,* 283-293.

Boring, E. G.; Bridgman, P. W.; Feigl, H.; Israel, H. E.; Pratt, C. C.; and Skinner, B. F. Symposium on operationism. *Psychol. Rev.,* 1945, *52,* 241-294.

Carnap, R. Logic. In *Factors determining human behavior,* Harvard Tercentenary Publications. Cambridge: Harvard Univ. Press, 1937.

Feigl, H. Logical empiricism. In Runes, D. D. (ed.) *Twentieth century philosophy.* New York: Philosophical Library, 1943.

Feigl, H. and Sellars, W. (eds.) *Readings in philosophical analysis.* New York: Appleton-Century-Crofts, 1949.

Hayakawa, S. I. *Language in action.* New York: Harcourt, Brace, 1941.

Israel, H. E. and Goldstein, B. Operationism in psychology. *Psychol. Rev.,* 1944, *51,* 177-188.

Joad, C. E. M. *A critique of logical positivism.* Chicago: Univ. Chicago Press, 1950.

Johnson, W. *People in quandaries.* New York: Harper, 1946.

Kattsoff, L. O. and Thibaut, J. Semiotic and psychological concepts. *Psychol. Rev.,* 1942, *49,* 475-485.

Morris, C. W. *Signs, language, and behavior.* New York: Prentice-Hall, 1946.

Reichenbach, H. *Elements of symbolic logic.* New York: Macmillan, 1947.

Chapter III. Theoretical Constructs

[Selection reference lists on pp. 85-86, 102, 111, 128-129.]

Boring, E. G. A psychological function is the relation of successive differentiations of events in the organism. *Psychol. Rev.*, 1937, *44*, 445-461.

Lewin, K. Constructs in psychology and psychological ecology. *Univ. Ia. Stud. Child Welf.*, 1944, *20*, 1-29.

London, I. D. The role of the unneutralized symbol in psychology. *J. gen. Psychol.*, 1949, *40*, 229-246.

London, I. D. The role of the model in explanation. *J. genet. Psychol.*, 1949, *74*, 165-176.

Prentice, W. C. H. Operationism and psychological theory: a note. *Psychol. Rev.*, 1946, *53*, 247-249.

Tolman, E. C. An operational analysis of "demands." *Erkenntnis* (*J. unif. Sci.*), 1936, *6*, 383-390.

Chapter IV. Levels of Explanation

[Selection reference list on p. 154.]

Goldstein, K. *The organism: A holistic approach to biology derived from pathological data in man.* New York: American Book Co., 1939.

Hebb, D. O. *Organization of behavior.* New York: Wiley, 1949.

Heider, F. Environmental determinants in psychological theories. *Psychol. Rev.*, 1939, *46*, 383-470.

Heider, F. Social perception and phenomenal causality. *Psychol. Rev.*, 1944, *51*, 358-374.

Lashley, K. S. Coalescence of neurology and psychology. *Proc. Amer. Philos. Soc.*, 1941, *84*, 461-470.

Loucks, R. B. The contribution of physiological psychology. *Psychol. Rev.*, 1941, *48*, 105-126.

MacLeod, R. B. The phenomenological approach to social psychology. *Psychol. Rev.*, 1947, *54*, 193-210.

Redfield, R. (ed.) *Levels of integration in biological and social systems.* Lancaster, Pa.: J. Cattell Press, 1942.

Tolman, E. C. A stimulus-expectancy need-cathexis psychology. *Science*, 1945, *101*, 160-166.

Chapter V. Theoretical Emphases

[Selection reference lists on pp. 169-170, 185-186.]

Allport, G. W. The psychologist's frame of reference. *Psychol. Bull.*, 1940, *37*, 1-28.

Klüver, H. Psychology at the beginning of World War II: Meditations on the impending dismemberment of psychology written in 1942. *J. Psychol.*, 1949, *28*, 383-410.

Lewin, K. The conflict between Aristotelian and Galilean modes of thought in contemporary psychology. *J. gen. Psychol.*, 1931, *51*, 141-177.

Sarbin, T. R. Clinical psychology—art or science. *Psychometrika*, 1941, *6*, 391-400.

Seward, J. P. The sign of a symbol: a reply to Professor Allport. *Psychol. Rev.*, 1948, *55*, 277-296.

Welch, L. An integration of some fundamental principles of modern behaviorism and Gestalt psychology. *J. gen. Psychol.*, 1948, *39*, 175-190.

Chapter VI. Lawfulness in Behavior

[Selection reference lists on pp. 202-203, 215-216.]

Brunswik, E. Thing constancy as measured by correlation coefficients. *Psychol. Rev.*, 1940, *47*, 69-78.

Brunswik, E. *Systematic and representative design of psychological experiments.* Berkeley: Univ. California Press, 1949. [Also in *Proc. Berkeley Symposium on Math. Stat. and Probability.* Berkeley: Univ. California Press, 1949.]

Chein, I. Behavior theory and the behavior of attitudes: some critical comments. *Psychol. Rev.*, 1948, *55*, 175-188.

Doob, L. W. The behavior of attitudes. *Psychol. Rev.*, 1947, *54*, 135-156.

Guthrie, E. R. The status of systematic psychology. *Amer. Psychol.*, 1950, *5*, 97-101.

Hull, C. L.; Felsinger, J. M.; Gladstone, A. I.; and Yamaguchi, H. G. A proposed quantification of habit strength. *Psychol. Rev.*, 1947, *54*, 237-254.

Hull, C. L. Behavior postulates and corollaries—1949. *Psychol. Rev.*, 1950, *57*, 173-180.

Chapter VII. Special Techniques: Logico-mathematical

[Selection reference lists on pp. 232-233, 255-256, 275-276.]

Anastasi, Anne. Faculties *versus* factors: a reply to Professor Thurstone. *Psychol. Bull.*, 1938, *35*, 391-395.

Boring, E. G. Statistical frequencies as dynamic equilibria. *Psychol. Rev.*, 1941, *48*, 279-301.

Brower, D. The problem of quantification in psychological science. *Psychol. Rev.*, 1949, *56*, 325-333.

Burt, C. *The factors of the mind: an introduction to factor analysis in psychology.* New York: Macmillan, 1941.

Estes, W. K. Towards a statistical theory of learning. *Psychol. Rev.*, 1950, *57*, 94-107.

Fitch, F. B. Symbolic logic and behavior theory: a reply. *Psychol. Bull.*, 1940, *37*, 817-819.

Graham, C. H. Behavior, perception and the psychophysical methods. *Psychol. Rev.,* 1950, *57,* 108-120.

Guilford, J. P. Factor analysis in a test-development program. *Psychol. Rev.,* 1948, *55,* 79-94.

Hall, E. W. Some dangers in the use of symbolic logic in psychology. *Psychol. Rev.,* 1942, *49,* 142-169.

Hilgard, E. R. Review of *Mathematico-deductive theory of rote learning: the psychological system. Psychol. Bull.,* 1940, *37,* 808-815.

Householder, A. S. and Landahl, H. D. *Mathematical biophysics of the central nervous system.* Bloomington, Ind.: Principia Press, 1945.

Kattsoff, L. O. Philosophy, psychology and postulational technique. *Psychol. Rev.,* 1939, *46,* 62-74.

Marhenke, P. Review of *Mathematico-deductive theory of rote learning: the logical system. Psychol. Bull.,* 1940, *37,* 815-817.

Miller, J. G. Symbolic technique in psychological theory. *Psychol. Rev.,* 1939, *46,* 464-479.

Perloff, R. A note on Brower's "The problem of quantification in psychological science." *Psychol. Rev.,* 1950, *57,* 188-192.

Rashevsky, N. *Mathematical biophysics.* Chicago: Univ. Chicago Press, 1948.

Spearman, C. *The abilities of man.* New York: Macmillan, 1927.

Stevens, S. S. On the theory of scales of measurement. *Science,* 1946, *103,* 677-680.

Thomson, G. H. *Factorial analysis of human abilities.* Boston: Houghton Mifflin, 1939.

Thurstone, L. L. Current misuse of the factorial methods. *Psychometrika,* 1937, *2,* 73-76.

Thurstone, L. L. Shifty and mathematical components. *Psychol. Bull.,* 1938, *35,* 223-236.

Thurstone, L. L. *Primary mental abilities.* Chicago: Univ. Chicago Press, 1938.

Thurstone, L. L. Current issues in factor analysis. *Psychol. Bull.,* 1940, *37,* 189-236.

Thurstone, L. L. *Multiple factor analysis.* Chicago: Univ. Chicago Press, 1947.

Weber, C. O. Homeostasis and servo-mechanisms for what? *Psychol. Rev.,* 1949, *56,* 234-239.

Wiener, N. *Cybernetics, or control and communication in the animal and man.* New York: Wiley, 1948.

Woodger, J. H. The formalization of a psychological theory. *Erkenntnis* (*J. unif. Sci.*), 1938, *7,* 195-198.

Zipf, G. K. *Human behavior and the principle of least effort.* Cambridge, Mass.: Addison-Wesley Press, 1949.

Chapter VIII. Special Techniques: Field-theoretical
[Selection reference lists on pp. 314-315, 323-324, 329-330.]

Boring, E. G. Human nature vs. sensation: William James and the psychology of the present. *Amer. J. Psychol.*, 1942, *55*, 310-327.

Boring, E. G. Mind and mechanism. *Amer. J. Psychol.*, 1946, *2*, 173-192.

Cartwright, D. and Festinger, L. A quantitative theory of decision. *Psychol. Rev.*, 1943, *50*, 595-621.

Chein, I.; Cook, S. W.; and Harding, J. The field of action research. *Amer. Psych.*, 1948, *3*, 43-50.

Festinger, L., *et al. Theory and experiment in social communication.* Ann Arbor, Mich.: Univ. Michigan Press, 1950.

Festinger, L.; Schacter, S.; and Back, K. *Social pressures in informal groups.* New York: Harper, 1950.

Kantor, J. R. Current trends in psychological theory. *Psychol. Bull.*, 1941, *38*, 29-68.

Kantor, J. R. An interbehavioral analysis of propositions. *Psychol. Rec.*, 1943, *5*, 309-339.

Kantor, J. R. *Problems of physiological psychology.* Bloomington, Ind.: Principia Press, 1947.

Kantor, J. R. *Psychology and logic.* Vols. I and II. Bloomington, Ind.: Principia Press, 1950.

Koffka, K. *Principles of Gestalt psychology.* New York: Harcourt, Brace, 1935.

Krech, D. Attitudes and learning: A methodological note. *Psychol. Rev.*, 1946, *53*, 290-293.

Krech, D. and Crutchfield, R. S. *Theory and problems of social psychology.* New York: McGraw-Hill, 1948.

Leeper, R. *Lewin's topological and vector psychology: a digest and a critique.* Eugene, Ore.: Univ. Oregon Press, 1943.

Lewin, K. Vorsatz, Wille, und Bedürfnis. *Psychol. Forsch.*, 1926, *7*, 294-385. [Translated as "Will and needs," in Ellis, W. D. (ed.), *A source book of Gestalt psychology.* New York: Harcourt, Brace, 1938, 283-299.]

Lewin, K. *A dynamic theory of personality.* (Trans. by D. K. Adams and K. Zener.) New York: McGraw-Hill, 1935.

Lewin, K. *Principles of topological psychology.* (Trans. by F. Heider and G. M. Heider.) New York: McGraw-Hill, 1936.

Lewin, K. Field theory of learning. *Natl. Soc. Stud. Educ.*, 41st Yearbook, 1942, Part II, 215-242.

Lewin, K. Formalization and progress in psychology. Studies in topological and vector psychology. *Univ. Ia. Stud. Child Welf.*, 1940, *16*, 19-42.

Lippitt, R. *Training in community relations.* New York: Harper, 1947.

London, I. D. Psychologists' misuse of the auxiliary concepts of physics and mathematics. *Psychol. Rev.*, 1944, *51*, 266-291.

Snygg, D. and Combs, A. W. *Individual behavior; a new frame of reference.* New York: Harper, 1949.

Chapter IX. Special Techniques: Psychoanalytic

[Selection reference lists on pp. 349-351.]

Alexander, F. A jury trial of psychoanalysis. *J. abn. soc. Psychol.,* 1940, *35,* 305-323.

Allport, G. W. *The use of personal documents in psychological science.* New York: Social Science Research Council, 1942.

Bellak, L. and Ekstein, R. The extension of basic scientific laws to psychoanalysis and to psychology. *Psychoanal. Rev.,* 1946, *33,* 306-313.

Boring, E. G.; Sachs, H.; Landis, C.; Brown, J. F.; Willoughby, R. R.; Symonds, P. M.; Murray, H. A.; Frenkel-Brunswik, Else; Shakow, D. Symposium: psychoanalysis as seen by analyzed psychologists. *J. abn. soc. Psychol.,* 1940, *35,* 3-55; 139-211.

Brown, J. F. Freud and the scientific method. *Phil. Sci.,* 1934, *1,* 323-337.

Ellis, A. An introduction to the principles of scientific psychoanalysis. *Genet. Psychol. Monogr.,* 1950, *41,* 147-212.

French, T. M. Interrelations between psychoanalysis and the experimental work of Pavlov. *Amer. J. Psychiat.,* 1933, *12,* 1165-1203.

Freud, S. *A general introduction to psychoanalysis.* (Trans. by Riviere.) Garden City, N. Y.: Garden City, 1943.

Heidbreder, Edna. Freud and psychology. *Psychol. Rev.,* 1940, *47,* 185-195.

Hendrick, I. *Facts and theories of psychoanalysis.* New York: Knopf, 1947 (2nd ed.).

Hull, C. L. Modern behaviorism and psychoanalysis. *Trans. N. Y. Acad. Sci.,* 1939, *1,* Ser. II, 78-82.

Kardiner, A. Psychoanalysis and psychology. A comparison of methods and objectives. *Phil. Sci.,* 1941, *8,* 233-254.

Landis, C. Psychoanalysis and scientific method. *Proc. Amer. Philos. Soc.,* 1941, *84,* 515-525.

Lewin, K. Psychoanalysis and topological psychology. *Bull. Menninger Clinic,* 1937, *1,* 202-211.

Lorand, S. (ed.) *Psychoanalysis today.* New York: Int. Univ. Press, 1944.

Tomkins, S. S. (ed.) *Contemporary psychotherapy.* Cambridge, Mass.: Harvard Univ. Press, 1943.

Chapter X. Perception

[Selection reference list on p. 386.]

Brunswik, E. *Wahrnehmung und Gegenstandswelt.* Leipzig and Wien: Deutick, 1934.

Brunswik, E. Psychology as a science of objective relations. *Phil. Sci.,* 1937, *4,* 227-260.

Brunswik, E. Distal focussing of perception: Size constancy in a representative sample of situations. *Psychol. Monogr.*, 1944, *56*, 1-49.

Koffka, K. *The growth of the mind.* New York: Harcourt, Brace, 1928 (rev. ed.).

Köhler, W. *The place of value in a world of facts.* New York: Liveright, 1938.

Köhler, W. *Dynamics in psychology.* New York: Liveright, 1940.

Köhler, W. and Dinnerstein, Dorothy. Figural after-effects in kinesthesis. *Miscellanea Psychologica Albert Michotte.* Louvain: Institut Superieur de Philosophie, 1947.

Köhler, W. and Emery, D. A. Figural after-effects in the third dimension of visual space. *Amer. J. Psychol.*, 1947, *60*, 159-201.

Köhler, W. and Held, R. The cortical correlate of pattern vision. *Science,* 1949, *110*, 414-419.

Chapter XI. Learning

[Selection reference lists on pp. 426-428, 452.]

Guthrie, E. R. *The psychology of learning.* New York: Harper, 1935.

Guthrie, E. R. *The psychology of human conflict.* New York: Harper, 1938.

Guthrie, E. R. Psychological facts and psychological theory. *Psychol. Bull.*, 1946, *43*, 1-20.

Hull, C. L. Mind, mechanism and adaptive behavior. *Psychol. Rev.*, 1937, *44*, 1-32.

Hull, C. L. *Principles of behavior.* New York: D. Appleton-Century, 1943.

Lashley, K. S. Experimental analysis of instinctive behavior. *Psychol. Rev.*, 1938, *45*, 445-472.

Lashley, K. S. Structural variation in the nervous system in relation to behavior. *Psychol. Rev.*, 1947, *54*, 325-334.

Lashley, K. S. and Wade, Marjorie. The Pavlovian theory of generalization. *Psychol. Rev.*, 1946, *53*, 72-87.

Skinner, B. F. *The behavior of organisms.* New York: D. Appleton-Century, 1938.

Skinner, B. F. Are theories of learning necessary? *Psychol. Rev.*, 1950, *57*, 193-216.

Thorndike, E. L. An experimental study of rewards. *Teach. Coll. Contr. Educ.*, 1933, No. 580.

Thorndike, E. L. *Selected writings from a connectionist's psychology.* New York: Appleton-Century-Crofts, 1949.

Tolman, E. C. *Drives toward war.* New York: D. Appleton-Century, 1942.

Tolman, E. C. Cognitive maps in rats and men. *Psychol. Rev.*, 1948, *55*, 189-208.

Tolman, E. C. The nature and functioning of wants. *Psychol. Rev.*, 1949, *56*, 357-369.

Tolman, E. C. There is more than one kind of learning. *Psychol. Rev.*, 1949, *56*, 144-155.

Tolman, E. C. The psychology of social learning. *J. soc. Issues, Suppl. Ser.*, 1949, No. 3.

Tolman, E. C. *Collected papers.* Berkeley: Univ. Calif. Press, 1951.

Chapter XII. Psychodynamics

[Selection reference lists on pp. 469-471, 497.]

Alexander, F. *Our age of unreason.* Philadelphia: Lippincott, 1942.

Alexander, F.; French, T. M.; and collaborators. *Psychoanalytic therapy.* New York: Ronald, 1946.

Alexander, F. and French, T. M. *Studies in psychosomatic medicine.* New York: Ronald, 1948.

Dollard, J. and Miller, N. E. *Personality and psychotherapy.* New York: McGraw-Hill, 1950.

Horney, Karen. *The neurotic personality of our time.* New York: Norton, 1937.

Horney, Karen. *New ways in psychoanalysis.* New York: Norton, 1939.

Horney, Karen. *Self analysis.* New York: Norton, 1942.

Horney, Karen. *Neurosis and human growth.* New York: Norton, 1950.

Maslow, A. H. Conflict, frustration, and the theory of threat. *J. abn. soc. Psychol.*, 1943, *38*, 81-86.

Maslow, A. H. A theory of human motivation. *Psychol. Rev.*, 1943, *50*, 370-396.

Maslow, A. H. and Mittelmann, B. *Principles of abnormal psychology.* New York: Harper, 1941.

Miller, N. E. Theory and experiment relating psychoanalytic displacement to stimulus-response generalization. *J. abn. soc. Psychol.*, 1948, *43*, 155-178.

Mowrer, O. H. *Learning theory and personality dynamics.* New York: Ronald, 1950.

Rosenzweig, S. A dynamic interpretation of psychotherapy oriented towards research. *Psychiatry*, 1938, *1*, 521-526.

Rosenzweig, S. An outline of frustration theory. In J. McV. Hunt (ed.) *Personality and the behavior disorders.* New York: Ronald, 1944, 379-388.

Chapter XIII. Personality

[Selection reference lists on pp. 516, 521.]

Allport, G. W. *Personality: a psychological interpretation.* New York: Holt, 1937.

Allport, G. W. *The nature of personality.* Cambridge, Mass.: Addison-Wesley Press, 1950.

Kluckholn, C. and Murray, H. A. *Personality in nature, society and culture.* New York: Knopf, 1948.

Murphy, G. The freeing of intelligence. *Psychol. Bull.,* 1945, *42,* 1-19.

Murray, H. A., *et al. Assessment of men.* New York: Rinehart, 1948.

Rogers, C. R. *Counseling and psychotherapy.* Boston: Houghton Mifflin, 1942.

Rogers, C. R. *Client-centered therapy.* Boston: Houghton Mifflin, 1950.

Chapter XIV. Social Interaction

[Selection reference lists on pp. 542, 549.]

Kardiner, A. and collaborators. *The psychological frontiers of society.* New York: Columbia Univ. Press, 1945.

Lewin, K.; Lippitt, R. and White, R. K. Patterns of aggressive behavior in experimentally created "social climates." *J. soc. Psychol.,* 1939, *10,* 271-299.

Lewin, K. Action research and minority problems. *J. soc. Issues,* 1946, *2,* 34-46.

Lewin, K. Frontiers in group dynamics. I. Concept, method and reality in social science; social equilibria and social change. *Hum. Rel.,* 1947, *1,* 5-41.

Lewin, K. Frontiers of group dynamics. II. Channels of group life; social planning and action research. *Hum. Rel.,* 1947, *1,* 143-153.

Lewin, K. *Resolving social conflicts.* New York: Harper, 1948.

Lewin, K. *Field theory in social science.* (D. Cartwright, ed.). New York: Harper, 1951.

INDEX

The following conventions are used: *auth.*, for authorship of selections; *ment.*, for mention not justifying more specific description; *quoted*, for quotation of at least one sentence; *ref.*, for bibliographic reference; *fn*, for footnote (immediately following page number).